The Quark XPress Book

3rd Edition

by
David
Blatner

Keith Stimely
and

Eric Taub

edited by
Stephen F.
Roth

AN OPEN HOUSE BOOK

PEACHPIT PRESS

The QuarkXPress Book, Third Edition
David Blatner, Keith Stimely, and Eric Taub
Edited by Stephen F. Roth

Peachpit Press, Inc.
2414 Sixth St.
Berkeley, California 94710
800/283-9444
510/548-4393 (phone)
510/548-5991 (fax)

Permissions
Pages 381, 384, 392, Figures 8-4, 8-7, 8-13, reprinted with permission of Special Collections Division, University of Washington Libraries (photo by Todd, negative no. 10511).
Pages 388, 399, Figures 8-10, 8-17, reprinted with permission of Special Collections Division, University of Washington Libraries (photo by A. Curtis, negative no. 4103).
Page 396, Figure 8-16, reprinted with permission of Special Collections Division, University of Washington Libraries (photo by A. Curtis, negative no. 30744.)

Trademarks
Many of the designations used by manufacturers and sellers to distinguish their products are claimed as trademarks. Where those designations appear in this book, and Peachpit Press was aware of a trademark claim, the designations have been printed in initial caps or all caps.

Notice of Liability
The information in this book is distributed on an "As Is" basis, without warranty. While every precaution has been taken in the preparation of this book, neither the authors nor Peachpit Press, Inc. shall have any liability to any person or entity with respect to liability, loss, or damage caused or alleged to be caused directly or indirectly by the instructions contained in this book or by the computer software annd hardware products described herein.

ISBN 1-56609-067-9
Printed and bound in the United States of America
0 9 8 7 6 5 4 3 2 1

PRINTED ON RECYCLED PAPER

Quark
XPress
Secrets

▼▼▼

When we introduced QuarkXPress back in 1987, we had no idea of the broad impact it would have on the world of publishing. Now, if you look at any random collection of magazines and newspapers, the chances are that many of them were produced using QuarkXPress. From high-end publishing to newsletters and brochures, the methods used to produce high-quality documents have changed completely in the space of only a few years. And QuarkXPress has been a major force catalyzing that change. The power of XPress rivals, and in some cases surpasses, the power of older, expensive, high-end publishing systems.

But, with this power came complexity. That is until the release of QuarkXPress 3.0. When we were developing 3.0, it was immediately apparent that we had to make a radical shift in the way the user interacts with the computer. We couldn't just tack on features at random and hope that the documentation writers could explain them. To add more features, we had to make using XPress simpler. The 3.0 user interface makes QuarkXPress both more powerful and easier to use. Now everyday layout tasks can be done in easy and obvious ways. Powerful new features and an intuitive interface make QuarkXPress 3.0 a radically superior page layout and design program.

Nevertheless, in developing documentation for the product, we take a very broad view of our audience. The XPress documentation takes you only so far. The uses of the product are as varied as the backgrounds of the users. To get all the information that everyone wants takes much more. That's where *The QuarkXPress Book* comes in.

When Keith and David asked me to write a foreword for *The QuarkXPress Book,* I thought, "Yeah, sure. I'll write something generic that says how nice the book is and that it will be a good addition to your library." Then, I actually got to read it. This is more than a good book on XPress. It is a great book. It explains everything about publishing with QuarkXPress in detail. Technical issues that you can read about nowhere else are discussed in depth.

But, this is also more than just a book on QuarkXPress. It is a book on Macintosh. The information that's covered has broader uses to anyone who owns a Mac. It explains lots of secrets about how the Mac really works. And with tips ranging from simple step-by-step procedures for creating fancy drop caps to advanced uses of ResEdit to customize your system, the information provided is invaluable. As far as I know, it has never been collected in one place before.

Users like David and Keith are one of the reasons that QuarkXPress has been successful. Making a great product takes more than just a bunch of clever people in research and development. It takes actual users telling us what we did right and what we did wrong. David and Keith both use XPress. This book was produced with XPress. Its quality is not a testament to what QuarkXPress can do; it is a testament to what QuarkXPress can do in the hands of skilled and knowledgeable operators. No matter what your level of expertise, this book will help you know more and work better. It will be one of the most useful books you own for XPress and the Macintosh.

Tim Gill
Founder and Senior Vice President
of Research and Development
Quark Inc.

The Amazon Explorers

▼▼▼

"You're doing what?"

"We've got one QuarkXPress document here to print the borders for each page, and then in this other document we have all the text in galleys. We tried to put them together, but because we don't know the program well enough, it's faster just to use our production people for pasteup."

"If you're just going to paste it up, why are you using QuarkXPress at all?"

"A consultant suggested we buy a Macintosh and Quark-XPress. But we haven't had a chance to really learn it. Besides, QuarkXPress lets us make really good borders."

It was a story both of us had heard before. Designers, ad agencies, small and large businesses bought Macintoshes and QuarkXPress with the idea that everything was going to be easier, faster, and cooler. All that can be true, but let's face it: QuarkXPress is not a magical solution. Desktop publishing on the Macintosh requires knowledge, experience, and expertise.

It seems there is a need for a consultant who not only knows the computer and graphic design, but also one who can sit there, patiently, and—at 11 P.M.—walk with you through building a better registration mark, making a drop cap, or explaining how master pages work. All for a $29 flat fee. That consultant is this book.

▼ ▼

The Early Days

But how did this book come to be? What possessed us to write 176,496 words, more or less, on a piece of computer software? Let's start at the beginning of our QuarkXPress story.

The early days of desktop publishing were much simpler than they are now. When a new program came out, we asked some basic, hard-hitting questions.

- Can you put text on a page?

- Can you put graphics on a page?

- Does the page print?

Once we had a satisfactory answer to those three questions, we could get down to brass tacks, ripping it to pieces to make it do all the things it wasn't designed to do. It was a wild time, much like trudging through the Amazon forests with only a machete and a match.

To be blunt, I'm not ordinarily the quiet type. So it is telling that, when I saw the first copy of QuarkXPress 1.0, all I could say was, "Wow." Here was, at last, a program to use instead of PageMaker. No more eyeballing the measurements, no more relying on built-in algorithms. Those were the days of PageMaker 1.2, and QuarkXPress was a glimmer of hope in the dark ages.

But it was the beginning of the Macintosh Way, and we were so gung-ho on not acting like IBM PC users anymore that we would do almost anything not to look in the manuals. Even if we had wanted to peek every once in a while, peer pressure was stiff. No, we had to play by the rules and learn QuarkXPress the hard way.

But perhaps all those years of system crashes and blank pages coming out of the printer paid off. While frequenting cocktail parties, we can blithely hint at the magnificent techniques we've come upon for using QuarkXPress in a networked environment. Our friends and family are amazed as we stand tall, knowing which menu to pull down to create style sheets. But is it really enough?

Making Pages

Even more important than fancy party talk has been the ability to use all our QuarkXPress tips and tricks to make good-looking pages quickly and efficiently. And back in 1990, we knew it was finally time to put finger to keyboard and get this information out to you, the real world users of QuarkXPress. To find even more tips, tricks, and techniques for Quark-XPress users, we searched the on-line systems, looked through back issues of computer magazines, and even resorted to books on other Macintosh software.

But books full of tips and tricks tell just half the story. And we think the simple menu-by-menu approach that most computer books use deserves the phrase "tastes filling, less great!" We knew there should be more.

So we sat down and listed all the ways in which we use QuarkXPress in our work: books, magazines, newsletters, flyers, and brochures. The most striking thing we found was that we rarely used QuarkXPress by itself. Aldus Freehand, Adobe Illustrator, PostScript programming, ResEdit, Microsoft Word, Adobe Photoshop, and numerous desk accessories and utilities all play a large part in our publishing process. We figured that if we weren't publishing in a vacuum, you probably weren't either. So we gathered up information about using those programs in conjunction with QuarkXPress.

Our idea was to roll together tips and tricks, a full overview of the program, and in-depth discussions of core concepts behind using QuarkXPress in a real world setting. So, we've included discussions on fonts, PostScript printing, color models, and much more, alongside examples of how we've been using QuarkXPress for the past six years. We also describe the way QuarkXPress operates and how to take advantage of its sometimes strange methods.

Of course, this is a lot of information for a single book. But what did you shell out $29 for? Chopped liver? No, this book is meant not only to be read, but to be used. We wanted to include a Post-It pad so you could mark the pages you'll use the most, but it didn't work out. But don't let that stop you.

▼ ▼

About this Book

We have purposely taken a wide spectrum of potential readers into account, from Macintosh beginners to seasoned professionals. We did this because we've found that those seasoned professionals are delighted to learn new tricks, techniques, and concepts, and people who have used the Mac very little sometimes surprise us with their intuitive grasp of the Big Picture.

Remember, this book was written for you. It's designed to work for you—as your personal consultant—whoever you are. It's also designed to help you get a sure footing on a sometimes uneven path and to help you make pages like the pros.

Organization

We have organized this book to reflect what we think Quark-XPress is all about: producing final camera-ready output from your computer. So we start with an overview of the program, move on to building a structure for the document, then discuss the basics—such as putting text and pictures on a page. Next we move into some fine-tuning aspects of QuarkXPress, and finally to printing. That's the speed-reading rundown; now here's a play-by-play of the chapters.

Introduction. In the Introduction we lay out QuarkXPress on the table, telling you what it is and what it does. We also run down each of the new features in versions 3.0 and 3.1.

Chapter 1: Structure and Interface. The first step in understanding QuarkXPress is learning about its structure from the ground up. This involves an investigation of QuarkXPress's menus, palettes, and dialog boxes. We also look at file management, navigating through your document, and the basics of the new libraries, grouping, and alignment controls.

Chapter 2: Document Construction. Without a sturdy foundation, your document won't be reliable or flexible when you need it to be. This chapter discusses the basics of making earthquake-proof infrastructures for your pages: opening a new document, creating master pages, and setting up column guides and linking for text flow.

Chapter 3: Word Processing. If you wanted a drawing program, you would have bought one. Words are what QuarkXPress is all about, and this chapter is where words start. We talk here about simple text input, the Find/Change feature, and spell-checking.

Chapter 4: Type and Typography. Once you've got those words in the computer, what do you do with them? Chapter 4 discusses the details of formatting text into type—fonts, sizes, styles, indents, drop caps—all the things that turn text into type.

Chapter 5: Copy Flow. You bought the computer, so why not let it do the work for you? This chapter explains how to use style sheets to automate aspects of copy processing, and how to use importing and exporting effectively.

Chapter 6: Pictures. Who reads text anymore? We like to look at the pictures. And pictures are what Chapter 6 is all about. We discuss every Macintosh graphics file format and how to work with each in your documents. We also cover rotating, skewing, and other manipulations of images.

Chapter 7: Where Text Meets Graphics. This is the frontier-land, the border between the two well-discussed worlds of type and pictures. Life gets different on the edge, and in this chapter we discuss how to handle it with grace—using inline boxes, paragraph rules, and the new text runaround features.

Chapter 8: Modifying Images. Here's where a good eye can help you improve a bitmapped image, and a creative eye can help you make those graphics do flips. In this chapter we look at brightness, contrast, gamma correction, and halftoning for bitmapped images such as scans.

Chapter 9: Color. QuarkXPress is well-known for its powerful color capabilities. Chapter 9 covers color models, building a custom color palette, applying colors, and the first steps in understanding color separation.

Chapter 10: Printing. This chapter is where everything we've talked about is leading: getting your document out of the machine and onto film or paper. In this chapter we cover every step of printing—from the Chooser to color separations. We also discuss the finer points of working with service bureaus and how to troubleshoot your print job.

Appendix A: PostScript. You don't have to be a tweak to make PostScript programming helpful in your work. This appendix is full of tips for searching through and modifying your PostScript files before you print them.

Appendix B: Resources. The second appendix is an extensive directory of Quark XTensions, software, hardware, and magazines and publications that we've found useful while working with QuarkXPress.

Appendix C: Using QuarkXPress 3.2. This appendix covers (in excruciating detail) every new feature in QuarkXPress version 3.1 and 3.2. We've also thrown in a bunch of tips and tricks that didn't make it into the first edition of the book.

Appendix D: EfiColor. EfiColor, a color management system that improves the correspondence between colors on screen, on color printer output, and on printed results from offset printing, is the single biggest new feature in QuarkXPress 3.2. It's covered in detail in this appendix.

Finding What You Need

There are many ways to read this book. First, there's the cover-to-cover approach. This is the best way to get every morsel we have included. On the other hand, that method doesn't seem to work for some people. As we said, this book is meant to be used, right off the shelf, no batteries needed.

We've done everything in our power to make it easy to find topics throughout this book. However, there's so much information that sometimes you might not know where to look. The table of contents breaks each chapter down into first and second level headings. So you can jump to a particular topic fast.

Note that almost all of the new, updated information on versions 3.1 and 3.2 in this third edition is in Appendix C.

If it's a tip that you're looking for, you can look through the tips list at the beginning of the book. We've also started the tips in the text with the word "Tip" to make them stand out. Finally, if you can't find what you're looking for, or are trying to find an explanation for a single concept, try the index.

Conventions

We love icons and other conventions of a graphic user interface. But we like them on a computer, not in a book. We've tried to avoid clogging up the space in this book as much as possible with unnecessary items that are difficult to understand without a crib-sheet. However, we did face one difficulty: identifying items in QuarkXPress, such as menus and menu items, dialog boxes, features, commands, and so on.

To make it easy, we've established one simple convention throughout the book. If we talk about a feature or item itself when we name it (for example, the General Preferences dialog box, the Libraries item, 200% page view), we don't do anything different with the phrase. If we don't identify the item directly, we put quotes around it (for example, zoom to "400%," select "Libraries," and so on). The only exceptions to this convention are the standard Macintosh commands (Save, New, Paste, etc.), which simply don't need identification.

▼ ▼

Acknowledgements

No book is an island. So many people have directly and indirectly contributed to this book's production that we would have to publish a second volume to thank them all. We do want to thank a few people directly, however.

First of all, a great thanks to the people at Quark who not only put out a great product, but also worked with us to get this book out to you with as much information in it as we've got. In particular, Tim Gill, Fred Ebrahimi, Elizabeth Jones, Becky "our fave" Lefebvre, Jay "the Guy" McBeth, Greg Morton, Ralph Risch, Kathleen "hold on, I'll check" Thurston, Peter Warren, and Dave Shaver.

Other folks: Dan Brogan, Peter Dako, Robert Hoffer, Scott Lawton, Sal Soghoian, Dacques Viker, and the mavens at EFI: Stephanie "stop processing" Arvizu, Adam Stock, and Danielle Beaumont.

And many thanks go to all the people who wrote, called, and e-mailed us their comments and suggestions. We've tried to incorporate their ideas into this second edition.

The People Who Made This Book

Guy Kawasaki wrote about Steve Roth in *The Macintosh Way*: "If you find an editor who understands what you are trying to do, brings the best out of you, and doesn't botch up your work, 'marry' him as fast as you can." I can't think of a better description of Steve, so that'll have to do. Steve's already married to Susie Hammond, who—along with Cindy Bell—was excellent in making sure our t's were dotted and i's crossed, and—most of all—making sure that we didn't sound like fools.

I also want to thank our publisher, Ted Nace. We gave it the wings, but he made it fly. Also, much appreciation and astonishment goes toward our excellent book designer Olav Martin Kvern, our wordsmith Don "reference-man" Sellers, and the Open House production staff, Don "not a minion" Munsil, Rebecca Wilkinson-Nickell, Neil Kvern, Glenn Fleishman, and other folks who helped poke and prod until it was done. The people at Harvard Espresso and Marketime, for mind- and body-sustaining espresso. Mike Arst for saving our butts and helping us get our figures in shape. Doug Peltonen, for help with technical edits. George Aldridge and the staff of Datatype and Graphics, and Chuck Cantellay and Jim Rademaker at Seattle Imagesetting for delivering this baby from the imagesetter(s).

And, finally, there are those people even further behind the scenes who helped us along the road. Vincent Dorn at LaserWrite in Palo Alto, who said, "Hey, let's go to Burger King." Steve Herold at LaserGraphics in Seattle, who said, "Meet Steve Roth." My entire family, Debbie Carlson, Leah Brass, and other friends who were such a support over the past few decades. It wouldn't have happened without you.

Thanks.

David Blatner

Overview

Contents

▼ ▼

▼ ▼

Tips

▼ ▼

▼ ▼

▼ ▼

Chapter 5   Copy Flow

Chapter 6   Pictures

▼ ▼

INTRODUCTION

Trying to figure out exactly what type of program QuarkXPress is sometimes reminds us of a scene from an old "Saturday Night Live" episode, when a couple bickered over their new purchase. "It's a floor wax," said one. "No, it's a dessert topping," replied the other. The answer was clear: "It's a floor wax *and* a dessert topping." QuarkXPress is a program with the same predicament. Some people insist it's a typesetting application. Others bet their bottom dollar that it's a word processor. Still others make QuarkXPress a way of life.

The truth is that QuarkXPress is all these things, and more. However, no matter how you use it, it is never more than a tool. And a tool is never more than the person behind it.

We like to think of machetes. You can use a machete as an exotic knife to cut a block of cheese. Or you can use it as your only means of survival hacking through the Amazon jungles. It's all up to you.

Here in the Introduction, we talk about the big picture: QuarkXPress and how it fits into the world of desktop publishing. We also talk about the new QuarkXPress, version 3, and how it's different from previous versions. Most importantly, we set the stage for the real thrust of this book: how to use QuarkXPress to its fullest.

▼ ▼

What QuarkXPress Is

QuarkXPress 3 combines word processing, typesetting, page layout, drawing, image control, and document construction in a single program. From text editing to typographics, page ornamentation to picture manipulation, it offers precision controls that you'll be hard pressed to find in other programs.

Who QuarkXPress is For

Just because it has all these powers, though, doesn't mean that only trained publishing professionals or graphic designers can or should use it. Anyone who can run a Macintosh ("the computer for the rest of us") can use it. In fact, many of the people who swear by QuarkXPress aren't even in the "publishing" business. They use it for internal corporate communications, product brochures, stationery, display advertisements, name tags, labels, forms, posters, announcements, and a hundred other things.

Of course, it does "real" publishing, too, and has become a top choice in that realm. It's used by book publishers such as Simon and Schuster and Peachpit Press; magazines such as *Newsweek, People, Playboy, Spy, Smart, Rolling Stone,* and *Premiere;* newspapers such as *The New York Times, USA Today, The Washington Times,* and *The Denver Post;* design firms, art studios, advertising agencies, and documentation departments throughout the world.

▼ ▼

What QuarkXPress Does

When it comes right down to it, QuarkXPress is built to make pages. You can place text and graphics as well as other page elements on an electronic page and then print that out in a number of different formats. But how can you do that? What tools are at your disposal? Before we spend the rest of the book talking about how to use QuarkXPress and its tools, we had better introduce you to them. And perhaps the best way to introduce QuarkXPress in real world terms is to provide a digest of some of its most basic options.

Page sizes. You can specify the page sizes for each of your documents, along with their margins. Page dimensions can range from 1 by 1 inch to 48 by 48 inches, and margins can be any size. QuarkXPress's main window presents you with a screen representation of your full page, and guidelines indicate margin areas. You can view pages at actual size or any scale from 10 percent to 400 percent. If your document consists of multiple pages, you can view them all by scrolling. If pages are larger than the maximum paper size handled by the target printer, QuarkXPress will *tile* the document, printing it in overlapping sections for you to assemble manually.

Page layout. QuarkXPress provides tools so you can design your pages by creating and positioning columns, text boxes, picture boxes, and decorative elements. There's a facility to set up "chains" for the automatic flow of text both around a page and between pages. QuarkXPress automates the insertion of new pages and new columns, the creation of elements that are common to all pages, and the page numbering/renumbering process itself.

Word processing. QuarkXPress's word processing tools let you type directly into pages and edit what you type, with your text appearing in either the full-page background (as on paper in a typewriter) or wrapping into overlaying text boxes that can be moved and resized. Text always automatically rewraps to fit new box boundaries.

Formatting type. You have full control over character-level formatting (font, size, style, etc.) and paragraph-level formatting (indents, leading, space before and after, etc.). You can also build style sheets for different types of paragraphs that include both character and paragraph formatting.

Importing text. Various import filters let you bring in formatted text from other programs (again, either onto full pages or smaller text boxes), while simultaneously reformatting, using style sheets.

Graphic elements. Drawing tools let you create lines, boxes, ovals, and polygons in different styles, sizes, and shapes, with different borders, fills, and colors.

Importing graphics. You can import computer graphics into picture boxes. These graphics can include scanned images, object-oriented and bitmapped graphics, in color, gray scale, or black and white. Once you've imported them into picture boxes, they can be cropped, fitted, rotated, skewed, and—with bitmaps—manipulated for brightness, contrast, and special effects.

▼ ▼

The New QuarkXPress 3

Following is a quick tour of the new features in QuarkXPress 3; this may be of most interest to experienced QuarkXPress users as a handy checklist. For these users, we have some good news and some bad news. The bad news is that you have a few habits to unlearn. The good news is that most of them are the things you loved to hate! So it's really not bad news at all. We've also rolled in some of the high points of version 3.1. But for a complete discussion of this newest version, see Appendix C, *Using QuarkXPress 3.1.*

Changes from previous versions are considerable, but Quark has taken great care to make the transition easy, keeping the same "look and feel." Experienced users will have a great time exploring the new nooks and crannies. If you are a novice you shouldn't feel overwhelmed by some of the terminology and references employed here; you'll soon be well-versed in them all.

Like all really good programs, QuarkXPress provides more than one way to get something done. For example, you have five different options for changing the size of a piece of type. You can choose the one which not only suits the occasion, but the one which suits your working style best.

Structure and Interface

Perhaps the biggest changes in this version of QuarkXPress are in the interface—the way in which you and QuarkXPress get your document made. Quark dropped some troublesome features from previous versions—like parent and child boxes—that really got in the way of making pages, and it's added dozens of features—notably the Measurements and Document Layout palettes—that make it much easier to get your work done.

What You See

Both the way in which you see your page and the way in which QuarkXPress is set up on the computer screen have changed.

The page. Now pages and page spreads are surrounded by an on-screen pasteboard area, allowing bleeds, experimentation with items, and temporary storage before placing them on your page. You can create multiple page spreads on this pasteboard (up to a total of 48 inches in width), and then view them as separate pages or as spreads.

Moving around. You can scroll through your documents either one screen or a full page at a time. Scrolling is aided by a new "live" scroll feature. And you can zoom out to 10 percent and in to 400 percent with a tool or a keystroke. Also, your QuarkXPress document is now viewable in a

Thumbnail mode. In fact, you can even manipulate pages while in this mode. If you've got the FeaturesPlus XTension (included in the QuarkFreebies 3.0 package), you can use a grabber hand to move pages around inside the window.

New palettes. The Tool palette now floats on the screen so that you can move it to suit your needs (owners of large screens can breathe a collective sigh of relief). The new Measurements palette is a stunner. It shows you relevant information about the text and picture boxes you've selected, including the items that are inside those boxes. Not only can you see this information, but you can alter it quickly and on the fly. Another built-in floating palette is the Document Layout palette, which allows you to add, delete, and move pages by dragging icons around—and also to assign master pages.

QuarkXPress 3.1 includes three additional palettes: Colors, Trap Information, and Style Sheets. Plus, several add-on XTensions add palettes to QuarkXPress's interface.

Libraries. Imagine meticulously labelled filing cabinets and storage trays right on your Macintosh screen—in fact, right next to your QuarkXPress document window. These are the QuarkXPress Libraries. You can use them to archive graphics and text boxes in palettes with WYSIWYG, scrollable views. Imagine just dragging library items to your document and back. Imagine being able to create as many libraries as you want, name them whatever you want, put up to 2,000 items in each, and have up to seven open at a time.

New Tools

While two tools were dropped from the Tool palette (the arrow making tools), several others appeared.

- The Zoom tool takes a place on the Tool palette, though it's more easily accessed through a keystroke.

- The Rotation tool lets you rotate text and picture boxes with great precision.

- The Polygon Picture Box tool lets you create picture boxes or graphic elements of any shape and complexity.

You can also use some "hidden" tools. For example, the arrow keys on your keyboard nudge items around in 1- or .1-point increments. The Control key is a quick route to zooming in and out of specific areas. And double-clicking with the mouse can take you to the Text or Picture Box Specifications dialog boxes or even to the Tool Preferences dialog box where you can set your own parameters for how the tools work.

Preferences

Besides setting preferences for tools, you now have more options available via new Preferences submenus. These options include a Typographic Preferences dialog box, a General Preferences dialog box, and—in version 3.1—an Application Preferences dialog box. These let you set many new defaults, such as automatic picture importing and picture greeking, and even items as esoteric as your screen scrolling speed.

One newsworthy fact that should have a warming effect on anyone who had to deal with parent and child boxes in the past is that QuarkXPress has made them optional. Yes, you can still have them if you want to, and for some purposes you will. It was never a bad idea. What was bad was that you couldn't turn the relationship constraints on and off. Now you can.

Numerical Specs

QuarkXPress has always been known for its precision. Now Quark has gone a step further and implemented unheard of measurement accuracy: almost every measurement can be specified to the thousandth (.001) of a point or the hundredth (.01) of a degree.

You can also type in values as equations in multiple measurement methods. For example, you can type "4p + .5"" as a single expression rather than try to convert inches to picas or vice versa.

Page Items

At every QuarkXPress 3 demo we've seen, the item and page manipulation features have elicited the most applause and gasps. First of all, you can now drag items across page boundaries. Secondly, you can drag whole pages around within a document. Thirdly, you can drag copies of pages or items from one document to another. Cutting and pasting are all very well and good, but this is truly interactive design.

Also well-implemented is the Space/Align Items dialog box, which lets you automatically align objects by their left sides, right sides, tops, bottoms, or centers, either vertically or horizontally. This alignment and distribution can be specified by a measurement value or a percentage of the original spacing.

You can now not only multiple-select items by Shift-clicking or by dragging a *marquee* (a square selection area denoted by a moving dotted line), but you can also group those items together. And once they're grouped, you can still modify each item separately if you want.

Objects such as text boxes, picture boxes, and rules can now have preferences "attached" to them. For example, you can specify that every text box you create will be transparent and surrounded by a 2-point frame.

Rotation

Text and picture boxes can be rotated to any degree. The text in the text boxes remains WYSIWYG and fully editable at all times. The pictures are also fully editable, just as they are in their nonrotated form. Lines can also be rotated from several points, including their start, end, or center-point.

▼▼

Document Construction

Making and editing your pages has never been easier. Quark has refined some clunky areas—such as the old "default pages"—making them smooth and effective.

Master Pages

What were "default pages" have now been revamped and renamed "master pages." Not only can you have up to 127 different master pages, accessible at the click of a mouse, but any changes you make to your master pages can be retroactively applied to the pages in your document. We get heart palpitations every time we think of those days when we manually scrolled through documents, making some minor change. Oy.

Multipage Spreads

Need to throw a quick three-page spread together in the middle of your magazine? It's just an icon's drag away. Multipage spreads can be enormous, containing anywhere from 2 to 48 pages.

▼▼

Text and Typography

Want to work with text? QuarkXPress's text handling has been streamlined to make typing and manipulating text as speedy as possible. QuarkXPress has also gone a step further in its finding, changing, and spelling features, allowing you to search a whole document rather than just a specific story. For example, you can now search for the word "brilliant" in 18-point Bookman Italic anywhere in your document.

When it comes to styling your text, QuarkXPress has taken several steps to add functionality and increase efficiency. Also, some long-awaited features such as vertical justification and automatic drop caps make their Macintosh debut in version 3.

Typographic Preferences and Measurements

We mentioned the Typographic Preferences dialog box. This is where you can specify how QuarkXPress builds its super- and subscript, small caps, and superior characters. The baseline grid, automatic leading, and automatic kerning controls also appear here.

And when we said above that you can enter measurements in the thousandth of any unit, that includes a thousandth of a kern/track unit, which are each $\frac{1}{200}$ of an em. Thus, kerning and tracking measurements are now applicable to the twenty-thousandths (.00005) of an em. You can specify point size and leading in .001-point increments (a favorite saying around here is, "Why would anyone want to do that?").

Special Characters

Three new special characters were added to QuarkXPress's line-up: the Indent Here, Discretionary New Line, and the Nonbreaking Em Dash. The Indent Here promises to be the hot item of the week. With it you can make text flow in ways you haven't even thought about yet.

Drop Caps

Someone finally brought automatic drop caps to the Macintosh. You can specify how many characters you want to drop and the number of lines you want them to fall, and QuarkXPress handles the alignment for you. Plus, they flow along with your text!

First Baseline Position

It's always nice to add a little precision here and there. Remember all the times you added 2-point blank lines and fiddled with weird leading just to move that first line around?

Now you can specify where you want the first line of a text box to fall.

Vertical Alignment and Justification

Before, you could only horizontally align paragraphs, making them left-aligned, right-aligned, centered, or justified. Well, now you can specify vertical alignment and justification as well within a text box. Text can flow from the top down (as usual), bottom up, center up and down, or be justified so that the first line falls at the top of the box, the last line at the bottom, and all the other lines evenly distribute between the two. Newspapers can rejoice over this one.

Widow and Orphan Control

Several new features aid in the elimination of widows and orphans from your documents. The first, the Keep with Next ¶ control, makes sure, as an example, that subheads stay with their subsequent paragraphs. Another, the Keep Lines Together feature, can help hold together an entire paragraph or a specified number of lines at a paragraph's beginning or end.

Copy Flow

QuarkXPress's Style Sheets feature has always taken full advantage of every available typographic control. Now you can import and export the full range of typographic attributes in an improved coded XPress Tags format so that you can work with QuarkXPress documents in any word processor or any computer system. We should also note that QuarkXPress has gotten better in how it handles styles and style sheets when working with text. It now works the way you'd want it to. Similarly, the Word 4.0 filter that was released with the Zapper 1.0 XTension is better than it was in the past.

▼ ▼

Pictures

We already mentioned that you can now create polygonal picture boxes, in addition to the oval and rectangular boxes that were in QuarkXPress version 2. But once you have the picture in the picture box, you can now do any number of new things to it.

Rotating and Skewing

Not only can you rotate the picture box itself and keep the picture modifiable, but you can rotate the picture independently of the picture box. You can also apply a horizontal skew to imported pictures. Either of these features can be applied to the hundredth of a degree.

Picture Usage and Automatic Updating

You can get an up-to-date account of your imported linked pictures with the Picture Usage feature. Have they changed since you imported them? Are they missing? Where are they located on your page, and your disk? If the picture has changed you can tell QuarkXPress to re-import it. You can also tell QuarkXPress to automatically re-import all pictures that have changed every time you open your document.

Picture Greeking

Now you don't have to wait for all those pictures to redraw while you scroll across the page. Instead, you can greek all pictures, making them gray boxes. Selecting the picture brings it back to life.

Save Page as EPS

This isn't really a feature about pictures as much as a feature that lets you make your QuarkXPress page into a picture. You can create an Encapsulated PostScript (EPS) document for any page in your file, specifying how large the EPS image should be and whether it should have a color or black-and-white PICT representation.

▼▼▼▼▼▼▼▼▼▼▼▼▼▼▼▼▼▼▼▼▼▼▼▼▼▼▼▼▼▼▼▼▼▼▼▼▼

Where Text Meets Graphics

It's a precarious area, where text meets graphics. But this is where QuarkXPress is made to work best. Quark has implemented several new features here, including anchored graphics and rules. They've also modified the text runaround feature to give you considerably more control over where text can and should flow.

Text Wrap

You won't see the Transparent or Runaround check boxes in any specifications dialog boxes anymore. The Transparent check box has been replaced by a more powerful Background color pop-up menu, and now text runaround has a Runaround Specifications dialog box of its very own. Text runaround can now be set to "None" (no runaround), "Item" (wrap around the box), "Auto Image" (wrap around the picture), and "Manual Image" (where you can set your own runaround by manipulating boundary lines). If you choose the Item runaround, you can now set a different text outset value for each of an item's four sides. You can also make text run inside a box (including a polygon) by choosing the Invert feature.

Anchored Elements

Inline graphics are finally here with the inclusion of anchored boxes and rules. You can copy and paste either text or picture boxes directly into text. This means they will flow along with body copy as you edit it or make changes to the page geometry.

Also, text paragraphs can be defined with rules above or below. These rules likewise flow along with the text. Plus, you can specify what kind of rules they are, and where QuarkXPress should place them.

Color

QuarkXPress has always been a leader in the field of color publishing. Now it adds built-in trapping to its list of abilities. You can specify color pairs to overprint, knock out, or trap using either a specific value or QuarkXPress's built-in algorithm. In version 3.1 you can go a step farther and control trapping on an object-by-object level.

QuarkXPress was already able to make color separations from EPS files, but now it can properly separate spot colors, including Pantone colors from any FreeHand or Illustrator Encapsulated PostScript file. Version 3.1 adds Open Prepress Interface (OPI) commenting and the ability to directly separate CMYK TIFF files.

Printing

Three new features enhance your control over the printing process. The first, "Suppress Printout," lets you choose whether an item (any item, including pictures, rules, and so on) will print out or not. Secondly, QuarkXPress now lets you choose between two registration mark settings: Centered or Off Center.

Perhaps the greatest enhancement to QuarkXPress's printing feature is the Spreads function. This lets you print a multipage spread on one piece of film, with one set of registration marks rather than breaking it up into multiple pages.

▼ ▼

XTensions

QuarkXPress allows for add-on modules called XTensions that add functionality to the program. Over 200 developers around the world are creating custom XTensions for either commercial sales or private use. However, two XTensions are worth mentioning right now: Zapper 2.0A, and the Quark-Freebies XTensions package (including FeaturesPlus and Network Connection). These modules were created by Quark and released for free.

The Zapper XTension fixes bugs that were discovered in QuarkXPress after its initial release. Zapper 2.0A (released in late November, 1990) includes the bug fixes that were in versions 1.0 and 2.0, so you only need the newest version. The Freebies 3.0 package includes seven incredibly helpful tools and utilities, plus fifteen customizable program defaults. The following list includes many of the highlights of the package.

- Automatic fraction formatting

- Grabber hand for scrolling

- Manual kerning removal

- Word space control

- Window selector

- Value conversion palette

We have included information about these XTensions throughout the book. If you are using QuarkXPress 3.0, we think you'd be crazy not to have them. If you've got version 3.1, don't bother with these—get the newest version.

The Freebies 3.1 features weren't finalized as of this writing, but we're sure there'll be even more cool stuff in it.

▼ ▼

Requirements

To take advantage of all these great new features in Quark-XPress, you need, at a minimum, a Macintosh IIfx with 32 megabytes of RAM, a 300-megabyte hard disk drive, twin removable hard drives, a 600-megabyte read/write optical drive and 2-gigabyte DAT tape storage system for secondary backup, a 32-bit color drum scanner, a high-res imagesetter with the new PostScript Level II RIP, a Printware LQ 1200-by-600-dpi laser (for rough comps), a QMS ColorScript thermal transfer printer, a 21-inch color monitor with 24-bit video and graphics accelerator cards, and, of course, an NTSC video capture board and genlock control panel.

Just kidding! All you really need is a Mac Plus system. But, as few things are more frustrating than being all psyched up to start something only to discover that you can't, for lack of an essential component, here is a résumé of the components you need to know about.

Hardware and System Software

QuarkXPress 3 will run on the Macintosh Plus—and any Mac subsequently released—which has 1 megabyte of RAM, a hard disk, and Apple's system software version 6.0 or later. Some features of QuarkXPress 3.1 are only available under System 7 or higher. No matter your Mac model, two megabytes of RAM is *highly* recommended. Otherwise, MultiFinder operation will be impossible, performance will suffer greatly, and you will be limited in your use of utility programs (inits, cdevs, and DAs), some of which can seem practically indispensable once you've employed them.

QuarkXPress will also run on the older Macs (the 128K and 512K models of 1984–1986) that have been upgraded to contain the 1 megabyte of RAM and 128K ROMs that became standard-issue with the Mac Plus. These older Macs must also be fitted with an 800K floppy disk drive, and a SCSI (Small Computer Systems Interface, pronounced "scuzzy") port for attaching a hard disk.

But let's be honest: we really can't recommend using QuarkXPress to its fullest on any Macintosh model under an SE/30 (unless you have an accelerator board). We should know. Keith uses a Mac Plus, and David owns an SE. You can do everything in this book on these models, most of the time even faster than you could with older versions of QuarkXPress. But the handling of color is, of course, very limited (even more so because QuarkXPress doesn't presently dither colors to grays). And most features work much more efficiently on faster Mac models than they do on the 68000-based machines.

Hard Disks

The Iron Law of Hard Disk Storage is that your needs expand to equal and then exceed the storage capacity available. Get the biggest hard disk you can. If you think you'll never need more than 40 megabytes of storage, then get double that. You may be sorry later if you don't.

Random Access Memory

RAM is good. Put as much into your computer as you possibly can afford. For a Mac Plus, SE, or upgraded early model, the limit is 4 megabytes. Other models can handle up to eight megs. If you're doing serious publishing, chances are you'll want to run QuarkXPress in MultiFinder along with several other applications. You'll want the extra RAM to move around smoothly when you have those programs open along with much-needed cdevs and inits such as ATM and Boomerang.

▼ ▼

Tip: Updating QuarkXPress. Quark sends out two versions of its upgrade packages: the Installer and the Updater. The Installer is made for people who purchase new versions. The Updater will upgrade an older version to 3.0, 3.1, or 3.2. The Updater requires that you have a copy of the older version present on your hard disk to update.

But what if you need to re-install your copy at some point due to a hard disk failure or some other obscure reason? Do you need to re-install version 2.12 and then update it? No. Just hold down the Option key before you click on the OK button (see Figure I-1). This installs a copy without an older version having to be around.

Figure I-1
Installing with
an updater

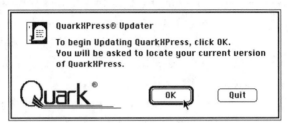

Hold down Option while clicking OK to install without having an older version on disk.

▼ ▼

Tip: Installing Zappers. As we mentioned above, Quark has released three Zappers as of this writing that modify your copy of QuarkXPress 3.0, getting rid of stray bugs (anomalies). Zappers may be available for version 3.1, too.

Installing a Zapper is easy; just drag it into the same folder as your copy of QuarkXPress and then launch QuarkXPress. As soon as the program is fully launched, the Zapper is finished with its work. You can then throw it away (though we suggest you keep it around on a floppy disk, just in case you need to use it again).

Some people (including some at Quark tech support) think that it's best to use the Zapper on a new, clean, never-been-used copy of QuarkXPress. We don't know if it's true or not, but we pass the suggestion on to you. We've had no problems ourselves, but if you do, try trashing your copy of QuarkXPress, re-installing the program (see "Tip: Updating QuarkXPress," above), and then zapping that version.

You can tell if your copy has been zapped by holding down the Option key while selecting "About QuarkXPress" from the Apple menu (see Figure I-2). A new copy of QuarkXPress displays "Subversion: 0." Zapper 1.0 changes it to "Subversion: 1," and Zapper 2.0A changes it to "Subversion: 3." If you're using QuarkXPress 3.0, you only need Zapper 2.0A (it fixes everything that Zapper 1.0 and 2.0 do, plus some).

Figure I-2
About QuarkXPress
Environment

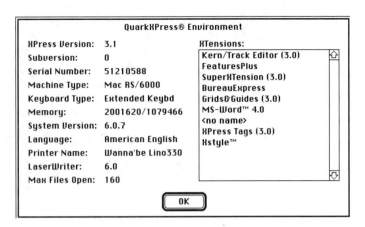

QuarkXPress® Environment

XPress Version:	3.1	XTensions:
Subversion:	0	Kern/Track Editor (3.0)
Serial Number:	51210588	FeaturesPlus
Machine Type:	Mac RS/6000	SuperXTension (3.0)
Keyboard Type:	Extended Keybd	BureauExpress
Memory:	2001620/1079466	Grids&Guides (3.0)
System Version:	6.0.7	MS-Word™ 4.0
Language:	American English	<no name>
Printer Name:	Wanna'be Lino330	XPress Tags (3.0)
LaserWriter:	6.0	Xstyle™
Max Files Open:	160	

OK

▼ ▼

QuarkXPress and You

Version 3 of QuarkXPress is clearly a pretty impressive package. But don't let it intimidate you. Remember, QuarkXPress is not only a machete, it's a Swiss Army machete. If you want to use it for writing letters home, you can do it. If you want to create glossy four-color magazines, you can do that too. The tool is powerful enough to get the job done, but sometimes—if you're trying to get through that Amazon jungle—you need to wield your machete accurately and efficiently.

Let's look at how it's done.

CHAPTER 1

STRUCTURE AND INTERFACE

Who ever thought that something called a "gooey" would ever be so important to the way we use a computer? While most of the world clutched their crib sheets to remember "how-to" keyboard codes for saving a document, moving to the end of a line, or drawing a box, a few visionary researchers came upon a simple idea: a *graphical user interface*, or GUI ("gooey"). "Why not," these researchers asked, "make using a computer more intuitive?" These researchers developed the underpinnings of the Macintosh GUI, which, in turn, laid the way for desktop publishing to take off.

The basics of the Macintosh GUI are simple: create an environment in which somebody can get the most out of a computer without having to remember too much, or even think too much in order to get the job done. The GUI comes between the person using the computer and the computer itself. For example, when you want to move a file from one disk to another, you click on it and drag it across the screen. The GUI handles all the internal computer stuff for you.

When you work with QuarkXPress, you work with the Macintosh GUI. You don't have to remember long codes or read a computer language, or even understand what's going on behind the scenes. We must say that it's been our experience that the more you know about how computers work, the better you can use them. However, this book is not meant for programmers. This book, like QuarkXPress, is—to steal a line from Apple—"for the rest of us."

We hear mumbling in the halls, "Who cares about gooey users and interfaces; we just want to use the program." Well, hold on; you can't tell the players without a program, and you can't effectively use QuarkXPress without understanding how it relates to you. So, we'll be the emcee and introduce the players: the members of the QuarkXPress interface.

▼ ▼

The Files

When you take QuarkXPress out of the package, you're faced with six disks. If you're like us, you bypass the manual entirely and just start shoving disks into the computer to see what there is to see. We suggest starting with Disk 1. Just put it in and double-click on the only file on that disk. If this is an update for an earlier version of QuarkXPress, the file on Disk 1 is probably an updater program (see "Tip: Updating QuarkXPress" in the Introduction). If this is a new purchase, the file is probably the QuarkXPress Installer. Both of these programs accomplish the same thing: they put QuarkXPress 3 onto your hard disk.

Registration

When you first install QuarkXPress, you are required to fill out a survey. The information you provide is saved onto a registration disk that you send back to Quark. There were myths going around saying Quark was secretly saving all sorts of other information on this disk, including what software you use and so on. This is not true. The registration disk *does* take one piece of information with it that it doesn't ask you for: your system configuration (what Macintosh model you use, what system, and so on). Theoretically, this information could help the people in technical support, should you ever talk to them about a problem.

Other Files

When the Installer or Updater is done, you will find a slew of files on your hard disk. These include several files for getting text from word processors, a dictionary, and several other files that help QuarkXPress do its business. Figure 1-1 shows a folder with all of Quark's programs and add-ons in it.

Figure 1-1
Our QuarkXPress folder

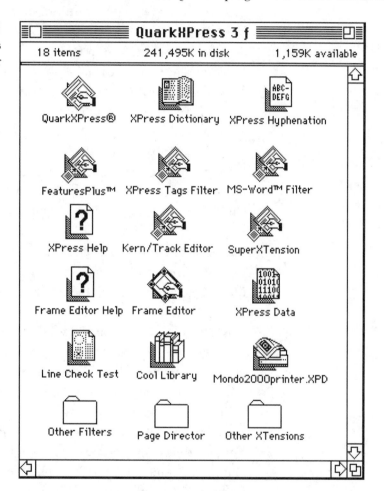

If you are new to QuarkXPress, you probably want to work through Quark's tutorials and look at their sample files. These supplemental materials comprise the two last disks in the package. Quark doesn't install them for you, so if you want to copy them to your hard disk, you must do it yourself by dragging them across from the original disks.

▼ ▼

Tip: Clean up Your Folder. Unless you have and use more software than we do (which is hard to imagine), you don't need all those files. We never seem to have enough room on our hard disks, so we have gotten in the habit of "throwing away" any files that we don't need. If you're never going to use the Frame Editor (we can't think of many reasons why you'd want to; it lets you create bitmapped frames), just throw it away, along with its help folder. If you only use Microsoft Word as your text editor, go ahead and throw away the MacWrite, WordPerfect, WriteNow, and MS-Works text filters. If you ever need to get them back, you'll find them on Program Disk 3 in the installation package.

However, if you really don't want to throw out those files, at least put the ones you don't use in the Other Filters folder. The more supplementary files you have floating around in QuarkXPress's folder, the longer QuarkXPress takes to launch.

▼ ▼

Tip: Where To Put All Those Files. Just a quick digression on the topic of hard disk management. Apparently, one of the most difficult techniques for Macintosh users to understand and control is the effective management of files on their hard disks. Now, we know that *you* wouldn't do something like this, but there are those who just toss their files and applications all over their hard disks, sometimes into folders and sometimes not. They are making their lives hard for themselves.

The Macintosh's folder system is designed to make life easy for you. We like to keep one folder called "Quark Folder" that contains the actual QuarkXPress application and all the filters and supplemental files we need. We have a folder inside of that one for keeping extra add-on modules and filters that we sometimes need. Then, in a different folder from the Quark Folder, we keep our QuarkXPress documents (usually a specific folder for each project we're working on).

If you aren't familiar with folders and how they work, we heartily suggest you look into the matter (see "File Management," below). You may not self-actualize from using folders well, but your life is sure to be the better for it.

▼ ▼

Faith

Just to be honest with you, there's almost no way to explain one feature in QuarkXPress without explaining all the rest at the same time. But that would make for a pretty confusing book. Instead, we're asking you to take minor leaps of faith along the path of reading this chapter. If we mention a term or function you don't understand, trust us that we'll explain it further in later chapters. If you are able to do that you will find that what we are discussing all makes sense. For example, we're not going to talk about the details of creating a new document until the next chapter, *Document Construction*. But since we need to talk about working with documents now, we ask you to trust us while we go over the details of opening, closing, and saving your files.

▼ ▼

File Management

Getting a good grasp on file management is essential to working most efficiently and happily with QuarkXPress. When we talk about file management with QuarkXPress, we are talking primarily about opening, closing, and saving your documents. These are pretty basic concepts, so if you've used other Macintosh programs you should feel right at home with it. If you haven't used a Macintosh before, you're soon to learn a great way of organizing computer files.

Opening Documents

Remember that QuarkXPress is not the same as your document itself. There is the program—QuarkXPress—and then there are files that you create with QuarkXPress. We won't talk in depth about creating new files until Chapter 2, *Docu-*

ment Construction. However, there are several QuarkXPress documents that are available to be opened on the Tutorial and Sample disks.

There are two ways to open an existing QuarkXPress document. If you're not in QuarkXPress, you can double-click on the document's icon, which launches QuarkXPress and opens the file. If you are in QuarkXPress, you can select Open from the File menu (or type Command-O). QuarkXPress then asks you if you want to view either documents, or templates—or both ("All Types"). We discuss templates and their function in "Saving Your Document," below.

▼ ▼

Tip: Launching QuarkXPress. When you launch QuarkXPress (double-click on the QuarkXPress icon) the program performs all sorts of operations while it's loading. For example, it figures out what fonts are in the system and which XTensions are available for its use. While it's doing all this, you don't see too much happening on the screen. You know that the computer is ready to go when you see QuarkXPress's menu bar across the top of the screen and the Tool and Measurements palettes appear.

▼ ▼

Closing Documents

After you have finished working on a document, you must close it. You have three choices for closing a document: clicking the close box in the upper-left corner of the document window, choosing Close from the File menu, or selecting Quit from the same menu. This last choice not only closes the file, but it also quits QuarkXPress. If changes have been made to the document since the last time you saved it, you'll see an alert box asking you if you want to save those changes.

Saving Your Document

Until you save your document to a disk, it exists only in the computer's temporary memory (called RAM), ready to disappear forever in the event of a power disruption or system crash. You should save any new document as soon as it opens, and make frequent saves during your work session. All it takes is Command-S. We suggest developing it into a nervous tic. We cannot tell you how many times our clients and we have lost hours of work because we didn't save frequently enough. David even made a little sign to post above his computer that said, "Save Every 10 Minutes."

Saving your document is so important, Quark gave you two different items on the File menu to do it: Save and Save As.

Save As. Selecting Save As from the file menu (or typing Command-Option-S), lets you save the document you're working on under a different name. For example, David often saves different versions of a document with each version number attached. The first one might be called "Brochure 1.1," the next "Brochure 1.2," and so on. Whenever he decides to create a new version, he chooses Save As from the File menu, which brings up the Save As dialog box (see Figure 1-2). He types in a file name (or edits the one that's there), then clicks on the Save button to save it to disk. If you decide to do this, remember to delete earlier versions as soon as you decide you don't need them anymore, or else your hard disk will be so full, it'll burst at the seams.

Like we said above, file management is an issue that too many people don't seem to "get." The Save As dialog box is a key ingredient in file management. The important issue here is that your document is saved to whatever folder is open in the Save As dialog box. If you want your document saved in a folder called Current Jobs, you must navigate your way to that folder. You have a few tools at your disposal for this. Table 1-1 shows several mouse and keyboard shortcuts.

Save. If you want to save your document with the same name that it already has, you can select Save from the File menu (or type Command-S). If you haven't yet saved your document, and it is unnamed, selecting Save automatically reverts to the Save As function.

Figure 1-2
The Save As dialog box

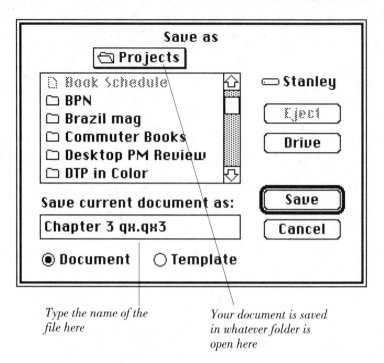

Type the name of the file here

Your document is saved in whatever folder is open here

Table 1-1
Navigating through the high seas

Do this...	To get here...
Up arrow	Move one item up on the displayed files list
Down arrow	Move one item down
Command-Up arrow	Move one folder "up"
Double-click	Open this folder
Enter or Return	When a folder is highlighted, open this folder; if no folder is highlighted, Save here

Templates

The concept of templates seems—to some people—shrouded in more mystery than the Druids of old. Here's an area that seems complicated because people make it complicated. But it's not. Really.

You have the choice of saving your document as a template when you're in the Save As dialog box. When a file is saved as a template, nothing changes except that you cannot accidentally save over it. For example, let's say you create a document and save it as a normal document called "Newsletter Template." Then, a couple of days later you go back into the document and create the newsletter: you make changes, flow text in, and place pictures. You then select Save from the File menu. The file, "Newsletter Template," is modified with the changes you made, and there is no way to "go back" to the original untouched file.

Okay, let's say you create that same "Newsletter Template," then save it as a template by selecting "Template" in the Save As dialog box. Then, when you make changes to that document and select Save from the File menu, QuarkXPress doesn't automatically erase the old file and replace it with the new one like it did above. Instead, it gives you the Save As dialog box and let's you choose a different name. In version 3.2 templates open as Untitled documents.

▼ ▼

Tip: Resaving Templates. If QuarkXPress gives you the Save As dialog box when you try to Save a document specified as a template, how can you change the template itself? Simple. You can replace the old template with a new one by giving it exactly the same name in the Save As dialog box (don't forget to select the Template button if you still want it to be a template).

▼ ▼

Revert To Saved

As we said above, no changes are permanent until you save them. If you want to discard all changes made to a document since the last save, you can do it by closing the document (choose Close from the File menu) and telling QuarkXPress that you don't want to save the changes. Or, if you wish to continue working on it without interruption, choose "Revert to Saved" from the File menu. For example, if—in the name of improvement—you have managed to mess up your document beyond redemption, you can revert to the version that you last saved.

Multiple Documents

QuarkXPress lets you open up to seven documents at a time, each in a separate window. However, the actual number and size of documents you can have open depends on both the amount of memory available and the number of files open (QuarkXPress internally opens more files than just the documents you work with; see "Tip: Too Many Files Open," below).

Window Management. In the olden days, it was a pain to move between one open document and another, especially if you had a small Mac screen. For those of you who don't know what we're talking about, the problem arises from having several windows open on your screen, but not being able to select them, because they're all stacked up on top of one another. The FeaturesPlus XTension in the QuarkFreebies 3.0 package, which you have no excuse not to own since it's free, finally provides a great way to manage multiple open documents. When that XTension is in your QuarkXPress folder, QuarkXPress adds a Windows submenu item at the bottom of the View menu (see Figure 1-3). This submenu lists the titles of each open document. To activate one document's window, select it from the list.

Figure 1-3
The Window submenu from the QuarkFreebies 3.0 package

The Window submenu has a default setting that makes it show the list of open windows in the order that they appear on the screen ("Front-To-Back Order"). That is, if you have four documents open, the Window submenu shows the "backmost" window at the bottom of the list, the "frontmost" window at the top of the list, and so on. You can switch this to an alphabetical listing by selecting "Alphabetical Order" from the submenu.

▼ ▼

Tip: Too Many Files Open. The Macintosh system lets you have a limited number of files open at one time. This number was determined for the original Finder, and—for some obscure reason—was never raised when MultiFinder was created. Obviously, the more applications you have running at a time, the more files you have open. This is especially true because many applications open "invisible" files that you don't ordinarily know about. For example, QuarkXPress opens one file for each XTension you have available in your QuarkXPress folder, plus a file for the XPress Dictionary, XPress Hyphenation, and so on.

When we ran two or more applications at a time, we found ourselves staring at warning dialog boxes that said we couldn't open another file, and listening to mysterious beeps when we tried to open a DA from the Apple menu. Then we learned that we could use a utility such as Fedit (or the option in Suitcase II) to increase Apple's limit. Any utility that lets you alter the boot blocks of your system should work fine. This is a very easy process. We set ours to 40 (which, for some technical reasons, actually means that we can have up to 200 files open), and we've never had another problem of this sort.

▼ ▼

Locking Documents

There's one final method of insuring against undesirable changes to documents: locking the file. This is a function of the Macintosh system rather than QuarkXPress. You can lock an entire document so that changes will never be saved by selecting the document while in the Finder (after quitting from QuarkXPress), choosing "Get Info" from the File menu, and clicking the Locked check box in the upper-right corner of the Get Info dialog box. Another way to lock a file is by using CE Software's DiskTop DA. You can select a file, type Command-I (for "Get Info"), then select the Locked button. This is handy for locking documents on the fly.

If you open a locked QuarkXPress document by double-clicking on it, you are told that this is a locked file and that you won't be able to save your changes. If you open the locked file from within QuarkXPress and later try to save it, you get a nasty, "Can't Save to Disk" error. The only way to save a locked file is to perform a Save As under a different name.

QuarkXPress's Interface

While working in QuarkXPress, you have access to its powerful tools and features through several areas: menus, palettes, dialog boxes, and keystrokes. Let's look carefully at each of these methods and how you can use them.

Menus

There are several conventions used with menus. One is the hierarchical menu, which we often call a submenu. These allow multiple items to be, literally, offshoots of the primary menu item. Another convention is the check mark. A check mark next to a menu item shows that feature is enabled or activated. Selecting that item turns the feature off, or disables it, and the check mark goes away. Figure 1-4 shows these two menu conventions. Other conventions are discussed as needed throughout the book.

We don't need to talk a great deal about menus and what's on them here, because we discuss their contents throughout the book. However, you should note that certain types of features fall under particular menus. Let's go through a quick rundown.

File. Items on the File menu relate to disk files (entire documents). Commands to open, save, and print disk files are located here.

Edit. The Edit menu contains features for changing items within QuarkXPress. The last section of the Edit menu contains features to edit internal defaults on a document or application-wide level, such as the color palette, the text style sheets, and specifications for each tool on the Tool palette (see "Tool Palette," below).

Style. The Style menu changes depending on what item you have selected on your document page. Selecting a picture box results in one Style menu, selecting a text box results in a different one, and rules (lines) result in a third menu. The items on the Style menu enable you to change specific style attributes of the selected item.

Item. Whereas the Style menu contains commands for changing the contents of a picture or text box, the Item menu's commands change the box or rule itself. For example, changing the style of a picture box's contents might involve changing the shade of a picture. Changing an attribute of the box itself may involve changing the frame thickness of the picture box.

Page. The Page menu is devoted to entire pages in your document. Controls for master pages (see Chapter 2, *Document Construction*) are located here, as well as several features for adding, deleting, and navigating among pages.

View. Almost every feature based on what you see and how you see it is located in the View menu. This menu also includes several other items, such as Show Guides, that involve QuarkXPress's interface. We'll be discussing these later in this chapter.

Utilities. This menu is, in many ways, a catch-all that contains assorted goodies for helping make pages. Spell-checking, libraries, and so forth are kept here. Also, most XTensions add items to the Utilities menu, so the more XTensions you have, the longer this menu is.

Figure 1-4
Menu conventions

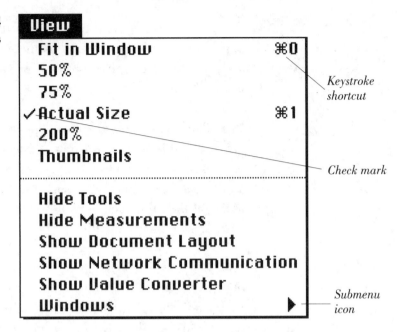

Keystroke shortcut

Check mark

Submenu icon

▼ ▼

Tip: Adding Your Own Keystrokes. This is *not* a paid political announcement. We love QuicKeys. To be fair, there are other macro-makers around, but we know QuicKeys the best and we're continually amazed at what it helps us do. For those who don't know what making macros is all about, let us elucidate. Macros are miniprograms that you can build that tell the computer to do something.

For example, if you use the Move to Front function from the Item menu often (we do), you may want to create a macro that selects "Move to Front" for you in a keystroke rather than having to pull down a menu yourself. We have one of these: Command-Control-F. This saves more time than you can imagine (or, if it doesn't, it at least feels like it does—which is just as good).

Macros don't have to be as simple as just selecting a menu item, though. For example, one macro we have selects a paragraph, applies a style sheet, puts an extra rule above the paragraph, and places a special character after the paragraph's last word. One keystroke sets the macro off and running.

On the simpler side of macros, there's another way to create keystroke "macros" for selecting menu items: ResEdit. David likes this method even more than QuicKeys because, when it comes to QuarkXPress, he's a tweak and likes to get into the guts of the program. ResEdit is a free program published by Apple that lets you search through and edit a file's resource fork. Most applications on the Macintosh have a resource fork that holds information about its menus, along with lots of other stuff. Let's say you wanted to add a keystroke that selects the Section feature from the Page menu.

1. Make a copy of QuarkXPress to work on (playing around in your only copy is beyond foolish).

2. Launch ResEdit. You should not currently be running QuarkXPress when you do this.

3. Open the QuarkXPress application. You may have to open several folders to get to it. When it's open, you can see a list of every resource type (they all have four-letter names).

4. Double-click on the MENU resource type from the list.

5. Find the resource that controls the menu that you want to change. This is not easy, because the menus are numbered rather than named. It's a game of trial and error. In the case of the Page menu, it's resource 1007.

6. ResEdit shows you the menu in a scrolling list (see Figure 1-5). Select the item from the menu (in this case "Section"). Then highlight the area labeled, "Cmd."

7. Type the key that you want to assign to that item. Don't hold down the Command key while you do this. Just the key. For example, if you want Command-8 to open the Section dialog box, just type 8.

8. Close that window (select Close from the File menu or type Command-W).

9. Quit ResEdit. If you are satisfied with your work, say

OK when it asks you if you want to save the changes you have made. If you don't like what you've done, click on No.

When you next run QuarkXPress, you can see the new keystroke on the menu.

This is an industrial strength tip, and is not to be fooled around with lightly. ResEdit can do wonders for seriously messing up your application and, possibly, your system. On the other hand, ResEdit lets you do things you could never do otherwise.

Figure 1-5
A QuarkXPress menu as shown by ResEdit. Your version of ResEdit may appear slightly differently.

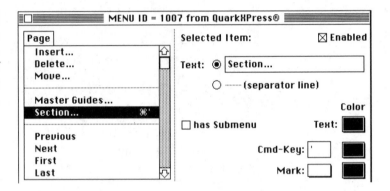

Palettes

There is a radically new item in QuarkXPress's user interface that makes life extraordinarily better for anyone with a large screen monitor: functional palettes. The analogy to a painter's palette is helpful insofar as a palette contains a selection of usable and changeable items that you can put wherever suits you best. A left-handed painter may hold a paint palette in her right hand, while a short ambidextrous painter might place the palette on the floor. QuarkXPress has several palettes, each with a different function, that can be placed anywhere you like on the screen. They're additional windows on the screen that—although they can overlap one another—never go "behind" a document window. Because of this, we call them *floating* palettes.

You can manipulate palettes in the same manner as you would move a Macintosh window. For example, to move a palette, drag the window from the top, shaded area. To close a palette, click in the Close box in the upper-left corner. Two palettes we'll talk about (the Document Layout palette and the Libraries palette have "zoom" boxes in their upper-right corners. Click in them once and the palette expands; again, and it reduces in size.

QuarkXPress comes with four basic palettes: the Tool palette, the Measurements palette, the Document Layout palette, and the Libraries palette (see Figure 1-6). When you first launch QuarkXPress, you can see two of these four: the Tool palette and the Measurements palette. QuarkXPress remembers which palettes are open or closed and where the palette is placed, so the location and the status of palettes remain from when you quit to when you next start up.

For information about the three new palettes in version 3.1, see Appendix C.

Figure 1-6
QuarkXPress's four
basic palettes

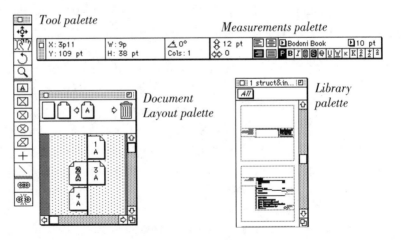

Let's take a look at each one of these palettes.

Tool palette. The Tool palette is the most elementary and functional of the palettes. There's not a lot you can do without it. Here you have the tools for making boxes in which you place your pictures and text, tools for rotating, tools for drawing lines, and tools for linking the text boxes together to allow the flow of text. Selecting a tool is easy: just click on it (see "Tip:

Keyboard Palettes," below). We won't go into each tool here, as we discuss them in "Using the Tools," later in this chapter.

Measurements palette. Like the Style menu, the Measurements palette is dynamic: it changes depending on what sort of item is selected on your document page. Text boxes have one type of Measurements palette, Picture boxes have a second type, and rules and lines have a third type (see Figure 1-7). Which tool from the Tool palette you have selected also has an effect on how the Measurements palette looks. The Measurements palette's purpose in life is to show you an item's vital statistics and save you a trip to the Style or Item menu for making changes to those page elements.

For example, if you select a text box, the Measurements palette shows the dimensions of the text box, the coordinate of its upper-left corner, the number of columns in the box, the rotation of the box, and the style, font, and size of the text you've selected in the box.

Not only does the Measurements palette display this information, but you can click on an item in the palette and change it. For example, if you want to rotate a picture box 10 degrees, you simply replace the "0" with "10" and then type either Return or Enter (pressing Return or Enter tells QuarkXPress that you've finished; it's like clicking on an OK button).

Note that the left half of a Measurements palette displays information about a page element (an "item"), and the right half displays information about the contents or the style of the item (see "Items and Contents," later in this chapter).

▼ ▼

Tip: Keyboard Palettes. You can access and select items on either the Tool palette or the Measurements palette by using keyboard commands. To select the next tool on the Tool palette (to move down one), type Command-Tab. To select the next higher tool, type Command-Shift-Tab. If you have closed the Tool palette, you can open it by entering either of these key commands.

You also can use the Tab key to move through the Measurements palette. You can jump to the first item on this

Figure 1-7

The Measurements palette changes depending on what type of page element you have selected

For text boxes

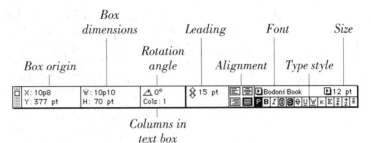

Columns in text box

For picture boxes

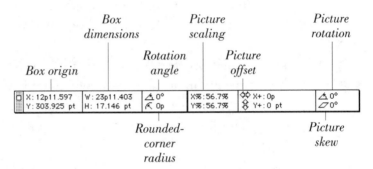

For lines (rules)

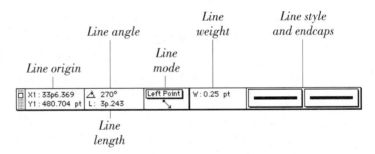

palette by entering Command-Option-M (this also opens the palette if it was closed).

David finds it much faster to toggle between items on the Tool palette using keystrokes, especially when moving between the Content tool and the Item tool. And he hardly ever uses the mouse to click in the Measurements palette, preferring to type a Command-Option-M, then tabbing through the items until he gets where he wants.

Document Layout palette. You can find the Document Layout palette by selecting "Show Document Layout" from the View menu. This palette displays a graphic representation of your document, page by page. When you first start using it, it's slightly weird, but the more you work with it, the more you realize how amazingly cool it is. We discuss the Document Layout palette in "Manipulating Your Document," later in this chapter, but—in a nutshell—you can use this palette for creating, deleting, and shuffling pages, assigning master pages, and creating multipage spreads. Generally, many of the functions of the Page menu can be performed by dragging icons in the Document Layout palette.

Library palette. Here's another QuarkXPress feature which we discuss in much greater detail later in this chapter (we're not trying to tease; we're just taking things one step at a time). The Library palette is a simple enough palette, but it has some very powerful uses. You can have more than one Library palette open at a time (each palette represents one Library file), and you are able to store up to 2,000 items in each library.

Dialog Boxes

You can perform almost every function in QuarkXPress with only the palettes and the menus. However, it is rarely efficient to work this way. Dialog boxes are areas in which you can usually change many specifications for an item at one time. For example, Figure 1-8 shows the Text Box Specifications dialog box. In this dialog box, you can modify any or every item quickly, then click on OK to make those changes take effect.

Here's a quick lesson in terminology, if you're unfamiliar with dialog boxes. The area in which you enter a value is called a *field*. Often times there are *check boxes* that can be set to on, off, or undefined. Many dialog boxes also contain *pop-up menus*, which act much like the menus at the top of the screen: just position the cursor on them, press the mouse button, and move the mouse upward or downward until you have selected the item you want. Then let go of the mouse button.

Figure 1-8
A typical dialog box

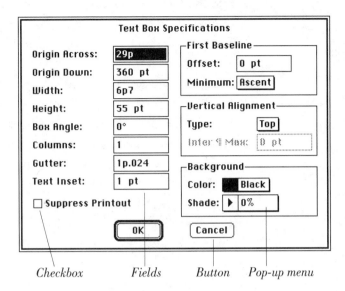

Checkbox   Fields   Button   Pop-up menu

Typically, dialog boxes have two buttons: OK and Cancel. Clicking on OK closes the dialog box and puts your changes into effect. Cancel closes the dialog box and ignores the changes you've made. Some dialog boxes have a Save option, which acts as OK. Other dialog boxes have an Apply button. Clicking on this button temporarily applies the settings you've made to the document so that you can see them. If you like what you see, you can then click OK. If you don't like it, you can usually type Command-Z to revert the dialog box back to the last setting. In any case, you can click on Cancel to rid yourself of the dialog box and the changes you've made, even after applying them.

▼ ▼

Tip: Pushing Your Buttons. Almost every button in Quark-XPress's dialog boxes can be replaced with a keystroke. The keystroke is usually the first letter in the button's name. For example, if a dialog box has Yes and No buttons, you can select them by typing Command-Y and Command-N. When you're checking the spelling of a story, you can select the Skip button by typing Command-S. Note that any button that is highlighted (has a darker border than a normal button) can be selected by typing Enter or Return (this is usually OK). Cancel is selected by typing Command-Period.

▼ ▼

Tip: Continuous Apply. As we said earlier, the Apply button temporarily applies the change you made in a dialog box. You can then decide whether you want to actually make that change, revert back, or cancel the operation entirely. Even though typing Command-A speeds up the process some, we often find it helpful to be in a Continuous Apply mode by typing Command-Option-A. Typing this highlights the Apply button (turns it black), as if you were holding the button down continually. Now, every change you make in the dialog box is immediately applied to your page item. You can still type Command-Z to undo the last change, or Command-Period to cancel the dialog box. To turn "Continual Apply" off, just type Command-Option-A again.

▼ ▼

Tip: Specifying Measurements. Unless you raise horses and measure everything in "hands," chances are that QuarkXPress and you share a common measurement system. QuarkXPress understands measurements in points, picas, inches, ciceros, centimeters, and millimeters. You can use these measurement units at any time, no matter what the default setting is (see "Changing Defaults," later in this chapter). Table 1-2 shows how to specify a value for each system.

You also can specify measurements with a plus or minus sign to build simple equations using one or more measurement units. For example, if a measurement was set to 10p, and you wanted to add 4cm, you could type 10p+4cm. Similarly, if you wanted to take away 1p2 (ever since calculators, our math skills have degenerated horribly), we could type 10p-1p2.

Table 1-2

Measurement systems

You can spec...	by typing...	For example...
points	pt or p	6pt or p6
picas	p	10p or 2p6 (2 picas, 6 points)
inches	"	6"
ciceros	c	2c or 6c3 (6 ciceros, 3 points)
centimeters	cm	3cm
millimeters	mm	210mm

▼ ▼

Using the Tools

Up to now, we have primarily talked about the general interface; this does this, that does that. Now our emphasis shifts toward the practical. The first step is learning about the tools on the Tool palette. If you used earlier versions of QuarkXPress, you'll note that the two arrow-making tools are missing from the lineup. Don't fear, they've been integrated with the normal line-making tools (which makes a lot more sense to us). There are three new tools that take their place, though: the Rotation tool, the Zoom tool, and the Polygon Picture Box tool. Let's look at each tool on the Tool palette in turn.

Items and Contents

If you only learn one thing from this chapter it should be the difference between items and contents. This is a concept that some people find difficult to understand, but it is really pretty simple. Moreover, the concept of items and contents is central to working efficiently in QuarkXPress.

Let's take it from the beginning. In order to put text on a page, you must place it in a text box. To put a graphic image on a page, you must place it in a picture box. Text boxes act as a sort of corral that holds all the words. There's almost no way a word can get outside the bounds of a text box. Picture boxes act as a sort of window through which you can see a picture. In both cases the content of the box is different from the box itself.

Boxes are *items*. What goes inside them is *content*. You can modify either one, but you need to use the correct tool at the correct time.

Item tool. The Item tool is the first tool on the Tool palette. It's used for selecting and moving items (picture and text boxes, rules, and so on). You can use the Item tool by either choosing it from the Tool palette or holding down the Command key while any other tool is selected (though you can't select or work with multiple items unless you actually have the Item tool selected). We discuss all the things you can do with items later in "Manipulating Items."

Content tool. The second tool on the Tool palette is the Content tool. This tool is used for adding, deleting, or modifying the contents of a text or picture box. Note that its palette icon consists of a text insert and a hand. When you have selected this tool from the Tool palette, QuarkXPress turns the cursor into one of these icons, depending on what sort of box you have highlighted (as we'll see in Chapter 6, *Pictures*, the hand is for moving images around within a picture box).

Text Boxes

In this chapter we're mostly talking about items, which we sometimes call page elements. The first tool we come to on the Tool palette that lets us make a page element is the Text Box tool. The method of creating text boxes is simple: choose the Text Box tool from the Tool palette, and then click and drag a text box. You can see exactly how large your text box is by watching the width and height values on the Measurements palette. Note that you can keep the text box a perfect square by holding down the Shift key while dragging.

Text boxes—as items—have five basic attributes: position, size, background color, columns, and text inset. They also have border or frame attributes, which we discuss later in this chapter.

Position and size. All boxes are positioned by their upper-left corner. This point is called their *origin*. The first two fields in the Text Specifications dialog box (select the box and type Command-M) and the text box Measurements palette are the "Origin Across" and the "Origin Down." The size of the box is then specified by its width and height (the distances to the right and down from the origin).

▼ ▼

Tip: Quick Accurate Boxes. Some people tend toward a visual approach to creating and sizing boxes in QuarkXPress, while others work with a more mathematical or coordinate-based method. Fortunately, both work equally as well. You can click and drag page elements out to the size you want them, if you prefer to make a decision based on seeing what it looks like.

Or, if you're working on a grid, you can draw a box to any size, and then go into the Measurements palette or Item Specifications dialog box to specify the origin coordinates, the width, and the height.

▼ ▼

Background color. The concept of transparency in earlier versions of QuarkXPress has gone the way of the wind. New to the scene is "Background Color." Every box can have a background color set to any color on the color palette (see Chapter 9, *Color*), or can have a background set to None. Any background color other than None can be set to a specific tint.

Note that 0 (zero) percent of a color is not transparent—it's opaque white. This background color reaches all the way to the inside edge of the frame around the box. There is a subtle distinction between going to the edge of the box and the edge of the frame: if you have specified a frame on a box, the background color only fills to the frame, rather than the edge of the box (see "Frames," later in this chapter). If you have not specified a frame around a box, however, then the background color fills the box up to the border.

Columns. While the last two items were applicable to both text and picture boxes, the columns attribute is text box-specific. Text boxes can be divided into a maximum of 30 columns. The size of each column is determined by the size of the *gutter* (blank space) between each column. You can set the gutter width only in the Text Box Specifications dialog box, although you can set the number of columns in either this dialog box or the Measurements palette.

Note that you cannot have columns that have negative widths. In other words, the number of columns you can have is determined by the gutter width. For example, if your gutter width is 1 pica and your text box is 20 picas, you cannot have more than 11 columns (that leaves only 9 picas for the columns; hardly enough for any text to fit on a line).

Text Inset. The last attribute particular to text boxes is "Text Inset." The Text Inset value determines how far your text is placed inside the four sides of the text box. For example, a Text Inset value of 0 (zero) places the text right up against the side of the text box. A text inset value of 3cm places the text no closer than 3 centimeters from the side of the box. The default setting is 1 point. We can't tell you why; we find it rather obnoxious. Later, in "Changing Defaults," we discuss how to change these default settings. We usually just change it to zero text inset. You can only specify the Text Inset value in the Text Box Specifications dialog box.

▼ ▼

Tip: That Ol' Specifications Dialog Box. We use the Specifications dialog boxes for picture boxes, text boxes, and rules so much that we're glad to have some variance in how we get to it. You can open a Specifications dialog box for a page element in three ways.

• Double-click on the page element using the Item tool (remember, you can hold down the Command key to temporarily work with the Item tool).

- Select the item with either the Content or the Item tool and type Command-M.

- Select the item with either the Content or the Item tool and choose "Modify" from the Item menu.

Once you're in the dialog box, you can tab through the fields to get to the value you want to change. After a while, you start to memorize how many tabs it takes to get to a field, and you can type Command-M, tab, tab, tab, tab, tab, enter the value, press Return, and be out of there before Quark-XPress has time to catch up with you. That's when you know you're becoming an XPress Demon.

▼ ▼

Picture Boxes

As we said above, picture boxes are made to hold pictures. That's part of the truth, but let's hold off on that subject for a bit. Chapter 6, *Pictures*, tells us all about importing pictures. QuarkXPress gives us four different tools for creating picture boxes. Each makes a differently shaped box: rectangles, rounded-corner rectangles, ovals, and polygons. Let's take a brief look at each of these and why you should use them.

Rectangular Picture Box tool. This is the basic, no frills picture box maker. As with the Text Box tool above, just click and drag a box to the size you want it. We use this box for 95 percent of the picture boxes we make.

Rounded-corner Picture Box tool. The Rounded-corner Picture Box tool makes rectangular picture boxes that have rounded corners. Is this of interest to you? Not to be biased, but some of the all-time worst designs that have come off a Macintosh use rounded-corner picture boxes. We really dislike them. But, then again, it's your design, and you can do what you like with it.

To be frank for a moment: this tool is redundant. Why? Any rectangular picture box can have rounded corners simply by an adjustment to the Corner Radius value in the Picture Box Specifications dialog box or the Measurements palette. Unless you use a lot of rounded-corner picture boxes (and if you do, we don't want to know about it), you probably could get by with just using the Rectangular Picture Box tool and adjusting the Corner Radius.

Oval Picture Box tool. When you need circles and ovals, the Oval Picture Box tool is the way to get them. Ovals are constrained to circles when you hold the Shift key down while dragging. Note that oval picture boxes are still defined by the rectangle that bounds them. That is, you modify an oval's shape by its height and width.

▼ ▼

Tip: Given a Radius of a Circle... Sometimes we find that we want to make a circle with a specific radius or diameter. Don't worry, you don't have to go back and relearn high-school geometry formulas. First, remember that a circle is as wide as it is tall. Then, remember that the diameter of a circle is its width (or height). The radius of a circle is half of its diameter. For example, if you need to make a circle with a radius of 2 inches, just drag out a circle picture box, and set its width and height to 4 inches (radius of 2×2 = a diameter of 4).

▼ ▼

Polygon Picture Box tool. This last feature is the newcomer of the bunch, showing up for the first time in version 3. And like many of the other new features in this version, this function is...Wow. The Polygon Picture Box tool lets you make a picture box in almost any shape you'd like. The key is that the shape must be made of only straight lines.

The basic method for creating this type of frame is to click on the Polygon Picture Box tool, click where you want your first point to be (it doesn't matter which corner of the frame you begin with), then keep clicking at successive corners to create the shape you want. You'll notice that when the mouse hovers over the first point on the line the cursor turns into a hollow circle. This indicates that it will close the path when you click and finish the polygon.

Polygonal picture boxes must have at least three points on them, but there's no limit that we can tell (and we've done some pretty complex picture boxes; see "Tip: Making Your Grayscale Picture Transparent" in Chapter 8, *Modifying Images*).

Once you have created a polygon, QuarkXPress places an invisible rectangular border around it. The corner handles of this border, like the bounding border of ovals, define the polygon's height and width. Whenever you select the polygonal picture box, you see these corner handles. You can use them to stretch the polygonal picture box, but not to reshape it. We cover reshaping and resizing polygons and other picture boxes in "Manipulating Items," later in this chapter.

Picture Box Attributes

Picture boxes are similar to text boxes in several ways. First, they are positioned according to their origin (upper-left corner of the box). Secondly, they are generally sized by their width and height. Thirdly, they have background color (see "Text Boxes," above, for a discussion of these three items). However, some picture boxes have two attributes that text boxes don't: Corner Radius and Suppress Picture Printout. We'll hold off on covering the latter until Chapter 6, *Pictures*.

The Corner Radius attribute is applicable to rectangular and rounded-corner rectangle picture boxes. We've already told you how we feel about rounded corners on picture boxes, but—just in case you still want to make them—you can use this value to set how rounded those corners should be. Literally, the "Corner Radius" defines the size of the radius of a circle tangent to the sides of the box (see Figure 1-9). You can change the corner radius of a rectangular picture box either in the Picture Box Specifications dialog box or in the Measurements palette.

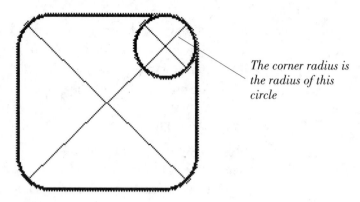

Figure 1-9
The Corner Radius
setting defines how
rounded the corners
should be

*The corner radius is
the radius of this
circle*

Transforming Picture Boxes

Once you have a picture box created, you can change it into another type of picture box by using the Picture Box Shape submenu under the Item menu (see Figure 1-10). For example, if you made a rectangular picture box on your page you could turn it into an oval by first selecting the picture box, and then selecting the oval picture box icon in the Picture Box Shape submenu.

Figure 1-10
Picture Box
Shape submenu

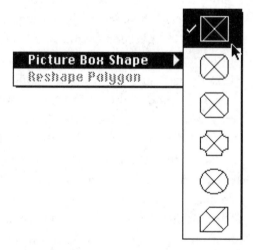

This submenu has two other preset picture boxes that you might find useful. One is a bevelled corner picture box, another is a photo-frame picture box. The "depth" of the bevel or the concave curve depends on the Corner Radius setting.

The last item on the Picture Box Shape submenu is an icon representing a polygonal picture box. When you select a picture box and then choose this last icon, the picture box does not change in any obvious way. However, this is an extremely useful technique for making slight modifications to a picture box as we'll see later when we discuss the Reshape Polygon feature.

Lines and Arrows

The Tool palette contains two tools to draw lines and arrows on your page. To be precise, you really only draw lines, but those lines can be in several styles and have arrowheads and tailfeathers. You can create these lines with any thickness between .001 and 504 points (that's a pretty thick line), and at any angle. The two tools are the Orthogonal Line tool and the Line tool.

Orthogonal Line tool. For those of you who aren't in arm's reach of a dictionary, *orthogonal* means that the lines you draw with this tool can only be horizontal or vertical. Drawing a line is easy: choose this tool from the Tool palette, then click and drag to where you want to go. This tool is somewhat redundant, insofar as you can constrain the movement of the Line tool orthogonally by holding down the Shift key. But, since most of the rules we make are horizontal or vertical, it's nice to have this option.

Line tool. The Line tool can make a line at any angle. If you hold down the Shift key while dragging out the line, you can constrain the line to 45 or 90 degrees. Don't worry if the line looks jaggy; that will smooth out when the file is printed.

Line Attributes

Once you have created a line, you can apply certain attributes to it, including line weight, style, endcaps, and color. Each of these can be specified in the Line Specifications dialog box. Several also can be specified in the Measurements palette.

Line weight. We always use the word "weight" rather than "width," which is what QuarkXPress calls the thickness of a line. The line weight is centered on the line. That is, if you specify a 6-point line, 3 points fall on one side of the line you drew, and 3 points fall on the other side. This value appears in both the Line Specifications dialog box and the Measurements palette. However, we never use mundane methods like that; instead, we type Command-Shift-\ (backslash) to bring up the Line Width dialog box (which, as we discuss later, you also can use for specifying type size). Table 1-3 shows several other ways to change a line's weight with keystrokes. Note that these are the same keystrokes as changing the size of type.

Table 1-3
Changing Line Weight

To change a line...	Type...
Increase weight by preset amount	Command-Shift-Period (>)
Increase weight by 1 point	Command-Shift-Option-Period (>)
Decrease weight by preset amount	Command-Shift-Comma (<)
Decrease weight by 1 point	Command-Shift-Option-Comma (<)

Color and shade. You can choose any color on your document's color palette (see Chapter 9, *Color*), then tint it to any value from 0 to 100 percent, in 1-percent increments (0 percent is white). This specification is only available in the Line Specifications dialog box.

Style and endcaps. Lines don't have to be boring; spice them up with a new style, or add endcaps to turn them into arrows. You can choose one of 11 different line styles and one of six endcap combinations by selecting them from two pop-up menus in either the Line Specifications dialog box or the Measurements palette (see Figure 1-11).

Figure 1-11
Line styles
and endcaps

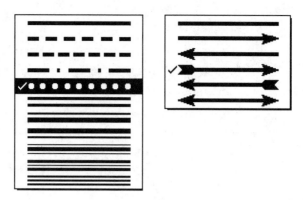

Six of the line styles are defined as multiple lines. The weight of each line of the group is determined by a ratio. For example, each line in the double line style is given a third of the total weight. So, if you specify the double line with a 12-point thickness, each black line is 4 points thick, and the white space between them is 4 points across.

Even though you have six to choose from, the endcap styles are limited: basically with arrowheads and tailfeathers or without them. Because QuarkXPress defines all its lines as going from left to right or top to bottom, you can control which side the arrow head should be on by choosing the proper endcap from the pop-up menu. For example, if your line was drawn from left to right, and you want the head of the arrow to be on the left end of the line, you should select an endcap that has the arrow pointing to the left.

Manipulating Items

Once you've created a page element (item) such as a picture box or a line, what can you do with it? A lot. In this section we talk about how to move, rotate, resize, reshape, lock, duplicate, and delete items. Remember that we're talking only about the items themselves here, so you need to select the items with the Item tool to perform most of these changes.

Moving Items

You can move an entire page element in several ways. First, by selecting the Item tool, then clicking on the object and dragging it. This sometimes gets tricky if you have many different overlapping objects on a page. For example, normally you can click anywhere within an empty picture box to select it. However, if you're trying to select a picture box that has a picture in it, you must click on the picture itself.

The second method for moving an item is by changing its origin coordinates. We find this method especially useful if we need to move the item a specific amount. For example, let's say we have a text box with its origin at 3 picas across and 3 picas down. If we want to move a text box horizontally 1.5 inches, we change the Origin Across coordinate in the Measurements palette to 3p + 1.5", then press Enter. The box is automatically moved over.

A third method for moving items is by selecting them and using the arrow keys on the keyboard. Each time you press an arrow key, the item moves 1 point in that direction. Pressing Option-arrow moves the item a tenth of a point.

▼ ▼

Tip: Techniques for Item Placement. If you have a style of placing and sizing your page elements—such as lines and picture boxes—that works for you, stick to it. To paraphrase, "a manner of picture box placement is a real possession in a changing world." Nonetheless, here are some basic guides that we've found helpful:

- Use pica/point measurements for everything except basic page size. This is the standard among designers and printers, and allows precision without having to deal with numbers like .08334 inches (which is 6 points, or half a pica). It also makes dealing with type on your page easier to think in terms of picas and points, since that's how type is generally specified.

- Try to use round numbers for most of your measurements. Creating a box while at the Fit in Window size usually gives you measurements that have coordinates out to the thousandth of a point, such as 6p3.462. It might seem like a picky detail, but, in the long run, it can come in handy to either create your boxes at Actual Size and then resize them if needed, or, if you must work at a reduced or enlarged view, go into the Measurements palette or the Item Specifications dialog box (double-click on the box or type Command-M) and change the coordinates and the sizes to round numbers.

- Use the oval or polygon shaped boxes only when you must have that shape. Using a rectangle or square box for the majority of your pictures can cut your printing time in half or even to a third of what it takes when you use ovals.

▼ ▼

Rotating Items

A new feature in version 3 is the ability to rotate page items. The rotation of an item is an attribute that can be specified in either that Item Specifications dialog box or the Measurements palette. Note that positive rotation values rotate the object counter-clockwise; negative values rotate it clockwise. Most objects are rotated from their center. This center may not be where you think it is, however. The center is defined as the middle of the object's bounding box. Figure 1-12 shows a sample of an object that's center is not where you might expect.

Lines are the main exception when it comes to the center of rotation. Lines are rotated differently depending on their Mode (see "Lines," below). For example, if a line is in Right Point mode when you specify a rotation, the line rotates around the right endpoint.

If you are more visually minded, you can rotate items using the Rotation tool.

1. Select a page item.

Figure 1-12
QuarkXPress rotates
from the center of an
object's bounding box

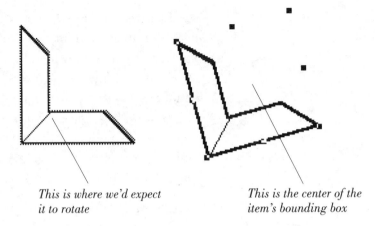

*This is where we'd expect
it to rotate*

*This is the center of the
item's bounding box*

2. Choose the Rotation tool from the Tool palette.

3. Click where you want the center of rotation.

4. Drag the Rotation tool. As you drag, the object is rotated in the direction you drag.

We don't like to use this tool, but that's just us and our bias. It may suit you well. However, it's significantly harder to control the rotation by using the tool rather than typing a specific rotation.

Resizing and Reshaping Items

Resizing an object is just about as simple as moving it. Reshaping it may be that simple, or it may be slightly more complex. Resizing and reshaping lines is a little different from resizing or reshaping picture or text boxes, so let's take them one at a time.

Picture and text boxes. Before we get into reshaping polygons, let's discuss the basics: resizing and reshaping rectangular and oval boxes. Once again, you have a choice between using QuarkXPress's interactive click and drag style or working in measurements. To resize by clicking and dragging you must place the screen cursor over one of the box's handles. Boxes have eight handles (one on each side, one on each corner) that you can drag to resize. Dragging a side handle resizes the box in one direction—horizontally or vertically. Dragging a corner handle resizes the box in two directions (horizontally *and* vertically). As long as "Reshape Polygon" is not selected from the Item menu (if it's selected, it has a check mark next to it), you can resize polygons using this same click and drag method.

In order to maintain an item's width and height ratio, you can hold down the Option and Shift keys while dragging. If you want to constrain the box into a square or circle, just hold down the Shift key while dragging (if the object were rectangular or oval, it would snap into a square or a circle).

The second method of resizing and reshaping picture and text boxes is by changing their height and width values. These values are located in both the Item Specifications dialog box and the Measurements palette. Unless you're a wizard at math, it's difficult to keep an object's aspect (width-to-height) ratio this way. Instead, this is a great way to make a box exactly the size you want it. For example, if you want an 8-by-10-inch picture box, you can draw one to any size you'd like, then change its width and height coordinates to 8 inches and 10 inches.

Polygonal picture boxes. Once you make that last segment of a polygon by clicking on its beginning/ending point, it seems as if the game is over. If the Reshape Polygon item is not selected from the Item menu, then QuarkXPress places a rectangular bounding box around the polygonal picture box and there's no way to move a corner or a line segment. The key there, of course, is the Reshape Polygon feature from the Item menu. If you select a polygonal picture box and then enable Reshape Polygon, each corner point has its own handle.

To move a corner point, simply click on it and drag it someplace else. You also can move an entire line segment, including the two points on either end of it, by just clicking and dragging it. To add a new corner point, you can hold down the Command key and click where you want it. Or, if you want to delete a corner point that was already there, you can hold down the Command key and click on top of it.

Lines. Most people define lines by their two endpoints. However, QuarkXPress can define any line in four different ways. Each line description is called a *mode*. The four modes are as follows.

- **Endpoints.** They describe the line by two sets of coordinates, X1,Y1 and X2,Y2. In the Line Specifications dialog box, these may be called the "Left Endpoint" and the "Right Endpoint," or the "Top Endpoint" and the "Bottom Endpoint," depending on how steep the line is.

- **Left Point.** In Left Point mode, QuarkXPress describes a line by three values: its left or bottom endpoint, its length, and its angle.

- **Right Point.** QuarkXPress uses the same three values for the Right Point mode, except it uses the right or top coordinate.

- **Midpoint.** The fourth mode, Midpoint, defines lines with its length and angle based on the coordinate of the most central point. That is, if a line is 2 inches long, QuarkXPress draws the line 1 inch out on either side from the midpoint.

You can define a line while in one mode, modify it with another, and move it with another. For example, let's say you draw a line someplace on your page. You then find you want to rotate it slightly. You have the choice to rotate the line from its left point, right point, or midpoint by selecting the proper mode from the Measurements palette or the Line Specifications dialog box, then changing the line's rotation value. If you want to move just the left point of the line over 3 points, you can switch to Endpoints mode and alter the X1,X2 coordinate.

Unfortunately, there is no way to resize a line by a given percentage.

▼ ▼

Tip: Constraining Lines. We all know that you can hold down the Shift key while you resize or reshape a line to hold the line horizontally and vertically. However, you also can constrain a line along its angle of rotation by holding down the Option and Shift keys together while dragging an endpoint. This is similar to constraining boxes to their width/height proportions.

▼ ▼

Tip: Making Line Joins Join. We're putting a bid in here for a Line tool that can draw more than one segment at a time (like a polygon that doesn't have to be closed up). Until then, however, we are forced to use single-segment lines, carefully joining them at their corners. Note that if you place two lines' endpoints together, they won't necessarily join properly. That is, if two lines come together at a 90 degree angle, and their endpoints are specified as exactly the same, the corner joint looks chiseled out (see Figure 1-13).

Figure 1-13
Lines don't always
join properly

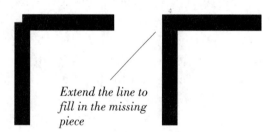

*Extend the line to
fill in the missing
piece*

You can fill this missing piece in by moving the endpoint of one of the lines half the line thickness. For example, if you are using 12-point lines, one of the lines should be extended 6 points farther. Remember, you can adjust the line mode and specify an endpoint coordinate as an equation (for example, 45p3.6+6pt).

▼ ▼

Locking Items

There are times when you want an item to stay how and where it is. For example, if you've painstakingly placed multiple text boxes on your page you probably don't want to move or resize them accidently. You can lock any page item down to its spot, making it invulnerable to being moved or resized with the Item tool. Just select the item with either the Item or the Content tool and choose "Lock" from the Item menu (or type Command-L).

If an item is locked, the Item tool cursor turns into a padlock when passed over it. You cannot move it by clicking and dragging either the item or its control handles. We find this feature especially helpful when we're working on a complex page and don't want an accidental click here or a drag there to ruin our work.

To unlock an item, select it and type Command-L again (or choose from the menu).

▼ ▼

Tip: Moving Locked Items. As usual, no matter how much we say you can't do something, there is a way to get around it. The one way you can move a locked item is by changing its Origin Across and Origin Down settings in the Item Specifications dialog box or in the Measurements palette (see "Resizing and Reshaping Items," above).

▼ ▼

Duplicating Items

The last set of features we discuss in this section on manipulating items revolves around duplicating items on your page. There are three ways of duplicating a page element such as a picture or text box—copy and paste it, duplicate it, and use "Step and Repeat."

Copy and paste. Selecting an item, copying it, and pasting it (Command-C and Command-V) is the Macintosh Way, though it's not always the most efficient or precise way. Many people get confused when they copy and paste picture and text boxes, because they don't use the correct tools. Remember, the Item tool is for working with items (boxes and lines), and the Content tool is for working with the *contents* of boxes. If you have the Content tool selected and you try to copy a text box, you only copy the text you may have inadvertently highlighted within the box rather than the box itself. The Item tool actually copies the text box.

When you paste the page item, the program places it in the middle of your screen, which is not always where you want it. Then you can use the methods we described earlier to move it around your page.

Duplicate. If you select an item with the Item tool or the Content tool, then choosing "Duplicate" from the Item menu (or typing Command-D) duplicates that item, displacing it from the original with the horizontal and vertical offsets last used in "Step and Repeat" (see below). You can then move the new item around to where you want it. The default setting for "Duplicate" is ¼ inch to the right and down from the original object.

Step and Repeat. The Step and Repeat feature can best be described as a powerhouse, and we wish every program had it. "Step and Repeat" (Command-Option-D) lets you select one or more objects and duplicate them with specific horizontal and vertical offsets as many times as you like. For example, if you want 35 lines, each 9 points away from each other across the page, you select the line, choose "Step and Repeat" from the Item menu, and enter "35" in the Repeat Count field, "9 pt" in the Horizontal Offset field, and 0 (zero) in the Vertical Offset field. After you use "Step and Repeat," you can type Command-Z to undo all of the duplications.

Both "Duplicate" and "Step and Repeat" have certain limitations. First, you cannot duplicate an item so that any part of it falls off the pasteboard. If you are working with constrained items, you cannot duplicate them so that any of the copies would fall outside of the constraining box. Any items you do duplicate from within a constrained group become part of that constrained group. However, duplicating an item from a set of grouped objects does not necessarily include the copy in the group.

▼ ▼

Tip: Clone Item. If you're an Aldus FreeHand user, you're probably familiar with the Command-= keystroke to duplicate an item without any offset. This is called *cloning*. QuicKeys lets us make QuarkXPress do the same thing. We built a macro that selects "Step and Repeat" from the Item menu, types "1-Tab-0-Tab-0" and clicks on OK. This makes a duplicate of an item that sits precisely on top of the original.

▼ ▼

Deleting Items

As we suggested above, there is a difference between deleting the contents of a picture or text box and deleting the box itself. When the contents of a box, such as a picture or text are deleted, the box still remains. When the box itself is deleted, everything goes. We think the easiest way to delete a page item is to select it (with either the Item or the Content tool) and type Command-K. This is the same as selecting "Delete" from the Item menu. The second easiest way to delete an item is to select it with the Item tool and press the Delete key on your keyboard.

A third way to delete an item is to select it with the Item tool and select Cut or Clear from the Edit menu. Of course, cutting it actually saves the item on the Clipboard so that you can place it somewhere else later.

The only one of these methods that works for deleting an item from a group is Command-K. That's because to remove this kind of page item, you must first select it with the Content tool (or else you end up deleting the entire group).

▼ ▼

Relationships Between Items

If you ask someone who used QuarkXPress in an earlier version than 3 what one feature they would have sold their grandmother to have gotten rid of, they would undoubtedly say "parent and child boxes." These parent and child boxes made it nearly impossible to be flexible with page design because boxes became "trapped" inside other boxes. These constraints were actually rather useful and accessible when you got accustomed to them. But there were many times when what we really needed was a choice of whether to enable it or not.

Our prayers have been answered. Version 3 takes the idea of parent and child boxes and expands it considerably by including a full implementation of multiple-item grouping and the option to turn parent and child box constraints on and off at will. In this section we talk about controlling the relationships between items: their layering, their grouping, constraining, and, finally, their position on the page relative to other page elements.

Layering Items

QuarkXPress, like most electronic publishing programs, handles multiple objects on a page by *layering* them. Each page item (picture boxes, text boxes, and lines) is always on a higher or lower layer than the other page items. This is generally an intuitive approach to working with page elements; it's just what you would do if each of the objects were on a little pieces of paper in front of you. The one difference is that, while you can have multiple objects on the same layer with each other on paper, each and every item is on its own layer on a QuarkXPress page. When you're placing objects on your page, you work from the bottom layer up. That is, the first object you place on your page is the back-most object, the second object "sits" on top of it, and so on.

If none of your page elements touches or overlaps another, then layering has almost no relevance to you. However, when they do touch or overlap in some way, you want to be able to control which objects overlap which. The primary methods for controlling layering are the Bring to Front and Send to Back commands in the Item menu.

"Bring to Front" and the "Send to Back" function as sweep-ing controls, moving a selected object all the way to the back or all the way to the front layer. There's no way to make something move just one layer back, for example, which makes working with multiple overlapping items sometimes difficult.

Grouping Objects

First the good news: for the first time in QuarkXPress history, you can select multiple items on a page. Now the even better news: those items can be grouped together to act as a single object. You can position and move a group of objects on the page with the Item tool, and still get in and modify single elements of the group using the Content tool.

Here's what you do.

1. Using the Item tool, select the items you want grouped. You can hold down the Shift key to select multiple items. Or, you can drag a marquee over or around the objects (any object that touches the mar-quee is selected).

2. Select "Group" from the Item menu (or type Command-G).

It's that easy. When the group is selected with the Item tool, a dotted line shows the bounding box of the grouped objects (see Figure 1-14).

Figure 1-14
Grouped objects

*Bounding box
shows the
grouped object*

To ungroup a bunch of objects, select the grouped object with the Item tool and select "Ungroup" from the Item menu (or type Command-U).

▼ ▼

Tip: Multilevel Grouping. Not only can you group multiple objects, but you can group multiple groups or groups and objects. This means that you can build levels of grouped objects. For example, on a catalog page you may have six picture boxes, each with a caption in a text box. You can group each caption box with its picture box, then select these six grouped objects and group them together. Later, if you ungroup the six objects, each picture box is still grouped with its caption box.

▼ ▼

Modifying Grouped Objects

As we mentioned above, once you have grouped a set of objects, you can still modify each one of them using the Content tool. Just select the element and change it. Each item can be rotated, resized, or edited just as usual. To move a single object in a grouped selection, hold down the Command key to get a temporary Item tool. Then move the object where you want it and let go of the Command key.

QuarkXPress lets you do some pretty nifty things with grouped items. If you select "Modify" from the Item menu (or type Command-M, or double-click on the group with the Item tool), QuarkXPress gives you a specifications dialog box for the group. If every object in a group is the same type of object (all rules, or all text boxes, etc.), it gives you a modified specifications dialog box for that type of object. The Origin Across and Down values are the measurements for the upper-left corner of the group, rather than any one object within the group.

If you change a value in one of these composite specifications dialog boxes, you change that value in every one of the objects in the group. For example, if you specify a background color to the grouped objects, the background color is applied to all the boxes in the group. If you apply a Picture Rotation value of 20 degrees to a group of picture boxes, the items in each of the picture boxes are rotated within their box (see Chapter 6, *Pictures*).

You also can change several specifications for a group of mixed-type objects. For example, you can specify "Suppress Printout" for a group, and each of the objects in the group is assigned "Suppress Printout." If you later ungroup the objects, the settings you make while they were grouped remain.

Note that if you have any lines (rules) in the group, changing the background color of the group affects the color of the line itself.

▼ ▼

Tip: Modifying Frames for Groups. If your grouped objects don't contain any other grouped objects, you can modify each and every frame in the group by selecting "Frames" from the Item menu (or typing Command-B). You can't select this when there are grouped groups.

▼ ▼

Tip: Watch Out for What You Group. We love the ability to drag a marquee out with the Item tool in order to select multiple objects. It's fast, it's effective, and it picks up everything in its path. Sometimes it even picks up things you don't want it to pick up. For example, let's say you have an automatic text box on your page and then place some picture boxes on it. If you drag a marquee across the page to select the picture boxes, chances are you'll select the text box, too. You may not notice this at first, but if you start dragging the group off into a library or someplace else, you'll be dragging the text box along for the ride. This spells havoc (press Command-Z quick to undo the last action).

So, just a quick lesson from people who've been there: watch out for what you select and group. And if you do select more than you want, remember that you can deselect items by holding down the Shift key and clicking on them (the same technique works for adding more items to a selection).

▼ ▼

Constraining

We talked a little about the parent and child box constraint relationships earlier in this section. If you never used Quark-

XPress before version 3, you were spared the horrible ordeal of brainwashing yourself to the point that these parent and child boxes made sense. If you were "brought up" with earlier versions of QuarkXPress you are probably finding yourself either breathing a hearty sigh of relief or cursing because you're brainwashed and you can't live without these constraints. Either way QuarkXPress has an answer for you.

Let's be clear here, for those not familiar with this feature. We're not talking about the type of constraining that Macintosh people usually talk about (and that we've mentioned earlier in this book) that refers to holding down the Shift key to constrain the movement of an object to a 45- or 90-degree angle. This is a different sort of constraint.

Whenever David thinks about parent and child box constraints, he thinks of a baby's playpen (this is probably some leftover childhood trauma, but he doesn't want to go into it). A playpen is basically a box that is a structure in its own right. However, you can place objects (or babies) into it, and they can't get out unless you physically take them out.

Similarly, a parent box is a text or picture box that has certain structural constraints so that any items that are created or placed inside its boundaries ("child" items) can't easily get outside those boundaries. For example, imagine a text box that was specified as a parent box. It acts as a normal text box. However, when you draw a line inside it using one of the Line tools, that line cannot be moved or resized to extend outside the text box. The only way you can get it out is by cutting it and pasting it elsewhere.

We know it sounds awful, but, like we said, there are some great applications. For example, building a table by adding vertical and horizontal rules to a text box is aided if those rules don't slip away when you move the box (child items move with their parents). Also, if you have a specific area in which all items must remain, creating a parental constraint makes sure that you don't accidentally mess up your specs when your eyes are bleary at three in the morning.

You can create parent and child box constraints in two ways: automatic constraints and manual constraints. Let's look at each of these in turn.

Automatic constraints. Automatic constraints were the standard for earlier versions of QuarkXPress. With automatic constraints on, all picture and text boxes act as parent constraint boxes. You can turn automatic constraints on and off with a click on the Auto Constraint button in the General Preferences dialog box. You can turn "Auto Constraint" on while you create boxes that you want to act as parent boxes and child items, and then turn it off to create "normal" boxes and items. This means that when you turn "Auto Constraint" off, the parent boxes only act as parent boxes to the child items that you created while "Auto Constraint" was on.

Note that the parent box and the child items are grouped when you select them with the Item tool. To unconstrain these items, see "Manual constraints," below.

Manual constraints. If you prefer, you can apply your own parent and child box constraints to a set of objects by manually constraining them. It's easy to do.

1. Make sure the page elements you want to be child items are totally within the boundaries of the box you want to be the parent box.

2. Make sure the soon-to-be-parent box is behind each of the objects that are soon-to-be-constrained. Parent boxes must be on a lower layer than their children. You can think of the playpen analogy: the playpen must be under—and surround—the child.

3. Group the child and parent objects and boxes together (see "Grouping," above).

4. Select "Constrain" from the Item menu.

Those objects that are on top of the parent box and are in that group are constrained to the boundaries of the parent box.

You can deconstrain this group of objects by clicking on the parent/child group with the Item tool and selecting either "Unconstrain" or "Ungroup" from the Item menu. "Unconstrain" removes the constraints, but leaves the items grouped. "Ungroup" removes both the grouping and constraining specifications (you cannot have parent/child constraints without grouping).

Aligning and Distributing Objects

Alignment and distribution, too, is a new feature for Quark-XPress 3. This feature lets you line up a bunch of page items or distribute them evenly across a given space. This is the feature that surprised us most in version 3, because we didn't know how badly we needed it until we started using it. Now we use it all the time.

Both alignment and distribution are covered in the same feature: the Space/Align function in the Item menu. Selecting this brings up the Space/Align Items dialog box (see Figure 1-15). This dialog box is broken down into Horizontal and Vertical sections, and you can use one or the other—or both—by clicking in their respective check boxes.

Figure 1-15
Space/Align Items
dialog box

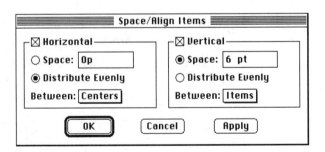

Because the controls are the same in each area (except you can select "Top Edges" and "Bottom Edges" in the Vertical section items rather than "Left Edges" and "Right Edges" in the Horizontal), we're just going to discuss the basics of each feature once (see Figure 1-16) for examples of alignment and distribution. The controls that appear in the Horizontal and Vertical areas are Between, Space, and Distribute Evenly.

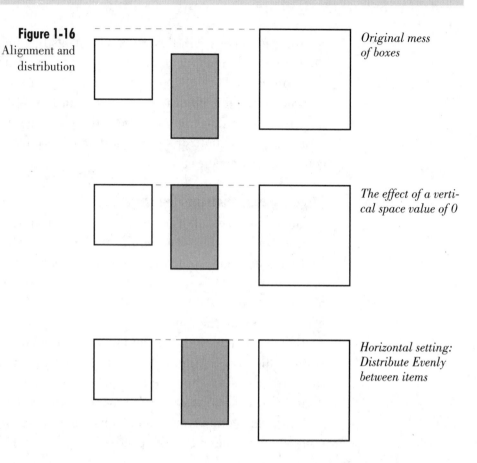

Figure 1-16
Alignment and
distribution

*Original mess
of boxes*

The effect of a vertical space value of 0

*Horizontal setting:
Distribute Evenly
between items*

Between. So you want to align or distribute two or more objects. But do you want to base this function on the centers of the objects, the left edges, or the right edges? Or do you want to base the movement on the edges of the items themselves. You can do any one of these by selecting it from the Between pop-up menu. As we mentioned above, "Left Edges" and "Right Edges" changes to "Top Edges" and "Bottom Edges," depending on whether you're in the Horizontal or Vertical section of the dialog box.

The concept of aligning or distributing objects based on "Item" is sometimes confusing to people. "Item" refers to the bounding box of the page element. So, for example, horizontally aligning two text boxes based on "Item" results in the right side of one being aligned with the left side of the second. And note we said that this is based on the bounding box of the object, which is the smallest rectangle that can enclose the entire object. This may result in alignment that you might not expect, especially when you're working with oddly shaped polygonal picture boxes.

Space. Enabling the Space value (by clicking in the round button in front of it) lets you align objects. The value in the Space field determines how far apart the objects should align. For example, let's say you are horizontally aligning two boxes and you have "Centers" selected in the Between pop-up menu. If you specify "0p" (zero picas) as the Space value, the center of the first box is centered exactly on the center of the second box. If you specify "5p" as the Space value, the center of the first box is placed 5 picas away from the second box.

But which box moves? The topmost or leftmost items stay stationary; they are the reference points for alignment. Other page elements move to align with them.

As we said, we use alignment all the time. If we have four text boxes that we want to line up on their left edges, we no longer have to select each one and make sure their horizontal positioning is equal. Now, we just select them all and align their left edges with the Space setting set to zero. Similarly, if we have multiple objects on the page, and we want to center all of them on top of each other, we can apply both a vertical and a horizontal alignment to them, with "Centers" selected in the Between pop-up menu.

Distribute Evenly. Instead of aligning objects, you can distribute them across an area. For example, if you have three picture boxes, you can move the center box so that the space between the center of the first box and the middle box is the same as the space between the middle box and the last box. We find distribution very helpful when we have a number of items that are all the same size, but are scattered around the page.

"Distribute Evenly" always takes the leftmost and rightmost or the top and bottom page elements that you have selected and uses them as the distribution boundaries. In other words, those objects don't move, while all the other objects that you selected for distribution do move.

Note that the Between pop-up menu has an effect on how page items are distributed. For example, QuarkXPress can distribute the items by their centers, left edges, right edges, and so on. The method that you use should be determined by the context.

▼▼

Getting Around Your Document

One of the first things a veteran of earlier QuarkXPress versions notices in version 3 is the pasteboard—an area that surrounds each of the pages in a document. This wide perimeter has many uses, including bleeding objects off a page, and temporarily storing boxes and lines. We also find it useful just for giving a better view of the page and how it will print.

However, unless you happen to work on an enormous screen, you never get to see much of the pasteboard—much less your entire page—at one time. Let's look at how you can move around to see different parts of a page, and different pages within your document.

Scrolling

The first step in moving around within your document is scrolling. *Scrolling* refers to using the horizontal and vertical scroll bars on the right and bottom sides of the document window to move your page (see Figure 1-17). If you click in the arrow at the top of the vertical scroll bar, you move a bit "up" your page (closer to the top). If you click in the left arrow in the horizontal scroll bar, you move to the left on your page, and so on. We find many people never get past this elementary level of scrolling. This is conceivably the slowest method you could use. We implore you to look at our alternatives, instead.

Figure 1-17
The document window

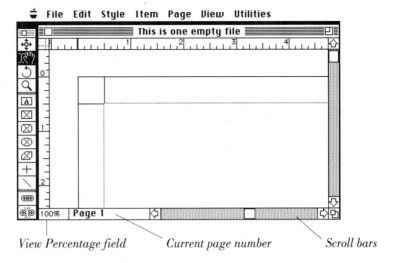

View Percentage field   *Current page number*   *Scroll bars*

You can shift large distances in your document by moving the little white box in the scroll bars up and down by dragging the box along the gray bar. Clicking in the gray area above the white box moves you up one screen; clicking below the box moves you down one screen, and so on. You also can use keystroke commands to move around the screen vertically. Table 1-4 shows you how.

Table 1-4
Moving around your document

To move	Type	On extended keyboards, type
Up one screen	Control-K	Page up
Down one screen	Control-L	Page down
Start of document	Control-A	Home
End of document	Control-D	End
First page	Control-Shift-A	Shift-Home
Last page	Control-Shift-D	Shift-End
Next page	Control-Shift-L	Shift-Page down
Previous page	Control-Shift-K	Shift-Page up

If you do use the scroll bar arrows to get around, you definitely want to examine the Scroll Speed feature in the Miscellaneous Preferences dialog box (available when you have the FeaturesPlus XTension from the QuarkFreebies 3.0

package). This feature lets you control how far each click in a scroll bar arrow takes you. For example, if you have the Scroll Speed set to "Fast," then one click in an arrow may move you an entire screen or more. If you have it set to Slow, a click may only move the screen 1 or 2 points. The Scroll Speed feature is only available when you have no documents open. We know this is a little like getting something when you least need it, but Quark was trying to make you realize the changes you make to this are application-wide rather than document-wide.

▼ ▼

Tip: "Live" Scrolling. When you drag the white box along the scroll bar, it's often difficult to tell how far on the page you've gone. This is because the vertical scroll bar represents the entire length of your document and the horizontal scroll bar represents the full length of the pasteboard. If you have multipage spreads in your document, the pasteboard can be very large (see more on spreads in Chapter 2, *Document Construction*). But if you hold down the Option key while you drag the white scroll bar box, the screen scrolls "with you," so you can see how far you're going (this is called *live scrolling*).

If you have the QuarkFreebies 3.0 package or Quark-XPress 3.1 installed, you can enable live scrolling on a permanent basis by placing a check mark in the Live Scroll check box in the Miscellaneous Preferences dialog box.

▼ ▼

Tip: Use the Grabber Hand. If (or when) you have the FeaturesPlus XTension (from the QuarkFreebies 3.0 package) or QuarkXPress 3.1, you have the option of turning your cursor into a grabber hand that lets you move around the screen in any direction. Just hold down the Option key, click somewhere on the page, and drag. The screen moves where you move the grabber hand. If you move the grabber hand to the left, the screen moves to the left (so you see farther to the right). Try it! We think it's one of the greatest methods for getting around the page.

▼ ▼

Tip: Adjusting Your Pasteboard. QuarkXPress 3.1 and the FeaturesPlus XTension, which comes with the Quark-Freebies 3.0 package, let you modify the width of your pasteboard. Note that the width—the area on either side of your page or spread—can change, though the area above and below the page is fixed (permanently a little small for our tastes). You can make this change by entering another Pasteboard Width value in the Miscellaneous Preferences dialog box (under the Edit menu). This value is specified in percentage of your page size. That is, 100 percent specifies that each side of the pasteboard should be the same size as a page. Thirty percent specifies a much narrower pasteboard.

▼ ▼

Zooming

If you have a brand new, 90-inch HDTV monitor, you may not need to read this section. For the rest of us, zooming is a necessity of life. When you zoom in and out of a page, you are using an electronic magnifying glass, first enlarging a particular area of a page, and then reducing your screen view so that you are seeing the entire page or pages at once.

QuarkXPress lets you magnify or reduce your screen view from 10 to 400 percent, in steps of .1 percent. You can jump between several preset views quickly by selecting them from the View menu or by using keystrokes. The menu lists scrolling values of 50 percent, 75 percent, Actual Size (100 percent), 200 percent, and Fit in Window. This last item adjusts the zoom percentage to fit whatever size window you have open at the time. If you're working with facing pages, then the scale is set to fit a two-page spread in the window.

There are two basic keystroke-and-click combinations that you can use to zoom in and out. Option-clicking on your page alternates between zooming out to "Fit in Window" and zooming in to "Actual Size." Command-Option-click on your page alternates your view between "Actual Size" and "200 percent." You also can type Command-0 (zero) to go to Fit in Window view, and Command-1 to go to "Actual Size."

Quark has added a Zoom tool on the Tool palette for your quick zooming pleasure. Sorry, did we say "quick?" We hardly find clicking in the Tool palette, then on our document, then back in the Tool palette "quick." However, we're in luck. If you hold down the Control key, you get a Zoom In tool, and if you hold down both the Control and the Option keys, you get a Zoom Out tool.

Each time you click on your page with the Zoom tool, QuarkXPress zooms in or out by a particular percentage. You can control the increments that it uses by changing the Zoom tool's default preferences (see "Changing the Defaults," later in this chapter).

▼ ▼

Tip: Alternate Zooming. Note that if you have the grabber hand feature enabled, the Option-click and Command-Option-click zooming tools don't work, because Option is being used to invoke the grabber hand. Here's a little undocumented feature to fix that: the grabber hand is disabled and the keystrokes re-enabled when the Caps Lock key is down. We've quickly gotten into the habit of pressing Caps Lock, Option-clicking, and then pressing Caps Lock back to off.

▼ ▼

Another one of our favorite methods for zooming in and out is by adjusting the View Percent field in the lower-left corner of the document window. Note that when you're in Actual Size, this field shows "100%." Whenever you zoom in or out, this field changes. Well, you can change it yourself by clicking in the field, typing a scaling percentage, and pressing Enter or Return.

But definitely our favorite zooming technique is to hold down the Control key (to get the Zoom tool), and dragging a marquee around a specific area. When you let go of the mouse button, QuarkXPress zooms into that area at the precise percentage necessary to fit it on your screen. That is, if you're at Actual Size and drag a marquee around one word, QuarkXPress zooms in to 400 percent and centers that word on your screen. You can use this to zoom out, too, by dragging a marquee that's larger than your screen (the screen scrolls along as you drag the marquee), but we don't find this as useful.

▼ ▼

Tip: Zoom Adjusting for Bitmaps. Let's say you have a 72-dpi bitmapped image scaled to 38.5 percent. At the low resolution of the computer screen (72 dots per inch), it's difficult to see the bitmap accurately. And if you zoom in a random percentage, the bitmapped image still looks odd, because the resolution of the bitmapped image does not have an integral relationship with the resolution of the screen. You can make sure you get a proper match and have your bitmapped image look normal by zooming in using the correct percentage. You can figure this percentage out by dividing the scaling percentage you used into 10,000. For example, in the example used above, the bitmapped image was scaled to 38.5 percent. Divide that into 10,000 (use a calculator!), to find that you should zoom in to 259.7 percent. If you have no idea what we're talking about here, don't worry: we discuss all this in Chapter 6, *Pictures*.

▼ ▼

Moving from Page to Page

In the last section we talked about moving around your page using scrolling and zooming. Because every page in your document sits on one big pasteboard, these same techniques work for moving around your document. That is, you can scroll from one page to another using the scroll bars and the Grabber hand, and so on. But let's be frank: this is not the fastest way to get around. It might help in moving around a 2-page spread, but not for moving around a 200-page book. Instead, there are ways to move by whole pages at a time or simply jump to the page that you want.

If you have an extended keyboard (we generally recommend these for serious desktop publishers), you can move one page forward or back by typing Command-Page Up or

Command-Page down (you can replace the Command key with the Shift key if you like). If you don't have an extended keyboard, Control-Shift-K and Control-Shift-L also moves one page at a time.

You may find yourself wanting to jump to the very beginning or the very end of your document. Again, on the extended keyboard, just press the Home or the End key. On nonextended keyboards, type Control-A or Control-D. You'll jump to the top or the bottom of the document, respectively. There is confusion just waiting to happen here. Jumping to the top or the bottom of the document does not ensure that you jump to the first or last page. Especially in the case of facing-page documents (see Chapter 2, *Document Construction*), you may find yourself out in the middle of a pasteboard, not knowing where the actual page is until you zoom out.

Instead of using the jump to top or bottom keystrokes, try Command-Home (Control-Shift-A) or Command-End (Control-Shift-D). These move you to the top of the first or last page in your document. Once again, you can substitute the Shift key for the Command key for these keystrokes.

If you're trying to get to a page somewhere in the middle of your document, there are three methods to get there quickly.

- You can select "Go to" from the Page menu (or, better yet, type Command-J. Note that this keystroke has changed from Command-G in earlier versions).

- You can double-click on the page icon in the Document Layout palette.

- If you have SuperXTension from the QuarkXTras package, you can select a page from a pop-up menu. Just click in the Page Number field in the lower-left corner of the document window, and then drag until you get to the page you want.

Note that for any of the keystrokes we've outlined here, there is a menu item in the Page menu. We think working with a mouse and menus is fast, but there is no doubt that once you start working with keystrokes, moving around your document becomes lightning fast.

▼ ▼

Manipulating Your Document

Okay, now that we've covered how you can move around your document, let's talk about how you can insert, delete, and move pages within your document. There are three good ways to handle these tasks in QuarkXPress: menu items, thumbnails, and the Document Layout palette. Let's look at each one of these.

Menu Manipulations

As we said much earlier in this chapter, the Page menu holds QuarkXPress's page manipulation tools. In this section we're primarily interested in the first three menu items: Insert, Delete, and Move. We're holding off on a discussion of inserting pages until the next chapter (see "Making Pages" in Chapter 2, *Document Construction*), so we'll talk about the last two.

When you choose "Delete" from the Page menu, Quark-XPress displays the Delete dialog box. This is a simple dialog box asking you which page or pages to delete. If you only want to delete one, just type it in the From field. If you want to delete consecutive pages, then type the page range in the From and To fields.

If you want to move a page or a range of pages, you can select the Move item from the Page menu. Here you have another simple dialog box, in which you can specify which page or pages to move, and where to move them (see Figure 1-18). For example, if you want to move pages 15 through 21 to after the last page in your document, you can type 15 in the first field, 21 in the second field, and click "At End of Document." You also can specify a move to before or after a specific page.

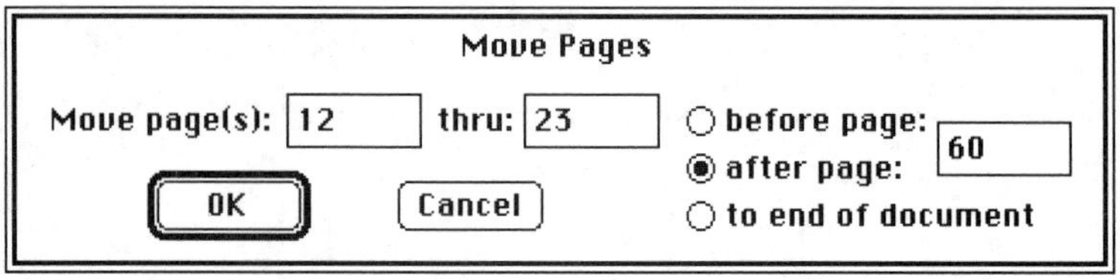

Figure 1-18
The Move Pages
dialog box

Thumbnails

Version 3 now includes a View mode called Thumbnails. You access it in the same way as you select any other specific percentage scaling view: from the View menu (or by typing "Thumb" into the Percentage Scaling field in the lower-left corner of the document window). Although you can use this to look at your document as thumbnails (like looking at it in 10 percent viewing mode), "Thumbnails" is actually more useful as a tool for moving pages.

To move a page in Thumbnails mode, simply select the page and drag it where you want it. While moving a page around in Thumbnails mode, you'll find the cursor turning into two different icons. The first looks like a little mini-page. If you let the mouse button go with this icon displayed, the page is moved, but it's added as a spread. That is, the rest of the pages won't shuffle and reflow (see "Multiple Page Spreads" in Chapter 2, *Document Construction*).

The second icon, a black arrow, appears when you move the cursor directly to the left of or under another page. This arrow means that the page will be placed directly before or under a specific page. Letting go of the mouse button when you have this arrow cursor reflows the pages in the document. This is the same as moving pages using "Move" from the Page menu.

▼ ▼

Tip: Moving and Deleting Multiple Pages. It's easy to select more than one page at a time while in "Thumbnails" or delete or move pages while in the Document Layout palette (more on the latter in the next section). If the pages are consecutive (from page 4 through 9, for example), just hold down the Shift key while you select each page or click on the first page in the range, hold down the Shift key, and click on the last page in the range. Every page is then selected between the two (this is just like selecting text).

You can select nonconsecutive pages (such as pages 1, 3, and 9), while in Thumbnails mode or in the Document Layout palette by holding down the Command key while clicking on each page.

▼ ▼

Document Layout Palette

The Document Layout palette is one of the key elements in working efficiently with multipage documents. You can move pages, delete them, insert new ones, create and apply master pages, and more, with a quick drag of an icon. Let's look at how you can use this palette to delete and move pages.

To open the Document Layout palette, select "Show Document Layout" from the View menu (see Figure 1-19). For our purposes right now, you only need to think about two areas in the palette: the page icons at the bottom, and the trash can in the upper-right corner. We'll get into more advanced uses (applying master pages, for instance) in Chapter 2, *Document Construction.*

Figure 1-19
The Document
Layout palette

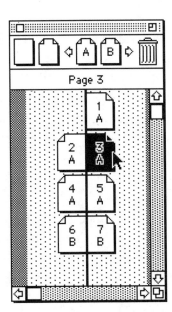

Moving pages within the Document Layout palette is just like moving them in Thumbnails mode, except that you can't see what's on the pages. Simply select the page or pages that you want to move, and drag them to their destination. Quark-XPress uses the same icons here as in Thumbnails mode. That is, the little page icon means that you're creating a spread, and the right and down arrow icons mean that you're moving the pages into the flow (the other pages displace to accommodate this page).

Deleting a page with the Document Layout palette is as simple as deleting a file while on the Macintosh desktop: just select it and drag it into the trash icon. However, do note that while you can retrieve a file that you placed into the desktop Trash, you cannot undo your actions and retrieve a page that you threw away in QuarkXPress. Obviously, it's worth being extra careful in this area.

Moving Items Between Documents

But you don't have to stop at moving items and pages just within your document. You can move them from one document to another faster than you can say, "Why-can't-I-open-more-than-one-document-at-a-time-with-PageMaker?"

To move a page item from one document to another, you must have both documents open and visible on your screen. This is sometimes difficult on small screens. You can usually resize one or both screens using the Resize area on the document window (that little icon in the lower-right corner). Then, select the item you want to move with the Item tool (or just hold down the Command key to get the Item tool temporarily), and drag it across.

If you pause between the document windows, you may find the first document start to scroll. Don't worry, it's just QuarkXPress not realizing that you want to move it all the way into the second document. Just move the item a little farther and the scrolling should stop. Once you let the mouse go, the item is copied over into the new document. Note that we say "copied." The item is not actually moved, rather it is copied from one into the other. If you want to get rid of it in the first document, just delete it (Command-K).

Of course, there is always the old standby method for getting items from one document to another: Copy and Paste. Here, you want to make sure that you have the Item tool selected while in both documents, or else QuarkXPress won't know that you want to copy or paste the item itself.

Moving Pages Between Documents

Earlier versions of QuarkXPress sported a Get Document function, which was extremely useful. First of all, it let you copy whole pages from one document to another. Secondly, it let you access pages from a different document without actually opening it (this was often helpful in retrieving corrupted files). Unfortunately, the Get Document feature is now gone.

Taking its place is a feature that lets you actually drag a page from one document into another, as long as both documents are in Thumbnails mode. This is especially handy if you like to see the pages that you're copying before you copy them.

▼ ▼

Tip: Moving Background Windows. If you're working on a small screen and you need to resize and move your document windows in order to drag across page items or even full pages, you might find it helpful to know that you can move a window without actually selecting it. That is, normally, if you click on a window, that window is brought to the front and highlighted. We say that it becomes *active*. You can move a window without bringing it to the front (activating it) by holding down the Command key while you click and drag the bar at its top.

▼ ▼

Linking

We need to introduce a concept here that is crucial to working with text boxes: linking. *Links*, sometimes known as chains, are the connections between text boxes that allow text to flow from one into the other. You can have as many text boxes linked up as you like. There are two ways to link text boxes together: have QuarkXPress do it for you automatically, or do it yourself manually. We cover automatic text links in Chapter 2, *Document Construction*. We cover manually linking here.

Linking Text Boxes

Let's say you have two text boxes and the text in the first is overflowing (a little box with an "x" in it in the lower-right corner indicates a text overflow), so you want to link it to the second box. First choose the Linking tool from the Tool palette (it's the one that looks like three links in a chain). Next click on the first text box, and then on the second text box. When you click on the first text box, a flashing dotted line should appear around it. Then, when you select the second text box, an arrow should connect from the first text box to the second. We call this the *text link arrow*. This happens even if the two text boxes are on different pages.

That's it. The boxes are now linked, and text flows between them. If you want to link another box to your text chain, just follow the same procedure: click on the second text box, then on the third, and so on. Note that you cannot link a box to another box that has text in it.

If you want to add a text box to the middle of a text chain, first click on a box that is already linked, and then click on the text box you want to add. The text now flows from the original chain, through your added text box, and back to the original chain (see Figure 1-20).

▼ ▼

Tip: Getting Rid of the Flashes. Many people seem to get flustered when they've selected a text box with the Linking tool and then decide they don't want to follow through and link the box to anything after all. The text box is just sitting there flashing, seeming to call for some special action. Nope, no special action required. You can either click someplace where there's no text box, or just switch tools, and the flashing stops.

Figure 1-20
Linked text boxes

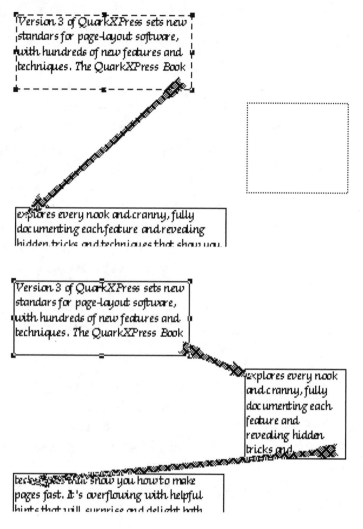

Unlinking Text Boxes

If you want to remove a link between two text boxes, use the Unlinking tool from the Tool palette. The process is simple. Let's say you have a link between two text boxes that you want to sever. First, click on one of the text boxes with the Unlinking tool. As soon as you click on it, you should see the gray arrow linking the two boxes. Then click on either the arrowhead or the tailfeathers of this text link arrow. The arrow disappears and the link is gone.

If other page items are on top of the text link arrow's arrowhead and tailfeathers, you may not be able to click on it. This always seems to happen at 1 A.M., after everything else has gone wrong on the project, and this is the last straw. Nonetheless, the way we solve this problem is to rearrange the layers using "Move to Front" and "Move to Back" or to temporarily shift the obstructing objects in order to get to one of the two.

Another problem some people encounter is that they can click and click on the arrowhead or tailfeather, but can't make it disappear. Quark has made it difficult to click on so that you don't accidently click on the wrong text link arrow. Try placing the cursor right over the very tip of the arrow or the point where the two tailfeathers meet.

▼ ▼

Tip: Unlinking a Text Box from the Middle of a Chain. If you unlink a text box from the middle of a chain by clicking on the arrowhead or tailfeathers with the Unlinking tool, the entire text chain is broken at that point. Instead, you can tell Quark-XPress to remove a text box from the text chain without breaking the rest of the flow by selecting the Unlinking tool, then holding down the Shift key while clicking on the box you want to remove.

▼ ▼

Guides and Rulers

When you are working on your document, you usually have rulers on the top and left sides of the window. This not only gives you a perspective on where you are on the page, but it's a great visual aid in selecting coordinates. Let's say you want to change the size of a picture box by dragging a corner handle. If you're visually inclined, you may not want to bother with referring to the Measurements palette while you drag. Instead, if you watch the rulers, you'll see that gray lines show the left, right, top, and bottom edges as it moves.

You can turn the rulers on and off by selecting "Show" or "Hide Rulers" from the View menu, or by typing Command-R. The only time you really need to turn the rulers off, though, is when you want to get a slightly larger view of the page. Otherwise, just leave them on.

You can specify which measurement system you want to use in your rulers in the General Preferences dialog box (from the Edit menu, or type Command-Y). The vertical and horizontal rulers don't have to use the same measurement system. For example, you can set "Horizontal Measure" to inches and "Vertical Measure" to picas. This just confuses us, so we generally keep both the same (we always use picas).

The values you choose in the General Preferences dialog box are not only used on the rulers, but also throughout the Measurements palette and Item Specifications dialog box. For example, if you change the "Vertical Measure" to Ciceros, then every vertical measurement shows up in ciceros and points. You can still type in measurements using other units (see Table 1-2, earlier in this chapter), but QuarkXPress always converts them.

Guides

Back in the good old days, before we started laying out pages by sitting in front of little plastic boxes, no one worked without guides. We had blueline guides on pasteup boards, straightedge guides on drafting tables for making sure we were aligning items correctly, and transparent rulers to ensure that we were measuring type and rules correctly. We certainly didn't throw any of that away when we bought our Macintoshes—they still come in handy often. However, QuarkXPress gives us all those tools electronically.

You can add a vertical or a horizontal guide to your page by clicking in one of the rulers and dragging it out onto the page. Note that the guide runs the length of the page from top to bottom or from side to side. However, guides won't cross over a spread (see "Tip: Longer Guides," below). Once you've placed a guide on your page, you can move it by clicking on the guide in an area where no other page items are (the page margin is often a good place for this) and dragging it to where you want it. The Measurements palette displays the coordinate of where the guide is while the guide is moving (unfortunately, once you let go of the guide, there is no way to find out the measurement of where it sits on the page without "grabbing" it again).

To remove a guide from your page, grab it in the page margin area or anyplace where there are no other objects, and drag it out of the window (either back into the ruler, or off to the right or bottom of the window).

▼ ▼

Tip: Longer Guides. As we noted above, if you drag a guide onto a page, the guide reaches from one side of the page to the other, and doesn't cross over a spread, or even onto the pasteboard. You can make a longer guide that reaches over both of these by dragging a guide onto the pasteboard, letting go, and then moving it onto the page. Another method is to click and drag out a guide from a part of the ruler not directly over or to the left of the page.

▼ ▼

Guides don't print, so it doesn't matter where you place them on your page. However, you may want to adjust the guides to fall in front of or behind opaque text or picture boxes. You can do this by changing the Guides setting in the General Preferences dialog box. Your two choices are "Behind" and "In Front."

Snap to Guides

One of the most important values of guides is that picture and text boxes can snap to them. All guides have this feature, including margin and column guides (we'll talk more about them in Chapter 2, *Document Construction*). You can turn "Snap to Guides" on and off by selecting it in the View menu. For example, if you have five picture boxes that you want to align, you can pull out a guide to the position you want it, and—if "Snap to Guides" is enabled in the View menu—as the picture boxes are moved next to the guides, they snap to that exact line.

On the other hand, there are times when you probably want to disable "Snap to Guides"—so just select it again from the View menu. For example, if you are working with a line very close to a column guide, it may snap to the guide when you don't want it to. Just turn it off. Generally, however, we leave this feature on.

The distance at which a guide pulls an item in, snapping it to the guide position, is determined by a control in the Miscellaneous Preferences dialog box. This dialog box is accessible if you have the QuarkFreebies 3.0 package installed on your system. The default value is 6 points.

▼ ▼

Tip: Vertical Leading Ruler. One feature QuarkXPress doesn't have is a customizable vertical ruler. "Why would anyone want that?" we hear you asking. Well, the best reason is to set a vertical ruler in increments of your body copy's leading (see Chapter 4, *Type and Typography*). That is, if the body copy leading is set to 11 points, it's nice to have a vertical ruler in increments of 11 points. This is especially helpful for aligning objects to your leading grid.

One way to get such a custom vertical ruler is to create one on the pasteboard. Follow these steps.

1. Draw a 1-pica-wide box as tall as your page (we would just draw a little box, then go into the Measurements palette and set the "Origin Across" and "Down" both to 0, the width to 1 pica, and the height to 8.5 inches or whatever). Make sure this box has no background color and a text runaround of None.

2. Place a 1-pica-wide line with a thickness of .5 point at the bottom or top of this box.

3. Step-and-repeat this line in increments of your body copy leading as many times as you need to reach from the top of the box to the bottom.

4. Select the box and every line in it (drag a marquee around them all with the Item tool), and group them together (Command-G).

5. Type Command-M to go to the Group Specifications dialog box, and enable "Suppress Printout" by clicking in its check box.

QuarkXPress 3.1 includes a Show Baseline Grid feature which—we admit—is often more useful than this tip (see Appendix C, *Using QuarkXPress 3.1*).

▼ ▼

Frames

There are times when you want to put a picture on your wall with a frame and there are times when you just tape it up frameless. When you're making pages, there are times when you want a frame around a text or picture box, and there are times when you don't. QuarkXPress lets you have your choice. All picture and text boxes default to a frame of width 0 (zero), which means there's no frame at all. You can add a frame to any picture or text box by selecting it and choosing "Frame" from the Item menu (or typing Command-B).

The Frame Specifications dialog box contains fields and pop-up menus that let you specify the weight, color, shade, and line style of your frame (see Figure 1-21). Color and shade are self-explanatory, but we need to talk a little about frame styles and their thickness.

Figure 1-21
Frame Specifications
dialog box

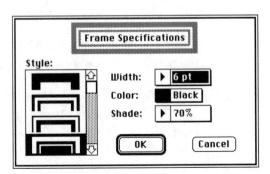

Frame style. The first seven styles in the Style scroll list are lines, double lines, triple lines, and variations on those lines. You can apply these frames to any kind of text or picture box. Any other frames on the list are frames that are considered "complex," and can only be applied to rectangular picture or text boxes. They are defined as bitmapped images (see Chapter 6, *Pictures*, for a discussion of bitmapped images versus object-oriented graphics). The ones that come with QuarkXPress are pretty good, because the frames consist only of vertical and horizontal lines. Any diagonal lines look jaggy when they print out, which is something we won't stand for (we're just snobs, that's all; some people don't mind).

All we can say is be careful with the frame you use.

Frame Weight

Quark calls the thickness of a frame its "width." We're used to calling it the "weight." No matter what you call it, it's the thickness of the frame. And, in a similar manner to lines, if the line weight is not thick enough, the frame style may not show up properly (a triple line set to .5 point comes out looking just like a single half-point line).

Frames can grow from the box edge in, or the box edge out. That is, a 10-point frame is measured from the edge of the box either out or in. This is different from lines: their weight is measured from their center (a 10-point line falls 5 points on one side of the line, and 5 points on the other).

You can control which side of the box edge the frame falls on with the Framing pop-up menu in the General Preferences dialog box (from the Edit menu, or type Command-Y). Choosing "Inside" from this menu places frames on the inside of a box; "Outside" places them on the outside.

Note that you can create a frame on a box while in the Inside mode, then change the mode to Outside, and subsequent frames are built on the outside of boxes (or vice versa). Existing boxes don't change when you change the preferences.

▼ ▼

Libraries

QuarkXPress 3 lets you keep libraries full of items: picture boxes, text boxes, lines, groups of objects, and so on. These libraries are saved as external files on a disk that you can move from one place to another. For example, while writing this book, we placed each piece of artwork, grouped with figure numbers, captions, and callouts, in a library. The artwork was later taken out of the library by the production team and placed on the QuarkXPress pages. This increased the chance that nothing too weird would happen when we were making pages, and decreased the time it took to produce a chapter.

Note that a library holds a page item, plus its contents. For example, you could place a text box with a particular headline in a particular style in a library. However, picture boxes in libraries don't necessarily fully contain their pictures. If a picture is in an EPSF, TIFF, or RIFF format, the library only remembers the link to the external file, rather than the file itself. So, although our artwork could be stored in a library, we still had to move many of our EPSF and TIFF files from disk to disk (if you are lost, don't worry; we talk about all these issues in Chapter 6, *Pictures*).

You can have up to seven libraries open at a time, and each library can hold up to 2,000 entries. You can even label each library entry for quick access. Let's look at how all of this is done.

Manipulating Libraries

To open a library, select "Library" from the Utilities menu. QuarkXPress brings up a dialog box asking you to find the library you want. If you want to create a new library, you can click "New." Once you choose a library, QuarkXPress brings it up on your screen as a palette.

As we mentioned earlier in this chapter, palettes work much like other windows (in fact, we often call them *win-*

doids). For example, like a window, you can close a palette by clicking in the close box in the upper-left corner. The palette floats, so you can move the palette wherever you like on your screen. You also can expand the palette by clicking in the zoom box in the upper-right corner of the box. Note that this type of zooming doesn't have anything to do with a percentage scaling view. The first time you click on it, the palette fills your screen. The second time, it decreases back to "normal" size. You also can resize the windoid by clicking and dragging the lower-right resizing box, just like a normal window.

Adding and Moving Library Entries

You'll hardly believe how easy it is to add and remove library entries. To add a page item to an open library, just click on the item with the Item tool (or hold down the Command key to get a temporary Item tool), and drag the item across into the library. When you're in the library, your mouse cursor turns into a pair of glasses (don't ask us why; all the librarians we know wear contacts), and two triangular arrows point to your position in the library. When you let go of the mouse button, the item you're dragging is placed in the library where these pointers are indicating. That is, you can position your page item anywhere in the library by dragging it into place.

You also can add an item to a library by using Cut or Copy and Paste. You need to use the Item tool to cut or copy an item from the page, but you can use either the Item or the Content tool to paste it in a library. Just click in the position where you want the item to go, then type Command-V (or select Paste from the Edit menu). When picking a place to paste the item, click between two items, so that you can see the positioning arrows. If you click on an item in the library before pasting, you are telling QuarkXPress to replace that item with this new one.

After you add an item to a library, then you can see a thumbnail-size representation of it (see Figure 1-22). Note that this representation is highlighted, and you won't be able to do any work on your page until you click someplace other than the library.

Figure 1-22
Adding an item
to a library

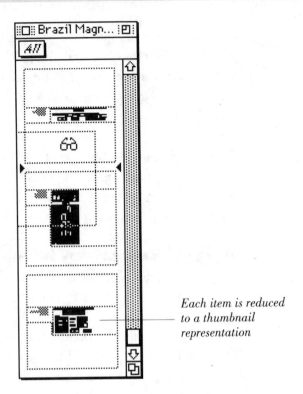

*Each item is reduced
to a thumbnail
representation*

You can move an item in a library from one position to another by clicking on it and dragging it to a new position. If you have more items in your library than fit in the palette, you may have some difficulty, because the library doesn't automatically scroll as you drag. We use one of two methods to get around this. First, you can cut and paste items as we described above. Secondly, you can click on the Zoom box to expand the size, then reposition the item, then rezoom the box down to a small palette.

Removing Library Items

To take an item from an open library and place it on a page, just click on it with either the Item or the Content tool and drag it out onto your page. This doesn't remove the item from the library; it just makes a copy of it for your page. If you want to delete an item from a library, click on it, then select "Clear" from the Edit menu (or press the Delete key). You also can use Cut from the Edit menu (Command-X), which removes the item and places it on the Clipboard.

Labelling Library Items

Imagine having 150 different items in a library and trying to find just the ones that are pictures of baby seals. Remember that all you can see on screen is a thumbnail representation of the items. Luckily, you have labelled each library item with a foolproof system, and you are just a pop-up menu item away from finding those baby seals.

Every item in a library may be labelled either for identification purposes or to group items together (or both). With your library items labeled, you can access the library items by a single label, multiple labels, and more.

To assign a label to a library item, double-click on its thumbnail representation. Up comes the Library Entry dialog box (see Figure 1-23). There is only one field in this dialog box for you to type the label in. Note that after you add one label to an item, the pop-up menu in this dialog box is enabled. This pop-up menu lists each of the previous labels you've assigned (see "Tip: Grouping Library Items").

Figure 1-23
The Library Entry
dialog box

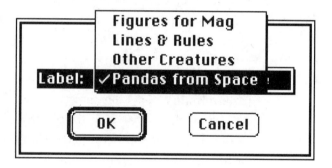

After you have labeled items in your library, you can select from among them with the pop-up menu at the top of the Library palette (see Figure 1-24). This acts as a kind of electronic card catalog. There are always two items in this pop-up menu: All and Unlabeled. Selecting "All" shows you every item in the library. Selecting "Unlabeled" displays only the items that have not yet been labeled. Any other labels that you have assigned to library items also appear on this pop-up menu. If you select one of these, you can see any item (or items) that have been assigned that label.

Figure 1-24

Selecting a subcategory
in the library

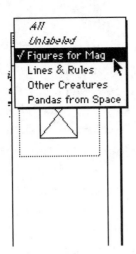

If you select a second label from the pop-up menu, that label is added to the category you're already looking at. The name on the pop-up menu changes to Mixed Labels, which tells you that more than one label is being displayed. You can deselect one label category by rechoosing it from the pop-up menu (that is, these labels in the pop-up menu act as on-and-off toggle switches). You can deselect all the subcategories by choosing All from the pop-up menu.

▼ ▼

Tip: Grouping Library Items. As we mentioned above, you can group library items together (this isn't the same as grouping items on the page). You do this by giving them the same label. For example, if you have a group of lines that you use a lot for one magazine, you might label them all "Mag Lines." Then, when you need one, you simply pull down the Library palette's pop-up menu and select that label. However, if each one of the item's labels isn't exactly the same, QuarkXPress won't know to group them together. Instead of typing the same label over and over again for each item, you can just type it once. Then use the pop-up menu in the Library Entry dialog box to choose that item each time you want to assign it to an item within the library. This is faster and you avoid typos.

▼ ▼

Saving Libraries

No matter how hard you try, you won't find a command to save the library file. This can be disconcerting, to say the least. What happens to all those items if you can't save them?

QuarkXPress normally saves a library only when you quit the program or close your current document. This is generally unacceptable, because people work for long periods of time without quitting or closing a document (during the production of this book one person lost over an hour's worth of work because of a system crash before the library was saved).

Fortunately, the QuarkFreebies 3.0 package includes an Auto Library Save feature in the Miscellaneous Preferences dialog box that makes QuarkXPress save a library every time you place a new item in it. This may slow down your work a little, if you're adding a number of items, but it could also save you lots of time if something should go wrong.

▼ ▼

XTensions

Here's an aspect of QuarkXPress that we think is so hot and amazing that we couldn't think of a nasty thing to say about it even if we tried. Quark has built in a system so that programmers can write add-on modules (XTensions) to work with QuarkXPress. There are over 100 developers around the world creating these XTensions. Some cost $5,000 and are designed for a very limited market, such as large newspapers. Others are free, and can (and should) be used by anyone using QuarkXPress. Appendix B, *Resources*, gives more information about how to get your hands on XTensions.

In order to use an XTension, all you have to do is place it in the same folder as QuarkXPress. When you start up QuarkXPress the XTension does its thing, whatever that may be. Usually, XTensions add an item to a menu, or even add a whole new menu. Most XTensions add items to the Utilities menu, because they are utilities. For example, Billy Ball released a free XTension called Asave (on electronic bulletin board systems and through computer user groups) that automatically saves your document every five minutes (or however often you choose). This XTension works behind the scenes for you, but you control it through an item on the Utilities menu.

We talked about another type of XTension in the Introduction: the Zapper. This type of XTension is released by Quark for the purpose of fixing bugs that were discovered after QuarkXPress's initial release. Zapper XTensions actually modify the QuarkXPress application the first time you start up the program. This means that after the first time you run QuarkXPress with them available, you can throw them away (although we recommend keeping them on disk somewhere just in case you need them again).

Changing Defaults

QuarkXPress 3 also gives you more options for customizing the internal default settings than ever before. A *default setting* is a value or a way of doing something that QuarkXPress uses unless you specifically choose something else. For example, a default setting for picture and text boxes is that they are created with no frame around them (see "Frames," earlier in this chapter). But you can change default settings. You can modify QuarkXPress so that every text box you create automatically is framed with a 2-point line.

Default settings range from how guides are displayed on the screen to how QuarkXPress builds small caps characters. There are three basic dialog boxes that let you specify your default settings preferences: General Preferences, Typographic Preferences, and Tool Preferences. The FeaturesPlus XTension from the QuarkFreebies 3.0 package adds two further dialog boxes: Miscellaneous Preferences and Fraction/Price Preferences. Each of these dialog boxes can be accessed through the Preferences submenu under the Edit menu. QuarkXPress 3.1 also adds the Application Preferences dialog box (see Appendix C).

We talk about Typographic Preferences and the Fraction/Price Preferences in Chapter 4, *Type and Typography*, and we cover several items from the General Preferences dialog box throughout the rest of the book, so we'll cover the "missing" areas in a quick rundown here.

General Preferences

Of the 13 default preferences in the General Preferences dialog box (see Figure 1-25), only one is not described elsewhere in this book: Points/Inch. Here's a list of where you can find information on the other 12 defaults.

Figure 1-25
The General
Preferences
dialog box

```
┌─────────────────────────────────────────────────────────────┐
│          General Preferences for True Life QK Stories        │
│                                                              │
│  Horizontal Measure:  [Inches]        Points/Inch:   [72  ]  │
│  Vertical Measure:    [Picas]      ☐ Render Above: [24 pt]    │
│  Auto Page Insertion: [End of Section]  ☒ Greek Below: [7 pt]│
│  Framing:             [Inside]        ☒ Greek Pictures        │
│  Guides:              [In Front]      ☐ Auto Constrain        │
│  Item Coordinates:    [Page]                                 │
│  Auto Picture Import: [Off]                                  │
│  Master Page Items:   [Keep Changes]  ( OK )    [ Cancel ]   │
└─────────────────────────────────────────────────────────────┘
```

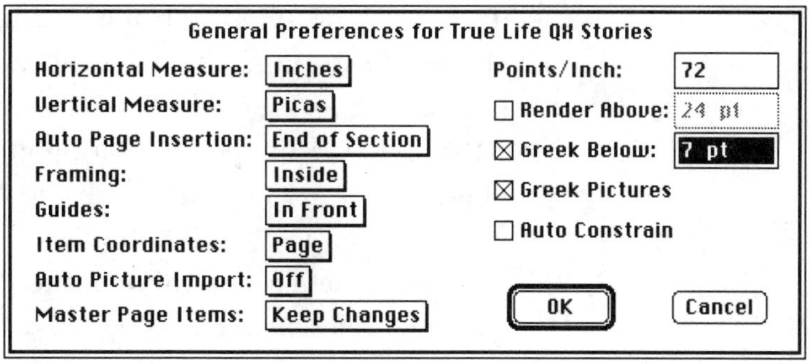

Horizontal Measure and Vertical Measure. See "Guides and Rulers," earlier in this chapter.

Auto Page Insertion. See "Automatic Page Insertion," in Chapter 2, *Document Construction*.

Framing. See "Frames," earlier in this chapter.

Guides and Item Coordinates. See "Guides and Rulers," earlier in this chapter.

Auto Picture Import. See "Picture Usage," in Chapter 6, *Pictures*.

Master Page Items. See "Changes to Document Pages" in Chapter 2, *Document Construction*.

Render Above. See "Type Rendering," in Chapter 4, *Type and Typography*.

Greek Below. See "Text Greeking," in Chapter 4, *Type and Typography*.

Greek Pictures. See "Greeking and Suppression," in Chapter 6, *Pictures*.

Auto Constrain. See "Constraining," earlier in this chapter.

Points/Inch. Somebody, sometime, somewhere along the line, decided that PostScript should measure 72 points to an inch. However, as it turns out, the printers and graphic designers have always measured just *over* 72 points to the inch. Quark-XPress, being the power-rich program it is, gives you the choice of how you want to measure points. If you have a burning need to work in a traditional measurement setting, you could change the value of the Points/Inch field in the General Preferences dialog box to 72.27. We tend toward forward progress and think that people should just throw out their old rulers and embrace a new standard. Thus, we leave it at 72 points per inch.

Tool Preferences

You may find yourself making the same change or changes repeatedly to a type of page item; for example, you always change the text inset for text boxes from 1 to 0 points, or always change your lines to ¼-point thickness after drawing them. These item attributes, as well as most other attributes for page items, are defaults that you have some say in.

You can use the Tool Preferences dialog box to change the default settings for any of the item-creation tools on the Tool palette, plus the Zoom tool (see Figure 1-26). To change a default for an item-creation tool (the tools that create picture boxes, text boxes, or lines), select the tool's icon in the dialog box, and then click on one of the three buttons to change some aspect of that tool: Modify, Frame, or Runaround.

Figure 1-26
Tool Preferences
dialog box

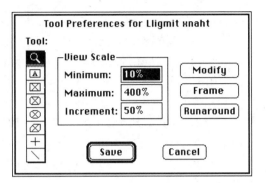

Modify. This button brings up the Item Specifications dialog box for the particular tool. As we discussed earlier in this chapter, a picture box has a different specifications dialog box than a text box, and so on. You can change any value in this dialog box that is not grayed out. For example, you can change the default corner radius of a rounded-corner rectangle picture box, but you can't change its default width or height. We rarely want our picture boxes to have a colored background, so we have changed our picture box tools' defaults so that the "Background Color" is set to "None."

Frame. You can specify an automatic frame for text or picture boxes by clicking on the Frame button. Let's say you specify a 1-point single-line frame for the Polygon Picture Box tool. After you click OK, every polygonal picture box you make has that frame. You don't have to keep the frame if you later don't want it (just remove it as you would any other frame: change it's width to 0). But this is the default setting for creating new ones.

Runaround. You also can change the text runaround value for boxes made with a tool. For example, you can set the Text

Box tool to make text boxes that have no runaround. Note that you can set any runaround that you normally could for a box or line except that you cannot set a picture box to "Manual Runaround."

▼ ▼

Tip: Get to Those Tool Preferences Quickly. As you probably can tell, we do almost anything to avoid actually making a selection from a menu. We just find other methods are faster for us, and they should be for you, too. For example, you can jump to the Tool Preferences dialog box by double-clicking on a tool in the Tool palette. This automatically highlights the tool you chose, and you're ready to make your change. Unfortunately, this is one dialog box in which you can't use the keyboard to "push" buttons.

▼ ▼

Tip: Document Defaults Versus Program Defaults. There's an important difference between changing your default preferences when you've got a document open and when you don't. If you have a document open when you change a default preference, that change is specific to that document. If no documents are open when you set a default preference, then you are setting new defaults for the whole program and that change is made to every new document you open from then on.

For example, if you set the increments on the Zoom tool to 100 percent while a document is open, the preference is logged for that document only. If you set it while no documents are open, that setting is made for every new document you create. However, documents that were opened using the original setting keep their defaults.

▼ ▼

Moving On

You now know the basics of how QuarkXPress relates to you, and the general concepts of how you can use its tools to make your pages. If you weren't familiar with these tools before, a little practice will turn you into a pro in no time. If you were familiar with them, we hope you now have increased your arsenal of high-caliber techniques. Either way, you should now be ready to move into the next chapter, in which we move away from a free-form, throw-it-all-on-a-page style of working and introduce you to systematic methods of building documents.

CHAPTER 2

DOCUMENT CONSTRUCTION

We find the design process particularly fascinating. The designer must meld rigid, mathematical specifications with flowing, flexible sensibilities. QuarkXPress works best when you use this mix. First, build the foundation of your document with precision. Second, place items on the page with creativity.

This chapter is about starting that process: building an infrastructure for your document. We call this *document construction*. It's just like the construction of a building. First you decide on the building's specifications—how tall and wide, and so on. Next, you lay a foundation and build structural supports.

In QuarkXPress it's very similar. First we decide on the specifications of the document—how tall and wide, whether it's double- or single-sided, and so on. Next, we build the structures of the page—repeating page elements, page numbering, and text flow. If you don't take these steps first, the foundation of your work will be unreliable—and your building might just fall down.

Step with us into the building mode. First stop is opening a new document.

▼ ▼

Building a New Document

When you open QuarkXPress under the program defaults, you'll see a blank screen underneath the menu bar, with the Tool and Measurements palettes showing. The first step in creating a new document is to choose "New" from the File menu (or type Command-N). This brings up the New dialog box, shown in Figure 2-1. It is here that you take the first steps in determining a document's page dimensions, page margins, number of columns, the spacing between columns, and whether the pages are laid out facing each other or not.

Figure 2-1

New dialog box

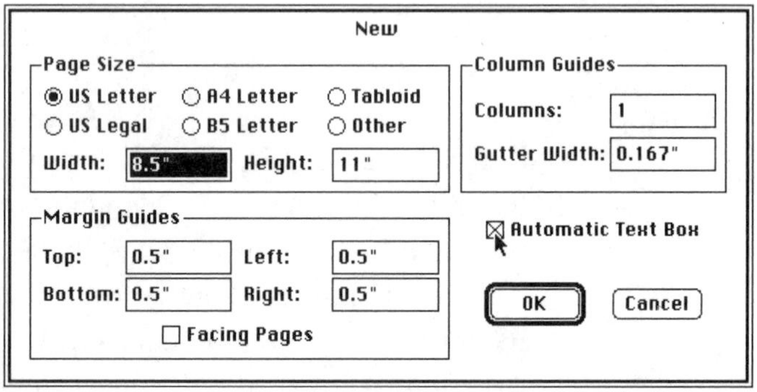

The New dialog box is the "Checkpoint Charlie" for entering the new document zone (walls may crumble, but metaphors remain). Note that there is nothing in the New dialog box that locks you in; you can make changes to these settings at any time within a document, even after you've worked on it a lot.

Let's take a look at each of this dialog box's items in detail.

Page Size

When you make your pass through the New dialog box on the way to creating a document, you have the opportunity to determine the dimensions of its pages. The *default setting*—the one QuarkXPress chooses for you if you make no change—is a standard letter-size page: 8.5-by-11 inches. You can choose among five preset choices, or you can choose a custom size page. Table 2-1 shows the measurements for each of the preset choices in three common measurement units.

Table 2-1

Preset page sizes

Name	In Inches	In Picas/Points	In Millimeters
US Letter	8.5 by 11	51p by 66p	216 by 279.4
US Legal	8.5 by 14	51p by 84p	216 by 355.6
A4 Letter	8.27 by 11.69	49p7.3 by 70p1.9	210 by 297
B4 Letter	6.93 by 9.84	41p6.9 by 59p.7	176 by 250
Tabloid	11 by 17	66p by 102p	279.4 by 431.8

Choosing "Other" lets you create any page size from 1 by 1 inch to 48 by 48 inches. You also can select another page size by simply typing the page dimensions into the Width and Height fields. Note that if you're using one of the preset radio button choices, these fields show the measurements for those pages.

▼ ▼

Tip: Page Size is Not Paper Size. "Page Size" in the New dialog box refers to the size of the pages you want as your finished output—not to the size of the paper going through your printer. These may or may not be the same. In the Page Size area, type in the page dimensions of the actual piece you want to produce. For example, if you want to create a book page 7 by 9 inches, enter these values in the Width and Height fields, even if you're outputting to a laser printer capable of only letter-size pages.

▼ ▼

Margin Guides

The Margin Guides area allows you to specify the margin sizes on all four sides of a page: "Top," "Bottom," "Left," and "Right." When you work with facing pages (see below), "Left" and "Right" change to "Inside" and "Outside." These margin guides can be used to define the *column area*. In the book and magazine trade, the column area is usually called the *live area*. It's the area within which the text and graphics usually sit (see Figure 2-2). The term "live area" may be slightly misleading, however, because everything that's on a page prints out, whether it's inside the margin guides or out-side—or even partially on the page and partially off it.

Figure 2-2
The column,
or "live" area

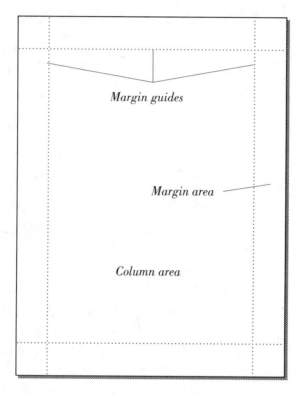

Margin guides

Margin area

Column area

Like almost every other measurement in QuarkXPress, you can type in the Margin Guide values in inches, picas, or any other measurement units. However, there are some qual-ities about margin guides that are less universal. Although margin guides resemble ruler guides both in form and func-tion, once you place margin guides you cannot change their position by dragging them. We look at making these kinds of modifications in "Making Pages," later in this chapter.

All pages in your document don't have to have the same margins. But they do until you create multiple master pages.

Once again, we defer discussion of this process until later in the chapter. For now, let's just concentrate on building one simple document.

Facing Pages

Although the Facing Pages feature is located in the Margins area of the New dialog box, it deserves some special attention. At this stage in the game, you have two choices for your document: single-sided or facing pages.

Single-sided pages. Single-sided pages are what most people generate from desktop-publishing equipment: a single-sided piece of paper. For example, handbills, flyers, posters, letters, memos, or one-page forms are all single-sided. In QuarkXPress a normal single-sided document looks like a series of pages, each positioned directly underneath the next (see Figure 2-3).

Facing pages. Facing pages are radically different in form and function from single-sided pages. Whereas nonfacing pages are destined to be single, facing pages are always married to another page (well, almost always). These two pages are adjacent to each other. For example, pick up a book. Open it in the middle. The left page (the *verso*) faces the right page (the *recto*). In many books (like the one you're looking at), the left and right pages are almost exactly the same. However, most books have a page with a slightly larger inside margin (*binding margin*) than they do an outside margin (*fore-edge margin*). This is to offset the amount of the page "lost" in the binding.

QuarkXPress displays facing pages directly next to each other on the screen (see Figure 2-4). For example, moving from page 2 to page 3 you must scroll "across" rather than "down." Note that page 2 is always a left page, and page 3 is always a right page. Even numbers fall on the left; odd numbers fall on the right.

Figure 2-3
Single-sided pages

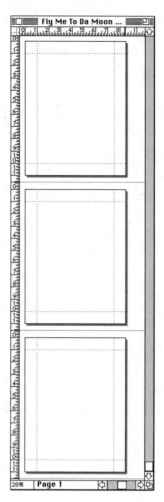

If you select "Facing Pages" in the New dialog box, Quark-XPress sets up two master pages: a left and a right page. These can be almost completely different from each another. Later in the chapter we'll see how.

Column Guides

There's another kind of automatic guide you can place on a page: column guides. The area within the margin guides can be subdivided into columns by selecting a value larger than 1 for the Columns field in the New dialog box. For example, if you want a page that ordinarily has three columns of text on it, you can specify a value of 3 (see Figure 2-5).

Figure 2-4
Facing pages

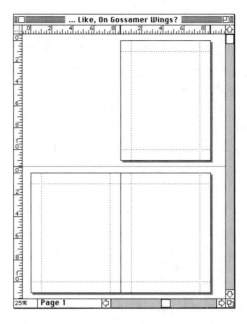

Your next decision is the amount of gutter space. This is a different "gutter" than people sometimes use to refer to the inside page margin. In QuarkXPress, the *gutter* is the blank space between column guides.

Note that these column guides don't print out. Nor do they limit what you can do on the page. They are simply part of the general infrastructure of the document, and are meant as

Figure 2-5
Column guides

guides. Not only can you change these guides at any time, but you can disregard them entirely.

Perhaps the best way to think about column guides is the concept of the page grid. Unfortunately, QuarkXPress can't create a true horizontal and vertical grid for your page. However, it can give you the tools to make one yourself. Column guides are the first part of that procedure: they allow you to place columns of space on a page. When "Snap to Guides" is selected from the View menu, items such as text boxes and lines snap to your column guides (see Chapter 1, *Structure and Interface*).

The Grids&Guides and Grid Layout XTensions can also be a great aid in creating page grids (see Appendix B).

Automatic Text Box

Here's a relatively easy choice: do you want your first page and all subsequent pages you add to have a text box already placed on them? If so, just check this box. The text box fills the page to the margin guides. This is clearly the way to go if you're working with documents such as books or flyers that are mostly text.

If you do select "Automatic Text Box," the text box that QuarkXPress makes for you is set to the same number of columns and gutter size that you specified in the Column Guides area.

▼ ▼

Tip: Check That New Dialog Box. QuarkXPress remembers what you selected in the New dialog box for the last document and gives you the same thing next time you start on a new document. This can be helpful or it can be a drag. You'll hear us say this throughout the book: verify each dialog box as you go. Don't just assume that you want every default setting. Pay attention to those details and you'll rarely go wrong.

▼ ▼

Two Construction Scenarios

We've sat down with so many people trying to get them to understand how QuarkXPress works that we could tell you stories that would knock your socks off. For example, let's look at the way two different people might attempt to create the same document.

The Nightmare Scenario

Bill is setting up his new document. This is what he thinks.

"Hmmm...I want to create a pamphlet whose pages are 4 inches wide by 7 inches tall. It'll be perfect bound with pages facing each other. So I guess I'll really need 8 by 14 inches as my page size, since I'll print two of those pages on one piece of paper. No, wait. I don't need to double both dimensions, because the height is constant at 7 inches. So I really need 14-inch width by 7-inch height, and that's what I'll type into Page Size. But wait! I guess I should leave the page size as the default 8.5 by 11—because that's the size of the paper going through my laser printer. Oh, and margins— I want 1-inch top margins and .5-inch margins for the other three sides. Does this mean I have to measure those from the outside edge of my 8.5-by-11-inch page? So am I really dealing with a 7.5-by-9-inch page, and do I type that in Page Size? And how much space do I need to leave for crop marks? Or do I...? Hunh?"

Folks, it's been known to happen, and we have bundles of unsworn testimony.

The Blissful Dream Scenario

Vicki is setting up her new document. This is what she thinks.

"My finished pamphlet will comprise pages that are 4 inches wide by 7 inches tall. Therefore, that's what I'll type as my custom page size. The pamphlet will be bound with facing pages, so that means I'll just check the Facing Pages check box. Margins will be 1 inch at the top, .5 inches for all the other sides. So those values are what I'll enter in the

Margins area. I can print the facing pages together on my 8.5-by-11-inch paper from my laser printer by printing it sideways (I'd better look at Chapter 10, *Printing*, about how to do that)."

The Lesson: When you're setting up your document, have faith that QuarkXPress exists to make your life easy, not hard. Each item in the New dialog box should be taken at face value as the value you want on the final page. Let QuarkXPress do its job, and yours will be a lot easier.

Master Pages: Elementary

In March 1990, traffic was disrupted and mini-riots occurred in major American cities as thousands of employees of graphic design firms, typesetting shops, service bureaus, and other businesses took to the streets spontaneously in joyous, drunken revels upon hearing Quark's announcement that version 3 of QuarkXPress would significantly improve the program's implementation of master pages.

Master pages is the means of establishing repeating elements common to multiple pages within a document. For example, if you have one master page in a single-sided document, then what's on that master page shows up on every new page you create. In facing-page documents there are two master pages, one for the left page and one for the right. Master page elements can be defined as common to all left or all right pages. Thus, in a facing-page document, all the left pages include all the elements on the left master page.

Master pages are great for a number of functions, including automatic page numbers, headers, footers, siders, borders, repeating graphics, or any other item that you want to show up on many different pages.

In versions of QuarkXPress prior to 3, "master pages" were called "default pages," and they had a big problem: they were set in stone, and we don't mean the Adobe typeface.

Once you formatted your default pages and began building a document, changes to the default page would not apply retroactively to the pages already created. In other words, document pages would not be updated when you changed a default page. We remember having made a typo in our header and having to manually fix it on every page in a book simply because QuarkXPress couldn't make the change for us.

But all that is in the past now. QuarkXPress's new implementation offers you not only the freedom to change your mind without penalty, but more flexibility in master page creation than any other Mac publishing program. But if you use other page-layout software, you should note that Quark-XPress's master pages differ significantly from their competition's versions in concept and function.

How the Other Guys Do It

In PageMaker, DesignStudio, and Ready,Set,Go, master pages interact "transparently" with actual document pages. It is common to describe them using the metaphor of transparent overlays on all pages, but really they are more like "underlays" beneath each page. In one of these other programs, like PageMaker, you create and edit the guts of the document on your document page, while PageMaker's master page underlay displays and prints underneath it. Speaking metaphorically, you can "slide out" this master page underlay at any time, change the page formatting, and then slide it back in.

In these programs, you can choose to base document pages on master pages or not—simply by turning the master on or off for specific pages. However, you cannot locally change any master page elements within actual document pages, because although they display and print there, they really exist only on the underlay—untouchable unless they are slid out. Nor can you choose to base pages on only certain of the elements on a master page; everything on the master page is either turned on or turned off. And you cannot have multiple master pages for a single document.

How QuarkXPress Does It

Master pages in QuarkXPress 3 is totally different. You get all the retroactive formatting power found in the other programs, plus more. Elements on QuarkXPress's master pages show up on regular document pages not as view-only elements existing on an underlay, but as real elements that you can edit just like any other page element. If you change master page formatting, you have the option of saving any "local" modifications you've made to those master-page elements on document pages.

You can base actual pages on a *formatted* or a *blank* master page (the latter is the QuarkXPress equivalent of turning a master page "off"). And you can have multiple master pages—up to 127—in any document, so you can base different document pages on different master pages. This is very useful if your document comprises multiple sections that require different looks.

We're going to stick to the basics in this elementary section on QuarkXPress's master pages, because to throw all the options and variables down on the table at once might make things seem more complicated than they really are. Working with master pages isn't complicated when taken step by step.

Your First Master Page

Two things happen simultaneously when you press OK in the New dialog box: QuarkXPress builds a master page called "Master A" and creates the first page of your document for you to work on. The master page and the document page are almost identical. If you specified "Facing Pages" in the New dialog box, QuarkXPress still only creates a single document page, but it makes two master pages: a left page called L-Master A and a right page called R-Master A.

You can move between viewing the master pages of a document and the document itself using three methods.

- **Document Layout palette.** The icons for the master pages are located at the top of the Document Layout palette.

To jump to the master page you want to view, simply double-click on its icon (see Figure 2-6).

Figure 2-6
Viewing a
master page

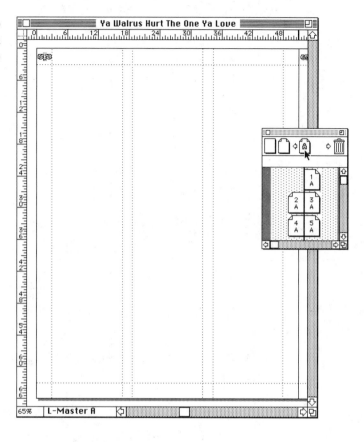

- **Display menu.** You can choose either your document or your master pages by selecting one of them from the Display submenu under the Page menu (see Figure 2-7).

- **Go-to pop-up page feature.** Clicking on the page number in the lower-left corner of the document's window gives you a pop-up menu on which you can select any document page or master page (see Figure 2-8). This feature is only available if you have the QuarkXTras package (see Appendix B, *Resources*).

Figure 2-7
Selecting a page
to look at

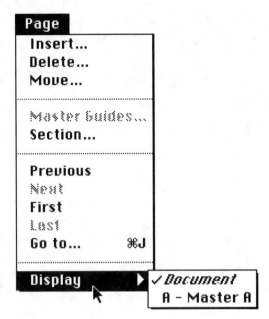

Figure 2-8
Go-to pop-up
page feature

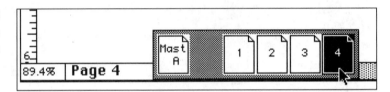

You can tell whether you're looking at a document page or a master page by three tell-tale signs.

- A page number indicator in the lower-left corner of the document window tells you that you are looking at a document page.

- An automatic text link icon is always in the upper-left corner of a master page. (We discuss what this is later in the chapter.)

- While viewing a master page, you won't be able to perform certain functions that are usually available. For example, the Go to (Command-J) feature is disabled, as well as "Insert." Often, even typing is impossible when a master page is displayed.

▼ ▼

Parts of a Master Page

Although master pages look very similar to normal document pages, there are some basic differences of which you need to be aware. These are the master guides, the automatic text link icon, and the automatic text link box. Each of these is integral to the construction of a well-built document. Note that "automatic text link icon" is our term for what Quark's documentation refers to as both the "Intact Chain Icon" and the "Broken Chain Icon." Similarly, our term "automatic text link box" is referred to as "automatic text box" in the Quark manuals. We think our terminology is more descriptive, so that's what we use. If you like theirs, then do a mental substitution.

Master Guides

We said above that you could change the margins and column guides after you set them in the New dialog box. The Master Guides dialog box is the place to do it. For those of you who are used to a previous version of QuarkXPress, this feature replaces the old Page Guides command. You can get the Master Guides dialog box by selecting "Master Guides" from the Page menu (see Figure 2-9).

When you use the Master Guides dialog box to change the margin guides or the column guides, only the master page that you have open changes. However, after you learn about multiple master pages later on in this chapter, you'll see that you can have a different set of margins and columns for each master page in your document.

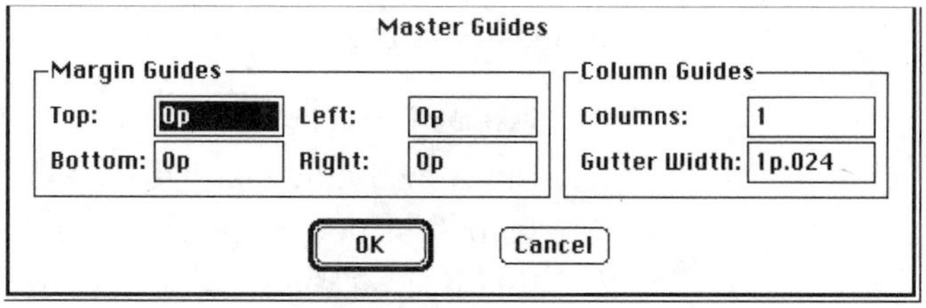

Figure 2-9
The Master Guides
dialog box

```
                          Master Guides
 ┌Margin Guides───────────────┐    ┌Column Guides─────────┐
 │ Top:    [0p]    Left:  [0p] │    │ Columns:      [1]    │
 │ Bottom: [0p]    Right: [0p] │    │ Gutter Width: [1p.024]│
 └─────────────────────────────┘    └──────────────────────┘

              ( OK )        [ Cancel ]
```

Automatic Text Link Icon

The automatic text link icon is the little picture of a chain link in the upper-left corner of every master page. It is the gateway to QuarkXPress's automatic text linking feature. This feature allows QuarkXPress to automatically link together text boxes that lie on each page. This process also can be accomplished manually but it is much slower. The automatic text link icon works in conjunction with the automatic text link box, which we discuss soon.

The automatic text link icon is always either broken (disabled) or linked (enabled). You can use the Linking and Unlinking tools while viewing your master pages to switch the automatic linking on and off (see below).

Automatic Text Link Box

Another item of importance to master pages is the automatic text link box. This is a text box that is linked through QuarkXPress's automatic linking mechanism. Automatic linking is the way that QuarkXPress links pages together. We know this sounds confusing. Let's look at an example.

Picture a one-page document with only one master page, Master A. If your text fills and overflows the text box on the first page, you can add a page by selecting "Insert Page" from the Page menu. If your Master A has an automatic text link box on it, then the overflow text automatically flows onto the newly added page. If there is no automatic text link box on the master page, then QuarkXPress does not link your first page text box to anything, and you have to link things manually (see Chapter 1, *Structure and Interface*).

There are two ways to get automatic text link boxes on your master page.

- **Automatic Text Box.** If you select "Automatic Text Box" in the New dialog box, QuarkXPress places a text box on your first document page and also on Master A. The text box on the master page is automatically assigned to be an automatic text link box.

- **Linking to the chain.** You can create your own automatic text link box by drawing a text box on your master page and then linking it to the automatic text link icon. First, select the Linking tool. Second, click on the automatic text link icon in the upper-left corner of the page, and then on the text box you want automatically linked (see Figure 2-10).

Figure 2-10

Creating an automatic text link box

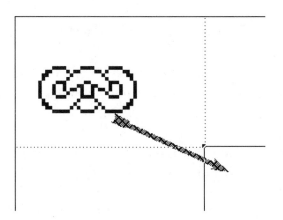

An automatic text link box is a special case text box. It is reserved solely for text that is typed in document pages, so you cannot type any text in it while on the master page. This is different from other boxes that are on the master page, which can contain text or graphics. We'll look at why you'd want these other types a little later on.

Modifying Automatic Text Link Boxes

While you cannot type in automatic text link boxes, you can make many formatting specifications on them. For example, you can specify the number of columns, width, height, background color, and frame. While QuarkXPress originally places automatic text link boxes so that they fill the area outlined by the margin guides, you can move and resize them to suit your needs.

▼ ▼

Tip: Assigning a Startup Font. Although you cannot actually type in an automatic text link box while in master page viewing mode, you *can* assign a character formatting to the box. Just select the text box with the Content tool and specify the font, size, style, and so on. Then, when you return to the document page, the text you type in that box appears in the font, size, and style that you chose. Text that is imported into that box does not necessarily appear in that font, however.

▼ ▼

Creating Multiple Automatic Text Link Boxes

You can actually have any number of automatic text link boxes on a master page. What you have to do is link them all in the order in which you want text to flow into them. You define the first box as automatic, using the procedures described above. Then you click in succession with the Linking tool on the boxes you want to define as automatic text link boxes. This defines them as part of the automatic text chain. You'll see the linking arrows shoot out with each new link that you create. To continue the link from a left master to a right master, click on the right master's automatic text link icon before joining any boxes found on the right master.

Delinking Automatic Text Link Boxes

The easiest way to discard an automatic text link box is to delete it (Command-K). But if you want to keep the box and simply negate its definition as an automatic text link box, you can do that using the Unlinking tool. First, click on the automatic text link icon with the Unlinking tool, thereby showing the linking arrow. Next, click on the tail of the linking arrow to break the chain and turn the box into a "normal" master page text box. In the case of multiple, successively linked boxes, the automatic linking is broken wherever you've broken the chain, though any other links you've created remain.

▼ ▼

Tip: Make Sure that You're Working with the Correct Pointer. It's very easy to attempt linking and unlinking only to find nothing happening—no arrows shooting out or changing course. In such a case, remember the wise words of Ship's Engineer Montgomery Scott, who has shouted many times to trembling trainees, "Use the right tool for the right job, laddies!" Hold down the Option key as you select the Linking or Unlinking tools (as your operation requires), so that they remain selected and so provide you with the correct pointer, without which you can't conduct these operations.

▼ ▼

Tip: Use Step and Repeat to Copy Page Geometry. Remember, there's no need to recreate boxes and graphic elements for the right side of a master page if you've already created the left side. Select each item to duplicate and use the Duplicate or Step and Repeat features (under the Item menu) to create copies. A "Step and Repeat" with a vertical offset of 0 (zero) ensures that the copies are at precisely the same vertical position on a page as the original. Remember that you can hold down the Shift key as you drag copies to constrain movement horizontally or vertically. After you move the items, then change the text content, and the character and paragraph formatting as is appropriate to your right master formatting plans.

▼ ▼

What to Put on a Master Page

Although your creativity in formatting master pages is unlimited, master pages' most common uses are for headers, footers, and siders. These typically contain such information as publication name, chapter or section title, author's name, date or number of the issue, and page numbering. These items are perfect for master pages because creating them for every page in your document would be a chore that Hercules would shudder at and Job would give up on.

- Headers are repeating sections at the tops of pages, usually in the margin area.

- Footers are headers that fall at the bottoms of pages.

- Siders are the same as headers and footers, except that they appear on the side margins of pages. Far less common than headers and footers, they are usually reserved for wide margins as you don't want them abutting regular text. In bound documents, they most often appear on the *outside* margin of each page, so that they don't disappear into the binding.

If you're used to working with a dedicated word-processing program, you know that the way to create and edit headers and footers in it is to call up a special window and type into it, thereafter choosing to hide or show the header/footer on scrolling pages as the particular program allows. There is no way to hide headers and footers in QuarkXPress. You create them directly on your master pages as standard text or picture boxes, and they show up everywhere you go. Figure 2-11 shows a master page with headers, footers, and siders.

Figure 2-11
Headers, footers, and siders

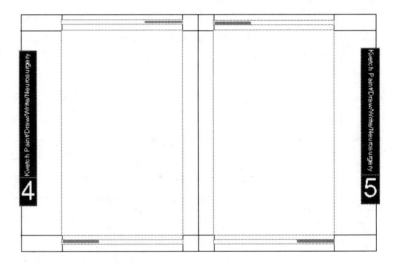

Automatic Page Numbering

Part of building a firm infrastructure in your document is making your document work for you rather than you work for your document. A perfect example of this is page numbering.

We have a confession to make: before we knew better, we would put "1" on the first page, "2" on the second page, and so on. When we deleted or added pages, we just took the time to renumber every page. That seemed reasonable enough. What else could we do?

QuarkXPress lets you set up automatic page numbering for an entire document. You don't actually type any number on the master page. What you type is the Current Box Page Number character (Command-3). This gives you a "number placeholder." This placeholder is replaced by the page number when you are looking at the document from the Document view. In master pages, the page number placeholder looks like this: <#>.

The number appears in whatever font, size, and style you choose on the master page. For example, if you make the <#> character 9-point Trump-Mediaeval all the page numbers come out in that style.

Remember, the Current Box Page Number character (Command-3) is simply a character that you type, manipulate, or delete using keyboard commands. You also can type it alongside other text, to form text blocks that read, "Page <#>" or "If you wanted to find pg. <#>, you found it."

These page numbers flow with your pages. For example, if you move page 23 to be your new page 10, every page in the document changes its position and numbering accordingly. Also, if you change the page numbering scheme to Roman numerals or whatever (see "Sections," later in this chapter), QuarkXPress automatically changes that style on every page.

Graphics and Master Pages

You can do anything with a graphic on a master page that you can do on a regular document page, including defining it for text runarounds. You can be subtle and put a small graphic in your header or footer, or you can put a great big graphic in the background of every page (see Figure 2-12).

The thing to remember when formatting master pages with graphics—whether as backgrounds or for runaround effects—

Figure 2-12

Placing a graphic on
your master page

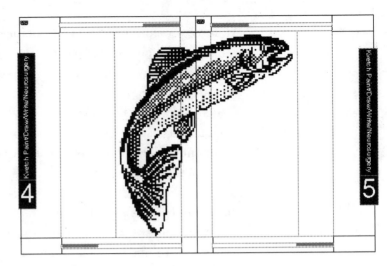

is that what you place on the master page appears on every
page of the document. If you only want a graphic on a few
pages in your document, you're best off either handling such
things on a page-by-page basis in the regular document view,
or creating different master pages to hold different graphics.

Changing Master Page Items

After you have created your master page, you can manipulate
the text and picture boxes in either master page or document
view. Which view you're in when you make a change determines what effect the change has on your document.

Changes on Master Pages

If you are in master page view when you make a change to a
master page item, the change is reflected on every page in
your document that is based on that master page—unless
that item has been changed on particular pages while in document view.

For example, let's say you have a header with the name of
the document and the page number. You have created a 30-
page document with this master page, so each page has that

header on it. If you change the header so that it reads differently, that change shows up on all 30 pages. However, if you changed the header on page 10 while in document view before reworking the header on the master page, the header on every page *except* page 10 is changed. Page 10 remains unchanged because your local page formatting overrides the master page formatting for that text box.

Continuing with this example, as long as no local page formatting changes are made, if you delete the header from the master page, the header is deleted from every page of the document. But, if a change had already been made locally to the header on page 10, then that header on page 10 is *not* deleted.

Taking this concept one step farther, if you actually delete a master page, the master items that appear on document pages are deleted, too, unless you have *locally* modified them in some way. For example, if you have a picture box on a master page, and page 3 is based on that master page, then the picture box appears on page 3. If you do not modify that picture box in some way, deleting the master page removes the picture box from page 3. This makes some sense if you think about it for a while, even though it's often frustrating.

Changes to Document Pages

Once back on the actual document pages, any changes made to master items (elements derived from the master page) affect only those actual pages; master pages themselves are not affected by local page formatting. To modify a master page, you have to go back into master pages view.

In "Advanced Master Pages," below, we discuss how to create multiple master pages and assign them to a page. But what happens if you assign one master page to a page that already has master items on it? Master items from the first master page are generally deleted and replaced by the new master items. The one exception is if you have already locally modified a master item.

The determining factor for what happens to master page items that have been modified locally (while in document view) is the Master Page Items feature in the Preferences dialog box (under the Edit menu). You have two choices.

Delete Changes. If "Master Page Items" is set to "Delete Changes," every master item on a page is deleted and replaced with new master items—even if changes have been made locally. If you have made changes, this is a great way to "reset" the page: reapply a master page to a document page while "Delete Changes" is set in the Preferences dialog box. All the locally modified items are deleted and reset back to the original master items.

Keep Changes. The alternative to deleting locally modified master items is keeping them. When "Keep Changes" is selected in the Preferences dialog box, QuarkXPress skips over any master items that you have modified (changed their position, size, shape, font, text, and so on). This is the default setting when you start a document.

Summing it Up

And that's really all there is to how the master page feature works. It's simple, and simply ingenious, and any more advanced things that you do with it are based on these operational principles.

▼ ▼

Master Pages: Advanced

If you've gotten this far, you've learned the hardest stuff about QuarkXPress's master pages. We're calling this the advanced section not because it's more complex or difficult, but because it simply represents a further level of control, by offering the following additional options.

- Creating new master pages

- Creating new master pages based on existing ones

- Naming and ordering master pages

- Applying master pages to document pages

- Deleting master pages

There are many ways to use multiple master pages. For example, most books are separated into several sections, including front matter, body text, and index. Each section is paginated and formatted differently from the body, with different (or no) headers or footers. You can create a master page for each of these sections. Multiple master pages are almost required for magazine production, where you may have a plethora of different sections: front matter, regular article pages, photo features, full-page ads, and small-ad sections, to name a few.

Multiple master pages are accessible primarily through the Document Layout palette. We introduced the Document Layout palette in Chapter 1, *Structure and Interface.* Now we're going to concentrate on how you can use it to work with your master pages.

Document Layout Palette

If you look at the Document Layout palette for the facing-pages document in Figure 2-13, you'll see that it is divided vertically into three parts: the blank document and master pages area, the master pages name area, and the document layout area.

Blank document and master pages area. At the top of the Document Layout palette is the blank document and master pages area. This is used for creating, storing, and deleting both document and master pages. Within this section are three control areas. The first contains blank single-sided and facing-page icons; the second control area contains the master page selection list; and the third has the trash can. You can create a new master page by dragging a blank single or facing-page icon into the master page selection list (see Figure 2-14).

Figure 2-13
Document Layout
Palettes for a single-
sided and a facing-
pages document

*Blank document and
master pages area*

Master pages name area

*Document layout
area*

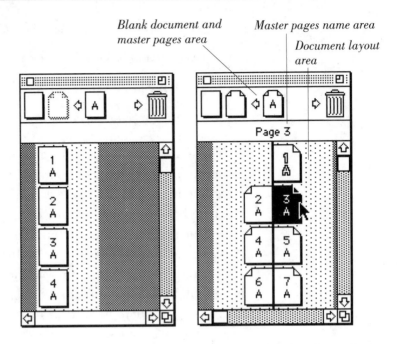

Similarly, you can delete a master page by dragging its icon into the trash can. Note that this trash can is *not* like the one on your Macintosh desktop. It doesn't bulge first and require a further action to get emptied. It is emptied immediately upon release of the mouse button; that is, once you put either your master or document page into it, it is deleted forever. This action is not reversible with Undo (Command-Z). So make sure you really want to do it.

▼ ▼

Tip: Retrieving Document Layout Deletions. If you've deleted a master page from the Document Layout palette, the only way to get it back is by selecting "Revert to Saved" from the File menu. This, of course, only works if you've saved your document recently. Bear in mind that this method wipes out all changes you've made since your last save, so pause a moment and reflect before you jump into this last resort.

▼ ▼

If you have more than two or three master pages, Quark-XPress lets you move them by clicking on the scroll arrows. Note that the second master page you create is called "Mas-

Figure 2-14
Creating a new
master page

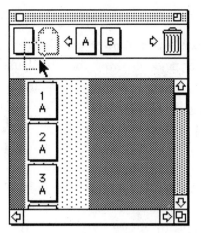

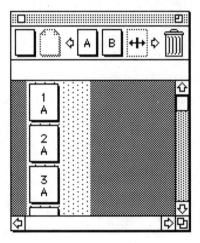

ter B," even if you place the icon in the master page selection list before Master A.

Master pages name field. Just below the blank document and master pages area is the master pages name area. You can assign a name to each master page by first selecting a master page from the master page selection area and then replacing the name "Master B" (or whatever) with your desired name. The name you assign is the name that appears in master page scroll lists and menus throughout the program.

▼ ▼

Tip: Master Naming Conventions. Note that although you can name a master page anything you like, QuarkXPress displays page icons with only a letter (A, B, C, and so on). We find it helps to name master pages with a letter as a prefix. For example, if Master A is a master page for the table of contents, we might label it "A-TOC." Our next page may be called "B-Front Matter," and so on.

To get a listing of all the master pages' names, select "Insert Page" from the Page menu, then click on the Master Page pop-up menu and, while holding the mouse button down, create a screen dump (type Command-Shift-3). You can then print out this screen dump as a reference guide.

▼ ▼

Document layout area. The largest area in the Document Layout Palette is the document layout area. This shows icons of the document's pages, numbered and positioned in the order of their actual appearance in the document (see Chapter 1, *Structure and Interface* for more on this area). Each page icon on the palette displays the master page that it is based on. When you first open a new document, only one page is visible and it is based on Master A.

Basing a New Master Page on Another

If you need a new master page but don't want to format it from scratch, you can base it on another that carries at least some formatting that you wish to retain. You do this by first creating a new master page as described above. Then, select the icon of the particular master page whose formatting you wish to copy and drag it over the icon of the just-created master page, releasing the mouse button when that icon is highlighted.

Applying Master Pages to Document Pages

You can apply the formatting of any master page to an existing document page, whether that page was already based on a master page or not. To do this, drag a master page icon on top of a document page icon. You can release the mouse button as soon as the page icon is highlighted. The document page assumes the formatting of that master page. Unmodified master items (from the old master page) are deleted. Items that you have modified may or may not be deleted (see "Changing Master Page Items," above).

▼ ▼

Making Pages

In Chapter 1, *Structure and Interface*, we discussed moving pages around and deleting them. Clearly, that was slightly premature as we haven't yet gotten to adding new pages to a document. We cover that procedure here.

There are two ways to add pages to your document—the Insert Pages dialog box, and the Document Layout palette.

Insert Pages

The first way you can add pages to your document is by selecting "Insert" from the Pages menu. This brings up the Insert Pages dialog box (see Figure 2-15). This dialog box is almost entirely self-explanatory, but we'll go over it piece by piece just to be sure.

Figure 2-15
The Insert Pages
dialog box

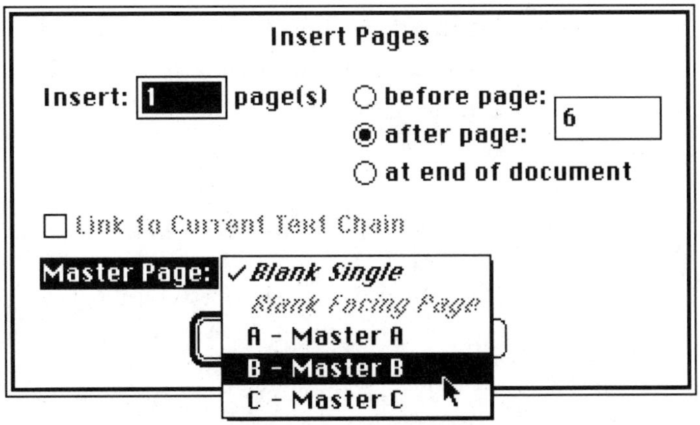

You can type the number of pages you want to add in the Insert field, and then select where you want those pages to be added. You have three choices: before a page, after a page, and at the end of the document. The first two require that you choose a page that the page(s) should be added before or after; the third requires no additional number, as it places the pages after the last page in the document.

Before you hit OK, though, you need to think about two other things in this dialog box: the Link to Current Text Chain check box, and the Master Page specification. Let's look at these in reverse order.

Master Page specification. You can choose which master page you want these pages to be based on by selecting one from the Master Page pop-up menu. Or, if you like, you can base the pages-to-be on blank single-sided or facing-page pages (you can choose the latter only if you're working with a facing-page document).

Link to Current Text Chain. If a text box is selected on your page and the master page you are basing your inserted pages on has an automatic text link box, then you have the option of having the inserted pages automatically linked with the text box you have selected. This is a potentially confusing concept, so let's look at it carefully.

Let's say you have a text box on a page, and it's overflowing with text. Let's also say that your master page C-Feature-Opener has an automatic text link box on it that is enabled (linked to the automatic text link icon).

1. Select the text box on the document page.

2. Select "Insert" from the Page menu.

3. Add a page based on master page C-FeatureOpener at the end of the document.

If you click on "Link to Current Text Chain" in the Insert Pages dialog box, then the text from your document page text box automatically links to your inserted pages. If you do not select "Link to Current Text Chain," then the pages are still added, but there is no link between your text box and the text boxes on those pages. You can, however, link them up manually using the Link tool.

Document Layout Insertions

The second method for inserting pages is to insert them via the Document Layout palette. Like everything else in this palette, adding pages is performed via dragging icons. To add a page based on a master page, drag that master page icon down into the position you want (before a page, after a page, at the end of a document, or as a page in a spread). If you don't want the page based on a master page, you can drag the single-sided or facing-page icon into place instead (as mentioned above, you can only drag a facing-page icon if you are working with a facing-page document).

If you want to add more than one page at a time, or want to add pages that are linked to the current text chain, then you must hold down the Option key while clicking and dragging the page icon into place. When you let go of the icon, QuarkXPress gives you the Insert Pages dialog box. You can select the appropriate items as described above.

▼ ▼

Modifying Your Pages

Fortunately for desktop publishers, you can change the foundation of your document significantly more easily than a construction worker can change the foundation of a building. Not only can you modify your master pages in all sorts of ways, as we've seen, but you can modify the underlying page size, margins, column guides, and more. Let's look at each of these controls.

Changing Page Size

Even after you've clicked OK in the New dialog box and begun adding pages to a document, you can still change the page size in the Document Setup dialog box (choose "Document Setup" from the File menu; see Figure 2-16). Note that this dialog box bears a striking resemblance to a portion of the New dialog box. The rules are just the same (see "Page Size," above).

Your only real limitation in modifying page size is the size of any objects you have already placed on the page. Quark-XPress won't let you make a page so small that page elements would "fall off" the pasteboard (the size of the pasteboard surrounding each page is determined by the size of your document page). If this is a limiting factor, you may be able to work around the problem by adjusting the width of the pasteboard (see "Tip: Adjusting Your Pasteboard," in Chapter 1, *Structure and Interface*).

Changing Facing Pages

You can change one other page feature with the Document Setup dialog box: facing pages. If you originally specified your document as single-sided, you can change to a facing-page document by clicking on the Facing Pages item in the Document Setup dialog box. Facing-page documents can have facing master pages (the facing-page icon is enabled in the Document Layout palette). However, you cannot change a facing-page document to a single-sided document if you have

Figure 2-16
The Document
Setup dialog box

```
                    Document Setup
 ┌─Page Size──────────────────────────────┐
 │  ● US Letter    ○ A4 Letter   ○ Tabloid │
 │  ○ US Legal     ○ B5 Letter   ○ Other   │
 │  Width: [8.5"]        Height: [11"]     │
 └─────────────────────────────────────────┘

            ☐ Facing Pages

        [ OK ]        [ Cancel ]
```

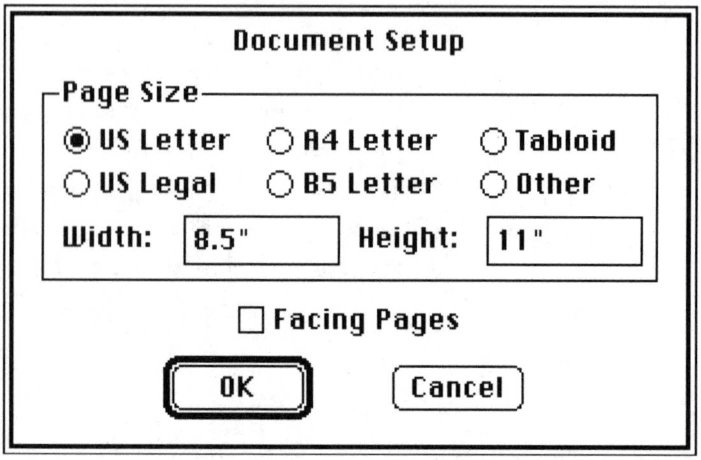

any facing master pages. If you need to change a facing-page document to a single-sided document, first delete all the facing master pages (drag them into the trash), and then deselect "Facing Pages" from the Document Setup dialog box.

Changing Margins

As we mentioned above, every page in your document has the same margins until you create multiple master pages, each with different margins. When you first open a master page, its margin guides are set to the values you specified in the New dialog box. You can change these margins by selecting "Master Guides" from the Page menu. Remember that the Master Guides menu item is only available when a master page is being displayed.

▼ ▼

Tip: Ignoring the Guides. Even without creating and applying different master pages, you can get "de facto" different margins within a document, since margin guides are only that—*guides*. If you want, you can simply ignore them. Draw out or resize a text or graphics box so that it is bigger or smaller than the margin-defined area, creating a custom "active area" for your page elements. But unless you're dealing with one-page documents, it's really best to handle multiple margin definitions by going ahead and changing the Master Guides settings.

▼ ▼

Changing Column Guides

Migrants from PageMaker should be aware that Quark-XPress's column guides cannot be repositioned by dragging them with the mouse. Instead, you change the Column Guides settings in the Master Guides dialog box. QuarkXPress lets you have a different number of columns and varied gutter sizes for each master page. If you want to have no column guides on a page, type "1" in the Columns field.

▼ ▼

Tip: Snap to Guides for Box Fitting. We often find it more helpful to draw separate text boxes for each column rather than use one large text box separated into columns. Column and margin guides make this process easy. If you have "Snap to Guides" turned on (under the View menu), you can quickly draw a text box that fills one column. This text box can be duplicated, then positioned in the next column, and so on, until each column is created. Keith sometimes decides he doesn't want the column guides cluttering up the page after he's drawn these text boxes, so he simply removes them from the master page using "Master Guides." David, having lived with clutter most of his life, just leaves the guides where they are.

Automatic Page Insertion

Importing a long text document can be a harrowing experience when you're working with automatically linked text boxes. Where does the rest of the text go when the first text box is filled? QuarkXPress lets you control this through the Auto Page Insertion pop-up menu in the General Preferences dialog box (under the Edit menu). You have four choices: "End of Story," "End of Section," "End of Document," and "Off." The default setting (the way it's set up if you don't change anything), is "End of Section."

End of Story. With this option enabled, QuarkXPress inserts new pages right after the page containing the last text box in a story, and they bear the master page formatting of the page that held that box. If, for instance, your story starts on page 1 and jumps to page 5, any text overflow from the page 5 text box causes pages to be inserted following page 5, not page 1.

End of Section. Under this option, pages are inserted following the last page in a section (see "Sections" and "Page Numbering," later in this chapter). Additional pages bear the master page formatting of the last page in that section. Thus, if your page 1 story jumps to page 5, and page 5 is part of a section that ends with page 8, new pages inserted because of text overflow appear right after page 8.

End of Document. This option causes pages to be inserted after the last page of the document, no matter how long it is and despite any sections you might have set up. Inserted pages bear the master page formatting of the last page of the document.

If you have only one story and one section in a document, then all three of these settings mean the same thing.

Off. When "Auto Page Insertion" is set to "Off," QuarkXPress never adds pages automatically. Instead, you must add pages manually (see "Making Pages," earlier in this chapter).

Text Linking

Remember, the Automatic Page Insertion feature only works if your master page has an automatic text link box. That makes sense, because otherwise pages are inserted based on text flowing through the automatic text chain. You cannot have *automatic page insertion* without an *automatic text link*, and you cannot have that without an *automatic text link box.*

▼ ▼

Multiple Page Spreads

When the rest of the world thought that facing-page spreads were pretty nifty, Quark came along and added the capability to build three-page spreads. In fact, you can quickly and easily build four-page, five-page, or any number of pages in a spread, as long as the combined width of the spread doesn't exceed 48 inches.

Once again, this is a job for the Document Layout palette. Spreads can be created in both facing-pages and single-sided documents by clicking on a page icon and dragging it to the right side of a right page or to the left side of a left page (single-sided documents, for this purpose, are made entirely of right pages). The pasteboard (represented by the dark gray area in the palette) automatically expands to accommodate the pages. Figure 2-17 shows an example of creating a three-page spread in a facing-page document.

Note that dragging a page to the left of a right page or to the right of a left page may result in reshuffling the file rather than building a spread.

Figure 2-17
A three-page spread

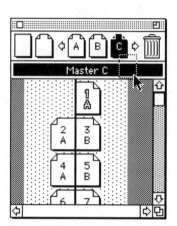 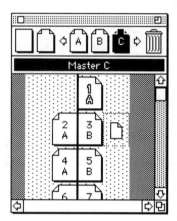

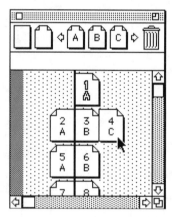

Sections and Page Numbering

Earlier in this chapter we discussed how to apply automatic page numbers to your document's master pages. Here we talk about how to customize those page numbers and create multiple sections within a single document.

Ordinarily, a QuarkXPress document has one section. Page numbers start with the Arabic numeral 1 and go up consecutively, page by page. However, you can change the starting page number, the style of page numbers, and add multiple sections that each have their own page numbering styles.

Changing Your Page Numbering

Let's say you're producing a book, and each chapter is saved in a separate QuarkXPress file. If the first chapter ends on page 32, you can tell QuarkXPress to start the page numbers in chapter two at page 33, and so on. To do this, go to the first page of the document (the one you want to change the numbering for), and select the Section item from the Page menu. Enable the Section feature by clicking in the box (an "X" should appear). Type the number at which you'd like your document to start, and click OK (see Figure 2-18).

Figure 2-18
Setting up a
new section

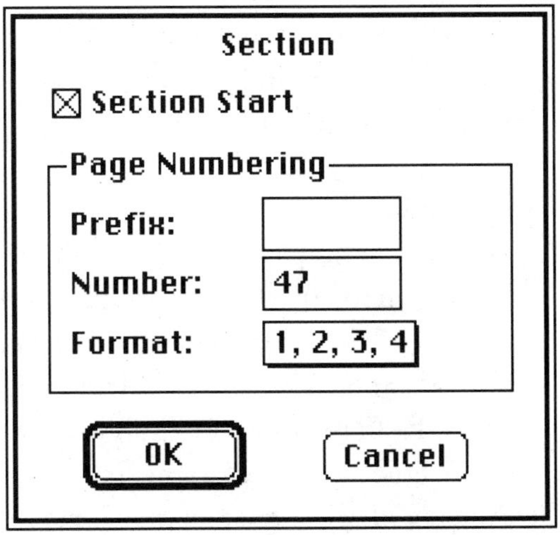

The first page of a new section always has an asterisk after its name. This doesn't print out. It's just a sign on the screen that this is a section beginning.

▼ ▼

Tip: Get to That Section Quickly. You also can modify the Section dialog box by clicking on the page icon for the first page in the section, and then clicking once in the master pages name area in the Document Layout palette.

▼ ▼

Changing the Page Numbering Style

QuarkXPress lets you choose among five formats for numbering pages.

- Arabic numerals (1, 2, 3, 4, etc.)

- Uppercase Roman numerals (I, II, III, IV, etc.)

- Lowercase Roman numerals (i, ii, iii, iv, etc.)

- Capital letters (A, B, C, D, etc.)

- Lowercase letters (a, b, c, d, etc.)

You can change the numbering style for a section by going to the first page in a section, selecting "Section" from the Page menu, and choosing a numbering format from the Format pop-up menu.

Prefixes

The automatic page numbers can contain more than just a number in the five formats listed above. You also can include a prefix of up to four letters or numbers to the page number. For example, you may want the page numbers in a book appendix to read A-1, A-2, and so on. The "A-" is a prefix to the Arabic numerals. You can type this sort of prefix in the Prefix field of the Section dialog box.

▼ ▼

Automatic "Continued..." Pagination

In magazines and newspapers, where stories can jump from page 6 to 96, it is often helpful to have a "Continued on Page

X" message at the bottom of the column from which text is jumping, and a "Continued from Page X" message at the top of the column to which it is jumping. These are sometimes called *jump lines*. QuarkXPress can't automate creation of the lines, but it can automate the placement and revision of the page numbers in them. This is useful because you may change links, or insert or delete new pages, and such actions could change the page numbers referred to. In such cases you won't have to go through and manually update the numbers.

To Create a "Continued on..." Message

It's easy to create these jump lines (see Figure 2-19).

Figure 2-19
Jump lines

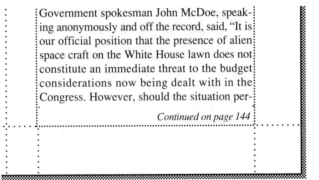

Government spokesman John McDoe, speaking anonymously and off the record, said, "It is our official position that the presence of alien space craft on the White House lawn does not constitute an immediate threat to the budget considerations now being dealt with in the Congress. However, should the situation per-

Continued on page 144

1. Make a text box the same width as the column or text box it concerns and move it on top of that text box (if this new text box is set behind the original text box, you can select "Bring to Front" from the Item menu).

2. Be sure its runaround is set to "Item" (see Chapter 7, *Where Text Meets Graphics*). This ensures that your jump line has its own space, and isn't jumbled in on top of the other text.

3. Type the text of your jump line (for example, "Continued on"), and, when you come to placement of the page number, type Command-4. This is the Next Text Box Page Number character. If you haven't added pages yet, the character as typed looks like this: <None>.

If your text links change, pages get shuffled, or an act of god is invoked, QuarkXPress always knows where your text is going and updates the "Next Box Page Number." Nonetheless, these jump lines can sometimes get confused. When QuarkXPress sees one of these jump lines, it looks at any text box that is behind the jump line. If there is more than one text box that is behind the jump line text box, Quark-XPress chooses the one that is "closest" to it; in other words, the text box that is on the next layer down.

To Create a "Continued from..." Message

You can create a "Continued from" jump line by following the same procedures for creating a "Continued to..." text box, but place it at the top of the column concerned. When you come to the page number, type Command-2, for the Previous Box Page Number character, which shows the page number of the previous text box in the chain. This number is also automatically updated as necessary.

Your messages don't have to read "Continued on/from..." You can type any words you want. For instance, "Started on page <None>" or even "If you really care about finishing this story, you'll have to flip past the bulk of this magazine and go all the way to page <None>, where you'll find it buried among the facial cream ads." What matters is that you type the relevant placeholder character somewhere in your message text box.

▼ ▼

Crop Marks and Print-Area Considerations

Crop marks, sometimes called "trim marks," sit just off the four corners of a page or page spread, indicating page edges. We'll hold off discussing them until Chapter 10, *Printing*. However, a couple of things about them are worth considering now. The two decisions you need to make are whether you want crop marks or not, and whether you want Quark-

XPress to make your crop marks automatically or you want to make them yourself.

To Crop or...

The decision of whether to crop or not depends on the sort of document you are producing and the output device you are using. If you're producing 8.5-by-11-inch or 8.5-by-14-inch letters, memos, reports, flyers, or newsletters on your laser printer for mass reproduction based on those printouts, you don't need trim marks (you won't be cutting the pages). If you're producing document pages that are smaller than the surrounding physical media on which they print—for example, printing to a roll-fed imagesetter—you'll need crop marks so that your lithographer knows exactly what to work with.

Who Crops What

Normally we just let QuarkXPress make the crop marks at the edges of our document pages, but we have run into at least two situations where we want to create them ourselves. These situations break down into two basic types.

- **Multiple-up copies.** When we use QuarkXPress to design and create business cards, we might step-and-repeat the final version two, four, or even eight times to create multiple-up copies on one letter-size page. Each one of these cards needs its own trim marks, and this is a situation where QuarkXPress cannot place them for us (see Figure 2-20).

- **Special service.** If we don't want the registration marks or QuarkXPress's job information for some reason, then we have to make our own crop marks. Note that crop marks should be a minimum of 6 points long, and preferably 1 to 2 picas from the actual page boundary. The Freebies 3.0 XTension lets you set how far you want the automatic registration and crop marks from the boundary.

Figure 2-20
Multiple-up copies

> **"No Flies" Food Prep Service, Inc.**
> *"The People People"*
> • **Leading the industry since 1990** •
>
> **H.L. Munchkin,**   122345 67th Avenue
> President, CEO, & Owner   Somewhere, USA
> *Sorry, no phone calls*

Tip: Watch Your Edges. No laser printer can print all the way to the edges of a page on any side—be it a letter-, legal-, or tabloid-size page. Normally, the print area of a letter-size page on a desktop laser printer is 7.67 by 10.14 inches—leaving a bit less than a half-inch all around as the "no print" boundary. You can enlarge the print area to 8 by 10.78 inches—leaving about a quarter-inch all around as the "no print" boundary—by selecting "Larger Print Area" from the Page Setup dialog box (see Chapter 10, *Printing*). This could be relevant to where you set your page margins and manually added crop marks for documents destined for laser printers.

▼ ▼

Foundations

You are now ready to build your pages with the understanding and confidence that you've got a strong infrastructure to hold the document up. You can use the tools discussed in Chapter 1, *Structure and Interface*, to build text and picture boxes on your master and document pages, and next we'll talk about how to start filling those boxes with text and pictures.

CHAPTER 3

WORD PROCESSING

When you think of Quark-XPress, you think of typography. But before you can set type in Quark-XPress, you have to get the words into your computer somehow. In the early days of desktop publishing, you'd usually write your stories in a word-processing program, and then import the files into a page-layout program. From its beginning, QuarkXPress was a capable word processor, and as it matured, it added more and more word-processing features. With version 3, QuarkXPress can easily be used to create and edit even the most complicated of documents.

However, all is not sweetness and light. In complex documents, QuarkXPress can become so slow that even a moderately skilled typist can get ahead of it.

In this chapter, we'll examine the strengths and weaknesses of writing in QuarkXPress, including its powerful Find/Change feature and its spelling checker. We'll also give you some tips for overcoming QuarkXPress's occasional sluggishness.

▼ ▼

Entering Text

The most basic aspect of entering text into a QuarkXPress document is making sure that what you type shows up where you want it. QuarkXPress novices often become flustered when they open a document and start typing, only to find that nothing is happening. That's because to enter text in a text box, you must use the Content tool, and you must have selected a text box.

So remember, before you can type anything, click on the Content tool (if it isn't already selected), then click on the box where you want your text to appear.

▼ ▼

Tip: Where Did the Rest of My Page Go? QuarkXPress novices, and even experienced users, often get a rude shock when working on complicated page layouts because of a feature of the Content tool. Whenever you select a text (or picture) box, any other page elements that overlap that box are hidden. This feature can be useful because it lets you edit the contents of a box free of any distractions caused by other page elements. However, the sudden disappearance of many or most of the elements on a page can panic even experienced users, particularly if they've turned off the display of guides, which also hides the borders of any nonselected boxes.

But of course these "vanished" elements are not lost, and can be quickly brought back to view by deselecting the box you're editing. Just click outside the page.

▼ ▼

Selecting and Navigating

As we mentioned in the Preface, you should be familiar with the basic mouse and editing techniques used by almost every Macintosh application. QuarkXPress adds many extras to the standard Mac ways of moving the insertion point and selecting text. Like most Mac programs, QuarkXPress gives you the flexibility of having more than one method for performing the same action; in the case of selecting and navigating, you can use either the mouse or the keyboard.

Using the Mouse

As with any Mac program, you can select a range of text by dragging the pointer diagonally up or down a text column, or you can select a word by double-clicking on it. But Quark-XPress has additional multiple-click selections (see Table 3-1). If you triple-click, you can select a line of text. Quadruple-clicking selects a paragraph, and quintuple-clicking selects all the text in the active box's text chain (this is the equivalent of typing Command-A).

Table 3-1
Effects of
multiple clicks

To Select	Click
A word, and contiguous punctuation	Twice
A line	Three times
A paragraph	Four times
An entire story	Five times

If you hold down the Shift key and click anywhere in your text chain, all the text from the previous location of the insertion point to the location of your click will be selected.

Note that if you select a range of text in a text box, then deselect the box and edit other boxes, QuarkXPress remembers the selection. When you again select the text box, the same text will be automatically selected.

▼ ▼

Tip: Extend by Word. If you continue to press down on the mouse button after your final click, you can extend your selection by dragging. If you've selected a word by double-clicking, you can drag to select more text, word by word. If you've selected a paragraph with four clicks, you can similarly drag to increase your selection paragraph by paragraph.

▼ ▼

Using the Keyboard

You can use the keyboard to duplicate most of the selections you can make with the mouse. You can also do many things with the keyboard that are not possible with the mouse alone (see Table 3-2).

To move to the	Type
Previous character	Left Arrow
Next character	Right Arrow
Previous line	Up Arrow
Next line	Down Arrow
Previous word	Command-Left Arrow
Next word	Command-Right Arrow
Start of line	Command-Option-Left Arrow
End of line	Command-Option-Right Arrow
Start of story	Command-Option-Up Arrow
End of story	Command-Option-Down Arrow

Holding down the Shift key in combination with any of the keyboard movement commands selects all text between the insertion point's original location and the location to which the key combination sends it. Again, to select all the text in a story, type Command-A.

The ability to quickly jump to the beginning or end of a story by using Command-Up Arrow or Command-Down Arrow is especially handy, as it can save you a lot of scrolling if you forget the exact page on which a story starts or finishes.

▼ ▼

Tip: The Lazy Man's Way to Follow a Text Chain. QuarkXPress has a simple feature that can help if you need to follow a story through your document, but you don't exactly remember the page to or from which the text chain is jumping. All you have to do is position the insertion point at the beginning or end of the story's text box on the current page. If you're at the beginning of the text box, use the Left Arrow key to move the insertion out of the current box to the previous box in the chain. If you're at the end of the box, similarly use the Right Arrow key to jump the insertion point to the next box in the text chain.

As soon as you move the insertion point out of the current box, QuarkXPress follows it, scrolling automatically to the page containing the text box to which you've moved the insertion point. If possible, QuarkXPress even nicely centers the box in the document window.

▼ ▼

Deleting Text

There are a number of ways of deleting text in QuarkXPress (see Table 3-3). You can, of course, use the Delete key to delete text to the left of the insertion point a character at a time, or to remove a text selection. QuarkXPress also lets you delete the character to the right of the insertion point by holding down the Shift key while pressing Delete. Similarly, Command-Delete gets rid of the entire word to the left of the insertion point, and Command-Shift-Delete removes the word to the right of the insertion point.

Table 3-3
Keyboard deletions

To delete the	Type
Previous character	Delete
Next character	Shift-Delete or Extended Keyboard Del key
Previous word	Command-Delete
Next word	Command-Shift-Delete
Any selected text	Delete

▼ ▼

Finding and Changing

QuarkXPress's powerful Find/Change feature is one of the reasons many desktop publishers prefer to use QuarkXPress as their word processor. You can use the Find/Change feature either to look for and change occurrences of any text you specify, regardless of attributes such as font, style, point size, and so on, or it can look for and change these attributes, with no regard to the actual words being modified. Or it can look for and change only occurrences of specified text with specified attributes.

As you read about the various options that can be set for the Find/Change dialog box, remember that you can change its defaults by opening it and modifying it with no document open. Any changes you make are stored in the QuarkXPress Data file and become the new defaults for your copy of QuarkXPress.

Where QuarkXPress Looks

QuarkXPress can check either the entire text chain connected to the active text box, or it can look for and change text everywhere in a document. If you have a text box selected, QuarkXPress searches through the story from the location of the insertion point to the end of the story. To search an entire story, you must have the insertion point at the very beginning of the story (press Command-Option-Up Arrow).

To have QuarkXPress check all the text in the document, you must make sure to have *no* text box selected at all, then choose the Find/Change command, and select the Document check box in the Find/Change dialog box. Only if no text boxes are selected can QuarkXPress reliably search all of a document's text. If you currently are displaying a document's master pages, this check box will be labelled "Masters," and you can use it to search all the document's master pages.

Specifying Text

To simply change all occurrences of text, regardless of attributes, you can use the Find/Change dialog box as it first appears when you select the Find/Change command from the Edit menu (see Figure 3-1). Enter the text you want QuarkXPress to find in the Find what field, then enter the new text you want in the Change to field.

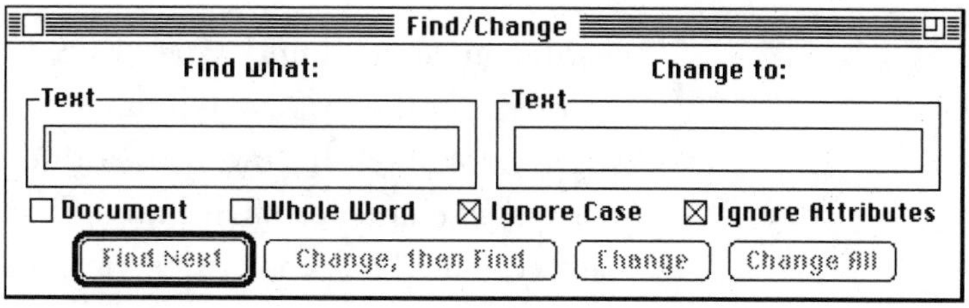

Figure 3-1
The Find/Change
dialog box

Special Characters. You can enter certain special characters in the Find what and Change to fields with the aid of the Command key. For example, if you want to search for all the new paragraph characters in a document (what you get when you press Return at the end of a paragraph), you select the Find what field, and type Command-Return. This appears in the field as \p.

Table 3-4 shows characters you can enter in these fields, how to type them, and how they appear in the fields.

Table 3-4
Special characters
in the Find/Change
dialog box

To enter this character in a field	Type this	And this appears
Tab	Command-Tab	\t
New paragraph	Command-Return	\p
New line	Command-Shift-Return	\n
New column	Command-Enter	\c
New box	Command-Shift-Enter	\b
Previous box page number	Command-2	\2
Current box page number	Command-3	\3
Next box page number	Command-4	\4
Wild card (single character)	Command-?	\?
Backslash	Command-\	\\

Note that the wild card character can only be used in the Find what field.

You can use the wild card character to represent any character. This is useful if you're looking for a word you may have spelled different ways, such as "EPS" and "EPSF." Instead of running two search operations to find all occurrences of this word, you could simply type "EPS\?" in the Find what field. You can get the "\?" by typing either Command-? or by typing a backslash followed by a question mark. To use the backslash character itself in the Find what or Change to text box, type the backslash twice, or Command-\.

Whole Word. Next to the Document check box you'll find another one labelled "Whole Word." Checking this box means that QuarkXPress only finds occurrences of the text in the Find what field if it's not bounded by other text or numerals. So a Whole Word search for "ten" would find the word "ten" when it's bounded by spaces, punctuation, or special characters such as new line or paragraph marks. It would *not* find "often," "tenuous," or "contentious." If you don't have "Whole Word" selected, QuarkXPress will find every occurrence of the text you entered, even if it's embedded in other text.

Ignore Case. If the Ignore Case box is checked, QuarkXPress finds all occurrences of the text in the Find what field, regardless of whether the capitalization of the text found in the document exactly matches what you typed into the Find what field. For example, if you entered "Help," QuarkXPress would find "Help," "HELP," and "help."

When "Ignore Case" is checked, QuarkXPress determines the capitalization it uses when it changes text based on how the text it finds in the document is capitalized. If the found text begins with an initial capital, QuarkXPress similarly capitalizes the first letter of the text in the Change to field when it's used at that location.

Similarly, if the found text is in all capitals, or all lowercase, QuarkXPress applies the same capitalization to the replacement text. If the found text doesn't match any of the above three cases, QuarkXPress capitalizes the replacement text exactly as you entered it into the Change to field.

For example, let's say you are searching for all examples of "QuarkXPress" and want to make sure the internal capitals are proper. If you leave Ignore Case on, and the program finds "quarkxpress," it does not capitalize the proper characters. Turn Ignore Case off, and XPress replaces it with "Quark-XPress," properly capitalized as you entered it.

Specifying Attributes

The Ignore Attributes box in the Find/Change dialog box lets you specify whether you want QuarkXPress only to look for and replace text, regardless of formatting attributes (font, size, style), or whether you want it to include attribute information in the criteria it uses for searching and changing. When the box is checked, QuarkXPress looks for all occurrences of the Find what text no matter how it's formatted, and replaces it with the Change to text, without making any changes to the character formatting at that location in the document.

When you deselect the Ignore Attributes box, the Find/Change dialog box expands (see Figure 3-2). In addition to text fields under the Find what and Change to headings, there are areas for specifying font, size, and style under each heading.

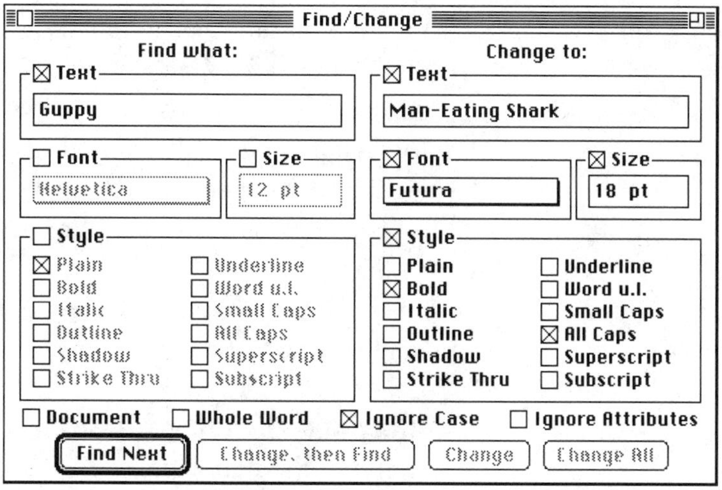

Figure 3-2
The Find/Change
Attributes dialog box

What to Find, What to Change

Notice that there's a check box next to the name of each area under the Find what and Change to headings. By checking and unchecking these boxes, and by modifying what's inside each area, you tell QuarkXPress just what attributes you're looking for, and what you want them changed to. There need be no parallel between what you specify in the Find what side and the Change to side. In fact, such "asymmetrical" searches offer some of the most intriguing possibilities for finding and changing.

You can easily, for example, add the bold style to every instance of the word "bold." If you're editing a revision of a document, you could indicate possible deletions by applying the strike-through style. Then, if the deletions are approved, use the Find/Change command to remove them quickly (search for strike-through, and replace with no text). You could also find all occurrences of a company name, and apply a special typeface or style to it.

The Text, Font, and Size areas are simple to use. If you want to specify something, make sure the area's box is checked. Then you simply enter the text or point size in the appropriate fields, and use the pop-up font menu to select the font to be found or changed. In the Find what side, the Font menu lists only the fonts actually used in the current document; on the Change to side, it lists all fonts currently available from your Mac's system.

If the document uses fonts that are currently not open in your system, QuarkXPress will list them in the Find what side, along with their font ID numbers. You can then use the Find/Change command to change the unavailable fonts to ones that are currently available (though you can expect the whole document to reflow, since the character widths vary so much between fonts).

Finding and Changing Character Styles

Specifying the many character styles available in Quark-XPress is a bit more complicated when you're using the Find/Change dialog box. The check boxes next to most of the Style choices can be either checked, unchecked, or grayed.

Click on an unchecked box once to check it; twice to make it gray, and a third time to uncheck it again (see Figure 3-3).

Figure 3-3

Check boxes in the
Find/Change dialog box

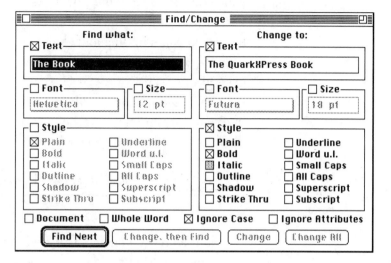

A checked box on the Find what side means that you want QuarkXPress to find text containing that style. An unchecked box means you *don't* want it to find text with that style. A grayed box means that it doesn't matter if the text contains that style; you want QuarkXPress to find text either way.

Similarly, checking a Style box on the Change to side means you want QuarkXPress to apply that style when it changes text it finds. An unchecked box means you *don't* want that style to be present in the changed text, and if it's there, QuarkXPress will remove it. A grayed box means that QuarkXPress doesn't do anything to that style. If it's already there, it will stay there; if it's not, QuarkXPress won't add it.

If you check the Plain style box, all other style boxes will be unchecked. The styles listed under Plain (Bold, Italic, Outline, Shadow, and Strike Through) may be checked, unchecked or grayed in any combination, but the styles on the right side of the Style lists operate as pairs. A word can't have both the Underline and Word Underline styles simultaneously. So checking on one unchecks the other, and graying one automatically makes the other gray as well. Small Caps/All Caps and Superscript/Subscript work together similarly.

Going to It

Now that you know how to specify what you want to find, what you want to change, and how to tell QuarkXPress where to search, you can use the four buttons at the bottom of the dialog box to begin finding and changing. When you first specify your Find/Change criteria, all buttons except "Find Next" are grayed out (see Figure 3-4). Click on "Find Next," and QuarkXPress searches for the first occurrence of text matching your specifications in the current story or document. It displays this text in the document window and selects it.

Figure 3-4
The Find/Change
control buttons

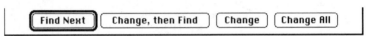

You then have a choice. Clicking "Find Next" again takes you to the next occurrence of text meeting your specifications, without changing the currently selected text. Clicking "Change, then Find" changes the selection as specified in the Change to side of the dialog box. QuarkXPress then looks for the next occurrence of matching text. The Change button changes the selected text and leaves it selected, and the Change All button has QuarkXPress search for and automatically change all occurrences in the story or document.

▼ ▼

Tip: Seeing Text as It Is Found. If you are one of the unlucky sods who has a small-screen Mac (we are among them), you'll find that the Find/Change dialog box fills the entire screen when you are searching or replacing attributes. Thus, when you click on "Find Next," you can't see what the program found. However, you can reduce the size of the dialog box considerably by clicking on the Zoom button in the box's upper right corner (see Figure 3-5). The reduced view shows only the buttons you need to navigate and change what you've specified. Clicking on the Zoom button again takes you back to the larger dialog box.

Figure 3-5
Shrinking the Find/
Change dialog box

| Find/Change |
| Find Next | Change, then Find | Change | Change All |

▼ ▼

Spell-Checking

Of course, once you've got your text written or imported into QuarkXPress, you wouldn't want to print it without first running it through QuarkXPress's spell-checker. QuarkXPress comes with an 80,000-word dictionary, and you can create your own auxiliary dictionaries as well. The Check Spelling command is on the Utilities menu, and allows you to check a selected word, a story, or an entire document (see Figure 3-6).

Figure 3-6
The Check Spelling
hierarchical menu

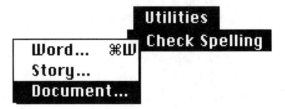

Checking a Word

To check a word, select it, and choose "Word" from the Check Spelling hierarchical menu (or type Command-W). The Check Word dialog box appears (see Figure 3-7), listing all words in the QuarkXPress dictionary (and the open auxiliary dictionary, if any), that resemble the word you selected. QuarkXPress calls this the suspect word. If the suspect word appears in a dictionary, it will appear in the scrolling list and be automatically selected. This means that, as far as Quark-XPress is concerned, the word is spelled correctly, and you can click the Cancel button and continue.

Figure 3-7
Checking a word

```
▓▓▓▓▓▓▓▓▓▓▓ Check Word ▓▓▓▓▓▓▓▓▓▓▓

Suspect Word: speeling

   ┌──────────┐    ┌──────────────────┬──┐
   │ Replace  │    │ speeding         │⬆ │
   └──────────┘    │ spelling         │  │
   ┌──────────┐    │ steeling         │  │
   │  Cancel  │    │                  │⬇ │
   └──────────┘    └──────────────────┴──┘
```

If the suspect word doesn't appear in an active dictionary, you can scroll through the list of words and select a replacement. Click on the word in the list, then click on the Replace button. The new spelling replaces the word in your story, and the Check Word box closes.

If QuarkXPress can't find any words that approximate the suspect word, it displays the message, "No similar words found." Click on the Cancel button to close the Check Word dialog box.

Checking a Story

To check a story, select the story's text box (any box in a linked chain will do) and make sure the Content tool is active. Select "Story" from the Check Spelling hierarchical menu (or type Command-Option-W). The Word Count dialog box appears, showing running totals as QuarkXPress scans the story, counting the total number of words, the total number of unique words (each word counted once, no matter how many times it occurs), and the number of suspect words—ones that QuarkXPress can't find in its dictionary, or in an open auxiliary dictionary.

When QuarkXPress is finished counting, click on the OK button. This returns you to your document if no suspect words have been found. If they have been, the button brings up the Check Story dialog box (see Figure 3-8). This dialog box displays suspect words one at a time, in the order they occur in the story. As each appears in the dialog box, Quark-XPress scrolls the document window to the word, and highlights it, so you can see it in the context in which it's used. If a suspect word is used more than once, QuarkXPress tells you how many times.

Changing the Spelling. If you know the correct spelling for a suspect word, you can enter it in the Replace with field, then click on the Replace button to have the new spelling replace the one in your document. If you want QuarkXPress to look for possible spellings in its dictionary, or in an open

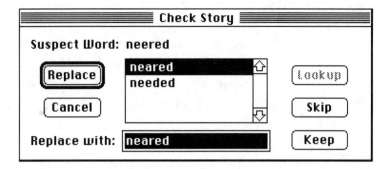

auxiliary dictionary, click on the Lookup button (or press Command-L). QuarkXPress displays a list of possible alternatives in the scrolling text field. You can select a spelling by clicking on it, then clicking on the Replace button. The new spelling replaces the suspect word in your document, and QuarkXPress moves on to the next suspect word in the story. If there are no more suspect words, the Check Story dialog box closes. You can also revert back to the original spelling by clicking on the Suspect Word in the dialog box.

Note that if QuarkXPress finds more than one occurrence of a suspect word, it will replace every occurrence of the word with the new spelling you choose.

Skipping and Keeping. To go to the next suspect word without changing the spelling of the current one, click on the Skip button (Command-S). To add the current suspect word to an auxiliary dictionary, click on the Keep button (Command-K). This button is only active when an auxiliary dictionary is open (see "Auxiliary Dictionaries," below).

Checking a Document/Master Page

You can check all the text in an entire document by selecting the Document command from the Check Spelling hierarchical menu. QuarkXPress counts and checks all the words in your current document, from first page to last. It displays the Word Count dialog box, then lets you change suspect words through a Check Document dialog box that is identical in layout and function to the Check Story dialog box.

Similarly, when master pages are displayed, the Document command on the menu becomes "Masters." By selecting this command you can check all the text on every master page in your document, using a Check Masters dialog box that works just like the Check Story and Check Document dialog boxes.

Auxiliary Dictionaries

You can't add words to or edit QuarkXPress's standard dictionary. You can, however, create and use auxiliary dictionaries, so you can have QuarkXPress's spell-checker take into account specialized words that aren't in the standard dictionary. Note that you can only have one auxiliary dictionary open at a time for each document.

Remembering Dictionaries. If you open or create an auxiliary dictionary with a document open, QuarkXPress automatically associates the two. Whenever you open the document, QuarkXPress also opens the dictionary, until you either close the dictionary or open a different one. You can also open a dictionary with no documents open at all; this dictionary will be applied to all documents you create subsequently. However, QuarkXPress may not be able to find an auxiliary dictionary if you move either the dictionary or a document associated with it, in which case, you'll receive an error message when you try to spell-check your document.

Creating or Opening an Auxiliary Dictionary. To open an existing auxiliary dictionary, or to create a new one, select the Auxiliary Dictionary command from the Utilities menu. This opens the Auxiliary Dictionary dialog box, which is a standard file-opening dialog box. You can locate a dictionary by looking through the folders on your mounted drives. Select it and then click on the Open button.

You can also create a new auxiliary dictionary by clicking on the New button, which brings up a file-saving dialog box that lets you specify the name and location of the new dictionary. Enter the name of the new dictionary in the text field, and click on the Create button.

Adding and Removing Words. When you create an auxiliary dictionary, it contains no words. You can add words to the dictionary by using the Keep button when you're spell-checking. This button adds the current suspect word to your auxiliary dictionary. Another way to add words is with the Edit Auxiliary item from the Utilities menu. This feature is only available when there's an open auxiliary dictionary.

When you select Edit Auxiliary, a simple dialog box appears, with a scrolling list of all the words in the currently open dictionary (see Figure 3-9). To add a new word, enter it in the text field and click on the Add button. Words added to the dictionary cannot contain any spaces or punctuation (not even hyphens). To remove a word from the dictionary, scroll through the list until you find the word. Select it by clicking on it, then click on the Delete button.

Figure 3-9
The Edit Auxiliary
Dictionary dialog box

▼ ▼

Tip: Editing Dictionaries with a Word Processor. QuarkXPress dictionaries are simply text files, with one word per paragraph. They have a "type" of TEXT and a "creator" of XPRS (you can change a file's type and creator with DiskTop, ResEdit, and several other programs). Because it's a text file, you can edit a QuarkXPress auxiliary dictionary with any word processor. Remember to save as text only.

▼ ▼

Tip: Adding Your Microsoft Word Dictionary. The user dictionaries that Microsoft Word creates are text files as well, and like Quark-XPress dictionaries, they have one word per paragraph. They're usually called "User 1." Since a Word dictionary is of type DICT, you have to use Word's Shift-F6 (the Open any file command) to open it. Once it's open, you can copy the contents and paste them into your QuarkXPress auxiliary dictionary.

Be aware that if you edit the Word dictionary and save it, you have to sort it in Word's special order, save it as text only, and then change the file type back to DICT before Word will recognize it as a dictionary.

▼ ▼

When Not to Use QuarkXPress

While QuarkXPress does have powerful word-processing features, as we've seen in the preceding sections of this chapter, there are reasons why you may not want to use it for most of the word processing in your documents. The main reason to use QuarkXPress is that you never have to worry about losing any formatting information when importing and exporting text. If your text stays in QuarkXPress, that isn't a problem.

But there are good reasons to consider editing and writing your text outside QuarkXPress. First of all, word processing programs tend to be much less expensive than QuarkXPress. If you're in a big office or workgroup, it may make more financial sense to do basic text entry on word processors, rather than a powerhouse page-layout program like QuarkXPress.

Another reason is that, powerful though QuarkXPress may be, it doesn't offer features available in the most powerful word-processors, such as outlining or automatic numbering of paragraphs. If you're working on a long, complicated document with sections that might require constant rearranging and reorganizing, you probably need the organizational power of a good outlining feature like Microsoft Word's. Since Word's style sheets work well with QuarkXPress's, Word is usually considered the best word processor to use with QuarkXPress (see Chapter 5, *Copy Flow*).

Slow Going

But perhaps the most important reason to consider *not* doing your word processing in QuarkXPress is speed. Or rather the lack of it. Sometimes writing and editing text in Quark-XPress can seem to slow to a crawl. Entering text becomes so sluggish that the program can't keep up with even a moderate typist, and, worse still, some typed characters seem to fall into a black hole while they're waiting to appear on the screen. So your normally excellent typing can suddenly appear riddled with typos.

Why does this happen? First, QuarkXPress often has to jump all over the document as you type, unlike a word processor, which simply scrolls top to bottom. Secondly, Quark-XPress has to do much more work than a typical word processor whenever it must reflow text. If you have specified complicated hyphenation and justification settings, if you've set the automatic kerning threshold so that it's active for most of the text in a story, if you've applied a lot of kerning or tracking effects, all these require QuarkXPress to perform extra calculations in order to determine where line breaks should fall whenever it reflows text. If you're working on a long story that goes through several pages of linked boxes, with many runarounds caused by other page elements, this complexity also adds to the computations that QuarkXPress must perform whenever you change or add text. So you can often get the feeling that you're physically pushing a heavy load of text along a tortuous path as you type. Here are a few suggestions for working around the problem of sluggish text entry in QuarkXPress.

▼ ▼

Tip: Use a Text-editing Desk Accessory. Veteran QuarkXPress users have discovered that, while characters may be lost when typing with speed problems into an QuarkXPress story, type pasted in from the Clipboard never gets lost or damaged. One way to quickly get text into the Clipboard is to type it in a simple text-editing desk accessory, and then copy and paste it into QuarkXPress. There are many such DAs on the market. You could even make do with Apple's bare-bones "Note Pad." Then there's the excellent shareware McSink, and the commercial programs Vantage and MockWrite (see Figure 3-10).

The disadvantage of using DAs is that whatever text you create in them can be only pure text. You must apply any formatting attributes after you've pasted the text into QuarkXPress.

Figure 3-10
The Vantage
text editing DA

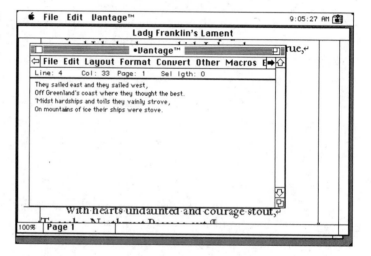

Modifying Preferences and Settings

You can quickly modify some of the things in QuarkXPress that affect the speed with which you can enter or edit text.

Hyphenation. Turn off hyphenation as much as possible in your document. If QuarkXPress doesn't have to determine if and where it should hyphenate a word whenever it breaks a line, it will be able to incorporate new or changed text into a story more quickly. Simply edit all of the H&J settings used in your document, and turn off hyphenation (see Chapter 4, *Type and Typography*). Turn hyphenation back on when you're ready to proof or print your document.

If you're using style sheets, you can streamline this process a bit. Instead of editing your H&J settings each time you want to turn hyphenation on or off, you can create a special hyphenation setting with hyphenation off, called, perhaps, NoHyphens. If you've based most of the styles in your document on the Normal style, all you have to do is edit the Normal style, and select the NoHyphens setting to turn off hyphenation in all styles based on Normal. To turn hyphenation back on, just reselect Normal's original H&J setting (we discuss style sheets in more detail in Chapter 5, *Copy Flow*).

Kerning. Turn off automatic kerning in your document. Go to the Typographic Preferences dialog box for your document (available from the Edit menu), and make sure the Auto Kern Above check box is not checked.

Note that the two suggestions above affect where line breaks fall and how text will appear when printed. You should make certain to return both the H&J and kerning settings to those you intend to use for final output before you check your document for widows, orphans, or loose lines.

Using Dummy Text Boxes

The problem with using a text-editing DA to type text is that you can't include any character formatting attributes. And if you modify the settings of your QuarkXPress document to speed things up, you may forget to change them back, and end up printing a document with incorrect hyphenation and kerning. Moreover, if you have complicated layouts, entering text into QuarkXPress will still be sluggish, even if you have turned off hyphenation and kerning, as QuarkXPress must still reflow the entire story as you enter or change text.

Another solution to the text entry problem is to create a text box in the pasteboard area of the page where you want to enter or change text. If you need to simply add text to the page, type the text into the box on the pasteboard area, copy or cut it, and then paste it into the correct location in the story's text box on the page.

If you need to edit text that's already there as well as add text, select the text to be modified from the page, and then copy and paste it into the box on the pasteboard. Make all the necessary edits there, then copy or cut the revised text, and paste it back to the same location on the page. Since QuarkXPress remembers the last selection you made in any text box, all you need to do is select the story's box on the page. It won't be necessary to reselect the text that you originally copied out. QuarkXPress does that for you automatically.

▼ ▼

Tip: Use a Dummy Document. If you must make many changes to a story, you could find it cumbersome to create boxes on each page's pasteboard area as described above. Another solution is to make a new document with a simple page layout, copy the entire story to be edited over to the dummy document, make all your changes there, then copy the story back to your original document.

1. Open the document with the story that needs editing.

2. Create a new, blank document using the New command from the File menu.

3. Using the Content tool, select a text box in the original document which contains part of the story to be edited.

4. Type Command-A (or click five times) to select all of the story in the text chain, and type Command-C to copy it.

5. Make the window for the new, blank document active. Select the default text box on the first page, and press Command-V to paste the entire story into it.

6. Make all your edits in the new document. Since there is only the simplest of layouts—a single rectangular box on each page—delays in reflowing text as you edit will be minimal.

7. After you've made your corrections, press Command-A to select all the text in the new document, and press Command-C to copy it.

8. Activate the window for the original document (the FeaturesPlus XTension makes this easy; just select the document from the Windows item in the View menu). Click in a text box belonging to the edited story. QuarkXPress should automatically highlight the entire story, just as it was the last time you selected the text box. If it doesn't, be sure to type Command-A to select the entire story again.

9. Press Command-V to paste the edited story back into its proper location in the original document. Because you had the original story selected in the last step, the Paste command replaces the entire story with the modified story.

There's one caveat to observe with this technique. Copying and pasting text brings over all the styles contained in the text to the new document, except for any that are already there. If you're starting a new, blank document, this means that the Normal style will already be present (along with any other default styles you may have defined), and may not match the Normal style in your original document. If you apply the Normal style to any text in the new, dummy document, it may not have the formatting attributes you want, and it will retain these attributes even after you paste the story back into the original document, where you'll have to remove and then re-apply the Normal style to make sure that paragraph has the correct formatting applied.

There are two ways to avoid this headache. The simplest is to remember not to mess around with styles when you're editing text in a dummy document. If you must work with styles when you're editing a story in a dummy document, save your original document with another name (perhaps even as a template). Then delete all the document pages, create a simple, new blank page, and use this new document as the dummy document into which you paste and edit text from your original. Bear in mind that you may have to repeat this process every time you make significant changes to the styles in your original document.

▼ ▼

Watching Your Words

By following the tips we've shown you here, you may not be able to have QuarkXPress write your documents for you, but you'll be able to get the very most out of the program's advanced word-processing features.

Next we'll see how you can take those blocks of plain text that you've created and turn them into type using Quark-XPress's extensive typographic controls.

CHAPTER 4

TYPE AND TYPOGRAPHY

There's an old husband's tale that says you can tell what a baby is going to grow up to become by the first real word she speaks. If she says "mama," she'll grow to be a loving parent. If she says "teevee," chances are she will be a couch potato. If she says "QuarkXPress," she'll become a typesetter.

There's no doubt, even if this tale is hogwash, that Quark-XPress is often the first word on a typesetter's lips when the topic of desktop publishing comes up. That's because no desktop publishing application handles typesetting as powerfully as QuarkXPress. In this chapter we will discuss the many typographic controls which QuarkXPress puts at your fingertips. We're going to start with basics: fonts and typographic principles. However, professionals should at least skim over this section (the fundamentals of fonts are rarely taught, and many people find themselves in deep...uh...water at some point because of it).

Next, we'll discuss control of both character- and paragraph-level styles, including—among many other items—kerning and tracking, hyphenation and justification, and typographic special effects.

If you're reading this book from cover to cover, expect to spend a while here in this chapter. We've got a lot to talk about, and we expect you'll find it rewarding.

▼ ▼

Macintosh Fonts

The word "font" now has several meanings. Historically, it refers to a set of characters in a given typeface and size. Typefaces are the general look of the character set. For example, Helvetica is a typeface, while 14-point Helvetica is a font.

However, for the sake of simplicity, we're following the path that has become popularized over the past few years, defining both *typeface* and *font* as synonyms: a font or a typeface is a set of characters that share a particular look. For example, the text you're reading is one particular font or typeface, while the headings for each section are in a different font or typeface. The more you learn about type and typography, the more you see its subtle nuances and personalities. But don't worry too much about that yet. Just start by seeing these basic differences.

Typefaces can be found cast in metal, carved from wood, or imaged on photographic negatives. In the case of the Macintosh computer, typefaces are represented digitally. That is, you can't see the typeface until you tell the computer to process the digital information and image a character to either the screen or onto paper or film. As it turns out, the Macintosh was built in such a way that it images fonts to the screen in a different way than it prints them. What does that mean for you? It means that what you see on the screen may not be exactly what you get on paper.

Adobe Type Manager

Since we're still at the beginning of the chapter, we're going to talk as if you aren't using Adobe Type Manager (ATM) on your computer. However, consider it homework to buy a copy of ATM by the end of this chapter. Why should you buy it? Primarily because it makes the fonts you see on the screen bear a greater resemblance to those you get from your printer. At any size. Figure 4-1 shows the difference between type on a Macintosh screen with and without ATM.

Figure 4-1
Screen type with
and without ATM

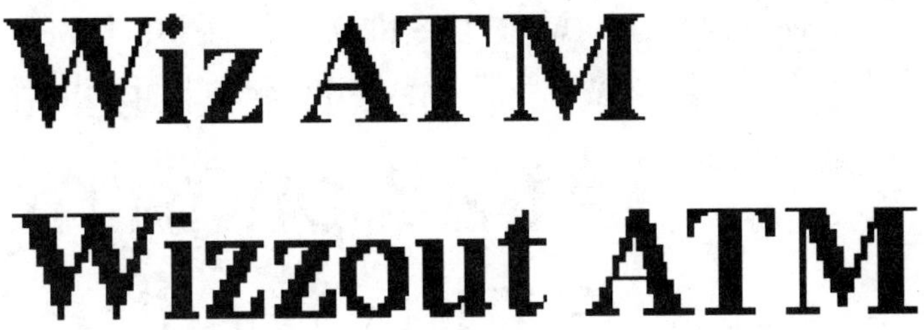

Wiz ATM

Wizzout ATM

Screen Fonts

Let's start simple: the Macintosh images fonts on the screen
using screen fonts. These fonts are collections of bitmapped
images—one bitmapped image for each character at each
size (if you don't know the differences between bitmapped
and outline graphics, take a quick peek at that section at the
beginning of Chapter 6, *Pictures*).

When you press a key on the keyboard, the computer
goes to the font file, extracts that character at the size nearest
to the one you want, then extrapolates the image to create the
specified size. For example, if you specify that you want to
type in 17-point Helvetica, the computer will get the nearest
screen font it has, let's say 12-point Helvetica, and then
scale it up. One look at Figure 4-2 and you can see this is an
ugly way of doing things. But, for the past six years, it was
the only way to do things.

Loading screen fonts. Screen fonts are stored in suitcases. This
is evident by their perpetually rumpled look, which some
people call "jaggy." There are two methods of taking fonts
out of their suitcases so you can use them. The first is by
using Font/DA Mover to move the fonts out of their suitcases
and into the System file (as an exercise, go ahead and open
your system folder and locate the System file; most people
don't know it's even there, but that's half of what makes the
computer go!). The second method is to use a utility such as
MasterJuggler or Suitcase II. The second method is much
preferred, as moving fonts around with Font/DA Mover can
screw up both the fonts and your system file in the long run.

Now is the time for 12 pt. type.

At 17 pt., there's still time.

At 28 pt. things take a turn for the worse.

At 40 point, allow me to suggest you consider ATM.

Printer Fonts

If screen fonts image on the screen, then printer fonts must image on printers. That's just the way of the world. And whereas the screen font is bitmapped, the printer font is made up of outlined characters that can be scaled, rotated, and skewed in all sorts of ways without the ugly extrapolation encountered on the screen.

The printer font is also sometimes used as a basis for screen fonts. We'll talk more about this process, called *rendering*, in "Type Rendering," below.

You usually don't have to worry too much about making sure it's the printer font and not the screen font that's used to print. Just make sure the printer font is in your system folder (that's different from the System file) where the Mac can find it when it needs to. We'll talk more about making sure printer fonts are available in Chapter 10, *Printing*. However, the key issue for you to understand is that the screen font is acting as a *representative* of the printer font. You see the bitmapped screen font on the screen, but it gets replaced with a nice, smooth, outline font on your printed output (see Figure 4-3), imaged at the resolution of the output device.

Figure 4-3
The screen font and
the outline font

Oooh-wah oooh-wah boop-boop bitty,
Talkin' 'bout the font from
Bitmap City

Bitmapped screen font

Bitmap City?
Can't say as I've been there.

Outlined printer font

You should note that there are presently two types of outline fonts available: Type 1 and Type 3. There was a myth for some time that Type 1 fonts were better quality. This is not true. However, the manufacturers of high-quality fonts generally use the Type 1 format for several reasons, including the fonts' compatibility with ATM (again, see "Type Rendering," later in this chapter). At any rate, Type 3 fonts are becoming less popular now.

Microsoft and Apple have developed a third type of font format, called TrueType (also known as "Royal"). TrueType fonts are not widely available at the time of this writing, but should be introduced with Apple's System 7 in 1991.

What Makes a Font?

Before we move on to how QuarkXPress handles fonts, let's just look a little further into the subject of fonts in general.

You can work with thousands of different typefaces on a Macintosh and a PostScript printer. Figure 4-4 shows four potential candidates. Note that the bold, italic, and bold italic versions of a typeface are actually entirely separate faces from the "base" or "Roman" font.

Figure 4-4
Four separate fonts

Adobe Garamond Roman

the same, **Bold**

one more time: *Italic*

and of course ***Bold Italic***

However, if a bold or italic (or bold italic, for that matter) version of the font is not available, the computer may generate its own version of that style. A bold will be created by printing double, an italic will be created by skewing—also known as slanting or "obliquing"—the font. Like many things the computer does on its own, these versions are pretty awful. They're usable in certain circumstances, but quite unacceptable for anything approaching traditional typeset quality.

▼ ▼

Fonts and QuarkXPress

Let's be clear here: we're not going to transform you into an amazing typographer in the course of one chapter. We may not even make a dent in the enormous learning curve that everyone must go through in learning about type. But we *will* give you the information you need to use QuarkXPress as a powerful tool when you do know what you want, and we will try to point out some important issues in desktop typography.

We're going to spend the rest of this chapter talking about QuarkXPress's basic font manipulation tools, and then move into more complex issues of typography and how to make your type look great.

▼ ▼

Tip: Use the Content Tool. The very first thing you need to know about the control of type in QuarkXPress is that you must have selected both the Content tool and the text box that contains the text you want to change. If you want to make a character-based change, you must have those characters you want to alter selected. If you want to make a paragraph-based change, you can select the paragraph (four mouse clicks), or a portion of the paragraph. You can even just have the cursor located anywhere within the paragraph. Just remember: if you want to change the contents of a text box, use the Content tool.

▼ ▼

Character Formatting

There are two types of typographic controls: character-based and paragraph-based. The character-based controls let you change the character formatting; the paragraph-based controls let you change the paragraph formatting. It's as easy as that. Let's talk about character formatting first.

The character-based controls are those that affect only the text characters that you select. If you have selected only one word in a sentence and apply a character style to it, that word and only that word will be changed.

Character styles include typeface, size, kerning, color, and a whole mess of other things. Let's look at each character-formatting control, how you can change it, and why you'd want to.

Selecting a Typeface

Picking a typeface can be a very personal thing, fraught with implication and the anxiety of decision. If someone tells you they want their document set in 10-point Courier, it may be better just to stay quiet. However, once the choice has been made, there is a number of ways to select the typeface. Let's look at each of them here.

The Style menu. Almost every typographic control can be accessed through an item on the Style menu. When you have the text selected that you want to change, you can select the typeface name from the Font submenu.

The Measurements palette. If the Measurements palette is closer within reach, or if you would rather avoid hierarchical submenus, you can select a typeface from the Measurements palette instead. Here you have two methods of selecting.

- You can click on the arrow button to bring up a menu of fonts. It is often quicker to select from this menu than from the Style menu.

- You can type the name of the typeface you want. Do this by clicking to the left of the first character of the typeface name shown in the Measurements palette, then typing a few characters of the typeface name you want. As soon as QuarkXPress recognizes the name it will type the rest of it for you. For example, if you want to change from Helvetica to Avant Garde, click just to the left of the "H" and type "Ava." By the time you type these three letters, chances are it will recognize Avant Garde (as long as you have that screen font loaded). This is clearly a boon to desktop publishers who have many fonts and are tired of scrolling down a list for five minutes just to select Zapf Dingbats.

You can use these two methods together to select a typeface from the Measurements palette. For example, if you're looking for Zapf Dingbats but can't remember how "Zapf" is spelled, you can simply type "Z" and then click on the arrow key button. You are transported directly to the end of the list as opposed to the beginning.

Character Attributes. The Character Attributes dialog box is the Style menu and half the Measurements palette rolled into one, and is a simple keystroke away (Command-Shift-D). Here you can change the typeface using the same methods as described in "The Measurements palette," above.

Find/Change and Font Usage dialog boxes. Let's say you have half your document in Helvetica and you want to change that copy to Futura. You can use the Find/Change or the Font Usage dialog boxes to search for and replace all instances of characters set in the Helvetica font with Futura. We discussed the Find/Change dialog box in some detail back in Chapter 3, *Word Processing*, and we'll discuss the Font Usage feature later in this chapter.

Font Size

Changing the size of the typeface is as easy as...well, just about as easy as changing the typeface itself. In fact, you use the same options for changing the type size as we described above: Style menu, Measurements palette, Character Attributes dialog box, and the Find/Change or Font Usage dialog boxes. In addition, you can use a set of keystrokes to make your selected text larger or smaller (see Table 4-1).

Table 4-1
Font sizing keystrokes

Hold down...	To get...
Command-Shift-Period	Increases point size through a preset range
Command-Shift-Comma	Decreases point size through a preset range
Command-Option-Shift-Period	Increases point size in 1-point increments
Command-Option-Shift-Comma	Decreases point size in 1-point increments

The preset range that we mention in Table 4-1 is the same range listed on the Size menu: 7, 9, 10, 12, 14, 18, 24, 36, 48, 60, and 72 points. When you increase through the preset range with a keystroke, your character size jumps from one to the next on this list.

▼ ▼

Tip: Precision Font Sizing. If you aren't satisfied with the preset font sizes, you can type in your own—in .001-point increments—in the Font Size dialog box. You can get to this dialog box by selecting "Other" from the Size submenu or by typing Command-Shift-\ (backslash).

▼ ▼

Type Styles

QuarkXPress has 13 built-in attributes that you assign at a character level. Figure 4-5 gives samples of each of these, plus examples of how to use them.

These type attributes can be assigned to selected text in four ways, which are similar to how you assign typefaces and type size.

Style menu. You can select a type style from the Type Style submenu under the Style menu (see Figure 4-6).

Measurements palette. Each of the type styles is displayed by an icon in the Measurements palette (see Figure 4-7). The icons either display a sample of the style or give a graphic representation of it. For example, Superscript is shown by the numeral 2 over an up arrow. To select a type style, just click on the icon. The icon acts as a toggle switch, so to turn the style off you simply click on it again. If you have several type styles selected, you can quickly rid yourself of them by clicking on the "P" (for Plain).

Keystrokes. Each type style can be selected by a keystroke, as shown in Table 4-2. Once again, the styles are toggled on and off with each keystroke. We find keystrokes especially useful

Figure 4-5
Type styles

Plain text
Boldface
Italics
Outline
Shadow
~~Strike-through~~
Underlined (everything)
Word underlining
LARGE & SMALL CAPS
ALL CAPS
Superscript (baseline shown as dotted line)
Subscript
Superior characters

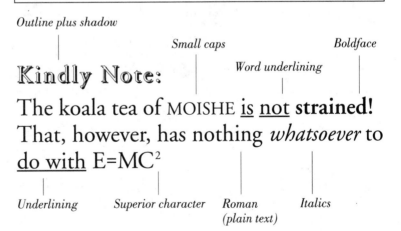

Outline plus shadow

Small caps   Boldface
          Word underlining

Kindly Note:
The koala tea of MOISHE is not **strained!**
That, however, has nothing *whatsoever* to
do with E=MC²

Underlining   Superior character   Roman   Italics
                                       (plain text)

Figure 4-6

The Type Style menu

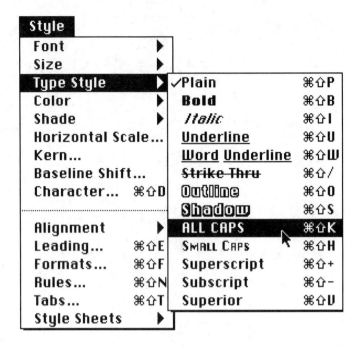

Figure 4-7

Measurement palette
type styles

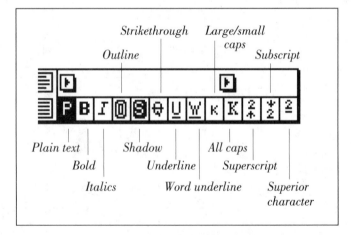

while typing directly into QuarkXPress; we can enter text and change styles while never taking our hands from the keyboard.

Character Attributes. Type styles in the Character Attributes dialog box (Command-Shift-D) are turned on and off by checking boxes. These check boxes can be in one of three states: on, off, or indeterminate.

Table 4-3 Type styles	Type...	To get...	Example
	Command-Shift-P	Plain text	Ecce Eduardus Ursus
	Command-Shift-B	Bold	**Ecce Eduardus Ursus**
	Command-Shift-I	Italic	*Ecce Eduardus Ursus*
	Command-Shift-U	Underline	<u>Ecce Eduardus Ursus</u>
	Command-Shift-W	Word underline	Ecce Eduardus Ursus
	Command-Shift-/	Strike through	~~Ecce Eduardus Ursus~~
	Command-Shift-O	Outline	Ecce Eduardus Ursus
	Command-Shift-S	Shadow	Ecce Eduardus Ursus
	Command-Shift-K	All caps	ECCE EDUARDUS URSUS
	Command-Shift-H	Small caps	ECCE EDUARDUS URSUS
	Command-Shift-+	Superscript	Ecce Eduardus Ursus
	Command-Shift-Hyphen	Subscript	Ecce Eduardus Ursus
	Command-Shift-V	Superior	Ecce Eduardus Ursus

- **On.** An "X" in the check box means the style is selected for the entire piece of selected text.

- **Off.** If the check box is blank, that style is not applied to any of the selected text.

- **Indeterminate.** A check box shaded gray means that some of the characters have that type style, and others don't. Check the box again, and the box goes to on. A third time turns it off.

Note that these three states are also used to display the type style in the Measurements palette. However, instead of an "X," the Measurements palette uses a reversed box.

Styling by Attributes Versus Font Choice

You can style text either by applying style attributes like those described above, or by choosing a styled font itself. For example, say you're working with the Bodoni font, and you want to italicize some selected text. You can either choose "Italic" as a style, or go to the Font submenu and choose the specific Bodoni Italic screen font (assuming you have it installed). That font will show up in the submenu as "I Bodoni Italic" (or something similar to this). Either way, you'll get the same results: Bodoni Italic on your screen and on the page.

Which method is better? Choosing by formatting attribute is certainly faster, especially if you do it with keyboard commands. And it has the advantage of being font-independent. For example, if you've applied an italic formatting attribute to a range of your Bodoni text, and later decide to change your text face to Galliard, the italic formatting is transferred as well.

On the other hand, if you choose the Bodoni Italic font for the emphasized range of text, when you make the changeover to Galliard, you get just Galliard and not Galliard Italic. Why? Because you simply switched from one font to another, and your text carried no format information. The original italicized range was an italic font with a Plain style attribute.

▼ ▼

Color and Shade

You can quickly and easily change the color or the tint (shade) of a piece of text. First, select the text and then select either the color from the Color submenu, or the tint value from the Shade submenu off the Style menu. The default color palette contains nine colors (see Chapter 9, *Color*, for information about adding and editing colors in this list). The default shades are 10 percent tints; you can assign a specific tint value by selecting "Other" in the submenu.

▼ ▼

Tip: Reversed Type. There is no specific command for reversed type—typically white-on-black type—as there is in Page-Maker. But that doesn't mean you can't achieve that effect. Simply select the text and choose "White" from the Color submenu or from the Character Attributes dialog box (Command-Shift-D). If you want the reversed type on a black background, either place a black box behind it, or color the text box's background under the Text Box Specifications dialog box (Command-M).

▼ ▼
Horizontal Scale

Imagine the characters in a typeface as being rubber and stretchable. Now imagine stretching a typeface that took hundreds of hours to laboriously design at a specific width to 60 percent of its size, warping the characters into something they were never meant to be. Now imagine the designer's face.

Okay, you get the idea: typefaces were designed to be a specific width and shouldn't be messed with unless you have some really good reasons. What are some good reasons? The best reason of all is that you want the typeface to look that way. If you're responsible for the typographic design, then you can make any choices you want. Note that we're not talking about your using 70 percent compression of Helvetica because you don't feel like buying another package from Adobe. We are talking about your using an 85 percent compression of Cheltenham because it looks cool.

Another good reason to play with the horizontal scaling is if you need to make some body copy fit a particular space. Here we're talking about changing the horizontal scaling of the text 2 or 3 percent wider or narrower, not 10 or 20 percent. We'd be surprised if anyone other than the designer could see the difference of a few percent, especially at small sizes. Scaling Times Bold to 50 percent of size to make it fit as a headline is a bad idea (see Figure 4-8).

If, after all that, you still want to play with the horizontal scaling of your type, you can do so using the Horizontal Scale feature found under the Style menu. Entering values under 100 percent will squeeze the text narrower; values over 100 percent will stretch it wider. Note that you don't have to type a percent sign; just the number will do.

Figure 4-8
Horizontal scaling
of type

Got a problem?
Check your compression.

20 pt. Helvetica Extra Compressed

(tracking: +2)

Got a problem?
Check your compression.

20 pt. Helvetica (horizontal scaling: 60%)

(tracking: −2)

Got a problem?
Check your compression.

20 pt. Helvetica bold (scaling: 60%)

(tracking: −2)

Times Bold with horizontal scaling of 50%, but with the inter-word spaces not compressed.

Rats! Squashed again!

Times Bold with horizontal scaling of 50%, with inter-word spaces also scaled to 50%. Tracking in both examples: -1.

Squashed! Rats again!

Times Roman 10/11 (normal scaling).
I began to experience an acute sense of panic when, despite everyone's assurances to the contrary, I began to approach the end of the line and found that I was not quite going to make it.

Times Roman (scaled to 99% with same line width)
I began to experience an acute sense of panic when, despite everyone's assurances to the contrary, I began to approach the end of the line and found that I was not quite going to make it.

You can also alter horizontal scaling through keystrokes: Command-] (close square bracket) makes selected text wider in 5 percent increments; Command-[(open square bracket) makes the selected text narrower in 5 percent increments (we remember the difference in an obscure way: the key on the left means narrow (or less), the key on the right means wider (or more).

▼ ▼

Kerning and Tracking

There are times in life when all those little letters on a page are just too far apart or too close together. The problem may be between two characters in 120-point display type, or it may be throughout an entire typeface. Whatever the case, QuarkXPress can control it through the use of kerning and tracking. They're similar, but let's look at them one at a time.

▼ ▼

Tip: Know Your Ems and Ens. Many typographic controls are specified using units of measure called *ems* and *ens*. These are not nearly as confusing as some people make them out to be. An em, in QuarkXPress, is equal to the width of two zeros side by side in the font size you're working in. This is usually close to the font size itself. Therefore, an em space in 60-point type is around 60 points wide. An en space is half of an em space, so it would be around 30 points wide. This is a very weird way of doing things (normally an em would be just the same as the point size), but it's the Quark Way, so we follow it.

If you're typing along and change point size, then the size of the em and en units changes as well. This can be a great aid. For example, if you change the size of a word after painstakingly manually kerning it, your kerning does not get lost or jumbled. The kerning was specified in ems, and therefore is scaled along with the type.

Note that because QuarkXPress figures its em spaces weirdly, an em space and an em dash are not equal. Oh well.

▼ ▼

Kerning

Adjusting space between character pairs is referred to as *kerning*. You'll sometimes find kerning defined as purely the removal of such space. In QuarkXPress, kerning can be the removal or addition of space—moving two characters closer together or farther apart. Figure 4-9 shows some examples of type, first unkerned and then kerned. The problem is made obvious here: too much space between characters can make words look uneven or unnatural.

Figure 4-9
Kerned and
unkerned type

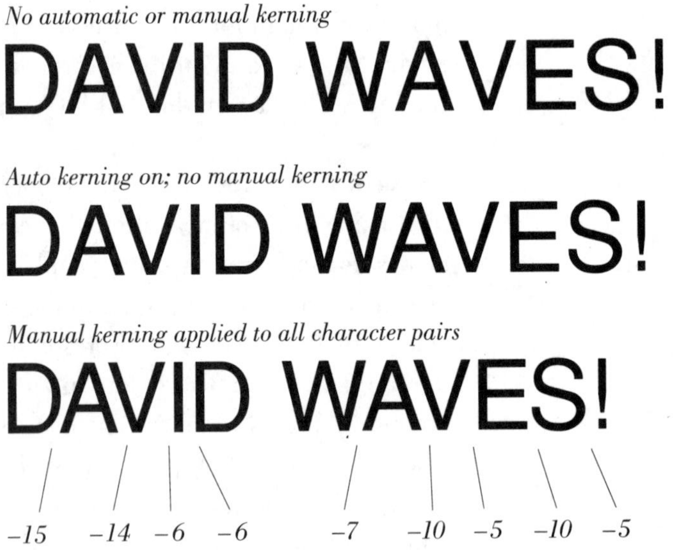

No automatic or manual kerning

DAVID WAVES!

Auto kerning on; no manual kerning

DAVID WAVES!

Manual kerning applied to all character pairs

DAVID WAVES!

−15   −14   −6   −6   −7   −10   −5   −10   −5

QuarkXPress supports two kinds of kerning: automatic and manual.

Automatic. When we say automatic, we mean automatic: all you have to do is turn the function on and QuarkXPress will make use of the font's built-in kerning pairs. It's up to font vendors to determine how many, and what, kerning pairs to include with a font, and what values to assign them. Most fonts come with anywhere between 100 and 500 such pairs.

There's almost no good reason to turn off automatic kerning altogether, but if you want to, the switch is in the Typographic Preferences dialog box, under the Edit menu. There is, however, very good reason to make judicious use of automatic kerning. The issue is speed; the more kerning pairs in a font, the slower it will display and print. Because of this, and because you really don't need kerning enabled for text smaller than 10 or 12 points, "Typographic Preferences" also allows you to set the smallest point size that automatic kerning will be applied to. We usually keep it set to 7 points (we can easily see the difference between kerned and unkerned text blocks at 8 points). If you're picky about your body copy and you're printing to a high-resolution imagesetter, you may want to lower this value to 4 or 5 points.

Manual. Figure 4-9 showed a word in three renditions: with no kerning, with automatic kerning, and with manual kerning in addition to automatic kerning. The last looks best, doesn't it? (Please agree.)

Manual kerning in QuarkXPress is the adjustment of space between character pairs on a case-by-case basis. You make each adjustment in increments of em spaces (see "Tip: Know Your Ems and Ens," above). Why anyone would want to kern to a precision of $\frac{1}{20,000}$ of an em space is beyond us, but QuarkXPress lets you do just that.

Manual kerning is usually reserved for larger type sizes for two reasons. First, it's harder to see poorly kerned pairs in smaller point sizes, so people say, "Why bother?" Secondly, you wouldn't want to go through a sizable amount of body text in the 8- to 14-point range, meticulously kerning pairs. It would take forever. Leave kerning of small type sizes to automatic kerning. If you don't like the built-in kerning pairs in a font, you can change them (see "Kerning and Tracking Tables," below).

▼ ▼

Tip: What To Do with These Numbers. We're going to throw a bunch of numbers at you like $\frac{1}{20}$ em, but the important thing to remember is how the type looks, not all the numbers that get you there. When we're working in QuarkXPress, we never think, "Oh, we're going to change the kerning $\frac{1}{20}$ em." We just say, "Oh, let's see how adding some kerning here would look." Focus on the methods, and you'll get the feel for it pretty quickly.

▼ ▼

Manual kerning is a character-level attribute, but with a distinct difference from other character styles. Instead of selecting the text you want to change, you only place the cursor between two of the characters before applying kerning (see Figure 4-10). If you select one or more characters you end up applying tracking rather than kerning (see "Tracking," below). You can then control the space between the characters in four different ways.

Figure 4-10
Cursor placement
for kerning

Correct cursor placement for manual kerning

Incorrect cursor placement for manual kerning, but right for tracking

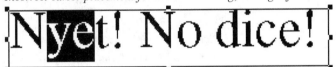

Kern. You can select the Kern feature from the Style menu, which brings up the Kern dialog box. Whole number values typed in here represent units of $\frac{1}{200}$ em. For example, typing in 10 adds $\frac{10}{200}$ ($\frac{1}{20}$) em of space, and typing -.1 removes $\frac{1}{2000}$ em of space (the minus sign—a hyphen—before the value makes a negative value).

Character Attributes. Changing the kerning value between two characters by using the Character Attributes dialog box (Command-Shift-D) works just fine, but it's probably the slowest method you could find.

Measurements palette. The Measurements palette contains a left arrow and a right arrow that can control tracking and kerning in text (they mean something different for pictures). Table 4-3 gives you a rundown on how to use them.

Table 4-3
Kerning control with the
Measurements palette

Clicking on...	While holding...	Does this...
Right arrow		Increases space 10 units ($\frac{1}{20}$ em)
Right arrow	Option key	Increases space 1 unit ($\frac{1}{200}$ em)
Left arrow		Decreases space 10 units ($\frac{1}{20}$ em)
Left arrow	Option key	Decreases space 1 unit ($\frac{1}{200}$ em)

Keystrokes. David hates to take his hands off the keyboard while he's working. He asks, "Why should I, when I can do just about everything I need through keystrokes?" He's got a point there. Table 4-4 shows the keystrokes you can use to control kerning.

Table 4-4
Kerning keystrokes

Holding down...	Results in...
Command-Shift-}	Increases space 10 units ($\frac{1}{20}$ em)
Command-Option-Shift-}	Increases space 1 unit ($\frac{1}{200}$ em)
Command-Shift-{	Decreases space 10 units ($\frac{1}{20}$ em)
Command-Option-Shift-{	Decreases space 1 unit ($\frac{1}{200}$ em)

No matter which method you use to kern, you can see the kerning value in the Measurements palette (just to the right of the left and right arrows), in the Kern dialog box, and in the Character Attributes dialog box.

▼ ▼

Tip: Kerning the Kerned. What shows up as the kern value when you want to kern a pair that is already kerned because of automatic kerning? Nothing. You'll still find a zero in the Kern Amount field. QuarkXPress regards the values applied in automatic kerning as the norm, so you don't have to worry about them.

However, if you have applied "manual kerning pairs" with "automatic kerning" switched one way, then later you switch it the other way, your kerning values may be way off.

▼ ▼

Tracking

QuarkXPress calls two different functions "tracking." They're similar, but we need to break them down for clarity. The first is a character-level attribute, and we're going to talk about it here. The second is a font-level attribute (changing this value changes the font as a whole, rather than just a set of characters), and we'll discuss it in great detail later in this chapter.

Tracking, as a character-level attribute, is the adjustment of space between a range of characters. It's sometimes called track kerning or kern tracking, though we think the best name for it is range kerning. The idea is simple: you can add or subtract space from between many pairs of characters all at one time by using tracking controls (see Figure 4-11 for examples of tracking). These controls are so similar to the kerning controls that we're not even going to waste time and paper going into much depth.

You can control tracking by selecting a range of type and using the Measurements palette, the Track feature from the Style menu, the Character Attributes dialog box, or the same keystrokes as kerning. The reason all the controls are virtually the same is that QuarkXPress "decides" for you whether to kern or track, based on what is selected in the text box. In fact, though, these controls have the same functions. One is applied to a single pair of characters; the other is applied to several or many pairs.

Figure 4-11
Tracking text

Tracking: +7

Art directors *everywhere* were ignoring me until I realized what I needed:

Much tighter tracking!

Tracking: –12

Tracking: 0. The art director threatens to fire you because this copy takes up three lines.

Hey, look, duuuuuude, you're, like, crowding into my space!

Problem solved! Tracking: –4.

Hey, look, duuuuuude, you're, like, crowding into my space!

▼ ▼

Tip: Tracking and the Single Word. The way tracking works, technically, is by adding or subtracting space to the right of each selected character. If you want to track a single word and don't want the space after the last character adjusted, you should select not the whole word, but only the characters up to the last letter. For example, if you want to apply a -10 unit track to the word "obfuscation," without changing the space after the "n," you would only select the letters "obfuscatio" and apply tracking.

▼ ▼

Note that kerning and tracking are totally separate items, even though they seem to be the same. One result of this is that kerning and tracking are cumulative. For example, if you kern a character pair -10 units, then apply a tracking of -10 units to those characters, the space between them ends up 20 units smaller than normal.

▼ ▼

Tip: Overcoming Kerning and Tracking Limits. QuarkXPress 3.0 allows you to type in a kerning or tracking value up to 100 (.5 em). For example, a line of text in 20 point could have up to 10 points of space between each character. However, you may need to space text out farther for a desired effect.

You can accomplish this by taking advantage of invisible spaces. Simply add an extra space or two between each character; the spaces add a constant amount of space between the characters (the width of the Spacebar plus the tracking applied that's to it). Figure 4-12 shows the result of these manipulations.

If you use QuarkXPress 3.1, you can track up to 500 units, and this tip is less important (see Appendix C).

Figure 4-12
Tracking above
the limits

MEPHISTOPHELES   *With no tracking*

M E P H I S T O P H E L E S   *Spaced to the*
                                  maximum
                                  tracking limits

M E P H I S T O P H E L E S   *Spaced even further*
                                  using extra spaces

▼ ▼

Tip: When To Track. Ah, we hear the reader sighing, "But what about some real world tips?" Okay, let's throw some rules out for you.

- If you're setting text in all capital letters, add between 5 and 10 units of space by tracking the word. Remember not to add the tracking to the last character of the word, or else the space character will be affected, too.

- Printing white text on a black background often requires a little extra tracking, too. We don't need to get into the scientific reasons for this; just try it and see.

- Larger type needs to be tracked tighter (negative tracking values). Often, the larger the tighter, though there are aesthetic limits to this rule. Advertising headline copy will often be tracked until the characters just "kiss." You can automate this feature by setting up dynamic tracking tables, which we'll discuss later in this chapter.

- A condensed typeface, such as Futura Condensed, could usually do with a little tighter tracking. Sometimes we'll add as little as -1 unit to a text block to make it hold together better.

Remember, however, that no matter how solid a rule, you are obliged to break it if the finished design will be better.

▼ ▼

Word Spacing

The QuarkFreebies 3.0 XTensions package adds one more capability to character-level attributes: adjustable word spacing. As we discussed above, tracking is the adjustment of space between characters; it's often called letter spacing. Word spacing, then, is the adjustment of space between words.

There are three conditions for adjusting word spacing over a selected range of text.

- You can only use keystrokes.

- You must have an extended keyboard.

- Quark's add-on XTension file must be in the same folder as your copy of QuarkXPress.

Table 4-5 shows the keystrokes you should use to adjust word spacing.

Baseline Shift

The final character attribute that we discuss here is baseline shift. The baseline is the line—if you will—on which the type sits. For example, each line of text you're reading is

Table 4-5

Keystrokes for word spacing

Type...	To get...
Command-Shift-Control-]	increase word spacing 10 units
Command-Shift-Option-Control-]	increase word spacing 1 unit
Command-Shift-Control-[	decrease word spacing 10 units
Command-Shift-Option-Control-]	decrease word spacing 1 unit

made of characters sitting on a baseline. You can shift a character or group of characters above or below the baseline using the Baseline Shift feature under the Style menu. The baseline shift is specified in points; negative values shift the character down, positive values shift it up. You can enter any value up to three times the font size you're using; for example, you could shift a character off the baseline by 30 points in either direction if that character were 10-point type.

Note that baseline shift is similar to kerning and tracking in an important way: even though you specify values in points rather than ems, the value of the baseline shift will change as the font size changes. For example, if you specify a 4-point baseline shift for some 15-point type, when you double the font size to 30 points, the shifted character is "reshifted" to 8 points (2 × 4).

The truth of the matter is that you can and will use the superscript and subscript type styles for almost every instance of raising or lowering a character. So what's the advantage of having a separate Baseline Shift control? Figure 4-13 shows several examples of how you might use baseline shift in your text.

Figure 4-13

Baseline Shift

I DON'T NEED NO BASELINE SHIFT.

I FEEL A NEED FOR A SUPERSCRIPT.

ME, I'D RATHER BE A SUPERIOR CHARACTER.

OY. I'M FEELIN' KINDA UNSTABLE, WHAT WITH ALL THIS BASELINE SHIFTING GOING ON.

Paragraph Formatting

Character formatting is all very well and good, but when it comes to how text flows in a column, it don't make Bo Diddley squat. To handle text flow on a paragraph level, we move to paragraph formatting. These controls include indents, leading, tabs, and hyphenation and justification, as well as some esoteric functions such as "Keep with Next ¶" and a widow and orphan control. We'll discuss each of these features and more. In addition, as usual, we'll give you lots of examples so you can see what we're talking about.

The central headquarters of paragraph formatting is the Paragraph Formats dialog box (see Figure 4-14). Let's discuss each feature in this dialog box in turn, branching off on tangents when we need to.

Figure 4-14
The Paragraph
Formats dialog box

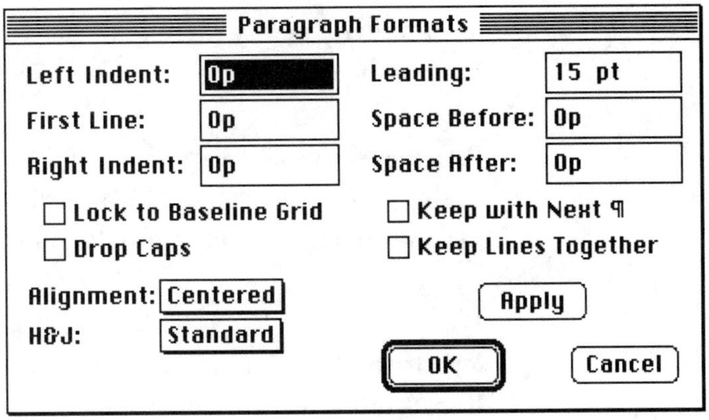

Alignment

Why not start with the most bold and blatant paragraph attribute—its alignment. Most people are familiar with the four horizontal alignment options: left-aligned, right-aligned, justified, and centered. We will discuss each of these first, then move on to a less-known feature: vertical alignment.

Horizontal Alignment

If you've been involved with desktop typography long enough (a day or two), you'll know that different sources have many names for the same thing. For example, what QuarkXPress calls "left-aligned," others may call "left-justified," "flush-left," or "ragged-right." We're not going to start naming names, but QuarkXPress's terms are simpler and make more sense. For one thing, "justified" means only one thing: text fitting flush on left and right. "Fully-justified" is redundant, and "left-justified" is...well, it just isn't. Figure 4-15 shows some examples of text with various horizontal alignments.

Figure 4-15
Horizontal alignment

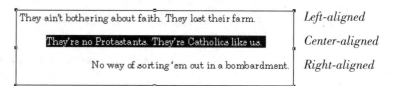

They ain't bothering about faith. They lost their farm.   *Left-aligned*

They're no Protestants. They're Catholics like us.   *Center-aligned*

No way of sorting 'em out in a bombardment.   *Right-aligned*

You can specify alignment for a paragraph using any of four methods.

Paragraph Formats. As we said above, the Paragraph Formats dialog box is always an option when you're changing paragraph formats. The control is a pop-up menu item (see Figure 4-16).

Style menu. You can select the horizontal alignment you want from a submenu labeled "Alignment" under the Style menu.

Keystrokes. Note that the Alignment submenu lists a keystroke for each style. These are easy to remember as they rely on a first-letter mnemonic ("L" for left, "R" for right, and so on).

Measurements palette. Perhaps the easiest alignment method of all is to use the Measurements palette. When you have an insertion point in a paragraph, QuarkXPress displays four icons representing the four horizontal alignment selections

Figure 4-16

Alignment control in
the Paragraph Formats
dialog box

```
╔══════════ Paragraph Formats ══════════╗

  Left Indent:    [0p        ]   Leading:         [auto      ]

  First Line:     [0p        ]   Space Before:    [0p        ]

  Right Indent:   [0p        ]   Space After:     [0p        ]

        ☐ Lock to Baseline Grid        ☐ Keep with Next ¶
        ☐ Drop Caps                    ☐ Keep Lines Together

  [Alignment:]  ┌─────────────┐        (  Apply  )
                │ ✓Left       │
  H&J:          │  Centered   │        ( OK )  ( Cancel )
                │  Right  ↖   │
                │  Justified  │
                └─────────────┘
```

(see Figure 4-17). To change a paragraph's alignment, just
click on the one you want.

While left-aligned, right-aligned, and centered paragraphs are relatively straightforward, justified text is more
complicated. However, we're putting off talking about
justification and hyphenation until later in this chapter.

▼ ▼

Tip: Limit Your Alignments. We're sure you would never do this.
We know that you're a designer of reputation and flair. But
we might as well mention this tip, just in case.

Don't use left-aligned, right-aligned, centered, and
justified text all on the same page unless you have a reasonable design sense and a signed note from your parent. Too
often people let all this highfalutin technology go to their
head and design their pages using every trick in the bag.
Remember that there is strength in subtlety.

▼ ▼

Figure 4-17

Horizontal alignment
in the Measurements
palette

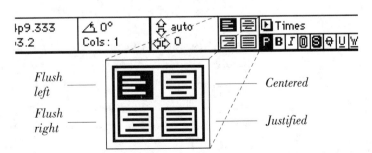

Vertical Alignment

Vertical alignment is not really a paragraph attribute, but rather an attribute of each text box. Nonetheless, as we're talking about alignment, we might as well bring this into the discussion.

Just as horizontal alignment is the horizontal placement of the text within a column, vertical alignment is the vertical placement of the text within its box. You can specify attributes similar to those used in horizontal alignment: top, bottom, center, and justified. The only place you can change this setting is in the Text Box Specifications dialog box (Command-M). Here you're presented with a pop-up menu for each selection (see Figure 4-18).

Figure 4-18
Vertical Alignment in
the Text Box
Specifications
dialog box

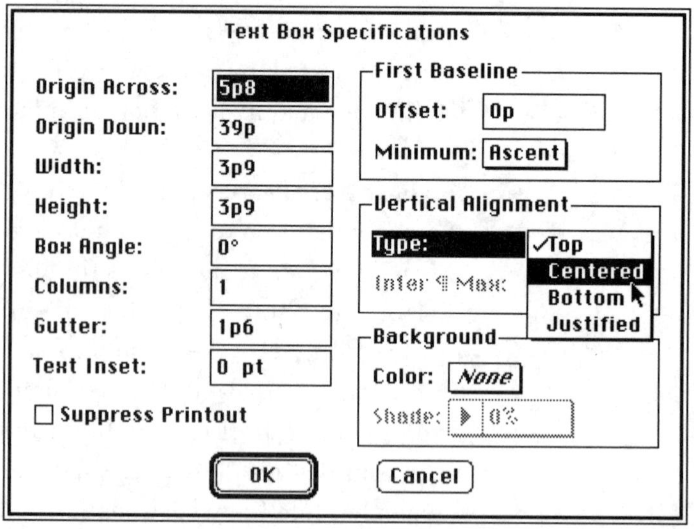

Let's look at each of the alignment possibilities briefly.

Top. This is the default setting for "text boxes." It's what you're probably used to if you use QuarkXPress regularly. The text starts at the top of the text box and, as you type, fills the box. Exactly where the text starts from depends on the first baseline control (discussed later in the chapter).

Bottom. By specifying "Bottom," you force the first line of text to be placed at the bottom of the box. Then, as text flows into the text box, each line pushes the type higher in the box. The last line of text in the box is always flush with the bottom of the box. Note that it is the bottom of the descender that is flush with the bottom of the box, rather than flush with the baseline.

Center. When "Vertical Alignment" is set to "Center," the text within the text box is vertically centered. That sounds trite, but we can't explain it any better than that. See Figure 4-19 for an example of this effect.

▼ ▼

Tip: Centering Text. Specifying either horizontal or vertical center alignment may not result in your text looking perfectly centered. Why? For two reasons. First, the mathematical horizontal centering of text may not look as "right" as an optical centering, especially if you have punctuation before or after the text. You can use invisible characters (colored white) or altered indentation (see "Indents," below) to change the way the text looks (see Figure 4-20). Remember, what looks right is more "right" than what the computer says.

In the case of vertical centering, text in all capitals or text in fonts such as Zapf Dingbats may not be centered correctly in the box. The reason for this is that QuarkXPress does not actually find the center of the characters you've typed. Rather, it uses the full height of the font, ascent and descent combined, to calculate proper placement. We suggest using baseline shift to move the characters around until they look the way you'd like them to.

▼ ▼

Justified. Justification here means that text will be flush with the top and bottom of the box. QuarkXPress will put the first line of the text box at the top, the last line at the bottom, and then add or delete space between interior lines. Leading settings will be overridden when necessary.

Figure 4-19
Vertical alignment

Edges of text box

Installing **KvetchWrite** is the absolute living essence of simplicity.

First, except on old S-100 systems, you will need to reformat your

hard disk. As you know, this is a short and simple procedure that anyone

can do.

Next, remove Disk 27 from its fireproof container. If you forget the

Vertical alignment: justified

Installing **KvetchWrite** is the absolute living essence of simplicity.
First, except on old S-100 systems, you will need to reformat your
hard disk. As you know, this is a short and simple procedure that anyone
can do.
Next, remove Disk 27 from its fireproof container. If you forget the

Vertical alignment: bottom

Installing **KvetchWrite** is the absolute living essence of simplicity.
First, except on old S-100 systems, you will need to reformat your
hard disk. As you know, this is a short and simple procedure that anyone
can do.
Next, remove Disk 27 from its fireproof container. If you forget the

Vertical alignment: top

Installing **KvetchWrite** is the absolute living essence of simplicity.
First, except on old S-100 systems, you will need to reformat your
hard disk. As you know, this is a short and simple procedure that anyone
can do.
Next, remove Disk 27 from its fireproof container. If you forget the

Vertical alignment: centered

Figure 4-20
When centering
is not centered

"Take your little brother swimming with a brick."

This is not visually centered because of the quotation marks.

"Take your little brother swimming with a brick."

This is adjusted by placing invisible punctuation on each line.

When Quark first announced that version 3 would support vertical justification, the press thought it was the greatest thing since the transistor. Our response is: if you set up your leading grids and "text boxes" correctly, you shouldn't need to have some computer going through your drawers, shuffling lines around. We wouldn't want a computer to marry our daughters (if we had any), and we don't want a computer changing our leading and paragraph spacing.

No matter how picky we are about correctly setting up our documents, we do admit that there are times when vertical justification comes in handy. For example, many newspapers use this feature constantly to "bottom out" their columns.

You can specify a maximum distance between paragraphs in a vertically-justified text box by changing the Inter ¶ Max value in the Text Box Specifications dialog box. A setting of "0" (zero), which is the default, tells QuarkXPress to distribute all space evenly by adding interline spacing (leading). A setting higher than 0 lets the program add extra space between paragraphs rather than change your leading. Figure 4-21 shows some examples of vertically-justified text with different Inter ¶ Max settings.

▼ ▼

Indents

Horizontal alignment depends entirely on where the left and right margins are. In a column of text, the margins are usually at the edges of the text box. However, you may want the

Figure 4-21

Varying the
Inter ¶ Max setting

Ior, auritulus cinereus ille annosus Raili, solus in silvae angulo quodam carduoso stabat, pedibus late divaricatis, capite deflexo de rerum natura meditans. "Cur?' cogitabat, modo "quemad-modum?'
Itaque Puo appropinquante Ior paulisper a meditatione desistere gavisus est ut maeste "Ut vales?' ei diceret.

Text is 10/11, nter ¶ Max setting is 0p. The leading is ignored completely.

Gray line represents the text box.

Ior, auritulus cinereus ille annosus Raili, solus in silvae angulo quodam carduoso stabat, pedibus late divaricatis, capite deflexo de rerum natura meditans.

"Cur?' cogitabat, modo "quemad-modum?'

Itaque Puo appropinquante Ior paulisper a meditatione desistere gavisus est ut maeste "Ut vales?' ei diceret.

Text is 10/11, Inter ¶ Max setting is 4 pt. The leading is adjusted slightly, while space is added between paragraphs.

Ior, auritulus cinereus ille annosus Raili, solus in silvae angulo quodam carduoso stabat, pedibus late divaricatis, capite deflexo de rerum natura meditans.

"Cur?' cogitabat, modo "quemad-modum?'

Itaque Puo appropinquante Ior paulisper a meditatione desistere gavisus est ut maeste "Ut vales?' ei diceret.

Text is 10/11, Inter ¶ Max setting is 1 pica. The leading is back to normal, and space is only added between paragraphs.

first line of every paragraph to be indented slightly. Or you might want the left or right margin to be other than the edge of the text box. You control each of these by changing the values for the paragraph indents.

▼ ▼

Tip: Watch the Text Inset. The default text inset for "text boxes" is 1 point, so your text will be indented one point from each side of the box automatically. Make sure to change the value in the Text Box Specifications dialog box (Command-M) if you don't want the 1-point indent.

▼ ▼

QuarkXPress lets you change three indenting values: left indent, right indent, and first line indent. All three controls are located in the Paragraph Formats dialog box (Command-Shift-F; see Figure 4-22). We'll discuss each one and then talk about how you can use them for special typographic effects.

Figure 4-22
Right, left, and first-line indents

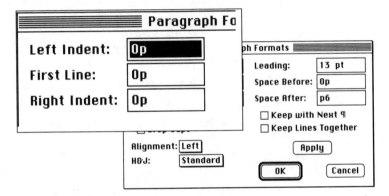

Left Indent. The Left Indent control specifies how far the selected paragraph will sit from the left side of the text box or column guide. The left indent does not take the Text Inset settings into account (see Chapter 1, *Structure and Interface*), so you should add those in yourself. For example, if you want your paragraph to be exactly 3 picas indented from the side of the text box, and your Text Inset setting is 4 points, then your left indent should be 2p8 (3 picas minus 4 points).

Right Indent. The Right Indent control specifies just the opposite of "Left Indent"—in other words, how far will the right edge of the paragraph be positioned from the right edge of the text box or column guide. For example, if you change the right indent to .5 inch, you can imagine an invisible line being drawn one-half inch from the right column guide. The text cannot move farther to the right than this line (see Figure 4-23.)

First Line. Whatever you do, wherever you go, don't type five spaces to indent the first line of each paragraph. If you must, use a tab. If you want to avoid the whole problem in the first place, use a first line indent. The First Line indent feature does exactly what it sounds like it would do: indents only the first line of each paragraph.

How far your indent should be depends primarily on your design and the typeface you are working with. If you are working with a typeface with a large x-height (the height of the lowercase "x" in comparison with the height of the capital letters), you should use a larger first line indent than if you are working with a low x-height typeface.

▼ ▼

Tip: Hanging Indents. You can use "Left Indent" and "First Line" to create hanging indents (used for bullet lists and the like) by typing a negative number as the first line indent. We

Figure 4-23
Right indent

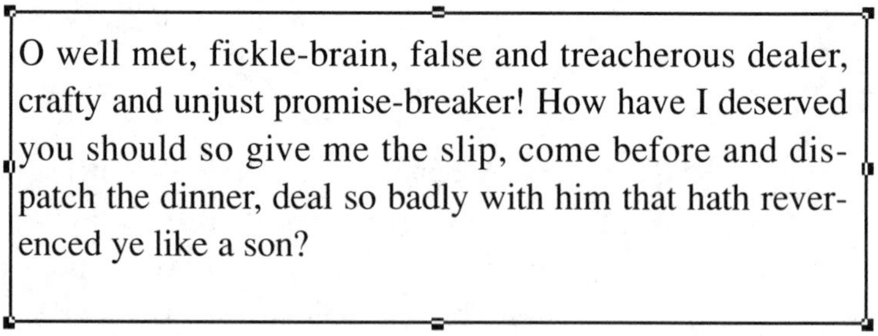

O well met, fickle-brain, false and treacherous dealer, crafty and unjust promise-breaker! How have I deserved you should so give me the slip, come before and dispatch the dinner, deal so badly with him that hath reverenced ye like a son?

No right indent

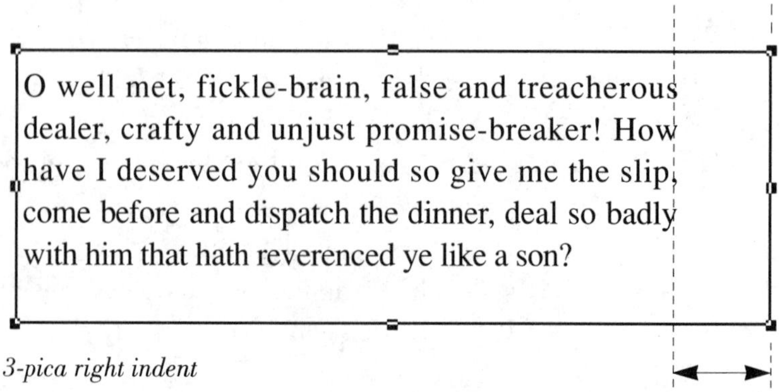

O well met, fickle-brain, false and treacherous dealer, crafty and unjust promise-breaker! How have I deserved you should so give me the slip, come before and dispatch the dinner, deal so badly with him that hath reverenced ye like a son?

3-pica right indent

often use 1p6 (one and a half picas) for a left indent and -1p6 for a first line indent. This places our first character (a bullet) at the zero mark, and the subsequent lines at the 1p6 mark (see Figure 4-24). In fact, typing a tab after the bullet skips over to the 1p6 mark whether or not we have a tab stop there (we'll discuss tabs and tab stops later in this chapter).

▼ ▼

Note that you don't have to specify any of the indents by typing numbers. While the Paragraph Formats dialog box is open, you are shown a ruler along the top of the active text box (see Figure 4-25). This ruler contains three triangle markers in it: two on the left, and one on the right. You can move these icons by clicking and dragging them along the ruler.

The right triangle is the right indent. The bottom-left triangle is the left margin. The top-left triangle is the first line indent. While moving these triangles around, the first line indent "moves with" the left indent. This is the same as Microsoft Word and other programs (though those programs let you move the left indent independently by holding down the Shift key). For example, if you set a ¼-inch first line indent, and then move the left margin triangle to ½ inch, the first line indent will move with it to the ¾-inch point (½ inch plus ¼ inch).

Figure 4-24
Hanging indents

Figure 4-25
The text ruler associated with the Formats dialog box

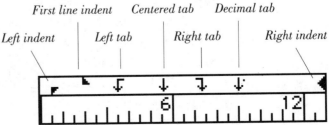

▼ ▼

Leading

If we could get any one concept across to you in this chapter, we'd want it to be: don't follow the defaults. By not following default values, you are forced to pay attention to how the type looks, rather than letting the computer do it for you. There is perhaps no better example of why this is important than leading.

Leading (pronounced "ledding") is the space between lines of text. The name originates from setting lead strips or blocks between lines (slugs) of metal type. QuarkXPress gives you considerable control over leading values for each paragraph, or it can "fly on automatic," specifying leading for you.

In this section we'll discuss the two modes and three methods for specifying leading. Pay close attention to the words "color" and "readability" in this section; they're the reasons we bother to be so meticulous.

Specifying Leading

Although QuarkXPress lets you use any measurement system you want, leading is traditionally measured in points. When talking type, most typesetters and designers say things like, "Helvetica 10 on 12," and write it out as "10/12." Designers who have grown accustomed to digital equipment (in other words, just about everybody), would say that 10/12 means setting 10-point type so that the baseline of one line is 12 points from the baseline of the next line (see Figure 4-26).

Leading is a paragraph-level attribute. That is, each paragraph can have its own leading value, but you can't change leading within a paragraph. You specify your leading in one of three places: the Paragraph Formats dialog box (Command-Shift-F), the Leading dialog box (Command-Shift-E), or the Measurements palette. Whereas in the first two you can only type in the leading value (more on this below), in the Measurement palette you can change leading in two ways (see Figure 4-27).

Figure 4-26
Specifying leading

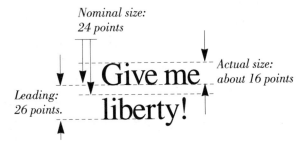

You can also use short cuts to change a paragraph's leading. Table 4-6 shows the four keystrokes.

- You can select the leading value and replace it with the value you want.

- Clicking on the up and down arrows next to the leading value increases or decreases the leading value in 1-point increments.

You can also use short cuts to change a paragraph's leading. Table 4-6 shows the four keystrokes.

QuarkXPress lets you specify leading values in three ways: absolutely, automatically, and relatively. Let's look at these.

Absolute. Setting your leading in an absolute form makes your leading as steadfast as Gibraltar. If you specify 14-point leading, you get 14-point leading—no matter what size text

Figure 4-27
Leading in the Measurements palette

Increase leading

| X: 13p8.8 | W: 14p2 | ⚓ 0° | ⇳ 18 pt | ≡ ≡ 🄳 AG⸱ |
| Y: 26p | H: 12p10 | Cols: 1 | | ≡ ≡ 🄿 B 🄸 |

Decrease leading

Table 4-6
Leading keystrokes

Typing...	Results in...
Command-Shift-'	Increases leading in 1-point increments
Command-Option-Shift-'	Increases leading in .1-point increments
Command-Shift-;	Decreases leading in 1-point increments
Command-Option-Shift-;	Decreases leading in .1-point increments

the paragraph contains. If your type is bigger than your leading, the type will overprint on preceding lines. When, as in the example given above, someone talks about 10/12 type, this is what they're talking about.

QuarkXPress lets you type any absolute leading value between .001 and 1,080 points.

Automatic. "Auto Leading" sets leading as a percentage of the largest font size on a given line. This percentage is usually 20 percent greater than the font size. For example, if the largest font size on a given line is 10 points, then your leading will be set to 12 points (10 plus 20 percent of 10). If you change the font size to 12 points, then the leading changes to 14.4 points. Note that if you change only one character on a line to a larger font size, then that line alone will have a different leading value, even though "Auto Leading" is a paragraph-wide feature (see Figure 4-28).

"Auto Leading" is built into QuarkXPress; it's the default setting of any new text box. However, to choose it specifically, you can type in either the word "Auto" or the number 0 as the leading value.

You can change the automatic leading percentage value in the Typographic Preferences dialog box (under the Edit menu). There are two things you should note about doing this, though. First, the change is document-wide; you can't change the automatic leading percentage for only one paragraph or text box. Secondly, you must specify clearly what

Figure 4-28
Using "Auto Leading" can result in irregular leading within a paragraph

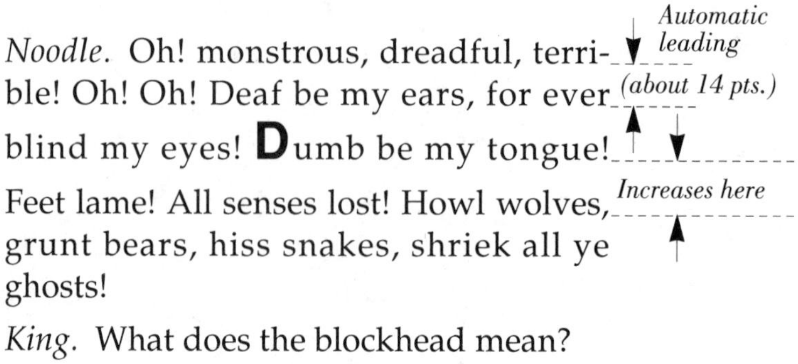

Noodle. Oh! monstrous, dreadful, terrible! Oh! Oh! Deaf be my ears, for ever blind my eyes! **D**umb be my tongue! Feet lame! All senses lost! Howl wolves, grunt bears, hiss snakes, shriek all ye ghosts!

King. What does the blockhead mean?

Automatic leading

(about 14 pts.)

Increases here

the automatic leading measurements are; that is, if you want a percent, you must type a percent sign. This is important because you can specify the automatic leading to be a relative leading value (more on relative values in a moment).

To be honest with you, we use automatic leading when we're typing up grocery shopping lists. But when we're working on a project professionally, we define it for ourselves using absolute or relative leading.

Relative. Whereas automatic leading generally determines the leading value based on a percentage of font size, relative leading determines leading by an absolute value. You specify relative leading by including the characters + or - (plus or minus/hyphen) before your leading value. For example, applying a leading value of +3 to 12-point type would result in 12/15 leading. If you changed the font size to 22 point, you would get 22/25 leading (22 plus 3).

By typing a negative relative value, you can tighten up the leading. However, you have a limit: the height of a capital on the lower line cannot move higher than the baseline of the upper line.

We often use relative leading when we are specifying leading "solid"—that is, when the leading equals the point size. Instead of keying in 30-point leading for 30-point type, we simply type +0. Then, if (or when) we change the font size, the leading changes with it.

Leading Modes

When specifying leading in QuarkXPress, you can work in one of two leading modes: word processing and typesetting. You can select which mode to use in the Typographic Preferences dialog box (under the Preferences submenu under the Edit menu). Selecting one or the other determines the method QuarkXPress uses to measure leading.

Word Processing. Let's be straight here: even if you are using QuarkXPress only as a word processor, you shouldn't use

Word Processing mode. There's just no point to it. Selecting Word Processing mode makes QuarkXPress use an ascent-to-ascent measurement. Ascent-to-ascent means that the leading value you specify will be measured from the top of a capital letter on one line to the top of a capital letter on the next line. The only reason Quark included this was because many word-processing programs use this method. But you shouldn't, because the leading will change depending on the typeface you're using.

Typesetting. As we noted above, the proper way to specify leading on the Macintosh is to measure from the baseline of one line to the baseline of the next. QuarkXPress calls this Typesetting mode. Make sure to enable that mode, then leave it alone.

▼ ▼

Tip: When Black and White Is Colorful. When designers and type-setters talk about the *color* of a page or the color of type, they probably aren't talking red, green, or blue. They're referring to the degree of darkness or lightness that the text projects, also called its *weight*. The color of text is directly related to the typeface, the letter spacing, word spacing, and leading. Other design elements, such as drop caps, graphic elements, or pullquotes, can have a significant effect on the color or weight of a page. It's usually a good practice to maintain an even and balanced color throughout your page, unless you're trying to pull the viewer's eye (as opposed to pulling the viewer's leg) to one area or another (see Figure 4-29).

One way to see the color of a page or a block of type is to hold the printed page at some distance and squint severely. You can also turn the page over and hold it up to light, so you can see the text blocks without being distracted by the text itself.

▼ ▼

Tip: Leading Tips. Here are a few tips and tricks for adjusting your leading. Remember, though, that ultimately it is how easily the

Figure 4-29
The color, or weight,
of text blocks

Eduardus ursus, amicis suis agnomine "Winnie ille Pu"—aut breviter "Pu"—notus, die quodam canticum semihiantibus labellis superbe eliquans

Bookman 10/11

Eduardus ursus, amicis suis agnomine "Winnie ille Pu"—aut breviter "Pu"—notus, die quodam canticum semihiantibus labellis superbe

Bookman Bold 10/11

Eduardus ursus, amicis suis agnomine "Winnie ille Pu"—aut breviter "Pu"—notus, die quodam canticum semihiantibus labellis superbe eliquans

Times-Roman 10/13

Eduardus ursus, amicis suis agnomine "Winnie ille Pu"—aut breviter "Pu"—notus, die quodam canticum semihiantibus labellis superbe eli-

Helvetica 10/13

Eduardus ursus, amicis suis agnomine "Winnie ille Pu"—aut breviter "Pu"—notus, die quodam canticum semihiantibus labellis

Palatino 0 tracking

Eduardus ursus, amicis suis agnomine "Winnie ille Pu"—aut breviter "Pu"—notus, die quodam canticum semihiantibus labellis superbe eliquans

Palatino -10 tracking

text reads and how comfortable the color is that counts. Figure 4-30 shows some samples for each of these suggestions.

- Increase the leading as you increase the line length. Solid leading may read fine with a line containing five words, but will be awful for a line containing 20 words.

- Generally use some extra leading for sans serif or bold type. It needs the extra room.

- Note the x-height of your typeface. Fonts with a small x-height can often be set tighter than those with a large x-height.

- Set display or headline type tightly. Big type can and should be set tightly, using either +0 relative leading or even absolute leading smaller than the point size you're using.

Figure 4-30
Leading techniques

Look, s'pose some general or king is bone stupid and leads his men up a creek, then those men've got to be fearless, there's another virtue for you. S'pose he's stingy and hires too few soldiers, then they got to be a crowd of Hercule's. And s'pose he's slapdash and don't give a bugger, then they got to be clever as monkeys else their number's up.

——— 9/9.5

9/11

The longer a line, the more leading you need

Look, s'pose some general or king is bone stupid and leads his men up a creek, then those men've got to be fearless, there's another virtue for you. S'pose he's stingy and hires too few soldiers, then they got to be a crowd of Hercule's. And s'pose he's slapdash and don't give a bugger, then they got to be clever as monkeys else their number's up.

The misery of this one woman surges through my heart and marrow, and you grin imperturbed over the fate of thousands!

The misery of this one woman surges through my heart and marrow, and you grin imperturbed over the fate of thousands!

Fonts with small x-heights can be set tighter

9/11.5

9/9.5

The best thing since sliced bread

36/31

Display type can be set tightly

Cagney Jads

48/39

Watch out for your ascenders and descenders

- When you're using really tight leading, be careful not to let the ascenders of one line touch the descenders of the line above it.

A corollary tip to all of these: break the rules if it makes the design look better!

▼ ▼

Space Before and After

Not only can you place interline space with leading, you can add space between each paragraph by using the Space Before and Space After attributes. You can find both of these controls in the Paragraph Formats dialog box (Command-Shift-F).

While it is entirely your prerogative to use both the Space Before and Space After attributes, you normally will only need to use one or the other. Think about it: if you add equal space before and space after a paragraph, it doubles the amount of space between each paragraph. Whichever you use is immaterial. David always uses "Space Before," and Keith likes "Space After." Each requires a slightly different way of thinking, but the concepts are ultimately the same.

We've seen more than one designer become flustered when applying "Space Before" to the first paragraph in a text box. Nothing happens. Remember that "Space Before" has no effect on the first paragraph in a text box. To add space before the first paragraph in a text box, use the First Baseline placement control (see "First Baseline," below).

▼ ▼

Tip: Adding Extra Space. Let's see if we can pound this idea into your head as strongly as we did with "Don't use multiple spaces between words or punctuation." Don't ever use an extra carriage return to add space between paragraphs. Not only will you offend the people at Quark who spent long hours implementing the Space Before and Space After features, but you will—nine out of 10 times—mess yourself up with extra blank paragraphs hanging out at tops of columns or in other places where you don't want them. If you want a full line of space between paragraphs, apply it through "Space Before" or "Space After" in the Paragraph Formats dialog box.

▼ ▼

First Baseline

The first line of a text box is always a tricky one for perfectionists. How far away from the top edge of the text box should the line sit? And how to get it there? Previous to version 3, we were forced to insert tiny 2-point-tall blank lines and then add space after, or change the leading, or some other horrible workaround. Fortunately, Quark has implemented First Baseline control in the Text Box Specifications dialog box (Command-M).

The key issue to remember here is that QuarkXPress places the first line of the text box according to one of three values: the size of the type, the Text Inset value, or the First Baseline Offset value. This is potentially confusing, so let's take it slowly. First, QuarkXPress compares the three values (type size, Text Inset, and First Baseline Offset). If the size of the type is larger than either the First Baseline Offset value or the Text Inset value, then the Text Inset value is used. If the First Baseline Offset value is larger than both the type and the Text Inset value, then it is used as the first line's placement.

If the Text Inset is the value used rather than the First Baseline Offset value, then a fourth factor is brought into the equation: the Minimum setting. The Minimum setting specifies where the top of the text is. You can choose three values for the Minimum setting: Cap Height, Cap + Accent, and Ascent (see Figure 4-31).

For example, if your text box has a text inset of 6 points and a first baseline offset of 3 picas (36 points), QuarkXPress places the first line 36 points down from the top edge

Figure 4-31
First baseline settings:
Minimum and Offset

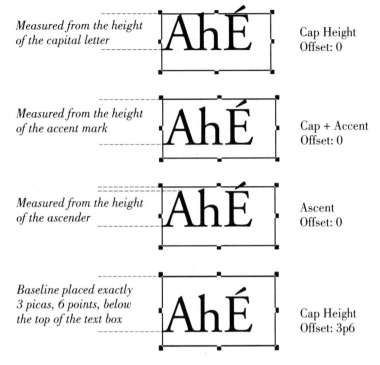

Measured from the height of the capital letter

Cap Height
Offset: 0

Measured from the height of the accent mark

Cap + Accent
Offset: 0

Measured from the height of the ascender

Ascent
Offset: 0

Baseline placed exactly 3 picas, 6 points, below the top of the text box

Cap Height
Offset: 3p6

of the box. On the other hand, if the type changes to 60 points, then QuarkXPress ignores the First Baseline Offset value and places the top of the text (as determined by the Minimum setting) at the Text Inset value.

Tabs

If you've ever typed on a typewriter, you've probably encountered tabs. A tab is a jump-to marker. For example, if you're typing along and hit the tab key, the text cursor jumps to the next tab stop along the line. You can place these tab stops anywhere you like across the text column; they are paragraph-specific, so each paragraph can have a different set of tab stops.

If you don't specify your own tab stops, QuarkXPress sets default stops every ½ inch across the text box. If you are setting up a table and you want to place tabs between each column, follow the same rule as spaces: don't place multiple tabs in a row to make your columns align. Set one tab stop for each column. Then just press Tab once to jump from column to column.

QuarkXPress 3.0 lets you set four types of tab stops using two different methods. Let's look at the types of tabs first. The four types of tabs are: left tab, right tab, center tab, and decimal tab.

- **Left tab.** This is the type of tab you're used to from type-writers. The text after the tab continues on as left-aligned.

- **Right tab.** Tabbing to a right tab stop causes the following text to be right-aligned. That is, it will be flush right against the tab stop.

- **Center tab.** Text typed after a center tab will center on the tab stop.

- **Decimal tab.** This is a specialized type of tab. It acts as a right tab until it encounters a decimal point (period). From that character on, it acts as a left tab.

Figure 4-32 shows examples of each of these types of tabs in a common example—a table. See Appendix C for a description of the new types of tab stops.

The easiest and most precise way to place your tab stops is through the Paragraph Tabs dialog box, which you can find by selecting "Tabs" under the Style menu, or by typing Command-Shift-T. When this dialog box is open, QuarkXPress places a ruler bar across the box of the text box you're working in. You can place a tab stop by first selecting the kind of tab stop you want from the Alignment choices, then either clicking in the ruler area or typing a tab stop value into the Position box. If you choose the latter, and simply type the value in, you must click either the Apply button or OK to make the tab stop appear in the ruler bar (see Figure 4-33).

Figure 4-32
Using tabs

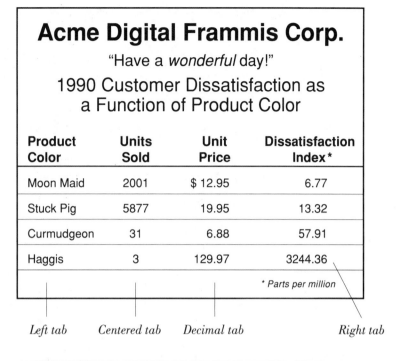

Product Color	Units Sold	Unit Price	Dissatisfaction Index*
Moon Maid	2001	$ 12.95	6.77
Stuck Pig	5877	19.95	13.32
Curmudgeon	31	6.88	57.91
Haggis	3	129.97	3244.36

Left tab   *Centered tab*   *Decimal tab*   *Right tab*

Figure 4-33
The Paragraph Tabs
dialog box
(this dialog box looks
different in Quark-
XPress 3.1; see
Appendix C)

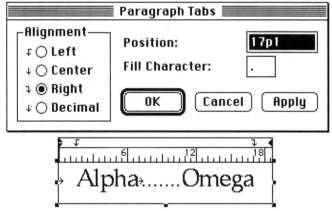

You can also add a leader to each tab stop. A leader fills the tab space with a repeated character, such as a period or a dash (see Figure 4-34). To add a leader to a tab stop which has not been created yet, set the alignment of the tab, type the leader character into the Fill Character field (we prefer the word "leader" to "fill character"), and then place the tab stop. To add a leader to a tab stop which has already been placed, click on the tab stop icon, type the leader in the

Figure 4-34
Tab leaders

Period used as leader character (18 pt.—same as other type on the line).

Moishe is ....not strange.

Oh yes. . . . . .he is too.

Tab character selected, reduced to 10 pt. with tracking value of 100.

It droppeth ----------------as the purple
rain from ⓡⓡⓡⓡⓡⓡⓡⓡⓡⓡ Hollywood

*Other characters used as tab leaders. In the second line, the point size of
the tab itself was reduced to 10 pt.*

appropriate box, and then click the Apply button. If you want
to place more than one tab with a leader, you must click on
the Apply button for each one. When you have placed the
tabs you want, click OK to save the changes to that paragraph. When you have placed the tabs you want, click OK to
save the changes to that paragraph.

The second method for applying tabs is through the
Paragraph Formats dialog box. However, in this instance,
you can only create left tab stops and you must place them
by clicking in the text box ruler (in other words, it's really a
very limited way to apply tabs to a paragraph).

You can go back and edit the tabs by dragging the tab
icons along the ruler in either the Paragraph Tabs or the
Paragraph Formats dialog boxes. Note that you cannot type
in a new value for a tab stop in the Position box (this just
adds a new tab rather than moving the old one). You can rid
yourself of an unwanted tab, by the way, by clicking on the
icon in the ruler and dragging it out of the ruler boundaries
(see Figure 4-35). And a click in the ruler with the Option
key held down erases all the tab stops for that paragraph.

Figure 4-35
Dragging away
a tab stop

▼ ▼

Tip: Don't Use Space Where You Really Want Tabs. Have you ever tried to align multiple columns using spaces? If you have, you have probably known frustration like no other frustration known to desktop publishers. We call it the "it-works-on-a-typewriter" syndrome. It's true; you can line up columns on a typewriter. But you shouldn't in desktop publishing. The reason has to do with fonts.

On most standard typewriters, the font you're using is a monospaced font. That means each and every character in the font is the same width. However, most typefaces on the Macintosh are not monospaced. Therefore, you cannot rely on an equal number of characters always being an equal distance. Figure 4-36 shows this phenomenon clearly. So, don't use multiple spaces when you're trying to align columns. In fact, don't use multiple spaces ever. Use tabs.

Figure 4-36
Using spaces
for alignment

Take one	from column "a"	and one	from column "b"
but here	you actually	have four	columns see?

Aligned with spaces (bad)

Take one	from column "a"	and one	from column "b"
but here	you actually	have four	columns see?

Aligned with tabs (good)

▼ ▼

Hyphenation and Justification

There are few items more dear to a typesetter's heart than hyphenation and justification—often called simply H&J. Proper hyphenation and justification of a document is often the most important single factor in the way a document looks. And if your H&J is bad...well, there's little that anyone can do (see Figure 4-37).

Figure 4-37
Hyphenation and Justification can make the difference

Doing a good job with the program involves knowing a little something about good hyphenation and justification settings. If y'ain't got the good settings, you don't got the good-looking type, either. This paragraph, for example, is simply atrocious.

Doing an *especially* good job with the program involves taking the time to learn about its hyphenation and justification controls. You'll be glad you did.

QuarkXPress has some very powerful controls over how it hyphenates and justifies text in a column. However, this is once more a situation where you won't want to follow along with its default settings. Let's take a look at what hyphenation and justification is all about, and then get into the details of how you can make it work for you.

The Basics of H&J

Although hyphenation and justification are entirely separate functions, they almost always go together. Almost always.

The idea behind both hyphenation and justification is to make text fit into a given space and still look as good as possible. It turns out that there are three basic ways to fit text without distorting it too much: controlling the spacing between each of the letters, controlling the spacing between the words, and breaking the words at a line break by hyphenating. Any one of these, if performed in excess, looks pretty awful. However, it is possible to mix them together in proper measure for a pleasing result.

▼ ▼

Tip: Check for Rivers. Often the first problem that arises when people set their text to justified alignment is that their documents start looking like a flood just hit; all these rivers of space are flowing around little islands of words. Too much space between words is disturbing to the eye. We told you in "Tip: When Black and White are Colorful," above, that turning the page over and holding it up to the light is a good way to check the color of a text block. It's also a great way to check for rivers in your text. This way your eye isn't tricked into actually looking at the words—just the spaces.

▼ ▼

Although you can't adjust the algorithms that Quark-XPress uses for H&J, you can change many variables that help in its decision-making. These values make up the Edit Hyphenation & Justification dialog box, found by first selecting H&Js from the Edit menu, and then clicking on the Edit button (see Figure 4-38).

Let's divide the controls in this dialog box into two groups and discuss them one at a time.

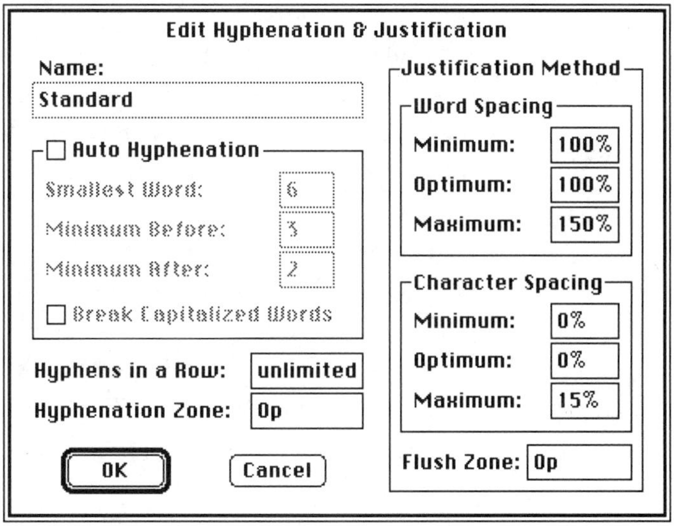

Figure 4-38
The Edit Hyphenation & Justification dialog box (this dialog box looks slightly different in version 3.1; see Appendix C)

Edit Hyphenation & Justification

Name:
Standard

☐ Auto Hyphenation
Smallest Word: 6
Minimum Before: 3
Minimum After: 2
☐ Break Capitalized Words

Hyphens in a Row: unlimited
Hyphenation Zone: 0p

OK   Cancel

Justification Method

Word Spacing
Minimum: 100%
Optimum: 100%
Maximum: 150%

Character Spacing
Minimum: 0%
Optimum: 0%
Maximum: 15%

Flush Zone: 0p

Auto Hyphenation

QuarkXPress can automatically hyphenate words at the end of a line, breaking them into syllables according to an internal algorithm. When you first start up the program, Auto Hyphenation is turned off, and QuarkXPress won't hyphenate any words unless you include hyphens or discretionary hyphens (see "Formatting Characters," below). You can turn Auto Hyphenation on by clicking in the Auto Hyphenation check box in the Edit Hyphenation & Justification dialog box. When you enable hyphenation, several items turn from gray to black. These features are the basic controls over QuarkXPress's internal hyphenating algorithms. Let's look at them one at a time.

Smallest Word. When QuarkXPress is attempting to hyphenate a line of text, it must decide what words are eligible for hyphenation. You can quickly discard most of the smaller words by specifying the smallest word QuarkXPress considers. For example, you might not want the word "many" to hyphenate at the end of a line. By setting the Smallest Word value to "5" or higher, you tell QuarkXPress to ignore this word, as well as any other word with fewer than five letters.

Minimum Before. The Minimum Before value specifies the number of letters in a word which must come before a hyphen break. Depending on your tastes and your pickiness level, you might set this to "2" or "3." Otherwise, words like "tsetse" (as in "fly") might break after the first "t."

Minimum After. The Minimum After value specifies the number of letters in a word that must come after a hyphen break. Again, this value is based on aesthetics. Some people don't mind if the "ly" in "truly" sits all by itself on a line. (*The New York Times* breaks "doesn't" after the "s.") For most quality work, however, you would want a minimum setting of "3."

Break Capitalized Words. This control is self-explanatory. You can tell QuarkXPress to either break capitalized words or not. The feature is there for those people who think that names should never be broken. We're picky, but not that picky.

Hyphens in a Row. One area in which we are *that* picky is the number of hyphens we allow in a row. For most work, we hate to see more than a single hyphen in a row down a justified column of text. QuarkXPress defaults to "unlimited," which is the same as typing 0 (zero). If you're creating newspapers, this might be appropriate. If you're making art books, be a bit more careful with your hyphens.

Hyphenation Zone. Another way to limit the number of hyphens in a section of text is the Hyphenation Zone setting. While relatively simple in function, this feature is one of the more complex to understand fully (it was for us, anyway). The idea is that there is an invisible zone along the right margin of each block of text. If QuarkXPress is trying to break a word at the end of a line, it looks to see where the hyphenation zone is. If the word before the potentially hyphenated word falls inside the hyphenation zone, then QuarkXPress just gives up and pushes the word onto the next line (does not hyphenate it). If the prior word does not fall within the hyphenation zone, then QuarkXPress goes ahead with hyphenating the word.

Normally, Hyphenation Zone is set to 0 (zero) picas. This setting specifies no hyphenation zone, so all lines can have hyphenation (up to the limit of the Hyphens in a Row value.

For example, if the words "robinus christophorus" came at the end of a line and QuarkXPress was about to hyphenate "christophorus," it would first look at the word "robinus" to see if any part of it fell inside the hyphenation zone. If it did, QuarkXPress would not hyphenate "christophorus" at all; if it didn't, QuarkXPress would use its standard hyphenation algorithms to break the word appropriately.

Justification

As we mentioned above, justifying text is the process of adding or subtracting space throughout a line of text to keep it flush on the left and right. You can alter several of the parameters QuarkXPress uses for determining justification by changing values found in the Edit Hyphenation & Justification dialog box. These values are controlled in three different areas: "Word Spacing," "Character Spacing," and the "Flush Zone." Let's look at each of these.

Word Spacing. As we described above in "Character Formatting," word spacing describes the amount of space between words. In the case of justification, it describes the spectrum of how large or small the spaces between words can be. You can specify Minimum, Maximum, and Optimum percentages of a normal space character. For example, a value of 80 percent allows a space between words that is 80 percent of a normal space.

We almost always specify a tight minimum and maximum, such as 85 percent and 105 percent, with an optimum value of 100 percent. We do this because we'd rather have tightly spaced lines than loose lines. (Depending on the typeface, we might even set "Optimum" to around 95 percent.)

Character Spacing. You can also set Minimum, Maximum, and Optimum percentages for the widths of characters. The percentages are based on the width of an en space (see "Formatting Characters," below). Whereas 100 percent was normal width for "Word Spacing," 0 (zero) percent is the normal width for "Character Spacing," and should almost always be used for the Optimum setting.

We generally don't give QuarkXPress much freedom in adjusting the tightness of characters because we think the typeface designer probably knows more about what character widths should be than we do (and certainly more than Quark-XPress does). For example, we might set "Minimum" to -1 percent, "Maximum" to 5 percent and "Optimum" to 0 (zero) percent. But here, again, is an area where you need to print out a few text blocks, preferably on an imagesetter, look at the color of the type, and decide for yourself.

Flush Zone. If you thought the Hyphenation Zone setting was obscure, you just hadn't heard about Flush Zone yet. The Flush Zone setting does one thing, but does it very well: It determines whether the last line of a paragraph gets force-justified or not. The value you type in the field is the distance from the right margin that QuarkXPress checks. If the end of the line falls into that zone, the whole line gets justified. Of course, in many instances, you could just use the Force Justify alignment setting in QuarkXPress 3.2.

▼ ▼

Setting Your Own H&J

Different paragraphs in your document may need different hyphenation and justification settings. For example, you may want each paragraph on one page to hyphenate regularly, but on another page to remain unhyphenated. You can use QuarkXPress's H&Js feature to set up multiple H&J settings to be applied later at a paragraph level.

Creating an H&J Setting

When you select "H&Js" from the Edit menu, the H&Js for Document dialog box appears (see Figure 4-39). You can add, delete, edit, duplicate, or append H&J settings. The list on the left side of the dialog box shows the names of each H&J setting. A new document only contains one setting: Standard. This is the default setting for all text paragraphs.

You can add a new H&J setting in two ways.

- Click on the New button to open a new H&J setting. Change the hyphenation and justification parameters as described above, then give the setting a name.

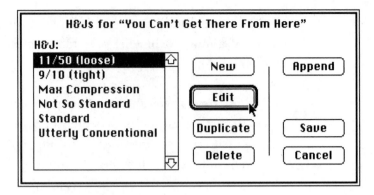

Figure 4-39
The H&Js for Document dialog box

When you are done, click on OK. The Edit H&Js dialog box you see when you click "New" is a duplicate of the Standard setting.

- Click first on a setting (such as "Standard"), and then on the Duplicate button. You can then edit a duplicate of the setting you first clicked on. This is helpful for basing one H&J setting on another.

To delete a setting, first click on its name, then click on the Delete button. If you have set up H&J settings in a different document, you can append them to your current document's list by clicking on the Append button, and then selecting the document to import from. If the names of any appended H&J settings are the same as settings in your open document, they are not imported.

Applying an H&J Setting

Once you have created more than one H&J setting, you can choose which setting to use on a paragraph-level by using the Paragraph Formats dialog box. With the cursor in a paragraph, or with multiple paragraphs selected, you can select an H&J setting from the pop-up menu in the Paragraph Formats dialog box (see Figure 4-40).

▼ ▼

Tip: Tighter and Looser H&Js. David almost always works with a minimum of three H&J settings in his document: Standard, Tighter, and Looser. First, he edits the Standard H&J setting,

Figure 4-40

Applying an
H&J setting

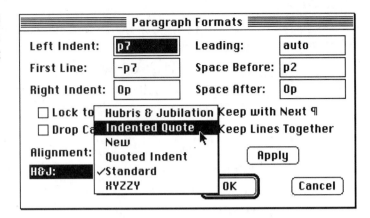

turning "Auto Hyphenation" on, and tightening up (lowering
the values) on the character and word spacing parameters.
The Tighter and Looser settings are for specialty cases. If a
line looks better with slightly tighter than normal H&Js, then
he applies "Tighter." If the Standard settings are too limiting
for a paragraph, and having looser spacing wouldn't hurt it,
then he applies "Looser."

One of the most important things to remember when fooling around with these types of settings is the color of the
page. If setting a tighter H&J makes one text block look particularly darker than the rest of the page, you may need to
manually alter the paragraph rather than let the H&J settings
do it for you.

Widow and Orphan Control

We mean no disrespect to widows and orphans, but when it
comes to typesetting, we must carefully control them, stamp-
ing out their very existence when we have the chance.

If you know what we're talking about already, bear with us
or skip this paragraph (or test whether you can remember
which is the widow and which is the orphan). A *widow* is the
last line of a paragraph that winds up all by itself at the top of a
column or page. An *orphan* is the first line of a paragraph that

lands all by itself at the bottom of a column or page. We sometimes also refer to a line of text comprised of only one word as an orphan. David likes the following mnemonic device: widows sounds like "windows," which are high up (top of the page), whereas orphans make him think of tiny Oliver (who was small, and thus, at the bottom of the page).

All typographic widows and orphans are bad, but certain kinds are really bad—for example, a widow line that consists of only one word, or even the last part of a hyphenated word. Another related typographic horror is the subhead that stands alone with its following paragraph on the next page.

Fortunately, QuarkXPress 3 has a set of controls that can easily prevent widows and orphans from sneaking into your document. The controls are the Keep With Next ¶ and Keeps Lines Together features, and you can find them in the Paragraph Formats dialog box (Command-Shift-F). Let's look at each of these.

Keep With Next ¶

The Keep With Next ¶ feature is perfect for ensuring that headings and the paragraphs that follow them are always kept together. If the paragraph is pushed onto a new column, a new page, or below an obstructing object, the heading follows right along (see Figure 4-41).

You may want to keep paragraphs together even in cases not involving subheads. For example, entries in a table or list that shouldn't be broken could each be set to "Keep with Next ¶."

Keep Lines Together

The Keep Lines Together feature is the primary control over widows and orphans for your paragraphs. When you click on the Keep Lines Together check box in the Paragraph Formats dialog box, QuarkXPress expands the dialog box to give you control parameters in this area (see Figure 4-42). Let's look at these controls one at a time.

Figure 4-41
Keep With
Next ¶ feature

Mephisto
Du
übersinnlicher
sinnlicher
Freier,
Ein Mägdelein
nasführet dich.
Faust
Du Spottgeburt
von Dreck und
Feuer!
Mephisto

Und die
Physiognomie
versteht sie
meisterlich:
In meiner
Gegenwart
wird's ihr, sie
weiß nicht wie,
Mein Mäskchen
da weissagt ver-
borgnen Sinn;

This paragraph style does not have Keep With Next ¶ set

Mephisto
Du
übersinnlicher
sinnlicher
Freier,
Ein Mägdelein
nasführet dich.
Faust
Du Spottgeburt
von Dreck und
Feuer!

Mephisto
Und die
Physiognomie
versteht sie
meisterlich:
In meiner
Gegenwart
wird's ihr, sie
weiß nicht wie,
Mein Mäskchen
da weissagt ver-
borgnen Sinn;

This paragraph style does have Keep With Next ¶ set

Figure 4-42
Keep Lines
Together feature

Paragraph Formats

Left Indent: `0p`   Leading: `auto`

First Line: `0p`   Space Before: `0p`

Right Indent: `0p`   Space After: `0p`

☐ Lock to Baseline Grid   ☐ Keep with Next ¶

☐ Drop Caps   ☒ Keep Lines Together

Character Count: `1`   ◉ All Lines in ¶

Line Count: `3`   ○ Start: `2` End: `2`

Alignment: `Left`

H&J: `Standard`

`Apply`

`OK`   `Cancel`

All Lines in ¶. You can keep every line in a paragraph together by selecting the All Lines in ¶ button. For example, if a paragraph is broken onto two pages, enabling "All Lines in ¶" results in that entire paragraph being pushed onto the next page to keep it together.

It's easy to confound a computer. Keith remembers a 1960s TV show in which a man forced a computer to commit suicide by instructing it to perform contradictory functions. Fortunately, QuarkXPress won't cause your Macintosh to blow up if you specify "All Lines in ¶" to a text block larger than your column. In cases like this, QuarkXPress simply goes ahead and breaks the paragraph, ignoring this control.

Start. You don't have to specify that all the lines in a paragraph should be kept together. Instead, you can control the number of lines that should be kept together at the beginning of the paragraph and at the end.

The value you type in the Start field determines the minimum number of lines that QuarkXPress allows at the beginning of a paragraph. For example, specifying a two line Start value causes paragraphs that fall at the end of a page to maintain at least two lines on the first page before it breaks. If at least two lines of that paragraph cannot be placed on the page, then the entire paragraph is pushed over to the next page.

The Start feature is set up to eliminate orphans in your documents. If you don't want any single lines sitting at the bottom of a page, you can specify a value of 2 for the Start control (some designers insist that even two lines alone at the bottom of a page is ugly and may want to adjust the Start value to 3 or greater).

End. The value specified in the End field determines the minimum number of lines that QuarkXPress allows to fall alone at the top of a column or after an obstruction. A value of 2 or greater rids yourself of unwanted widowed paragraphs (if a widow occurs, QuarkXPress "pulls" a line off the first page onto the second page or column).

▼ ▼

Tip: Other Orphan and Widow Controls. It's all very well and good to let QuarkXPress avoid widows and orphans for you, but for most documents you still need to painstakingly peruse each page, making adjustments as you go. You have many other tools to help you avoid widows and orphans. Here are some of our favorites.

- Adjust tracking by a very small amount over a large range of text. Nobody can tell if you've applied a -0.01 tracking to a paragraph or a page, but it might be enough to pull a widow back.

- Adjust horizontal scaling by a small amount, such as 99.5 percent, or 100.5 percent.

- Make sure "Auto Hyphenation" and "Auto Kern Above" are on. Kerning can make a load of difference over a large area of text. And remember that you can set up different hyphenation and justification settings for each paragraph. You might apply a tighter or a looser setting for a range of paragraphs.

If none of these works for you, don't forget you can always just rewrite a sentence or two (if it's yours to rewrite). A quick rewrite of a sentence can fix up just about any problem.

▼ ▼

Baseline Grid

In typography, the smallest change can make the biggest difference in a piece's impact. For example, look at a high-quality magazine page that has multiple columns. Chances are that each line matches up with a line in the next column. Now look at a crummy newsletter. Place a rule across a page and you'll see lines of text all over the place. What's missing is an underlying grid. You can create a grid and lock each line of text to it with QuarkXPress's Baseline Grid feature.

Each document has its own Baseline Grid setting, which is pervasive throughout every page. However, whether a block of text actually locks to that grid is determined on a paragraph level. You can set the Baseline Grid value for the document in the Typographic Preferences dialog box (from the Preferences submenu under the Edit menu, or just type Command-Option-Y). You have two controls over the Baseline Grid: the Start value and the Increment value. The Start value determines where this grid begins on the page, measured from the top of the page. Set it to start at the first baseline of your body copy.

The Increment value determines the distance from one horizontal grid line to the next. Generally, this value is the same as the leading in the majority of your body copy. For example, if your body copy has a leading of 13 points, then you should type 13 pt as your Increment value.

To lock a paragraph to the baseline grid that you have established, click on the Lock to Baseline Grid control's checkbox in the Paragraph Formats dialog box (Command-Shift-F). Note that the baseline grid overrides paragraph leading. That is, if your paragraph has a leading of 10 points, when you enable Lock to Baseline Grid, each line snaps to the Increment value (13 points, in the example above). If your paragraph has a leading larger than the Increment value, each line snaps to the next grid value. In other words, your leading never gets tighter, but it can get very loose. If your Increment value is 13 points and your leading is 14 points, each line snaps to the following grid line, resulting in 26-point leading.

There is no doubt that a careful study and practice of baseline grids can make your document better looking. However, you can get the same quality from being careful with your leading and text box placement.

▼ ▼

Fine-tuning Type

Almost everything we've talked about in this chapter has been at a character or paragraph level. Here we're going to talk about making typographic adjustments on a document level. You have control over several areas at a document level, including how superscript, subscript, superior, and small caps characters are "built," and what words will hyphenate. You can also create custom automatic tracking and kerning tables, and run through an automatic check for typographic "problem areas."

Let's look at how you can use each of these controls in your documents.

Typographic Preferences

By selecting "Typographic" under the hierarchical Preferences submenu (under the Edit menu), you can alter QuarkXPress's default settings for superscript, subscript, superior, and small caps characters (see Figure 4-43). We talk about these items here, as well as the Character Widths setting. You can find a discussion of baseline grid and of leading preferences in "Leading" and a discussion of Auto Kerning in "Kerning," both earlier in this chapter.

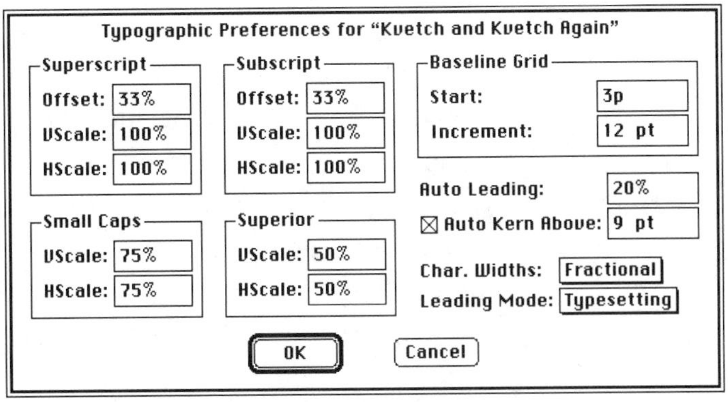

Figure 4-43
The Typographic Preferences dialog box (this looks slightly different in version 3.1; see Appendix C)

Typographic Preferences for "Kvetch and Kvetch Again"

Superscript		Subscript		Baseline Grid	
Offset:	33%	Offset:	33%	Start:	3p
UScale:	100%	UScale:	100%	Increment:	12 pt
HScale:	100%	HScale:	100%		

Auto Leading: 20%

Small Caps		Superior	
UScale:	75%	UScale:	50%
HScale:	75%	HScale:	50%

☒ Auto Kern Above: 9 pt

Char. Widths: Fractional
Leading Mode: Typesetting

OK   Cancel

Superscript and Subscript. Few people ever bother to get into the nitty-gritty of type styles, but the controls are here if you ever want them. Both the Superscript and the Subscript controls are the same: Offset, VScale, and HScale.

- Offset. You can determine how far from the baseline your superscript or subscript characters should move by altering the Offset amount. You specify "Offset" as a percentage of the text size. For example, if the offset for "Subscript" were set to 50 percent, then a subscript character would move 9 points down for 18-point type.

- VScale and HScale. These terms are short for "Vertical Scale" and "Horizontal Scale," which are responsible for how tall and wide the super- or subscript text is. The controls default to 100 percent, which we find much too large. We generally set both to a value between 70 and 80 percent, so that a superscript or subscript character doesn't stand out too much against the rest of the text.

Superior. You don't have to worry about the offset for superior characters because they are automatically set to be flush with a capital letter in that font. So the only modifications you can make here are to the vertical and horizontal scaling of the character. This is clearly an area of aesthetic choice. We tend to like the 50 percent default that QuarkXPress gives us.

Small Caps. You can also set the vertical and horizontal scaling of all small caps characters in a document. Though it would be nice to be able to set the characteristics of small caps on a paragraph or story level, these controls are usually good enough.

There are times when adjustable small caps are even better than traditional small caps (fonts designed especially to be used as small caps). For example, we know a designer who recently specified that all small caps in a book's body copy should be 9.5 points tall. The body text was 10-point

Palatino, so the company producing the templates just changed the small caps specifications to 95 percent in the horizontal and vertical directions (95 percent of 10-point type is 9.5-point type). A traditional small cap would not achieve this effect.

Character Widths. QuarkXPress can display and print text using one of two methods—Integral and Fractional character widths. Integral character widths ignore the true widths of characters in a font, rounding them off to the nearest point. Does this seem like something we'd recommend? No. Unless you always use QuarkXPress to print to a dot-matrix printer such as the ImageWriter II, keep the Character Widths setting to Fractional.

▼ ▼

Kerning and Tracking Tables

As we noted earlier in this chapter, most fonts include built-in kerning tables of 100 to 500 pairs. However, you can modify these pairs or add your own by using Quark's Kern/Track Editor XTension (it's free and comes with QuarkXPress). You must make sure that this XTension is located in the same folder as your copy of QuarkXPress.

Modifying tracking and kerning tables is different from many of QuarkXPress's typographic controls in that it is font-specific. For example, if you alter the kerning table for Avant Garde, those changes will be in effect whenever you use Avant Garde in any QuarkXPress document.

The modifications you make are stored in the XPress Data file, so you aren't really altering the font itself. Note, though, that this means you have to be doubly careful that you include your XPress Data file if you move a document from one machine to another.

Kerning Tables

To modify a font's kerning table, choose Kerning Table Edit from the Utilities menu. This brings up the Kerning Table Edit dialog box, which presents a scrolling list of available fonts (see Figure 4-44). The list lets you choose Plain, Bold, Italic, and Bold Italic variants of each installed font.

Figure 4-44
The Kerning Table
Edit dialog box

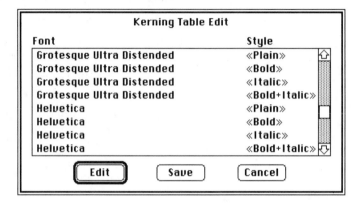

The fonts appear in styles such as "Janson Text," "B Janson Text Bold," "I Janson Text Italic," and so on. Modifying a Bold version of "B Janson Text Bold" won't help you any. Instead, choose "B Janson Text Bold" in its Plain style.

You have to edit kerning tables for one font at a time. This means that you cannot edit Palatino in its Plain style and expect all the Bold, Italic, and Bold Italic variants to be altered as well. Altering the kerning tables for font families that have been harmonized does, however, affect the entire family.

After selecting a font from the list, click OK to move to the Kerning Values dialog box (see Figure 4-45). Here you can edit an existing pair, add a new pair to the list, or delete a pair. You can also import and export lists of these kerning pairs in a text file format. Let's look at how each of these operations is performed.

Adding a pair. You can add a new kerning pair to Quark-XPress's list in three steps.

1. Type the two characters in the Pair field.

Figure 4-45
The Kerning Values
dialog box

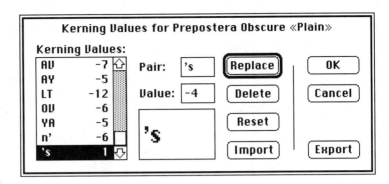

2. Type a kerning amount into the Value field. This value is specified in ½₀₀ of an em (see "Tip: Know Your Ems and Ens," earlier in this chapter). You can see a graphic representation of the kerned pair in the window below the Value field.

3. Click on the Add button.

That's all there is to it.

Editing a pair. You can adjust kerning pairs that you have created or that come predefined in the font by clicking on a pair in the Kerning Values table, and then modifying the value in the Value field. Once you have set the value you want, click on the Add button to add it back to the table.

Deleting or resetting a pair. If you don't like a kerning pair that you added, or you want to get rid of one that was built in, simply select the pair from the list and click on the Delete button. If you have altered a kerning pair and want to reset it back to its original value, click on the pair and then on the Reset button.

Import/Export. There are those who know kerning pairs so well that they'd rather just type up a mess of them in a text-editing program and then import them all at once into QuarkXPress. You can do this by creating a text-only file within any text editor (such as Microsoft Word, Vantage, or MacWrite) in the following format.

1. Type the kerning pair (the two letters).

2. Type a space.

3. Type the kerning value in QuarkXPress's kerning units (1/200 of an em). Negative numbers mean negative kerning.

Next, click on the Import button to bring this text file in.

If you want to edit the kerning values that are already built into the font, you can first export those values by clicking on the Export button. Then edit them and re-import them.

▼ ▼

Tip: Quick Kerning for Families. Applying kerning pairs to a number of faces can be very time consuming and tiresome. You can speed up this process by using the Import feature to apply the same kerning tables to several typefaces. Once you've imported the kerning tables, you can go back and edit them to make up for specifics of that typeface.

▼ ▼

Tracking Tables

Most fonts need to have tighter tracking applied to them in larger point sizes. In the past, we've just gotten used to changing the tracking for various display fonts, because font vendors do not build supplemental tracking values into their fonts. Fonts come with only one tracking value: the normal letter spacing of the font, as determined by the type designer. However, QuarkXPress lets you create custom tracking tables for each font you use.

A tracking table tells QuarkXPress how much tracking to apply at various sizes of a font. This, too, is part of the Kern/Track Editor XTension that comes with QuarkXPress, and you must have this XTension file in the same folder as your copy of QuarkXPress for it to work.

Here's an example to illustrate this feature. Let's say you're creating a template for a new magazine. You've decided to use Futura Bold for your headers, which are at a number of different sizes. You know that your largest header is 60 points and has -20 tracking, and the smallest header is 12 points and has no tracking. Here's what you do.

1. Select "Tracking Edit" from the Utilities menu.

2. Choose the font that you want to edit—in this case Futura Bold—and click on the Edit button. In font families that are not merged, you have to create tracking settings for each style variation. For example, one tracking table for Bodoni, another for B Bodoni Bold, and so on. If you select a merged font family (a typeface family merged with some utility), the tracking table is applied to all four basic style variations (Plain, Bold, Italic, and Bold Italic).

3. You see the Tracking Values dialog box (see Figure 4-46). The vertical axis represents tracking values from -100 to 100 in increments of $\frac{1}{200}$ em. The horizontal axis represents type sizes from 0 to 250 points. The farther to the right on the grid, the larger the type. The default setting is a horizontal bar at the zero tracking level. In other words, all point sizes have a zero tracking value.

4. Click on the line at the 2-point size (on the far left). As you hold down the mouse button, you can see the graph values shown in the dialog box. Note that clicking on the graph places a new point on it. You can have up to four corner points on each graph. This first point is the anchor at the zero tracking level.

5. Click on the line at the 60-point size and drag the graph line down to the -20 tracking level. Figure 4-46 shows these two points making up the entire graph. If

we saved this now, then whenever you used Futura Bold, all point sizes larger than 2 points would have negative tracking applied to them.

6. You can add a third control handle at the 12 point type size and set it to zero tracking. Now all type larger than 12 points has tracking applied.

To save your changes, click OK. Then, if you're done with your tracking table edits, click Save.

While editing a font's tracking table, you can start over by clicking on the Reset button. You can always go back (even after you've saved), and click on the Reset button to get the horizontal bar graph back.

Note that these tracking values are only applied to a font when "Auto Kern Above" is turned on. In fact, the tracking tables only apply to font sizes above the automatic kerning limit which has been entered in the Auto Kern Above value field in the Typographic Preferences dialog box.

Also note that if you edit the tracking tables for any fonts in your document and then send the file to someone else (for example, to a service bureau for printing), you must include your XPress Data file. This is because custom tracking tables are stored in the XPress Data file as opposed to in the document or with the screen font. For the same reason, text exported from QuarkXPress does not maintain this tracking either.

Figure 4-46
A tracking table graph

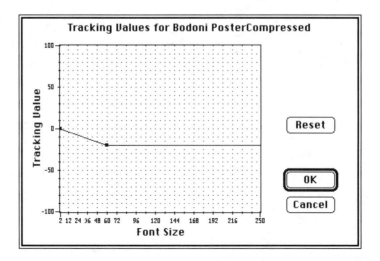

▼ ▼

Hyphenation

QuarkXPress gives you two other tools for controlling hyphenation: the Hyphenation Exceptions and the Suggested Hyphenation features. Let's look briefly at each of these.

Suggested Hyphenation

The entire life's work of the Suggested Hyphenation feature is to help you figure out how QuarkXPress is going to hyphenate a word. First select "Suggested Hyphenation" from the Utilities menu (or type Command-H). Once you have a word selected, or have the cursor somewhere within or immediately to the right of a word, QuarkXPress shows you how it would potentially hyphenate a word (see Figure 4-47).

Figure 4-47
Suggested Hyphenation

QuarkXPress uses an algorithm to hyphenate words, and it takes all sorts of things into account, including the parameters set within the Edit Hyphenation & Justification dialog box, such as the number of entries in "Break Capitalized Words," "Minimum Before," and so on. For example, when "Minimum After" is set to "3," the word "wildly" does not appear hyphenated in the Suggested Hyphenation dialog box. However, if you change "Minimum After" to "2," it does.

Hyphenation Exceptions

You can control the hyphenation fate of particular words by setting your own specific hyphenation in the Hyphenation

Exceptions dialog box, which you access by selecting "Hyphenation Exceptions" from the Utilities menu (see Figure 4-48). You can then add or delete words at will from the Hyphenation Exception list.

When you first open the dialog box, it is empty. To add a word, just type it in the available space, including hyphens where you want them. If you don't want a word to hyphenate, don't put any hyphens in it.

Once you've created some hyphenation exceptions, you can edit them by clicking on them, making the necessary changes, and then clicking the Replace button (note that the Add button changes to a Replace button in this case). You can also delete items on the list by selecting them and clicking the Delete button.

Hyphenation exceptions are stored in the XPress Data file, which is in the same folder as the QuarkXPress application. The changes you make are global: they affect each and every document on that machine when you create or open them. On the other hand, like other information stored in the

XPress Data file, they won't follow your document around onto other people's machines. If you send the document file for use elsewhere with another copy of QuarkXPress—like the one at your favorite service bureau—you must send your copy of XPress Data along, too. This changes in version 3.1 of QuarkXPress (see Appendix C, *Using QuarkXPress 3.1*).

▼ ▼

Tip: Watch Those Hyphens. There's nothing like giving your document a good once over before you print it out. One of the things you want to look for is a badly hyphenated word. Remember that QuarkXPress uses an algorithm to hyphenate words rather than a look-up dictionary like some other programs. Because of this, it can hyphenate more words than other programs, but it doesn't always do it right. For example, QuarkXPress hyphenates the word "Transeurope" normally as "Transeur-ope" rather than "Trans-europe." (We're happy, however, to say that it hyphenates "therapist" after the "r.") If you find these problem words, you can either change them manually (by adding discretionary hyphens), or make a global change using "Hyphenation Exceptions."

▼ ▼

Line Check

David can remember the day—no, days—when his final task before taking a 530-page book to the service bureau was to scroll laboriously though his QuarkXPress files, looking for and fixing any last-minute widows, orphans, and badly hyphenated words. Of course, each fix caused a reflow of all text that followed, and so on. Would that he had Quark's XTras package, which includes an XTension called Line Check that automatically searches for "typographically undesirable" lines. It can search through a document looking for widows, orphans, automatically hyphenated words, manually hyphenated words, "loose" lines (justified lines with too much space in them), and "text boxes" that have overflowed.

It won't fix them for you, but it sure does make cleaning up documents at the last minute a less harrowing experience. Unfortunately, the XTras package doesn't come free with QuarkXPress. However, the Line Check XTension, along with the other XTensions in the package make the already low-priced package really a bargain.

Special Characters

If you're using QuarkXPress to type letters to your mother, you probably don't need this section. If you're doing just about anything else with it, stand by.

When you look at your Macintosh keyboard, you see between 50 and 100 characters represented on the keys. What you don't see are the hundreds of special characters you can access with just a few keystrokes. In this chapter we'll look at what some of those characters are, including invisible "utility" characters, dingbats, math symbols, and special punctuation. By no means do you have to memorize most of these; instead, you may want to refer back to the tables we've included when you're working on documents.

Formatting Characters

The first set of characters we'll look at are invisible characters that are used for special formatting in your document. Several of these characters are visible when you select "Show/Hide Invisibles" from the View menu. However, a few are not; you just have to remember where you put them. Let's take a look at what these characters are (see Table 4-7 for more information on each character).

Return. Sometimes known as a "carriage return" or a "hard return," this is the key to press when you're at the end of a paragraph. In fact, the Return character delineates paragraphs from each other. Most people don't think of the

Name	Keystroke
Return	Return
Soft Return	Shift-Return
Tab	Tab
Indent here	Command-\
Discretionary new line	Command-Return
Discretionary hyphen	Command-Hyphen
Nonbreaking hyphen	Command-Equal
Nonbreaking space	Command-Spacebar
New column	Enter
New box	Shift-Enter
En space	Option-Spacebar
Nonbreaking en space	Command-Option-Spacebar
Flex space	Option-Shift-Spacebar
Nonbreaking flex space	Command-Option-Shift-Spacebar
Current page number	Command-3
Previous text box page number	Command-2
Next text box page number	Command-4

Table 4-7
Invisible formatting
characters

Return key as a character, but you can actually see it and select it with "Show/Hide Invisibles" turned on.

QuarkXPress is great at wrapping characters onto their next line, so don't press Return after each line like you would on a typewriter. Also, don't press Return twice in a row to add extra space between paragraphs. Instead, use "Space Before" and "Space After" (see "Space Before and After," above).

Soft Return. Holding down the Shift key while typing Return results in a soft return, often called simply the "new line" character. A soft return forces a new line without starting a new paragraph with all its attendant attributes—space before and after, first line indent, paragraph rules, and so on. For example, we use soft returns for tabular text or for forcing a line break in justified text. This is a character that takes some getting used to, but we recommend you play with it until you do, because it really comes in handy.

Tab. People also rarely think about the Tab key as a separate character, but that's just what it is. We talked somewhat about tabs in "Tabs," above, so we don't need to go into it now, other than to say you should really know your tabbing and never (never) use the Spacebar to align columns.

Indent Here. New to QuarkXPress 3 is an invisible formatting character, Command-\ (backslash) called "Indent Here." Typing this character causes the rest of the lines in a paragraph to indent over to that character. We find this feature particularly useful for hanging punctuation or inline graphics, drop caps, or headings (see Figure 4-49).

Figure 4-49
The Indent
Here character

How do I love thee? Let me count the ways: ¶

1) This is the first one. I can't remember quite what it is, but I'm sure I mean well.¶

2) Here's the second one. Hmmm. Can't quite remember it, either, but now at the very least I know exactly how to ↵ use the Indent Here character.

Arrows indicate positions of Indent Here characters

How do I love thee? Well, don't you think that's a bit of an impertinent question? I mean, if I'd asked *you* that, you'd have every right to throw me out. I mean, such nerve . . .

"We, the curmudgeonly, having solemnly sworn to

Discretionary New Line. You can place the Discretionary New Line character, a Command-Return, within a word to suggest places to break the word if QuarkXPress needs to. For example, if you type an en dash and feel comfortable about the surrounding words breaking at a line end, you can type a Command-Return after the en dash (en dashes won't break without this). If QuarkXPress determines that it needs to break the line at this point, it does. If it doesn't need to break the line there, it doesn't break it (and the character, being invisible, has no other effect on your text). Figure 4-50 shows an example of this character in action.

Figure 4-50
The discretionary
new-line character

Whilst shaving at
Schenectady–on–Thames, the cat
ran into the room. *En dashes don't break*

Whilst shaving at Schenectady–on–
Thames, the cat ran into the room.

*Discretionary new line character here
allows the line to break differently*

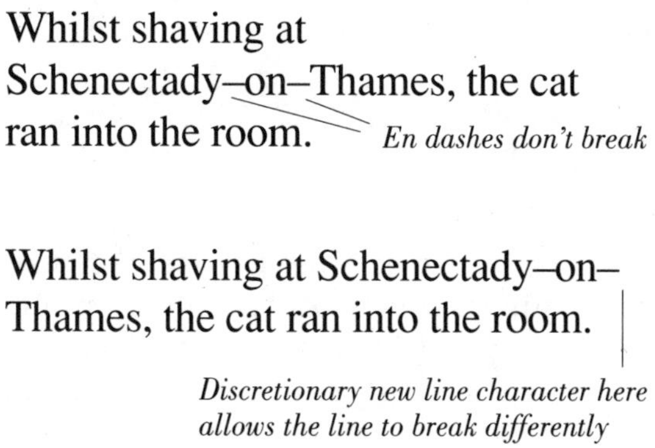

Discretionary Hyphen. The Discretionary Hyphen character (Command-Hyphen) acts in the same manner as the Discretionary New Line character, but if the line needs to break at that point, QuarkXPress adds a hyphen at the break. This is the only way to suggest hyphenation for a particular word.

Discretionary hyphens also play another role in QuarkXPress. If you place a discretionary hyphen before a word, that word will never hyphenate at the end of a line. In other words, the discretionary hyphen can also act to turn hyphenation off for a single word.

▼ ▼

Tip: Adding Hyphenation. When you need to add your own hyphenation to some text, don't go in and add regular hyphens. Why? What would happen if the text had to reflow for some reason (like you added a word)? All of a sudden you would have hyphens scattered throughout your text (see Figure 4-51). Instead, use discretionary hyphens (Command-Hyphen). These will break into real hyphens if they need to, but will "disappear" when they're not needed (even Find/Change ignores the character).

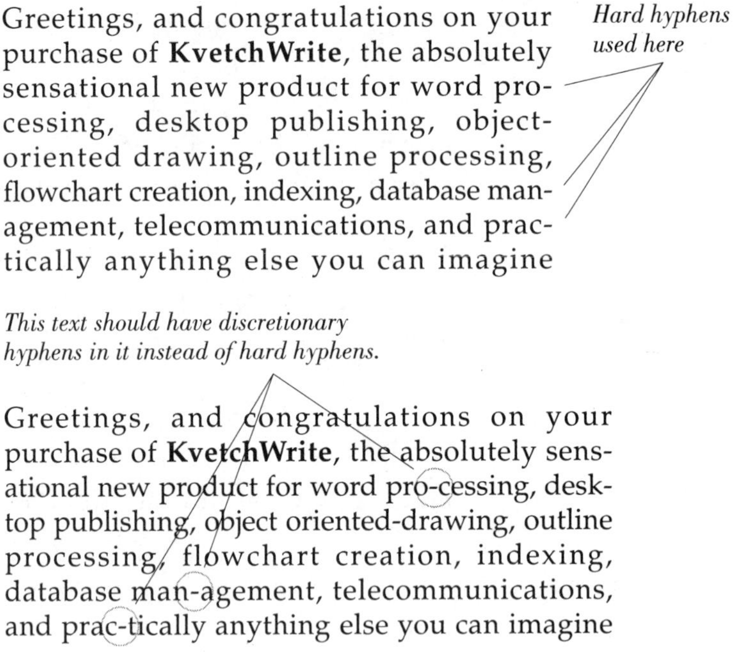

Figure 4-51
Reflowed hyphens

Greetings, and congratulations on your purchase of **KvetchWrite**, the absolutely sensational new product for word processing, desktop publishing, object-oriented drawing, outline processing, flowchart creation, indexing, database management, telecommunications, and practically anything else you can imagine

Hard hyphens used here

This text should have discretionary hyphens in it instead of hard hyphens.

Greetings, and congratulations on your purchase of **KvetchWrite**, the absolutely sensational new product for word processing, desktop publishing, object oriented-drawing, outline processing, flowchart creation, indexing, database man-agement, telecommunications, and prac-tically anything else you can imagine

Nonbreaking Hyphen. You will probably come upon a word which should be hyphenated, but shouldn't be broken at the end of a line. A nonbreaking hyphen is placed within text by typing Command-= (equal sign).

Nonbreaking Space. A nonbreaking space looks just like a normal space character. However, it will never break at the end of a line. A great use of this is in company names which include spaces, but shouldn't be broken over several lines (unless you absolutely have to).

New Column and New Box. If your text box contains multiple columns or is linked to other text boxes, you can use the New Column and New Box characters to force text to jump from one to the next. Typing Enter forces a text jump to the next column. If the character is placed in the last (or only) column of a text box, it will force a jump to the next linked text box. Otherwise, typing Shift-Enter forces a jump to the next linked text box.

En Space. As we mentioned earlier in the chapter, an en is half an em, which—to QuarkXPress—equals the width of two zeros. With a quick calculation we find that an en space must equal the width of one zero. Typing Option-Spacebar results in an en space, which acts just like a space character. Command-Option-Spacebar gives you an en space that doesn't break at the end of a line. Note that because of the way QuarkXPress defines an en, an en space is rarely the same width as an en dash.

Flex Space. The documentation calls this character a half en space, but because Quark has released XTensions that let you adjust its width, a more appropriate name is "Flex Space." The flex space has a default value of one half an en space, which is similar to the width of punctuation marks.

Page Numbers. QuarkXPress lets you use three characters to display page numbering (see Table 4-8). As we noted in Chapter 2, *Document Composition*, these are not only page-dependent, but also text box-dependent. For example, you can place a text box with the "Next Text Box" character (Command-4) on top of a linked text box and the page number will register the link of the text box under it.

Punctuation and Symbols

A typographer shouldn't feel limited using a Macintosh. The typefaces from the major vendors (Adobe, Bitstream, Monotype, and so on) are loaded with the characters you need to

Table 4-8	Type...	To get the page number of...
Page numbering characters	Command-2	The previous text box
	Command-3	The current text box
	Command-4	The next text box

create excellent type, including proper quotation marks, ligatures, and em dashes. If you aren't already a typographer, you'll want to pay careful attention to the tips and examples we show. Using some simple techniques may make the difference between a piece that looks like it was desktop published (in the worst sense of the phrase) and a piece that is professional.

We can't discuss every special character that appears in a font, but we'll hit on a few of the important ones. Table 4-9 shows how to type each of these, plus a good number of additional characters.

Em and en dashes. An em dash, typed with an Option-Shift-Hyphen, should be used in place of double hyphens to indicate a pause or semi-parenthetical. For example, don't do this: "Villainous-looking scoundrels--eight of them." An em dash is named for how long it is (one em).

An en dash (Option-Hyphen) should generally be used for duration and distance such as in "August–September," and "the New York–Philadelphia leg of the trip." It's half as long as an em dash, so it doesn't stand out quite as much.

Note that QuarkXPress will break a line after an em dash in wraparound text, but not an en dash.

Ligatures. Ligatures are to type what diphthongs are to language. That is, they slur characters together by connecting them. Whereas many classic typefaces would contain up to 10 ligatures, most typefaces on the Macintosh include two basic ligatures, but most people don't bother to use them, for some obscure reason. It's a pity, because they really can help a piece of text look great.

Name	Looks like	Keys to press
Opening double quote	"	Option-[
Closing double quote	"	Option-Shift-[
Opening single quote	'	Option-]
Closing single quote	'	Option-Shift-]
em dash	—	Option-Shift-Hyphen
en dash	–	Option-Hyphen
Ellipsis	…	Option-;
Fraction bar	/	Option-Shift-1
Vertical bar	|	Shift-\
Capital ligature AE	Æ	Option-Shift-'
Small ligature ae	æ	Option-'
Ligature fi	fi	Option-Shift-5
Ligature fl	fl	Option-Shift-6
Bullet	•	Option-8
Copyright	©	Option-g
Registered	®	Option-r
Trademark	™	Option-2
Degree	°	Option-Shift-8
Section	§	Option-6
Paragraph	¶	Option-7
Dagger	†	Option-t
Cents	¢	Option-4

The two ligatures are the "fi" and the "fl" combinations. They can be typed with Command-Shift-5 and Command-Shift-6. Figure 4-52 shows these ligatures in action.

Although using ligatures may make your type look nicer, they may make your life harder. For example, QuarkXPress doesn't presently understand words with ligatures in them. That is, those words come up as "wrong" during spell checking, they improperly hyphenate, and are difficult to search for. Perhaps these problems will change with time, but for now, working with ligatures is a trade-off.

Figure 4-52
Common ligatures

But why *not* flaunt the finest of encyclopedias?

No ligatures (utterly, utterly déclassé . . .)

But why *not* flaunt the finest of encyclopædias? (ENCYCLOPÆDIÆ?)

With "fl", "fi", and "ae" ligatures

▼ ▼

Tip: Finding and Replacing Ligatures. We often hold off to the last minute to find the "fi" and "fl" combinations in our documents before replacing them with the proper ligatures. If you use ligatures, make sure you're careful about replacing them. Especially make sure you turn off "Ignore Case" from the Find/Change dialog box. If you don't, capitalized "Fi" or "Fl" combinations get changed, too!

▼ ▼

Quotation Marks. The first tip-off that someone is green behind the ears in desktop publishing is his or her use of straight quotes instead of proper, "printer's quotes." Straight quotes, which is what you get when you press the ' and " keys, should be used for notation of measurements (inches and feet) or for special typographic effect (some fonts' straight quotes look great in headline type). Printer's quotes, or curly quotes, should be used for English/American quotations.

Registration, Copyright, and Trademark. The registration, copyright and trademark characters are found in the Option-r, Option-g, and Option-2 keys. We have only one thing to say about using these characters: be careful with your sizing and positioning. We recommend immediately assigning the superior type style to the character, then determining whether it should be kerned or not (see Figure 4-53).

Figure 4-53
Special symbols

KvetchWrite™ is a product of No Accounting For Taste, Eh?® Documentation © Copyright 1990 No Class Productions.

Trademark and registration characters re-done as superior characters

KvetchWrite!™ is a product of No Accounting For Taste, Eh?® Documentation © Copyright 1990 No Class Productions.

Registration mark kerned +12 to give it a little room to breathe

Result without kerning: Eh?®

▼ ▼

Tip: Key Caps. Anyone who can remember every character in a font, including all special symbols and characters, is no one to borrow money from. We can never remember most of the characters we need, so we use the Key Caps DA. Key Caps comes free with your system, and shows you a keyboard map for every character in any font you choose (see Figure 4-54). To use Key Caps, first open the Key Caps DA from the Apple menu, then select the font you want to see from the Key Caps menu. When you press the Shift key, you see the map of all the uppercase characters. If you press the Option key, you see the Option characters, and so on.

Figure 4-54
The Key Caps DA

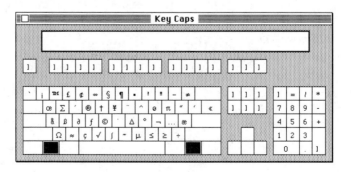

▽ ▽

Foreign Punctuation and Accents

Working in a foreign language is really a trip. Foreign languages have a different word for everything. Many foreign languages, such as French and Spanish, contain accented characters that are built into fonts from the major type vendors. For example, you can type *élève* without moving to some obscure other font. Table 4-10 lists the characters that you would most likely use in a foreign language.

Many people don't fully understand how to type these characters. Several of them aren't as easy as just hitting a key, or even a key with Option or Shift held down. For example "é" is typed by first typing Option-e, then typing the letter "e." It's a two-stroke deal.

▼ ▼

Tip: Get it Right for Overseas. We, in the United States, grew up with the ethnocentric viewpoint that the way we write and typeset is the way everybody does it. Not so. For example, double quotation marks are used in America where single quotation marks are used in Britain. In other European countries, our quotation marks are replaced with guillemets («, », ‹, and ›—Option-\ and Shift-Option-\, and Shift-Option-3 and Shift-Option-4). The Spanish language sets a question or an exclamation point at both the beginning (upside down, keyed with Option-Shift-/ or Option-Shift-1) and at the end of sentences. Figure 4-55 shows examples of each of these styles.

Other languages, such as Hebrew, Farsi, Russian, and Greek, must be typed using a font specific to that language,

Figure 4-55
Foreign punctuation

¡Mi llama se llama Spot!

¿Dónde está la casa de Pépe?

Il dit «La fromage, ça va bien?»

Spanish inverted exclamation and question marks

European guillemets

"He said, 'totally, dude' and walked off into the sunset."

'He said, "totally, dude" and walked off into the sunset.'

American (left) and British (right) quotation marks

Table 4-10

Foreign accents and
punctuation

Name	Looks like	Keys to press
Left guillemets	«	Option-\
Right guillemets	»	Option-Shift-\
Left single guillemets	‹	Option-Shift-3
Right single guillemets	›	Option-Shift-4
Base double quote	„	Option-Shift-W
Base single quote	‚	Option-Shift-0
Question mark down	¿	Option-Shift-?
Exclamation point down	¡	Option-1
Acute vowel	áéíóúÁÉÍÓÚ	Option-E, then vowel
Umlaut vowel	äëïöüÄËÏÖÜ	Option-U, then vowel
Grave vowel	àèìòùÀÈÌÒÙ	Option-~, then vowel
Circumflex vowel	âêîôûÂÊÎÔÛ	Option-I, then vowel
Cedilla C	Ç	Option-Shift-C
Cedilla c	ç	Option-C
Capital slashed O	Ø	Option-Shift-O
Small slashed o	ø	Option-O
Deutscher double s	ß	Option-S
Dotless i	ı	Option-Shift-B
Tilde	˜	Option-Shift-M
Tilde N	Ñ	Option-N, then Shift-N
Tilde n	ñ	Option-N, then N
Circumflex	^	Option-Shift-N
Macron	¯	Option-Shift-,
Breve	˘	Option-Shift-.
Ring accent	°	Option-K
Ring a	å	Option-A
Ring A	Å	Option-Shift-A
Dot accent	·	Option-H
Pound sterling	£	Option-3
Yen	¥	Option-Y

and may require specialized software. QuarkXPress is presently available in 14 different languages, including Japanese
and German.

▼ ▼

Math Symbols and the Symbol Font

QuarkXPress is the wrong program in which to produce a mathematics textbook. You can use utilities such as Expressionist or MacΣqn to help you create equations, but they're not really set up for doing heavy-duty math typesetting as in FrameMaker. Nonetheless, you can still do a pretty good job in QuarkXPress, as long as you don't have to produce 2,000 different equations in a document.

The key, besides the typesetting control, is the symbols themselves. Most typefaces come with a wide variety of built-in math symbols. Table 4-11 provides a list of the most common of these and how to type them.

If you want to typeset an equation of any complexity (such as multiplication), you will quickly want to learn about the Symbol font. Symbol is a Greek and math font that comes with your Macintosh system. It includes such characters as a true multiplication sign (×), which you can create by typing Option-Y. Use the Key Caps DA mentioned earlier to examine the other characters in this typeface.

Table 4-11

Commonly used math symbols found in most fonts

Name	Looks like	Keys to press...
Division	÷	Option-/
Plus or minus	±	Option-Shift-=
Greater or equal	≥	Option-.
Lesser or equal	≤	Option-,
Approximate equal	≈	Option-X
Not equal	≠	Option-=
Infinity	∞	Option-5
Partial differential	∂	Option-D
Integral	∫	Option-B
Florin	ƒ	Option-F
Capital omega	Ω	Option-Z
Capital delta	Δ	Option-J
Product	Π	Option-Shift-P
Summation	Σ	Option-W
Pi	π	Option-P
Radical	√	Option-V
Per thousand	‰	Option-Shift-E

▼ ▼

Tip: One-stroke, One-character Font Change. QuarkXPress has so many keystrokes and shortcuts that we can never remember them all. Here are two that Keith uses all the time but David always forgets about: typing Command-Shift-Q will set the next character you type in the Symbol font, while typing Command-Shift-Z sets it in Zapf Dingbats. After you type the character, QuarkXPress automatically reverts back to the typeface you were in.

▼ ▼

Dingbats

Letters, numbers, and symbols do not a funky design make. Ofttimes you need Dingbats. Dingbats, or pi fonts, are collections of interesting and useful shapes, pictures, graphics, and so on. The most popular dingbat font by far on the Macintosh is Zapf Dingbats, which is included in almost all PostScript laser printers (except Steve's; he still uses his original LaserWriter from 1985). Table 4-12 shows a listing of about a third of the Zapf Dingbats typeface and how to type them. The other two-thirds are mostly variations on what is shown here.

Other examples of dingbat or pi fonts are Carta, Morbats, and Pi (see Figure 4-56 for a few examples of Carta).

Figure 4-56
Some other dingbats

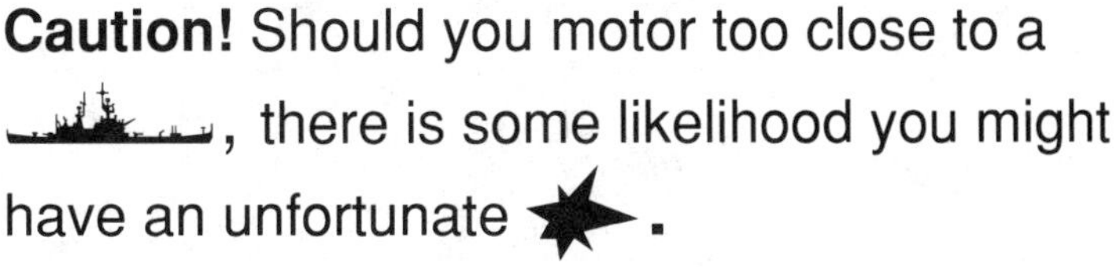

Caution! Should you motor too close to a ⚓, there is some likelihood you might have an unfortunate ✦.

You can use these fonts for fun, but you'll more likely want to use them in a very functional way. Most people use them for bullets (those round Option-8 bullets get tiring to look at pretty quickly). David's favorite for this function is the lowercase "v" from Zapf Dingbats (❖).

Table 4-12

Useful Zapf Dingbats characters

Name	Looks like	Key to press after Command-Shift-Z
Shadow ballot box up	❑	O
Shadow ballot box down	❐	P
3D ballot box up	❑	Q
3D ballot box down	❒	R
Filled ballot box	■	N
Hollow ballot box	☐	N (apply outline style)
Opening great quote	❝	Shift-]
Closing great quote	❞	Option-N
Opening single great quote	❛	Shift-[
Closing single great quote	❜	Shift-\
Great bullet	●	L
Great hollow bullet	○	L (apply outline style)
Great shadow bullet	◯	M
Filled arrowhead	➤	Option-Shift-E
Right arrow	→	Option-]
Fat right arrow	➡	Option-Shift-U
3D right arrow	⇨	Option-Shift-I
Speeding right arrow	⯈	Option-Shift-7
Triangle up	▲	S
Triangle down	▼	T
Love leaf	❦	Option-7
X-mark	✘	8
Check-mark	✔	4
J'accuse	☞	Shift-=
Victory	✌	Comma
Scissors	✂	Shift-4
Pencil straight	✐	/
Pen nib	✎	1
Telephone	☎	Shift-5
Cross	✚	Shift-;
Star	★	Shift-H
Quatrastar	◆	Shift-F
Octastar	✳	Shift-W
Big asterisk	✺	Shift-Z
Circled sun	☉	B
Snowflake	❄	D

You can also use these characters as graphics on your page. Don't forget you can shade and color type to act as a background or foreground graphic.

▼ ▼

Tip: Ballot Boxes and Custom Dingbats. Up until now, the best way to create blank "ballot" boxes has been either to type a Zapf Dingbats lowercase "n" and set it to outline style, or to buy a separate font package such as Caseys' Page Mill's Bullets and Boxes. The problem with the first method is that image-setting the outline often resulted in a hairline that was too thin to reproduce well. The only problem with the second method was that it cost something to buy it (the package itself is great, though). Nonetheless, version 3 of Quark-XPress now gives us a better option.

1. Create a picture box of any size.

2. Give the picture box a border (Command-B); we like to use .5 points.

3. Using the Item tool, cut the box and paste it onto the Clipboard.

4. Using the Content tool, select where in the text you want the box to go, and then paste the box in.

5. Resize it to suit your needs.

Not only can you make box characters this way, but also any polygon, or anything else you can create within the application. Also, by importing a graphic into the picture box before you cut and paste it, you can create your own custom dingbats (see Figure 4-57).

▼ ▼

Figure 4-57
Custom dingbats

And re<u>mem</u>ber! 🧑 The *"cornier"* your Presentation, the less likely it is to be *Taken Seriously!*

Custom dingbat created by placing an EPS (Encapsulated PostScript) file within an anchored picture box. The picture box was resized, and its base-line shifted, until the block of text looked appropriately corny.

☐   *Ballot box made with an outlined Zapf Dingbat ("n")*

☐   *Ballot box made with an anchored (square) picture box having a 0.3-pt. frame.*

▼ ▼

Typographic Special Effects

QuarkXPress is not a special effects program, such as Type-Styler or LetraStudio. But this doesn't mean that it can't give you the power to create many exciting effects with your type. In this section, we're going to look at a few of the possibilities, like drop caps, rotated text, shadowed type, and type as a picture. But we can't cover everything that you can do. Here, especially, is an area in which to play around.

Chapter 7, *Where Text Meets Graphics*, covers a few other special effects that you can create using QuarkXPress, such as text runaround.

Fractions

Desktop publishing isn't so young that it doesn't have some hallowed traditions. One of the most hallowed is groaning in pain at the mention of creating fractions. But, as with most traditions, you shouldn't let that frighten you off. The "fraction problem" in desktop publishing arises because most Macintosh fonts do not come with prebuilt fraction characters.

You can create your own fractions five different ways. Let's take a look at each of these, and discuss why you'd want to use some and avoid others.

Pseudo-fractions. You can create pseudo-fractions by just typing in numbers separated by a slash. Let's be frank: they look awful, and are considered bad form. But in some cases, such as simple word-processed documents or manuscript text, they're perfectly acceptable. Opinion varies on how best to type these characters, especially when you have a fraction following a number. We generally like to add a hyphen between a number and its fraction. For example, one and one-half would be typed "1-1/2."

Don't try to use the "fraction" character (Option-Shift-1) for this kind of fraction. It almost always bumps into the second number and looks *shmatta* (like junk).

Proper fractions. You can create proper fractions—such as ½, ¾, or $^{29}\!/_{32}$—by applying specific character-level formatting to each character in the fraction. The following example shows you how.

1. Type the pseudo-fraction, such as 3/8. In this case, you should use the fraction bar character (Option-Shift-1) rather than the normal slash character.

2. Select the numerator—in this case, the 3—and set it to "Superior."

3. Select the denominator—in this case, the 8—and change its size to match the numerator. You can figure out what this size is by checking the Superior settings in the Typographic Preferences dialog box. For example, at the default Superior settings of 50 percent, you would need to change a 12-point denominator to 6 points.

4. Kern the fractions as desired. The spaces between the numerator and the fraction bar, and the fraction bar and the denominator almost always need to be tightened up.

You can change the size of the numerator by changing the Superior settings in the Typographic Preferences dialog box.

But remember to reset your denominator to the proper point size. Differently sized numbers in a fraction look very weird.

When a proper fraction follows a number, you probably don't want any sort of hyphen or even a space (see Figure 4-58).

Figure 4-58
Fractions

A pseudo-fraction

They tell me getting there is 3/8 of the fun.

A pseudo-fraction, followed by one created via the method noted in the text (see "Proper Fractions")

I went to see *8-1/2* but only stayed for ¾ of it.

A fraction generated by the Make Fraction function of the Freebies 3.0 XTensions—plus some manual kerning within the fraction.

About ¼ of the time, I won't even give him a dime.

Fractions XTension. The QuarkFreebies 3.0 XTensions package contains a feature that creates fractions for you. It essentially acts as a macro, performing the procedure outlined above. To let QuarkXPress make the fraction for you, follow these steps.

1. Type the fraction as two numbers separated by a slash. The fraction must have a space character before and after, or QuarkXPress includes any adjoining characters in the finished fraction.

2. Place the cursor either in the fraction or just to the right of it.

3. Select "Make Fraction" from the Type Style submenu (under the Style menu)

Stacked fractions. QuarkXPress also lets you create stacked fractions, such as ¼ and ¾. Here's a quick formula for making them.

1. Type the numerator and denominator, separated by an underline (Shift-Hyphen).

2. Change the point size of these three characters to 40 percent of original size. For example, 12-point type gets changed to 4.8-point type.

3. Select the numerator and the underline, and apply a baseline shift equal to the point size (40 percent of original).

4. Leave the numerator and underline highlighted and apply -90 units of tracking.

5. At your discretion, apply extra kerning between the characters to achieve a more precise look. You may want to zoom to 400% or print a test sheet.

You may need to adjust the numbers we provide for different typefaces and number combinations. Note that this method of creating stacked fractions only works when both numbers are single digits.

Fonts and utilities. Some fonts, such as EmDash's Hfraction, consist entirely of fractions. Usually, these fonts are set in Times or Helvetica, so unless you're using those typefaces, they won't perfectly match your text.

You can also create your own fraction fonts with a utility program such as ParaFont, Fontographer, or FontStudio. This method allows you to use any font that you're already using to generate custom fraction characters.

Initial Caps

Initial Caps are enlarged characters at the start of a paragraph. They lend a dramatic effect to chapter or section openings. There are four basic types of initial caps: raised, dropped, hanging, and contoured. Each of these styles is now considerably easier to create, due to two major new features in version 3—automatic drop caps, and the Indent Here character (Command-\).

Let's look at several initial caps and how they are made.

Standard raised caps. Raised caps can be created as simply as just enlarging the first letter of the paragraph (see Figure 4-59). It's important to use absolute leading when creating standard raised caps. If you don't, the first paragraph's leading gets thrown way off.

Figure 4-59
Standard raised caps

Unaccustomed as I am to public speaking . . . but that never did prevent me from running off endlessly at the mouth . . . you, sir! Stop that hideous snoring! But I digress . . .

14-pt. copy with a 30 pt. cap.

Hung raised caps. A spin-off of the standard raised cap is the hung raised cap (see Figure 4-60). You can hang the letter "off the side of the column" by placing an Indent Here character after it or creating a hanging indent with indents and tabs. The rest of the text block's lines all indent up to that point.

Figure 4-60
Hung raised caps

Unaccustomed as I am to public speaking . . . but that never did prevent me from running off endlessly at the mouth . . . you, sir! Stop that hideous snoring! But I digress . . .

14 pt. copy with a 30 pt. cap. Indent Here character has been placed to the immediate right of the raised cap.

Standard drop caps. QuarkXPress 3 includes a new feature that lets you make drop caps quickly and painlessly. The Drop Caps control is located in the Paragraph Formats dialog box (see Figure 4-61). To create a drop cap in a paragraph, just place the text cursor in the paragraph, and enable "Drop Caps" by clicking in its check box. You can then modify two parameters for this feature: "Character Count" and "Line Count."

The character count is the number of characters that are made to drop. The line count is the number of lines that they drop. For example, specifying "3" in "Character Count" and

"4" in "Line Count" would make the first three characters of the paragraph large enough to drop four lines down. You don't have to worry about sizing the character, aligning it, or specifying the space between the drop cap and the rest of the text. In this example, the baseline of the drop cap aligns with the fourth line down, and the ascent of the drop cap aligns with the first line's ascent. Note that some fonts have ascents that are taller than their capital letters. This may make the process slightly more difficult, depending on what effect you're trying to achieve.

Note that you can change the amount of space between the initial cap and the text that is flowing around it by kerning the space directly after the drop cap character.

Figure 4-61
Standard drop caps

Let it never be said that the Koala tea of Moishe is not strained. Should this be said, it is entirely possible that the very fabric of civilization would fall utterly into the hands of the

Note what happens in the Measurements palette when you place the cursor at the very beginning of such a text box or select (highlight) the drop cap. If you call up the "Font Size" dialog box, it will also show "100%."

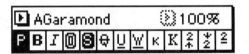

Hanging drop caps. This effect is achieved the same way as the hanging raised caps: just place an Indent Here character (Command-\) directly after the dropped character (see Figure 4-62). You can adjust the spacing between the drop cap and the following text by adjusting the kerning value between the drop cap and the next character (in this case, the Indent Here character).

Scaled drop caps. You have one hidden feature on drop cap characters and drop cap characters only: percentage scaling. After creating a standard drop cap (as described above), you can

Figure 4-62
Hanging drop caps

3-line drop cap with Indent Here character placed here, creating hanging drop cap

L et it never be said that the Koala tea of Moishe is not strained. Should this be said, it is entirely possible that the very fabric of civilization would fall utterly into the hands

select the drop cap character(s) and change the point size to a percentage of the original drop cap size. For example, Figure 4-63 shows a paragraph first with a standard drop cap, and then with the drop cap scaled to 150 percent. You can change the percentage of the drop cap character(s) to anything you want, and the baseline will always align with the Line Count line.

Figure 4-63
Scaled drop caps

The same, with the capital "L" enlarged to 150% of its normal size

L et it never be said that the Koala tea of Moishe is not strained. Should this be said, it is entirely possible that the very fabric of civilization would fall utterly into the

The Measurements pallette reflects the change — again as a percentage of the normal drop cap size (not in points).

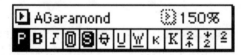

Anchored raised caps. Another way of making a raised cap is to create it in a separate text box, then anchor that box to the beginning of the paragraph (we discuss anchored text and picture boxes in Chapter 7, *Where Text Meets Graphics*). The raised cap in Figure 4-64 is actually a separate text box containing a large capital letter on a tinted background. The character is also centered horizontally and vertically within

We fully recognize that the message "Now formatting your hard disk. Have an *exceedingly* nice day," appearing during the **KvetchPaint** installation, is a bit alarming. Rest assured that it is a harmless prank by one of our programmers — who is, you can also rest assured, no longer with us. As soon as we can break the encryption he used, we will certainly eliminate this silly

the frame. We also applied other formatting to the initial cap, such as kerning and baseline shift.

Anchored drop caps. After creating an anchored raised cap, you can make it "drop" by selecting "Ascent" in the Anchored Text Box Specifications dialog box (select the anchored box and type Command-M, or double-click on the anchored box). Figure 4-65 shows an example of this, along with an anchored drop cap which has been "hung."

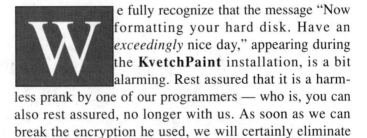

We fully recognize that the message "Now formatting your hard disk. Have an *exceedingly* nice day," appearing during the **KvetchPaint** installation, is a bit alarming. Rest assured that it is a harmless prank by one of our programmers — who is, you can also rest assured, no longer with us. As soon as we can break the encryption he used, we will certainly eliminate

Wraparound dropped caps. When using letters such as "W" or "A" you may want to wrap the paragraph text block around the letter (see Figure 4-66). While there is no way to do this using automatic features, you can still use the methods learned from earlier versions of QuarkXPress.

1. Copy the first letter of the paragraph into a new, smaller text box.

2. Size the initial letter approximately to fit the number of lines you want.

3. Set both the background and the runaround of your text box to "None."

4. Place your initial cap text box over your paragraph text box. The paragraph should not reflow if you've set "Runaround" to "None."

5. Draw a line or a polygon around the initial cap, creating a border where you want the text to wrap.

6. If you drew a line, change its shade to 0 (zero) percent.

7. Make sure the wraparound object is on top of the paragraph, but under the initial cap.

This is only one of many variations on a theme for creating wraparound drop caps. Another is to use an initial cap brought in from a draw or illustration program (as any sort of graphic file). You can then use QuarkXPress's automatic runaround or manual runaround features to control the text runaround (we discuss text runaround in detail in Chapter 7, *Where Text Meets Graphics*).

Figure 4-66
Wraparound drop caps

As literally dozens screamed with the blood lust and *ennui* to which the Romans of those times were so often given, without fear an unrepenting Androgynous strode onto the filthy floor of the Desultorium, there to meet his fate before the sinister person of GLUTEUS MAXIMUS, vice-tonsil of Rome, one of the not-nicest guys ever to pack iron in the Big SPQR.

Illuminated caps. We've just seen the use of graphics "disguised" as text. Figure 4-67 shows a graphic-as-text, but with no disguise at all. This fancy illuminated capital letter was found in an art book, scanned, and brought into a picture box as a TIFF image.

Figure 4-67
Illuminated caps

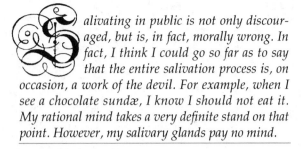

alivating in public is not only discouraged, but is, in fact, morally wrong. In fact, I think I could go so far as to say that the entire salivation process is, on occasion, a work of the devil. For example, when I see a chocolate sundæ, I know I should not eat it. My rational mind takes a very definite stand on that point. However, my salivary glands pay no mind.

Mixed font caps. We've already cautioned you about using too many fonts on a page. But if there was ever a time to break the rules, it's with initial caps (see Figure 4-68). If you want your initial caps in a different font, simply change the font for those characters. However, note that when you change the initial cap's typeface, the character may not align properly with the rest of the text.

Figure 4-68
Mixed font initial caps

Zapf Chancery   *Adobe Garamond*

Sconce, call you it? So you would leave battering, so I would rather have it a head. And you use these blows long, I must get a sconce for my head, and ensconce it too, or else I shall seek my wit in my shoulders. But, I pray, sir, why am I beaten?

Multiple initial caps. "Character Count" in the Drop Caps feature lets you drop up to eight letters in your paragraph. So a drop cap could be a drop word, if you like (see Figure 4-69).

Playing with initial caps. Like we said, initial caps are great opportunities to play and come up with creative ideas. Can you recreate the initial cap examples in Figure 4-70?

Figure 4-69
Multiple initial caps

5-character drop cap with horizontal scaling of 75%. Font size changed from 100% to 87.5%.

Comma scaled down to 75% of normal font size, not 87.5% (it's less obtrusive that way).

What, gone in chafing, and clapped to the doors? Now I am every way shut out for a very bench-whistler; neither shall I have entertainment here or at home. I were best to go try some other friends, and ask counsel what to do.

Figure 4-70
More initial caps

A POOR MAN IS OBSERVED STARING in admiration at the large and ornate tombstone of the richest man in town. He shakes his head slowly and mutters, "Now, that's what I call living!"

O f course, the last time I went to one of those big banquets, I lost my wallet. I went up to the microphone and announced "Ladies and gentlemen, I've lost my wallet, with eight hundred dollars in it. Whoever finds it will get a reward of fifty dollars!"

Then a voice from the back of the room yelled out, "I'll give seventy-five!"

Shadowed Type Alternatives

Applying the "Shadow" type style to any range of selected type creates a generic shadow that cannot be customized. For example, you cannot change its thickness, shade, or offset. Although this is a perfectly nice shadow effect and is useful for many purposes, you may occasionally want more control over your shadows.

You can have total control over your shadows by using duplicate text boxes. Here's one way to do it (see Figure 4-71).

1. Create a text box with a line of solid black text in it.

2. Duplicate the text box (Command-D).

3. Select the text within the second text box and modify it (change its color or tint, etc.).

4. Send the second text box to the back (choose "Send to Back" under the Item menu).

Make sure that the topmost boxes have their Runaround and Background Color set to None. You can then move the second text box around until you have it placed where you want it. You might also want to group the two text boxes together in order to move them as if they were one item.

Figure 4-71
Alternative shadows

Pricing

The Freebies 3.0 XTension lets you automate one other common text formatting function: pricing. It's simple to make a number into a "price." Just type the value, place the cursor within the number or just to the right of it, then select "Make Price" from the Type Style submenu under the Style menu. You have several options for how QuarkXPress formats the character, including whether it should take out any decimal point you've included and if the numbers after the decimal point (the "cents") should have an underline or not. These controls are located in the Fraction/Price Preferences dialog box, which is only available from the Edit menu when no documents are open.

▼ ▼

Text Handling

The focus of this chapter—and this book, for that matter—is high-quality printed output. However, before you can get there you do a lot of staring at a computer screen. In this chapter we're going to look at two features that make this phase of your production a little easier: type rendering and type greeking.

Type Rendering

Adobe Type Manager (ATM) caused a revolution in Mac screen typography almost overnight—finally fulfilling the promise of WYSIWYG font display without the need for separate bitmapped (screen) fonts in each size used. Whenever you choose a different font size, ATM goes out to your system folder, finds the PostScript outline fonts, and builds screen bitmaps on the fly for the size you've requested.

However, ATM only works with Type 1 fonts (most vendors now create fonts in this format). It won't do any good with Type 3 fonts, and you may have some of those around. Serious desktop publishers don't want to limit themselves to Type 1 fonts. What to do then, if you want to use Type 3 but don't want to revert back to the days of inaccurate, jaggy type rendering?

Here, as in so many other areas, QuarkXPress comes to the rescue. It can do for Type 3 fonts what ATM does for Type 1: create screen bitmaps on the fly while you type. Between ATM and QuarkXPress, you can achieve clean screen fonts for almost any typeface in the PostScript universe.

The key to QuarkXPress's rendering ability is "Render Above," found in "General Preferences" under the Edit menu. You can turn rendering on and off by clicking in the appropriate box. When the feature is enabled, you can specify a minimum point size for rendering. The default value is 24 points; any text set below 24 points will appear on screen using an available screen font rather than a rendered bitmap. You have the choice to specify a minimum Render Above size from 2 to 720 points, in .001 point increments.

With such a great feature, why ever turn it off? And, while it's on, why limit the sizes at which it's functional? The reason is speed. Screen fonts that are installed using Font/DA Mover, Suitcase II, or MasterJuggler will image on the screen significantly faster than it takes for QuarkXPress to render nice smooth outlines. If you're working with a page full of body text 12-points tall, you don't want QuarkXPress to take the time to render all those characters. Chances are, you only want it to take the time to give you nice smooth outlines for display or headline type. And, if you're in a hurry, you may not even want it to do that.

There are three key points to remember about the QuarkXPress rendering function.

- It works only with Type 3 fonts, just as ATM works only with Type 1 fonts. Use it in conjunction with ATM for the best of both worlds: accurate rendering of all fonts of either type.

- You must have a screen font of at least one size installed with either Font/DA Mover or a utility program such as Suitcase II. This is because QuarkXPress needs to recognize the font and place it on the program's font menu when you first start up.

- The printer's PostScript fonts must be available for QuarkXPress to find. This means they should be in either the system folder or—if you are using a font juggling utility—in the same folder as the screen font.

Text Greeking

After all this talk about making text look better on the screen and on your printed output, you probably need a relief from type. Let's talk about how to make type go away.

Designers have long worked with a concept known as greeking. Greeking is a method of drawing gray bars to represent blocks of text, rather than taking the time to image them all on the screen. QuarkXPress can greek text under a specific size limit, which you define in the General Preferences dialog box (Command-Y). The default value for text greeking is 7 points; you can set it from 2 to 720 points.

Unless you really want to see every character of every word at every size, there's hardly any reason to turn text greeking off. However, depending on what your page design is like, you may want to adjust the Greek Below values at different times.

▼ ▼

Tip: Go Ahead and Change Your Mind. Because you can set both "Text Greeking" and "Text Rendering" as preferences, you can adjust them as you work. For example, if you start your document with "Text Rendering" off, then realize you want to use it, go ahead and turn it on. Or if you want to adjust the minimum text greeking size to sometimes see particular areas of text and sometimes not, you can change these values on the fly.

▼ ▼

Tip: Checking Your Layout. When we need to get an idea of how a page's design and balance is looking, we often set our minimum text greeking size to a size large enough to include everything on our page except headlines or display type. This way we can see the page itself without being bothered by either text redraw or the particulars in the text.

▼ ▼
Putting It Together

If you got through this entire chapter and are still not too bleary-eyed to read this, you must really be a QuarkXPress die-hard. After having learned about QuarkXPress's word-processing capabilities in the last chapter and what you can do to those words in this chapter, you're ready to move on to the theory and practice of style sheets and copy flow. You don't need to know everything that's in Chapter 5, *Copy Flow*, to work with type in QuarkXPress, but we think it's a good idea to learn it. There's working with type, and then there's working hard at type. We're trying to get your work to be as easy as possible.

CHAPTER 5

COPYFLOW

s you've learned in preceding chapters, you can do all sorts of wonderful things to type in QuarkXPress. But there's more to the intelligent handling of your copy in QuarkXPress than simply setting it in exquisite type. You have to get the document produced on time.

In the development of a publication, copy is almost never static. For any number of reasons, you may have to make drastic changes in the formatting or content of the copy (usually at or beyond the last minute). Your success in meeting deadlines (and getting paid) can often depend on how carefully you've anticipated such changes. If you don't plan from the very beginning to manage the flow of your document's copy, it will surely end up managing you, and in ways you won't like.

Managing Copy

QuarkXPress has two very powerful tools for automating the formatting and management of your document's copy: Style Sheets and XPress Tags. Use these tools wisely, and you'll soon make your copy jump through hoops at the snap of your fingers (or the click of your mouse). Use them poorly, or not at all, and you'll be the one jumping through the hoops, probably at three in the morning before a major job is due. In this chapter, we'll tell you how to make the best use of these features. The key is learning to work smart.

Working Smart

Simply put, there are two ways to handle your copy in Quark-XPress: the dumb way and the smart way. What's the main difference between the two? Working the smart way, you make the computer do your work as much as possible. Working the dumb way, you take it on yourself to do the kind of mindless, repetitive tasks computers were meant to take off your hands—in this case the repetitive formatting and reformatting of copy.

It takes a bit more time at first to set up a document to take advantage of QuarkXPress's automation, but it is well worth it if you ever need to make even the simplest document-wide change in the way your text is formatted. Of course, if you're the kind of person who always gets everything right the first time, you'll never, ever need to change any formatting once you've entered it, so you may not find this chapter of much use. The rest of you should pay careful attention.

The dumb way. The dumb way to format your copy is the way you most likely learned earliest; by selecting text and directly applying various characteristics. Should a paragraph be centered? Go to the Style menu and center it. Need to change the typeface? Go to the Font menu and do it.

"What's so dumb about that?" you may ask. It's not that there's anything inherently wrong with applying formatting directly to your copy; it's just that by doing so, you doom yourself to performing the same selecting and modifying actions over and over again whenever you need to format another text element with the same formatting, and whenever you need to make major changes to your document. For instance, if the paragraphs you centered now have to be made flush left, you must select and change each paragraph individually.

Another way of working dumb is to carefully format your text in QuarkXPress, and then, when heavy editing is required, export the copy to a word processor, edit it, then re-import it into QuarkXPress. Suddenly you may notice that you've lost most of your special QuarkXPress formatting (such as horizontal scaling, superior characters, kerning, etc.), and it's time for another long, painstaking formatting pass through your document.

The smart way. The smart way to handle your copy is to take the time to be lazy. Make QuarkXPress's features work for you. Whenever you create a new paragraph format, for any reason at all, assign a style to the format. The next time you need to make another such paragraph, you can simply apply the appropriate style, and QuarkXPress will instantly apply the correct formatting.

And if you've been religious about creating and applying styles for all your document's paragraphs, you can then make sweeping formatting changes throughout your document with only a few keystrokes. Also, be sure to use XPress Tags in exporting your text. This will keep your formatting information intact, even if you must send stories out to be edited on a dreaded DOS computer. The following sections reveal the best ways to work smart with QuarkXPress.

▼ ▼

Style Sheets—What They Are, and Why You Need Them

A "Style Sheet" is simply the name QuarkXPress gives to a collection of formatting attributes applied to a paragraph. For every paragraph in your document, QuarkXPress keeps track of whatever information you've specified for fonts, type style and size, leading, alignment, indents, and much more.

Warning: A Style Is a Style Sheet Is a Style

For some reason, Quark decided not to follow accepted terminology when it named its Style Sheet feature. It is commonly understood in desktop publishing that the group of formatting attributes for a particular type of paragraph is called a "style." Furthermore, the list of all the styles in a document is called a "style sheet." In QuarkXPress, each paragraph has its own "Style Sheet" and the collection of these is simply referred to as the "Style Sheets." Generally, we'll use the more commonly accepted terminology, as the usual distinction between style sheets and styles is a useful one. However, when you see the term "Style Sheet" with initial caps, we will be referring to that particular feature of QuarkXPress.

And Now—Back to the Show

Whether you've actually used style sheets before or not, you already think in terms of styles as you create a document every time you decide that a particular paragraph needs to be formatted differently from those around it—even if the change is something as simple as centering a heading.

"Style Sheets" in QuarkXPress lets you assign a unique name to any group of formatting commands for a particular type of paragraph. You can create a style name for titles, for different levels of subheads, for footnotes, or for any type of paragraph you care to. Once you've defined a style, you can quickly apply it, with all its attributes, to any paragraph, saving yourself many trips to QuarkXPress's Style menu.

Even better, whenever you make a change to a particular attribute within a style, those changes are automatically applied to every paragraph that uses that style. So if you've had the foresight to define and use styles conscientiously when creating your documents, you won't be fazed by last-minute requests to change the size, font, and alignment of every picture caption in a book. Because you've had the foresight to create a "caption" style which is applied to every caption in your book, you need only change the attributes of that style to change the style of every caption. Otherwise, you're in for a long, tedious stretch of hunting down and manually changing every caption in your book.

Tagging

We've mentioned that you must give a style a name. Another word for a style name is a *tag*. Here's how it works. If you know that you'll need to have two kinds of subheads in your document, you can make styles named, for example, SubheadA and SubheadB, and apply them to the appropriate paragraphs. The process is called *tagging*. It's important to remember that there's a difference between a style's name (its tag), and a style's formatting.

As you work on a document, be sure to tag each paragraph by clicking in it with the Content tool and choosing a style from the Style Sheets menu (see Figure 5-1). After a paragraph is tagged, you can easily change its appearance by modifying its style. Therefore, when you begin to work on a document, it's not really that important what formatting is associated with each style, since you can always change the formatting later. Once you've tagged all the paragraphs in your text, you can experiment by modifying the formatting of their styles at your leisure.

Local Formatting Versus Style Formatting

Another point to remember about QuarkXPress styles is that the character formatting contained in a style is applied to an entire paragraph. If the style calls for Times Roman, the entire paragraph will be in Times Roman. You can override the style's font for specific text within the paragraph. This "local" or "hard" formatting will remain, even if you apply a different font to the paragraph's style, or apply a different style to the paragraph. (But if a paragraph has the Quark-XPress option No Style applied to it, *all* local formatting will be wiped out when you apply a style to it. See "Normal Style and No Style," below.)

Local formatting is the *only* way to format just part of a paragraph; QuarkXPress doesn't have styles that can be applied to selected characters. Some programs, such as Frame-Maker and the IBM version of Microsoft Word, have both paragraph and character styles. This can be extremely useful for

Figure 5-1
The Style Sheets menu

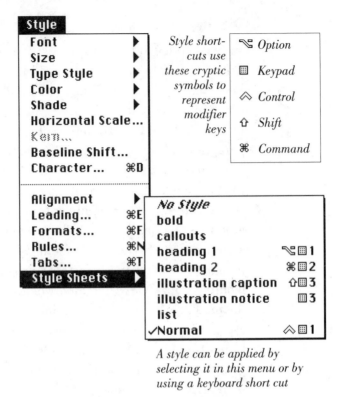

A style can be applied by selecting it in this menu or by using a keyboard short cut

applying specific formatting to elements within a paragraph, such as bold run-in heads at the beginning of a paragraph.

Unfortunately, there is one instance in which Quark-XPress will lose track of local formatting. If you apply a style to a paragraph which contains the same formatting information as you've used in local formatting, and then you apply a style with different formatting, your original local formatting will be lost.

For instance, assume you have a paragraph whose style calls for plain text (that is, neither bold nor italic), and you've made a few words in the paragraph bold. Now you apply a style that makes *all* the text bold, and then you apply a style that *isn't* bold. All of the text in the paragraph will no longer be bold, including the text to which you originally applied the bold formatting. This doesn't just apply to making text bold or italic, but to any local formatting which can also belong to a style.

It seems that QuarkXPress simply says to itself, "Aha, this text which once contained local formatting should now have the same formatting as all the text around it. So I don't have to remember the local formatting anymore." And it doesn't (see Figure 5-2).

Defining Styles

To create or edit styles in a QuarkXPress Style Sheet, use the Style Sheets command on the Edit menu. This calls up the Style Sheets dialog box (see Figure 5-3). If you call up this dialog box when a document is open, you'll see all the styles for that document. You can use this dialog box to

Figure 5-2
How QuarkXPress loses local formatting

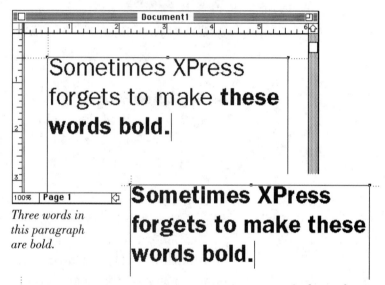

Three words in this paragraph are bold.

Apply a style which calls for all text to be bold.

Now apply a style that calls for plain text. See your local formatting disappear.

create, edit, and delete styles, and, by using the Append button, import the style sheet of another QuarkXPress or even Microsoft Word document. If you use this dialog box with no open documents, you'll be able to edit and add to QuarkXPress's default style sheet list, which will be automatically included in all new documents.

Figure 5-3
The Style Sheets
dialog box

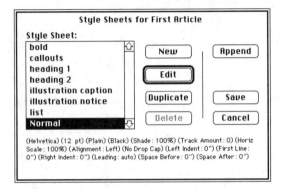

Creating a New Style

To create a new style sheet, click on the New button in the Style Sheets dialog box. The Edit Style Sheet dialog box appears (see Figure 5-4). In the Name field, enter the name of the new style you want to create. If you want to define a keystroke combination that will automatically apply the style, click in the Keyboard Equivalent field, and press the combination you want. It's often a good idea to use a key in combination with the Control key, because keystrokes defined this way won't conflict with any of QuarkXPress's other key commands, none of which use the Control key.

▼ ▼

Tip: Keys You Can Use for Style Short Cuts. You can only use certain keys for applying styles—the F keys (F1 through F15) and the numbers on the numeric keypad. In combination with the Control, Command, Shift, and Option keys, that provides for a lot of short cuts.

There's no way to print a listing of what keystrokes go with what styles (see Tip: Printing Your Style Sheet) so we just print a screen shot of the Style Sheets submenu and tape

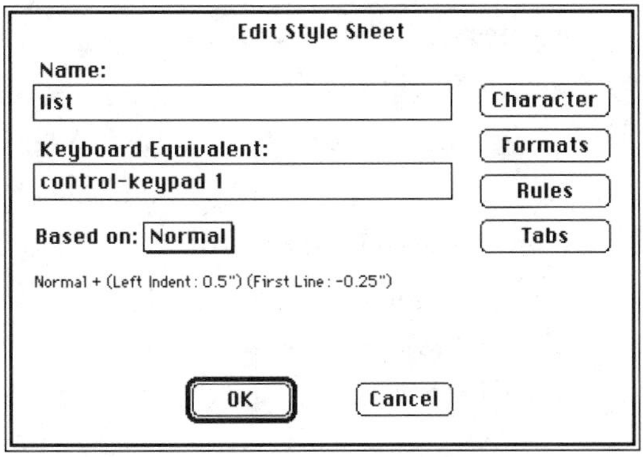

Figure 5-4
The Edit Style
Sheet dialog box

```
                    Edit Style Sheet
    Name:                              ┌───────────┐
    ┌──────────────────────────┐       │ Character │
    │ list                     │       └───────────┘
    └──────────────────────────┘       ┌───────────┐
    Keyboard Equivalent:               │  Formats  │
    ┌──────────────────────────┐       └───────────┘
    │ control-keypad 1         │       ┌───────────┐
    └──────────────────────────┘       │   Rules   │
                                       └───────────┘
    Based on: ┌────────┐               ┌───────────┐
              │ Normal │               │   Tabs    │
              └────────┘               └───────────┘

    Normal + (Left Indent : 0.5") (First Line : -0.25")


            ┌────────┐      ┌──────────┐
            │   OK   │      │  Cancel  │
            └────────┘      └──────────┘
```

it to our wall. If you have a really long style sheet, you may have to take a couple of screen shots.

▼ ▼

Once you've named a style, you can define it by clicking on the Character, Formats, Rules, or Tabs buttons. Each of these buttons calls up dialog boxes with the same names as those available from the Style menu for text. You can use these boxes to define your new style, just as you would to format any paragraph of text.

When you're finished defining the style, click on OK, and you'll be brought back to the Style Sheets dialog box. Click on the Save button. Hold the mouse button down when you select "Style Sheets" under the Style menu, and you'll see your new style listed and ready to be applied.

Normal Style and No Style

Every QuarkXPress document has a default style, the Normal style. This is the style that is automatically applied to all the text in a document if you don't specifically apply a style. You can edit the Normal style just like any other.

"No Style" is different. Applying "No Style" removes *all* style information from a paragraph. All the formatting is then treated as local, hard formatting. Normally, local formatting doesn't change when you apply a style to a paragraph. However, if the paragraph has "No Style" applied to it, applying a style overrides all local formatting.

Appending Styles

The Append button in the Style Sheets dialog box (brought up by choosing "Style Sheets" from the Edit menu) lets you import styles from other documents into your QuarkXPress document. You can import styles from other QuarkXPress documents, as well as from Word 4 and 3 files. Clicking on the Append button brings up a standard directory dialog box, which you can use to choose the file whose styles you want to import.

Another way to move styles from one QuarkXPress document to another is to copy text containing those styles. You can either use the Copy and Paste commands, or simply drag a box containing the text from document to document.

It's important to remember that you can only import styles that *don't* have the same names as ones already used in your document. So if you already have a style named "Body Text" in a document, you can't import any "Body Text" style from another document. QuarkXPress simply ignores the styles with matching names, and imports the styles whose names don't match any already in the document.

Furthermore, when you bring in text that has the same style names as existing styles, but different formatting, QuarkXPress does an odd thing. It brings in the text with its source formatting intact, but as local, hard formatting. The style name is still there, but it doesn't do you any good. You have to apply "No Style," then reapply the style, losing *all* local formatting in the process.

For example, let's assume that the Normal style in the original document calls for 12-point Helvetica, and the Normal style in the target document is set for 10-point Palatino. If you move text from the originating document to the target, any "Normal" text you bring over won't change to 10-point Palatino. It will remain 12-point Helvetica (local, hard formatting). Even though these paragraphs are tagged with the Normal style, you'll have to re-apply the tag by applying "No Style" and then Normal again to these paragraphs in order for the correct formatting to appear.

▼ ▼

Tip: QuicKeys Styles. Style sheets are powerful, but we don't always find them accessible enough. So we've created macros using QuicKeys (our favorite macro-making program) to automate two actions that QuarkXPress doesn't provide keyboard short cuts for.

- Selecting "No Style" from the Style Sheet submenu.

- Opening the Style Sheets dialog box.

You can also use ResEdit to assign a keystroke to the Style Sheets item on the Edit menu (see Chapter 1, *Structure and Interface*).

▼ ▼

Tip: Creating Styles by Example. Instead of using the Edit Style Sheet dialog box to define the format of a style, you can create a style based on an existing paragraph in your document (see Figure 5-5). This way you can format a paragraph just the way you want it, and then create a style that has all those attributes.

To create a style based on an existing paragraph's formatting, position the insertion point anywhere in the paragraph, then create a new style. When you get to the Edit Style Sheet dialog box, you'll see all of the formatting that's applied to the current paragraph listed at the bottom of the box. All you have to do is then name the new style, click on OK, and save your changes.

▼ ▼

Basing One Style on Another

A powerful feature of QuarkXPress's "Style Sheets" is its ability to base one style on another. By basing many styles on, say, the Normal style, you can quickly change many elements in your document by simply changing the Normal style.

For example, let's say you want all your subheads to be the same as the Normal style, only bold and in larger type. By basing the subhead style on the Normal style you can

Figure 5-5

Creating a style
by example

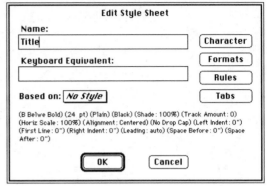

Place the insertion point in a paragraph

When you click on
the New button from
the Style Sheets
dialog box, you'll see
an Edit Style Sheet
dialog box listing all
the attributes of the
selected paragraph

ensure that every change you make to the Normal style is
instantly reflected in the subhead style. If you change the
Normal style's font from Helvetica to Franklin Gothic, the
font of the subheads based on the Normal style automatically
changes from Helvetica to Franklin Gothic as well. The subheads retain their larger size and boldness, however.

To base one style on another, use the pop-up Based on
menu in the Edit Style Sheet dialog box to select the style upon
which you want to base your new style (in this case, Normal).
Next, use the buttons in the dialog box to change only those
attributes you want to be different in the new style (in this
case, increasing the type size, and making it bold). Notice that
the text at the bottom of the Edit Styles dialog box shows the
style that your new style is based on, along with all the additional formatting you've applied to the new Style Sheet.

If you plan your style sheets carefully, you can use this
based-on feature to create nested hierarchies of styles based
upon one another, so that a simple change to one style will be
applied to all the styles based on it, and the styles based on
those, ad infinitum. This "ripple effect" is a great time-saver,
so it's well worth your while to carefully plan your styles to
take greatest advantage of this effect.

▼ ▼

Tip: Use Shift-Option-click to Copy Styles from One Paragraph to Another. In addition to using the Style Sheets menu and keyboard short cuts to apply a style to a paragraph, you can also use a neat short cut to copy formats from one paragraph to another. Click in the paragraph whose format you want to change. Then Shift-Option-click on any other paragraph whose format you want to copy. Not only is the paragraph's style copied, but any local changes to the paragraph's formatting (margins, tabs, leading, etc.) are also applied to the destination paragraph. No local character formatting in the destination paragraph is changed.

▼ ▼

Tip: Use Search and Replace to Fake Character Styles. Although QuarkXPress doesn't have character styles, it is possible to use the powerful search and replace feature to achieve some of the functions of character styles. If you regularly use text with specific local formatting within your paragraphs, with a specific font, size, and weight, the Find/Change command can save you a lot of keystrokes. Use it to replace a unique, easily applied style (such as outline or shadow) with formatting that can require multiple keystrokes or trips to the Style menu (such as 12-point New Baskerville Bold).

1. In your word processor, assign a seldom-used character style, such as underline, outline, or shadow, to the text to which you want to apply your special local formatting.

2. Bring the text into QuarkXPress.

3. Select the Find/Change command from the Edit menu. Deselect the Ignore Attributes check box by clicking in it. Click on the appropriate boxes to replace the style you originally applied with the new formatting you want.

4. Click on the Change All button.

Unfortunately, you can't use this method to apply the more sophisticated of QuarkXPress's typographic controls, such as tracking or horizontal scaling.

▼ ▼

Combining Paragraphs For Run-in Heads

Another way to fake character styles—this time to create run-in heads—is by combining paragraphs. If you have two consecutive paragraphs with different text formats, and you combine them by deleting the carriage return that separates them, the text within the new paragraph will retain the formatting of the paragraph it originally belonged to. For example, you could create a head using a paragraph style calling for 14-point Futura Bold, and follow it with a body paragraph whose style calls for 12-point Garamond Three. By deleting the return after the Futura Bold paragraph, you'll end up with the Futura Bold text as a run-in head for the body text set in Garamond Three.

Note that if you put some special character or series of characters at the end of heads that you want to be run-in, you can use the Find dialog box (Command-F) to get rid of the carriage returns. (Remember: \p is the code for carriage returns in the Find/Change dialog box.)

There are a few drawbacks to this paragraph combination trick, however. You must be aware that you're basically fooling QuarkXPress. When you combine two paragraphs, QuarkXPress applies all the settings for the first paragraph to the new, combined paragraph. QuarkXPress also applies the style for the first paragraph to the new paragraph. So in our example, QuarkXPress thinks that the 14-point Futura Bold is the default font for the entire new paragraph, even though part of it appears as 12-point Garamond Three. QuarkXPress doesn't consider the Garamond Three formatting to be local, hard formatting, and if you apply a new style to this paragraph, *both* the Futura and Garamond will be changed to the font called for in the new style.

Since the fake character styles created by this technique are rather fragile, you should probably not use this technique unless you're certain that you won't have to ever change the style that's applied to the combined paragraph.

▼ ▼

Importing Text

An important part of controlling the flow of copy is getting your copy into QuarkXPress in the first place. You do this with the Get Text command in the File menu. In order to access this command, you must have the Content tool selected, and a text box active. To bring text into the active text box, follow the steps below.

1. Position the insertion point where you want the text to be brought into the text box.

2. Choose Get Text from the File menu (Command-E).

3. When the Get Text dialog box appears (it looks very similar to a standard Macintosh directory dialog box), select one of the files listed. It displays all files that are in a word-processing format that Quark-XPress can import.

4. Press Return, or click on the Open button.

If you'd like QuarkXPress to automatically convert straight double and single quotes (",') to curly double and single quotes ("", "), and to convert double hyphens (--) to true em dashes (—), check the Convert Quotes box in the Get Text dialog box.

If you're importing a Microsoft Word file, and you want QuarkXPress to include the file's style sheets, check the Include Style Sheets box. Also, if you're importing an ASCII (text) file that uses XPress Tags to contain formatting and style sheet information, you must also be sure to check the Include Style Sheets box (more on XPress Tags later).

What Filters Are, and How To Use Them

QuarkXPress uses files called filters to contain the information which it uses to convert text to and from word-processing formats. The formats QuarkXPress can understand are MacWrite, MacWrite II, Microsoft Word (Mac), Microsoft Works, Microsoft Write, WordPerfect (Mac) and WriteNow, as well as ASCII text using XPress Tags. In order for Quark-XPress to understand these file formats, you must have the appropriate filter in the same folder with QuarkXPress. If you don't need a particular filter, move it out of that folder so the program will load faster.

▼ ▼

Tip: Style Tags Versus XPress Tags. Do not under any circumstances have both the Style Tags and XPress Tags filters in the same folder with QuarkXPress. You can have one or the other, but if both are there (at least in subversion 2), you have a good chance of crashing.

▼ ▼

When It Is OK and Not OK To Use QuarkXPress As Your Word Processor

As we saw in Chapter 3, *Word Processing*, QuarkXPress has very powerful word-processing features. Its search and replace function, in particular, is far more powerful than that found in many word processors. For small documents, you can easily dispense with the fairly standard desktop publishing procedure of writing your text in a word processor and then importing it. Instead, you can simply use QuarkXPress to create your text as well as flow it into pages.

However, there is a pitfall. With medium-size and long documents that have long text chains flowing through complicated multipage layout, writing and even heavy-duty editing can become very slow, even on fast Macs. QuarkXPress seems to reflow its text with almost every keystroke. If you're a fast typist, you may find yourself having to deliberately slow way down to prevent characters you've typed from getting lost as they slowly make their way into QuarkXPress. If you run into this frustrating problem, you should consider exporting your text to a word processor, editing it there, and then re-importing it to QuarkXPress (see "Exporting Text," below).

Alternately, you could create a blank QuarkXPress document with a single large text box on each page (see Chapter 3, *Word Processing*, for a more detailed description of how to do this). Typing and editing in this text box is faster because QuarkXPress doesn't work as hard to flow your text.

What Word Processor to Use?

Although QuarkXPress can import formatted text from several word processors, it can only interpret the style sheets of Microsoft Word files. Since style sheets are so important to the proper management of your copy, Word automatically becomes the best word processor for working with Quark-XPress. (Unless you decide to work exclusively with XPress Tags, which can be used, albeit awkwardly, by any word processor that can import and export ASCII files—that is to say, nearly all word processors).

Another plus for Word is that QuarkXPress will correctly import pictures contained in Word files as inline graphics, and can even export inline graphics to the correct location in a Word file.

How QuarkXPress's Style Sheets Work with Word

When you bring a Word document into QuarkXPress, and you've checked the Include Style Sheets box, QuarkXPress will take every style from the Word file into its own Style Sheet, incorporating as much of Word's formatting as Quark-XPress can handle.

QuarkXPress can import a great deal of Word's own formatting. All of the character styles available in Word can be carried over into QuarkXPress, with the exception of double and dotted-line underlines. QuarkXPress ignores whatever values you've entered for super- and subscripts, instead applying whatever values you've specified for them within your QuarkXPress document (in Typographic Preferences). Word's expanded and condensed type settings are converted to tracking values in QuarkXPress. Since you specify these values using points in Word, and QuarkXPress uses two-hundredths of an em, there is usually only a very rough correlation between how tightly type is set in Word, and what you get when you bring it into QuarkXPress.

For paragraph formats, QuarkXPress brings in most available Word settings, except that it ignores the Page Break Before setting, and only the top and bottom rules set for boxed paragraphs will be imported (though QuarkXPress does a good job of interpreting the correct size and weight of rules). QuarkXPress ignores any values you've set for space between rules and their paragraphs.

Any of Word's attributes which can be applied to styles can be successfully imported as styles by QuarkXPress, with the exceptions noted above.

If you import a Word file which has styles with the same name as styles already in the QuarkXPress document, those Word styles won't be imported, and the style already within QuarkXPress will be applied instead. The QuarkXPress styles predominate. However, any local formatting you've applied in the Word document will be imported.

This ability to replace Word styles with QuarkXPress styles is very important, as you can use Word's style sheets to tag paragraphs with style names, and have QuarkXPress apply the appropriate formatting as soon as you import the text. The QuarkXPress styles take over from the Word styles with the same names. So you can create styles in QuarkXPress using all of its sophisticated formatting, secure in the knowledge that none of that style sheet formatting will be lost if you ever have to export the text back to Word for editing; the QuarkXPress formatting will be waiting patiently for the copy's return.

▼ ▼

Tip: Don't Worry About Word Styles. Remember that QuarkXPress overrides Microsoft Word's formatting for style sheets. That is, if your Microsoft Word document's Normal style is 18-point Helvetica and your QuarkXPress document's Normal style is 12-point Palatino, the text that is tagged as Normal appears in Palatino (like you'd want). The implication of this is that you never really have to worry about what the styles look like in Word. For example, in this book, our Microsoft Word text was all in Helvetica and New York, but when we imported the text files into QuarkXPress, they came out in the fonts you're reading (Bodoni and Futura).

▼ ▼

Exporting Text

After you go through all the trouble of bringing copy into QuarkXPress and formatting it, why would you want to then export it? Aside from administrative reasons (backups, etc.), there are two major situations in which exporting text can be important.

If you encounter sluggishness when working with text in QuarkXPress, you should consider exporting your text into a word processor, editing it there, and then re-importing it back into QuarkXPress.

Moreover, if you work in a busy workgroup-publishing environment, you may find it absolutely necessary to pull text out of QuarkXPress so that editors can work on it while you continue to refine a newsletter's or magazine's layout.

How to Export Text

Exporting text from QuarkXPress is pretty much the opposite of importing it.

1. With the Content tool, select a text box containing the story you want to export.

2. Choose "Save Text" from the File menu. The Save Text dialog box will appear.

3. Enter the name you'd like the exported text to be saved under. Select either the Entire Story or Selected Text button.

4. Use the pop-up Format menu to choose the format for the exported file. The formats listed in the menu will depend on which filter files you have in the Quark-XPress folder.

5. Press Return, or click on OK.

Pitfalls

The most important consideration when bringing text out of QuarkXPress and then back in is how to accomplish this without losing all the formatting you've applied within QuarkXPress. No current word processor can handle horizontal scaling, for instance, and such formatting could easily be lost during the export/re-import process. There are ways to keep this formatting intact no matter where your Quark-XPress text ends up, however, by using style sheets or XPress Tags.

Exporting to Word

One solution is to export to Microsoft Word. Word files made from QuarkXPress contain style sheet information, and, as mentioned above, the appropriate formatting will be automatically applied when you bring the text back into QuarkXPress. But using Word is only a partial solution to the formatting problem, since only formatting that's applied to an entire paragraph can be stored in style sheets. If you've applied special local formatting to individual characters or words (such as, for instance, superior type, tracking, kerning, or scaling), it will be lost during the export/re-import process, even if you use Word and take full advantage of style sheets.

▼ ▼

Tip: Exporting Styles. We often use QuarkXPress's Export feature to export all our styles to Microsoft Word. This saves us having to recreate every style name on Microsoft Word's style sheet. To do this, create one little one-line paragraph for each style. Apply the style, then export that text in a Word format. When you open the file in Word, all the styles are there.

▼ ▼

Tip: Printing Your Style Sheet. We can't find any way to print out a listing of every style on our style sheet along with descriptions from QuarkXPress. However, if you export the styles as described in the last tip, you can print out the styles from Word. When you've opened your Microsoft Word document with each of the styles, go to the Define Styles item under the Format menu (or type Command-T), and select Print from the File menu (Command-P).

▼ ▼

A Solution: XPress Tags

There is a solution to the problem of losing formatting when exporting and re-importing text, however: export the file in the special ASCII format called XPress Tags. XPress Tags uses special—and complicated—coding that can record every single one of QuarkXPress's text formatting attributes, from style sheets to local formatting (see Figure 5-6).

You may find an ASCII file with XPress Tags confusing to look at, with its multitude of arcane numbers and codes. However, there are many reasons why XPress Tags is the best format to use when you need to edit and then re-import copy.

Why Use XPress Tags?

Not only do files using XPress Tags contain all of a story's QuarkXPress formatting, but because ASCII is a universal file format, these files can be edited by virtually any word processor—Mac, MS-DOS, or UNIX. Although the coding

Figure 5-6
XPress Tags

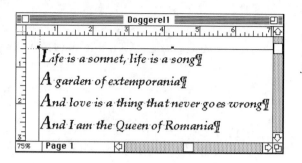

When you save this file in XPress Tags format...

...the text file looks like this

```
@Normal=<*L*h"Standard"*kn0*kt0*ra0*rb0*d0*p(0,0,0
,0,0,0,g)*t(0,0," "):¶
Ps100t0h100z24k0b0c"Black"f"BI Palatino
BoldItalic">¶
@Normal:<*L*h"Standard"*kn0*kt0*ra0*rb0*d0*p(0,0,0,
0,0,0,g)*t(0,0," "):¶
Ps100t0h100z36k0b0c"Black"f"BI Palatino
BoldItalic">L<z24>ife is a sonnet, life is a song¶
<z36>A<z24> garden of extemporania¶
<z36>A<z24>nd love is a thing that never goes wrong¶
<z36>A<z24>nd I am the Queen of Romania¶
```

may appear daunting if you're used to the WYSIWYG world of the Macintosh, professional typesetters have been working with code-based systems for years, and tagged files can be easily integrated into such an environment.

So if you find yourself regularly needing to export Quark-XPress stories with sophisticated text formatting, XPress Tags is clearly the way to go. While it may take a while to get used to editing an XPress Tags file, it's a lot less work than having to painstakingly reformat your copy every time you bring it back into your QuarkXPress document. Table 5-1, found at the end of this chapter, is a comprehensive list of the codes used in XPress Tags.

▼ ▼

Tip: Automate Your Copy Processing with XPress Tags. Once you're familiar with the coding format used by XPress Tags, you can easily set up a QuicKey to apply formatting codes to an ASCII file in your word processor. If you're more ambitious and handy with database programs, you can design a report format that creates a file that incorporates XPress Tags, and which you can then bring into QuarkXPress fully formatted.

▼ ▼

Tip: Importing Text from Ventura Publisher. If you look closely at the filters that came with QuarkXPress, you'll notice a filter called Style Tags. This was the original filter used by QuarkXPress to generate tagged ASCII text. Style Tags doesn't contain all the QuarkXPress formatting information that XPress Tags does, so for most purposes, Style Tags has been superseded by XPress Tags. But there's one important exception. Style Tags uses the same coding format as that powerhouse of DOS-based desktop publishing, Ventura Publisher. That's right, if you export a tagged, coded ASCII file from Ventura Publisher, you can use the Style Tags filter so QuarkXPress interprets and uses most of the formatting that was created in Ventura. Similarly, Style Tags can be used to bring formatted text from QuarkXPress to Ventura.

Note, however, that many Ventura files are based heavily on Ventura styles that cannot be imported into QuarkXPress. So you'll need to create your style sheets in QuarkXPress first.

▼ ▼

Automate Your Production with CopyFlow

If you find yourself frequently needing to export and re-import text from your QuarkXPress document, you should consider purchasing the CopyFlow XTension (no relation to this chapter!) from North Atlantic Publishing Systems (NAPS). You can use CopyFlow to record a name and editor for every story in your QuarkXPress document, and specify a folder on your Mac (or on a network server) from which the story should be imported, and to which it should be exported (see Figure 5-7).

Once you've named and specified folders for stories, you can, with a single command, automatically export individual stories, or every named story, to the export folder. You can export to any word processing file supported by QuarkXPress, or to XPress Tags, Style Tags, or NAPS's own tagging format.

Figure 5-7
CopyFlow

This floating windoid gives you information about the name, creator, and editor of the current story

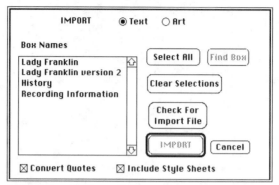

This dialog box lists all the stories in a document

If you use NAPS's own tagging format, it can actually combine every story into a single large tagged file, so you (or your editor) can easily edit all the text in a document. Once the copy's been edited, CopyFlow can automatically re-import the stories into their text boxes, untouched by human hands. If you've exported all your text to a single concatenated file, CopyFlow will automatically split up the file and send each story to the correct text boxes.

An add-on to CopyFlow, CopyFlow Reports, automatically creates a QuarkXPress document listing all the named stories and pictures in a document, along with their lengths and the last time they were edited.

NAPS has also developed an interesting product called CopyBridge, for large magazines and newspapers, which provides automated links between DOS computers running XyWrite for writers and editors, and Macs running Quark-XPress for page layout. This linking system actually allows writers and editors using XyWrite to see onscreen exactly where line breaks will fall on their stories when they are imported into QuarkXPress layouts on the Macintosh. The XyWrite users can also see how much text must be added or removed to make a story exactly fit its story boxes.

Getting Your Stories Straight

Once you've taken advantage of some, if not all, of these features of QuarkXPress, you may still find it necessary to burn the midnight oil making last-minute changes. But at least you'll have the full power of QuarkXPress on your side, not buried within a user's guide. Get to know styles, import and export filters, and especially XPress Tags, and you can go a long way toward being lazy: make your computer do the work, rather than having to do it yourself.

Table 5-1

XPress Tags codes

Note: All codes that are in angle brackets can be combined within one set of angle brackets. For example, <BI*d(1,3)> changes the formatting to bold, italic, and with an initial cap.

Character Formats	
Style	**Code**[1]
Plain	<P>
Bold	<B>
Italic	<I>
Outline	<O>
Shadow	<S>
Underline	<U>
Word underline	<W>
Strikethrough	</>
All caps	<K>
Small caps	<H>
Superscript	<+>
Subscript	<->
Superior	<V>
Type style of current style sheet	<$>

[1]*These codes act as toggle switches; the first time they're encountered, the format is activated. The second time, the format is deactivated. Note the similarity to formatting keystrokes.*

Table 5-1

XPress Tags codes
(continued)

Attribute	Code[2]	Value set in...
Typeface	<f"name">	Name of font
Size	<z#>	Points
Color	<c"name">	Name of color (the four process colors and white can be specified by C, M, Y, K, and W, without quotes, as in <cY>)
Shade	<s#>	Percentage
Horizontal scale	<h#>	Percentage
Kern next 2 characters	<k#>	½₀₀ em
Track	<t#>	½₀₀ em
Baseline shift	<b#>	Points

[2]*In these codes, "#" should be replaced with a number. This number can be set to the same precision as QuarkXPress's measurements (tenths, hundreths, or thousandths of a unit). The measurement units used are shown. If you replace "#" or any other code value with a dollar sign ($), QuarkXPress uses the formatting of the current style sheet.*

Paragraph Formats

Attribute	Code[3]	Value
Left-align	<*L>	None
Center-align	<*C>	None
Right-align	<*R>	None
Justify	<*J>	None
Paragraph formats	<*p(#,#,#,#,#,G or g)>	Left indent, First Line, Right indent, Leading, Space before, Space after, Lock to baseline grid. G=lock, g=don't lock.
Drop cap	<*d(chars,lines)>	Character count and line count
Keep with next ¶	<*kn1> or <*kn0>	1=keep with next, 0=don't keep with next
Keep together	<*kt(A)> or <*kt(start,end)>	"A"=all; start and end are number of lines
Set tab stops	<*t(#,#,"character")>	Position, Alignment (0=left, 1=center, 2=right, 4=decimal, 5= comma), Fill character[4]

Table 5-1 XPress Tags codes (continued)	H&J	<*h"name">	Name of H&J spec-ification
	Rule above	<*ra(#,#,"name",#,#,#,#)>	See "Rule below"
	Rule below	<*rb(#,#,"name",#,#,#,#)>	Width, Style (from 1–11), Name of color, Shade (percent), From left, From right, Offset (if you specify Offset as a percentage place a percent sign after the number)

[3]*In these codes, "#" should be replaced with a measurement in points. If you replace "#" or any other code value with a dollar sign ($), QuarkXPress uses the formatting of the current style sheet. If the code requires multiple values, every value must be present and delineated by a comma.*
[4]*Align on is specified by replacing the alignment number by the character contained within quotation marks.*

Special Characters

Character	Code
Return	<\n>
Discretionary return	<\d>
Discretionary hyphen	<\h>
Indent Here	<\i>
Previous text box page #	<\2>
Current text box page #	<\3>
Next text box page #	<\4>
New column	<\c>
New box	<\b>
@	<\@>
<	<\<>
\	<\\>
ASCII character	<\#decimal value>[5]
Standard space	<\s>[6]
en space	<\f>[6]
Flex space	<\q>[6]
Punctuation space	<\p>[6]

[5]*Note that the number sign must precede the ASCII character value.*
[6]*Precede these codes with an exclamation point to make them nonbreaking. For example, <\!s>.*

Table 5-1
XPress Tags codes
(continued)

Style Sheets		
Description	**Code**	**Values**
Define style sheet	@name=	Name of style sheet; follow the equal sign with definition
Use Normal style sheet	@$:	
Use "No Style"	@:	
Apply style sheet	@name:	Name of style sheet

CHAPTER 6

PICTURES

We've been talking a lot about text and rudimentary graphic elements such as arrows and ovals, but let's not forget that, ultimately, QuarkXPress is designed to integrate not only text and lines, but also graphics from other programs, and it contains many powerful features to aid in this task. QuarkXPress handles line art and images such as four-color photographs with a power and feature set previously only attainable by using several programs in conjunction.

Version 3 adds many new features to QuarkXPress's already powerful picture-handling capabilities.

- Full independent rotation of pictures and picture boxes

- Precision placement of all images and picture boxes

- Horizontal skewing of graphic images

- Automatic re-importing of modified pictures

- Picture greeking

Here are the three basic steps of importing pictures into your documents.

1. Create a picture box.

2. Bring in a picture by either pasting from the Clipboard or using the Get Picture feature (similar to the Place command in other programs).

3. Manipulate the image until you like the way it looks on the page.

But what types of pictures are available for use? And how to accomplish the desired look? In this chapter we explore the full range of possibilities for bringing graphics in from other applications and manipulating them on the page. In Chapter 8, *Modifying Images*, we'll talk about some of the effects you can achieve by modifying graphics once they're ready to be printed.

Let's first take a close look at the different types of pictures on the Macintosh applicable to QuarkXPress users.

▼ ▼

Macintosh Graphic Formats

If there is a question we're asked more often than "why won't my file print?" it's "what's the difference between all those different graphic formats?" The question refers to a host of formats with names such as EPS, EPSF, EPSP, TIFF, RIFF, PICT, PICT2, PNTG, compressed TIFF, MacPaint, and Draw. No one can be blamed for being confused when faced with such a list! Some of these are different names for the same thing, others are subtly different, and a few represent totally, to-the-core different concepts altogether.

The fundamental question when considering a graphic file on the Macintosh is whether it is a bitmapped or object-oriented file.

Bitmaps

Bitmapped images are the most common type of file format. When you use a scanner and scanning software, you are generating a bitmapped image. When you use an image-editing and painting program such as Adobe Photoshop, MacPaint, or ImageStudio, you are working with and generating bitmapped images. However, no matter how ubiquitous bitmapped images are, you are still strictly limited as to how you can use them.

Bitmapped images are just that: images made of mapped bits. A *bit* is a small piece of information. To begin with, let's think of it as a single pixel, or dot, which can be turned on or off. When you look very closely at the screen of a black-and-white Macintosh, you can see that the screen image is made up of thousands of these tiny bits. Some are turned on (black), and some are off (white). The *map* is the computer's internal blueprint of what the image looks like: "bit number 1 is on, bit number 2 is off," and so on (see Figure 6-1).

There are three primary pieces of information which are relevant to any bitmapped image: its size, resolution, and pixel depth.

Figure 6-1
Each pixel sits
on the grid

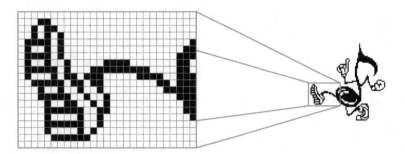

Size. The bitmap is a rectangular area which describes every dot (pixel) in and around the image. This area is broken down into a grid of many square pixels. Every pixel is whole and not fractured. You can describe the size of the gridded area in several ways, but it is most often specified in the number of squares or pixels per side, or in inches per side.

Resolution. The resolution of the bitmapped image is usually defined as the number of pixels, or squares, per inch on the grid (of course, this is different in countries using the metric system). A low-resolution bitmapped image may have 72 pixels per inch (called dots per inch, or dpi). A picture described using only 72 dots per inch looks very rough. Such low-resolution images are often called *jaggy*. A higher resolution bitmapped image may be 300 dots per inch or above (many slide scanners scan images at over 4,000 dpi!). These images, when printed, are much crisper and cleaner, with fewer jaggies (see Figure 6-2).

Pixel depth. Each pixel, then, is specified as a specific color. The range of colors available is determined by the type of bitmapped image it is (see "File Types," below). In the simplest bitmapped images, each pixel is defined as either black or white. These are called bilevel or 1-bit images because each pixel is described with one bit of information, and as we mentioned above, that one bit can be either on or off (1 or 0). Bilevel images are *flat*; they have little depth. More complex bitmapped images are *deep* because they contain pixels that are defined with multiple bits, enabling them to describe many levels of gray or color. For example, an 8-bit image can describe up to 256 shades of gray for each pixel (those of us in the Northwest, having to look at gray a great deal, can identify and name most of those shades). A 32-bit image can describe over 16 million colors (see Figure 6-3).

Manipulating bitmapped images. The limitations inherent in bitmapped images become most clear when you manipulate the picture in some way, such as enlarging it significantly. The key is that the picture's resolution is related directly to its size. If you double the size of a bitmap, you cut its resolution in half; if you reduce the size of the picture to

Figure 6-2
Low-resolution versus
high-resolution
bitmapped line art

72 dpi   *300 dpi*

1-bit (2 shades)

4-bit (16 shades)

one-quarter, you multiply its resolution by four. For example, a 72-dpi 1-bit graphic when enlarged 200 percent becomes a twice-as-rough 36-dpi image. However, when reduced to 50 percent, it becomes a more detailed 144-dpi image (see Figure 6-4).

A gray-scale or color image, when enlarged, becomes "pixelated," rather than looking "rougher." That is, you begin to see each square pixel and its tonal value (see Figure 6-5).

Object-oriented Graphics

Instead of describing a picture dot by dot, object-oriented files specify each object in a picture on a coordinate system. Therefore, whereas a bitmapped picture could take an enormous amount of space describing one circle, an object-oriented file could describe it in one line: "draw a circle of this size with a center at X,Y." The computer knows what a circle is and how to create it. Different object-oriented formats can describe different things, but most can

Figure 6-4
Scaling a bitmap
affects its resolution

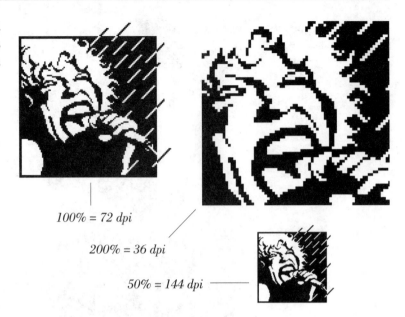

100% = 72 dpi

200% = 36 dpi

50% = 144 dpi

Figure 6-5
Pixelation from
enlarging a
gray-scale image

*72-dpi, 4-bit
gray-scale TIFF
at 100%*

*72-dpi, 4-bit
gray-scale TIFF
at 400%*

easily specify objects such as lines, curves, and type, as well as attributes such as shading and object rotation angle.

Most object-oriented graphics can also contain bitmapped objects as objects in their own right, though you may or may not be able to edit those bitmaps with a paint program. These files are almost always created by an application such as MacDraw, FreeHand, or Illustrator.

The magic of object-oriented graphics is that you can stretch them, rotate them, twist them into a pastry, and print them on various resolution printers without worrying about how smooth the lines will print. That is, when you print on a 300-dpi plain-paper laser printer, you get a full 300 dpi, and when you print to film with a 3,000-dpi printer, you get beautifully smooth lines at 3,000 dots per inch! There is no inherent limit of information for the picture, as there is in bitmaps (see Figure 6-6). Theoretically, there are no inherent limits to the number of gray levels in an object-oriented picture. Realistically, however, each format has upper limits.

Figure 6-6
Object-oriented
graphics versus
bitmapped images

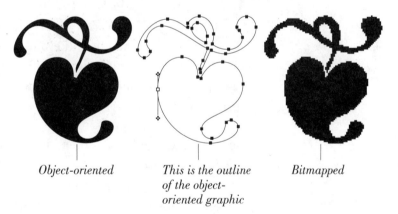

Object-oriented   *This is the outline*   *Bitmapped*
                          of the object-
                          oriented graphic

File Types

On the Macintosh, all files are identified by their "types." When we talk about file types in this book we're talking about two things: how the information is formatted within the file, and how the file is saved to disk. The common usage of file type—such as Paint or MacPaint—refers to the way in which the information is formatted. Then there is the way the

Macintosh system names files when it saves them to disk; it gives every file an actual, technical, four-letter file type. For instance, files generally referred to as Paint or MacPaint files are type PNTG. For the sake of simplicity, we use the terms *type* and *format* interchangeably.

You can examine the file type of files using several different utilities, such as CE Software's DiskTop (our favorite utility for this sort of task; see Figure 6-7). It's important to understand and identify file types for the discussion below, where we cover the main graphic file formats used with QuarkXPress.

Paint/PNTG. The Paint format is ultimately the most basic of all graphics formats on the Macintosh. When the Mac first shipped in 1984, it came with two programs: MacWrite and MacPaint. The latter was a very basic painting program that let you paint bitmapped images, cutting and pasting these pictures into MacWrite files or saving them as Paint-format (PNTG) files.

Paint files are black and white (1-bit), 72 dots per inch, 8 by 10 inches (576 by 720 dots). That's it. No more and no less. Even text is handled like bitmapped graphics; the only way to edit it is to edit the pixels that make it up. Clearly, this format has some stringent limitations which restrict the usability of the images.

PICT graphics. The PICT format, also a part of the original Mac system, but first made easy-to-use with MacDraw, tackles graphic images on an object-level as opposed to a bitmap level. However, a PICT image can contain bitmaps either alongside object-oriented drawings, or as its only object. Unlike most programs, QuarkXPress understands bitmap-only PICT files, and lets you manipulate them as such.

PICT images can be of any size but only in black and white (gray levels, just as in MacPaint documents, are handled by a dithered bitmap pattern to simulate gray). PICT2

Figure 6-7
CE Software's
DiskTop

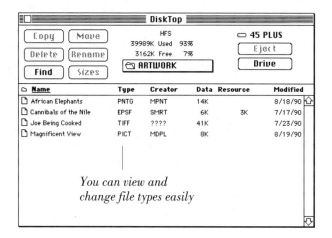

*You can view and
change file types easily*

images, which because of their ubiquity are simply called PICT images, now support color and gray scales.

Ultimately, the biggest problem with the PICT format is its unreliability in several respects. For example, line widths can change when moving a picture from one program to another, and text spacing can change, sometimes drastically. Also, printing to high-resolution printers (1200+ dpi) can be spotty. Remember that when you print a PICT to a PostScript imagesetter, the computer has to convert from one object-oriented language to another. We trust these conversions about as far as we can throw them. Nonetheless, PICT (including PICT2) is the primary format for printing to non-PostScript devices.

For the sake of completeness, we should note that it is also possible to attach a PostScript description of the image (see "Encapsulated PostScript/EPSF," below) to a PICT image (see "Pasting from the Clipboard," below).

Encapsulated PostScript/EPSF. Encapsulated PostScript format (EPSF or EPS) is certainly the most reliable format for putting images on paper or film. PostScript is a powerful object-oriented page-description language, though its files may contain noneditable bitmaps as well. Although it has built-in font-handling features, it ultimately treats type as a graphic made of lines and curves. This makes working with fonts in a PostScript environment a joy, with many possibilities. It is easy to create a PostScript file on the Macintosh, but to print it out you must have a PostScript-compatible printer.

EPS images come in three basic varieties: EPS without a preview, EPS with a preview, and EPSP. This last one isn't PostScript for psychics, but instead the primary format for preview-enclosed EPS images on the PC side of things (we won't be discussing this format until QuarkXPress for the PC comes out).

The preview-enclosed feature in many EPS files allows you to bring that file into QuarkXPress and see a low-resolution representation of the image on the screen. When the file is printed to a PostScript printer, however, the bitmap is ignored and the underlying PostScript is used. If a preview image—which is generally a PICT or TIFF file—is not available, then you just see a big gray box on the screen, which may contain some basic information, such as the file's name.

TIFF. The Tag Image File Format (TIFF) is another form of bitmap. However, it has significantly more potential for high-quality images. First off, instead of the standard 8-by-10-inch, 72-dpi, black-and-white PNTG image, a TIFF file can be created at any size and resolution, and include gray-scale or color information. It is important to remember, especially when we move into image-editing and color separation work in later chapters, that these images are still just big bitmaps, and therefore only contain a finite amount of information.

Nonetheless, because of the flexibility of TIFF files, most scanning and image-editing programs such as DeskScan, ImageStudio, Photoshop, and Quark's own Apple Scanner XTension save and open the TIFF format.

TIFF files can seem simple until you really need to work with them in a variety of environments. As it turns out, there are several different TIFF formats, including compressed and uncompressed, TIFF-5, and RIFF (Raster Image File

Format; this isn't really a TIFF file, but for the sake of brevity, we've included it here). QuarkXPress imports both standard TIFF and RIFF images, as well as LZW-compressed TIFF files.

▼ ▼

Importing Pictures into QuarkXPress

Now that we know the types of pictures we'll be dealing with, let's look at how we'll deal with them. As we mentioned, the first step in importing a graphic from another application is to create a picture box within your QuarkXPress document. This is covered in Chapter 1, *Structure and Interface*, in the discussion of rectangles, ovals, and polygons. When you have an empty picture box on your page, you can see an "X" in the middle of it. At this point you're ready to bring a picture into the box.

Note that we're bringing a picture *into* the box, rather than replacing the box or even "melding" the two together. The picture box is one entity and the picture is another. You might think of the box as being a window frame through which you can see the picture. You can manipulate either the picture box or the picture, or both.

The two primary ways to bring a picture in are pasting from the Clipboard and using the Get Picture feature. In order for either of these methods to work, you must have the Content tool selected. This, of course, makes some inherent sense: if you're trying to manipulate (in this case, import) the contents of a picture box, you want to use the Content tool.

The Clipboard

The Macintosh system has a storage area called the Clipboard that lets you take information from one place and put it in another. Whenever you cut, copy, or paste, you're using the Clipboard. Thus, you can cut or copy a picture from one application into the Clipboard, and then paste it from the Clipboard into another application.

The only real problem with cutting and pasting is that the Clipboard only handles certain types of picture formats between multiple applications. If you are trying to bring an outline illustration over from Aldus FreeHand, for instance, you cannot simply cut and paste because outside applications (for example, QuarkXPress) don't understand FreeHand's outline format. They do, however, understand the PICT/EPS format, among other types. You can create a PICT/EPS version of an object within Illustrator or FreeHand and add it to the Clipboard by holding down the Option key while selecting Cut or Copy from the menu.

You can also use the Scrapbook in conjunction with cutting and pasting to bring over several objects at a time by cutting or copying an object, opening the Scrapbook, pasting it in, and then repeating the process for each object you want. If you have copied an object from FreeHand or Illustrator using the Option key technique described above, it is not necessary to hold down the Option key to copy it out of the Scrapbook and back onto the Clipboard.

To get your picture from the Clipboard into the picture frame, select the frame with the Content tool, then select Paste from the Edit menu (or use the Command-V short cut). QuarkXPress places the picture in the upper-left corner of the picture box (if you can't see the picture, then see "What Happened to My Picture?" below).

▼ ▼

Tip: Turning Text to Pictures. You can bring text into Quark-XPress as a PICT image by using a feature of Microsoft Word. Select the text you want in Word and type Command-Option-D. This converts the text to a PICT and places it in the Clipboard. Then move into QuarkXPress, select a picture box, and type Command-V (Paste). The picture (text) may look odd and bitmapped on the screen, but it will print out much smoother. You can also manipulate the picture, rotating or scaling it, as described later in this chapter.

▼ ▼

Get Picture

When creating almost all your high-quality documents you will be working with EPSF and high-resolution TIFF images. These, of course, output as gray-scale halftones for photographs, with smooth edges at any resolution, and—for EPS pictures—clean and dependable type at any size. With the possible exception of importing small pictures or type directly from an illustration program, you should use "Get Picture" from the File menu, rather than copying and pasting via the Clipboard. "Get Picture" assumes that a file has already been created and is located on disk somewhere.

With your picture box created, and the Content tool selected, you can select "Get Picture" from the File menu (or be like the pros and type Command-E). A directory dialog box appears, allowing you to find the file which you wish to import. Remember your retrieval short cuts here: up and down arrows move up and down the list, Command-up arrow moves into the next folder up, and double-clicking on a folder opens it.

When a file of a type that QuarkXPress recognizes (see "File Types" above) is selected, the file's type and size are displayed. New to version 3 is the Picture Preview window, which you can turn on or off. When on, you can see a thumbnail view of that file's pictures as long as there is a PNTG or PICT version available (if none of these is available, no image appears). This feature is, of course, a great help in finding a particular picture when you're not sure of the file's name. However, it does slow down the process, especially for files with complicated images, such as large color PICT files. Clearly, judicious use of "Picture Preview" can save you time.

Once the file is selected in the dialog box, click on the Open button or just double-click on the file, and the file appears in your picture frame. Note that QuarkXPress shows you its progress in the lower-left corner of the window, so if you're importing a three megabyte file on your Mac Plus, you can see how quickly (slowly) it is processing (perhaps this is the best time of the day to go out for an espresso).

▼ ▼

Tip: Grab That Pencil. You will undoubtedly find yourself in a situation at some point where you want to manually re-import a picture or import a new picture into an already used picture box. Problem: you lose the specifications for the original picture box (scaling, offset, rotation, and so on)! This is a case where you can use the most technologically advanced tools available to humankind, but all you really need is a simple notepad and a pencil. Just jot down all the specs for the previous picture (nice of QuarkXPress to show them to you in the Measurements palette), then, after you bring the new picture in, retype the original specs in (remember, if you have multiple changes to the picture box, it's usually quicker to make them in the Picture Box Specifications—Command-M—dialog box all at once).

▼ ▼

What Happened to My Picture?

When you import a picture, you may not see exactly what you were expecting or wanting in the picture box. It may be that you see only a gray box with some type, or that the image is misplaced, or even that you can't see it at all. Remember the First Rule of Computer Anomaly: Don't Panic.

Can't see the picture at all. The first thing to check for is whether or not the big "X" is still in the picture box; if it is, then "Get Picture" failed to retrieve the picture. Try again.

If what you see is just a blank frame, then the picture is probably somewhere in the box but you can't see it yet. The Get Picture feature automatically places the image in the upper-left corner of the bounding box of the frame. Note that we say the "bounding box" and not the box itself. The bounding box is the smallest rectangle which completely surrounds the frame. It's what you see when you are looking at your frame with "Reshape Polygon" (under the Item menu) off (see Figure 6-8). If you have an oval or a polygonal box, and the image is rather small, then you may have to move the object into the frame (see "Moving Your Pictures Around," later in this chapter).

There's no picture—just a gray box. If the image you imported was an EPS file with no PICT or TIFF image attached for a screen representation, then QuarkXPress represents the image as a gray box with the note "PostScript Picture" and the name of the file directly in the center of the gray box. This gray box shows the bounding box of the image, as defined in the header of the EPS document (see "Tip: Creating or Changing EPS Files").

Another cause of the gray box effect is looking at a complex picture from too far back. That is, when you look at the page from "Fit in Window" (under the View menu), it looks like a muddled gray box, but when you go to "Actual Size," it looks like what you were hoping for.

The third cause of the gray box effect is that the picture you imported was, in fact, a gray box. In this case, we can only suggest you think carefully about whether or not you

Figure 6-8
Polygons have
rectangular
bounding boxes

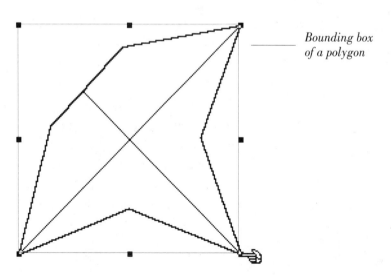

*Bounding box
of a polygon*

really consider a gray box an exciting enough graphic for your publication.

Working with Your Picture

Now that you have brought something (which may or may not look like the graphic you wanted) into the picture box, you can manipulate it in more ways than you ever could in previous versions, and certainly in more ways than in any other page-makeup program.

Moving Your Picture Around

In Chapter 1, *Structure and Interface*, you learned about moving your picture and text boxes around on the page. You can also move the picture itself around within the picture box. You may want to do this for two reasons: for picture placement and for cropping a portion of the image. Several methods for moving your image within (or even outside of) the box follow. Remember that even though the picture is inside the frame, they are two different entities and you can move and manipulate them using different tools.

Centering. Often the first thing you'll want to do with a picture, whether or not you can see it on screen, is to center it within the picture box. Designers and computer hackers alike have muddled through various tricks to center graphics perfectly within boxes, with equally varying degrees of success. We suggest you just type Command-Shift-M and let QuarkXPress do it for you. QuarkXPress centers the picture within its bounding box; that is, its lower-left and upper-right corners. Therefore, pictures which are oddly shaped (for example, an L-shaped picture; see Figure 6-9) may not be centered exactly where you'd expect them to be at first glance.

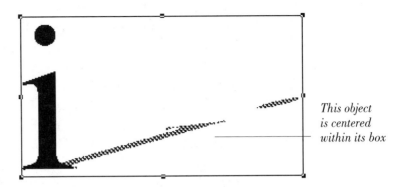

Figure 6-9
Centering an
oddly-shaped graphic

*This object
is centered
within its box*

Moving the picture. If you want the image somewhere other than the upper-left corner or in the center, you can use the Content tool (which switches to a Grabber hand when placed over the picture box) to move the picture around. Anyone who has ever done this can tell you that if the image is a large one it can take quite some time for the picture to respond to the hand movements. You may want to zoom in for precision alignment when you get close to where you want it, but remember that what you're looking at is still only a low-resolution (36- or 72-dpi) rendition of the real picture, which may be slightly different here and there.

If you know exactly how far you want to move the picture, you can type in the offset amounts in either the Measurements palette or in the Picture Box Specifications dialog box (type Command-M or hold down the Command key while double-clicking on the picture). This method is a real godsend when precision is the key, but there are some pitfalls to look out for. One such pitfall is expecting to know where the graphic image is either by the screen representation or the original placement (thinking it's up against the left edge of your box). In the first case, again remember that you're only looking at a 72-dpi image, and in the second case, remember that an EPS image almost always has some white space surrounding it. Therefore, when you import it, the image itself is slightly farther to the right than the left edge of the picture box. Until QuarkXPress is released on a Display PostScript system, when working with this method you're probably better off printing the page out and then measuring how far you want the image to be moved (see Figure 6-10).

▼ ▼

Tip: Minimoves. When you have the Content tool selected and have selected a picture box, you can "nudge" the picture within the box in tiny increments by clicking on the arrows in the Measurements palette. Each click moves the image one point in that direction. Holding down the Option key while clicking moves the picture in one-tenth of a point (.1pt) increments.

▼ ▼

Cropping. If you only want a portion of the picture, then you can "cut out" the unwanted areas by reducing the size of the box and moving the picture so that you only see the area you want (see Figure 6-11). However, there are those who crop out 90 percent of the image in order to use one flower in a bouquet! Then they duplicate that image 12 times and wonder why their file doesn't print (don't laugh too loudly; we've seen highly paid professionals do this!). Remember that QuarkXPress doesn't get rid of or forget the parts of the picture that aren't shown. That's why you can always go back and change your cropping or picture specifications. But the upshot of this is that it still has to process the entire image, which can take quite some time. So remember to use crop-

Figure 6-10
Minor picture offsetting
within the box

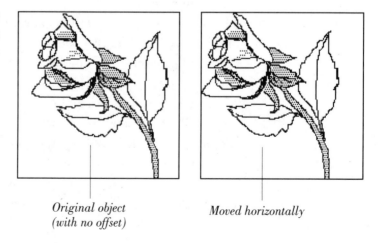

Original object
(with no offset)

Moved horizontally

Figure 6-11
The edge of the picture
box crops the picture

*This area
cropped out*

Visible area

ping judiciously. If you only want a small portion of the file, then use an editing program such as DeskPaint or Photoshop to cut out the other parts before you import the image.

▼ ▼

Tip: Precision Placement. One way to achieve better precision in placing EPS graphics from FreeHand or Illustrator is to build crop marks around the image before importing it into QuarkXPress. Once you import it, you can adjust the placement of the picture so that the crop marks lie just outside the picture box frame.

▼ ▼

Resizing your picture. After placing the graphic image where you want it, you may want to scale it to some desired size. QuarkXPress allows you to resize the image within the picture box, stretching or compressing it in the horizontal and/or vertical directions. Most often we find ourselves wanting to enlarge or reduce the picture the same amount in both directions in order to best fit the available space.

If the picture box you created is just the size you want your picture to be, you can quickly and automatically resize the picture to fit the box by typing Command-Shift-F. However, because this usually stretches the picture disproportionately (adjusting the horizontal and vertical sizing measures differently in order to fill the box), you probably want to type Command-Shift-Option-F (that's a handful!), which makes the picture as large as it can be within the box without distorting it. Note that if you've rotated or skewed the picture first (see "Rotating, Skewing, and Distorting" below), auto-resizing may not work exactly as you'd expect it to.

David almost never uses the simple and quick keystroke method, however, preferring to type the particular percentages he wants into the Measurements palette or into the Picture Box Specifications dialog box (Command-M). Of course, you can use a combination of these two methods, or even use a third: resizing the picture box.

Usually when you resize the picture box it has no effect on the image which is in it, other than possibly cropping out areas of the picture. However, if you hold down the Command key while resizing (clicking and dragging on one of the control handles), the image resizes along with the box (see Figure 6-12). As usual, holding down the Shift key constrains the picture box (and image) to a square or circle; holding down the Option key along with the Command and Shift keys constrains the picture box (and image) to its proper proportions.

Figure 6-12
Resizing a picture by dragging the picture box handles

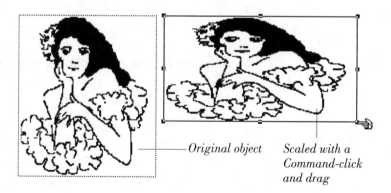

Original object

Scaled with a Command-click and drag

Resizing for better print quality. As we mentioned earlier, changing the size of a bitmapped image can significantly alter its
appearance, either for the better or for the much worse. In
general, reducing the size of a bitmapped image, especially
if it's a low-resolution graphic, such as PNTG, improves its
output quality by effectively increasing its resolution (a 72-
dpi image printed at 50 percent becomes a 144-dpi image).
However, sometimes even a slight reduction can make a big
difference. Bilevel images which contain repeating patterns,
such as a gray level, when imageset on a high-resolution
printer can come out in plaid patterns (see Figure 6-13).
This is due to the incongruity between the resolution of the
image and the resolution of the printer, and can be easily
rectified by slightly scaling the image by a specific percent.
The appropriate reduction can be determined by the following equation.

(Picture resolution ÷ Output resolution) × Any whole number
    × 100 = Scaling percentage

You can use the chart in Table 6-1 to determine the best
reduction for you, or you can create your own chart using the
equation above.

Figure 6-13
Nonintegral scaling
ratios can cause
patterning

Table 6-1

Integral scaling for
bitmapped images

When printer resolution is	Scale 72-dpi images to any of
1270 or 2540	34.02%
	56.69
	79.37
	96.38
	102.05
	119.06

When printer resolution is	Scale 72-dpi images to any of
300 or 600	12.00%
	24.00
	48.00
	72.00
	96.00
	120.00

When printer resolution is	Scale 300-dpi images to any of
1270 or 2540	23.62%
	47.24
	70.87
	94.49
	118.11
	141.73

Rotating, Skewing, and Distorting

QuarkXPress 3 has such amazing graphic manipulation tools that you may never need to use an illustration program to distort images again. For example, let's look at two other modification techniques: rotating and skewing.

Rotation. QuarkXPress lets you easily rotate your imported pictures to a degree unheard of (and certainly rarely needed): one-thousandth of a degree. Once again, you are able to set the rotation of the image in several ways.

The first question you'll want to ask yourself is whether you want to rotate the frame, and along with it the image, or just rotate the image itself. You can accomplish either of these by typing in the rotation angle in the appropriate place in the Measurements palette or the Picture Box Specifications dialog box (see Figure 6-14).

▼ ▼

Tip: Rotating Your Picture Boxes. Rotating the frame rotates the image, too! The quickest way to "straighten out" your image is to rotate it back by the same amount. That is, if you rotate your box 28 degrees but you want the picture to be straight, then rotate the image -28 degrees.

▼ ▼

Figure 6-14
The Picture Box
Specifications
dialog box and the
Measurements palette

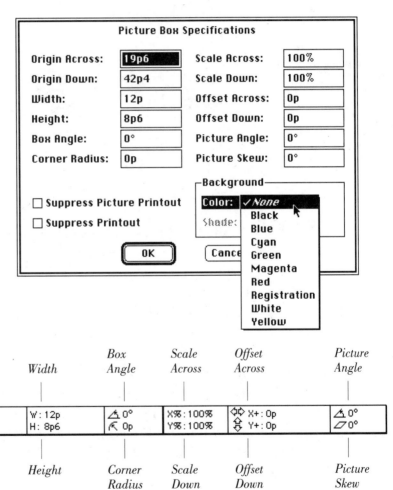

Skewing. Technically, skewing is the process of rotating the two axes differently, or rotating one and not the other. That is, if you rotate just the Y-axis (vertical axis) of the coordinate system to the right, everything you print out is "obliqued" (see Figure 6-15). QuarkXPress only allows you to skew in the horizontal direction (rotating the Y-axis), which is not a hindrance, as vertical skewing (or "shearing" as it is often referred to) is rarely required. Clearly, skewing an item is not called for every day, but it can be of great use in certain situations, enabling you to create interesting effects.

Figure 6-15
Skewing rotates the
vertical axis

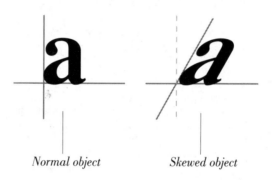

Normal object   *Skewed object*

You usually use only one of these effects at a time, perhaps in conjunction with scaling (resizing), but using all three together can make a graphic look quite unusual (see Figure 6-16).

One of the great advantages of these features is that they're not incremental. That is, unlike FreeHand or Illustrator, when you've rotated something 60 degrees, to change that rotation to 55 degrees, you just type 55 degrees rather than adjusting -5 degrees. This makes it incredibly easy to get back to where you started with an image when you've distorted it beyond recognition: just reset the scaling to 100 percent, and the rotation and skewing to 0 degrees.

Figure 6-16
Using all of the tools

Actual size

Across: 84%
Down: 149%
Rotate -30 degrees

Scale across: 84%
Scale down: 149%

Scale across: 84%
Scale down: 149%

*Scale across and
scale down: 170%
Rotate -20 degrees
Skew -50 degrees*

▼ ▼

Tip: Faking Perspective. To make a picture look like it's lying horizontally, change the picture rotation to -15 degrees, the picture skew to 45 degrees, and the vertical scaling to 70 percent (see Figure 6-17).

▼ ▼

Tip: Making Multiple Changes to Your Picture. If you know you are going to make multiple changes to your graphic image—changing the skewing, rotation, scaling, and offset, for example—you can speed up your formatting by making those changes in the Picture Box Specifications dialog box (Command-M or by double-clicking on the object while holding down the Command key) so that QuarkXPress will process all changes at once rather than one at a time.

▼ ▼

Figure 6-17
Pseudo-perspective

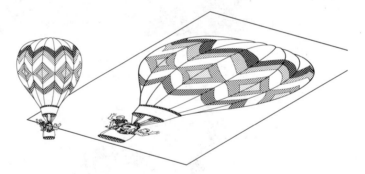

▼ ▼

Picture Management

Possibly the worst nightmare of a desktop publisher is arriving at the local service bureau to pick up 300 pages of film negative output, only to see that every illustration has come out as a low-resolution bitmap. Throwing away a thousand dollars is one way to learn some basics of picture management. Reading this section is another.

To Represent

The verb "to represent" means to stand in place for or to act as a placeholder. It is important to note that QuarkXPress represents high-resolution images (including TIFF, RIFF, and EPSF) as low-resolution pictures on the screen when you import them using "Get Picture." When it's time to print, QuarkXPress searches to find the original high-resolution image and uses it to automatically replace the low-resolution image. It looks first in the folder where the document was originally imported from, then in the same folder as the document you're printing, and finally in the system folder. If QuarkXPress is successful in this search, your output will look beautiful. If it cannot find the original, it uses the bitmapped 36- or 72-dpi representation for printing. In this case your output will look ugly.

Here are a few items to keep in mind when you use these sorts of pictures.

- Don't trash your file after importing it, assuming that it's placed for all time.

- Don't import your picture and then move the picture file into another folder titled "Picture Folder" (though doing the reverse of this is probably all right).

- Do be sure you know where your picture files are.

- Do keep your picture files together if possible, to avoid confusion if you need to move your document someplace (like a service bureau).

- If you send your document to a service bureau (or anywhere else, for that matter), put the document and all its high-resolution (EPSF, TIFF, or RIFF) pictures together either in the same folder or on the desktop. You may want to visually segregate the document from its pictures, but keep them in the same folder (see Figure 6-18).

Figure 6-18

Sending your disk to a service bureau

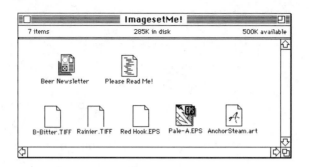

Picture Usage

Submitted for your approval: you've just completed a 600-page document with FreeHand illustrations on every page. The day before sending it to the imagesetter you realize that you have to make changes to every other picture. Tearing your hair out in clumps, you stay up all night changing all the pictures and recreating new EPS documents to replace all the old ones. But now it's dawn and you have to send it off or risk ruining the whole office's schedule. How will you re-import all those graphics in time? What about replacing and rotating and skewing them all to the correct positions? What will you do? What *will* you do?

Fortunately, you remembered to bring along your copy of QuarkXPress 3, which can automatically re-import every image which has changed since the last time you saved the document. QuarkXPress keeps a running tally of all the pictures that you bring into a document, including when they were last modified. If you have "Auto Picture Import" set to "On" in the Preferences dialog box, each time you open the document, QuarkXPress checks to see if any of the files has been modified. If they have, QuarkXPress brings the new copy in transparently and seamlessly. You won't even know that anything has changed.

Clearly, sometimes not knowing what QuarkXPress is doing behind the scenes is disconcerting or frustrating. You have another option here, which is to set your document preference to "On (verify)." With this selected, QuarkXPress checks for modified or missing files and, if it finds any, asks you whether you want to re-import them. As with all Quark-XPress features, there is no one "right" way to set up your documents; in some situations you want verifiable auto-importing, and in some you want none at all.

No matter how you have the Auto Picture Import feature set, you can always see a list of which pictures you have imported into your QuarkXPress document. The menu item to access this information is "Picture Usage" under the Utilities menu. The Picture Usage dialog box lists the pictures used, where they were originally found (their hierarchical disk path, starting from the disk and moving folder-to-folder, down to the file), the page number of the document where the picture is located, and the status of the picture—OK, modified, or missing (see Figure 6-19).

Figure 6-19
The Picture Usage
dialog box

OK. This is what you always hope for, especially before printing. QuarkXPress looks for the picture file first in the same place as the file was imported from, then in the same folder as the document, and finally in the system folder. If it finds it in any of these places you receive the OK notation.

Modified. If the file has been changed in any way since you imported it, you see the Modified notice in the status column. You have two options at this point.

- You can ignore the "problem." Remember that because QuarkXPress uses the external file for printing, the document will print with the updated version rather than the original. In other words, it will probably print the way you want it to, as long as you want the modifications which were made to the picture.

- You can update the image. All this really means is that you bring in a new representation image for your document. This approach may help you avoid the annoying dialog box at print time, "Some pictures have been modified or missing." To update the file, just select the name and click on the Update button.

Missing. If QuarkXPress cannot find a file with the same name anywhere it looks, it tells you that the file is missing. Again, you have two options.

- You can ignore it. This method is appropriate if you are trying to get some wild artsy effect using low-resolution printing, but is inappropriate for anyone trying to achieve a normal, good looking, high-resolution print.

- You can update the image. If the picture has just been moved to another folder, you can update the link by selecting the file and clicking on "Update." Here, you're not just bringing in a new representation, but actually relinking the "missing" picture with the document.

"Picture Usage" is also valuable when you want to jump to a particular image if you aren't sure where it is. For example, if you have many figures on many pages, and you want to go to the page which contains Figure 28-b, you can select that item in the Picture Usage dialog box and click on the Show Me button. This results in the document displaying the appropriate page and highlighting the picture box which contains that figure. This also works for graphics which have been anchored to text and have flowed to unknown places.

▼ ▼

Tip: Relinking with a New Picture. When you update an image in the Picture Usage dialog box, you don't have to relink with the same picture! You can relink with any other picture, and that image comes in using the same picture specifications as the original (scaling, skewing, and so on).

▼ ▼

Note that if you have a document which was created with a version of QuarkXPress earlier than 3, the Picture Usage dialog box only shows the EPS and TIFF images of that document. If you re-import or start with a new document in version 3, then you can see the full range of graphic file formats, including PICT and PNTG. However, pictures do not appear if they were pasted into their picture box, rather than imported using "Get Picture."

A dagger (†) appearing next to the page number in the Picture Usage dialog box signifies that the picture is on the pasteboard as opposed to on the page itself.

Greeking and Suppression

There are times when we'd really rather not see all those pictures. Perhaps the screen redraw or printing time is taking too long. Or perhaps we want to use the picture for placement only in the electronic document and don't want it to print out. Or perhaps we just hate the pictures. Whatever the case, QuarkXPress has a solution for you.

Picture greeking. New in version 3 is the Greek Pictures feature. Previous to this, you could only greek text below a certain point size. Now with "Greek Pictures" you can basically replace anything with a gray box. The primary benefit of doing this is speeding up screen redraw: it takes much longer to redraw specific type or a detailed picture than it does to just drop in a gray box where the type or picture should be. Another benefit is found in designing your pages. Sometimes having greeked in type and pictures allows you to see the page layout, including its balance and overall tone, better than if you are looking at "the real thing."

To greek the pictures in your documents, click on the Greek Pictures item in the General Preferences dialog box (Command-Y for a short cut to this dialog box). Note that with this selected, all picture frames except for empty and selected frames are greeked. Selecting a frame with either the Item or the Content tool ungreeks the picture.

▼ ▼

Tip: Invisible EPS Images. There are times when you not only don't want to see the images on the screen, but don't even want to see the grayed-out box described above. For example, you might want to place a particular image on your master pages that needs to print out, but doesn't need to be shown on the screen. You can create a screen-invisible EPS document (one which doesn't show on the screen but prints out properly) by using ResEdit.

1. Copy the EPS file (when working with ResEdit, always use a copy of the file).

2. Use a paint program such as DeskPaint or MacPaint to select a white rectangular area of the paint document and copy it into the Clipboard.

3. Open the copy of the EPS file within ResEdit.

4. Open the file's PICT resource by double-clicking on it.

5. Select "Clear" from the Edit menu.

6. Create a new PICT resource by typing Command-N, then paste the white square into it.

7. Go to the Get Info dialog box by typing Command-I; change the PICT's number to 256.

8. Save the changes to the file.

Now when you import this EPS file into your Quark-XPress document, you won't see anything, but it will successfully print out.

▼ ▼

Suppression of pictures. In the instances when you want the picture on the screen but not on your printouts, you can select "Suppress Picture Printout" in the Picture Box Specifications dialog box (type Command-M, double-click using the Item tool, or go the easy route: select "Modify" from the Item menu). You can also select "Suppress Picture Frame" in this dialog box, which suppresses both the picture contents and the frame itself.

▼ ▼

Page as Picture

David worked on a book recently which required taking illustrations which had been created in QuarkXPress and bringing them into PageMaker (horrors!). This is not an uncommon thing, of course; there are many times when you'd like to move text or graphics from QuarkXPress into other applications, or even bring a page of a QuarkXPress document into another QuarkXPress document as a picture. Version 3 now allows you to take care of these situations with a Save Page as EPS feature.

"Save Page as EPS" from the File menu brings up a dialog box in which you can select a page of your document and save it as a separate EPS file. You can adjust the scaling of the page (for example, make the page 25 percent of full size), and choose between a color or a black-and-white screen image. The page size is displayed in the dialog box so that you know how large the bounding box of the EPS image is. You can adjust this by changing the scaling. Remember that because this is PostScript, you can scale your EPS page down to 10 percent, bring it into another program, scale it back up to original size, and you won't lose any quality in your output (though your screen image may look pretty awful). Figure 6-20 shows a sample of a QuarkXPress page which was saved and brought back into another Quark-XPress document.

Figure 6-20
QuarkXPress page as
EPS document

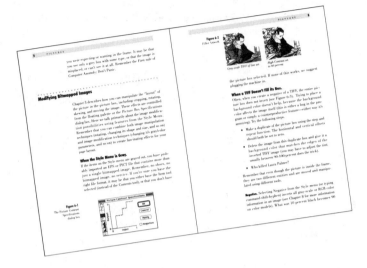

A word of warning here about EPS files from Quark-XPress. We don't mean to be pessimistic when we say that it would be foolish to expect saving a full-color QuarkXPress page as EPS, exporting to Illustrator, saving, then placing on a PageMaker page, and only then to send it through Spectre-Seps PM for final color separations, to work. Each of these programs was written by a different group of people and, consequently, handles color, type, and graphic elements differently. Even though, theoretically, the above process should work (PostScript is PostScript, right?), there is almost no way that it ever would (if you can do it, send us a copy!). So, be careful and prudent when you combine programs; the Macintosh platform is not as stable as it sometimes seems.

▼ ▼

Tip: Suppressing Pictures in EPS Pages. There are times when you don't want to see a graphic or have it print, but you still want it in the proper place in the document. For example, you've got a low-resolution scan set up for the text runaround, and you'll create an EPS file of the QuarkXPress page, placing the higher resolution scan in another program. Creating an EPSF file of a page with a graphic which has been suppressed does not suppress the screen image of that graphic (although it still suppresses the printing of the picture). If you don't want to see the screen placement picture, you can cover it with another picture box (a rectangle or a polygon perhaps) with a background color set to 0 percent black (nontransparent) before creating the EPS file.

▼ ▼

CHAPTER 7

WHERE TEXT MEETS GRAPHICS

It's a curious place, the wild frontier. Whether it's the border between Mexico and the United States, or the border between our tiny planet and the great unknown of Space, we humans strive to conquer and control. This book takes a slightly more microcosmic stance: we're only trying to conquer and control the text and graphics on a page. Nonetheless, it's a task that has been known to make designers shudder. This chapter will show you how this seemingly hostile frontier can be easily subdued.

In QuarkXPress, putting text and graphics together on a page can yield four results.

- They can be positioned so that they don't interact at all.

- They can intrude on one another, with either the picture or the text prevailing (the text flows on top of the graphic or the graphic sits on top of the text).

- They can bump into one another with the text keeping its distance (called *text runaround*).

- One can become embedded in the other and move wherever the other goes.

QuarkXPress allows for each of these possibilities with features such as transparent boxes, text runaround, and anchored boxes. In this chapter we look at each of these features and how they affect your pages.

So, let's take a step forward into those vast frontiers where text meets graphics.

▼ ▼

Transparency

The concept of transparency was first brought up in Chapter 1, *Structure and Interface*, when we talked about layering objects in QuarkXPress. The point we want to stress here is that where earlier versions of QuarkXPress tied the transparency and text runaround features together as a unit, version 3 separates them into two (or more) items.

It's easy to make a text or picture box transparent. Just give it a background color of "None" in the Text or Picture Box Specifications dialog box (double-click on the box with the item tool, or select it with either tool and type Command-M).

If one transparent picture box sits on top of another picture box, you can see the second picture box behind it (unless there's a picture in the way). On the other hand, if a transparent picture box sits on top of a text box, the text can do two things: it may freak out and run around the picture or the picture box, or it may sit there quietly and be trounced on (in which case you'd be able to see the text behind the picture box). Once again, this is different from QuarkXPress 2.12, where if a picture box were transparent, text would never flow around it.

▼ ▼

Text Runaround

Text flowing around a graphic element is controlled entirely by the Runaround Specifications dialog box, found by selecting a text or picture box and choosing "Runaround" from the Item menu (or typing Command-T). Text runaround is an attribute of a particular text or picture box. You must apply the runaround setting to the box around which the text should flow. For example, if you want text to wrap around a picture box, you should apply a runaround setting to the picture box.

Figure 7-1 shows the Runaround Specifications dialog box for a picture box. Note that each picture or text box has its own text runaround specification. The Runaround Specifications dialog box gives you four text runaround options for picture boxes and two options for text boxes. Text boxes have the option of either "None" or "Item." Picture box options are "None," "Item," "Auto Image," and "Manual Image." Let's look at each one of these options in detail, as they can give you radically different effects.

Figure 7-1
The Runaround
Specifications
dialog box

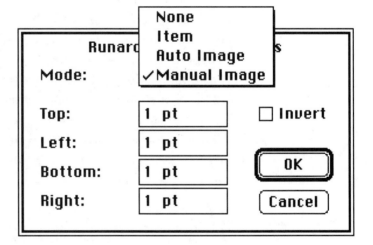

None

When you specify "None" as the Runaround mode, text that is "behind" a picture box flows normally. No text is offset, nothing is different. You may not be able to see much of the text behind the picture, but...hey, that may be your design choice (see Figure 7-2). This option is available for both picture and text boxes.

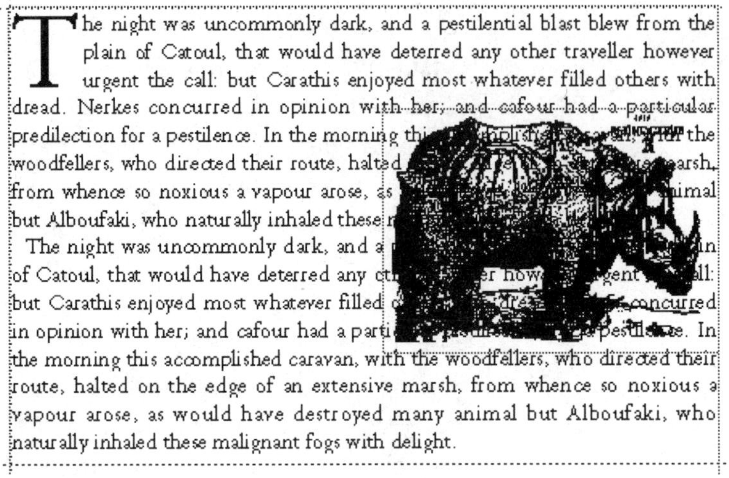

Figure 7-2
Text Runaround
Mode: None

The night was uncommonly dark, and a pestilential blast blew from the plain of Catoul, that would have deterred any other traveller however urgent the call: but Carathis enjoyed most whatever filled others with dread. Nerkes concurred in opinion with her; and cafour had a particular predilection for a pestilence. In the morning thi... woodfellers, who directed their route, halted ...arsh, from whence so noxious a vapour arose, as ...imal but Alboufaki, who naturally inhaled these ...

The night was uncommonly dark, and a ...in of Catoul, that would have deterred any ot... er how ...ent all: but Carathis enjoyed most whatever filled ... concurred in opinion with her; and cafour had a parti... pestile...ce. In the morning this accomplished caravan, with the woodfellers, who directed their route, halted on the edge of an extensive marsh, from whence so noxious a vapour arose, as would have destroyed many animal but Alboufaki, who naturally inhaled these malignant fogs with delight.

Item

The Item runaround specification is also available for both text and picture boxes. The key here is to remember that "Item" refers to the box itself. That is, it doesn't matter what's in the box. Any text that bumps into it flows around the edges of the box (see Figure 7-3). When you have "Item" specified in the Mode pop-up menu, you can change how far away the text should flow from the box on each of its four sides. This distance is called the *text outset*.

Those of you who have worked with earlier versions of QuarkXPress remember that in the olden days we had to go

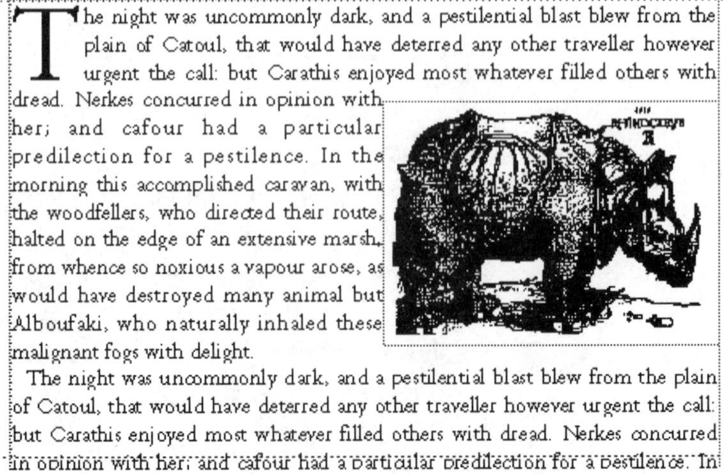

Figure 7-3
Text Runaround
Mode: Item

The night was uncommonly dark, and a pestilential blast blew from the plain of Catoul, that would have deterred any other traveller however urgent the call: but Carathis enjoyed most whatever filled others with dread. Nerkes concurred in opinion with her; and cafour had a particular predilection for a pestilence. In the morning this accomplished caravan, with the woodfellers, who directed their route, halted on the edge of an extensive marsh, from whence so noxious a vapour arose, as would have destroyed many animal but Alboufaki, who naturally inhaled these malignant fogs with delight.

The night was uncommonly dark, and a pestilential blast blew from the plain of Catoul, that would have deterred any other traveller however urgent the call: but Carathis enjoyed most whatever filled others with dread. Nerkes concurred in opinion with her; and cafour had a particular predilection for a pestilence. In through all sorts of machinations in order to adjust our text offset. Now we can control it quickly and with great precision.

Auto Image

The Auto Image text runaround mode is available only for picture boxes (that's why the word "image" is in the title). This is just like the text runaround that was available in earlier versions of QuarkXPress. You can specify the text offset for the runaround, and QuarkXPress automatically determines where the image is and how the text should flow around it (see Figure 7-4).

Figure 7-4
Text Runaround
Mode: Auto Image

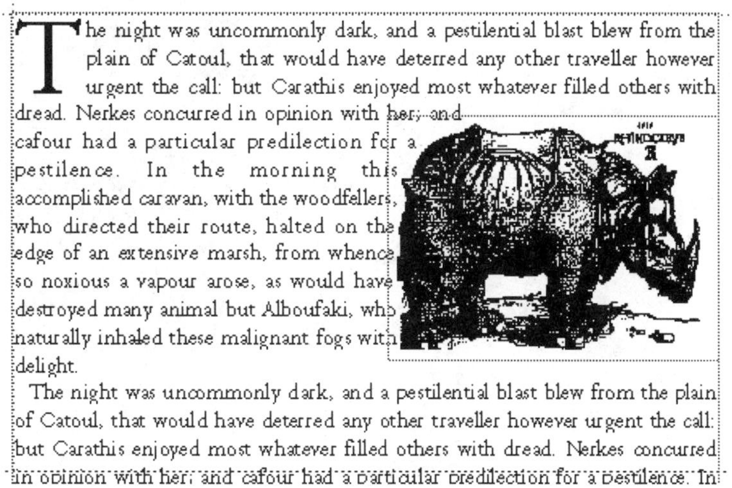

The night was uncommonly dark, and a pestilential blast blew from the plain of Catoul, that would have deterred any other traveller however urgent the call: but Carathis enjoyed most whatever filled others with dread. Nerkes concurred in opinion with her; and cafour had a particular predilection for a pestilence. In the morning this accomplished caravan, with the woodfellers, who directed their route, halted on the edge of an extensive marsh, from whence so noxious a vapour arose, as would have destroyed many animal but Alboufaki, who naturally inhaled these malignant fogs with delight.

The night was uncommonly dark, and a pestilential blast blew from the plain of Catoul, that would have deterred any other traveller however urgent the call: but Carathis enjoyed most whatever filled others with dread. Nerkes concurred in opinion with her; and cafour had a particular predilection for a pestilence. In

The image is defined by its screen representation. That is, if you have an EPS picture with a PICT representation, QuarkXPress uses the low-resolution bitmapped image to figure out where the text should run around. If the EPS picture has no screen representation and you only see a gray box, QuarkXPress cannot figure out what the image looks like "inside" the gray box. In this case, it just uses the gray rectangle as the runaround boundary.

Although TIFF images are defined by a rectangle, QuarkXPress treats white space as "blank" space. That is, if you have either a black-and-white or gray-scale TIFF image that has a lot of white space around the edges, QuarkXPress "sees" the boundary of the nonwhite image. However, even a single gray pixel apart from the main image can cause havoc with text runaround because QuarkXPress sets the text to run around that pixel, too (see Figure 7-5). Sometimes increasing the contrast of an image can help remove unwanted stray pixels (see Chapter 8, *Modifying Images*).

Figure 7-5

A couple of misplaced pixels in a TIFF file can throw off the runaround

Manual Image

New to version 3 is the Manual Image text runaround feature. This is one of the coolest features in the program. It lets you specify exactly where you want a runaround to be using a *text runaround polygon*. These polygons are similar to the polygonal picture boxes we discussed in Chapter 1, *Structure and Interface*, except that they are used only for text runaround purposes. Figure 7-6 shows an image with a manually set text runaround. Note the handles and dotted line specifying the corners and segments of the text runaround polygon.

It's important to remember here that QuarkXPress is creating a second box that specifies the text runaround path. This box is tied inherently to the picture box. If you move the picture box, the text runaround polygon moves, too.

However, you can resize or reshape either the polygon or the picture box without affecting the other.

Figure 7-6
Text Runaround
Mode: Manual Image

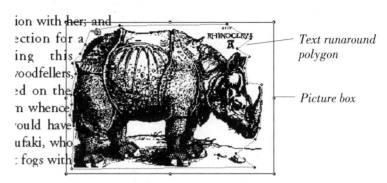

Text runaround polygon

Picture box

For those of you who were in such a hurry to get into the book that you skipped Chapter 1, *Structure and Interface,* here is a quick rundown of the necessary concepts and tools for working with polygons.

- Polygons are made up of segments joined by corner points.

- You can move a corner point by clicking on it and dragging it.

- You can also move a segment line of a polygon by clicking on it and dragging it. This moves the corner points at both ends of the segment.

- Moving corners or line segments while holding down the Shift key constrains the movement horizontally or vertically.

- You can add a corner point by holding down the Command key and clicking on a line where you want the corner point. When you hold down the Command key, the cursor turns into a hollow circle.

- You can delete a corner point by holding down the Command key and clicking on it.

- On text runaround polygons, you can delete the entire polygon by holding down the Shift and Command keys and clicking on the polygon. This deletes just the text runaround polygon, but not the picture box or the picture itself. The picture box then has no runaround assigned to it.

When you specify "Manual Image" for a picture box's runaround specification, QuarkXPress gives you the text runaround polygon that it uses internally for the Auto Image specification. You can then alter the polygon using the techniques outlined above so that the text runaround meets your design needs. Don't worry about getting it perfect the first time; you can always go back and change it.

Note that even though the text runaround polygon and the picture box are linked together when you move them, the picture box in no way restrains the movement of the polygon. For example, corner points and segments can be placed inside or outside the picture box (see Figure 7-7). In fact, you can use the Content tool to drag a picture and its text runaround polygon anywhere you want on the page (the picture "disappears" outside the picture box, but the text runaround polygon is still visible and active).

Figure 7-7
The polygon is
not restrained by
the picture box

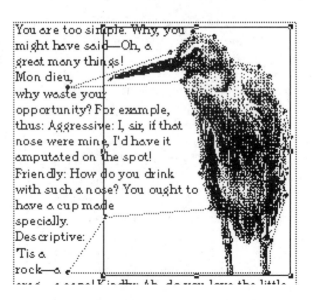

▼ ▼

Tip: Speed up Polygon Editing. Every time you change a corner or a line segment of a text runaround polygon, QuarkXPress redraws the polygon and recomposes the text to go around it. This quickly becomes tedious. You can make the program hold off on reflowing the text until you've finished editing by holding down the Spacebar. When you're finished, just let go of the Spacebar, and QuarkXPress reflows the text.

▼ ▼

Tip: Picture Wrap with No Picture. After you have built a text runaround polygon around a graphic image, you can delete the picture and the polygon remains. Remember to delete the picture while the Content tool is selected or else you'll delete the picture box (and the picture and polygon with it) instead of just the contents of the box.

▼ ▼

Tip: Polygons from Empty Boxes. If a picture box is empty when you apply Manual Image text runaround, the text runaround polygon is created in the shape of the picture box itself. We find this handy for creating quick, custom text runaround paths that don't necessarily have anything to do with a graphic. It's useful, for example, to force a block of text to justify at an angle or wrap around a large drop cap (see Figure 7-8).

▼ ▼

Inverting the Text Wrap

Each of the types of text runaround we've discussed is based on wrapping text around the outside of an object or polygon. The text flows on one side of the object only, whichever side is the wider and fits more text. However, you can also flow text inside a text runaround polygon (see Figure 7-9). This is called inverting the text wrap.

The trick in understanding how to quickly and easily invert the runaround is to remember that text flows where it has the most space to flow. First, select the picture box and give it a Manual Image text runaround (Command-T). Before

Figure 7-8

Text runaround polygons with no images attached

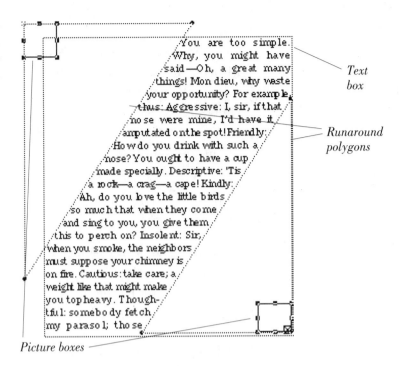

Text box

Runaround polygons

Picture boxes

Figure 7-9

Text flowing inside a text runaround polygon

You are too simple. Why, you might have said—Oh, a great many things! Mon dieu, why waste your opportunity? For example, thus: Aggressive: I, sir, if that nose were mine, I'd have it amputated on the spot. Friendly: How do you drink with such a nose? You ought to have a cup made specially. Descriptive: 'Tis a rock—a crag—a cape! Kindly: Ah, do you love the little birds so much that when they come and sing to you, you give them this to perch on? Insolent: Sir, when you smoke, the neighbors must suppose your chimney is on fire. Cautious: take care; a weight like that might make you top heavy. Thoughtful: somebody fetch

Text flows in the widest area, which in this case is outside the picture box

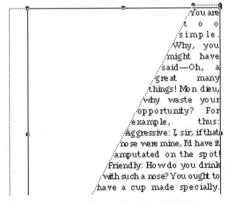

You are too simple. Why, you might have said—Oh, a great many things! Mon dieu, why waste your opportunity? For example, thus: Aggressive: I, sir, if that nose were mine, I'd have it amputated on the spot! Friendly: How do you drink with such a nose? You ought to have a cup made specially.

Here the text flows into the runaround polygon because it is larger than the area outside the picture box

you click OK in the Runaround Specifications dialog box, click on the Invert button to make it possible to invert the runaround. When you click OK, your text may or may not run inside the text runaround polygon. If there is more space for the text to run outside the picture box, it'll do that.

To ensure that the text runs on the inside of the text runaround polygon, first confirm that the Invert button is checked. Then resize the picture box (not necessarily the runaround polygon) so that the text has little or no room to flow around it.

▼ ▼

Tip: Disappearing Runaround Text . Remember that text runaround is based entirely on box layering. A picture box must be on top of a text box in order for Auto or Manual Image text runaround to have any effect. One problem many seasoned veterans of QuarkXPress have is that they forget they can assign a runaround to a picture box while the box still has an opaque background. If you assign a text runaround and find that you can't see the text behind the picture box, make sure your box has a background color of "None."

▼ ▼

Anchored Boxes

You probably don't think we can come up with a decent encore after those cool manual-image text runaround polygons. Well, here's another cool effect that is new to version 3: anchored boxes. Many programs let you paste graphic images directly into text. This is usually called *inline graphics*. QuarkXPress takes the concept of inline graphics one step farther by letting you paste either a picture or a text box directly into the flow of text. These picture or text boxes become anchored to the point where they have been pasted. In other words, as you type, they flow along with the text in the same position.

Anchored boxes can be used in many situations, such as placing small pictures in text as icons, creating picture drop caps, and allowing tables and figures to keep their place in text. Let's look at how these anchored boxes are created and how to work with them.

Turning a Box into a Character

We like to think of anchored boxes as turning a picture or a text box into a character that can be manipulated in a text block. This proves to be a useful model for working with anchored boxes. There are two steps involved with turning a picture or text box into an anchored box character.

1. **Cut or Copy.** The first step in creating an anchored box is to cut or copy the picture or text box using the Item tool. Click on the picture or text box and select Cut or Copy from the Edit menu (or type Command-X or Command-C). Because you're using the Item tool rather than the Content tool, the box itself is being cut or copied rather than just what's in it.

2. **Paste.** The second step is to paste the box into the text using the Content tool. Select the text box and place the cursor where you want your anchored text box to sit, then select Paste from the Edit menu (or type Command-V). Because you're using the Content tool, the box is pasted in as a character in the text block rather than a separate box.

What you can't do. QuarkXPress prohibits you from making certain objects into anchored boxes. First of all, you cannot anchor a group of objects. Secondly, anchored boxes are just that: boxes. Therefore, you cannot anchor something that can't be defined as a box, like a line. And, even though QuarkXPress calls polygons and ovals "boxes," it doesn't really let you anchor them (it turns them into rectangular picture boxes). A third function the program won't allow is anchoring text boxes that have anchored boxes within them.

Modifying Anchored Boxes

While anchored boxes can do many things that normal picture and text boxes can't do, they sacrifice some abilities as well. For example, you cannot select and drag an anchored box to a new location. Nor can you rotate anchored boxes (unless you rotate the text box that they are pasted into). And you can only resize anchored boxes using the sizing handles on the right and bottom sides.

But don't let all these "no-can-do's" dishearten you. There's still lots you can do.

The root of every change you can make with anchored boxes is the Anchored Box Specifications dialog box (there is one for picture boxes and another for text boxes; see Figure 7-10). Selecting the anchored box with either the Item or the Content tool and choosing "Modify" from the Item menu (or double-clicking on the box with the Item tool, or typing Command-M) brings up the appropriate dialog box for the type of box that is anchored.

Figure 7-10

The Anchored Box Specifications dialog boxes

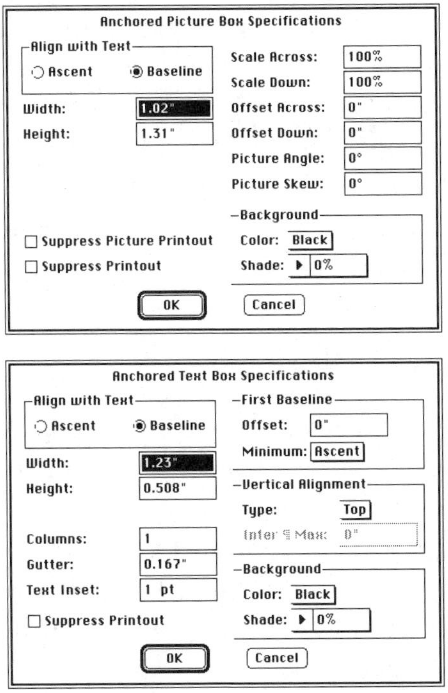

Resizing. You can resize anchored boxes by either dragging one of the three handles or by specifying a width or height in the Anchored Box Specifications dialog box or the Measurements palette. Remember that anchored picture boxes are just like normal picture boxes in most ways. For example, you can scale both the picture box and its contents by holding down the Command key while dragging one of the three control handles.

Contents modification. Both anchored text boxes and picture boxes are fully functional. That is, you can edit, import, or reformat the contents of any anchored box. To alter the contents of an anchored box, you must use the Content tool, just as if you were altering a normal box.

There are several features you cannot take advantage of, however. One thing you can't do is change an anchored box's text runaround specification. The text runaround for an anchored box is determined primarily by its alignment within the text box (see "Alignment," below). Another prohibited function is text linking: you cannot link to or from an anchored text box.

▼ ▼

Tip: Blend in Anchored Boxes. Note that the background color for an anchored box is not necessarily equal to the text box that it is located in. For example, if your text box is set to 10-percent gray and you anchor an opaque picture box into it, the anchored picture box most likely doesn't match its surroundings. If you can think of a better word than "tacky" to describe this, let us know. Instead, be sure to specify "None" for the background in all anchored boxes.

▼ ▼

Alignment. You can align an anchored box in two ways: "Ascent" or "Baseline." When you specify an anchored box to align by "Ascent," the top of the box aligns with the ascender of the tallest font in that text line. The rest of the figure drops down and text wraps around it. This is most commonly used for creating drop cap-like initial characters.

When you specify an anchored box to align by "Baseline," the bottom of the box aligns with the baseline of the line it's on. This is very helpful if the anchored box is attached within a line of text and is acting as if it were a special text character. How the text in previous lines accommodates this baseline alignment depends on the leading in the paragraph. If you specify absolute leading, the anchored box may overlap the text above it (see Figure 7-11). If you are using automatic or relative leading, the space between lines is widened to accommodate a larger anchored box. Again, the model of the anchored box as text character is particularly fitting, as these are exactly the effects you would achieve by using an oversized character in a text block (see Chapter 4, *Type and Typography*).

When using a baseline-aligned anchored box that acts as a character within a line, we recommend that you use absolute leading for your paragraph. Otherwise, all hell can break loose and text is shoved all over the place (however, see "Tip: Anchored Figures on Their Own Line," below).

You can choose the anchored box's alignment in two places: the Anchored Box Specifications dialog box or the Measurements palette. To change the alignment using the Measurements palette, click on one of two icons on the far left of the palette. The top icon represents "Ascent," and the bottom icon represents "Baseline."

Figure 7-11
Anchored box
alignment

Upwards and onwards, into the breach of contract he jumped, pen in hand and gas pedal under foot, ☞ whizzing along the Los Angeles freeways and bylaws.

Aligned by baseline. Text has absolute leading.

Upwards and onwards, into the breach of contract he jumped, pen in hand and gas

pedal under foot, ☞ whizzing along the Los Angeles freeways and bylaws.

Also aligned by baseline. Text has automatic leading.

▼ ▼

Tip: Anchored Figures on Their Own Line. You might use anchored boxes within a line of text for symbols, complex dingbats, or company logos, but more frequently you'll use them as single "characters" within their own paragraph. You can quickly get your page into a muddle unless you're careful with paragraph leading. We know we said we hated automatic leading and that you should never use it, but here's an exception. Setting the paragraph that contains the anchored box to "Auto Leading" ensures that there is enough space above the image so that it doesn't overlap any text. The anchored box's alignment should be set to "Baseline," too (see Figure 7-12).

▼ ▼

Tip: Aligning Anchored Text Boxes. If you're trying to align the baselines of text in an anchored text box with text that surrounds it, you need to make sure of three things.

• The leading in the anchored text box and the surrounding text box must be equal.

• The anchored text box must be set to 0 (zero) text outset in the Runaround Specifications dialog box. Note that this is *not* the same as selecting "None." Because you cannot specify runaround for a box once it's anchored, you should set this before you cut and paste it.

• The anchored text box must have a text inset of 0 (zero). You enter this value into "Text Inset" in the Anchored Text Box Specifications dialog box.

▼ ▼

Tip: Anchored Boxes as Initial Caps. In Chapter 4, *Type and Typography*, we implied that you could use anchored boxes as initial caps simply by pasting them in as the first character of a paragraph and setting their alignment to "Ascent." However, you may run into a problem. At the time of this writing there is a bug in QuarkXPress that still has not been fixed. The bug is that if your paragraph has any sort of left indent, some text lines that wrap around the anchored box are indented from the anchored box itself (see Figure 7-13).

Figure 7-12

Set anchored boxes to
"Auto Leading" to
prevent the graphic
from overlapping text

The night was uncommonly dark, and a pestilential
blast blew from the plain of Catoul, that would have
deterred any other traveller however urgent the call:
but Carathis ⌐ s with dread.
Nerkes con⌐ cafour had a
particular pr⌐ morning this
accomplished⌐ directed their
route, halted⌐ from whence
so noxious a⌐ troyed many
animal but A⌐ se malignant
fogs with del⌐

The night was uncommonly dark, and a pestilential blast
blew from the plain of Catoul, that would have deterred any

Absolute leading

The night was uncommonly dark, and a pestilential
blast blew from the plain of Catoul, that would have
deterred any other traveller however urgent the call:
but Carathis enjoyed most whatever filled others with dread.
Nerkes concurred in opinion with her; and cafour had a
particular predilection for a pestilence. In the morning this
accomplished caravan, with the woodfellers, who directed their
route, halted on the edge of an extensive marsh, from whence
so noxious a vapour arose, as would have destroyed many
animal but Alboufaki, who naturally inhaled these malignant
fogs with delight.

The night was uncommonly dark, and a pestilential blast
blew from the plain of Catoul, that would have deterred any

Automatic leading

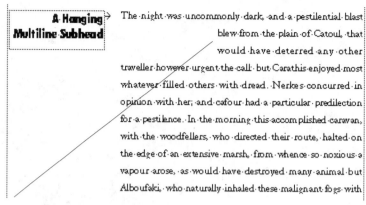

Figure 7-13
Anchored boxes can cause problems

The text is indented from the anchored box (this is a bug)

You have three choices for fixing this problem.

- Don't use left-indented text.

- Don't use anchored boxes for left-indented text.

- Use the Indent Here character (Command-\). This works only if your anchored box is supposed to be hanging in the margin.

▼ ▼

Working with Anchored Boxes

David had a professor once who maintained that when some-one reaches perfection, the skies open and he or she is lifted into the heavens in perfect bliss. Given that you're reading this book, you probably haven't reached that pinnacle yet. So what happens if you don't place the anchored box perfectly where it should be? Or what if you decide to change your mind and delete the anchored box?

Don't worry, we've got answers for all of that (even though the skies aren't opening here, either).

Moving Anchored Boxes. As we said earlier, you cannot move an anchored box by just dragging it around, like you would any other box. There are two ways to move an anchored box: the way that the documentation says you can, and the way that makes most sense. Quark's documentation says you must select the anchored box with the Item tool, select Cut from the Edit menu, and then switch to the Content tool to position the cursor and paste it. This is consistent with the way that anchored boxes get placed in text in the first place. However, using the model that once an anchored box is placed in a text block it behaves like a text character, we prefer to move this anchored box "character" by cutting and pasting it with the Content tool alone. This just seems more intuitive to us, and it works just fine.

Deleting Anchored Boxes. We'll say it just one more time: anchored boxes are just like text characters. Do you delete text characters with the Delete function from the Item menu (or type Command-K)? No, a character is not an item; it's a character, and should be treated as one. If you want to stamp out the measly existence of an anchored box, place the cursor after it and press the Delete key—or before it and press Shift-Delete.

Also, once you've turned a box into a character to anchor it, you can't just cut it and paste it somewhere else as a stand-alone graphic.

▼ ▼

Tip: Getting an Anchored Box out Again. We like to say, "There's always a workaround." As it happens, there are actually two ways to get an anchored box out as a stand-alone graphic. The first way is by selecting it with either the Content or the Item tool (we mean clicking on the box rather than dragging over it like a character) and selecting "Duplicate" from the Item menu (Command-D). This makes a copy of the box, but in a standard (nonanchored) form. The second method is to select the anchored box with the Item tool and copy it, and then paste it elsewhere (while still using the Item tool). This is the one instance where it does no good to think of the anchored box as a character. Oh well, models can't always be perfect.

▼ ▼

▼ ▼

Anchored Rules

While it's true that you cannot paste rules (lines) into text to anchor them, you can actually produce anchored rules using a different method. You can set anchored rules through paragraph-level formatting in text, and build them into style sheets. Unlike so many other features in QuarkXPress, you can only set anchored paragraph rules in one way. Unfortunately, these rules can only be horizontal (see "Tip: Vertical Rules," later in this chapter).

Rule Above/Rule Below

The one way to set anchored paragraph rules is via the Paragraph Rules dialog box. While your text cursor is in a paragraph or highlighting it, you can select "Rules" from the Formats menu (or type Command-N). You then have the choice whether to place a rule above the paragraph, below it, or both. When you select one of these rule positions, QuarkXPress expands the dialog box to give you more choices (see Figure 7-14).

The expanded Paragraph Rules dialog box gives you many options over the placement, size, and style of your horizontal rule. Let's look at each element of the dialog box.

Style. The right side of the Paragraph Rules dialog box contains the style specifications for the rule. You can choose the

Figure 7-14
The Paragraph
Rules dialog box

line style, width (thickness), color, and shade for the rule using the pop-up menus. You can also type in your own value for the Width and Shade fields, to the thousandth of a point or a tenth of a percent.

The line-styles available are the same styles available for all lines (see Chapter 1, *Structure and Interface*).

Length. You can specify the length of the rule and its horizontal position using the Length pop-up menu and the From Left and From Right controls. The initial decision you need to make is whether you want the rule to stretch from the left indent of the paragraph to the right indent (select "Indent" in the Length pop-up menu) or only to stretch as far as the text (select "Text" in the Length pop-up menu). Figure 7-15 shows examples of these settings.

Figure 7-15
The Length setting in "Rule Above/ Rule Below"

Length set to "Text"

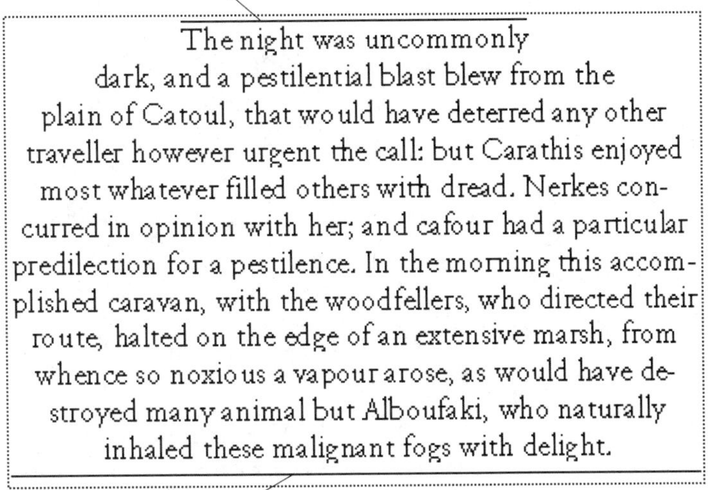

The night was uncommonly dark, and a pestilential blast blew from the plain of Catoul, that would have deterred any other traveller however urgent the call: but Carathis enjoyed most whatever filled others with dread. Nerkes concurred in opinion with her; and cafour had a particular predilection for a pestilence. In the morning this accomplished caravan, with the woodfellers, who directed their route, halted on the edge of an extensive marsh, from whence so noxious a vapour arose, as would have destroyed many animal but Alboufaki, who naturally inhaled these malignant fogs with delight.

Length set to "Indents"

Horizontal offsets. The next considerations in determining the length of the rule are its offsets from the left and right. You can specify how far from the left or right the rule should start (or end) by typing a measurement into the From Left and/or the From Right fields. Your only limitation in offsetting the rule is that the rule cannot go outside the text box. If your paragraph is set to a left indent of 1p6, the minimum left offset you can type is -1p6.

Vertical position. The third specification you can make for an anchored paragraph rule is its vertical position relative to the paragraph to which it is attached. This concept is a little tricky, and Quark's documentation doesn't do a lot to help clarify the idea. Let's break it down into pieces.

The vertical positioning of the rule is set in the Offset field. We don't like the word "offset," as it confuses the issue. We prefer the term "positioning," so that's what we'll use. Just remember that these values go in the Offset field. You can specify positioning with either an absolute measurement or a percentage. QuarkXPress handles each of these very differently.

Let's take absolute positioning first. An absolute measurement for a rule above is measured from the baseline of the first line in the paragraph to the bottom of the rule. An absolute measurement for a rule below is measured from the baseline of the last line in the paragraph to the top of the rule (see Figure 7-16).

Specifying the vertical position of a rule by percentage is slightly more complex. The first thing to remember is that the percentage you are specifying is a percentage of the space

Figure 7-16
Vertical positioning
of rules

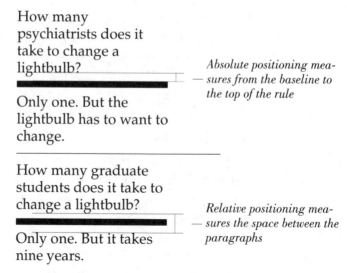

How many
psychiatrists does it
take to change a
lightbulb?

Absolute positioning measures from the baseline to the top of the rule

Only one. But the
lightbulb has to want to
change.

How many graduate
students does it take to
change a lightbulb?

Relative positioning measures the space between the paragraphs

Only one. But it takes
nine years.

between the paragraphs. This space is measured from the descenders of the last line of a paragraph to the ascenders of the first line of the next paragraph.

Let's look at an example. If you position a rule below a paragraph to 60 percent, QuarkXPress measures the distance between the two paragraphs (descender to ascender) and places the top of the rule 60 percent of that distance down. The rule grows *down* from that position as you increase its weight. A rule above a paragraph is placed with its bottom in the appropriate position, rather than the top, and the rule grows *up* from that position.

To us, percentage-based positioning is equivalent to automatic leading: we don't like it or its kind. We don't think it should be run out of town, because there's always a place for that kind of feature, but—in general—we don't like to use it. Why? There are some problems with percentage-based rules. For example, if a paragraph is specced to have a rule 30 percent above it, the rule doesn't show up if that paragraph sits at the top of a text box. A paragraph with a rule set some percentage below it won't appear if that paragraph is the last paragraph in the text box. It is nice that positioning a rule based on a percentage ensures that the rule doesn't overlap any text (it pushes the paragraphs away from each other if it needs to). But all in all, we would rather have complete control over where the rule always is, and feel sure that the rule is there no matter what happens to the paragraph.

▼ ▼

Tip: Reversed Type in Rules. This is one of the oldest tricks in the book. You can make reversed type that is anchored to text by assigning a thick rule above or below a paragraph and setting the type in the paragraph to white. You need to specify a vertical positioning for the rule so that it "overlaps" its own line. Out of habit, we always use a rule above about four or five points larger than the text size, and specify a -2 or -3-point offset (vertical position). You can use this same technique to create multiple-tinted tables (see Figure 7-17).

▼ ▼

Figure 7-17

Type in a rule

SPRING—1624		
Spread	750	1000
Full page	600	800
Half page	400	500
Quarter page	275	375
Spot	175	250

——— *Rule Above with -2-point offset*

These are rules, too!

▼ ▼

Tip: Vertical Rules. Nope, there's no way to cajole, coerce, or configure QuarkXPress to paste or place an anchored vertical line in a text block. Or is there? We work around this problem with the following technique.

1. Create a picture box as thin (or thick) as you want your rule.

2. Give the picture box the background color you want the rule to be (for example, 80-percent magenta).

3. Copy and paste this empty picture box into the text block as described in "Anchored Graphics," above. You'll probably want to paste it either at the beginning of a paragraph or on a line on its own.

4. Set the anchored box to Ascent alignment, and the text in the text box to absolute leading, so it wraps around the picture box/rule.

Figure 7-18 shows a sample vertical rule made using this method. Note that in this example, the rule appears as if it is set off from the left text margin. Actually, the text is set off from the rule using a 9-point left indent together with a -9-point first line indent. The picture box/rule is the first character in the paragraph.

▼ ▼

Tip: Return of Vertical Rules. If you need a vertical rule thinner than 1 point, you're out of luck with the last tip. One point is the minimum thickness of a picture box. It's obviously time to resort to drastic measures: build the rule in another program and then import it into a picture box before anchoring it

Figure 7-18
Anchored vertical rule

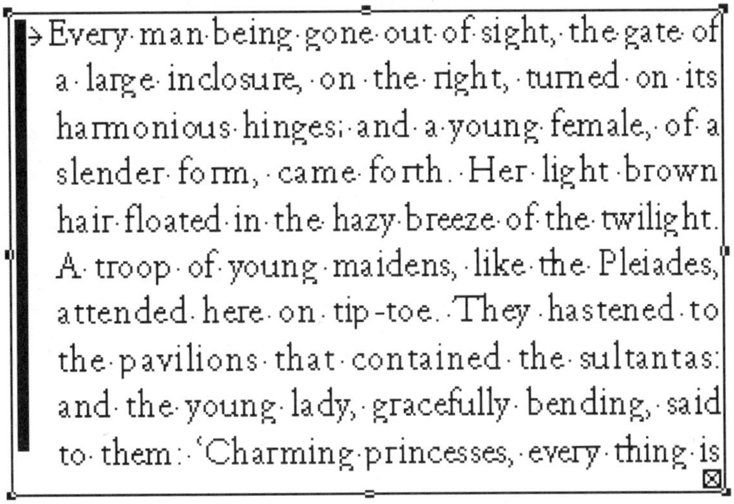

> Every man being gone out of sight, the gate of a large inclosure, on the right, turned on its harmonious hinges; and a young female, of a slender form, came forth. Her light brown hair floated in the hazy breeze of the twilight. A troop of young maidens, like the Pleiades, attended here on tip-toe. They hastened to the pavilions that contained the sultanas: and the young lady, gracefully bending, said to them: 'Charming princesses, every thing is

in a text box. If you need to lengthen or shorten the rule, just change the vertical scaling of the picture.

Poking and Prodding

Where text meets graphics. Like we said, it's a wild, woolly frontier just waiting to be mastered. We've explored how different boxes and page elements can interact, but these are mysterious regions where there is no substitute for poking and prodding about on your own.

The next two chapters deal with a few of the more detail-oriented features in QuarkXPress: modifying bitmapped images and working in color. After that, you'll be able to create any page known to humankind (and a few that aren't).

MODIFYING IMAGES

To be honest, many of you will never need to read this chapter, but we think you should anyway. Although image modification is an aspect of QuarkXPress which can only be described as fine tuning, we cover some important areas here, including an in-depth discussion of halftoned images.

In Chapter 6, *Pictures,* we discussed several graphic file formats, how to bring them into your QuarkXPress documents, and how to do basic manipulations with them, such as rotating, skewing, and scaling. In this chapter we look at how you can use QuarkXPress in place of other image-editing software to modify the imported image itself. Bear in mind that we're not talking here about image *editing.* You can't actually change the contents of imported graphics in QuarkXPress. You can, however, change some of their overall parameters, such as contrast, color, and halftone screen.

We start this chapter off by examining the types of images we can modify, and then we move into how to modify them. Much of this is potentially confusing, but bear with us, read carefully, and you'll be an inexorable image-modifier faster than you can say "phylogeny recapitulates ontogeny."

▼ ▼

The Picture File

In this chapter, we are *only* concerned with bitmapped images. Bitmapped images, as far as QuarkXPress is concerned, are black-and-white, gray-scale, or color, and are found in TIFF, RIFF, PNTG, and PICT files. In the case of PICT files, however, note that when it comes to image control, QuarkXPress only recognizes bitmapped-only PICTs. That means that no object-oriented graphics are recognized for the purpose of image modification. But let's be frank: you'd be foolish to be using PICT images anyway. They're very unreliable, and nearly impossible to do color separations with. Due to the nature of object-oriented PICT and EPSF files, QuarkXPress can import them (see Chapter 6, *Pictures*), but does not allow any modifications such as contrast control to be performed on them. Use TIFF files whenever possible, though Paint files are fine for small black-and-white images.

Bitmapped Images

You may want to take this opportunity to refresh your memory from Chapter 6, *Pictures*, about bitmapped images and the particular file types of PNTG and TIFF. Here are the highlights.

- Bitmapped images are simply rectangular grids of pixels (dots).

- The resolution of the image is the number of these dots per inch.

- Each pixel is assigned to be black, white, a level of gray, or a color. This color is represented by a number; for example, black might be 256 in a 256 gray-level file.

- Scaling the image has a direct effect on the resolution of the image. Enlarging the picture 200 percent cuts the resolution in half, which may result in jaggies or pixelation. Reducing the image 50 percent doubles the resolution, which may improve image quality (see Figure 8-1).

Figure 8-1
Scaling a bitmapped image has an effect on its resolution

50%

100%

400%

- A PNTG (Paint-type) file has a fixed size of 8 by 10 inches at 72 dpi (576 by 720 pixels), and each pixel can be only white or black. These are said to be "flat" or bilevel bitmapped images.

- A TIFF file can be any size rectangle with any number of dots per inch, and each pixel can have any level of gray or color which is definable by the color models described in Chapter 9, *Color*. TIFF files are said to be "deep" if they contain 4 or more gray levels (over 2 bits per sample point).

Modifying Images

It is rare that a scanned image prints the way you want it to without some modification, especially if you've scanned it in directly using Quark's Apple Scanner XTension (see Appendix B, *Resources*). You may also want to apply image-modification techniques to synthetic pictures created with a paint program. QuarkXPress lets you alter an image in several ways. Here's what you can do.

- Replace its contrast curve with preset high-contrast or posterized effects.

- Apply a custom gamma curve.

- Invert the image.

- Change the picture's screen or printed resolution.

- Apply a color or tint to the picture.

- Change the picture's halftoning parameters.

Each of these features is not only related, but fully interdependent on the others. Let's take a look at these controls and how you can use them to your benefit.

Welcome to the world of image modification!

Importing High-resolution TIFF Graphics

The first alteration you can make to your file is to upgrade or downgrade high-resolution TIFF files. This control is available only when you first import the picture (see "Get Picture" in Chapter 6, *Pictures*), so we had better cover it quickly before we move on.

Upgrading screen quality. QuarkXPress normally brings in a screen representation of a high-resolution TIFF or RIFF file at 36 dpi. This low-resolution screen image provides for a relatively quick screen refresh rate (when, for example, you move around the page). However, the image on the screen may look rougher than you'd like. You can double the screen resolution by holding down the Shift key while clicking the Open button in the Get Picture dialog box. This won't have any effect on your printed output, but do note that this may slow down your screen redraws (those of you who have a Mac IIfx or a 040 machine can stop chuckling).

Changing TIFF/RIFF types. If you are heavily into image editing and control, you will undoubtedly want to change the TIFF/RIFF type of an image at some point. Following are two tricks for changing the type at importation.

- Holding down the Option key when clicking Open in the Get Picture dialog box changes a TIFF line-art (two-bit) image into an 8-bit gray-scale image.

- Holding down the Command key when clicking Open in the Get Picture dialog box changes TIFF or RIFF gray-scale images to line art (1-bit), and TIFF color images to gray scale.

▼ ▼

The Style Menu

Chapter 6, *Pictures*, describes how you can manipulate the "layout" of the picture in the picture box, including cropping, rotating, skewing, and moving the image. These effects are controlled from the floating palette or the Picture Box Specifications dialog box. Here we talk primarily about the image modification possibilities using features from the Style menu. Remember that you can combine both image-manipulation techniques (rotating, changing its shape and size, and so on) and image-modification techniques (changing its gray/color parameters, and so on) to create fascinating effects for your page layout.

▼ ▼

Tip: When the Style Menu Is Gray. If the items on the Style menu are grayed out, you have probably imported an EPS or PICT file that contains more than just a single bitmapped image. Remember, no shoes, no bitmapped image, no service. If you're sure you have the right file format, it may be that you either have the Item tool selected (instead of the Content tool), or that you don't have the picture box selected. If none of this works, we suggest plugging the machine in.

▼ ▼

Color. We cover color fully in Chapter 9, *Color.* So at this point, suffice it to say that changing the color of the image using QuarkXPress's color feature effectively replaces all black pixels with ones of a particular color. For example, if you have a black-and-white image and you change the color to red, you then have a red-and-white image. Contrary to some forms of logic, selecting "White" from the menu does not have the same effect as reversing the image; it just makes all the pixels in the image white, and—believe us—there are easier ways of making fully white boxes!

▼ ▼

Tip: Making Your Gray-scale Picture "Transparent." The simple answer to "How do I make my gray-scale TIFFs transparent?" is you can't. Gray-scale TIFFs are not and can not be transparent. The reason for this is that every pixel has been assigned a gray level (whereas, in black-and-white, 1-bit TIFFs, the "white" pixels *are* transparent). However, you can fake a transparent look in some situations by importing the picture into a polygon which just wraps around the edges of the graphic. The best way we've found to do this is to import a graphic into a rectangular picture box, trace the edges using the Polygon Picture Box tool, then cut the graphic out of the first box and into the new picture box (see Figure 8-2).

▼ ▼

Figure 8-2
Making a fake
transparent
gray-scale TIFF

happiness runs in a circular motion; life is like a little boat upon the sea; everything is a part of everything anyway; you can have everything if you let yourself be; happiness runs in a circular motion; little boat upon the sea; part of every-thing everything if you let runs in a circle like a little boat upon is a part of every can have everything be; happi-ness run in a circular motion; life is like a little boat upon the sea; every-thing is part of everything anyway; you can have everything is you let

Shade. In the same spirit as changing each pixel's color, you can change the gray value for each pixel in the image. The method varies depending on whether you're working with flat or deep bitmapped images. With flat, bilevel, bitmapped images, you can select one of the percentages from 10 percent to 100 percent from the hierarchical menu, or choose "Other" and type in a tint value in 1 percent increments. This alters the printed output—every place there was a black pixel in your graphic, a gray pixel prints.

Because the proper way to change the "shading" of deep gray-scale or color images is through the Other Contrast dialog box (see "Other Contrast," below), the Shade menu item is grayed out when you are manipulating these sorts of images. Note that with either type of image, Mac screens which are able to show color and gray scales show a grayed screen representation of the image. However, 1-bit screens (such as those on a Mac SE) do not become grayed out unless you select 0 percent, in which case the image goes all white.

Negative. Selecting "Negative" from the Style menu (or typing Command-Shift-Hyphen) inverts all gray-scale or RGB color information in an image (see Chapter 9, *Color*, for more information on color models). What was 10 percent black becomes 90 percent black, what was 20 percent red becomes 80 percent red, and so on. For some obscure reason, this feature does not work with 1-bit (black-and-white) images (see "Tip: Making a Negative of Paint and PICT Bitmapped Images" below).

Note that the documentation released with QuarkXPress 3 maintains that selecting "Negative" here only changes the tonal values from the original picture; that is, contrast adjustments (see "Other Contrast," below) are ignored. For this once, the program does what it should and the docs are mistaken. Choosing "Negative" reverses all tonal values, and is equivalent to inverting the gray or RGB contrast curve (we discuss contrast curves later in this chapter).

▼ ▼

Tip: When a TIFF Doesn't Fill Its Box. Often, when you create a negative of a TIFF, the entire picture box does not invert (see Figure 8-3). Trying to place a background color doesn't help, because the background color affects the image itself (this is either a bug in the program or simply a counterproductive feature—either way it's annoying). Try the following steps.

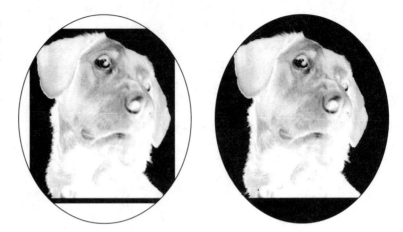

1. Make a duplicate of the picture box using the Step and Repeat function. The horizontal and vertical offsets should both be set to zero.

2. Delete the image from this duplicate box and give it a background color that matches the edges of the inverted TIFF image (you may have to adjust the tint; usually between 90 and 100 percent does the trick).

3. Send the duplicate box behind the original picture and change the original picture box's background color to "None" (transparent).

This also works to blend noninverted images into the background.

▼ ▼

Tip: Making a Negative of Paint and PICT Bitmapped Images. There must be a reason why QuarkXPress disallows bilevel (1-bit) images to be inverted with the Negative feature. We don't know what it is, though. However, we have found a quick workaround. Just select the item, change the shade to 0 percent, then change the background color to some shade of black (such as 100 percent).

▼ ▼

▼ ▼

Contrast

The Style menu also possesses the ability to change the contrast of gray-scale and color images. If you are working with a 1-bit (black-and-white) picture, these elements are inaccessible.

Contrast refers to the relationships among the tonal values of a picture. A high-contrast picture divides up the gray shades or color saturation of an image into a few sharply distinct tones; a low-contrast picture has little differentiation between tones, and looks grayed-out. You should try to strike some balance between these two, though you may want to create an unnatural-looking image by altering the contrast controls drastically.

The basic concept to remember regarding contrast controls is "input/output." For example, David likes to think of these controls as a machine into which he is inserting his TIFF or PICT images, and out of which comes what is going to print on the page. Other people sometimes think of this process as that of a filter through which the image is poured each time the page gets printed. Remember, though, that neither you nor QuarkXPress actually alters the picture file itself whatsoever; you only alter the "filter" or the "machine." Let's look at the controls QuarkXPress offers.

Normal Contrast. This filter "leaves well enough alone" and doesn't affect the image at all. This is the default setting for every gray-scale and color picture you import.

High Contrast. Selecting "High Contrast" from the Style menu has the immediate effect of making your gray-scale pictures look like they were badly scanned at a 1-bit (black-and-white) setting, and your color pictures look like poorly designed psychedelic flyers. The literal effect of this filter is to change all values under 30 percent gray to white, and all gray values 30 percent or above to black. Color images are affected in the same way: the saturation levels are broken down so that all colors with over 30 percent saturation are transformed to 100 percent, and so on (see Chapter 9, *Color* for a more in-depth discussion of color and its saturation levels). Why Quark chose the 30 percent mark is beyond us; it makes for some really ugly looking images. We'll look at how to change this "breaking" point later in this chapter.

Posterized. Whereas the High Contrast setting breaks down the image into only two gray or saturation levels—0 percent and 100 percent—"Posterized" divides the tonal values into six levels of gray or color saturation: 0, 20, 40, 60, 80, and 100 percent. Gray levels or color saturation in the original picture are mapped to these levels based on what they're closest to (for example, a 36 percent saturation of a color maps to the 40 percent level). Posterization is a common technique in image editing, though it should be used carefully (see Figure 8-4).

Other Contrast. The ultimate contrast control within Quark-XPress comes from the Picture Contrast Specifications dialog box, which you can get by selecting "Other Contrast" from the Style menu. This dialog box shows you the mechanism or the filter through which you are putting the picture. If you select "Other Contrast" after selecting "High Contrast" or "Posterize" from the Style menu, you see the contrast curve for those items. Otherwise, with "Normal Contrast" selected, you see a 45-degree line on the graph (see Figure 8-5).

Looking carefully at the graph we see that the axes are labelled Input and Output, and each is defined from zero (percent) to 1 (hundred percent). Tick marks are shown in increments of 5 and 10 percent.

The basic 45-degree Normal Contrast line defines a filter which makes no change to gray levels. For example, a gray level of 20 percent in the input picture is mapped (output) to

Figure 8-4
Posterization of a gray-scale TIFF image

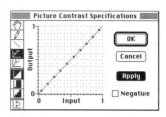

Normal contrast
Normal screen

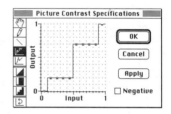

Posterized contrast
Normal screen

Figure 8-5
The Picture Contrast Specifications dialog box

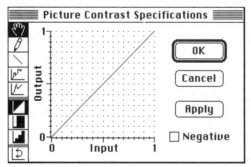

20 percent, 40 percent to 40 percent, and so on. By changing this line, we can change the mapping of the gray levels, affecting the contrast and shading of the printed picture.

Following are some basic tips and tricks to help you when you're modifying images using the Picture Contrast Specifications dialog box.

▼ ▼

Tip: Applying Your Changes. The Apply button is one of the all-time most helpful features that we've ever had the pleasure to use, especially on a large screen (anything larger than 9 inches). You can move the Picture Contrast Specifications dialog box out of the way of the picture you're working on by selecting the top portion of the dialog box and dragging. You can then make changes to the curve and click on the Apply button (or type Command-A) to see the change take place. If you don't like that effect, change the curve again or type Command-Z to undo that change. Selecting OK puts the most recent change into effect, but clicking on Cancel (or typing Command-Period) cancels any changes you've made.

▼ ▼

Tip: Continuous Apply. You can also type Command-Option-A for a continuous apply. This feature applies every change you make right after you make it. Sometimes it'll slow you down, but use it once and you'll find yourself becoming addicted to it. Typing Command-Option-A again turns continuous apply off. Remember: applying a change does not make it permanent; that only happens when you click OK or press Return (and even then you can go back and change it if you want!).

▼ ▼

Picture Contrast Specifications Dialog Box

As we mentioned above, the Picture Contrast Specifications dialog box (Command-Shift-C) is the representation of the overall contrast filter through which the picture is processed. The nine tools in this dialog box enable you to create all sorts of filters for both gray-scale and color images. These controls still aren't up to the caliber of programs like Photoshop and Enhance, which are designed for the purpose of image editing, but they do give you a good bit of control.

You can use the tools to change the contrast curve into either a straight line or a curve. By definition, any contrast curve which is not a straight line is a *gamma curve*. There's nothing mysterious about a gamma curve: it's simply a nonlinear curve with a fancy name.

Why would you want to apply a gamma curve to an image? The immediate answer is, "So you can create really far-out and wild images" (see Figure 8-6). However, perhaps more importantly, you can use gamma curves to correct for poorly scanned images, or to boost certain tonal values in a picture. Let's look at how this is done.

Figure 8-6

Gamma curves can be used for subtle or not-so-subtle contrast modification

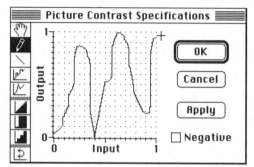

Hand tool. You can use the Hand tool to move the curve (or straight line) around on the contrast graph by selecting it, positioning it over the graph, and clicking-and-dragging with the mouse. You can constrain to either horizontal or vertical movements by holding down the Shift key while dragging (usually you'd want to hold down the Shift key before clicking and dragging, but it'll usually work even if you hold down the Shift key after you've started moving). The Hand tool is the easiest way to make adjustments to the contrast curve as a whole. For an example, see "Tip: Adjusting the Break Point on a High-contrast Image" below.

Pencil tool. If you've ever used the MacPaint painting program, you're already familiar with the Pencil tool. By selecting this tool and dragging over the curve, you can make both large and small adjustments. With the Pencil tool you can draw smooth gamma curves which adjust for problems in the original scan (see Figure 8-7). Or you can draw wild and bizarre roller-coaster curves which map the gray levels in weird ways. You can also make small corrections in the curve by carefully drawing over areas (see "Tip: Correcting Errors in the Curve," below). Remember, though, that you don't need to have a perfectly smooth curve all the time; slight bumps and dips have little effect on the final output.

Straight Line tool. If you can't figure out that the Straight Line tool draws straight lines, we wish you the best of luck with the program. However, it is not so obvious what these straight lines are good for. Think of the slope of a line in the same way as you think of the steepness of a hill. A steep slope steepens very quickly; a small slope steepens slowly. You can draw steep and gentle slopes easily with the Straight Line tool.

The steeper the slope, the higher contrast the image has. The gentler the slope, the less contrast; that is, the "grayer" the picture looks. However, remember that by using the

Figure 8-7

Gamma curve created with the Pencil tool

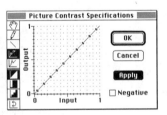

Default settings

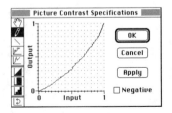

With a gamma contrast curve

straight line rather than a curved line, you are always losing tonal values. A steep, contrasted line loses the highlights and the shadows; a flat, low-contrast line loses midtones (see Figure 8-8).

Figure 8-8
Straight-line contrast curves often lose tonal values

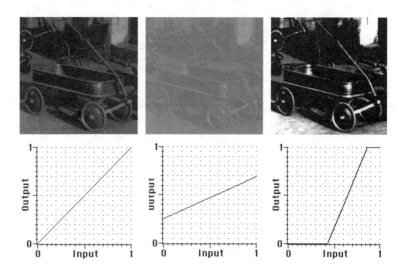

Posterizer tool. As we described earlier, posterization is the act of cutting out or dividing an image's gray or color levels into a few basic tonal values. By selecting "Posterize" in the Style menu, QuarkXPress divides the gray or color levels into six tonal values. When you select the Posterizer tool, QuarkXPress adds handle points to your line or curve at 10 percent increments. By moving these handles, you flatten and move that entire 10 percent area. By lining up multiple handles, you can easily create posterized effects with any number of levels up to 10 (see Figure 8-9).

Spike tool. Whereas the Posterizer tool places handles between the 10 percent marks and levels out (flattens) that 10 percent area, the Spike tool places handles directly on the 10 percent marks and has no affect on the area between the handles other than to adjust the lines to keep them contiguous.

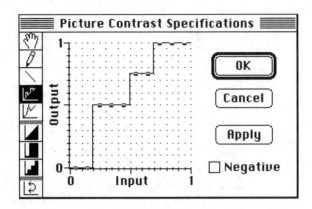

Figure 8-9
The Posterizer tool
adds handles
to your curve

Spiking a line is good for boosting particular tonal values; for example, if you wanted a 60-percent gray area to appear black, you could spike it up to 100 percent. Similarly, if you wanted to drop out all the dark areas of the cyan, you might use this tool. We usually use the Spike tool for drastic changes in the image, but sometimes it's just the thing for a quick minor adjustment. Also, if you are uncomfortable with the Pencil tool, you can approximate the curve path you want by clicking on the Spike tool and adjusting the spike handles.

Normal Contrast tool. Clicking on this reverts the contrast curve back to its initial 45-degree straight line.

High Contrast tool. Clicking on this switches the curve to the standard bilevel high-contrast "curve" as described above. The break point is set to 30 percent.

Posterized tool. When you click on this tool, the curve you're working on switches to the standard posterized curve. Tints under 10 percent go to white, over 90 percent go to black, and other tints round off to the nearest 20 percent.

Inversion tool and Negative check box. Contrary to popular belief, these two items in the Picture Contrast Specifications dialog box do not perform the same task, though in many instances you may achieve the same result. By clicking on either of these, for example, you can fully invert all gray-scale files. That is, where there was white, there is black, where there was 20 percent black, there is 80 percent black, and so on. Switching to negative and inverting the curve also creates the same effect while altering all three RGB values at once (see "Color," below for more on the RGB contrast curve).

However, inverting color images while using other color models can give you varying effects. Simply put, clicking on the Inversion tool on the tool palette flips the curve you are working on. Clicking on Negative has the same effect as selecting the Negative option in the Style menu (see "Negative," above).

▼ ▼

Tip: Adjusting the Break Point on a High-contrast Image. As we described above, the cutoff point on a high-contrast image is 30 percent, which does hardly anyone any good. Using the Hand tool in the Other Contrast dialog box, you can adjust this point horizontally to anywhere on the scale. Try moving the vertical line over to around 60 percent. This cuts out most of the lower gray values and gives you a clean and recognizable image for many gray-scale or color pictures (see Figure 8-10). This technique is also of great help when working with line art which was scanned as a gray-scale image. By adjusting the cutoff point, you can alter the line thicknesses in the artwork (see Figure 8-11). Remember that holding down the Shift key while using the Hand tool constrains the movements to horizontal or vertical.

▼ ▼

Tip: Applying a Shade to a Gray-scale or Color Picture. Remember that the Shade item is grayed out (unusable) for gray-scale and color TIFFs and PICTs. However, you can adjust the shading through the Picture Contrast Specifications dialog box. Use the Hand tool to move the contrast curve vertically (see Figure 8-12). Moving the whole curve up makes the image darker, and down makes it lighter (lower gray levels).

Note, however, that when you move the curve up or down, you're likely to cut out possible gray levels. If you make the

Figure 8-10
Adjusting the high-
contrast break point
for a gray-scale image

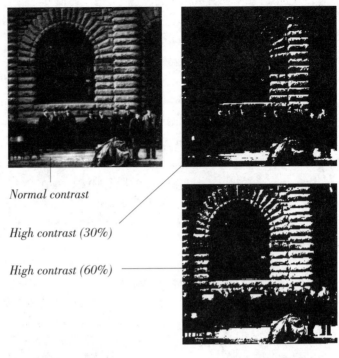

Normal contrast

High contrast (30%)

High contrast (60%)

Figure 8-11
This line art was
scanned as a
gray-scale image

High contrast (30%)   *High contrast (60%)*

image darker, for instance, dark areas go black; make it
lighter, and light areas go white. In either case, you lose
detail. Because of this, you may want to adjust the curve to
an appropriate gamma curve using the Pencil tool instead, as
described above.

▼ ▼

Tip: Correcting Errors in the Curve. You can make changes to the
contrast filter at any time. This means that if you are using

the Pencil tool and you can't keep your hand steady (we sure can't), you can smooth out the curve by going back over the rough parts after you've finished the basic line. It also means that if you don't like the change you made in the dialog box, you can type Command-Z to revert to the last state. It also means that if you hit OK and then decide that the image looks like crud, you can type Command-Z to revert, or just

Figure 8-12
Shading a
gray-scale TIFF

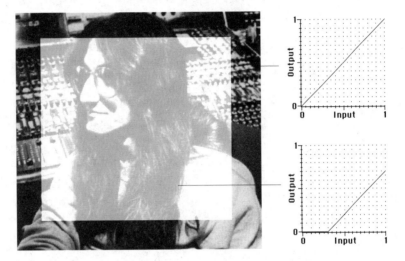

select "Normal Contrast" from the Style menu to get back to the picture's original state (at time of importing).

▼ ▼

Color

If you aren't familiar with working with color and the various color models that QuarkXPress supports, you may want to skip over this section until after you've read Chapter 9, *Color*. In this section we discuss contrast modification of color images using the various color models and their components.

QuarkXPress allows you to modify color bitmapped TIFF and PICT images using the same tools as you use with gray-scale images, except you can alter one color at a time. This clearly allows significantly greater control over the way your images print. Let's look at the steps you can take to modify these pictures.

Model. This item in the Picture Contrast Specifications dialog box appears when you are modifying a color bitmapped image. You can work with four different color models: HSB, RGB, CMY, and CMYK. When you select between the models, the image resets back to "Normal." Thus, you cannot make changes to an image in more than one color model.

Color. When you select one of the color models QuarkXPress prompts you with the appropriate color selection buttons. That is, when you select "HSB," Hue, Saturation, and Brightness buttons appear. Selecting "CMY" gives you Cyan, Magenta, and Yellow buttons, and so on. Each button can be selected on or off, and you can have any number of buttons selected at one time (when a button is on, it has an "X" through its check box).

The theory is simple: whatever buttons you have selected are the items which change when you alter the contrast control curve. In the RGB, CMY, and CMYK models, Quark-XPress gives you color buttons. If you select "Magenta" and "Yellow," for example, and change the contrast curve using the tools described above, you change the curve for only those two colors. Everything else remains the same.

The HSB model's buttons have slightly different functions. Changing the contrast curve with only "Hue" selected maps various colors to other colors. This can be seen on a color screen by examining the color spectrum on the horizontal and vertical axes as well as the curve itself. The Saturation button lets you map various saturations from 0 to 100 percent, and the Brightness button maps the brightness levels (levels of black) to other brightness levels. Once again, you can adjust each of these separately, in pairs, or all at one time.

▼ ▼

Halftones

Let's face it. Every high-resolution imagesetter on the market prints only in black and white. And almost every low-resolution laser printer prints only in black and white. There's clearly a lot to be said for black and white. What we need to realize, however, is that black and white is not gray. Real laser printers don't print gray (at least not the ones we're going to talk about).

So how do we get a picture with grays in it into the computer and out onto paper? The answer is halftones. The magic of halftoning is that different levels of gray are represented by different sized spots, which, when printed closely together, fool the eye into seeing the tint we want.

Take a look at any photograph in a newspaper, and it's easy to see the halftoning. Notice that the spacing of the spots doesn't change; only their size changes. There are large spots in dark areas, small spots in light areas. Let's take a look at the elements that make up digital halftones.

Dots. A laser printer prints pages by placing black dots on a white page (remember, this is the simple approach, and we're not getting into film negs and whatnot yet). Each and every dot on a 300-dpi printer is going to be $\frac{1}{300}$ of an inch in diameter (or thereabouts). That's pretty small, but it's still 8.5 times larger than what you can achieve on a Linotronic 300 ($\frac{1}{2540}$ of an inch, which is almost too small for the human eye to see). The primary factor concerning how large the dot is is the *resolution* of the printer (how many dots per inch it can print).

Spots. As was said before, a halftone is made up of spots of varying sizes. On a black-and-white laser printer or imagesetter, these spots are created by bunching together anywhere between 1 and 65,000 printer dots. They can be of different shapes and, to be redundant over and over again, different sizes. We'll look at several different types of spots later in the chapter.

Screen frequency. In the traditional halftoning process, a mesh screen is placed in front of the photograph to create the desired effect of spots (albeit rather square ones) all in rows. Keeping this process in mind can help you understand this concept. The *screen frequency* of a halftone is set by the mesh screen, and is defined as the number of these rows per inch. The lower the screen frequency, the coarser the image looks. The higher the screen frequency, the finer the image looks (see Figure 8-13).

Figure 8-13
Various screen
frequencies

20 lpi   *75 lpi*   *120 lpi*

To complicate issues a bit, the screen frequency of a halftone is often called its *line screen*. Whatever you call it, it's still calculated in the number of lines per inch (lpi). See Table 8-1 for information about when to use a particular line screen.

▼ ▼

Tip: Gray Levels in Your Halftones. Picture this: each spot is made up of tiny dots, and different gray levels are achieved by turning various dots on and off (at a 10-percent tint, 10 percent of the dots within a spot's cell are turned on). Okay, now remember that the lower the screen frequency, the bigger the spot, and the more dots are used per spot. The higher the frequency, the fewer dots are used. Thus, the higher the screen frequency, the fewer possibilities for levels of gray there are.

To find out how many levels of gray you can achieve, divide the resolution by the screen frequency, square it, and add one. For example, you can get 92 levels of gray when you print a 133-line screen at 1,270 dpi (($^{1270}/_{133}$)^2+1), but only 6 levels of gray when you print a 133-line screen at 300 dpi (($^{300}/_{133}$)^2+1). The output is clearly posterized. To get 92 levels of gray on a 300-dpi laser printer, you would need to print at

30 lines per inch! It's an unfortunate fact, but this is one of the inherent trade-offs in digital halftoning.

Output	Lines per inch
Photocopier	50–90 lpi
Newspaper quality	60–85 lpi
Quick-print printer	85–110 lpi
Direct mail pieces	110–150 lpi
Magazine quality	133–185 lpi
Art book	185–300 lpi

▼ ▼

Angle. The halftone screen does not have to be horizontal or vertical. It can rotate to other angles as well (see Figure 8-14), which can be of great use in both special effects halftoning and color separation (see Chapter 10, *Printing*). For reference sake, 0 and 180 degrees are horizontal, 90 and 270 degrees are vertical (some types of spots look the same in all four of these, and others look very different at each angle). A 45-degree angle is used most commonly, primarily because it is the least distracting to the eye. Remember that changing the angle of the halftone screen doesn't change the angle of the picture itself!

Making Halftones Work for You

Once again, just to be clear: any graphic image that contains gray requires halftoning. Even a simple box with a 10-percent tint comes out as a halftone. There's no other way to render grays on a black-and-white output device. With bitmapped images, QuarkXPress lets you change the parameters of the halftones: spot type, line screen, and angle.

The first four items in the screen section of the Style menu (see Figure 8-15) are preset combinations for you to choose. By choosing the fifth item, "Other Screen," you access the Picture Screening Specifications dialog box, which allows you to input your own choices, giving you the greatest amount of flexibility.

Figure 8-14
Rotating the halftone
screen to 0, 30, and
-45 degree angles

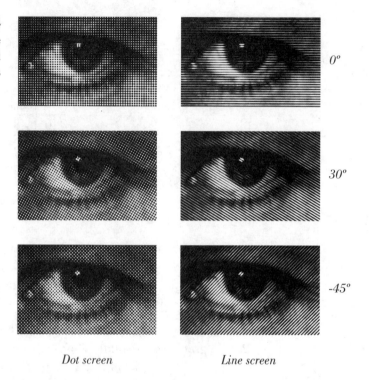

0°

30°

-45°

Dot screen   *Line screen*

Preset Screen Combinations

Let's look at QuarkXPress preset screen frequency and angle combinations first. Figure 8-16 shows a sample picture for each setting.

Normal Screen setting. Normal, in this case, means default. This is the setting all pictures automatically print in unless you specifically change them. The spot is a round dot (see further description of the round dot shape below), the angle is 45 degrees, and the screen frequency is whatever you chose in the Page Setup dialog box (move like the pros: type Command-Option-P). In most cases you will find yourself using the Normal Screen setting.

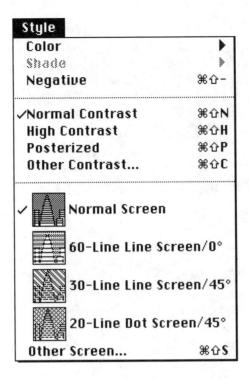

60-Line Line Screen, 0° setting. Why conform to "Normal Screen" when you have a choice like this? This screen setting uses a line screen, which is made up of halftone spots. These are lines rather than dots. We often call this a "straight-line screen" just to differentiate it from screen frequency, which, as mentioned above, is also sometimes called "line screen." This particular straight-line screen is set at a screen frequency of 60 lines per inch (lpi), each line being set to a 0 degree angle (horizontal). Printing at 60 lpi is coarse enough for the eye to easily see each line, but fine enough so that a casual observer won't notice it immediately. Nonetheless, the picture definitely looks different than if you used a round spot.

30-Line Line Screen, 45° setting. We're now in the realm of a very coarse straight-line screen. If you look too closely at this picture you won't even be able to tell what it is. This is a popular screen for special effects, though an angle of -45 (or 315) degrees is often used instead (see below on how to change the

Figure 8-16
The halftoning presets

 **Normal Screen**

 **60-Line Line Screen/0°**

30-Line Line Screen/45°

 **20-Line Dot Screen/45°**

angle). Because it's easy to see where the lines in the straight-line screen get fatter and thinner, the eye holds longer on how the image was created than what the image is itself.

20-Line Dot Screen, 45° setting. Here's another potentially confusing term. Here we have a "dot screen," which just means a spot which is round (the dots which make up the spot haven't changed any). A screen frequency this low can really only be used for special effects, unless you're printing on a billboard or other signage which won't be looked at up close.

Other Screen Option

We now come to the powerhouse behind QuarkXPress's screen features. Using the Other Screen feature under the Style menu (Command-Shift-S), we can choose between five screen patterns, and select any screen frequency or angle we like. Well almost any. Because of limitations in PostScript and the laser printer hardware, there are certain screen frequencies and angles which cannot be achieved (see the book *Real World PostScript* listed in Appendix B, *Resources*, for a detailed discussion of this problem). When this occurs, the printed output is as close as possible to what you requested.

Following is an in-depth description of these settings.

Screen. David's dream is to print out a halftone image at a line screen of 1, with each spot having a diameter of one inch. He doesn't have a particular reason for this; he just thinks it would be neat. Unfortunately, PostScript won't presently handle anything below 8 lpi, and QuarkXPress won't accept any value under 15. The upper range of 400 lpi is less of an inconvenience, though you may never have the urge to approach either of these limits. Select the screen frequency you want by typing it in, or type "0" (zero) or "default" to defer to the setting that is assigned in the Page Setup dialog box.

Angle. We discussed angles several sections ago, and we'll discuss them again in Chapter 10, *Printing,* when we talk about color separations, so we won't discuss them here. Just type in a number between 0 and 360 (or 0 to -360 if you think backwards). Once upon a time when you specified a particular angle, the angle would not rotate along with a page printed transversely (see Chapter 10, *Printing,*). This caused much consternation for people using coarse screens. We're happy to say that this is no longer the case, and when you specify an angle you get that angle no matter how you print it.

Pattern. Pattern here refers to the spot shape. You have five shapes to choose from (see Figure 8-17).

- Dot pattern. This is the round spot which you see in almost all PostScript output. At low tint values it's a round black spot which gets larger until nearly 50 percent, when it converts to a square, then inverts to a progressively smaller white spot for higher tint levels.

- Line pattern. Straight-line screens seem to go in and out of fashion, but they're always good for waking up your audience and, if you use too low a line screen, making eyeballs fall out. The line is thick at high tint values and thin for low values.

- Ellipse pattern. No, this is not a traditional elliptical spot. Printers have used elliptical spots for years and customers have grown accustomed to asking for them by this name, even though the shape of the spot is more of a rounded-corner diamond. The spot which QuarkXPress creates is an oval. We haven't found any good use for this.

- Square pattern. Here's another funky special effect spot which may come in handy some day. Each of the spots is square; low tint values are little squares, high values are big squares. Try some really coarse screen frequencies for this one.

Figure 8-17

Various halftone spot shapes (patterns)

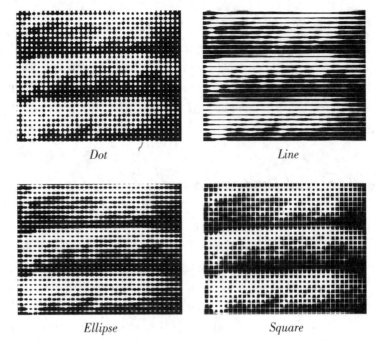

Dot   *Line*

Ellipse   *Square*

- Ordered Dither pattern. This spot shape is actually an attempt to go beyond traditional halftoning. It's more of a dither pattern optimized for printing on 300-dpi laser printers. Because the dithered pattern adjusts to the resolution of the laser printer, you shouldn't use this if you're planning on printing to an imagesetter (you'd get a dither at over 1,000 dots per inch, which could not be reproduced). The Ordered Dither pattern is also not optimal for offset printing. When should you use this? QuarkXPress maintains that you should use it when you are printing to a QuickDraw (non-PostScript) laser printer for making multiple copies on a photocopier. Don't even bother if you have a Post-Script printer; it looks terrible. Well, we guess it's nice to have the option.

Display Halftoning option. In most programs on the Macintosh, you cannot see the halftoning settings you choose until you print out a page. However, QuarkXPress can display a representation of the halftone if you click on the Display Halftoning check box. How well it displays the halftone type depends primarily on the resolution of your screen. You almost never need this to be turned on, unless you're working with low screen frequencies for special effects. Once again, it's sometimes nice just to have the option.

Many Colorful Shades of Gray

We've taken a pretty good look at the options you have for working with images in your QuarkXPress documents, from rotating them to changing their halftone spot shape. Next we go to the world of color and discuss how to bring color onto your pages. Finally, we'll move on to what is perhaps the culmination of all we have learned in this book: printing our documents out.

CHAPTER 9

COLOR

ook around you. Unless you're fully color-blind, everything around you has color. It's not surprising that people have wanted to work with color in their documents since...well, since people were creating documents! What *is* surprising is how complicated working with color can be, especially with all this computer equipment that's supposed to make life easy for us.

The complicated issues in desktop color range from specifying the color you want, to getting that color to print out on either a color or—more likely—a black-and-white laser printer, to producing separated films ready for offset printing. Desktop color has come a long way in the last year, and at the time of this writing, it's finally becoming satisfactory for a production environment. In another year, everything may have changed and achieving quality color from your Macintosh may be as easy as turning the computer on; but for now, we have some work cut out for us.

We begin this chapter with an overview of some basic theories of color, including the various color models (ways in which you specify color on the computer). This leads us into the color components of QuarkXPress's feature set, including building a color palette and building traps for better print quality. Although we discuss the fundamentals of color separation here, we'll cover the area of actually generating color separations of your documents later, in Chapter 10, *Printing*.

Welcome to the wild and weird world of color!

What You See and What You Get

Before we even begin talking desktop color, it's important for you to know that the color you see on the screen is almost never what you'll get out of your color printer or slide recorder, much less what you can expect to see off a printing press. Why? The primary reason is the difference in medium. Colors are displayed on the screen by lighting up phosphors, which emit colored light, which then enters your eyes. This is significantly different from colored printed material, which depends on other light sources to reflect off of it into your eyes. If you use a different method of showing color, you'll see different colors.

Pantone colors are a great example of this: take a Pantone swatch book and pick a color. Hold that color up to the screen next to QuarkXPress's Pantone color simulation. Chances are it'll be a totally different color. Even color proofs created from your final film aren't completely reliable (though they're the best predictor you can hope for). What comes off press may look different.

Another reason for the difference in color correspondence is that representing four process color plates with three (red, green, and blue) colors just doesn't work. The eye sees and processes the two differently.

Want more reasons? Okay, how about the monitors and imaging devices themselves. Take a color document on your color Macintosh and bring it to someone else's computer; it almost undoubtedly looks different, especially if the monitor is a different brand. Take that a step farther and image the document using a high-end slide recorder: the device uses light, just like your monitor, but the colors you get off it are very different from what you see on your computer.

Some monitors are better than others at displaying certain colors. And a monitor with a 24-bit color card is probably one step more accurate than an 8-bit video card. Some companies such as Radius sell monitor calibration systems to adjust the screen colors so that they'll more closely match your printed output. However, many of the best calibration systems are cost-prohibitive for most people.

Whatever you use, remember that what you see is *rarely* what you get.

The solution to all this uncertainty is to specify your colors from a swatch book. Look at the book, see what color you want, and spec it. If possible, create your own swatch book, and print it on whatever your final output device is—offset press, color printer, slide recorder, whatever. If you're printing process color, spec your colors from a process swatch book. If you're printing PMS color, use a PMS book.

▼ ▼

Tip: Taking a Color Reality Check. Russell Brown, senior art director at Adobe Systems, has some interesting things to say about working in color. To begin with, here are some questions to ask yourself before you consider working in color.

- Do I really want to do my own production?

- Will I save time?

- Will I save money?

- Am I using color as a design solution?

- Am I crazy?

Clearly, the last question is the most relevant one. Jumping into desktop color is like roller skating on the seven hills of San Francisco: if you don't really know what you're doing, it'll get ugly.

▼ ▼

▼ ▼

Tip: Color on Monochrome Monitors. Quark has decided that, for the time being, color should be shown on monochrome screens by its tint value rather than its brightness. What this means is if you specify a 100 percent yellow, you see 100 percent black. When printing, you can set the colors to print as various shades of gray, but on screen it always looks black.

This drives us crazy, as we do much of our work on a Mac SE and a Mac Plus. So while we're creating a document, we often tint every color, and only when we're ready to print do we go back and change to solids.

▼ ▼

Describing Color

In a perfect world you should be able to say, "I want this object to be burnt sienna," and your computer, service bureau, and lithographer should know exactly the color you mean. Outside of picking Crayola crayon colors, however, this just can't be done. Everyone from scientists to artists to computer programmers has been trying for centuries to come up with a general model for specifying and recreating colors. In the past 50 years alone these color models have been created: HSB, NTSC, CMYK, YIQ, CIE, PAL, HSL, RGB, CCIR, RS-170, and HSI, among others. (And we thought that Macintosh graphic file format names were far-out!)

QuarkXPress presently handles four color models, plus one color matching system (we'll describe the difference later): RGB, CMYK, CMY, HSB, and Pantone. Because these color models are intimately connected with printing and other reproduction methods, we'll first discuss the particulars of printing color, then move into each color model in turn.

Spot Versus Process Colors

When dealing with color, either on the desktop or off, you'll need to understand the differences between process or spot color. Both are commonly used in the printing process. Both can give you a wide variety of colors. But they are hardly interchangeable. Depending on your final output device, you may also be dealing with composite colors. Let's look at each of these, one at a time.

Process color. Look at any color magazine or junk mail you've received lately. If you look closely at a color photograph or a tinted color box, you'll probably see lots of little dots making up the color. These are color halftones (see Chapter 8, *Modifying Images,* for further information on halftones) made up of one to four colors: cyan, magenta, yellow, and black. We'll talk about this color model (CMYK) a little later on; what's important here is that you see that many, many colors are being represented by overlapping four basic colors. The eye blends these colors together so that ultimately you see the color you're supposed to.

Cyan, magenta, yellow, and black are the process colors. The method of separating the millions of colors into four is referred to as creating *process color separations.* Each *separation,* or plate, is a piece of film or paper that contains artwork for only one of the colors. Your lithographer can take the four pieces of film, burn metal plates from each of the four pieces, and use those four plates on a four-color press.

Don't get us wrong: process color is not just for full-color photographs or images. If you're printing a four-color job, you can use each of the process colors apart or together to create colored type, rules, or tint blocks on the page. These items appear as solid colors to the untrained eye, but are actually made from "tint builds" of the process colors.

Spot color. If you are printing only a small number of colors (three or fewer), you probably want to use spot colors. The idea behind spot colors is that the printing ink (or light source, if you're going to color slides) is just the right color you want, which makes the need to build a color using the four process colors unnecessary. With spot color for example, if you want some type colored teal blue, you print it on a plate (often called an overlay) which is separate from the black plate. Your lithographer prints that type using a teal blue ink—probably a PMS ink (see "Pantone," below) like PMS 3135 or 211, and then switches to black to print the rest of the job.

Once again, the difference between process and spot colors is that process colors are built using four separate colors printed closely together, while spot colors are printed using just one colored ink (the color you specify). In either case, your lithographer runs the page through the press once for each color's plate, or uses a multicolor press that prints the colors successively on a single pass.

Mixing the two together. There is no reason why you can't use both spot and process colors together in a document, if you've got the budget for a five- or six-color print job. Some lithographers have five- or six-color presses, which can print the four process colors along with one or two spot colors.

Composite color. If your final output is created on a film recorder (slides or transparencies) or a color printer, you may well encounter what we call composite color. Composite color is color which falls between spot colors and process colors. For example, most film recorders print using the RGB format (more on this format a little later on) whether your color is specified as CMYK or RGB or anything else QuarkXPress allows you to do. Similarly, the QMS Color-Script 100 represents both spot and process colors alike using either a pseudo-RGB or a pseudo-CMYK, depending on what type of wax transfer colors you have loaded.

The key here is that the colors you specify are being represented using some color model which you may not have intended. If you know that you are printing on such a device, you should refer to the service bureau and/or the owner's manual for tips on how to work best with that device.

Color Models

Before we jump into how to specify the colors you want, let's talk a bit about each of the color models that QuarkXPress 3.0 handles and what each is good for (see Appendix C for more information on color models in version 3.1).

RGB. Color models are broken down into two classes: additive and subtractive systems. An *additive* color system is counterintuitive to most people: the more color you add to an object, the closer to white you get. In the case of the RGB model, adding 100 percent of red, green, and blue to an area results in pure white. If you have a color television or a color monitor on your computer, you have already had a great deal of experience with the RGB model. These pieces of equipment describe colors by "turning on" red, green, and blue phosphors on the screen. Various colors are created by mixing these three colors together.

- Black: zero percent of all three colors

- Yellow: red + green

- Magenta: red + blue

- Cyan: green + blue

Color TIFF files, such as color scans of natural images, are saved using RGB specs. Most slide recorders image film using this method.

CMY. *Subtractive* colors, on the other hand, become more white as you subtract color from them, and get darker as you add more color. This is analogous to painting on a white piece of paper. CMY is a subtractive color model: the more cyan, magenta, and yellow you add together, the closer to black you get.

The connection between RGB and CMY is interesting: they are exact opposites of each other. In other words, you can take an RGB color and mathematically invert each of the RGB values and get the same color in the CMY model. If this doesn't come intuitively to you (it doesn't to us), don't worry. The theory behind this is much less important than what it implies.

The implication in RGB and CMY having an inverse relation is that colors in either model should be easy to convert. This is true. They are easy to convert. The problem is that the CMY model has few practical applications because cyan, magenta, and yellow don't really add up to make black in the real world. They make a muddy brown. Thus, lithographers over the years have learned that they must add a black element to the printing process to be useful.

CMYK. The color model that results when black is added to the CMY model is called CMYK. And, whereas the RGB is a standard for phosphorous screens, CMYK is the standard in the printing world, and the basis of color separations. It breaks every color down into four colors: cyan, magenta, yellow, and black ("K" is used in the acronym rather than "B" to avoid confusion with "blue"). However, the conversion between RGB and CMYK is nowhere near as precise as one could hope. In fact, different programs use different conversion algorithms, so an RGB color from QuarkXPress prints differently from what it would from another application.

You can describe many colors using this method. The following is how Quark describes a few, to the nearest percent.

- Red: 100 percent magenta, 30 percent yellow

- Green: 77 percent cyan, 100 percent yellow

- Blue: 100 percent cyan, 96 percent magenta

Almost every full-color job that gets printed on paper uses the CMYK process.

HSB. Rather than breaking a color down into subparts, the

HSB model describes a color by its hue, saturation, and brightness. The *hue* is basically its position in a color spectrum, which starts at red, moves through magenta to blue, through green to yellow, and then through orange back to red. The *saturation* of the color can be described as the amount of color in it. Or, conversely, the amount of white in it. A light pink, for example, has a lower saturation than a bright red. The color's *brightness* reflects the amount of black in it. Thus, that same bright red would, with a lower brightness, change from a vibrant red to a dark, dull, reddish-black.

You could also say that mixing a color (hue) with white produces a *tint* (a degree of saturation). Mixing it with black produces a *tone* (a degree of brightness).

HSB is not easy to understand intuitively, especially when it comes to specifying colors. For example, here are the hue values for the same colors specified above.

- Red: 0

- Green: 21,845 (QuarkXPress specifies this as 33.3 percent)

- Blue: 43,690 (QuarkXPress specifies this as 66.7 percent)

You may find HSB speccing useful if you're creating slides on a film recorder or the like, but it's not of much use for print publishing.

Pantone. One of the many subsidiaries of Esselte, the largest graphic design supplier in the world, is Pantone, Inc., whose sole purpose in life (and business) is to continue to develop, maintain, and protect the sanctity of the Pantone Color Matching System (PMS for short).

Printers and designers alike love the PMS system for its great simplicity in communicating color. As a designer, you can look in a Pantone-approved color swatch book, pick a color, then communicate that color's number to your printer.

He or she, in turn, can pull out the Pantone color mixing guidelines, find that color's "recipe," and dutifully create it for you. Almost all spot color printing is done with PMS inks.

Bear in mind that you can simulate many PMS inks using combinations of process inks. Some simulations are better than others. A pale blue is fairly easy to simulate with process inks, for instance; a rich, creamy, slate blue is almost impossible; and you'll never get anything approaching copper or gold with CMYK.

Pantone, knowing a good thing when it sees it, has licensed its color library to Quark so that you can specify PMS colors from within QuarkXPress (notice that there are even process equivalents for the Pantone colors). However, the color you see on the screen may have little correlation to what the actual PMS color is on paper. A computer screen is no substitute for a swatch book (we'll talk more about this later).

There are three problems with PMS color.

- Only certain colors are defined and numbered. If you want a color which is slightly lighter than one described, but not as light as the next lightest color in the Pantone book, you have to tell your lithographer to tweak it.

- Color specification books are never fully accurate or alike. David works with a Pantone book which is almost totally different from his printer's, due mostly to the difference in the age of the books, the ink types, and the paper types the books are printed on.

- We've never met anyone who actually understood the PMS color numbering scheme. For example, PMS 485 and PMS 1795 are very similar, though every number in between is totally different.

On the other hand, some designers use Pantone colors to avoid some pitfalls that process colors create. For example, the Understanding Company's road maps are often designed and printed using one to five different Pantone colors in various tints and combinations. This minimizes both the potential moiré patterning (see Chapter 10, *Printing*) and the possible loss of detail in small colored type.

Remember that the Pantone system is really designed for color matching rather than describing a color abstractly like these other color models do.

▼ ▼

Specifying Color

We've discussed applying colors to objects in previous chapters. Here we'll discuss how to create colors in QuarkXPress over and above the nine which come as default settings.

The Color List

Before you can use a color in QuarkXPress, you have to create it, so it appears in your document's color list. QuarkXPress allows up to 127 different colors on this list, including the six colors which must be present: Cyan, Magenta, Yellow, Black, White, and Registration (we'll talk about this last "color" later in this chapter). You can access this list—and thereby add, delete, and modify colors—by selecting "Color" from the Edit menu.

The Colors dialog box (see Figure 9-1) contains the color list (you can scroll through it if there are more than eight entries), plus several buttons to manipulate the colors. Let's discuss each feature, step by step.

▼ ▼

Tip: Making Your Colors Stick Around. You can alter the default color list—the list with which all new documents open—by adding, deleting, and modifying colors while no document is open. These changes stick around forever, or at least until you either change them again or reinstall QuarkXPress. Changing the color list while a document is still open only

Figure 9-1
The Colors dialog box

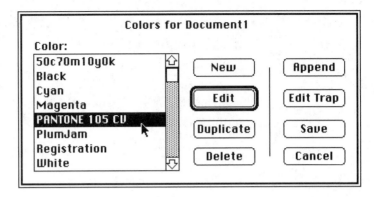

changes that document's color list, and does not affect any other documents.

▼ ▼

New

Clicking on the New button brings you to the Edit Color dialog box (see Figure 9-2). The name that you type in the Name box appears on the Color scroll list and the color lists in other menus throughout the program.

You can call your color anything you want. For example, when David is working with process colors, he usually defines the color he wants using CMYK (see "The Right Way" below on how to do this), then names it something like "10c80m0y20k." It's a bit cryptic at first, but he seems to like it. Keith, on the other hand, likes to just call the color by

Figure 9-2
The Edit Color
dialog box
(this dialog box is
slightly different in
version 3.1)

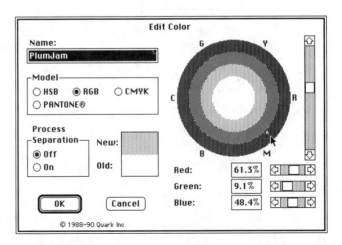

Figure A
This video image was captured using the ColorSnap 32+ XTension. Additional modifications were made using Adobe Photoshop.

DON SELLERS

Figure B
A CMYK TIFF file can be separated directly from QuarkXPress 3.1. Here you can see the final piece, plus each separate plate.

GREG VANDER HOUWEN

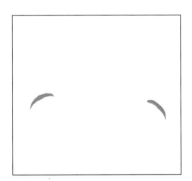

Figure C

A color swatch for
Trumatch colors

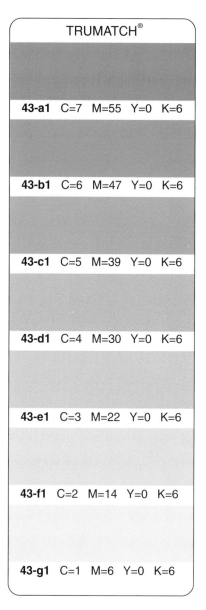

TRUMATCH®

43-a1	C=7	M=55	Y=0	K=6
43-b1	C=6	M=47	Y=0	K=6
43-c1	C=5	M=39	Y=0	K=6
43-d1	C=4	M=30	Y=0	K=6
43-e1	C=3	M=22	Y=0	K=6
43-f1	C=2	M=14	Y=0	K=6
43-g1	C=1	M=6	Y=0	K=6

Figure D

Linear color blend with
an EPS image over it

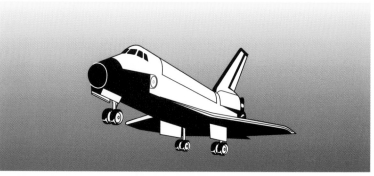

Figure E

Rules are trapped by placing an overprinting thicker and longer line between the rule and the background color.

Page objects such as picture and text boxes are trapped by adding a stroke around them. In this example, a third object was added that has a frame colored a particular trapping color.

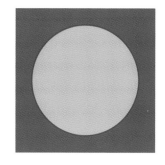

Type is trapped by stroking the character with either the foreground color or the background color. The gray outline shown here has been included for presentation purposes only.

You can trap a picture in a picture box by adding a frame to it. In this example, a black frame is added that overprints both the inside and the outside of the picture box.

Figure F
Duotones created with
Adobe Photoshop 2.0
and separated directly
from QuarkXPress

Figure G
This video image was
shot with a handheld
camera and captured
using the ColorSnap
32+ XTension. Here we
see the original image.

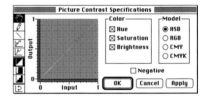

You can enhance
the image by altering
the color contrast
curve in the Picture
Contrast Specifications
dialog box.

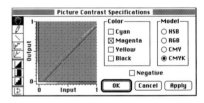

If you make major
modifications to the
contrast curves, the
image becomes
surrealistic.

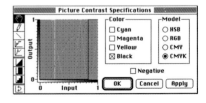

some name; for example, he might have a palette full of "fuchsias," and "royal blues," and so forth.

If you use Keith's way for spot color, you'll want to be sure you know what the corresponding color in your color swatch book is. For example, if you use the name "Copper," you'll want to remember that it represents PMS 876 so that you can communicate this to color identifier your printer. If you use the name "PMS 876," on the other hand, that's what prints out on the edge of the sheet when you pull seps. "Copper" would print out otherwise.

You also have two other elements to decide: the color model to use, and whether the color is a spot color or will be separated into process colors at print time. Each of these choices requires simply pressing a button. Note that you can create a Pantone color—which usually would be specified as a spot color—as a process color, thereby forcing it to separate into four plates at print time. What results is a process simulation of the Pantone color. Similarly, you could create a CMYK color which would print as a spot color on its own plate. The first example has some usefulness; the second has almost none.

You can specify a color in three ways.

The Wrong Way. You can use the mouse to click on an area on the color wheel. Note that the farther towards the center of the circle you go, the less saturated the colors are. In the center, all colors have zero saturation; they're white. You can choose a pink color by clicking in the red area (near the label "R") and then moving the pointer left until you find a saturation level you like. When you have the general hue and level of saturation you want, you can specify the level of brightness by using the scroll bar to the right of the wheel. The lower the box in the scroll bar goes, the darker the image you get (remember, the lower the brightness, the higher the concentration of black).

This is the wrong way because what you see on the screen probably has no relation to what you'll actually get on paper or film. We should add a caveat here, though. We call this method the wrong way only because amateurs and professionals alike are easily fooled into believing that what they see on the screen is what they're going to get off the press. They (we know you wouldn't) use this method to create process-separating colors, but they shouldn't.

You can, however, use this color-picking method for coming up with spot colors, if you're careful. For example, in a job we finished recently, we knew we wanted a greenish background printed with a Pantone color, but we didn't know which one. So we picked a color which looked about right on the screen, and set it to a nonseparating spot color called Kelly Green. We then discussed the color choice with our lithographer, and decided on a Pantone ink. This is a fine way of working with color. But, as we've said, it's too often used wrongly.

The Right Way. You can type in the value for each aspect of the model you're working with. When you are working in RGB, QuarkXPress shows you the percentages of red, green, and blue in the lower-right corner of the dialog box. When working in CMYK, QuarkXPress displays the cyan, magenta, yellow, and black values, and so on. As an alternative to typing in your own percentages in these boxes, or you can use the scroll bars to raise or lower the values.

This is the right way because what you specify is pretty close to what you get. Don't get us wrong: it's not easier this way by any means. You need to have a color swatch book for the color model you're working with, so that you can find the color you want in the swatch book and then type the values in. It's a hassle, but it works.

Another Right Way. Because Pantone colors are based on a matching system, you can also use a swatch book to determine a PMS color. When you have Pantone selected as the color model, you can select the color by either clicking on the color in the Pantone Color Selector box (see Figure 9-3) or by typing the desired PMS number into the Pantone No. box. When you type the number in, QuarkXPress automatically jumps to that color. In fact, if you type "312," it'll jump to that number, then when you type another "5" it'll jump to PMS 3125.

Figure 9-3
The Pantone Color
Selector box

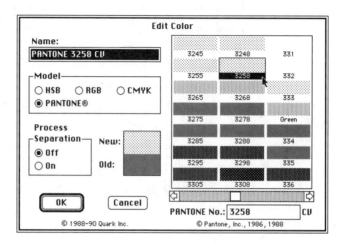

But remember two things when working with Pantone colors. First of all, never trust the screen to give you an accurate representation of the color, and secondly, even your swatch book may be "wrong" due to fading, a bad batch of ink, or some other act of god.

▼ ▼

Tip: Make Your Pantones Look Right. If you're working with spot colors, you can change the color specs for any Pantone color to make it look better on screen or on a color printer. The color specs have no effect when you print the spot overlays; they come out as black, like they should.

▼ ▼

Tip: Multiple Models. We include this tip with a caveat: it's fun and somewhat educational to play with color on the screen, but as we've said repeatedly, it often has little relationship to what you get on final output.

Sometimes you get a color just the way you want it in RGB, except you want a slightly darker tone. At this point you can switch to the HSB model by clicking on the appropriate button, then simply lower the brightness level slightly. The same applies for any combination of models. For example, start with a Pantone color, then get the CMYK values for it by clicking on the CMYK button, alter it, then translate to RGB for further changes. Every color model can be translated into the others.

▼ ▼

The final element in the Edit Color dialog box is the New/Old preview. When you are creating a new color, the lower half of this rectangle remains white (blank), as there was no "old" color to show. When you specify a color using one of the methods described above, the upper rectangle shows what that color looks like. You can specify a color, look at this preview window, then change the specifications, and actually see the change in the way the color looks.

When you have the color the way you like it, clicking OK closes this dialog box and adds your color to the palette.

▼ ▼

Tip: Color Tricks the Eye. Placing a colored object next to a different colored object makes both colors look different from what each would if you just had one color alone. Similarly, a color can look totally different if you place it on a black background rather than on a white one. These facts should influence how you work in two ways. First, when you're selecting colors from a swatch book, isolate the colors from their neighbors. We like to do this by placing a piece of paper with a hole cut out of it in front of a color we're considering (see Figure 9-4). Secondly, after you've created the colors you're going to work with in your document, try them out with each other. You may find that you'll want to go back and edit them in order to create the effect you really want.

▼ ▼

Figure 9-4
High-tech color
isolation tool

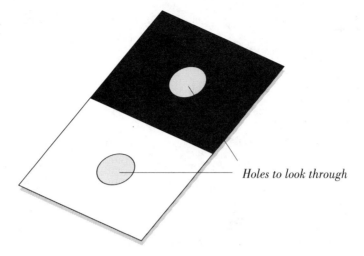

Holes to look through

Edit

Once you have a color on the color list, you can edit it by clicking on that color's name in the Color scroll list, then clicking
Edit (or just double-clicking on the color's name). In the
default color list (the one that's there when you first open
QuarkXPress) you can edit four of the colors: Red, Green,
Blue, and Registration. The other five colors, which include the
four process colors plus White and Black, cannot be edited.
When you edit a color, you see the same Edit Color dialog box
as described above, but with several basic differences.

- The name of the color already appears in the Name box.
  Changing this changes the color's listing in the Color
  scroll list, and retroactively changes the color name of
  each object you painted with the previous name.

- Both the upper and lower halves of the New/Old preview rectangle fill with the color. When you change the
  color specifications using the methods described
  above, only the upper half—the New preview—
  changes. In this way, you can quickly see a representation of the old versus the new color.

- The model is set to the model of the original color. For example, if the color was last modified using CMYK, it appears based on the CMYK model.

- The color's RGB and process color breakdown specifications are displayed.

You can change any of the color's specifications using the same methods described above. When you like the new color, click OK to save these changes to the color palette.

Duplicate

Let's say you love the color blue. We do. You want a new blue color that's really close to the one which is in the color palette, but you don't want to change the one already there. Click on the color Blue, then on "Duplicate." This opens the Edit Color dialog box, just as if you were editing the color, but the name of the color is changed to "Copy of..." In this case—Copy of Blue. As long as you don't change the name of your new color back to its original (or any other color already specified), you can change the specifications, and save it onto the Color scroll list without replacing the original color.

Unfortunately, QuarkXPress won't allow you to replace a color on the Color scroll list with another of the same name. In other words, if you want to replace all instances of Blue with Red, you must go in, edit Blue, and then change its name.

Delete

Is this button self-explanatory enough? Click on the color you most hate, then click "Delete." It's gone. Gone almost forever. Note that you cannot delete the four process colors, or Black, White, or Registration. Also note that when you delete a color that has been already used within your document, QuarkXPress asks you if you really want to delete it. If you say OK, then objects of that color are changed to Black. In version 3.2 when you delete a color that has been used in the document, you are prompted for a replacement color.

Append

When you click on the Append button, QuarkXPress lets you find another QuarkXPress file. Then, when you click on Open, that document's colors are added to your color list. Note that colors with the same names as colors that you already have are not appended. We think this is unfortunate; you should at least have the option.

▼ ▼

Tip: One More Way to Append a Color. If you want just one or two colors from another file, and don't want to append the entire list, you can copy and paste, or drag across an object filled with that color from another document. The color and its specifications come across too, and are added to the Color scroll list.

▼ ▼

Tip: Libraries of Colors. Here's one more way to save your colors so that you can bring them into a new document. Place an object (even just a picture box with a colored background) in a Library file. David has a Library file named "David's Colors" into which he places colors he knows he'll use in various documents, but which he doesn't want to place in the default color list. When he wants a particular color, he'll open the library, pull that color's object out onto the document page, and then delete it. The object is gone, but the color stays in the color list. Within the Library file, you can group your colors into types such as "Warm Colors," "Cool Colors," or "Newsletter Colors" using the Library's labeling feature.

▼ ▼

Edit Trap

Selecting the Edit Trap option in the Colors dialog box brings up the Trap Specifications dialog box. Trapping is a whole other *mishegoss* (Yiddish for "craziness"), so we'll put it off for now and discuss it at some length later in this chapter.

Save

When you are finished with adding, deleting, or editing your colors, you can click on Save to save those changes to your document's color list. Remember that even when you save the changes you can still come back and edit them later. These changes only apply to the document's color list, not to the default color list.

▼ ▼

Tip: Adding Document Colors to the Default List. Frequently you'll find that you want to add a color that you have created in a document to the default color list. Unfortunately, there's no easy way to transfer the color. We suggest Uncle Izzy's Notepad Method: open the color using the Edit button, write down the CMYK or Pantone values on your handy-dandy notepad, close the color, the color list, and all your documents, and then add the color back into the color list with no documents open. Boring procedure. But it works.

▼ ▼

Cancel

Almost every dialog box in QuarkXPress has a Cancel button. This one works the same as all the rest: it cancels your entries without saving any changes.

▼ ▼

Tip: Recovering from Color Boo-boos. We've found that working with the color list can seem intimidating to some people. It always seems as if something could go terribly wrong somehow. What if you delete a color by accident? Or change a color that should remain the same? Or create some really obscure colors, then remember that you don't have a document open and saving them would save the entire list to the default color list? Whatever you do, don't panic. Remember your friendly neighborhood error-catcher buttons: Cancel and Revert.

You can click on Cancel anytime before clicking on Save, and all your changes are...well, cancelled. This goes for both the Color scroll list and the Edit Color dialog box. On the other hand, don't accidently click on this after spending an hour perfecting a color, or else your work is lost. If you have clicked on Save but then decide you want to go back to the way colors looked before, you can select "Revert to Saved" from the file menu. Note that this reverts the entire file, not just the colors, back to the version last saved.

▼ ▼

Special Colors

QuarkXPress has two special colors that aren't really colors. They are "Registration," which we have mentioned above, and "Indeterminate," which we'll talk about soon in "Trapping" below.

Registration

This "noncolor" appears in the Color scroll list and on all color selection lists throughout the menus. When you color an object or type with this, it appears on every color separation plate you print. It's especially nice for job identification marks, and for registration or crop marks (if you are creating your own rather than letting the program do it for you; see Chapter 10, *Printing,* for more information on these special marks).

For example, David often prefers to bypass Quark-XPress's regular crop mark feature and draws his own crop marks in the border around the finished piece. Then he colors these "Registration," and they print out on every piece of film that comes out for that job. Note you can do the same thing by hanging pictures off the edge of the page (see "Tip: Additional Job Information" in Chapter 10, *Printing*).

▼ ▼

Tip: Editing the Registration Color. You can use the Edit feature described earlier to change the on-screen color of "Registration" to anything you like. However, note that you can only use the color wheel to choose colors for "Registration." Also, because "Registration" is originally black, the Edit

Color dialog box appears with the brightness scroll bar down to zero. Just raise the brightness to the level you want, and then change the color.

No matter what color you specify, it'll always print out on every plate. Changing the color changes nothing but the screen representation for that color.

▼ ▼

Tip: Unique Registration Colors. Use a color that is distinctly different from anything else in the document you're creating. That way you always know at a glance what's normal black stuff and what is colored "Registration."

▼ ▼

Indeterminate

When QuarkXPress looks at a selection and finds that either several colors are specified within that selection, or that it's a color picture, it calls this an Indeterminate colored background. This is not something you can change in any way. It's just a definition that the program uses to tell you there are several colors in the selection. In the next section on trapping we'll see the great benefits of the Indeterminate "color."

▼ ▼

Trapping

Nothing is perfect, not even obscenely expensive printing presses. When your print job is flying through those presses, each color being added one at a time, the paper may shift slightly. Depending on the press, this could be an offset of anywhere between .003 and .0625 inches (.2 to 4.5 points). If two colors abut each other on your artwork and this shift occurs, then the two colors may be moved apart slightly, resulting in a white "unprinted" space. It may seem like a $^3/_{1000}$-inch space would look like a small crack in a large sidewalk, but we assure you, it could easily appear to be a chasm. What can you do? Fill in these potential chasms with traps and overprints.

The concept and practice of traps and overprints contain several potential pitfalls for the inexperienced. Up until now, most designers just let their lithographers and strippers handle it. There is a school of thought that says we should still let them handle it. But you know these desktop publishers; they always want to be in control of everything. The problem is that designers weren't trained to do trapping! Let's look carefully at what it's all about.

Overprinting. Picture the letter "Q" colored magenta on a cyan background. Normally, when creating color separations, the cyan plate (we'll talk more about color separations and plates in Chapter 10, *Printing*) has a white "Q" *knocked out* of it, exactly where the magenta "Q" prints. This way the cyan and the magenta don't mix (see Figure 9-5). You can, however, set the magenta to overprint on the cyan. This results in the "Q" not being knocked out of the cyan; the two colors *overprint* in that area—resulting in a purple "Q" on a cyan background.

Figure 9-5
Knocking out and
overprinting

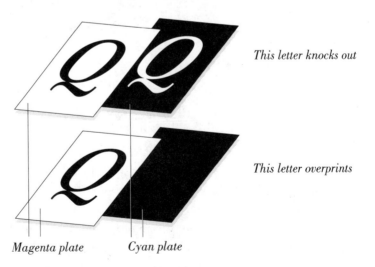

This letter knocks out

This letter overprints

Magenta plate   *Cyan plate*

Trapping. A trap is created by very slightly overprinting two colors right along their borders. Then, if—or when—the paper shifts in the printing press, the space "between" the colors is filled in with the additional trap color (see Figure 9-6). The trap can be created using two methods: choking and spreading. *Choking* refers to the background area getting smaller. *Spreading* refers to the foreground object (in the above example, the "Q") getting slightly larger.

Simple idea, right? But not necessarily a simple process when you're just beginning. Trapping and overprinting are new features with version 3, and we'll cover them in some detail.

Figure 9-6
Trapping two
colored objects

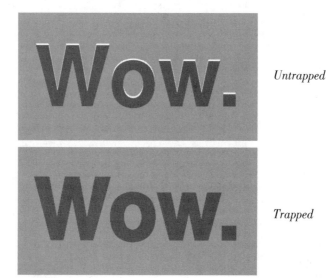

Untrapped

Trapped

Edit Trap

You can control all of QuarkXPress's trapping and overprinting features in the Trap Specifications dialog box, which is found by clicking the Edit Trap button in the Colors dialog box. The key to these features is that you are creating trapping and overprinting parameters for *pairs* of colors: the foreground and the background color. For example, picture some red type on top of a blue area. The blue is the background color; the red is the foreground color.

You can edit the trapping and overprinting parameters for background/foreground pairs by selecting the *foreground* color from the Color scroll list and clicking on "Edit Trap." You are then shown the Trap Specifications dialog box for that color (see Figure 9-7). The list on the left side of the dialog box is the pairing list: each of the colors is a potential background color.

Note that the color Indeterminate is listed. This "color" refers to three cases: a color picture in the background, a background where several different colors are present, or an item only partially covering a background color. If you leave this set to "Automatic," then QuarkXPress 3.0 doesn't include trapping at all in these circumstances (see Appendix C for more information about how version 3.1 handles this).

You can edit one, some, or all foreground/background pairs with three buttons: Automatic, Overprint, and Trap.

Figure 9-7
The Trap Specifications
dialog box

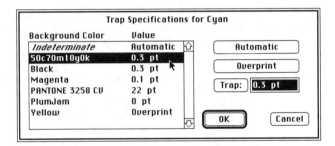

Automatic. When you first open the Trap Specifications dialog box for a color, each of the colors on the background list is set to Automatic trapping. If you change the trapping parameters with the tools described below, you can change a color pair back to "Automatic" by clicking on this Automatic button. "Automatic" refers to the following built-in trapping algorithm.

- Translate each color to its CMYK values.

- Note the black content of each color.

- If the foreground color has less black, then spread it, so that it slightly overlaps the background color.

- If the background color has less black, then choke it, so that it slightly "underlaps" the foreground color.

- If neither color contains black, don't trap.

This algorithm is based on the rule that in trapping, lighter colors should encroach on darker ones. That way the dark element defines the edge, and the lighter color overlapping doesn't affect that definition (see Figure 9-8).

If the background color is black and its shading is set to 95 percent or greater, then the automatic trapping algorithm sets black to fully overprint the color beneath it. In all other situations, though, the amount of trapping that the automatic algorithm uses ranges between 0 and 1 point of trap; the greater the difference between the amount of black in each color, the greater the trap. Again, see Appendix C for more information on how QuarkXPress 3.1 handles this.

Figure 9-8

Traps should go from light colors into dark colors

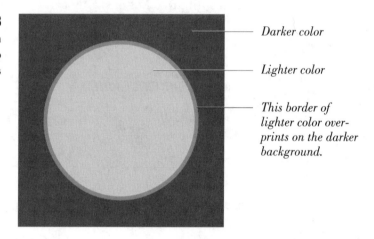

Darker color

Lighter color

This border of lighter color overprints on the darker background.

To get technical for a moment, the way QuarkXPress determines the size of the automatic trap is by dividing the two black values and multiplying that value by one point. For example, if the background color has 80 percent black and the foreground object has 20 percent black, then the background chokes by .4 point (.8 ÷ .2 = .4 × 1 point = .4 point) This is the default, anyway; you can change a lot about QuarkXPress's automatic trapping.

If we're going to get opinionated here, we should tell you that we don't think using the Automatic trapping feature is a good idea. Why? Again, it comes down to control. We don't like the computer making decisions for us on items such as trapping. Trapping is a delicate control and is often determined by what printing press, paper, and ink the lithographer will use. Check with your printer first.

Auto Trap Preferences

If you have QuarkXPress 3.1 or the Freebies 3.0 XTensions package, you can set several auto trap preferences. In the Miscellaneous Preferences dialog box under the Edit menu, you'll find a section labeled "Auto Trap Preferences" (see Figure 9-9). You have two basic choices here: absolute versus proportional, and blackness versus darkness. Let's look at what these obscure and mysterious names mean.

Figure 9-9
Auto Trap Preferences
(Most of these controls
are included in
QuarkXPress 3.1's
Application Pref-
erences dialog box;
see Appendix C)

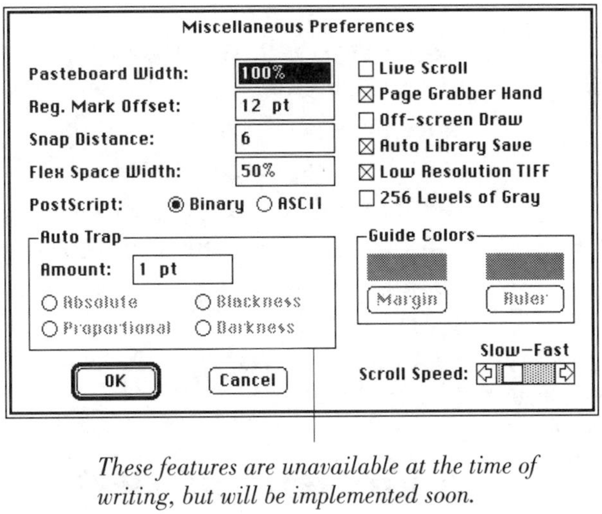

These features are unavailable at the time of writing, but will be implemented soon.

Absolute/Proportional. We discussed the algorithm that Quark-XPress uses to determine how much trap to apply to objects. This is a proportional algorithm. In other words, how large the trap is depends on several items, including the largest potential trap. QuarkXPress's default setting is a 1-point maximum. The trap can be anything from 0 to 1 point. Absolute trapping doesn't take any other factors into account. The trap value you specify is the trap value you get.

Blackness/Darkness. The blackness of a color is the amount of black in it, while the darkness of a color is generally how dark it is. Picture the colors blue and yellow next to each other. The yellow might actually have more black in it and still be lighter (on a darkness spectrum) than the blue.

Darkness is really a matter of how the eye sees a color rather than how the color is made. Because of this human element, it's impossible to make an algorithm that is as good as an eye. However, Quark has done its best, and this option may work better than a Blackness setting in some situations.

All in all, adjusting these settings can generally help when you're working with automatic trapping, but they're still not going to make your document look as good as just using common sense and manual trapping.

▼ ▼

Tip: Trapping Small Type. You can run into trouble when you're using small type, especially serif type, in a color document. Since the type is so fine—especially the serifs—even a small amount of trapping can clog it up. The counters can fill in, and the serifs can get clunky (see Figure 9-10). Bear this in mind when you're setting up your trapping preferences, and when you're specifying colors for type.

Figure 9-10
Serif type can clog up
and the serifs can get
clunky when trapped

Monsieur de Bergerac
Untrapped

Monsieur de Bergerac
Trapped

▼ ▼

Overprint. As we described above, telling QuarkXPress to overprint a color pair has the effect of printing the background color with no knocked-out white space. The foreground color fully overlaps the background color.

There are a few very important times when you'll want to overprint colors. If you overprint red on blue, for instance, you get purple, which is probably not what you intended. The most important of these times, perhaps, is printing fine black lines or type on a colored background. In fact, almost any time you have a black foreground object, it should overprint the background.

To set a color pair to "Overprint," select the background color from the list and click on the Overprint button.

▼ ▼

Tip: An Overprinting Black. There are times when we want black to overprint and times when we don't. To give ourselves the option, we added a color to our color palette called "OverprintBlack," which is a duplicate of the color black. We then edited the trapping specifications for each of the blacks: black would always knock out and sometimes trap, and "Overprint Black" always overprints.

A large black box printing over a multicolored background may look mottled if it overprints, so we'd use black. However, fine black type over the same background will probably look just fine, and we'd use "Overprint Black."

▼ ▼

Tip: Four-color Black. Even better, you can create a much richer black color by defining a separate black in your color palette which contains a bit of other process color in it. The standard rich black that color strippers use is 100 percent black along with 40 percent cyan. Keith sometimes likes to get complicated, though, and adds 20 to 30 percent each of magenta and yellow, too. When a plain black (100 percent K) object overlaps colored objects, it can look mottled. Adding color to your blacks solves the problem.

This trick works not only for achieving richer black off a printing press, but also better blacks from a thermal color printer. However, if the thermal color printer is your final destination, you might boost the additional colors between 50 and 100 percent each.

Note, though, that you should think carefully about how you apply this rich black. A potential problem lurks behind this technique: the cyan can show up from behind the black if (or when) the printing press misregisters. See Appendix C for a workaround to this problem.

▼ ▼

Trap. If you want to set your own specification for a trap, select the background color you want to apply the trap to, then type the amount of trap you want into the space provided. You can select any value between -36 and 36 points, in .001-point increments (why anyone would want a trap over 1 or 2 points is beyond us). A positive value spreads the foreground object (make it slightly larger by drawing a line around it). A negative value leaves the foreground object alone and chokes the background object. Don't select OK yet, though: you must first click the Trap button to activate the change (this last step has been the downfall of many a trapper).

The amount of trap you need depends a great deal on your lithographer. No printersworth their salt would say that their printing presses are dead on and that you don't need to build in any trapping. Chances are that a value between .2 points and 1 point is adequate. Just as a reference, for almost every color job we do, we set all the trap values to .3 points.

One fine point on trapping: if you are familiar with trapping using illustration programs such as FreeHand or Illustrator, you know that when you apply a trapping stroke to an object, your trap is really only one half of that thickness (the stroke falls equally inside and outside the path). If you're in the habit of typing 2 points when you want a 1-point trap, break it when you use QuarkXPress. This program handles the conversion for you.

Color from Outside Sources

Up until now in this chapter we have concentrated our discussion on color items—text, boxes, rules, and so on—which are built entirely in QuarkXPress. But what about bringing color EPS graphics in from other programs? And although we discussed modifying color bitmapped images in Chapter 8, *Modifying Images,* what about being prepared for creating color separations? We'll address these points now.

One area you won't read about here is working with color PICT images. Why? First, because we think they're kludgy (that's pronounced "cloodgy"), and so unreliable that we wouldn't use them for our own QuarkXPress documents (see Chapter 6, *Pictures*, for a slightly longer discussion of this format). Secondly, because the only thing you can really do well with a color PICT image is print it on a color laser printer or film recorder which handles QuickDraw well (or as well as could be expected). You have a little more flexibility with PICT2 bitmapped images, but there's currently no product that can separate them.

Color TIFFs

QuarkXPress 3.0 has no built-in method for creating separations of color bitmapped images (see Appendix C for the good news in version 3.1). It gladly prints a gray-scale representation of the entire picture, but when it comes to pulling it apart, it gives the big "no dice, dog lice." You can, however, separate color bitmapped images by using another application or XTension in conjunction with QuarkXPress.

You have two choices for the process of separating color bitmapped images: preseparating the picture using a program such as Adobe Photoshop, or separating the entire file after you have the image placed with Aldus PrePrint or Pre-Press Technologies' SpectreSeps QX XTension. Although we'll really be talking about color separation in detail in Chapter 10, *Printing*, let's explore these two methods briefly here.

Preseparating. Adobe Photoshop allows you to separate a color bitmapped image and save it to disk in what's called the Desktop Color Separation system (DCS)—called PostScript-5 by some.

When you preseparate color bitmaps, you end up with five files—one for each of the process colors, plus one which includes a pointer to each of those other files and supplies a low-resolution representation of the image. This last file is the one that you import into your QuarkXPress document. When you go to print, QuarkXPress sees the pointers and goes in search of the preseparated files, one at a time.

We searched in vain throughout both Quark's and Adobe's documentation for instructions on this process. Perhaps their feeling was that this was too technical for their readers. Let's look at the process and then you can decide for yourself.

1. With your image opened in Adobe Photoshop, switch the viewing mode to "CMYK" (under the Mode menu).

2. Select "Save As..." from the File menu.

3. Select "EPS" from the File Format menu in the Save As dialog box.

4. Name the file and click OK.

5. Check the Five Separate Files button to on (so it has an X through it). If you don't do this, QuarkXPress is still able to separate the file, but you'll get one enormous EPS file instead of five smaller ones.

6. Click OK.

7. Import the master file into QuarkXPress. The master file is the file that contains the color PICT representation of the four-color image along with the pointers to the other files.

8. Print your separations from QuarkXPress as described in Chapter 10, *Printing*.

That's it. No fuss, no dishes to clean up, nothing. Of course, we've already said that color separation is not as easy as clicking a button. If you're looking for quality color, you had better really know Photoshop well enough to work with its undercolor removal and color correction settings. Remember that QuarkXPress cannot apply any image modification on the EPS files that you import. All of that must be done before importing the picture.

Postseparating. The second method relies on Pre-Press Technologies' SpectreSeps QX XTension to provide the separations for you. You need not do anything special aside from properly importing your pictures and making sure you keep the files around so that SpectreSeps QX can later find them.

Another method of postseparating your QuarkXPress files is through Aldus's PrePrint application. However, there is a caveat: the truth of the matter is that, while Quark has insisted that QuarkXPress outputs PostScript in a format readable by PrePrint (the format is called Open Prepress Interface, or OPI), it really didn't until version 3.1. Appendix C describes this process in detail.

Which of these methods results in the superior separation? Here we get to the aesthetics of color separation, and we wouldn't want to sway your opinion (which is the nice way of saying that, for this once, we're not going to preach our opinions).

Color EPS Files

We've avoided the subject of object-oriented graphic files for several chapters, but now it's time to delve back in. Designers frequently generate color artwork using draw programs such as Adobe Illustrator or Aldus FreeHand, saving it as encapsulated PostScript (EPS). QuarkXPress can not only import files from these programs, but can also generate color separations of them. Once again, the details of generating color separations (or "seps," as they're often called) is covered in Chapter 10, *Printing*. But while we're talking about color on the desktop, we need to cover some general information about using these programs with QuarkXPress. We'll tackle this discussion one color method at a time: process first, and then spot (we're including Pantone colors in the spot color discussion, though you can also create process simulations of Pantone inks).

Process color. QuarkXPress can create color separations of illustrations which contain process colors built in FreeHand or Illustrator. Period. All you have to do is specify your process colors in either application, save them as EPS, and import them into your QuarkXPress document using "Get Picture." Nice and easy.

Note that we say you must use "Get Picture." If you use Option-Copy and Paste to paste an EPS graphic into a picture box, QuarkXPress won't separate it (holding down the Option key while copying from Illustrator or FreeHand copies the graphic in EPS format). In fact, while we're on the subject, we should note that QuarkXPress may not be able to separate color EPS files from applications other than Illustrator and FreeHand. It depends entirely on whether those applications create EPS files according to Adobe's color specifications.

▼ ▼

Tip: Matching EPS and QuarkXPress Tints. For various reasons (including dot gain compensation, which we'll talk about in Chapter 10, *Printing*), QuarkXPress sometimes changes the tint value of gray or colored objects when printing. For example, if you tint some text to 50 percent, it may actually print out at 40 percent. When you import an EPS file that contains tints, those gray levels are not adjusted from within QuarkXPress. A 50 percent gray tint comes out as 50 percent (all things being constant).

Because of this, trying to match the tints of objects created in QuarkXPress and those created elsewhere becomes a tricky proposition. If you find that you have a discrepancy, we suggest the following procedure.

1. While in QuarkXPress, create an object colored the tint you want to use.

2. Print that QuarkXPress document to disk and figure out what tint QuarkXPress is specifying. Chapter 10, *Printing*, tells how to print to disk. Appendix A, *PostScript*, shows how to find the tint value.

3. Use this value as the tint for your EPS picture (modify it from FreeHand or Illustrator or wherever).

4. Now re-import the modified EPS image into QuarkXPress.

The tints now match when you print.

Note that before you go through all this *mishegoss* you should try printing a sample of the two tints (the Quark-XPress-generated object and the EPS object from within QuarkXPress) on your final output machine. This advice comes from personal experience: we have made the mistake of getting all upset that the tints were different on our laser proofs, only to find that they print just fine on the imagesetter.

▼ ▼

Spot color. The key to working with spot colors brought in from either FreeHand or Illustrator is being careful with your naming. Two scenarios should make our point clear to you.

First, let's say we've created a color illustration in Free-Hand using process colors and one spot color, which we called "PlumJam." We exported our illustration as EPS and then imported it into a picture box in our QuarkXPress document. When we print color separations of this file, no PlumJam spot color plate appears (again, more on color separation in Chapter 10, *Printing*). In fact, in this scenario, though we specified the color as a spot color in FreeHand, it separates as a process color in QuarkXPress.

Second scenario: let's say we've created a similar illustration in FreeHand (or Illustrator, for that matter), naming the one spot color the same thing. But this time, after we bring the picture into our QuarkXPress document, we create a new color in our QuarkXPress color palette called—guess what—"PlumJam." Now when we print our separations, the proper spot color plate appears, apart from the process color plates.

Obviously, the trick is to have spot colors with exactly the same names in both the illustration program and Quark-XPress. Whether or not the colors actually are defined the same is irrelevant for color separations to print correctly. The same goes for the Pantone colors. If you use a Pantone color in your Illustrator file, just make sure it's named the same thing in your QuarkXPress file and it'll print fine. Fortunately, all three applications name their Pantone colors the same.

Specifications in EPS Files

QuarkXPress prints exactly what is specified in every EPS file. In fact, QuarkXPress has no way to change them: encapsulated PostScript files are totally self-contained and cannot easily be modified from outside sources. All the halftoning information for objects and bitmapped images, all the trapping and tinting information, and all the color specifications are set in hard packed mud (we like to think that you at least have a chance with hard packed mud; "stone" is a bit too final).

All this means that you must take a little more control into your own hands. You must specify your own trapping from within FreeHand or Illustrator, and make sure that these EPS images contain traps for their surroundings in QuarkXPress documents. Luckily, all overprinting specified in Illustrator or FreeHand (or any other program which handles its color PostScript properly) is handled correctly when generating color separations from QuarkXPress. Conversely, if an object's color is not set to "Overprint," it knocks out any background colors or objects within QuarkXPress.

Note that QuarkXPress's trapping controls do not have any effect on any colors or objects in EPS files. For example, if your EPS picture contains a spot color, PMS 345, and you have set up the equivalent spot color in QuarkXPress as described above, any trapping or overprinting assignments you make to PMS 345 in the Trap Specifications dialog box do not (and actually cannot) make any difference to the EPS file. They do, however, make all the difference to any objects created within QuarkXPress that are colored with PMS 345.

▼ ▼

Deciding to Work in Color

We started this chapter with a comment from Russell Brown, so we think it's only fair to end with what he considers to be the most logical steps to successful color publishing.

1. Complete a black-and-white project with text only.

2. Complete a black-and-white project with text and graphics.

3. Complete a project with several spot colors.

4. Complete a project with process color tints.

5. Finally, attempt the use of color photography.

We couldn't agree more. The Macintosh, no matter how powerful a tool, is still no substitute for experience. Work slowly and carefully, and you will become a raging color pro in time.

P R I N T I N G

Once upon a time, probably somewhere at some university, someone had an idea and named it "the paperless office." People wouldn't be bothered anymore with having to store the thousands (or millions) of pieces of paper which come through their offices each year. Instead, the information would all be placed on some sort of storage medium, easily referenced by computer. It was a magic concept; everyone agreed that it would make life easier, more efficient, and certainly more fun.

Go ahead and ask people who have been involved with electronic publishing for a while if they have seen any sign of the paperless office. As an example, in our offices, the ratio of expended paper to normal refuse is such that we empty our small garbage cans every couple of weeks and the voluminous paper recycling boxes weekly. When it comes right down to it in our business, every piece of work that we do is based, ultimately, on a printed page or an imaged piece of film (which will probably be used to print on paper later).

How do we extract the digitized information on disk to print onto paper? Many people mistake the process as being as easy as clicking on Print and OK. In this chapter we'll discuss what's behind those two actions, and go into some depth on how to get the most efficient and best quality print you can from your document. We'll also touch on tips for working with service bureaus and printers—both the mechanical and the human types.

Before we get into anything too complex, though, let's deal with two simple, yet crucial issues in most people's print jobs: PostScript and fonts.

PostScript

To put it simply, PostScript is what makes desktop publishing with QuarkXPress possible. PostScript is a page-description language—a bunch of commands that PostScript laser printers understand. When you tell QuarkXPress to print a page, it writes a program in PostScript describing the page, and sends that program to the printer. The printer (or imagesetter), which has a PostScript interpreter inside it, interprets the PostScript describing the page, and puts marks on the paper (or film) according to that description.

This chapter is dedicated, in part, to Chuck Geschke, John Warnock, and the other people who created PostScript. And we need to say one thing up front: we're not talking PCL here. We're not talking CORA or even SGML. These also are languages designed for putting marks on paper or film. In this chapter, however, we're talking PostScript.

Actually, we do talk about QuickDraw some, too, since it's integral to the Macintosh system. But mostly we're going to assume you're working with an Adobe PostScript printer. If you're working with a clone interpreter, such as the RIPS, Freedom of Press, or GoScript, we take no responsibility for what comes out on paper (or film, for that matter). The only reason we use clone interpreters is to laugh at the mistakes they make. Things change fast in this business, of course; there may be some good clones out there by the time you read this.

▼ ▼

Fonts

Almost everyone uses QuarkXPress at some point to work with text. It's a given. When you work with text, you work with typefaces. Choosing a particular font was covered in Chapter 4, *Type and Typography*. Printing that font is covered here.

If you don't fully understand how bitmapped and outline fonts work together, we recommend that you go back and look over the beginning of Chapter 4, *Type and Typography*. Working with each of these requires slightly different approaches to the printing process and results in drastically different printed pages. For those of you who kind of remember, but need a reminder, here's a recap.

Bitmapped Versus Outline

When you're working with the Mac and PostScript printers, you need two kinds of fonts—bitmapped screen fonts and outline printer fonts. You install the screen fonts into your System (or load them with Suitcase II or MasterJuggler); the printer fonts you drop into your system folder. The screen fonts display on screen; the printer fonts are used for printing.

Bitmapped fonts are to outline fonts as bitmapped images are to object-oriented images (see Chapter 6, *Pictures*), and what goes for bitmapped images goes for bitmapped fonts. For example, scaling has a direct effect on the resolution of the image, and rotation can cause severe changes in the placement of the bits.

Some bitmapped-only fonts are Chicago, Monaco, New York, Geneva, and San Francisco. In fact, it would be safe to say that almost every typeface named after a city is a bitmapped font. On the Mac desktop when viewing by icon, bitmapped fonts look like a suitcase with an "A" on it.

▼ ▼

Printer Fonts

Bitmapped fonts work in tandem with outline fonts. QuarkXPress automatically replaces the bitmapped screen font with the outline font at print time. But to be able to make this switch, it must be able to find the outline printer font—either in the printer's permanent memory, or in a file on disk.

David thinks of downloading as sending the font file *down* the AppleTalk lines to the printer (especially because his printer sits *down under* his desk). Any way you think of it, the action is the same. First, QuarkXPress tries to find the outline information, which is encapsulated in the printer font file. This file should be in the system folder (or if you're using Suitcase or MasterJuggler, in the same folder as the screen font).

Next, assuming that QuarkXPress can find the printer font, it downloads the font information to the laser printer along with your document. PostScript laser printers have memory allocated for font storage. However, printer models vary in their memory allocations—and thus, the number of fonts they can hold. For example, the old LaserWriters could only keep three or four fonts in memory at a time, while an Apple LaserWriter IINTX can keep around 12 or 13 fonts in memory. Exceeding the amount of memory available causes a PostScript error, flushing your job and restarting the printer. (We talk about PostScript errors later in this chapter.)

Note that you don't need the outline printer fonts in your system folder for any font that is resident in your printer. For example, all PostScript printers come with Times, Helvetica, Courier, and Symbol encoded directly into the printer's memory, so you don't need a printer font to use these typefaces. The Apple LaserWriter II comes with several other fonts, including Palatino, Bookman, and Zapf Chancery. The page that prints out when you start up your printer usually can tell you which fonts are resident.

Printing Ugly

When you have neither a printer font nor a printer-resident font available, QuarkXPress has two options.

- Print using the Courier typeface. This happens when your document contains an EPS file with fonts that you don't have available.

- Print the text using the bitmapped screen font. Quark-XPress prints the text almost exactly as it appears on screen.

We're not sure which of these is uglier. We tend to break into hives at the sight of either. However, perhaps Oscar Wilde said it best when he noted, "For those who like that kind of thing, that is the kind of thing they like."

More Font Downloading

Ordinarily, when your printing job is done, the fonts that you used are flushed out of the printer's memory. Then, next time you print the document, QuarkXPress has to download the fonts all over again. Downloading one time may not seem a long process, but having to download the fonts repeatedly starts to make chess look like a fast sport.

But you don't have to wait. You can do something about your predicament. You can download the fonts yourself.

Manual downloading. You can download a typeface to your printer and make it stay there until you turn the printer off. There are several utilities that let you do this. We like LaserStatus because it's a DA and because it's from CE Software (the makers of some of the world's coolest utilities). However, you can also use Adobe's Font Downloader or Apple's LaserWriter Font Utility.

Downloading a font manually is particularly helpful for typefaces which you use many times throughout the day. If Goudy is your corporate typeface, you can manually download it from one computer at the start of each day. And, as long as no one resets the printer, you can use it to your heart's content from any of the computers hooked up to the network (whether or not they have Goudy's printer font on their hard disks).

Hard disk storage. If you have a hard disk connected to your printer, you have one more option: downloading a printer font to the printer's hard disk. Once you download a font this way, it stays there until you erase it (or drop the hard drive on the ground). Downloading utilities such as Adobe's Font Downloader and Apple's LaserWriter Font Utility have the extra features necessary for this task. If you have some odd sort of printer, you may have to get special software from the manufacturer.

▼ ▼
Choosing a Printer

We're going to leave the choice of lithographers up to you. If it's MinutePress, good luck. If it's a really good printer, just listen to what they tell you and follow obediently. Instead, we want to talk here about what electronic-imaging device you use to output your document.

Clearly, the most important feature of a printer is its imaging resolution. Whereas many high-resolution imagesetters offer a variety of resolutions, most desktop laser printers are only happy when they're printing 300 dots per inch. Table 10-1 lists several printers with their resolutions.

We, like most people, use a desktop laser printer to print proof copies of our QuarkXPress documents before we send them to a service bureau to be imageset onto RC paper or film. Every once in a while we meet someone who prints first to an ImageWriter II or other QuickDraw printer, and then uses a service bureau to get PostScript laser proofs made. If you haven't got a laser printer yourself and are forced to do this, then so be it, but be sure to take some precautions.

Table 10-1

Resolution choices for
some imaging devices

Device	Printing resolutions in dpi
Apple ImageWriter II	72, 144
Desktop laser printers	300
Varityper VT-600	600
Linotronic 300/500	635, 1270, 2540
Compugraphic CG9400	1200, 2400
Linotronic 330/530	1270, 2540, 3386
Agfa Matrix SlideWriter	2000, 4000

The first thing to do is be aware of how your Chooser is set. The Chooser is a DA—part of the Macintosh system software that lets you choose what kind of printer you want to use. You can also specify which printer, if there is more than one on a network. You can access it by selecting "Chooser" from the Apple menu (see Figure 10-1). The icons on the left are the types of printer drivers you have installed in your system folder (printer drivers tell your computer how to drive your printer). When you click on one, the computer asks you for more pertinent information in the rectangle on the right.

Figure 10-1

The Chooser DA

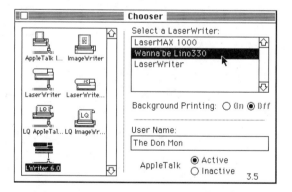

For example, if you click on an ImageWriter icon, you are asked which port the ImageWriter is attached to. If you click on the LaserWriter icon, you'll be asked which LaserWriter you want to use (even if only one printer is attached, you still need to select it by clicking on it before closing the DA). If you have a large AppleTalk network which is split up into zones, you may have to select a zone before selecting a printer in it. The changes take effect as soon as you close the Chooser window.

If you are working with just PostScript laser printers, you hardly need to worry about the Chooser. Just set it once and forget it, except when you want to switch between PostScript printers on the network. However, if you are printing to a QuickDraw printer (for example, an ImageWriter) with the aim to later print to a PostScript printer for final output, see "Tip: Switching Printer Types" below.

▼ ▼

Tip: Switching Printer Types. If you are creating a document on a machine with one type of printer attached to it and printing to a different printer for final output, make sure that you create your document with a printer driver compatible with the final output device. For example, if you are proofing on an ImageWriter II and will later print to a Linotronic imageset-ter, create your entire document with a LaserWriter driver selected in the Chooser (you don't actually have to own the laser printer or have it on hand to use its driver). Then, when you want to print your document, switch to the ImageWriter driver, and don't change your Page Setup dialog box settings. Call it superstition, or what you like, but it has taken care of some major printing problems in the past for us.

▼ ▼

Every time you make a different selection in the Chooser DA, you receive a dialog box noting that you should be sure to check your Page Setup dialog box (see "Page Setup" below). There are several reasons for this, the most important of which is that when you switch printer types, QuarkXPress needs to register that you've done this. It can then calculate the imageable area and other important controls. Otherwise, QuarkXPress sends a set of instructions to the printer which may be totally incorrect.

▼ ▼
Page Setup

Okay: you've got your document finished and you're ready to print. But wait! Don't forget to check the Page Setup dialog box. Some people choose the Page Setup feature by selecting it from the file menu. However, when we're doing demos, we like to look like pros and confuse the audience by just typing Command-Option-P (see Figure 10-2).

Figure 10-2

The Page Setup dialog box

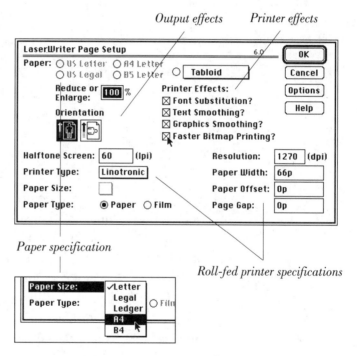

Output effects   Printer effects

Paper specification

Roll-fed printer specifications

The Page Setup dialog box is divided into five areas, although the dialog box itself doesn't delineate them very well. The areas are: paper specifications, printer effects, output effects, roll-fed printer specifications, and options. Let's take a look at each of these in turn.

Paper Specifications

The paper specifications feature is unavailable for printers that are able to print odd-size pages—primarily imagesetters (see "Printer Type" and "Roll-fed Printer Specifications," below). Contrary to popular belief, the paper size that you choose in this area is not necessarily the page size of your document. It is, instead, the *paper* size onto which you want to print your document (see Table 10-2). For example, if your newsletter is set up on a regular 8.5-by-11-inch page, you can have it printed onto as large as a tabloid-size area, or as small as a Number 10 envelope.

Table 10-2

Paper sizes available in the Page Setup dialog box

Name	Inches
US Letter	8.5 by 11
US Legal	8.5 by 14
A4 Letter	8.3 by 11.7
B5 Letter	9.75 by 6.45
Tabloid	11 by 17
A3 Tabloid	11.7 by 16.5
Number 10 Envelope	3.8 by 9.1

The page size you choose determines the printing area. So, if you choose a Number 10 envelope from the pull-down menu (the one that's usually set up for "Tabloid"), but your document is actually larger than an envelope, your page is cropped down to 23 by 54.5 inches. (This also leaves a ⅛-inch border around the edge of the envelope; so no bleeds!) Selecting a page size does not, however, determine where the automatic crop marks are placed (see "Registration Marks," later in this chapter).

Whatever the paper size you choose or the page size of your document (as determined in your Document Setup dialog box; see Chapter 2, *Document Construction*), the upper-left corner of your page is matched to the upper-left corner of the printed page. Confusing? Take a look at Figure 10-3 for a visual explanation of this.

Printer Effects

This field encompasses four basic features, described below.

Figure 10-3
Your printed page size
is determined by the
paper size you select

*If you specify
Number 10 enve-
lope as the paper
size, QuarkXPress
only prints this
much of your page*

All four default to On, but none of them has any conse-
quence unless you're printing to a PostScript printer.

Font Substitution. Remember that New York, Geneva, and
Monaco are not outline fonts, and print out as bitmapped
images on a PostScript printer (read: "ugly"). Checking
"Font Substitution" allows QuarkXPress to substitute Times
Roman for New York, Helvetica for Geneva, and Courier for
Monaco. While these typefaces, as far as graphics snobbery
is concerned, are still not the most beautiful choices of fonts,
they are significantly nicer than the jaggy bitmaps they're
replacing. However, do note that because the character
widths for each font are different, your text almost always
prints with the wrong character widths (see Figure 10-4).

Text Smoothing. If you must use a bitmapped font on a
PostScript laser printer, you may want to enable "Text
Smoothing." (If you're using a non-PostScript printer, see
"Tip: Smoothing on Non-Apple Printers" below). This fea-
ture tells the printer to attempt to smooth out the bitmaps, so

I, sir, it that nose were mine,
I'd have it amputated on the spot. "

Typed in New York

I, sir, if that nose were mine,
I'd have it amputated on the spot!

*Typed in New York, printed
with "Font Substitution" on*

I, sir, if that nose were mine,
I'd have it amputated on the spot!

Typed in Times Roman

they don't look too jagged. We've seen both excellent and awful results with this. It works best with small-size fonts with few "stair-stepped" areas, and it's terrible with fonts that are out of their size ranges (that is, if you have a bitmapped font which was designed for 14 point and you're using it at 39 point). In general, if it looks okay on the screen, it'll look at least decent in the output.

On the other hand, if you want the jaggy look of a bitmapped font, then be sure to disable the Text Smoothing feature. Many designers use the bitmapped quality as a design element, and the Text Smoothing feature makes their artwork look awful.

Graphics Smoothing. As the name would suggest, the Graphics Smoothing feature does to bitmapped graphics what "Font Smoothing" does to bitmapped fonts. The QuarkXPress documentation mentions that this is effective for "some bitmap pictures." What that means is it only works for Paint-type (PNTG) graphics (see Chapter 6, *Pictures*, for more information on this file format). Many people who are creating newsletters or flyers use this feature to smooth out inexpensive Paint-type clip art. There's no doubt that this helps a bit (okay, sometimes more than just a bit), but don't expect to get really smooth curves or diagonals from this method. Also, if there are gray areas or patterns in the art, smoothing can really mess them up.

▼ ▼

Tip: Smoothing on Non-Apple Printers. The four printer effects in this section are actually not QuarkXPress features, but instead functions of Apple's LaserPrep file (more on what this is later in this chapter). As it turns out, Apple programmed these feature so that they would only work on Apple printers (pretty sneaky, huh?). If you work on a non-Apple PostScript printer which is based on the Motorola 68000 chip (most desktop laser printers at this time of writing are), and would like to use these features, you can use ResEdit to change your LaserPrep file. Remember, when you're using ResEdit to work on a file, make a copy of that file first! You never know how badly you can mess up a file by typing the wrong key at the wrong time. When you're in ResEdit, follow the instructions below.

1. Open the LaserPrep file in your system folder by double-clicking on it.

2. Open the POST resources by double-clicking on the word POST.

3. Scroll down the list of POST resources until you get to -8192 (it's usually the last one on the list).

4. Use ResEdit's Find ASCII menu item to search for *{0}ifelse* and replace it with *{2}ifelse*.

5. Close the POST resources and the file (click on OK when it asks you if you want to save your changes).

Now, when you print with either of the smoothing features selected, it should work on your printer. We're not promising beautiful results, but it's nice to have the option.

▼ ▼

Faster Bitmap Printing. We can't be sure, but we think "Faster Bitmap Printing" is a feature that someone at Apple thought would be funny, so Apple included it in their LaserWriter driver (again, more on drivers later). Hey, who wouldn't want their bitmapped images to print faster? Why would anyone ever want to turn this off? In fact, turning it on does seem to speed up printing time from anywhere between .003 and 1 second on every test we conduct. There is slightly more speedup if your bitmapped images have an integral relationship with the printer's resolution (for example, 75-dpi bitmapped images sometimes print better and faster than 72-dpi images, because 75 goes evenly into 300; though sometimes they won't). Whatever the case, the whole thing makes us nervous—always has—and we automatically turn it off when we print.

Output Effects

You have control over five overall document printing effects in this section of the Page Setup dialog box: reduction/enlargement, orientation, halftone screen, printer type, and paper size. Again, we'll cover them one at a time.

Reduce or Enlarge. Changing this number affects the scaling of the document when you print. You can enter any whole number (no decimal points) between 10 and 400 percent. This is especially nice when printing proofs of a larger format document, or when trying to create enormous posters by tiling them (you could create a 4-by-4-foot poster in QuarkXPress and then enlarge it to 400 percent so that when that last page printed out of your printer and you'd tiled all 439 pages together, you'd have a poster 16 feet square). Table 10-3 shows several page-size conversion settings.

Orientation. Remember back to the first day of high school when they had Orientation Day? The idea was to make sure you knew which way you were going while walking around the school grounds. Well, this Orientation is sort of the same,

Table 10-3

Converting page sizes

To print this sized page	Onto this sized page	Reduce/Enlarge to
legal	letter	78%
tabloid	letter	64%
A4	letter	94%
letter	tabloid	128%

but different. The idea is to make sure QuarkXPress knows which way you want your document to go while it's walking through the printer. You have two choices: portrait and landscape. Luckily, this feature has its own icons so that you don't have to think too hard about which to choose. We've included some samples in Figure 10-5 so you can see what each does.

▼ ▼

Tip: Save the RC Trees. When you're printing onto a roll-fed imagesetter (more on these later), you can save film or paper by printing your letter-size pages landscape rather than portrait. That way you only use around 8.5 inches on the roll rather than 11. It may not seem like a great difference, but those three and a half inches really add up when you're printing a long document. For example, a hundred-page file will save an average of 30 inches of film or paper. Printing the pages landscape also makes it easy to cut them apart and stack them. Check with your service bureau to see if they'll give you a discount for the time and energy you've saved them.

▼ ▼

Halftone Screen. We talked at some length about halftones and halftone screens back in Chapter 8, *Modifying Images*. In the Page Setup dialog box, this specification determines the halftone screen frequency of every tint in your document (except for those graphic images which you have set using the Other Screen features, and EPS graphics that have their screen specified internally). This includes gray boxes, tinted type, screened colors, and so on. The default value for the halftone screen (the one that QuarkXPress uses unless you specify something else) is 60 lines per inch. On a 300-dpi

Figure 10-5
Tall versus
Wide Orientation.
The left column
is Tall, the Right
column is Wide.

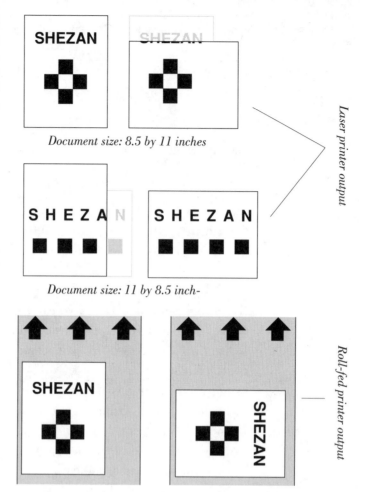

Document size: 8.5 by 11 inches

Document size: 11 by 8.5 inch-

Laser printer output

Roll-fed printer output

Document size: 8.5 by 11 inches

laser printer, this almost always gives you an actual screen frequency of 53 lpi. That's just the way it works. You can type your own setting from 15 to 400 lines per inch. Raising the screen frequency nets you "smoother" grays, but you'll find you have fewer of them to work with.

You should note that changing the screen frequency in one document, saving the document, then opening a new document may retain the original screen frequency. Thus, it is advisable to always check the Page Setup dialog box, just to make sure you're getting a proper halftone screen (what if the last person to use the computer set it to a 15-lpi screen?).

▼ ▼

Tip: A Colorful Shade of Gray. A couple of caveats to this tip, before we really get to it: this is helpful primarily if you're printing proofs which won't be reproduced, and if you don't need a wide spectrum of gray values in your output. That said, we think a great screen frequency to use for printing to a 300-dpi printer is 106. Go ahead and try it. We think you'll like the tone of the gray.

▼ ▼

Printer Type. Specifying the type of printer you'll be printing to with this pop-down menu lets QuarkXPress optimize the way it prints your document. It also determines several other factors in the print job, including activating or deactivating the Roll-fed Printer Specifications features (see below). To explain here what changes are made to each printer would probably not be productive; just pick one and take a leap of faith that it's really doing something. Do note, though, that changing the printer type here does not change the Chooser selection. The type of driver selected in the Chooser should properly reflect the printer selected here.

If the type of printer you're using is not listed on the menu, you can call Quark to see if they have a printer description file for you (these are different from the PPD files that come from Adobe). If your printer is basically the same type of printer as the one listed, go ahead and use the one that's there. For example, David prints to his Ricoh PC 6000/PS using the LaserWriter II selection because both printers are 300-dpi desktop laser printers of comparable speed, and so on. An Agfa Matrix SlideWriter is not comparable to a ImageWriter I, so call Agfa first.

Paper Size. Wait, didn't we already talk about paper size? We did. However, when it comes to printing on a printer that can take odd-size paper (for example, roll-fed printers, tabloid-size printers, and so on), the Paper Size section at the top of the menu is grayed out. In this case, you select a paper size from the Paper Size pull-down menu. Different printers have different page sizes available to them (the choices are determined by information in the printer description files or internally in QuarkXPress). Once again, you don't need to select a paper size that is consistent with your document's size (though the paper size must be larger than your page size). This only determines the imageable (or printable) area.

Roll-fed Printer Specifications

These features apply only to—you guessed it—roll-fed printers. These are imagesetters such as those in the Linotronic, Compugraphic, and Varityper lines (and color printers like the QMS ColorScript), that feed paper and film off rolls rather than one sheet at a time. The five choices available to you when you have a roll-fed printer selected in the Printer Type menu are paper type, resolution, paper width, page gap, and paper offset.

Paper Type. At last a nice, easy specification that you hardly have to think about. Just click on "Paper" or "Film," depending on which you are printing to. What difference does it make? Well, the truth of the matter is that it usually doesn't make any difference whatsoever if you're using the default setup. However, you can use the Printer Calibration XTension to adjust for dot gain for paper and film separately (more on this later in this chapter). QuarkXPress checks "Paper Type" to know which calibration chart to use.

Resolution. Don't change this number with the expectation that it has any major significance to how your job prints. It doesn't determine the resolution at which your job prints. It does, however, determine some important issues when printing bitmapped images. Paint- or 72-dpi PICT-type bitmapped images can be smoothed with Quark's proprietary bitmap smoothing algorithms, which depend on knowing the resolution of the image. Also, bitmapped images that have a very high resolution may print significantly faster when you include the right printer resolution. For example, QuarkXPress internally reduces the resolution of a 600-dpi line art image when it prints to a 300-dpi printer. The printer doesn't need any more than 300 dots per inch anyway, and you save time because QuarkXPress only has to download half as much information (and the PostScript interpreter has to wade through only half as much).

Gray-scale halftones are "resolution reduced" to two times their screen frequency. For example, a gray-scale TIFF really only needs 266 dots per inch when printing at 133 lines per inch. So do yourself a favor and let QuarkXPress help you out: type the correct printer resolution in this field.

Paper Width. The Paper Width specification is not an actual control so much as a description of the device you'll be printing to. A Linotronic 300, for example, can image to 11.7 inches (70p2 or 70 picas, 2 points). A Compugraphic CG9400 images to 14 inches, and a Linotronic 500 images to 17.5 inches. Whatever the case, and whatever the measurement style, just replace the default number with the proper paper width.

David fondly recalls the time when he printed several pages with "Paper Width" set to 11p7 (11 picas, 7 points, or 139 points), instead of 11.7 inches. Everything on each page was cut off at exactly 11p7 from the left edge. The rest of the page was blank. He wasn't happy, and has been studiously monitoring this feature ever since.

Paper Offset. This feature controls the placement of your document on the paper or film. The printer's default paper offset, even when set to zero, is actually enough so that you don't have to worry about changing the value of "Paper Offset" here. For example, on a Linotronic imagesetter, when "Paper Offset" is set to zero inches, the file is printed ¼ inch from the edge. If you want it farther from the edge, change this value.

However, the Paper Offset setting shouldn't exceed the document height subtracted from the paper width (that is, if you have a 10-inch tall document printing on 14-inch paper, your offset certainly should not be more than 4 inches, or else weirdness is sure to ensue).

Page Gap. The last roll-fed printer specification determines the amount of blank space between each page of the document as it prints out on the roll. Initially, this value is zero. We recommend changing this to at least ¼ inch (1p6) so you can cut the pages apart easily. If your document contains spreads, this gap between pages is placed between the spreads (more on printing spreads later), not between each page within the spread.

Options

This last set of Page Setup features is again direct from Apple's LaserWriter driver. You access this "second page" by clicking on the Options button from within the Page Setup dialog box (see Figure 10-6). The hallowed halls of Macintosh folklore may someday be cluttered with speculation on what particular animal is shown on this dialog box's page representation. While the consensus seems to be dog, we prefer the rare moof (half dog, half cow). Whatever the case, this is the animal to watch when it comes to five out of six of features in "Options."

Figure 10-6
The LaserWriter
Options dialog box

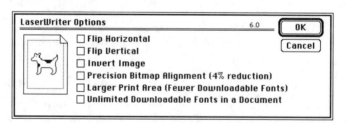

Flip Horizontal/Flip Vertical. We'll meld these two into one description, as they are really doing the same thing. Flipping an image is used primarily for creating from imagesetters either wrong- or right-reading film or film with emulsion side up or down. The differences? Let's look at what happens when you print onto film.

As the film moves through the imagesetter, the side of the film that is coated with a photographically-sensitive emulsion is exposed to a beam of laser light. If you have neither "Flip Horizontal" nor "Flip Vertical" selected, the film is imaged wrong-reading, emulsion down (which is right-reading, emulsion up). This means that when you are holding the film so that the type and graphics look right ("right-reading"), the emulsion of the film is facing you. If you select either "Flip Horizontal" or "Flip Vertical," the film emerges right-reading, emulsion down. To look at it in a different way, this means that when you hold the film with the emulsion away from you, the text and graphics look correct ("right-reading"). See Figure 10-7 for a quick graphical reference.

If you want to know why you'd ever care whether the emulsion is up or down, check with your lithographer (and then talk to a screen printer; you'll see they need different film output for similar but different reasons).

Invert Image. Clicking on this feature inverts the entire page so that everything that is set to 100 percent black becomes 0 percent black (effectively, white). It is the same as selecting the Inversion tool from within the Contrast Specifications dialog box, except that it affects the entire page.

▼ ▼

Tip: Negatives of Low Screen Frequency Halftones. If you are printing halftones or tints at very low screen frequency (anything coarse enough to actually see the spots), you should be aware of an important fact about "Invert Image." This feature does not actually invert pixels from black to white or white to black. It inverts gray levels. For example, a 70 percent black elliptical spot does not actually become a white elliptical dot 70 percent "large," but instead a white elliptical dot 30 percent large. It seems like a minor point, but it has caused enough difficulties around our offices. In cases like these, we now print to film positive and then take it to a stat house to get a negative shot of it.

▼ ▼

Figure 10-7
The effects of "Flip Horizontal" and "FlipVertical"

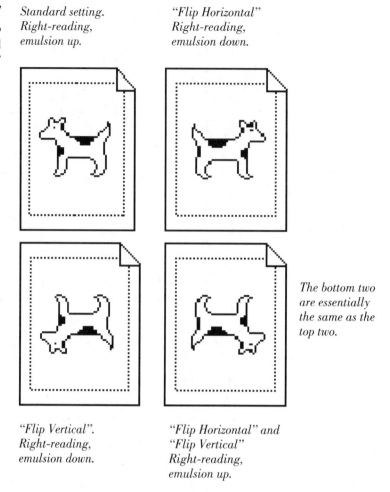

Standard setting.
Right-reading,
emulsion up.

"Flip Horizontal"
Right-reading,
emulsion down.

The bottom two
are essentially
the same as the
top two.

"Flip Vertical".
Right-reading,
emulsion down.

"Flip Horizontal" and
"Flip Vertical"
Right-reading,
emulsion up.

Precision Bitmap Alignment (4% reduction). We talked about printing bitmapped images back in Chapter 6, *Pictures*. The problem, in a nutshell, is that bitmapped images that don't have an integral relationship with the printer's resolution often print out with ugly tiled patterns. This is especially a problem with dithered black-and-white scans. For example, a 300-dpi printer attempting to print a 72-dpi picture has to resolve a discrepancy of .17 points per inch (300 ÷ 72 = 4.17). When you select "Precision Bitmap Alignment," the entire document is scaled down 4 percent, which raises the effective resolution of the bitmapped image to almost 75 dpi, and that image now prints with few or no ugly patterns.

The problem is that now the rest of your document has been scaled down 4 percent. If you're printing a small company newsletter and you don't care how good it looks, this might make no difference to you. Otherwise, it would be unwise to use this feature. Besides, QuarkXPress's ability to perform scaling on images makes the Precision Bitmap Alignment feature obsolete (few of your images are 72 dpi after you've scaled them, so the feature doesn't help anyway). Just reduce the graphic images and leave well enough alone. For more information on integral scaling of bitmapped images, see Chapter 8, *Modifying Images.*

Larger Print Area (Fewer Downloadable Fonts). When you print a page to a desktop laser printer, you are only able to print up to approximately ½ inch from the page edge because of the limited memory within the PostScript printer. The largest chunk of memory is reserved for storing the actual bitmapped image of the page. If you're working with a 300-dpi printer, it has to store around 7.5 million bits of information for each page it prints. The rest of the printer's memory is split up between the amount of space required to process the job (interpret the PostScript data) and to store the needed fonts.

By checking the Larger Print Area box, you tell Quark-XPress to alter the memory allocation slightly, giving a bit more memory to the imageable area and a bit less to the font area. You can then print out to the very minimum ¼-inch border, but you have less room to store your downloadable fonts, so the number of downloadable fonts you can use on a page is reduced. In other words, a page which may print fine without the Larger Print Area box checked may now cause an overload in printer memory and a PostScript error.

Unlimited Downloadable Fonts in a Document. Checking this feature is a last resort when you really have too many fonts on a page to print it successfully. The issue here is time. Normally, QuarkXPress downloads all the fonts it needs for a job as it needs them. If the printer's memory runs out, then it runs out, and you get a PostScript error telling you that you can't print the job.

If you have the Unlimited Downloadable Fonts in a Document feature enabled, QuarkXPress downloads the font when it needs it, then flushes it out of printer memory. Next time the document needs the font, QuarkXPress downloads it again. The problem is, that might be 10 times on a single page, making your job print very slowly. So, while you gain the ability to print as many fonts as you want, you pay a hefty price in printing time.

Also, just to be precise, it's not QuarkXPress that is using such a slow method here; it's the Apple LaserWriter driver. Well, someday someone will build some intelligence into these things.

▼▼▼

Printing

Once you've got the proper values specified in the Page Setup dialog box, you can move on to the actual Print dialog box, again found under the File menu (see Figure 10-8). Here you are confronted with even more buttons, controls, and special features designed to tweak your print job to the point of perfection.

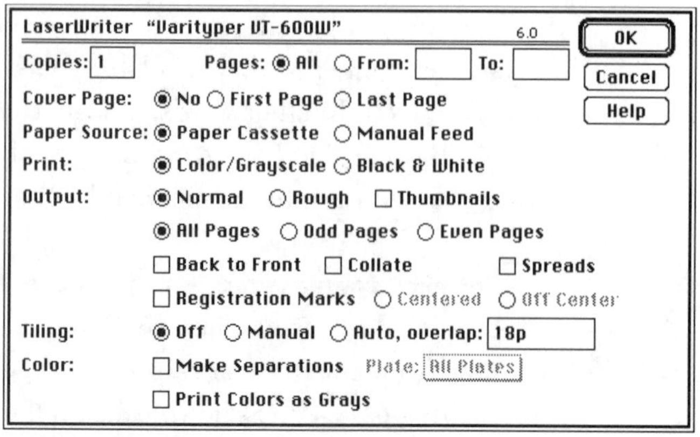

Figure 10-8
The Print dialog box
(This dialog box
may look different,
depending on
which QuarkXPress
version or Laserwriter
driver you have.)

In this section we'll take the dialog box apart and look at each feature to show how you can use it most effectively.

Print Dialog Box, Part 1

The first four rows in the Print dialog box are pretty standard, and you have seen them before if you've printed from other Macintosh applications. This is because they're actually connected directly to Apple's LaserWriter driver (if you use a different driver, these items may change). Let's look at each item at a time.

Copies. We might as well start with the simplest choice of all. How many copies do you want printed of your document? Let's say you choose to print a multiple-page document, specifying four copies. The first page prints four times, then the second page prints four times, and so on. In other words, you may have a good deal of collating to do later (see "Collate," below).

Pages. You can specify to print all pages in a document, or a range of pages. The values you type in for the From and To range must either be exactly the same as those in your document or be specified as absolutes. That is to say, if your document starts on page 23, you can't type From Page 1; it must be either From Page 23 (or whatever page you want to start from) or From Page +1 (the plus character specifies an absolute page number). Similarly, if you are using page numbering in an alphabet system (such as a, b, c, etc.), or using a prefix (see "Section and Page Numbering Systems" in Chapter 2, *Document Construction*), you have to type these sorts of numbers into the slots.

▼ ▼

Tip: From Beginning or End. If you want to print from the first page to a specified page, you can leave the From field empty in the Print dialog box. Similarly, if you leave the To field empty, QuarkXPress assumes you want to print to the end of the document.

▼ ▼

Cover Page. This feature is usually set to No, and we almost never change it. But then again, we don't work in large workgroups. Each cover sheet includes the name of the person who sent the job—determined by the name set in the Chooser DA—and a date/time stamp, among other information (see Figure 10-9). If you have several (or many) people printing to one printer, using cover sheets can be a real lifesaver. Not only does the cover page act as a label for each print job, but it separates each job so that one page from one document doesn't get mixed up with pages from the next document.

Figure 10-9

A print job's cover page

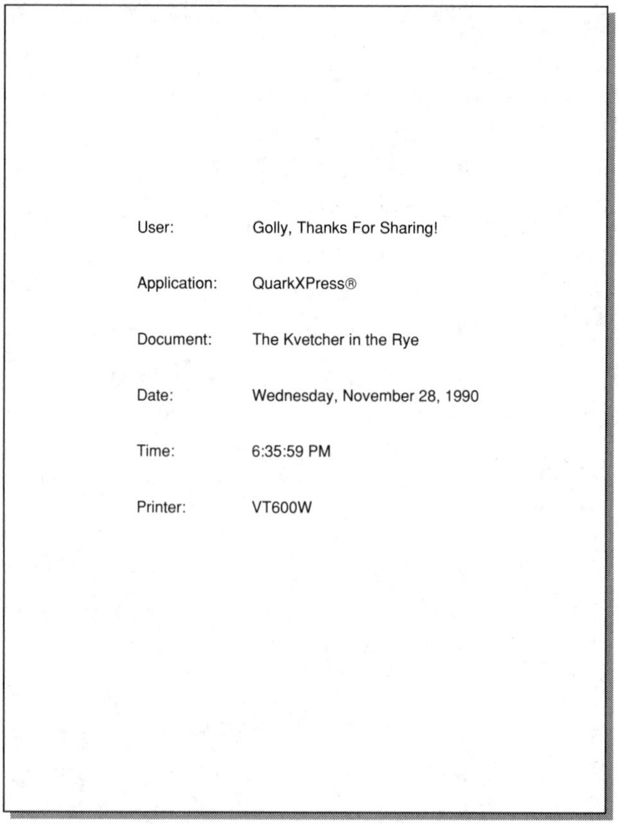

User:	Golly, Thanks For Sharing!
Application:	QuarkXPress®
Document:	The Kvetcher in the Rye
Date:	Wednesday, November 28, 1990
Time:	6:35:59 PM
Printer:	VT600W

Note that you can set the cover page to print either before the first page or after the last page. Take your pick, depending on whether your printer dumps paper face up or face down. But, if you're in a workgroup situation, you probably want everybody to use the same setting to avoid confusion.

On the other hand, why use extra paper if you don't need to? If you're the only person using the printer, and you don't need to document each print cycle, just leave this feature off.

Paper Source. This feature specifies where you would like the printer to get its paper. Normally, you'd have this set to "Paper Cassette." However, if you are using a printer that can take manual feed pages, you may want to select this at various times—for example, when you print onto a single sheet of special stationery or onto an envelope.

When "Manual Feed" is selected, the printer waits for a designated time—usually 30 seconds or a minute—for you to properly place the sheet of paper at the manual feed slot. If you don't place the page in time, the PostScript interpreter returns a time-out error and flushes the rest of the print job.

Print. The last of Apple's standard Print dialog box settings determines the type of printer you are using. Note that this is a relatively new item (at the time of printing), and you will not see it if you are using a LaserWriter driver earlier than version 6.0. You have two choices here.

- Color/Grayscale. Use this when printing to a printer capable of color or gray-scale tones; for example, the QMS ColorScript or the Océ Color Printer. Why Apple determined that this was the default setting, we'll never know (see "Tip: Changing to Black and White," below).

- Black & White. Here's the setting for the rest of us, when printing to a black-and-white printer, such as just about anything you'd ordinarily print to. The difference is often negligible, but we recommend doing it to appease your computer.

▼ ▼

Tip: Changing to Black and White. If you use Apple's LaserWriter driver 6.0.x, you are faced with the unwieldy and unending chore of manually clicking the Black-and-White button every time you want to print to your desktop laser printer. Paul Cozza, author of the SAM antivirus utilities, came up with a patch to the driver to set "Black and White" as the default rather than "Color/Grayscale."

Use Fedit or some other sector editor (Symantec includes a good one in their SUM Toolbox) to search the LaserWriter driver file (in your system folder) for the hexadecimal string below.

377C001700047801

Replace the third 7 with an 8. The hex should look like the string that follows.

377C001800047801

Then save the file back to disk. This will save lots of time and hassles (unless you're one of the unfortunate people who always prints to a color printer). We strongly recommend that you make this change to a copy of the LaserWriter driver. The technique is safe, but you can easily screw the file up if your finger slips at the wrong time.

▼ ▼

Print Dialog Box, Part 2

The second half of the Print dialog box is specific only to QuarkXPress (where the first half was common to all Macintosh programs). We break the discussion of these features down into three areas: output, tiling, and color. Appendix C covers the new printing features in QuarkXPress 3.1.

Output

Output covers the details of how QuarkXPress prints your job: what style, more detailed page selection, what order the pages should print, and whether or not you want registration marks. Let's go over each one in order.

Normal. What can we say about Normal? It's normally how you'd want your normal documents to print out. This is the default setting in the Print dialog box, and the only times you change it are when you want special printing effects like those listed below. You get just what you created, no better, no worse.

Rough. If your document has many illustrations or special frames in it, you may want to print your proof copies with "Rough" selected. This feature automatically replaces each picture in your document with a giant "X," and every complex frame with a double line of the same width (see Figure 10-10). Clearly, the pages print significantly faster than with "Normal."

Figure 10-10
Page printed with
the Rough feature

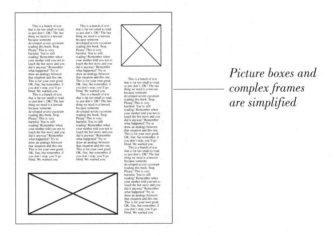

*Picture boxes and
complex frames
are simplified*

Thumbnails. Selecting "Thumbnails" shrinks each page of your document down to 12.5 percent of its size and lines up each page next to each other. It then fits as many as it can onto each printed page. This is great for an overview of your file, though the output you get is usually too small to really give you much of an idea of anything except general page geometry (see "Faster, Larger Thumbnails," below). Note that on PostScript printers, it takes just as long to print this one sheet of many pages as it does to print every page individually, so plan your time accordingly. If you just want to look over the pages, it would probably be faster to see them on screen in Thumbnail view. Remember that you don't have to print all your pages when you select "Thumbnail." We often find it helpful to just print one or two pages at a time to see how they're looking.

▼ ▼

Tip: Faster, Larger Thumbnails. We find the size that "Thumbnails" usually gives us pretty useless; they're just too small! And if we have pictures on the pages, the job takes too long to print. So we use this feature in conjunction with two others: "Rough" and "Reduce or Enlarge." "Rough" is nearby in the Print dialog box. Just make sure this is checked, and your thumbnails print with "Xs" through the pictures, and with simplified frames. The Reduce or Enlarge feature is found in the Page Setup dialog box and is covered above in that section. Change "Enlarge" to 200 percent, and your thumbnails are printed at 24 percent instead of a little over 12 percent. This is just about the right size for most letter-size pages.

▼ ▼

Tip: Two Thumbnails per Page. If you want your thumbnails much larger, you can up the scaling factor to 375 percent and turn the page landscape in the Page Setup dialog box. With this value, you can get two letter- or legal-size pages on one page. You can get two tabloid-size pages on one letter-size landscape page with an enlargement of 300 percent. If your document is made of two-page spreads, then you can print letter- and legal-size pages up to 400 percent (the maximum allowed for enlargement), and tabloid-size pages up to 350 percent.

▼ ▼

All Pages. This is the default position for printing pages from QuarkXPress. It means "all pages that you have selected above." In other words, if you have selected a page range from 23 to 28, having "All Pages" selected won't counteract your desires; it'll just print all those pages.

Odd/Even Pages. These two choices are mutually exclusive. We sometimes joke about this feature when we're working on jobs with several strangely designed pages: "Just print the odd ones, and leave the rest." The only real value we've ever gotten out of this feature lies in the tip below, "Printing Double-sided Documents."

▼ ▼

Tip: Printing Double-sided Documents. You can print double-sided pages with the following technique.

1. Print all the odd-numbered pages using the Odd Pages feature.

2. Place these pages back into the printer, face down.

3. Select "Back to Front" (we discuss this feature later in this chapter).

4. Print all the even pages.

If everything is set up right, the second page should print on the back of the first, and so on.

You can use this same technique to print documents when photocopying onto two sides of a page (if your photocopier handles automatic two-sided copying, then ignore this). Print the odd-numbered pages first, then the even-numbered pages, then ask your local Kinko's person what to do next.

▼ ▼

Back to Front. The problem with talking about printing from QuarkXPress is that each PostScript printer model is slightly (or not-so-slightly) different from the next. For example, when you print a multiple-page document on your laser printer, does the first page come out face up or face down? Some printers do one, some the other, and some give you a choice. If the pages come out face up, you'll love the Back to Front feature. Selecting "Back to Front" prints the last page from your page selection first, then prints "backwards" to the first page. The stack of pages that ends up in the output tray will be in proper order.

Note that you can't select this feature when you are printing spreads or thumbnails (if you want a good brain twister, try to think of how pages would print if you could select these together).

Collate. We said earlier that when you printed multiple copies of your document you would receive X number of the first page, then X number of the second page, and so on, leaving you to manually collate all the copies. You can have QuarkXPress collate the pages for you, instead, so that the full document prints out once, then again, and again, and so on, by selecting the Collate feature.

The problem with "Collate" is that it takes much longer to print out your complete job. This is because the printer cannot "remember" what each page looked like after it goes on to the next page, and so it has to reprocess the entire document for each new copy. How long this takes depends on the number of fonts and pictures you use, among other things. On a long document, the time difference becomes a toss-up: do you take the time to collate the pages yourself or have the printer take the time to process them?

Spreads. This is a powerful but potentially dangerous feature, so it should be used with some care. Selecting "Spreads" from the Print dialog box tells QuarkXPress to print spreads as one full page rather than as two or three pages. For example, printing a two-page, facing-pages spread with registration marks normally results in one page printing with its set of crop marks, then the next page, and so on. When "Spreads" is turned on, both pages abut each other and sit between the same crop marks. This is useful in a number of instances, perhaps the best of which is printing a spread that has text or a graphic across the page boundaries (see Figure 10-11).

However, there's a potential problem lurking behind the Spreads feature. Let's say you're laying out a magazine with a standard facing-page format, except in the middle of the document you have a fold-out, resulting in two three-page spreads. You send the file off to be imageset, specifying that "Spreads" should be checked On. When you get the film or paper back you find everything worked just like you thought it would: two-page spreads spread across two pages, and the two three-page spreads spread all the way across three pages (never mind that this is definitely not how you'd want to print a magazine; it would be a stripping nightmare).

Figure 10-11
Printing spreads

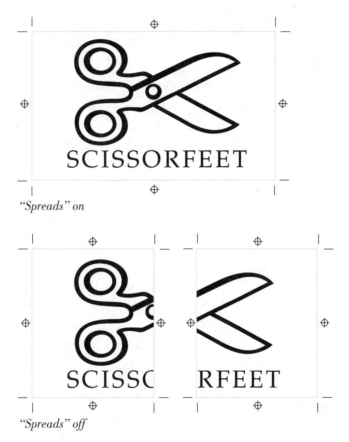

"Spreads" on

"Spreads" off

But when you get your bill, it's hundreds of dollars more than you expected. What happened? What went wrong? This is the dangerous part of printing contiguous spreads. When you specify "Spreads," QuarkXPress tells the roll-fed imagesetter to advance the film the width of the widest spread in the page range specified. So in the example above, each two-page spread actually took three pages of film; hence it was much more expensive.

▼ ▼

Tip: Printing Spreads in a Document. Don't waste paper or film when you print contiguous spreads from a multiple-page document; if for no other reason, it's expensive. If you have a multiple-page spread crossing pages 45 through 47, have your service bureau print the pages from 1 through 44 and 48 through the end as single pages, and then print the three-page spread on a separate pass.

▼ ▼

Tip: Printing for Saddle-stitched Binding. You can use the Spreads feature in conjunction with the Document Layout palette to "strip" together pages which will be double-sided and saddle-stitch bound. We think this is one of the coolest things you can do with the Document Layout feature anyway. Just follow these steps.

1. Create your document as usual, but with no facing pages (see Chapter 1, *Structure and Interface*).

2. When you're finished, use the Document Layout palette to move the last page to the left of the first page. Then the second to last page (which has now become the last page) up to the right of the second page (which is now the third page). Then the next last page to the left of the next single page, and so on.

3. When you're done, every page should be paired with another page, and the last pages in the document should be the middle-most pages. For example, in an 8-page booklet, the final pages would land up being the spread between pages 4 and 5.

4. Make sure the Spreads feature is selected in the Print dialog box when you print the document page.

Note that this method won't work if you are using automatic page numbering (because you're moving pages around; for example, the final page ends up being page 1).

If you're in need of more complex impositions, you might look into Impostrip (see Appendix B, *Resources*).

▼ ▼

Registration Marks. In addition to the text and graphics of the pages themselves, your printer (we're talking about the human lithographer here) needs several pieces of information about your camera-ready work. One fact is where the sides of the printed page are. If you're printing multiple colors, another piece of information your printer needs is how each color plate aligns with the other (we'll talk about creating color separations later in this chapter). Additional job and page information may be helpful also. Selecting the Registration Marks feature answers all of these needs—QuarkXPress places crop marks, registration marks, and page information around your document (see Figure 10-12).

Crop marks specify the page boundaries of your document. They are placed slightly outside each of the four

Figure 10-12
The Registration Marks feature places items around your page

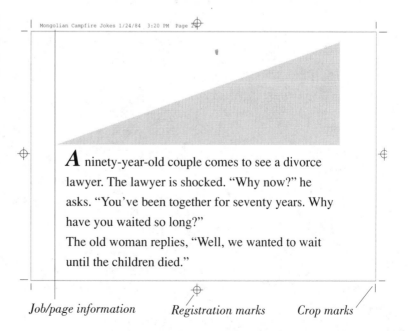

Job/page information   *Registration marks*   *Crop marks*

corners so that when the page is printed and cut to size, they will be cut away.

Registration marks are used primarily for color separation work, but you get them even if you just need crop marks on a one-color job. These are used by your printer's stripper to perfectly align each color plate to the next (see "Tip: Better Registration Marks," below).

The page and job information that is printed in the upper-left corner of the page includes your file name, a page number, and a date and time stamp. If you want more job information than is listed here, see "Tip: Additional Job Information," below.

Centered/Off Center. This feature of the Print dialog box refers to the placement of registration marks, and is only available when you have "Registration Marks" On. With "Centered" On, each registration mark is centered exactly in the center of each side of the printed page. This is where most strippers need it. Others, because of their pin-register systems, need the crop marks slightly off center. Ask your printer.

▼ ▼

Tip: Better Registration Marks. The registration marks that QuarkXPress creates for you are okay, but not great, and certainly not optimal from a stripper's point of view. This is how you can make a "better" registration mark directly in QuarkXPress (you can also make one in FreeHand or Illustrator and bring it in as EPS; see Figure 10-13).

1. Draw a line about ½ inch long. Set it to .25 points thick, with midpoints selected (in the Measurements palette).

2. Use the Step and Repeat feature from the Item menu to create one copy with no horizontal or vertical offset.

3. Make this second line perpendicular to the first by adding or subtracting 90 degrees from the line angle in the Measurements palette. Color the lines "Registration" (see Chapter 9, *Color*).

4. Draw a square picture box about ¼ inch large (hold down the Shift key to maintain a square) and center it over the lines. You could center it by either using the Space/Align feature (see Chapter 1, *Structure and Interface*) or by just aligning the box's handles directly over the lines. We prefer the latter, only because it's quicker for us.

5. Give the box a background color of 100 percent "Registration."

6. Select the two lines and step and repeat both of them once with no offsets. Bring these lines to the front, if they're not already there.

Figure 10-13
A "better"
registration mark

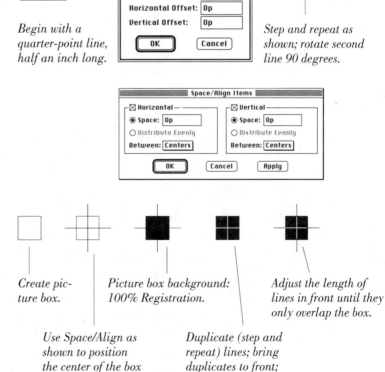

Begin with a quarter-point line, half an inch long.

Step and repeat as shown; rotate second line 90 degrees.

Create picture box.

Picture box background: 100% Registration.

Adjust the length of lines in front until they only overlap the box.

Use Space/Align as shown to position the center of the box directly over the lines' intersection.

Duplicate (step and repeat) lines; bring duplicates to front; color them white.

7. Color the second set of lines white, and shorten them so that they only overlap the box.

The great benefit of this registration mark is that when you print to negatives, your printer can still align black cross hairs on a white background.

Going this route is clearly more work, as you need to build your page larger than necessary, then add your own crop marks and registration marks (and job info, if you want it), but it could be rewarding, depending on your situation.

▼ ▼

Tip: Additional Job Information. The new pasteboard effect in QuarkXPress 3 allows a great deal of flexibility to printing in the area "outside" the crop marks. We discussed bleeds in Chapter 1, *Structure and Interface*, as items which are mostly on the page, but bleed slightly off it. But you can also create items that are mostly off the page, and only slightly on it. This is ideal for adding additional job information on your documents. As long as at least a bit of a picture or text box is on the page, it will be printed along with what's on the page.

Note that the page size that you have specified in the Page Setup dialog box is the limiting factor to how far off the page you can print these notes. Anything outside these boundaries is simply cut off.

▼ ▼

Tiling

What's a person to do with a 36-by-36-inch document? Printing to paper or film is…well, almost impossible (to be thorough we should mention it can be done through the Scitex VIP interface to an ELP printer or on Colossal System's giant 300-dpi electrostatic printer). You can break each page down into smaller chunks that will fit onto letter-size pages. Then you can assemble all the pages together (keep your Scotch tape nearby). This process is called tiling, and is controlled in the Print dialog box. The three options for tiling are Manual, Auto, and Off.

Off. Off is off. No shirt, no shoes, no tiling. QuarkXPress just prints the upper-left corner of the page.

Auto. Selecting the Auto Tiling feature instructs QuarkXPress to decide on how much of your document to fit onto each printed page. You do have some semblance of control here: you can decide how much overlap between pages you would like. Remember that you have a minimum of ¼-inch border around each page (at least on most laser printers), so you'll probably want to set your overlap to at least ½ inch to get a good fit. We generally use a value of 4 picas, just to be safe.

Note that QuarkXPress does not make an intelligent decision as to whether it would be more efficient to print the pages landscape or portrait, so you'll want to be careful to set this appropriately in the Page Setup dialog box (see Figure 10-14).

Manual. Most people seem to overlook the value of "Manual Tiling," skipping over it to "Auto Tiling." But there are times

Figure 10-14
Tiling your document

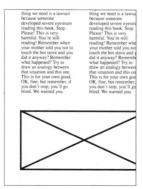

to trust a computer and times not to, and when it comes to breaking up our pages into manageable sizes, we generally prefer to make the choices ourselves.

When "Manual Tiling" is selected, QuarkXPress prints only as much of the page as fits on the page selected, starting at the ruler coordinate 0,0. You can then move the 0,0 coordinate to some other place on the page (see "Rulers" in Chapter 1, *Structure and Interface,* for more on this) and print the page again. In this way you can manually perform the same task as "Auto Tiling" does, or you can be specific about what areas of the page you want to print. Note that if you have a six-page document and print using "Manual Tiling," you receive (for example) the upper-left corner of each of the six pages before the printer stops. If you only want one page or a smaller range of pages, use the From/To specifications at the top of the Print dialog box.

We should point out that where you place the 0,0 point is usually not where QuarkXPress starts printing. It actually tries to give you a little extra room so that the area you selected prints on the imaged area of the printer. For example, if you're printing to a desktop laser printer with "Larger Print Area" turned off, QuarkXPress actually moves your starting point a couple of picas up and to the left. This is another area where QuarkXPress tries to be helpful, but ends up just being confusing and difficult to predict.

▼ ▼

Tip: Printer as Magnifying Glass. You can use "Manual Tiling" and "Enlarge" to blow up a particular area of the page for inspection (when 400 percent magnification on the screen still doesn't suit you). Change the enlargement factor in the Page Setup dialog box to 400 percent (or whatever enlargement you desire), then move the 0,0 point of the rulers to the area which you want to inspect. Now print that page with "Manual Tiling" on. Voilà! A super-size sectional.

▼ ▼

Tip: Assembling Your Tiled Pages. This really has nothing to do with the use of QuarkXPress, but when it comes to assembling tiled pages, we find it invaluable. The idea is simple: when fitting two tiled pages together, use a straight-edge to cut one, then use the other blank border area as a tab.

▼ ▼

Color Separations

We come now to the last area of the Print dialog box, which, as a subject, deserves a whole section of the book to itself—color separation. The concept behind color separation is simple, and QuarkXPress does a pretty good job of making the practice just as easy, but the truth is that this is a very complicated matter which, in the space of this book, we can only touch on briefly. Let's take a look at what color separation is all about, then move on to how QuarkXPress and various third-party products handle the process.

The Basics of Color Separation

A printing press can only print one color at a time. Even five- and six-color presses really only print one color at a time, attempting to give the paper (or whatever) a chance to dry between coats. As we discussed back in Chapter 9, *Color*, those colors are almost always process colors (cyan, magenta, yellow, and black), or they may be a spot color, such as a Pantone ink. Colors that you specify in your QuarkXPress documents may look solid on the screen, but they need to be separated and printed onto individual plates for printing. If you print color separations for a job with only process colors, you output four pieces of film for every page of the document. Adding a spot color adds another plate to the lineup.

Print Colors as Grays

Before we go any farther, we should jump to the last, but certainly not least, item in the Print dialog box. This is the Print Colors as Grays feature. Be sure to click on this if you are proofing your color document on a black-and-white printer.

This prints each color as a shade of gray rather than a solid black or white. You don't have too much control over which shades of gray go with which color, so subtle differences in colors (such as between a pink and a light green) may blend together as one shade of gray, but it's better than printing the file out as a page of solid black (see Figure 10-15).

Figure 10-15
Printing colors
as grays

With "Print Colors as Grays" turned off

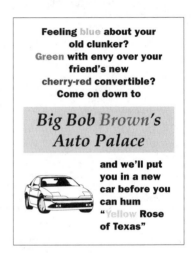

With "Print Colors as Grays" turned on

Another Look at Colors

If you haven't read Chapters 8 and 9, *Modifying Images* and *Color* respectively, we recommend you go back and look them over before getting too in-depth with color separation. But given that you probably have as busy a schedule as we do, here's a quick rundown of the most important concepts.

- Process colors are colors that may look solid on the screen, but will break down into varying tints of cyan, magenta, yellow, and black when printed as separations. We call these separating spot colors.

- Nonseparating spot colors are colors which don't separate at print time. Instead, they print on their own plate. These are typically Pantone (PMS) colors which will be printed with PMS inks.

• Each of the four process colors are printed as halftones (if you don't understand the fundamentals of halftoning, we *really* recommend you look at Chapter 8, *Image Modification*). By overlapping the screened tints, a multitude of colors is created.

Printing Color Separations

Let's start with the most basic method of printing color separations, and then move on to the more complicated concepts.

To print color separations, you check the Make Separations feature in the Print dialog box. This activates the Plates pop-up menu, giving you a choice of which color plates you want to print. By default, it's set to "All Plates," which includes the four process colors plus any nonseparating spot colors you have defined.

Even if you have "All Plates" selected, QuarkXPress will only print plates for the colors that are actually used in your document. If you create custom nonseparating spot colors, but don't actually use them in your document, they appear on the Plates menu. But don't worry: they won't print when you specify "All Plates."

We can't really call it a bug when the documentation goes right ahead and says that it is supposed to work this way, but the fact that QuarkXPress prints a black plate when you select "All Plates" even when you don't have anything black on the page is really annoying, if not downright crazy. But that's the way it goes, and the only way around it is to print each separate plate one at a time, selecting only the plates that actually are necessary.

The Rosette

When the process color plates are laid down on top of each other, the halftones of each color mesh with each other in a subtle way. Each plate's halftone image is printed at a slightly different angle, and possibly at a different screen frequency as well. The result is thousands of tiny rosette patterns (see Figure 10-16). If this process is done correctly, the separate colors blend together to form one smooth, clean color. If the angles or screen frequency are slightly off, or the registration (alignment) of the plates is wrong, then all sorts of chaos can ensue. Both of these problems can come about from errors on the lithographer's part, but more likely they are problems with your imagesetting process.

Figure 10-16
A simulated process
color rosette

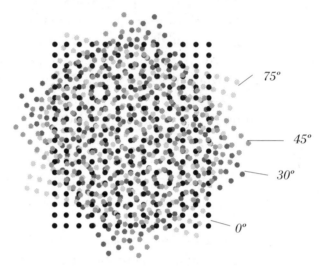

The most common effect of the above problems is a patterning in the color called a *moiré pattern*. There's almost no good way to describe a moiré pattern: it's best to just see a few of them. They might be pretty subtle, but it would behoove you to learn to identify them and learn how to make them go away. Figure 10-17 shows an outlandish example of this patterning caused by the screen frequency and angles being set completely wrong.

QuarkXPress uses the following angle values for process colors: black, 45 degrees; cyan, 75 degrees; magenta, 105 degrees; yellow, 90 degrees. These are pretty standard values, and they create a nice rosette, generally free of moiré patterns. However, note that you may not get what QuarkXPress asks for when it comes to angles and screen frequencies. This is a problem between PostScript and the physical limitations of laser printers. For an in-depth discussion, see Chapter 10 on halftoning in *Real World PostScript.*

Figure 10-17
Moiré patterning

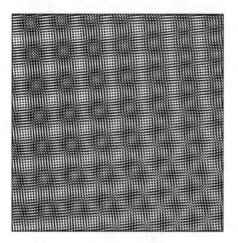

▼ ▼

Tip: Changing the Color Sep Angles. If you don't want to use the angles that QuarkXPress sets up for you, you have two choices: go into the PostScript code and change them yourself (we'll tell you how in Appendix A), or use Quark's Adobe Screen Values XTension. If you have this XTension in the same folder as your copy of QuarkXPress, you have the choice of getting Adobe's suggested screen/angle combinations for your color separations. These are values such as 71.5651 degrees at 94.8683 lines per inch. There is some speculation as to where these numbers came from. We've been told two stories. First, that the line screen/angle combinations were developed using highly advanced mathematical techniques, taking decimal rounding and other variables into consideration. Second, that it was totally trial and error (apparently Adobe's walls were covered with Cromalins at one point). All we can say is that sometimes they help and sometimes they don't. Besides, Adobe has come up with several different releases of these values; who's to say which is better?

▼ ▼

Dot Gain and Printer Calibration

It's easy to confuse the concepts of dot gain and printer calibration. They both have the same effect. To put it simply, both of these have to do with why the tint levels you specify in your files are not always what come out of the imagesetter or off the printing press. For example, you might specify a 40 percent magenta, and your final printed output will look like 60 percent. Don't kick yourself for typing 60 when you meant 40; remember that the problem could be in three places: dot gain, printer calibration, or your glasses might just be dirty. Let's look at each of these carefully and then explore what we can do about them.

Dot gain. Dot gain occurs while your artwork is actually on the press, and ink is flying about. The primary factors are the amount of ink on the press and the type of paper you're printing on (or, to be more specific, your lithographer is printing on). If there's too little ink on the press, your tints may print too lightly. If there's too much ink or if you're printing onto very absorbent paper, such as newsprint, your tints may print much too dark. A good lithographer can control the ink problem, but the issue of what kind of paper you're printing on must be kept in mind while you're outputting your finished artwork.

Printer calibration. Just to be clear, we're talking here about imagesetter calibration. The idea is this: when the imagesetter's density knob is cranked up to high so type looks nice and black, and the film processor's chemicals haven't been flushed and replenished in two weeks, your delicate halftoned color separations are going to print less than optimally. All this equipment is so nifty that we sometimes forget that we're actually dealing with precision instruments designed to be able to produce very high-quality artwork. If you or your service bureau doesn't understand how to take care of the equipment, the artwork suffers.

Glasses. The third possibility listed above is dirty glasses. In this busy world of contact lenses and corrective eye surgery, you have to stop yourself and ask: why am I wearing these things, anyway? Then remember that if your computer explodes, the shattering glass will harmlessly bounce off those plastic lenses. But remember to keep them clean, or no matter what you do about dot gain and printer calibration, the colors will still look muddy.

Adjusting for Dot Gain and Printer Calibration

We live in a less than perfect world, and so we require adjustments to compensate for reality. What exactly can we, as QuarkXPress users, do to ensure high-quality printed output?

First of all, we highly recommend that whoever is doing your imagesetting use a calibration utility such as Kodak's Precision Imagesetter Linearization Software. Proper use of this keeps the output from the imagesetter relatively consistent on a day-to-day basis. You can then be freed to concentrate on your efforts to compensate for the natural dot gain your art experiences while on the press.

The primary method of adjusting for dot gain is Quark's Printer Calibration XTension. We find using this for imagesetter calibration (which it seems to be intended for) useless unless you have an imagesetter inhouse and cannot use a utility like the one described above. However, as a tool to combat dot gain, it's just great. The problem, though, is cost.

To successfully adjust your printed output for the dot gain on various papers, you need to output the sample calibration guide which comes with the QuarkXTras package on a *calibrated* imagesetter (see Figure 10-18). Then—and this is the expensive part—have your lithographer print this guide onto a sample of the stock you plan to use. Take density readings of this printed sample and then adjust QuarkXPress's internal printer settings by following the directions for printer calibration in the QuarkXTras package.

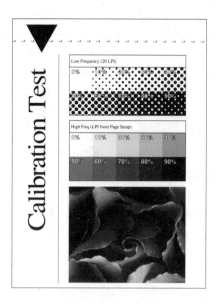

Figure 10-18
The printer
calibration guide

Working with a Service Bureau

The existence of service bureaus with imagesetters has mushroomed over the past five years, and the phenomenon grown from a storefront where you could rent a Mac and print on a laser printer to a specialty service where you can send your files to be imageset on a number of medium- and high-end imagesetters. Alongside this growth has developed standard etiquette and rules spoken only in hushed voices (and usually after the customer has left the shop). In this section we bring these rules out into the open and take you through, step by step, how to best send files to your service bureau, and how to ensure that you'll receive the best quality output from them.

The first thing to remember when dealing with service bureaus is that they don't necessarily know their equipment or what's best for your file any better than you. That's not to say that they are ignorant louts, but we are of the opinion that good service bureaus are few and far between, and you, the customer, have to be careful and know what you're doing.

The principal relationship we talk about in this section is that of you, the customer, sending your QuarkXPress files to

a service bureau to be imageset. We'll talk first about sending the actual QuarkXPress file, and then about sending a
PostScript dump of the file. Many of our suggestions may be
totally wrong for the way your particular service bureau
works, so take what works and leave the rest. Some prefer
PostScript dumps, for instance, while others opt for the
QuarkXPress files themselves.

▼ ▼

Tip: Does Your Service Bureau Have a Densitometer? A densitometer is another piece of expensive equipment that you may
not wish to spring for. Generally, you shouldn't have to; it's
the responsibility of the service bureau to check their output regularly (at least daily) to make sure the density of
their paper or film is correct, and that when you specify a
20 percent tint in your document, you get a 20 percent tint
out on your film (unless you're adjusting for dot gain, as
described above).

If you are working with halftones or tints (and especially
color separations) going to film, make sure your service
bureau owns a *transmission densitometer* (as opposed to a
reflective densitometer), knows how to use it, and does so
frequently, especially when moving between film and paper.

▼ ▼

Tip: Some More Questions for Your Service Bureau. Here is a list of a
few more questions, which you may want to ask when shopping for a service bureau.

- What imagesetters do they have available and what
  resolutions can I imageset at?

- Do they have dedicated equipment just for film, and
  do they calibrate it?

- Do they have an inhouse color proofing system?

- What type of film and processing do they use?

- Do they have a replenishing processor, or do they use
  the same chemicals continually?

- Do they inspect their film before it is sent out?

There are no right or wrong answers to any of these. However, asking the questions not only tells you a lot about the service bureau, but also teaches you a lot about the process they're going through to get you your film or RC paper.

You should make decisions about where to run each print job. For example, if a service bureau doesn't calibrate their equipment, you probably don't want to use them for halftoning or color separation work. If their top resolution is 1270 dpi, you may need to go elsewhere for gray-scale images. You can weigh these items against the cost of the film or paper output, the distance from your office, the friendliness of the staff, and so on.

▼ ▼

Sending Your QuarkXPress File

You have two basic choices in transporting your QuarkXPress document to a service bureau to be imageset: sending the file itself or sending a PostScript dump of the file. Let's be clear right off the bat that we strongly recommend sending a Post-Script dump. Why? Mostly because we want to be in control of our document's printing.

When we send the file off to be printed using someone else's system, we don't know whether their fonts are different, whether the text will reflow, whether they'll forget to set up registration marks, or whether they'll print the file at the wrong screen frequency. By sending them a PostScript dump (see "Sending a PostScript Dump," below) you put yourself in the driver's seat: you can control almost every aspect of the print job.

Sending QuarkXPress Files

Though we prefer to send PostScript dumps, we know of service bureaus that prefer to receive the actual QuarkXPress file. And the truth is that many people don't want to be responsible for checking all the buttons and specifications necessary to create a PostScript dump. If you find yourself in either of these situations, you'll need to know what to do in order to optimize your chances of success. Let's look at the steps you need to take.

Check your fonts. We can't tell you how important it is to keep track of which fonts you've used and where they are on your disk. Make sure that your service bureau has the same screen fonts as you, and has the printer fonts (downloadable fonts) that correspond to each and every font you've used in your document. We sometimes send our own screen fonts along with our job to the service bureau because we believe that sometimes screen fonts that are supposed to be the same simply aren't. Either they've gotten corrupted, or it was a different release, or something. But we'd rather be overcareful than have film come back totally wrong.

Chooser and Page Setup. We mentioned that this was possibly just superstition, but we've always found it helpful to make sure we've got a LaserWriter driver selected in the Chooser and that we've at least checked the Page Setup dialog box once before proceeding to the next step.

Look over your document. Take the extra time to perform a careful perusal of your entire document. If you need to, zoom in to 200 percent and scroll over the page methodically. Many problems with printing occur not with the printing at all, but with that one extra word that slipped onto its own line, or the one image that was "temporarily" set to "Suppress Printout," and then never switched back.

Print a proof. If you can print the document on a desktop laser printer, chances are the file will print at your service bureau. That's not a guarantee, but it's usually a pretty good bet. When you print this proof, go over it, too, with a fine-toothed comb. You might have missed something in the on-screen search.

Include the XPress Data. When you transport your file to the service bureau, don't ever just give them your one file. Always include a copy of the XPress Data file that is in the same folder as QuarkXPress. XPress Data contains information on tracking, kerning, and custom frames that you've used. It's a good idea to send this file even if you haven't used any of these features. You don't need the XPress Data file for QuarkXPress 3.1 (see Appendix C).

Include Your Illustrations. If you have imported TIFF, RIFF, or EPS pictures into your document by using the Get Picture feature, you need to include the original files on the disk with your document. Remember that QuarkXPress only brings in a representation image for the screen and then goes to look for the original at print time. You can use the Picture Usage dialog box to see which graphic images you imported and whether they are missing or present.

The idea is to send your service bureau a folder rather than just a file. Give them everything they could ever think of needing, just in case.

▼ ▼

Tip: Catching All the Fonts and Pictures. This is the age of desktop publishing; who has time to write down all the fonts and pictures that they used, one at a time? We often take snapshots of the screen using Exposure or ImageGrabber, piece them together, and print them out. To tell you the truth, it's often no quicker than just writing them down, but it's usually more fun.

▼ ▼

Tip: Check Your Compatibility. Fonts change, colors change, everything changes except change itself (if you've seen one cliché, you've seen them all). If you're working with a service bureau regularly, you'll want to make sure that their equipment and system setup is compatible with yours. One way of doing this is for you to use the same files. That is, copy every file off their disk onto yours. This is clearly tedious and never-ending. Another way to go is to perform periodic tests; you can use a test sheet. On this sheet should be the fonts you regularly use, a gray percentage bar, some gray-scale images, and perhaps some line art (just for kicks). The idea is to see whether anything changed much between your system and the service bureau's. If fonts come out different, the tints are off, or the density is too light or dark, you can either help them correct the problem or compensate for it yourself.

▼ ▼

Checklists for sending QuarkXPress files. We find checklists invaluable. Not only do they improve your method by encouraging you to do the appropriate task in the right order, they're satisfaction guaranteed every time you can check an item off the list, which in itself, is a boon to flagging spirits as a deadline looms. Below are examples of checklists we use before sending files to a service bureau.

Fonts

- What fonts did you use in your document?

- Does your service bureau have your screen fonts? (If not, send them.)

- Do they have your printer fonts? (If not, send them.)

Printer Type

- Chooser setting to LaserWriter or other appropriate driver?

- "Page Setup" to appropriate printer?

- Printer options checked in Page Setup dialog box? LaserWriter Options "second page" dialog box?

Document Check

- Check for boxes set to "Suppress Printout."

- Check for text box overflows.

- Check for missing or modified pictures (Picture Usage dialog box).

- Check for widows, orphans, loose lines, bad hyphens, and other typographic problems.

Proof

- Print a proof on a laser printer.

- Check it carefully. Is it what you want?

Relevant files

- Did you include the XPress Data file?

- Did you include EPS, TIFF, and RIFF files?

- Did you include the document itself? (Don't laugh, sometimes this is the one thing people *do* forget after a long day.)

Calibration

- Check calibration for gray levels?

Sending a PostScript Dump

It's probably clear that we not only don't trust many service bureaus to do the right thing, but we also don't trust ourselves to always remember everything we need to while standing at the service bureau counter. Because of this, we strongly urge you to use PostScript dumps. A PostScript dump, otherwise known as a print-to-disk, when performed correctly, almost always ensures a better print, and is generally preferred by your service bureau.

In fact, many service bureaus now give big discounts to people who bring in PostScript dumps as opposed to the actual files (our neighborhood service bureau cuts five dollars a page off their single-page price). Instead of having to open your file, make sure all the correct fonts are loaded, check all your settings, and then print it, they can take the PostScript dump and send it directly to their imagesetters.

The biggest difference is that you now have the responsibility for making sure your file is perfect for printing. However, this isn't as difficult as it may seem. Let's go through the steps you need to take to create the perfect PostScript dump. At the end we'll include a checklist that you can copy or recreate for your own use.

System setup. Make sure you have enough memory on your disk to save the PostScript dump. It will automatically be saved in the same folder as your copy of QuarkXPress (well, actually, sometimes it is arbitrarily saved into the system folder or someplace else, but usually it'll go into the QuarkXPress folder). PostScript dumps are often not small. They may take anywhere from 10K to 900K (or larger if you're creating color separations).

Chooser setup. Because you're printing to a PostScript device, you need to have the LaserWriter driver checked in your Chooser. You also need to have "Background Printing" turned off. It doesn't matter whether you have a PostScript printer hooked up or not.

Page setup. Check your Page Setup dialog box. The proper printer should be selected in the Printer Type menu. This determines how large the printed page should be. Be sure to set the halftone screen frequency you want; this is an area where many people screw up. Read over "Page Setup," above, for more details.

Fonts. You must have the screen font loaded for every font you use in your document. One way to check which fonts are in your document is with the Font Usage feature in the Utilities menu. However, this method won't always give you fully accurate results, so it's best to keep a running list of fonts you use. If you don't have the screen font for a document, try to get it; without it you run the risk of having your document printing in Courier. In addition, all your line spacing will be messed up due to a difference in character widths.

▼ ▼

Tip: Telling Fonts Not to Download. When QuarkXPress prints a PostScript file to disk, it attempts to include any outline printer font information it can find. For example, if you used Courier in your file and have the Courier printer font in your system folder, QuarkXPress will include that font's information in the file. However, if your service bureau already has the font, you don't need to include it in your PostScript file.

There are two ways to make sure QuarkXPress doesn't include any printer fonts you have floating about. The first option is to move the printer fonts some place where QuarkXPress can't find them. This means putting them anywhere but in the system folder, the QuarkXPress folder, and the folder where you keep your screen fonts. This is another instance where CE Software's DiskTop seems impossible to live without. With it, you can quickly move these files anywhere you want, then return them after you create the print-to-disk.

However, moving files around is not always the easiest nor quickest task. FontStopper is a DA that lets you pick which fonts you want accessible at any time. When you are ready to create your PostScript dump, you can use FontStopper to make particular printer fonts "disappear." Be aware, though, that it changes the file type and creator for all those downloadable fonts, and when it changes them back it changes them all to ASPF—the Adobe creator. So once you've used FontStopper, you can't tell Adobe from non-Adobe fonts by looking at the creator.

▼ ▼

Pictures. Check your Picture Usage dialog box to see if all the pictures you used in your document are available. This is a suggested step, but is not crucial, because if you don't do this, QuarkXPress checks for you at print time and then gives you the opportunity to find any that are missing.

Print. The most common mistakes in creating PostScript dumps are made in the Print dialog box. Be careful with the buttons and menus here. If you want registration marks you must turn them on here. If you want multiple copies (not likely, for high-resolution output), choose your value here.

But if you only want one copy of each page, make sure that you specify "1" here! We've had friends who've gotten 10 copies accidently back from their service bureau simply because they didn't check this carefully. Expensive mistake.

Be careful, too, with the Tiling features. You may be printing to a roll-fed imagesetter that can handle a full tabloid-size page and if you were printing tiled proof copies earlier, "Manual" or "Auto Tiling" might have been left on.

If you're making color separations, read over the color separation section above.

The F key. When you are finally ready to print the file, click on OK, and immediately press down on the F key on your keyboard. Hold down this key until you see the message "Creating PostScript file." If you start to see messages such as "Preparing Data," you waited too long to press the F key. Cancel and try again. Some people like to press the mouse button down, then press the F key, then let go of the mouse button. This way they ensure that they'll catch the computer in time.

The K key. If you are transferring the PostScript dump to a non-Mac machine before printing, or are printing to a printer that doesn't have Apple's LaserPrep downloaded to it, you should type the K key rather the F key. When you type the K key after clicking OK, QuarkXPress includes Apple's LaserPrep information at the beginning of the file. This information is vital to the way that your PostScript file runs. However, most service bureaus that use Macintosh computers already have the LaserPrep information downloaded to their printers. If you're unsure of your service bureau, ask them.

The PostScript0 File. We mentioned above where the file would be saved to, but not what it would be called. The first time you do a PostScript dump, the file is called PostScript0. The second time, PostScript1, and so on. After PostScript9 the computer starts over, erasing PostScript0 and replacing it, and so on. We recommend that after you create your dump, you immediately change the name to something intelligible,

like "Herbie'sBrochure.ps" (the ".ps" suffix is widely recognized as signifying a PostScript file as opposed to some other
sort of file). We sometimes work with a shareware program
called Laserfix (available through user groups and online
services), that allows us to name the PostScript file anything
and place it anywhere we like, but we've had some compatibility problems and so we are careful when we use it.

▼ ▼

Tip: When Your File Is Too Big. It's easy to make PostScript dumps
that are too big to fit onto a floppy. Add a TIFF or an EPS here
and there, forget to turn off access to printer fonts (see "Tip:
Telling Fonts Not to Download," above), or even just try to
print a large file. Don't fret: there's always a workaround.

First of all, if you're going to work with the Macintosh,
you must own a copy of StuffIt. It's shareware, which means
that you can get it almost anywhere (users group, dealer,
online service), but if you use it more than once, you are
honor-bound to send Raymond Lau his money (about $18).
StuffIt has become a standard on the Macintosh for compressing files. Some TIFF files can compress as much as 90
percent, although most files only compress around 30 to 60
percent. You can also use StuffIt to break up files into several
disks, then join them up again to fit back onto a hard disk.

There are also several other compression packages which
have gotten rave reviews recently, including DiskDoubler,
PackIt III, and StuffIt Deluxe. Sometimes the issue is not
which is better to use, but which program the person on the
receiving side owns.

If you're going to be sending lots of large files to your service bureau, we recommend a removable hard disk, such as
SyQuest or Bernoulli. Make sure the type you get is compatible with what your service bureau uses. These removables
can hold up to 45 or 50 megabytes of information. They're
also great for backing up your data.

When all else fails, you can use the HDBackup program
that ships with Apple's system software. In fact, many people

prefer this method. We don't. But we did hear of someone who did once.

▼ ▼

Checklist for sending PostScript dumps. Your service bureau will appreciate you for this one.

System and Font Setup

- Do you have enough memory on your disk to save the PostScript dump?

- Do you have the proper screen fonts loaded for the fonts that are in your document? EPS files?

- Have you disabled the printer fonts, so that they don't get included in the PS dump?

- Is your XPress Data file available?

Chooser and Page Setup

- Do you have the LaserWriter or other appropriate driver selected in the Chooser?

- Do you have the proper settings in the Page Setup dialog box? LaserWriter Options "second page" dialog box?

Pictures

- Do you have all the EPS, TIFF, and RIFF files available? Check the Picture Usage dialog box.

Print Dialog Box

- Are all the proper settings made? Registration marks? Page range? Color separations?

- Do you want to press the F key or the K key?

Sending the file

- Do you want to compress or segment the file?

- Rename the file to something appropriate.

▼ ▼

Troubleshooting

After all of this, printing should be a breeze, right? Well, we wish it were. Too often, we get phone calls from our service bureaus saying, "Your job wouldn't print." Back in the good old days, a service bureau would offer to fix it for you. Now life has gotten busy for them and they expect you to do the fixing. Here are some tips that we've found to work over the years.

Graphics Look Awful

One of the most common problems with print jobs from QuarkXPress has never had anything to do with QuarkXPress itself. The problem is with the person sending their files. Remember that QuarkXPress does not actually suck in any EPS or TIFF files that you have imported. It only brings in a low-resolution representation for the screen image, and maintains a link with the original file. If that file changes or is missing when QuarkXPress tries to print it, the graphic will look different from what you expected.

Two notes to write on your forehead follow.

- If you're going to send your QuarkXPress document, then send a folder, not a file. The folder should include the document, all EPS and TIFF images you used, and the XPress Data file (see Appendix C if you're using QuarkXPress 3.1). You might even consider sending along your screen fonts.

- If you can, send PostScript print-to-disk files (PS dumps) instead of the document itself. The PostScript dump *does* contain the TIFF and EPS files, as well as all the information QuarkXPress needs from the XPress Data file and screen fonts, and so on.

Memory Problems

QuarkXPress has gotten a bad rep in the past for causing PostScript errors at print time. Almost all of these errors are the result of printer memory problems (called VMerror), and almost all of them can be avoided with a few tricks.

Reset the printer. Our favorite technique for avoiding memory problems is simply to turn the printer off, wait a few seconds, and turn it back on again. This flushes out any extraneous fonts or PostScript functions that are hogging memory. It's sort of like waking up after a good night's sleep, but different.

If you're sending a PostScript dump created with the F key (see "The F key," above), remember to make sure that the LaserPrep file is downloaded first (resetting the printer gets rid of it). A PostScript dump created with the K key includes the LaserPrep information.

Use minimum settings. Using the minimum settings means turning off all the printer options in the Page Setup dialog box, including the LaserWriter Options "second page" dialog box.

Take care in your fonts. If you play around with a lot of different fonts trying to find one you like, you may inadvertently leave remnants of old fonts lying around. For example, a space character may be set to some font that you don't use anyplace else. Nonetheless, QuarkXPress must download that font along with every other font you use. This takes up memory that could be used for something else. Try using the Font Usage dialog box to see which fonts are sitting around in your document. Then purge the ones you don't need.

Use Unlimited Downloadable Fonts. If you must have many fonts on a page, you might want to enable the Unlimited Downloadable Fonts feature in the LaserWriter Options dialog box under Page Setup. See the section on this earlier in the chapter.

Print fewer pages at a time. We have successfully coached long documents out of an imagesetter by printing two to 10 pages at a time rather than trying to get all 500 pages out. This is obviously a hassle, but it's better than not getting the job printed at all. Much of the work can be done early by creating multiple PostScript dumps, then queueing them up on a spooler at the service bureau.

Remove enormous graphics. One of the great promises of desktop publishing was that we could print an entire page out with every graphic and text block perfectly placed. Remember that promises are often broken. Case in point: large graphics (or even small graphics) sometimes choke the printer. These graphics often will print all by themselves, but when placed on a page they become the chicken bone that killed the giant. Yes, using every trick possible you might get the page out, but is it worth the time? Perhaps it's more efficient to just let your printer or stripper handle that graphic. Or, god forbid, just hot wax that puppy and paste it down yourself.

Make sure you're zapped. The first version of QuarkXPress 3.0 that came out had a bug that caused many memory problems in printing. The first Zapper XTension fixed the bug in a jiffy. Like we said back in the Introduction, you should definitely be at subversion 1 or 2 (hold down the Option key while selecting "About QuarkXPress" from the File menu to see what subversion you're at).

PostScript Problems

There are some PostScript problems that aren't memory-related, even though just about everyone at Quark will tell you they don't exist. One is the infamous stackunderflow error. Another is the undefined command error. These are significantly harder to track down and fix. However, here are a few things you can try.

Save as. Logically, resaving your document under a different name doesn't make any sense, but it does work sometimes.

Selective printing. You can try to pinpoint what page element is causing the error by printing only certain parts of the page. For example, turn "Rough" on in the Print dialog box to avoid printing any pictures or complex frames. If the page prints, chances are one of the graphic images is at fault. You can also use "Suppress Printout" to specify a single image not to print.

If the page still doesn't print after printing a rough copy, try taking out a text box at a time, or changing the fonts you used. If you are printing color separations, try printing a single plate at a time.

Shrink the page size. For technical reasons we don't need to get into here, some pages avoid PostScript errors when printed at a smaller size. You can use the Reduce or Enlarge setting in the Page Setup dialog box to print the page at 25 or 50 percent of size. Of course, this will rarely help you in the long run. This method is only for really complex graphics or pages.

Re-import. If the problem turns out to be a graphic you've imported, you might try re-importing it. If the image is in a PICT format, you might have better luck using "Get Picture" rather than using Paste. Even better, convert the PICT into a better format, like TIFF (for bitmaps) or EPS (for object-oriented graphics). Then re-import it.

Check printer type. Make sure you have the correct printer type selected in the Page Setup dialog box. Often, this won't have any effect on your output, but it's worth checking.

md dict. The *md dict* is the collection of procedures in the LaserPrep file. When you print a file directly from within QuarkXPress, Apple's LaserWriter driver checks to see if the md dict is present. If it isn't, it gets downloaded automatically. However, if you're sending PostScript dumps to a printer, you may end up with undefined command errors because QuarkXPress can't find the proper procedure. The easiest way to download the LaserPrep information is to print a single blank page from almost any Macintosh application (*not* Aldus PageMaker).

Big Ugly White Gaps Appear Between Colors

You've output your four-color separations and sent the file off to your lithographer. A few days later you show up for the press check and you see, much to your surprise, big ugly white gaps appearing between each of the colors. What happened? You forgot about traps. It's easy to do, believe us. The remedy? Go read the section on trapping in Chapter 9, *Color*, and redo your negatives.

Wrong Screen Frequency

QuarkXPress can't read your mind nor the mind of your lithographer. If you print your file out with the default halftone screen frequency setting of 60 lines per inch, that's just what you'll get. This is coarse, but fine if you're just going to photocopy your page. However, it looks pretty awful compared to 120 or 133 lines per inch (or higher), which is used in most print jobs. Check with your lithographer for what screen frequency to use, then check your Page Setup dialog box before you print your job. Note that this is not a function that your service bureau can change if you provide a PostScript dump.

Not Enough Space Between Pages

If your pages are printing too close together from a roll-fed printer, you may have to adjust the Page Gap value in the Page Setup dialog box. Note that QuarkXPress prints your document only as wide as it needs to. For example, if your page is 4 by 4 inches, QuarkXPress only tells the imagesetter to print four inches of film. This is a great saving for film or RC paper, but sometimes it's a hassle to handle the output.

Word Spacing or Custom Frames Are Wrong

We don't want to tell you how many times we have heard people say, "After painstakingly setting all the type and kerning pairs and everything, I sent my QuarkXPress file to the service bureau and it came back looking awful!"

The problem? They didn't send their XPress Data file along with their QuarkXPress document. Remember that all the custom kerning pairs, hyphenation exceptions, tracking tables, and complex frames are stored in the XPress Data file, not in your document. In fact, there are other features which are stored directly in your QuarkXPress application, and may never show up on someone else's machine. This is one more good reason to send PostScript print-to-disk files (PS dumps) rather than the document itself.

Fonts Come Out Wrong

Don't forget that you have to have the printer fonts loaded for every font in the document available to QuarkXPress and the printer when you print. That means the fonts you selected, those that were imported, and those that are stuck somewhere in an EPS document. Available means that they should be in your system folder or—if you're using MasterJuggler or Suitcase II—in the same folder as the screen font.

Also, watch out for EPS files nested inside of EPS files nested inside of EPS files. Depending on which application created each EPS file, QuarkXPress may or may not be able to dig deep enough to find every font used.

Registration Problems

Imagine the Rockettes, kicking their legs to chorus line stardom in perfect synchronization. Then imagine the woman at one end having no sense of rhythm, kicking totally out of synch with the others. This is what happens when one color plate is misregistered with the others. When a sheet of paper is rushed through a printing press and four colors speedily applied to it, there is bound to be some misregistration—sometimes up to a point or two. However, you can help matters considerably by making sure that your film is as consistent as possible.

Whenever we are told that a job printed great "except for one plate that was off register," we immediately ask if that plate was run at a different time than the others. The answer is almost always yes. We realize that it's expensive and time-consuming to print four new plates every time you want to make a change to a page, but it is a fact of desktop life that you can almost never get proper registration when you reprint a single plate. Why? The weather, roll stretch, alignment of the stars...all sorts of reasons contribute to this massive hassle.

"Job Finished"

As we said way back at the beginning of the book, don't give up until you get it to work. If you run into difficulty, there is almost always a workaround solution. Working through to that solution almost always teaches a valuable lesson (as grandma used to say, "it builds character"). However, remember that the solution is sometimes to just print the job in pieces and strip them together traditionally. It feels awful when you have to clean off your drafting table and dust off your hot waxer, but efficiency is often the name of the game.

One last note: when the last page comes out of the imagesetter, don't forget to thank your computer, QuarkXPress, the service bureau, and yourself for a job well done.

POSTSCRIPT

Seven years ago, very few people understood how much a new, little-known computer programming language called Post-Script would change the world. The language, developed by Chuck Geschke and John Warnock at Adobe Systems, enabled computer users to place precise graphic images alongside text on a page with an ease not previously known. Those who did recognize the significance of this, including companies such as Apple Computer and Aldus Corporation, were quick to develop the tools to take advantage of PostScript.

Application software such as QuarkXPress, PageMaker, Ready,Set,Go, Illustrator, and FreeHand made use of the power in PostScript, thus creating a "friendly" interface between the user and the computer and laser printer. No longer was a knowledge of arcane computer coding or computer programming essential to imagesetting, for with a click and drag of a mouse, lines, curves, and text could be manipulated and then "magically" output to a printer.

But what if what you want is beyond the capabilities of the application you are using? Your options are limited: go back to pencil and paper, or learn a bit of PostScript. For the latter, we recommend Ross Smith's *Learning PostScript*.

However, you don't actually have to learn to program in order to achieve some powerful effects with PostScript.

Below, we outline several tricks for playing with PostScript and QuarkXPress, including finding out information about your QuarkXPress document and imported EPS images that you can't obtain otherwise, and writing PostScript code directly into your QuarkXPress documents.

▼ ▼

Getting to the PostScript

The first trick to working with QuarkXPress's PostScript is to get it in a readable form. There are two ways to do this: PostScript print-to-disks (dumps) and Save as EPS. We discussed PostScript dumps in Chapter 10, *Printing*. The method is simple: hold down the "F" key immediately after pressing OK in the Print dialog box. You must hold down the key until you see a notice that the computer is creating a PostScript dump.

The computer saves your PostScript file in the same folder as the QuarkXPress application, and names it Post-Script0. Your next dump will be called PostScript1, and so on. The file is plain text, and can be opened with any text editor such as WordPerfect, Microsoft Word, or Vantage.

If you're working with the System 7 LaserWriter driver, you can simply select PostScript File in the Print dialog box instead. When you press OK, the Macintosh lets you name the PostScript file anything you want and place it in any folder on your hard disk.

See Chapter 6, *Pictures*, for a discussion on saving a page as EPS.

What You See

The structure of QuarkXPress's PostScript files is pretty basic. At the top of the file is the header—a set of comments that define the page and the PostScript file. Next comes a long set of procedures that QuarkXPress uses to describe your page (all those words that start with "/xp" are names of procedures).

Then, finally, comes the body of the page description. This section is where you can find all those /xp procedures in action. Let's look at each of these sections in a little more detail.

Header. When you open your PostScript dump in a text editor, the first thing you see is a set of structuring comments.

```
%!PS-Adobe-2.0
%%Title: MyDocument
%%Creator: QuarkXPress®
%%CreationDate: Saturday, March 1, 1972
%%Pages: (atend)
%%BoundingBox: ? ? ? ?
%%PageBoundingBox: 0 0 612 792
%%For: The Human Potential
%%IncludeProcSet: "(AppleDict md)" 70 0
%%EndComments
%%EndProlog
%%BeginDocumentSetup
```

The PostScript interpreter (the computer in the printer that reads and understands QuarkXPress's PostScript) ignores any text after a percent sign (%), so all of these structuring comments are built in to help you or some other program understand what's going on in the file.

For example, the %%BoundingBox comment shows how large the page is, including crop marks and anything else that is being printed. The measurements that follow describe the lower-left and upper-right corners of the page. So, 0 0 612 792 means that the lower-left corner is at coordinate 0,0 and the upper-right corner is at 612,792. All measurements are in points, so this describes an 8.5-by-11-inch page. In the example above, the four question marks show that QuarkXPress has not told the Apple LaserWriter driver how large the page should be.

Procedures. Following the structuring comments come the procedures—the heart of QuarkXPress's page description. These don't do anything by themselves. They're more like mini-recipes that can be called on to carry out certain tasks. For example, there is one procedure for drawing lines, another for placing text on the page, and another for handling bitmapped images.

By changing these procedures, it's possible to alter the way in which your page prints. It is also possible to simply make the page unprintable. PostScript is a rather strict language; you have to make sure you have no typos, that all characters are in their proper case (upper or lower), and that a strict syntax is maintained.

The Body. Following the procedure definitions come the %%EndDocumentSetup and %%Page: ? 1 comments. From here until the end of the file is where the actual work is being done: the text and graphics on your page are included here along with the calls to the /xp procedures.

Here's where you can have the most impact on changing the way your page is printed. You can even add or delete text and graphics at this point (although it's really easier to just add these in QuarkXPress, if you can).

▼ ▼

Tip: Regularizing Lines. If you have a number of thin lines next to each other, some may appear thicker than others on a low-resolution printer (such as a 300-dpi desktop laser printer). If you need them to look the same, insert the following code directly after the header (before the line "md begin").

```
/_R {.25 sub round .25 add} bind def
/_r {transform _R exch _R exch itransform} bind def
/moveto {_r moveto} bind def /lineto {_r lineto} bind def
```

▼ ▼

Tip: Finding the Fonts. Every once in a while we find ourselves with an EPS image on our hands without knowing what fonts are in it. Of course, we need to know the fonts to ensure that we have the printer fonts available for it to print properly.

You can find out what fonts are in most EPS files in two ways. The first way is to open the file itself in a text editor. In Microsoft Word, you have to hold the Shift key down while selecting Open to be able to read the EPSF file type. The fonts are probably listed at the beginning of the file after the structuring comment %%DocumentFonts. If it says "atend," look at the end of the PostScript file.

If you've already printed a QuarkXPress file that includes an EPS image, you can find this same information by searching through the PostScript for the word "EPS." The %%DocumentFonts comments are probably not too far away.

▼ ▼

PostScript Escape Font

If you're a PostScript programmer (or just feel like playing around with some PostScript programming), you must get your hands on the PostScript Escape Font. This tiny font allows you to type PostScript code directly into a Quark-XPress text box. Any text in a text box that is assigned the PostScript Escape font is hidden (invisible). However, when you print the document, the PostScript code you typed (or imported) is included in QuarkXPress's output.

Note that any PostScript you include is sandwiched between a save and a restore (if you don't understand these terms, you shouldn't worry, but you also shouldn't expect your code to print).

▼ ▼

Changing Tints and Fonts

Remember, a PostScript dump from QuarkXPress contains a full description of how the page should print. This means you can search for and change particular items. Normally, you wouldn't need to do this, as QuarkXPress gives you so much flexibility from within the program itself. However, you may need to change a tint value or a typeface here and there. QuarkXPress describes all this information in the document body section, after the header and procedure definitions.

You can change a font within a document by searching and replacing its PostScript name. For example, if you have a sudden emergency at your service bureau and you realize that one headline should be Times Bold rather than Times Roman, you can search through the PostScript dump and replace all instances of "Times Roman" with "Times Bold." Be careful to use a font's PostScript name rather than its screen name. That is, you must use names such as "AvantGarde-DemiOblique" rather than "Avant Garde Bold Italic." If you don't know a font's PostScript name, you can download it to a printer and then use a program such as FontDownloader or LaserStatus to get the names of all the PostScript fonts on the printer.

We feel a bit reticent about telling you how you can change your fonts, because in truth, any changes you make are almost sure to end up looking pretty awful. Why? Because the character widths, kerning information, and other typographic settings may be significantly different from typeface to typeface. If there's any way to change the font from within QuarkXPress rather than in the PostScript dump, do it.

You may, on occasion, want to view and/or change a tint value of an element (text, box, line, etc.). You can do this easily. The difficult part is finding the PostScript definition of the object itself within a long page description. For example, finding a single 50 percent gray box within a full page may take some time. However, if it is the only 50 percent gray box, you can search for ".5 setgray" (don't include the quotation marks). If you want to change this to a 40 percent gray, change the line to ".6 setgray" (don't include the quotation marks). Note that the number you type before the command *setgray* is the amount of white. For example, 1 means 100 percent white, while .2 means 20 percent white (or 80 percent black).

Tip: Changing Halftones. QuarkXPress uses a standard dot half-tone spot when it tints type, rules, boxes, and other elements on the page (everything except halftoned bitmapped images, which you can control; see Chapter 8, *Modifying Images*). You can change the type of halftone spot that QuarkXPress uses by modifying the PostScript print-to-disk file. Search for "xpspot0 setscreen" (don't include the quotation marks). It should be somewhere near the beginning of the body of the file (after the %%EndDocumentSetup comment). The first two numbers on that line are the screen frequency and the angle. The screen frequency should be the same as what you specified in the Page Setup dialog box. The angle should be 45 degrees. You can change both of these to whatever you want them to be.

If you change the word "xpspot0" to "xpspot1," your halftones are printed with a straight-line spot; "xpspot3" is a square spot. If you are working with a screen frequency over 30 or 40, you probably won't be able to tell the difference between any of the spots, so this is mainly for special effects at low frequencies.

You can add your own spot functions by replacing the word "xpspot0" with a procedure. For example, you can create a tri-angular spot by replacing "xpspot0" with "{1 exch sub exch 1 exch sub sub 2 div}" (don't include the quotation marks).

Note that if your PostScript file has multiple color separations in it, each plate has its own setscreen command.

Tip: QuarkXPress's Coordinate System. If you know PostScript and you want to start playing around with PostScript dumps or the PostScript Escape Font, you should be aware that the coordinate system that QuarkXPress uses is significantly different from what you're probably used to. The 0,0 coordinate is in the upper-left corner of the printed page, and the entire page is inverted (1-1 scale). The biggest problem you'll encounter is that it's difficult to pinpoint where the 0,0 coordinate is on the page, as it depends on whether you're using crop marks, bleeds, and so forth. However, if you're persist-ent in your searches, you'll work it out.

▼ ▼

Just the Beginning

These are just the tips of the iceberg (pun intended). You can use a knowledge of PostScript to create all sorts of special effects within your QuarkXPress documents, including textured and patterned backgrounds and lines, blends (graduated fills), and graphic images—even effects which cannot be created even with programs such as Illustrator 3.0 and FreeHand. As we've tried to show you throughout this book, you definitely don't need to know PostScript programming to use QuarkXPress effectively. However, we like to spread the word that there's always more that can be done with computers and PostScript.

RESOURCES

We've always suspected that appendices chock full o' resources are only included in books under the orders of the greedy Publishing Trust—just to increase bulk and to justify a book's hefty price. We can't speak to the veracity of that suspicion for other books (especially from publishers we don't write for), but it couldn't be less true here.

As any QuarkXPress demon knows, and as we've tried to make clear throughout the book, QuarkXPress is not an island. We don't use QuarkXPress for everything, and we don't expect you to, either. And even if you do, there are many add-on XTensions from Quark and other developers that increase your power and efficiency in making pages.

We list here almost every software item we've discussed throughout the book, plus some that we think you should at least be aware of. The last section of this appendix is devoted to books and magazines that we find useful in our work. Perhaps you will, too. Good luck!

▼ ▼

XTensions

We first covered XTensions and how they can add functionally to QuarkXPress back in the Introduction. We mentioned several commercial vendors, but there's no way we could talk about them all. Below is a list of XTensions along with some general descriptions of what they are, how they work, and why we like them.

Note that we're not necessarily endorsing the use of these XTensions. They're ones that we've worked with or know the most about. There are many more XTensions out there that are worth looking into. To find out more about other available XTensions, contact the XChange at the address below. You can also find many freeware or shareware XTensions on electronic bulletin boards, such as America Online and Compuserve.

QuarkPrint
QuarkFreebies (free)
includes FeaturesPlus and NetworkConnection
QuarkXTras (only for 3.0)
includes SuperXTension
Zapper 2.0A bug fix (free; only for 3.0)
PM Filter (free)
CoolBlends
Photoshop™ Plug In
Bob (free)
Son of Bob (free)
Quark Inc.
1800 Grant St.Denver, CO 80203
(303) 894-8888
Product Information Line: (800) 788-7835

We've said it throughout the book, and we'll say it again: although versions 3.1 and 3.2 contain many of the features in previous XTensions, if you're working with an older version, the FeaturesPlus XTension from the QuarkFreebies package is essential. The NetworkConnection is a nice add-on in the Freebies package, but has a limited use, even in a networked situation (it has no use if you're not on a network). The Zapper 2.0A is also a must if you're working with version 3.0. Note that these are free from on-line services or from user groups. Quark adds a shipping and handling charge if you order directly from them.

QuarkPrint. The only XTension on the list that isn't free is the QuarkPrint package. QuarkPrint's predecessor, QuarkXTras, was also a commercial product, but it only works with version 3.0. QuarkPrint's mission in life is to make printing QuarkXPress documents easier for you. It let's you create named sets ("jobs") of Page Setup, Chooser, and Print dialog box settings. It also has some cool extra features like printing discontiguous pages (like 1, 5, 9–12).

PageMaker Filter. The PM Import filter is an XTension that lets you open files that were built in PageMaker 4.0 or 4.01. Note that it probably won't work for any PageMaker version later than that. In fact, it may not even work at all (different people have varying degrees of success). Although it has some limitations, it's great for transferring page geometry. Text is brought in properly, but some typographic values are lost in the translation. Moving text around is probably still performed better by exporting and importing Microsoft Word files. If you do use this XTension, remember to open the PageMaker file first and perform a Save As before attempting to import it into QuarkXPress.

CoolBlends. CoolBlends XTension is now included with QuarkXPress 3.2, though it's still a separate file in the QuarkXPress folder. This wild XTension lets you create five new types of blends: Mid-Linear, Rectangular, Diamond, Circular, and Full Circular. See Appendix C, *What's New in QuarkXPress 3.2*, for more information.

Photoshop™ Plugin. The Photoshop Plugin XTension is supposed to let you acquire images and place them directly into picture boxes. For example, you should be able to scan something and have it placed immediately into a picture box. Unfortunately, we've never gotten it to work. Maybe you can.

XTension of the Month Club
XPress XPerts XChange (X³)
The XChange
P.O. Box 270578
Fort Collins, CO 80527
(800) 788-7557
(303) 229-0620
Fax (303) 229-9773
CompuServe: 75300,2337
America OnLine: XChange

If great companies develop out of great needs, then the XChange is destined to fly. One of the biggest problems with getting quality XTensions has been where to go for information, sales, and technical support. The XChange is now here on the scene to help. They've made arrangements with most of the commercial XTension developers to be XTension Central: they'll market and sell XTensions (the developers love this because they're usually small shops without the resources to get the word out). And they'll also be handling tech support for many of the XTensions (what they don't know, they know how to find out).

If you need an XTension, but don't know who makes it, or if it even exists, call the XChange. If they don't know of it, they'll pass the idea on to a XTension developer who might create it down the line (or do a custom job for you).

The XChange also has an XTension of the Month Club. As a subscriber, each month you get a free XTension, a demo version of new or existing XTensions, and other software. They'll even send you a newsletter with all sorts of XTension information in it.

The XChange is also the central hub of the XPress XPerts XChange, an international users group for peole using QuarkXPress. At the time of this writing, X³ ("ex-cubed") is in its initial formation stages, but it looks like it will be a great place to acquire QuarkXPress information.

xdata

xtags

xstyle

Em Software

Here are three very different XTensions with very different applications. One for anyone publishing data, the second for anyone doing serious work with XPress Tags, and the third is for…anyone!

xdata. Xdata is a powerful XTension that formats information coming out of a database or a spreadsheet. Its uses vary. For example, David once built a 270-page, 17,000-name-and-address directory by importing information from a mainframe computer into QuarkXPress. Xdata automatically formatted each record the way he wanted it (name was bold, address was a smaller and different typeface, and so on). It's also handy for catalogs, financial sheets, and even mail merge.

xtags. Xtags does everything that XPress Tags does (see Chapter 5, *Copy Flow*), and more. The primary additions are creating and filling in-line anchored text and picture boxes, applying master pages, and translating user-defined tags upon import. It also includes error handling, which is sorely missed in Quark's XPress Tags. This last feature can be especially useful.

xstyle. Xstyle is an XTension that makes style sheets more accessible, and it works beautifully. It adds three new floating palettes to QuarkXPress (though you don't have to have them open all the time): Paragraph Styles, Character Styles, and Style Editor. Note that the character styles palette doesn't offer character-based styles. However, it does let you quickly change character formatting that isn't available in the Measurements palette.

ƒaceIT
a lowly apprentice production

Finally, an XTension for QuarkXPress that makes character styles! ƒaceIT is not a perfect XTension, but it does its job pretty well—better than anything else we've seen. Character styles, like paragraph styles (style sheets), let you name a group of character formatting attributes and then apply them all at once. Then, when you want to change those attributes, you can change them in the ƒaceIT dialog box, and your text gets changed throughout your document (see Figure B-1). This also contains other minor but helpful features. Joe Bob Blatner says Check it Out.

Scitex Document Reports
Scitex Fractions
Scitex Grides & Guides
Scitex Image Tools
Scitex Layers
Scitex Precision Tools
Scitex Corpration

You've all heard of Scitex, right? Million-dollar high-end imaging systems, and so on. Well now you can buy some of their expertise for much less than a milllion bucks. Most of the Scitex XTensions are really, really cool (the others are just plain cool), and can be extremely useful. Let's take a quick look at what they do.

Scitex Layers. This XTension lets you organize the various components on your pages, grouping and ungrouping quickly and easily. What's really great about Layers is that you can make layers disappear and appear at will. Invisible layers also don't print, so you can use Layers to create one document with varying pieces. For example, you could make one document with two different lanuages on the same page. When you want to print the English version, you can turn the French layer off, or vice versa.

Figure B-1
ƒaceIT XTension's
character styles

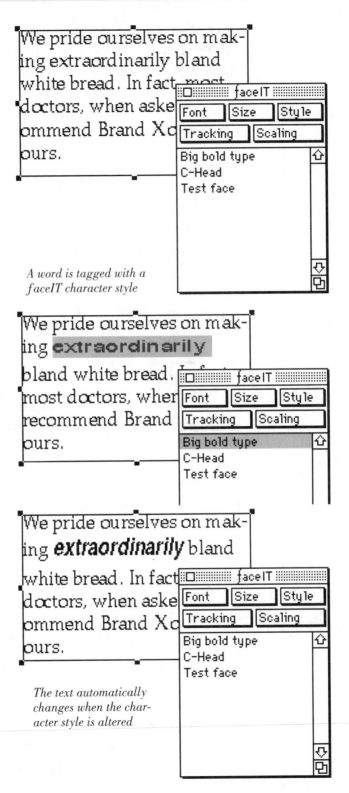

*A word is tagged with a
ƒaceIT character style*

*The text automatically
changes when the char-
acter style is altered*

Scitex Precision Tools. The Precision Tools XTension lets you do a number of things, including powerful aligning and measuring of items, magnifying areas of your page up to 1600 percent, precision nudging, and fast locking of multiple items in your document. In our judgement, the alignment and measurement tools are the best thing about this package.

Scitex Fractions. If you work with text that contains a lot of fractions, you'll love the Fractions XTension. It lets you create fractions quickly and intuitively. Most people will be happy enough with the free Make Fraction feature from Quark, but for others, this hands-on approach will be the cat's meow (see Figure B-2).

Figure B-2
Scitex Fractions

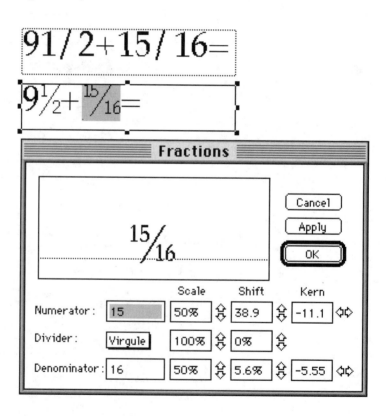

Scitex Grids & Guides. The Grids & Guides XTension from Scitex is the most powerful guide-making XTension that we've seen. It's also the most expensive (certainly a matter of "you get what you pay for"). If you work with a lot of page guides and don't use this XTension, you probably don't know what you're missing.

Scitex Image Tools. The Image Tools XTension from Scitex consists of four parts: blends, silhouettes, picture scaling, and quick proof. If you thought Cool Blends was great, you need to see Scitex Blends, which lets you create complex, multi-colored blends (like from red to blue to yellow at the rate you specify). The silhouette tool is extremely powerful for creating complex polygons around pictures and has built-in links to high-end high-resolution Scitex silhouetting tools. We sometimes use QuickProof when we've got a lot of high-resolution images on our page. It prints the page using screen-resolution images instead of sending the whole kit and kaboodle.

CopyFlow
CopyFlow Reports
CopyBridge
Overset
CopyFlow Geometry
Relink
Publication Locking
North Atlantic Publishing Systems, Inc.

Now here's a company with a mission: to help out the editorial process with as many XTensions as possible! CopyFlow, CopyFlow Reports and CopyBridge are three XTensions designed for groups of people working together on a project. CopyFlow lets you import and export stories from your documents very quickly and efficiently. This is a great aid to any publication that's being edited by one person while another person is doing page layout.

Add-ons to CopyFlow. CopyFlowReports is an add-on XTension that can give you detailed information about all the stories and pictures in your document. This information can be imported into a spreadsheet program for quick reference.

CopyBridge is an XTension designed for publishers who are using XyWrite or Microsoft Word extensively, and need a good translator for their QuarkXPress documents.

Publication Locking. Publication Locking also works in conjunction with CopyFlow. It lets you lock text and picture boxes in various ways. This is extremely helpful in tight production situations, when text and pictures are moving to and from editorial and production workstations.

By the way, don't let the workgroup concept deter you from looking into CopyFlow or Publication Locking; if you wear many hats in your job—from editor to production manager—this could still help you.

More XTensions. Relink and CopyFlow Geometry are two of the more esoteric XTensions we've come upon, but they can be extremely useful in certain situations. Relink lets you move page spreads and text boxes around and then relink a text chain automatically to flow the way you'd want it to. CopyFlow Geometry lets you build QuarkXPress page geometry by way of an ASCII text file. As it turns out, the ASCII codes are the same as in the program PC News Layout.

Overset. Overset is a little XTension in the genre of SetInset (see "SetInset" below): it does only one thing, but it does it well. Overset lets you see the text that won't fit into the text box you're working with. Once you turn this XTension on, when you click on that little "x" that indicates an overflow, Overset pops open another text box and flows the additional text into it. As soon as this auxiliary text box is empty, it handily disappears.

Sonar Bookends
Sonar TOC
Virginia Systems, Inc.

The Sonar Bookends XTension purports to create indexes and tables of contents. In our minds, this is more marketing hype than truth. What Bookends does really well is searching. It can search faster than bare feet move on hot asphalt. Not only can you search for things like "storm" throughout multiple documents, but you can search for all the instances of "storm" that are within four words of "warning" but aren't on the same page as "Billy Joel." It also creates a great concordance, and can be a good aid in cross referencing.

To be fair, there are many people who are happy with SonarBookends as an indexer. These people seem to fall into two categories: those who use the XTension as a starting point for their own indexes, and those who just don't care if they have a machine with no intelligence build their indexes.

Sonar TOC can create a pretty good table of contents, but it's a little clunky in how it works. Before you get too excited about these, check out the other index and table of contents XTensions that we talk about later on.

Tableworks
Tableworks Plus
Npath, Inc.

For those of you who follow the discussions on nationwide electronic bulletin board systems, you probably know that more people ask about a table-making XTension than anything else. To fill the need, Npath software has released Tableworks, a powerful table creation and editing tool. Tableworks adds a new menu and a new tool to the tool palette which lets you build a table quickly and efficiently. Well, maybe we shouldn't say "quickly"; QuarkXPress has never been good at handling a large number of text or picture boxes at any great clip. But it's certainly faster than having to do it by hand.

Tableworks also has many table manipulation features. For example, groups of cells can be merged to create straddle-column or row heads, and column and row heads can be treated differently when defining lines and when importing text. These heads can also be automatically repeated when a table carries over to a new page. Tables created with Table-works can be a fixed size or can be set up to dynamically grow horizontally or vertically, depending on the text brought into them.

Brad Walrod of High Text Graphics in New York has used Tableworks a lot more than we have. He says, "Tableworks is a must for anyone creating anything but the simplest tables in QuarkXPress. And Tableworks+, available later this year, promises to be a tool to please even the most jaded typesetter used to the tools of a dedicated typesetting system."

PinPointXT
Cheshire Group

Like Steve Werner, David dreams in PostScript. However, sometimes his dreams turn to nightmares when he encounters PostScript errors in printing jobs. Usually these errors flash on the screen quickly, then disappear, and the print job just dies. But that's where PinPoint XTension comes in handy. When PinPoint is turned on, QuarkXPress downloads some special PostScript code with your print job. This code "catches" any PostScript errors and tells you exactly what's going wrong and where. This XTension is very helpful for service bureaus who try to troubleshoot problems, or for PostScript hackers who are playing with QuarkXPress's code. Also see "Tip: Laserchecking with LaserCheck" in Appendix C, *What's New in QuarkXPress 3.2.*

SxetchPad
Datastream, Inc.

We never though we'd see the day when we could actually draw bezier curves in QuarkXPress and then curve type around them. Well, believe it or not, that's exactly what SxetchPad lets you do. But wait: there's more! You can also convert type to outline, and then fill and stroke those out-lines with colors or fancy blends. Plus, you can edit the curve points at any time (see Figure B-3).

Figure B-3

SxetchPad XTenion

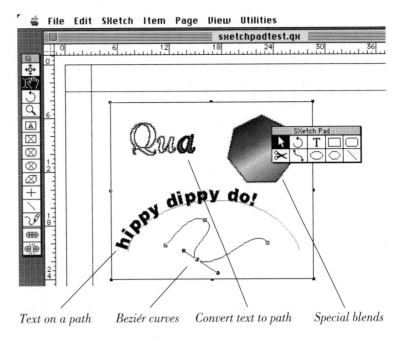

| Text on a path | Beziér curves | Convert text to path | Special blends |

SetInset
InsertSpace
XTend, Inc.

SetInset. SetInset is a shareware XTension that lets you define the inset for a text box on the left, right, top and bottom sides of the box. This overrides the single "all-sides" Text Inset value in the Text Box Specifications dialog box.

InsertSpace. XTend's commercial product, InsertSpace, brings to QuarkXPress a feature that traditional typesetters have been asking about for years. InsertSpace adjusts the tab stops for a line of text so that columns of text have equivalent amounts of space between them.

Azalea Barcode XTension
Azalea Software, Inc.

Jerry Whiting, king of barcodes, has finally developed an XTension to automatically create all sorts of high-quality EPS bar codes directly within QuarkXPress—UPC, ISBN, and many, many more. They're really cool.

Missing Link

NavigatorXT

Vision Contents

IndeXTension

ResizeXT

Textractor

and lots more!

Visions Edge

This may be the last company to be listed in this appendix, but it's *far* from being the least important or the least cool. Dacques Viker is creating some of the most useful utility XTensions on the market today. Here are descriptions of just a few (call the XChange for information on the others).

Missing Link. The Missing Link XTension lets you do all sorts of things you've wanted to do for years with linked boxes in QuarkXPress. For example, you can copy a text box out of the middle of a text chain and retain the text that's inside it. To us, the best thing is the ability to link together two chains of text boxes, each of which contain text (see Figure B-4).

Figure B-4
Missing Link XTension

*Two text chains
(before)*

*Chains linked together
with MissingLinkXT*

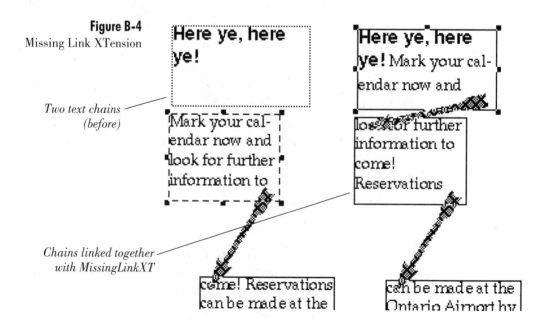

NavigatorXT. We often find ourselves working on a document zoomed in to 200 percent view. Then, when we want to edit a different part of the page we zoom out to Fit in Window and zoom back in to where we want to go next. This is time consuming, to say the least. That's when we go buy NavigatorXT, which lets us move quickly to various areas of the page without zooming out first. We simply bring up the Navigator palette and click on the area of the mini-page that we want to go to (see Figure B-5).

Figure B-5
NavigatorXT

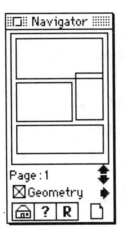

Vision Contents. Vision Contents is the table of contents maker that we've been waiting for for a long time. You can quickly create a table of contents based on style sheets, even over multiple documents. It even pulls out run-in heads if you want it to. Plus, as an added bonus, it can renumber sets of documents. For example, you can build a list of documents, tell it in what order they should flow, and then Vision Contents changes the opening page numbers for each document automatically.

IndeXTension. Ben Taylor originally developed this great indexing XTension for Future Publishing, but now Vision's Edge is expanding it even farther into cool realms. IndeXTension lets you create an index the way most people work: marking words and phrases on your document pages. You can also mark the words from within a word processor such as

Microsoft Word. If you have to create an index from a QuarkXPress document, you really should check this out.

ResizeXT. When David gives seminars in various places around the world, he has to answer lots of questions, but the one that almost always comes up is, "How can I resize a group of objects all at the same time?" His answer every time is "Call the XChange and get ResizeXT." This simple utility XTension is designed to resize pictures, text, lines, and frames quickly and exactly to the size you want them (see Figure B-6). Like many of Vision Edge's XTensions, it'll probably show up in the program itself someday, but until then this is the best we can hope for.

Figure B-6
Resize XT

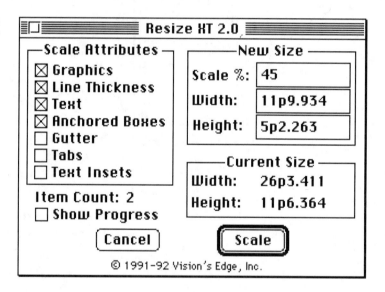

TeXTractor. If you need to pull text out of your QuarkXPress documents—whether for archival, text manipulation, or whatever—you should take a good look at the TeXTractor XTension (gotta' love these names, eh?). It's a powerhouse text extractor, letting you export the text in your document all at once, or by the criteria you specify.

▼ ▼

Software

FontDownloader
Illustrator
Photoshop
Adobe Dimensions
Adobe Type Manager
Adobe Systems Inc.
1585 Charleston Road
P.O. Box 7900
Mountain View, CA 94039-7900
(415) 961-4400

StuffIt
Aladdin Systems, Inc.
Deer Park Center, Suite 23A-171
Aptos, CA 95003
(408) 685-9175

FreeHand
PageMaker
PrePrint
Aldus TrapWise
Aldus Corporation
411 First Avenue S., Suite 200
Seattle, WA 98104
(206) 622-5500

MasterJuggler
ALSoft Inc.
P.O. Box 927
Spring, TX 77383-0927
(713) 353-4090

Fontographer
Altsys Corporation
269 W. Renner Road
Richardson, TX 75080
(214) 680-2060

LaserWriter Font Utility
ResEdit
Apple Computer, Inc.
20525 Mariani Avenue
Cupertino, CA 95104
(408) 996-1010

Bitstream Fonts
Bitstream, Inc.
215 First Street
Cambridge, MA 02142-1270
(617) 497-6222

Bullets and Boxes
Caseys' Page Mill
6528 S. Oneida Court
Englewood, CO 80111
(303) 220-1463

DiskTop
LaserStatus
QuicKeys
CE Software
801 73rd Street
Des Moines, IO 50312
(515) 224-1995

FontStopper
Compumation, Inc.
820 N. University Drive
State College, PA 16803

Electronic Border Tape
EBT Frame Mover
Computer Support Professionals
4545 N. 12th
Phoenix, AZ 85014
(800) 678-8848

ParaFont
MathType
Design Science
6475B E. Pacific Coast Highway
Suite 392
Long Beach, CA 90803
(213) 433-0685

EfiColor Profiles
Electronics for Imaging
2855 Campus Drive
San Mateo, CA 94403
(415) 286-8600

Fraction Fonts
EmDash
P.O. Box 8256
Northfield, IL 60093
(708) 441-6699

Suitcase II
Fifth Generation Systems, Inc.
1120 Industriplex Boulevard
Baton Rouge, LA 70809
(800) 873-4384

PlateMaker
In Software
2403 Conway Drive
Escondido, CA 92026
(619) 743-7502

Precision Imagesetter Linearization Software
Kodak Electronic Printing Systems, Inc.
164 Lexington Road
Billerica, MA 01821-3984
(508) 667-5550

Enhance
Micro Frontier
7650 Hickman Road
Des Moines, IO 50322
(515) 270-8109

Microsoft Word
Microsoft Excel
Microsoft
1 Microsoft Way
Redmond, WA 98052-6399
(206) 882-8080

Monotype Fonts
Monotype, Inc.
2500 Brickvale Drive
Elk Grove Village, IL 60007
(708) 350-5600

Super Boomerang
Now Utilities
319 SW Washington St.
11th Floor
Portland, OR 97204
(503) 274-2800

Mac-in-DOS

Pacific Micro

201 San Antonio Circle, C250

Mountain View, CA 94040

Exposure Pro

McSink

Vantage

Preferred Software, Inc.

5100 Poplar Avenue, Suite 706

Memphis, TN 38137

(800) 446-6393

ImageGrabber

Sabastian Software

P.O. Box 70278

Bellevue, WA 98007

(206) 861-0602

DiskDoubler

Salient

3101 Avalon Court

Palo Alto, CA 94306

(415) 852-9567

MacΣqn

Software for Recognition Technologies

55 Academy Drive

Rochester, NY 14623

(716) 359-3024

LaserCheck

Advanced PostScript Error Handler

Systems of Merritt, Inc.

2551 Old Dobbin Drive East

Mobile, AL 36695

(205) 660-1240

Color Calibration Software for Postscript Imagesetters
Technical Publishing Services, Inc.
2205 Sacramento
San Francisco, CA 94115
(415) 921-8509

Images with Impact
3G Graphics
11410 N.E. 124th Street
Suite 6155
Kirkland, WA 98034
(206) 367-9321

Impostrip
Ultimate Technographics, Inc.
4980 Buchan Street
Suite 403
Montreal, Quebec PQ H4P 1S8
Canada
(514) 733-1188

DeskPaint
DeskScan
Zedcor
4500 East Speedway, Suite 22
Tucson, AZ 86712
(800) 482-4567

Hardware and Other Entities

Matrix SlideWriter
Agfa Compugraphic
One Ramland Road
Orangeburg, NY 10962
(914) 365-0190

QuarkXPress Users International
P.O. Box 170
1 Stiles Road, Suite 106
Salem, NH 03079
(603) 898-2822
Fax (603) 898-3393

Thunder/24 Graphics Accelerator
SuperMac
485 Potrero Avenue
Sunnyvale, CA 94086
(408) 245-2202

Magazines and Publications

PostScript Language Reference Manual
PostScript Language Program Design
PostScript Language Tutorial and Cookbook
(also known as the Red, Green, and Blue books)
Addison-Wesley Publishing
6 Jacob Way
Reading, MA 01867
(617) 944-3700

Digital Prepress Book
Agfa Compugraphic
200 Ballardvale Street
Wilmington, MA 01887
(508) 658-5600

Real World PageMaker
Bantam Computer Books
666 Fifth Avenue
New York, NY 10103
(212) 765-6500

MacWeek
Coastal Associates Publishing Company
P.O. Box 5821
Cherry Hill, NJ 08034
(609) 461-2100

Step-By-Step Electronic Design
Dynamic Graphics
6000 N. Forest Park Drive
Peoria, IL 61614-3592
(309) 688-8800

The Form of the Book
Hartley & Marks, Inc.
79 Tyee Drive
Point Roberts, WA 98281

Desktop Communications
International Desktop Communications
48 E. 43rd Street
New York, NY 10017
(800) 966-9502

U&lc
International Typeface Corporation
2 Hammarskjold Plaza
New York, NY 10017
(212) 371-0699

The PostScript Type Sampler
MacTography
702 Twinbrook Parkway
Rockville, MD 20851
(301) 424-3942

Macworld
Macworld Communications, Inc.
501 Second Street
San Francisco, CA 94107
(800) 234-1038

Before and After
PageLab
331 J Street, Suite 150
Sacramento, CA 95814-9671

Real World Scanning & Halftones
QuarkXPress Visual Quickstart Guide
QuarkXPress Tips & Tricks
Learning PostScript
The Little Mac Book
The Macintosh Font Book
The Mac is not a typewriter
Real World FreeHand
and many, many others
Peachpit Press
2414 Sixth St.
Berkeley, CA 94710
(800) 283-9444
(510) 548-4393
Fax: (510) 548-5991

Publish!
501 Second Street
San Francisco, CA 94107
(800) 274-5116

Seybold Report on Desktop Publishing
Seybold Publications
P.O. Box 644
Media, PA 19063
(215) 565-2480

Desktop Typography with QuarkXPress
TAB Books
Blueridge Summit, PA 17294-0850
(800) 233-1128

Verbum
Verbum, Inc.
P.O. Box 15439
San Diego, CA 92115
(619) 233-9977

EC&I
Youngblood Publishing Company, Limited
505 Consumers Road, Suite 102
Willowdale, Ontario M2J 4V8
Canada
(416) 492-5777

Design Tools Monthly
1332 Pearl Street
Boulder, CO 80302
(303) 444-6876

MacUser
Ziff-Davis Publishing Company
950 Tower Lane, 18th Floor
Foster City, CA 94404

WHAT'S NEW IN QUARKXPRESS 3.2

Everything changes. The seasons change, the interest rate changes, even the matzoh-brei at Rose's Deli in Portland has changed (they said it'd never happen). Fortunately, at least one thing has changed for the better: QuarkXPress. Version 3.0 was good, 3.1 was better, and 3.2 is, well, grrreat. We can't be sure, but it sometimes seems like versions 3.1 and 3.2 of QuarkXPress have all the great features that Quark's software engineers really wanted to put into version 3.0 but didn't have the time for. We can understand that: we have a pile of tips, tricks, and useful production techniques sitting here that didn't make it into the first edition of the book.

In this appendix we're going to fully cover every feature that's been added to QuarkXPress since version 3.0, plus we're going to throw in a bunch of these great tips. Some of what we discuss here will seem to cover the same ground as what we talked about through the rest of the book, but we've tried to minimize this and just give you the essentials for working with the latest version of QuarkXPress.

Note that some of the features we talk about here are found only in version 3.2, whereas others are also in version 3.1. Most of the new 3.2 features are detailed in Table C-1, and you'll find "New in 3.2!" markers in the margins throughout this appendix to flag the latest features. We've also added a bunch of tips that have turned up since we wrote the appendix for the second edition. They're tagged with "New Tip" markers in the margins.

Table C-1	**New feature**	**See page...**
New features in QuarkXPress 3.2 (continued)	Renaming style sheets	591
	Revert to last autosave	567
	Smart quotes	567
	Speed scroll	561
	Stacking windows	554
	Tiling windows	554
	Trapping Preferences	609
	Unlimited open documents	554
	Vertical scaling	586
	QuarkXPress for Windows	631
	Windows submenu	554

Note that this appendix is structured in much the same way as the book's chapters: from *Structure and Interface* (Chapter 1) through *Printing* (Chapter 10). This should make it easy for you to quickly find the information you need.

▼ ▼

Scripting and EfiColor

There are two major areas of improvement in 3.2 that aren't covered in this appendix (or are only covered in passing)—scripting with Apple Events, and the EfiColor color management system.

EfiColor. EfiColor is a combination of an XTension and a background processor that improves the relationship between the colors you see on screen and what comes out of a printer or off a printing press. We discuss EfiColor in Appendix D.

Apple Event Scripting. Scripting—the ability to control QuarkXPress with programs written in AppleScript, Frontier, QuicKeys, and the like—is arguably the most important new feature in version 3.2.

We don't cover it here at all.

The technology was simply too changeable at press time, so we couldn't even include a command reference and be confident that it was correct. And there are few things more frustrating than trying to program something with an incorrect command reference. Plus, we don't want to simply provide the same information you'll get (probably in a ReadMe file) with QuarkXPress 3.2. We want to show you how to *use* scripting, including providing a bunch of cool scripts that you can use and modify to your own ends.

So we decided to hold off, and provide the scripting information on the disk you can get from Peachpit by sending in the card at the back of the book. In addition to all sorts of cool utilities, we'll provide a complete scripting guide that you can print out, and scripts to make XPress do double back flips.

▼ ▼

Structure and Interface

QuarkXPress had a significant facelift during the upgrade to 3.0 (see Chapter 1, *Structure and Interface*). Subsequently, Quark took a breather and didn't change the graphical user interface (GUI) too much. However, they did listen carefully to their users' wish lists and added some really cool features, like three new palettes, a bunch of new preferences, nifty commands for arranging windows, and some subtle differences in magnifying parts of a page. Let's look at each new change.

Installing and Upgrading

Let's start from the very beginning. Installing and upgrading QuarkXPress 3.2 is a snap (see "Tip: Updating Quark-XPress" in the introduction, page 17). Quark has added a few new procedures to this process: dialog boxes that ask you which file sets, text filters, XTensions, and other files you want to install (see Figure C-1).

Figure C-1

The XTension
Selection dialog box

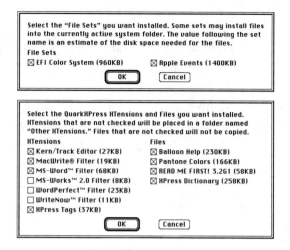

The File Sets dialog box, the first you see after you begin the installation, basically just gives you the option of installing the EfiColor color management system and/or the AppleEvents system. Selecting the EfiColor checkbox installs the EfiColor XTension in the same folder with QuarkXPress, the EfiColor DB folder (which contains the device profiles that come with your copy of QuarkXPress), and the EfiColor Processor in your System folder's Extensions folder. If you don't check this box, the EfiColor files won't be installed at all.

Note that the installer/upgrader still installs all the XTensions and filters, but the items that aren't checked in the second dialog box are placed in a separate folder. At least this helps keep your QuarkXPress folder tidy, and speeds up launching XPress, though it doesn't save any disk space. And (it had to come sooner or later) you can now tell the Installer not to install that infamous Frame Editor. All the better, in our book.

Note that Quark recommends that you turn off all your extensions and control-panel devices before you install QuarkXPress. You can do this by holding down the Shift key while restarting your Mac (hold it down until you see the dialog box that says "Extensions Off").

A major post-3.0 change is that the XPress Hyphenation and XPress Data files are gone. Don't fret; the functionality is still there. First, Quark just incorporated XPress Hyphenation into the QuarkXPress application. Then they did something really drastic: they did away with the XPress Data File (see "Saving the XPress Data," below). If you go a-searchin', you'll find that now there's an XPress Preferences file in either your QuarkXPress folder or the Preferences folder in your System folder. That's where it should be, so leave it alone.

About That About Box. After you've finished installing Quark-XPress 3.2, you may from time to time need to check the About box to double-check your serial number, find out about various XTensions you've loaded, and the like. There are a few changes here in version 3.2 to make it easier for you and Quark to keep track of your configuration (see Figure C-2).

Figure C-2
The QuarkXPress
Environment dialog box

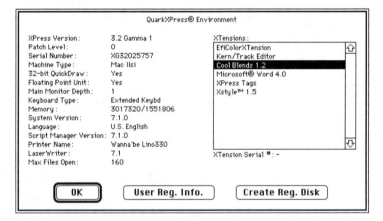

When you hold down the Option key and select About QuarkXPress from the Apple menu, the dialog box you get tells you familiar information about your own Mac's system and your version of QuarkXPress, as with previous versions. But also, if you click on a listed XTension name, you'll see the XTension's serial number (if it has one). And there's a button for displaying your own user registration information, and another for creating a registration disk with that information that you can send back to Quark. Quark uses these disks to plug your information directly into its customer-support database.

Why create a registration disk if it's already created as part of the installation process (see page 22)? Sometimes Quark receives registration disks that have been damaged in transit. Until now, there was no way they could ask you to easily recreate such a damaged disk; once you installed and mailed in your disk, it was *gone!* Now you have the option of creating a new one. Kind of obscure, rarely needed, but a lifesaver when you gotta do it.

▼ ▼

Tip: If You Sell Out. Why you'd ever want to sell your copy of QuarkXPress is beyond us. However, in case you do, you'd better know Quark's rules about such things. First of all, you have to notify Quark that you want to sell their product (the closest thing to this that we've encountered in real life is someone telling their parents that they wanted to buy birth control pills). Quark's customer service will send a Transfer Request form to you, and a License Agreement to the person to whom you're selling. After both of you sign the forms and send them back, Quark updates their databases and the deed is done. The only reason we even bring this up is that we've heard of people getting into weird situations 'cause they didn't follow the rules. So now you know.

▼ ▼

The New File And Library Commands

There's something new about Quark's New command. It's hierarchical. Look under the File menu, and you'll see a small submenu attached to the New command. You can either create a new document or a new library file from this submenu.

There's a logic to this. Since the two kinds of files you can create from within QuarkXPress are either documents or libraries (not counting the many kinds of files you can export from a document), it makes a certain sense to group the commands for creating these files under the New command.

Of course, you can always use the Command-N shortcut to make a new document and avoid the submenu, or Command-Option-N for a new library.

Also note that the Library command is gone from the Utilities menu. Now in version 3.2, you simply open Library files via the Open command, as you would any other QuarkXPress file. How do you know whether a file displayed in the Open dialog box is a document, a library or a template? Easy. Click on the document's name, and the file's type appears at the bottom of the dialog box, along with the type's small icon.

▼ ▼

Tip: Preview When Opening. One of the neat things about saving a document as a template is the handy preview of the document's first page you see whenever you select the template in QuarkXPress's file-opening dialog box. We always loved this feature, and wondered why Quark didn't simply implement it for *all* documents, not just templates. Well, as of version 3.2, they have. Note that QuarkXPress 3.2 can't preview documents saved in earlier versions of the program. You have to open them and use Save As first. To save a document with a preview, check Include Preview in the Save As dialog box.

▼ ▼

Screen Redraw

If there's one thing that QuarkXPress users can always use more of, it's speed. And Quark, knowing where their bread is buttered, is always trying to keep the customer happy. They've figured out how to make redrawing the screen much faster—sometimes up to five times as fast. You may or may not perceive the redraw speedup on your system, actually. Or the speedup might be negligible, depending on what you do. Two of the areas that have been considerably accelerated are drawing at smaller view scales, and drawing text that contains a lot of tabs. Because Quark uses a form of bitmap caching, scrolling around the screen is much faster, especially when you have Speed Scroll turned on in the Application Preferences dialog box.

Palettes

If you've worked with version 3.0 much, you know how great those floating palettes are. You can have them open or closed, move them around the screen, and get lots of functionality in very little space. Version 3.2 has three additional palettes: Trapping Information, Style Sheets, and Colors. We'll discuss in detail the Colors and Trapping Information palettes in "Color," and the Style Sheets palette in "Copy Flow," later in this chapter. There are some additions to the Measurements palette, and Quark also dramatically revamped the Document Layout palette, which we'll describe in "Document Construction."

For now, suffice it to say that each of these can be shown or hidden by selecting items in the View menu. Oh, and by the way, for you 3.0 users who have been creating QuicKeys to drag the palettes around the screen to where you like to have them, QuarkXPress now remembers where they were when you quit or closed them, and puts each palette in the right place when you open it.

Measurements Palette Changes. The changes to the Measurements palette are minor, but as the palette's so vital to your day-to-day use of QuarkXPress, we'll mention them here briefly.

First, when you have the Content tool active and a text or picture box selected, you'll notice two new small icons: to the left of the scaling fields for a picture box, and to the left of the leading and tracking/kerning fields for a text box. You can use these icons to flip the contents of these boxes horizontally or vertically (see "Flipping Out," later in this chapter).

When you have the Content tool active and a text box selected, you'll see a fifth justification mode icon, for the new forced-justification mode, which we'll explain in "Type and Typography," below.

▼ ▼

Tip: Jump to Fonts. If you've ever wondered how the Research and Development department at Quark decides what features to put into QuarkXPress, this might amuse you. Tim Gill, founder and senior vice president for R&D at Quark, attended the first annual Quark Users' International Conference in New York city back in 1991. In the middle of a question-and-answer session, someone stood up and asked if there was a way to change quickly from one font to another. He thought about it for a few moments and replied, "How about a keystroke that places you in the font field of the Measurements palette?" After a round of applause, he said, "Okay, it'll be in the next version." That keystroke, I'm proud to report, is Command-Shift-Option-M (the same as jumping to the Measurements palette, but add the Shift key).

▼ ▼

By the Numbers

QuarkXPress has always stood out for its ability to use numeric specifications—you can type in numbers for positioning, scaling, and the like. Of course, this feature has often required that you keep the good ol' Calculator DA open to do mundane arithmetic tasks (so when you needed to make a box exactly two-thirds of its current size, you could figure out just what number to enter in the appropriate field). Or, if you were a low tech type like some of us, it's meant keeping paper and pencil (or fingers) handy. Well, you can almost kiss your calculator (or pencil or fingers) good-bye.

QuarkXPress now performs simple arithmetic operations for you. Just use those basic arithmetic operators (+, -, * and /), and you're in business. So if you have a text box that measures 4.323 inches, and you want to make it two-thirds as wide, just add *2/3, to the right of the inch mark.

Note that arithmetic works in almost any field in any dialog box.

▼ ▼

Tip: Mix and Match Measurements. Even better, when you're adding or subtracting values, you can mix and match any measurement system that QuarkXPress recognizes. Even if you've specified in Preferences that inches be the measurement unit used for horizontal dimensions, you're not restricted to using inches in any horizontal measurement box. If you want to make our hypothetical 4.323-inch-wide text box three picas narrower, all you have to do is type -3p after the inch mark. It doesn't get much easier than this!

▼ ▼

More Better Shortcuts

We've always loved the many keyboard shortcuts built into QuarkXPress. With Version 3.2, there's much more to love. You might note that we've added a set of keystrokes inside the covers of this book. If that isn't enough, though, Table C-2 lists the many new shortcuts that Quark has added. Note that the Function keystrokes we list here aren't listed anywhere else in this book.

Stacking

Some of QuarkXPress's new features are subtle, but powerful in a production environment. For example, stacking items on the page: QuarkXPress now lets you move items forward or backward one layer at a time (instead of only all the way to the front or all the way to the back). When you hold down the Option key while selecting the Item menu, the Send to Back and Bring to Front items become Send Backward and Bring Forward. It's not as powerful as the way layering is done in FreeHand 3 or Illustrator 5, but it's a great start.

▼ ▼

Tip: Grab Down Deep. You can now select page items that are covered up by other page items. In previous versions, for example, if you wanted to select a picture box that was behind a text box, you had to move the text box first, then select the picture box. Now you can just hold down the Command-Option-Shift keys while clicking with the Content tool to select the picture box. One click selects the object one layer down, the second click selects the object on the next layer down, and so on.

▼ ▼

Type	To...
Control-V	Jump to magnification field
Command-W	Close window
Command-Option-W	Close all documents
Command-Option-E	Save Text
Command-L	Spell-check word
Command-Option-L	Spell-check story
Command-Option-Shift-L	Spell-check document
Command-, (comma)	Space/Align
Command-Shift-M	Force justify
Command-Option-Shift-Y	Application preferences
Command-Option-H	H&Js
Command-Option-Shift-P	Document Setup
Command-Option-Shift-S	Save as EPS
Control-' *or* "	Straight/Curly quotes
Command-5 *or* Control-Space	Nonbreaking space
F5	Bring to Front
Option-F5	Move Forward
Shift-F5	Send to Back
Shift-Option-F5	Move Backward
F6	Lock/Unlock
F7	Show/Hide guides
Shift-F7	Snap to Guides
Option-F7	Show/Hide baseline grid
F8	Show/Hide Tools palette
Shift-F8	Next tool
Shift-Option-F8	Previous tool
F9	Show/Hide Measurements palette
Shift-F9	Font field
Option-F9	Next font in list
Shift-Option-F9	Previous font in list
F10	Show/Hide Document Layout palette
F11	Show/Hide Style Sheets palette
Shift-F11	Edit Styles
Shift-Option-F11	Edit H&Js
F12	Show/Hide Colors palette
Shift-F12	Edit Colors

Type	To...
Shift-Option-F12	Trapping Preferences
Option-F12	Show/Hide Trap Information palette
F13	Font Usage
Shift-F13	Picture Usage

Box Skew

Here's another terrific feature we've been eagerly awaiting. Box Skew lets you skew text and picture boxes and their contents (we talk about skewing on page 332). You can skew a text box, and all the text within the box is skewed to the same angle—and you're still able to edit the text. By combining QuarkXPress's ability to skew and rotate text boxes, you can create some interesting effects, like a 3-D cube with angled text on each side (see Figure C-3).

Figure C-3
Box skew

Text Box Skew. To skew a text box and its contents, just select the box and choose the Modify command on the Item menu. In the Text Box Specifications dialog box (Command-M, or double click with the Item tool), go to the Box Skew field, and enter the number of degrees you want the box to be skewed (it only lets you enter values between -75 and 75 degrees). Enter a positive number to skew the box and its contents to the right; a negative number skews them to the left.

Picture Box Skew. You've been able to skew the contents of picture boxes in QuarkXPress since version 3.0, but now you can skew the box *and* its contents, all in one fell swoop. Just go to the Picture Specifications dialog box and enter a Box

Skew value exactly as described above for text boxes. The only difference is that you can still skew the *contents* of a picture box independently of the box itself, using the Picture Skew field in the dialog box or Measurements palette.

Of course, if you're really bored, you can even play dueling skewing by setting values in Box Skew and Picture Skew that cancel each other out.

▼ ▼

Tip: The Polygon Blues. Here's a quick one that can help you out of a jam. If you're drawing a complex polygon and can't find the first point of the polygon, don't fret, and—whatever you do—don't restart your Mac! You've got two reasonable choices. First, you can type Command-period to cancel the polygon operation. However, that kills the polygon entirely. The second choice is better: just double-click somewhere. Double-clicking automatically closes the polygon for you.

▼ ▼

Flipping Out

Here's another dream come true. It used to be that if you wanted to flip a picture or text along the vertical or horizontal axis—so that you could mirror it on facing pages, for instance—you had to dive into a graphics program, flip the image, save it as a picture, then bring it into your QuarkXPress document.

Well, no longer. Just select the object, then go to the Style menu and choose Flip Vertical or Flip Horizontal (we think these commands are dandy candidates for addition to your QuarkXPress QuicKeys set). Not only does this command let you flip pictures and text, but flipped text remains fully editable (to do this, you have to practice reading the newspaper in the mirror).

You can also use the new icons for flipping contents in the Measurements palette (see Figure C-4). The top icon controls horizontal flipping; the lower one controls vertical flipping. Note that Flip Vertical and Flip Horizontal only flip the contents of boxes, not the boxes themselves (subtle difference).

Figure C-4

Flip horizontal/vertical

No Flip

| X: 0.667" | W: 2.931" | ⊿ 0° | | ⧩ auto | Palatino | 12 pt |
| Y: 0.847" | H: 0.278" | Cols: 1 | | ⧩ 0 | | |

Vertical Flip

| X: 0.667" | W: 2.931" | ⊿ 0° | | ⧩ auto | Palatino | 12 pt |
| Y: 1.972" | H: 0.278" | Cols: 1 | | ⧩ 0 | | |

Horizontal Flip

| X: 0.667" | W: 2.931" | ⊿ 0° | | ⧩ auto | Palatino | 12 pt |
| Y: 3.097" | H: 0.278" | Cols: 1 | | ⧩ 0 | | |

Vertical and Horizontal Flip

| X: 0.667" | W: 2.931" | ⊿ 0° | | ⧩ auto | Palatino | 12 pt |
| Y: 2.597" | H: 0.278" | Cols: 1 | | ⧩ 0 | | |

Interactive Text Resizing

For quite a while you've been able to scale a picture box and its contents by holding down the Command key while dragging on a handle. Ever caught yourself attempting to do the same to a box of display type that just needs a little bit of tweaking? Now you don't have to feel sheepish, because you actually can scale text within a box by Command-dragging on its handles. As you resize the box, the text size increases or decreases to fit your changes. Depending on how you reshape the box, the type size changes, as well as the type's horizontal or vertical scaling (see Figure C-5).

Figure C-5

Interactive text resizing

All the rules for resizing and scaling picture boxes now apply to text boxes. In addition to Command-key scaling, Shift-Command turns rectangular boxes into squares (scaling contents appropriately), and Shift-Command-Option scales the box and its contents but maintains existing horizontal and vertical proportions. And if you wait half a second after you click on a handle before you begin to drag, you can see the type change on screen as you drag (see "Viewing Changes as You Make Them," below).

There are two catches to this neat new feature. First, it only stretches type to the limits you could ordinarily. For example, you can't stretch type wider than 400 percent, because horizontal scaling won't go any further than that. Second, this scaling only works on unlinked text boxes, not on text boxes that are part of a longer story, as it's intended for use on headline and display type. Think about how easily you could mess up the formatting of a long story, if by resizing a text box through which it flowed, you ended up scaling some (but not all) of the text in a paragraph. Although we're sure that someone out there will take issue with us, we agree wholeheartedly with Quark's decision to limit this feature to unlinked boxes!

Viewing Changes as You Make Them

Another relatively subtle but extremely helpful change is the ability to view page items while moving, cropping, rotating, or sizing them. You might remember that previously you were only shown the outline of a picture or text box while you altered it. Now, if you hold the mouse button down on a picture box handle for half a second before dragging it, you can see the picture crop (or scale, if you have the Command key held down, too) as you move the handle. Similarly, if you move or rotate the box, you can see the text or picture rotate while dragging if you simply pause for half a second before starting to drag. No, you don't have to count out half a second; just wait until you see the object flash quickly before you start dragging.

Doing Windows

Nope, we're not talking about the new version of QuarkXPress that runs under that other operating system, but rather how version 3.2 now lets you play with documents more than ever. You can open a whole mess more document windows at once, limited mainly by memory considerations. Goodbye seven-window limit! However, having so many document windows open at once could mean massive clutter and confusion (especially for Eric, who thinks that the Mac's "desktop metaphor" was created to let him make his virtual desktop as messy as his physical one); fortunately, Quark has provided two solutions.

First, under the View menu, the new Windows submenu lists all open document windows (including the Clipboard and Help and Find/Change windows). Just selecting a window makes it active, which is particularly convenient if the window you want happens to be hidden beneath a slew of other windows.

Second, there are two items in the Windows submenu: Stack Documents and Tile Documents (see Figure C-6). The Stack Documents command arranges your windows somewhat like a slightly fanned hand of cards. There's always at least a tiny smidgen of each window showing, even the hindmost one, so you can select any window by clicking on it.

If you've ever sprained your mousing wrist moving and resizing windows in order to drag items between documents, you'll really love Tile Documents. Tiling resizes every

Figure C-6
Tiling windows

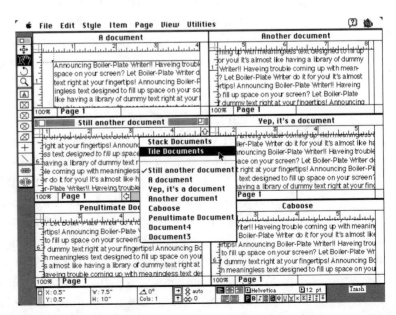

document window so that each takes up an equal portion of your Mac's screen. So if you have three document windows, tiling sizes and arranges them so that each takes up one-third of your screen. We often use this when dragging objects or pages from one document to another.

▼ ▼

Tip: Tiling to Multiple Monitors. If you're lucky enough to have more than one monitor attached to your Mac, you can have QuarkXPress tile documents so that the tiling spreads across all your available monitors. So if you have two monitors, and four open documents, two documents will appear in each monitor. You can turn on this feature by checking the Tile to Multiple Monitors box in the Application Preferences dialog box. If you leave this box unchecked, QuarkXPress will tile all its open documents within your main monitor only (the one that's displaying the menu bar).

▼ ▼

Tip: Windows Menu Shortcut. The Windows submenu sure is useful, but getting to its hierarchical commands is a pain in the mouse, especially since Quark has placed it right in the middle of the View menu. Fortunately, Quark has also added an easy and eminently logical shortcut. Hold down the Shift key and click on the title of your active document window, and up pops an exact replica of the Windows menu, from which you can select any window, or stack or tile them all. What better place for a Windows menu than in a window itself, anyway?

▼ ▼

Tip: Full-Screen Documents. You've probably noticed that whenever you open a document or make a new one, the document window sizes itself nicely to the size of your screen, except that it leaves some room at the left and bottom edges for the default locations of the Tools and Measurements palettes. If you click on the window's Zoom box, it expands to fill your entire screen, even the areas covered by these two palettes.

Now you can tell QuarkXPress how you want it to behave when you zoom a window. In the Application Preferences dialog box, under the Display section, there's a checkbox labeled Full-screen Documents. Check the box (the default is unchecked), and whenever you open or create a new document, or zoom a document window, it'll fill your entire screen. Leave it unchecked, and zooming will respect the default location of the Tools and Measurements palette.

▼ ▼

Page View

It always frustrated us that when we chose Fit in Window (or some other magnification percentage) from the View menu, it would just zoom in or out, but wouldn't alter the position of the page on the screen. Now, QuarkXPress not only zooms to the percentage you want, but it centers the current page in your window. If you have two facing pages showing in your document window when you select Fit in Window, QuarkXPress fits and centers that entire spread in the window.

▼ ▼

Tip: Fitting More in Your Window. Here's a quick tip for zooming in and out. If you select Fit in Window (or type Command-zero) from the View menu, QuarkXPress fits the current page to the window. However, if you hold down the Option key while selecting Fit in Window, it zooms to fit the entire width of the pasteboard into the window. However, note that you can't just type Command-Option-zero to get this view. Apple apparently reserved this keystroke for the Open dialog box (don't ask us why; we know it's weird). You could set up a QuicKey for this logical shortcut.

▼ ▼

Quark has an even cooler feature that centers a selected page item when you select a zoom percentage from the View menu. To be precise, QuarkXPress centers any selected page item if any part of the page that contains that item is in your document window, or—if the item is on the pasteboard—if any part of that item is shown in the document window.

For example, if you select a short rule on a page while viewing at Fit in Window size, and then select Actual Size, QuarkXPress zooms in and centers that rule on your screen. If the selected item is a text box and you have the Contents tool selected, then Quark centers on where the cursor is or on whatever text is highlighted. This makes zooming in and out on a page much easier: if you're editing some text, you can use Fit in Window to see the "big picture," then select 100 percent to zoom back to where your cursor is in the text.

Ultimately, we still like to use the Control-drag shortcut (see Chapter 1, *Structure and Interface*, pages 75–77) to zoom to where we want to go, but these new features are often helpful in bouncing quickly back and forth between percentage views.

▼ ▼

Tip: Jump to View Percent. Version 3.2 adds another handy keyboard shortcut: pressing Control-V selects the View Percent field of your active Quark window. To change your magnification, just type in any value between 10 and 400, and press Return or Enter. You can also enter T to get Thumbnails view.

▼ ▼

Copying Linked Text Boxes

The ability to easily copy objects between documents was one of the greatest new features put into QuarkXPress 3.0. The only problem was if you were trying to copy a linked text box, in which case QuarkXPress would refuse to let you copy or cut it to the Clipboard, or drag it to another page. In version 3.2, this problem has almost been solved.

Copying Single Linked Text Boxes. You can copy a single linked text box to a new document, and QuarkXPress copies, along with it, the entire text chain, from that box on. None of the text preceding that box in the chain moves to the target; only the text from the ensuing linked boxes (and any overflow text, which wasn't in any boxes).

Also note that if you have Automatic Page Insertion turned on, and your new document's master page has an automatic text box, QuarkXPress creates as many new pages as necessary to contain all of the copied story. So if you move a box that's part of a long story, you may end up with quite a stack of new pages to deal with. It'd be nice if QuarkXPress could automatically break the chains when you copy, bringing to the new document only the text within the box you're moving (if you'd like, that is), but we have to leave Quark *some* refinements to work on for the next version.

Copying Groups of Linked Text Boxes. Believe it or not, you can now also easily copy as a group text boxes that are linked to each other. But if you want to copy multiple text boxes that are linked to each other, *as well* as to boxes that you haven't selected, QuarkXPress will still refuse to copy or move them, giving you instead the familiar "This text box or a text box in the group has linkages that can't be duplicated." If you're in Thumbnails mode, and copy multiple pages from one document to another, links between boxes on different pages are also maintained in your target document.

Ruler Guides

For those of you who use a lot of rulers, you'll be happy to know that Quark has made it easier to move those puppies around. In previous versions of QuarkXPress, you could only move a guide by clicking on it in the margins or somewhere else where there were no page items, like picture or text boxes, in the way. Now, if you have the Item tool selected, you can move a guide by clicking on it anywhere you want. Of course, to click on the guide it has to be visible, so you may need to have the Guides control in the Preferences dialog box (Command-Y) set to In Front.

▾ ▾

Tip: Getting Rid of Ruler Guides. No matter how easy it is to move guides around, it's always a hassle to add twenty guides to a page and then remove them one at a time. Well, take a shortcut: hold down the Option key while clicking once in the horizontal ruler, and all the horizontal guides disappear. Option-clicking in the vertical ruler has the same effect on vertical guides. This works in version 3.0, too.

▾ ▾

One other subtle change in the area of rulers that you might like: Rulers are now visually accurate. What does that mean? It means that when a box or a rule looks like it is directly over a tick mark in the ruler, it really is. For example, if you want to visually place a box at the 2-inch mark (as opposed to using the Measurements palette), you can follow the gray lines in the rulers as you drag the box. When the gray line is over the 2-inch mark, the box is truly at 2 inches, even when you're at a view other than 100 percent, or if you've changed the Points/Inch value. This might not seem like a big deal, but in earlier versions, you could never really be sure unless you checked the Measurements palette or the Item Specifications dialog box. It might be at 1.998 or 2.01 inches.

▼ ▼

Tip: Dashed Guides. Did you know that if you change Quark-XPress's ruler guides to the color black in the Application Preferences dialog box, the guides change into dashed lines? They do. Some people like 'em that way, it turns out. If you want solid black guides, set the color to 99 percent black or the like.

▼ ▼

Application Preferences

You thought you could set a lot of preferences before! Now, Quark has included a new Application Preferences dialog box, which you can access by selecting Application from the Preferences submenu under the Edit menu (see Figure C-7). Any selections you make in this dialog box are application-wide; that is, they aren't just for the document you have open. Many of these controls may be already familiar to you if you used the FeaturesPlus XTension from the QuarkFreebies 3.0 package, or the many "Bob" XTensions Quark's distributed for free since then. Either way, let's jump in and discuss each element.

Guide Colors. The controls in the upper left corner of the Application Preferences dialog box let you change the colors of QuarkXPress's three types of guide lines: Margin, Ruler,

Figure C-7

The Application
Preferences dialog box

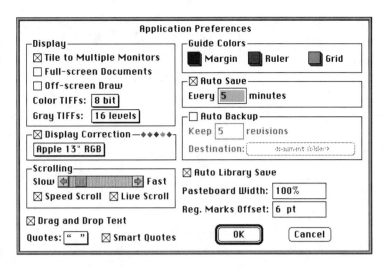

and Grid. The margin guides are the lines that show where the page margins are. The ruler guides are the guides you can pull out onto the page. And the grid guides are the lines that the program shows you when you have Show Baseline Grid enabled (see "Type and Typography," below). Note that this control is only available when your monitor is set to a minimum of 256 levels of gray or color.

The shareware XTension, Default Settings, from a lowly apprentice production, lets you set several other colors, including the highlight color, the page-edge color, and the background color for dialog boxes. As with most XTensions, we recommend you use the latest version (the one made for version 3.2), or else it may not work.

Live Scroll. Steve, our editor, keeps telling us not to be redundant in our writing. And since we already gave our shpiel about Live Scroll (as it was embodied in the FeaturesPlus XTension) back in Chapter 1, *Structure and Interface* (page 74), we'll just say: yes, this is a great feature, and it's great to have it built right in, but it's nowhere near as cool as the Page Grabber Hand.

Speed Scroll. Here's another wonderful enhancement in 3.2 that makes us want to bow down and give thanks in the general direction of Denver (where Quark lives). If you turn on

Speed Scroll, QuarkXPress automatically greeks the display of pictures, graphics and blends as you scroll through a document. Only when you stop scrolling does it take the time to properly display these elements. This may not sound like a big improvement at first, but if you've died of boredom while scrolling through a long document with lots of big four-color TIFFs, you'll appreciate how much time Speed Scroll can save you (that is, unless you *liked* taking a coffee break while you were scrolling).

Scroll Speed. Yep, now there's Speed Scroll *and* Scroll Speed. It's not confusing, is it? Scroll Speed controls how fast QuarkXPress scrolls when you use the scroll bars. Note that the default Scroll Speed control setting is pretty slow. Increasing the speed (by clicking on the right arrow) can make a drastic difference in how quickly you can make your pages (although this won't speed up your redraw any).

Page Grabber Hand. Back in Chapter 1, *Structure and Interface*, we talked about the Page Grabber Hand feature of the FeaturesPlus XTension (hold down Option and drag; see page 74). Like some other features, this was incorporated into version 3.1—and then incorporated right out again in 3.2! The Page Grabber hand is still there in 3.2, but it's permanently on; there's no option to turn it off in the Application Preferences dialog box. We can't imagine why you'd want to, anyway.

Tile to Multiple Monitors. As described back in the "Doing Windows" section, here's where you tell QuarkXPress whether or not you want it to consider *all* the monitors you have plugged into your Mac when it tiles open documents.

Full-screen Documents. Again, we covered this earlier in "Doing Windows." Checking this box lets you zoom windows to fill your entire screen; unchecking it leaves room for the Tools and Measurements palettes.

Off-screen Draw. We can't find any good reason to use Off-screen Draw other than personal preference. If you don't have this on, you can see QuarkXPress redraw each page object one at a time when you scroll around the page. If you enable Off-screen Draw, QuarkXPress redraws all the items "behind the scenes" and shows them to you all at once. It takes just as long either way, so it really comes down to how you like your computer to behave.

Color TIFFs/Gray TIFFs. These controls first saw life as a simple checkbox in version 3.1 that would allow you to choose whether, on 8- or 24-bit monitors, imported grayscale TIFFs would be displayed using 256 or 16 levels of gray. This proved to be so popular that the interface was revised (it's a pop-up menu now) and similar choices extended to color TIFFs. Specifically, you can select 16 (4-bit) or 256 (8-bit) levels of gray for gray-scale TIFFs, and 256 colors (8-bit), thousands of colors (16-bit), or millions of colors (24-bit) display for color TIFF images. These color choices offer a major change over how color TIFFs display in documents; before version 3.2, you could display imported TIFFs as 8-bit images only, regardless of the color depth of the TIFF itself.

Once again, it's a time-versus-quality issue. The lower the bit depth, the faster your screen redraw will be; the higher the bit depth, the better the onscreen display. You can recoup some of the performance hit from higher-quality image displays by selecting "Speed Scroll," above.

Of course, if you don't have 8-, 16-, or 24-bit images, you can't display them in those modes, anyway. Note that these features don't affect the images themselves or how they print—just how they're displayed on the screen.

Auto Library Save. As we said back on page 97, libraries are generally only saved when you close them. Enabling Auto Library Save makes QuarkXPress save the library every time you add an item to it. This slows down production a little, but it's worth it as a safety measure.

Low Resolution TIFF. This preference item first appeared in version 3.1, and then disappeared in version 3.2. Back in 3.1, when you had Low Resolution TIFF checked, imported TIFF images would shown on the screen at 36 dpi. This is the way QuarkXPress has always done it (unless you hold down the Shift key while importing them; see Chapter 8, *Modifying Images*, page 374). However, in version 3.2, the opposite is now the default. TIFFs come in at 72 dpi (screen redraws take longer) unless you hold down the Shift key, in which case you get 36 dpi. The Default Settings XTension from a lowly apprentice production lets you change the import resolution to anything you want.

Display Correction. If you've installed the EfiColor XTension and system (see Appendix D, *EfiColor*), you'll see a checkbox entitled Display Correction in the Application Preferences dialog box. This lets you turn on or off the part of EfiColor that attempts to match your onscreen display of color to match what's available from your selected printer. When you turn on Display Correction, you can select your monitor (if you have a profile installed for it) from a pop-up menu of monitors your EfiColor system knows about. We explain this process in more detail in Appendix D, *EfiColor*.

If you haven't installed EfiColor, but you *have* installed the Pantone Professional Color Toolkit control panel, you'll see the checkbox called "Calibrated Pantone" as your display choice, instead.

Calibrated Pantone. If you don't have EfiColor installed and you turn on the Calibrated Pantone option, QuarkXPress uses the color-matching powers of the Professional Color Toolkit control panel, if it's installed on your system. (It's available for free from Pantone, and from the usual nefarious sources.) Once you've specified your monitor and printer in the Toolkit control panel, it handles color matching of Pantone colors on screen and on printout (the Pantone spot colors being of special importance, since they're hard to simulate with CMYK inks).

It's arguable that EfiColor provides better screen representations of Pantone inks than Pantone's Toolkit does. Both base their screen colors on CIE values, but rumor has it that the Toolkit's CIE values aren't very good (there's an update in progress as we write this). For color-printer output, the Toolkit might provide better output, because it bases printing on CMYK values that are hand-tuned for each color and each printer. There's no need for color correction on separation, of course, because Pantone colors are printed with—you guessed it—Pantone inks.

Another advantage of using the Toolkit instead of EfiColor is speed; if you're just creating spot-color (read: "PMS") jobs, there's usually no reason to suffer the processing overhead that EfiColor imposes.

Pasteboard Width. That pasteboard around each of our document's pages is great, but we usually find it a little too large (and—depending on the job—occasionally too small). Fortunately, we can control how wide the pasteboard is by specifying a percentage in the Pasteboard Width field. The default value of 100 percent tells QuarkXPress to make each side of the pasteboard the same width as one page in the document. That is, if you have an 8½-by-11-inch page, each side of the pasteboard is 8½ inches wide, too. Changing the Pasteboard Width to 50 percent makes the pasteboard half that width. Unfortunately, there's still no way to change the pasteboard space above and below each page.

Reg. Marks Offset. We don't know about you, but if we were operating a two-ton paper-cutting machine on a tight schedule, we wouldn't always make cuts within three or four points (.055 inch) of accuracy. That's what QuarkXPress is asking your printer to do when it prints its registration marks only 6 points from the edge of the page (see Chapter 10, *Printing*, page 473). However, you can adjust how far out you want the registration marks to print with the Reg. Marks Offset control in the Application Preferences dialog box. We generally set this to between 12 and 18 points.

Auto Save. At first glance, Auto Save looks like a yawner. As it turns out, it's anything but. There are plenty of commercial and shareware utilities that will automatically save a document you're working on, as you're working on it. QuicKeys and Now Utilities' NowSave both come to mind.

But all these utilities work by generating the equivalent of QuarkXPress's Save command at predefined intervals. Now suppose you mistakenly delete all of a story; then, before you can undo your deletion, QuicKeys or NowSave kicks in, saving your document—and your mistake—for all eternity (or until you fix your mistake, or lose your job because of it!). For this reason, we've stayed away from autosaving utilities.

Until now. The folks at Quark really got the design of this feature right. You turn Auto Save on by checking the box, and you can specify any interval you want, in minutes, between saves (the default is every five minutes). But—and here's the great part—autosaves don't automatically overwrite your original file. That only happens when you use the Save command. So if you use the Revert to Saved command, you revert to the last saved version of your original file—just as you would expect—*not* to the last autosaved one.

Auto Save exists to help you recover from a dreaded system crash or network communications failure (when you lose the connection to your file server, and QuarkXPress refuses to let you do a "Save As.") After you have a crash, you can restart QuarkXPress and open the autosaved file.

Whenever QuarkXPress does an autosave, it creates a file in the same folder as your document that keeps track of every change you've made since the last time you saved the document. Whenever you save your document, QuarkXPress deletes that incremental file, and starts over again.

The problem with Auto Save is that it creates a file the same size as the one you're working on. If your file is twelve megabytes large, then you'd better have at least twelve megabytes available on your hard drive when you turn Auto Save on. It's a nice system, but far from perfect.

▼ ▼

Tip: Revert to Last Mini-save. Auto Save goes by another name, too: PageMaker calls these things mini-saves. Sometimes you want to use a mini-save as something other than crash insurance. Now you can actually revert to the last autosave instead of going back all the way to the last full save (for instance, if you like the changes you made ten minutes ago, but not the ones you made five minutes ago). Just hold down the Option key when you select Revert from the File menu.

▼ ▼

Auto Backup. Until now, revision control with QuarkXPress has been strictly up to you. If you wanted to keep previous versions of a document, you had to be sure to copy them to another location, or use "Save As" frequently, slightly changing the name of your file each time (we always name our files with version numbers—1.1, 2.4, etc.).

With version 3.2, those days are gone. You can use the Auto Backup function to tell QuarkXPress to keep up to 100 previous versions of your document on disk (the default is five). By clicking on the Destination button, you can specify exactly where you want revisions to be stored. The default, "<document folder>," is simply the folder in which your original document resides. If you ever need to open a previous version of a file, just look in the destination folder. The file with the highest number appended to its name is the most recent revision.

Smart Quotes. This option both turns on the Smart Quotes feature and lets you specify which characters will be used for open and closed quotes. Smart Quotes works by looking to the left of the insertion point to determine if an open or closed quote character should go there. If the character to the left is a white space character, such as a spaceband, tab key, or return, QuarkXPress enters an open single or double quote when you press the ' or " key.

The pop-up menu lets you choose some alternative quote characters, including all closed quotes, Spanish alternatives, and inside and outside guillemet combinations, all of which

"This is an example of Smart Quotes," he said.

"This is a different kind of Smart Quotes," he added.

„Here's yet another kind of Smart Quotes," he continued.

«These quotes are called guillemets,» he went on.

»So are these, but they're reversed,« he concluded.

can be useful if you're formatting foreign-language documents (see Figure C-8).

Tip: Toggling Quotes. Smart Quotes are really cool if you type a lot in QuarkXPress. However, if you ever want to enter a single or double "neutral" straight quote character, it's a hassle to turn Smart Quotes off first. Instead, hold down the Control key when typing the quote (single or double). When Smart Quotes is on, you get a straight quote; when it's off, you get a curly quote.

Drag and Drop Text. We thought drag-and-drop text editing was pretty cool when it was introduced to the Mac world in Microsoft Word 5.0. We think it's even cooler now that it's in our favorite program, introduced in version 3.2. Drag and drop is simply an easy way of copying or moving text from one location in a story to another.

To use drag-and-drop text editing, select some text, then drag the selection to another location in the text chain. As you move the mouse, you'll see an insertion point move along with it. When the insertion point reaches the place where you want the selected text to go, release the mouse button, and presto, your text is cut from its original location, and placed at the insertion point. If you want to copy a selection (instead of just moving it), hold down the Shift key as you drag. Note that any text you drag-move or drag-copy also gets placed in the Clipboard (replacing whatever was there). Also, at least for now, you can't drag-copy text between unlinked text boxes, or between documents—only within continuous text chains.

Trap. Version 3.1 had trap preferences as part of the Application Preferences dialog box. In 3.2, they're broken out into their own dialog box, which we'll discuss in "Color," below.

Saving the XPress Data

As we said earlier, QuarkXPress no longer ships with an XPress Data file. For those of you who don't know what this is, the XPress Data file was the place where QuarkXPress stored all custom (user-defined) kerning tables, tracking tables, frames, and hyphenation information (see Chapter 4, *Type and Typography*). If you moved your document from one machine to another (like sending it to a service bureau), you often had to include the XPress Data file with which it was created. But those days are gone now. We're really broken up about it, too (insert sarcasm here).

Now, when you create a kerning table (or a tracking table, a custom frame, or hyphenation exceptions) while in a document, the information is stored in two places: in XPress Preferences (essentially the same as XPress Data, but with a different name), and *within the file itself*. If you bring that file to another machine with a different XPress Preferences file, that machine alerts you that something is different (the tables in the Preferences file are different from those in the document). It then asks you whether you want to use the information that was stored with the document or not (see Figure C-9). If you respond that you don't want to use the document's original information, QuarkXPress reflows your pages using this new XPress Preferences information. If you respond that you do want to use the document's original information, it is used and continues to be saved right along with that file.

This means that when you send your QuarkXPress documents to a service bureau, you no longer need to include that

Figure C-9
QuarkXPress saves
some information with
the document

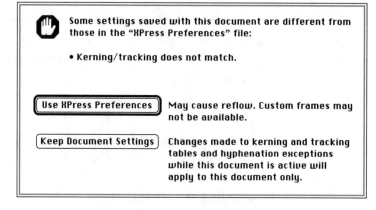

Some settings saved with this document are different from those in the "XPress Preferences" file:

• Kerning/tracking does not match.

Use XPress Preferences — May cause reflow. Custom frames may not be available.

Keep Document Settings — Changes made to kerning and tracking tables and hyphenation exceptions while this document is active will apply to this document only.

elusive XPress Data file. The service bureau just tells the program to use the document's information, and no text reflow occurs.

Version 3.2 also adds an important bit of information to each document that 3.0 and 3.1 inadvertently left out. If you've defined any special trapping information, that is now also contained in documents. So there'll be no more nasty trapping surprises when you look at your press run (or fewer, anyway).

Suppose you create custom information for a document, but don't want that information to be used in the next document you create. When you save and close that first document you can reset kerning or tracking tables, or clear out the hyphenation exceptions dictionary for the next document. If you don't clear and reset these controls, the XPress Preferences file remembers them, and they are used for each document that you create.

▼ ▼

Tip: Resetting and Switching Preferences. The truth of the matter is that the XPress Preferences file is basically the same as the XPress Data file; they just changed its name. If you delete the XPress Preferences file (or move it out of the System folder and the QuarkXPress folder), then QuarkXPress creates a clean, new one for you. This is a great method for starting over from scratch with the default tracking and kerning tables, and with no items in hyphenation exceptions.

If you have two or more XPress Preferences files with varying information, you can move them in and out of your QuarkXPress folder or System folder (preferably with a DA like DiskTop). However, you do have to quit and relaunch QuarkXPress for the new items to take effect.

▼ ▼

Don't worry about your old XPress Data files. They're obsolete, but you can still use them. Just put them in your QuarkXPress folder, make sure there are no XPress Preferences files floating around, and start QuarkXPress. The XPress Data file is magically transformed into an XPress Preferences file!

The Q Measurement

The problem with writing books about computer software is that we often have to send the books to press before the product is even completed. And with computer software, you never know when a feature will be added or removed at the last minute (especially with a company like Quark; they love to add new, cool features whenever possible). That said, we'll tell you about the Q measurement, even though we've been warned that it might disappear in the final release.

No, Q doesn't refer to the character on *Star Trek: The Next Generation* (although people at Quark like this television show so much that the upper management even dressed up in Star Trek uniforms last year at a meeting of high-end, high-volume users). It refers to a little-known measurement used mostly in Japan and Korea, and is exactly a quarter of a millimeter. Although there's almost no chance that Q will show up in the Vertical and Horizontal measurements pop-up menus, hopefully you'll be able to type any measurement as a Q in the palettes and dialog boxes (either upper or lower case is okay).

▼ ▼

Document Construction

Way back at the beginning of this appendix, we noted that everything changes. Well, here we go contradicting ourselves again. One thing that never changes is the need to create good, solid infrastructures for your documents. Out of all the tools available to do this, only a couple of things have changed since version 3.0. The first is that you can now print master pages by selecting Print while having the master page displayed in the document window. No, unfortunately, you can't print all the master pages at once, just one spread at a time. The second is the Document Layout palette.

Document Layout Palette

While the construction of documents hasn't changed much, the Document Layout palette has undergone significant changes in version 3.2.

Goodbye Trashcan. The first thing you'll notice about the palette is just how much its appearance has been changed (see Figure C-10). There's no Trashcan, and the left and right arrows for scrolling through your master pages are gone. Let's take a quick guided tour.

At the top of the palette, just below the title bar, are the two familiar icons for generic blank single-sided and double-sided pages, which you can use to create new master pages. To their right are two new buttons, Duplicate and Delete, whose functions we'll get into shortly. Below these buttons is an area for displaying master pages. Notice that now the master page icons are displayed one below each other, rather than left to right as before. With the 3.0 layout palette, if you had many master pages and wanted to see the icons for all of them, you had to make the palette window very, very wide, which was wasteful of your precious screen space, and ugly, too.

Now, if you need to see multiple master pages, you can easily enlarge the master page area by dragging down on the little black bar that separates the master page area's scroll

Figure C-10

The new Document
Layout palette

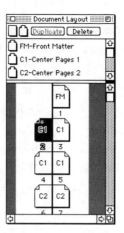

bar from the document page area's scroll bar. Another benefit of this redesign is that you can now see the name of each visible master page, instead of only the master page you've selected.

Naming Master Pages. QuarkXPress's default names for master pages are M1-Master 1, M2-Master 2, and so on. The characters to the left of the hyphen are the names' prefixes. When you apply a master page to a document page, the prefix shows up in the document page's icon, so you know what master's been applied to it. It's easy to rename a master page. Just click on the page's name, and type away. Type to the left of the hyphen to change the prefix, or to the right of the hyphen to change the actual name. Be careful not to wipe out the hyphen; if you do, QuarkXPress assumes everything you've entered is the master page name, and automatically adds a default prefix.

New Pages, Duplicating Pages. As before, you can make a new master page by dragging a blank single- or double-sided page icon into the master page area. You can create a new document page by dragging a master page into the document page area. The technique for creating new master pages based on an existing masters has changed, however. First click on the master you want to copy, and then click the Duplicate button.

Applying a Master Page. Here's another big change in version 3.2. To apply a master page to an existing document page, select the document page, then hold down the Option key and click on the master page you want to apply. In version 3.0 and 3.1, you simply dragged the master page icon on top of the document page.

Why the change? Although there was a certain drag-and-drop elegance to the old method, a slight slip of the mouse could result in your adding a new page when you really wanted to apply a different master to an existing page. Furthermore, you couldn't apply a master page to multiple document pages at once. The new technique makes this simple. Click with the Shift or Command key to select multiple pages, then Option-click on the master page. Similarly, if you want to apply a master page to an existing master page (replacing all its items with those of the source master page), you select the target master page, then Option-click on the source.

Deleting Pages. With the Trashcan replaced by the Delete button, you can be sure that deleting procedures are different in version 3.2. To delete a page or pages, just select what you'd like to delete, then click on the Delete button. (Big surprise, eh?) Option-click on Delete to avoid the dialog box asking if you *really* want to delete the page.

Sections. Creating a new section is also slightly different in the new palette. To start a new section, you can bring up the Section dialog box by clicking on the page number displayed under a document page's icon (see Chapter 2, *Document Construction*).

▼ ▼

Tip: Big Page Numbers. The problem with checking thumbnails on screen is that you can hardly ever figure out what page number is what. Carole Wade notes that she sometimes adds big automatic page numbers (Command-3) that hang off the edge of the pages onto the pasteboard for the left and right master pages (see Figure C-11). You can set these text boxes to have no runaround and turn Suppress Printout on, and

QuarkXPress acts as if they aren't even there. However, even at tiny sizes, you can see them attached to each page.

▼ ▼

Tip: Copying Master Pages. Have you ever wanted to copy a master page from one document to another? Kinda' difficult, isn't it? Well, no, not really. Put both documents into Thumbnail viewing mode and drag a page from the first document into the second. The master page that was assigned to that page comes over along with the page itself. Then you can delete the page itself, and the master page stays in the second document.

▼ ▼

Word Processing

There's one major change to version 3.2's word processing features: drag-and-drop text editing. Three other changes (new find/change and tab-setting capabilities) were introduced in 3.1, all of which make working with text significantly easier than in 3.0.

Drag and Drop Editing

We mentioned this earlier, in "Application Preferences," so here's a quick recap. When this option is active in the Applications Preferences dialog box, you can move selected text by simply dragging it to another location within its text chain. Holding down the Shift key as you drag copies the selected text.

Find/Change

If you use Microsoft Word, you probably know that when you search for text, when the program gets to the end of a document it asks you if you want to circle around and start from the beginning again. That way, if you started your search from the middle of the file, you'll get the first half of it on the second pass. QuarkXPress could never do this, which was a source of constant frustration and amazement to us. We always had to place the text cursor at the beginning of a text

Figure C-11
Thumbnail page
numbers

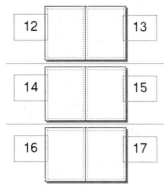

file and do the Find/Change from there. However, now there's an even quicker workaround.

When you have the Find/Change dialog box open, you can hold down the Option key to change the Find Next button to a Find First button. Clicking on the Find First button takes you to the first instance of your search string in that chain of text. You can also just press Option-Return or Option-Enter to activate Find First.

▼ ▼

Tip: Speed Spell-Checking. If you've ever tried to spell-check an enormous document, you've probably too often found yourself waiting for the screen to redraw. Only after the screen redraws can you decide to move on to the next word. Bob Martin points out that the process goes more quickly if you first reduce the window size considerably and then zoom in to 400 percent. QuarkXPress hardly has to redraw anything on the screen each time. Plus, the found text is almost always more visible in the small window.

▼ ▼

New Tabs

When you think of lining up a column of text, you should immediately think of tabs. We can't tell you how often we see people frustrated while trying to add a bunch of spaces between columns. Just type one tab, and set a tab stop. Quark-XPress version 3.1 changed the Paragraph Tabs dialog box slightly and added two more kinds of tab stops, as well as a new kind of tab (see Figure C-12). Let's look at each of these.

Figure C-12

Two new tab stops
and a new tab

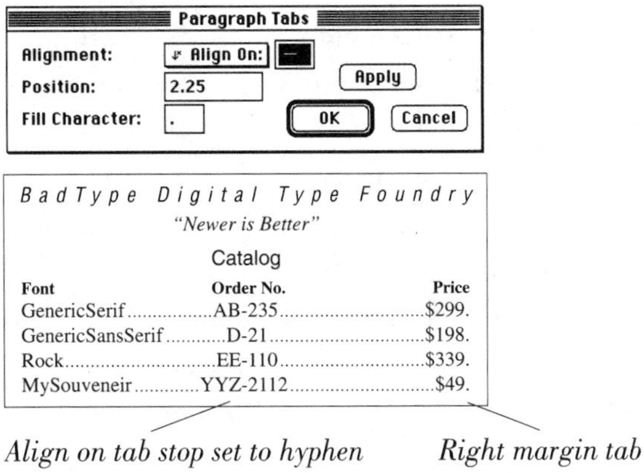

Align on tab stop set to hyphen   *Right margin tab*

Right indent tab. Trying to set a tab stop exactly at the right margin can be very frustrating. Even worse, if your right margin or the size of your text box changes, your tab stop doesn't follow along. Now you can type Option-Tab to insert a Right indent tab. This type of tab acts as though you've placed a right tab stop flush with the right margin of your paragraph. Plus, it moves as you adjust the margin or the text box. (We can hear the handful of people who "get it" sighing appreciatively in the background. Those of you who don't, just try it once and you'll understand.)

The Right indent tab acts just like a tab character (you can even search for it the same way, using "\t"), though there's no way to set its own leader (what QuarkXPress calls a "fill character"). It picks up the same leader as the last tab stop in the paragraph. Note that you won't see a tab stop in the Tab dialog box's ruler: it's always set to the right margin, wherever that is. Also, you should note that Option-Tab jumps past all other tab stops in that paragraph, all the way over to the right margin.

Comma tab stop. If you're reading this in Europe or anyplace else where it's common to type a decimal using a comma rather than a period (as we usually do here in North America), you'll like the new Comma tab stop. It acts just like the decimal tab stop (see "Tabs," on page 220), except that it uses a comma.

Align On tab stop. Actually, tab stops aren't limited to the period or comma characters anymore. Now you can align tabbed text at any character by choosing Align On from the new Alignment pop-up menu in the Paragraph Tabs dialog box. When this tab stop style is selected, QuarkXPress adds a small text field in which you can type the character to which you want the tabbed text to align. The default character is a period. (This is the same as a QuarkXPress 3.0 decimal tab stop; however, decimal tabs are now slightly different; see below.) If you change it to a dollar sign, the tabs line up at that dollar sign (see Figure C-13).

▼ ▼

Tip: Hanging Tabs. There's another subtle change introduced in QuarkXPress 3.1 which you'll love if you ever create balance sheets. The decimal tab doesn't just line up decimals any more. In fact, QuarkXPress now thinks of any non-number that falls after a number to be a "decimal point," and aligns to it. For example, if you type "<tab>94c2.44" on a line with a decimal tab, QuarkXPress aligns to the "c" rather than the period. We thought this was a bug, until we realized how handy it could be. For example, if you are lining up numbers in a column, the negative-balance parentheses hang outside of the column. You can even create hanging footnotes, as long as they're not numbers (see Figure C-14).

▼ ▼

Tip: Formatting Tabs Quickly. Barry Simon pointed out to us that you can sometimes format tabs for a number of lines more easily by just working on a single line. If you set the proper tab settings for the first line first, you can quickly apply those settings to the rest of the lines by selecting all the lines

Figure C-13
Align On tab

> **Public Contributions to the**
> **Chavez Private Museum**
> **of Private Art**
>
> *"All the art for some of the people"*
>
> Los Angeles ....US$45M
> Toronto................................CAN$23.3M
> New York ....US$136M
> Sydney.................................AUS$3M
> Liberia..................................LIB$18.1M

Grazing Goose Records
"It's a cadillac, dear."

Securities	$223
Properties	152[A]
Cash	(148)[B]
Shoebox fund	33

[A]This month's rent is paid
[B]We owe that guy for the pizzas

(including the first one), opening the Tabs dialog box (Command-Shift-T), and clicking OK (or pressing Return). The tab setting for the first line automatically gets applied to all the rest of the lines.

▼ ▼

Type and Typography

There's no denying that QuarkXPress remains the typographic standard against which all other programs are measured. Quark could have sat around on its laurels, but it didn't. QuarkXPress 3.1 added several exciting new features to help when you're wrestling with type, including Show Baseline Grid, adjustable Flex Space width, and increased kerning and tracking limits. Typographic enhancements added in version 3.2 are subtle, but welcome: control over whether accents appear over text formatted with the All Caps character style, Smart Quotes, vertical as well as horizontal scaling, and forced justification.

Automatic Ligatures

This might not seem like such a big deal to you, but our favorite new typographic feature, added in 3.1, is automatic ligatures. Ligatures (in case you don't remember from Chapter 5, *Type and Typography*, page 254) are specially designed characters that look like two letters touching. For example, if you type "fi" in most typefaces, the "i" bumps into the "f" and you get what we in the publishing business call "ugly." Instead, in many cases it's a good practice to replace the "f" and the "i" with the "fi" ligature.

QuarkXPress can now automatically replace the "fi" and the "fl" combinations with their respective ligatures *as you type them*. The key here is the Ligatures pop-up menu in the Typographic Preferences dialog box (Command-Option-Y). This pop-up menu contains three items: Off, On, and On (not ffi or ffl). Off is pretty self-explanatory: QuarkXPress won't replace any characters for you. If you select On, QuarkXPress turns the automatic replacement of every instance of "fi" or "fl" into a ligature (if your typeface has those ligature characters). The third choice, On (not ffi or ffl), is for some finicky folks who think that those particular combinations should not get the ligature treatment. We disagree (see "Tip: Pull Those Ligatures Tighter," below).

The first wonderful thing about automatic ligatures is that they work at all (see Figure C-15). The second wonderful thing is that you can edit them. That is, once you have characters that are turned into a ligature, you can still select among the characters or edit one of the characters, and so on.

Figure C-15
Ligatures

Officially, the finalists were affluent flounder

Without ligatures

Officially, the finalists were affluent flounder

With ligatures

The Ligatures feature in the Typographic Preferences dialog box includes a small text field off to the right that becomes active when you turn automatic ligatures on. The number in this field tells QuarkXPress the tracking or kerning level above which to break the ligature apart. For example, when the number in the field is 1, if the ligature is kerned or tracked more than 1 unit, the ligature breaks apart, becoming separate characters. If you change the number to 5, then QuarkXPress maintains the ligature until tracking or kerning has reached 6 units.

This is an important feature because you don't want two characters stuck together in "loose" text (it stands out too much). This kerning and tracking limit also applies to justified text. That is, if a text block is justified by adding space between characters, the ligatures break apart when necessary.

The third wonderful thing about automatic ligatures is that they solve the age-old problem of searching for and spell-checking text. For example, in previous versions of QuarkXPress, if you changed the word "official" to include a ligature (in the way described back in Chapter 4, *Type and Typography*), you could no longer search just for the word "official." You had to type the word with the special ligature symbol into the Find text field.

Likewise, when you went to spell-check your document, QuarkXPress wouldn't know the word, because it didn't understand what a ligature was. Hyphenation was also a problem for the same reason. Now, if you use automatic ligatures, all these problems go away because you're not typing any weird Option-Shift-5 or -6 characters.

Note that some typefaces don't have built-in ligatures, and others have them but QuarkXPress doesn't "see" them (this is especially true with some older Type 3 fonts). So the system's not totally foolproof, but it's still pretty good.

▼ ▼

Tip: Pull Those Ligatures Tighter. Ligatures make pages generally nicer looking, and automatic ligatures make life generally nicer to live. There are still two instances (actually there are many more, but we'll just focus on two here) where you need to look carefully at your ligatures: the "ffi" and the "ffl." As we mentioned above, you can turn automatic ligatures off for these character combinations, but we really can't see why you'd want to do this. Instead, we sometimes like to go in and pull the two "f's" slightly tighter together, often so that the crossbars touch (see Figure C-16). This gives the impression of a three-character ligature. However, many typefaces aren't malleable enough to do this. Either you have to kern in so tightly that the letterspacing looks odd, or you end up with the serif of the first "f" bumping into the second "f," and the whole thing looks even uglier than before. Therefore, in this tip, as in so many others, we urge you to take care with your typography; look closely, and keep your fingers on the Command-Z (Undo) keystroke.

▼ ▼

Figure C-16
The ffi and ffl ligatures

The Affluent Officer
The Affluent Officer

New Preferences

Other than automatic ligatures, QuarkXPress lets you set several other new preferences. Some of these you'll never touch, but it's good to know about them anyway.

Accents For All Caps. A typographic refinement added in version 3.2 lets you specify whether accents appear on accented characters to which you've applied the All Caps character style. Depending on the design of your document or what language you're working in, you may want to turn this feature—found in the Typographic Preferences dialog box—on or off.

Ciceros/Centimeter. We all know that 72 traditional points don't really measure an inch, right? However, a 72-to-the-inch point has quickly become a standard in the industry. Therefore, back at the end of Chapter 1, *Structure And Interface*, we noted that we just leave the points/inch control in the General Preferences dialog box (Command-Y) set to 72. QuarkXPress 3.1 added the option of changing the number of ciceros per centimeter in the same dialog box.

A cicero, in case you're like us (*Americanus Stupidus*), is a measurement in the Didot system, used primarily in France and other continental European countries. Just as a pica equals 12 points, the cicero equals 12 points. The difference? Differently sized points. A Didot point equals .01483 inch instead of the American-British .01383 inch. Anyway, the only really important thing about all this is that QuarkXPress defaults to 2.1967 ciceros per centimeter. This is close enough to a traditional cicero (you can do the math)....

Note that this control doesn't change the points-per-inch value any; if you're working in any measurement system other than ciceros, just ignore this control.

Alternate Em. Quark has always defined an em space as the width of two zeros of the current typeface. However, almost no one else in the world defines an em like that. Quark has promised us that in the final release of version 3.2, you will be able to turn on an Alternate Em setting. The Alternate Em sets the em space (and therefore all the settings based on it, such as kerning, tracking, and so on) to the size of the typeface you're using. For example, if you're typing in a fourteen-point typeface, QuarkXPress's em space (with Alternate Em turned on) is fourteen points wide. If they don't include this in the first release of QuarkXPress 3.2, scream loudly in the general direction of Quark.

Flex Space Width. When you type Option-Shift-Space you get what's called a flex space. This is just like a spaceband but you can specify how wide you want it to be (it flexes to your will). Also, once you specify its width, this space is fixed; it won't change width, even in justified text.

The control for this character's width is in the Typographic Preferences dialog box (Command-Option-Y). The percentage is based on the width of an en space. Therefore, the default value, 50 percent, is half an en space. 200 percent makes the flex space an em space. However, note that em or en spaces created with the flex space probably won't be the same widths as em or en dashes in a font (see "Tip: Know Your Ems And Ens," on page 189). Also note that when you change the width of a flex space in the Typographic Preferences dialog box, QuarkXPress changes the widths of flex spaces throughout that document.

Maintain Leading. If you don't use baseline grids (see page 235), but still want to maintain consistent leading on your page, you might want to look closely at the new Maintain Leading feature. This feature—which we usually just leave turned on in the Typographic Preferences dialog box— ensures that each line in a text box is placed according to its leading value when another object (such as a picture box or a line) obstructs the text and moves text lines around.

When Maintain Leading is turned off, two things happen. First, the line of text following an obstruction abuts the bottom of that obstruction (or its text runaround, if the runaround value is larger than 0 points). Second, the rest of the lines of text in that text box fall on a different leading grid than do those above the obstruction. This is much easier to see than to read (or write) about, so check out Figure C-17. This feature has no bearing on paragraphs that are already set to lock to baseline grid.

Figure C-17
Maintain Leading

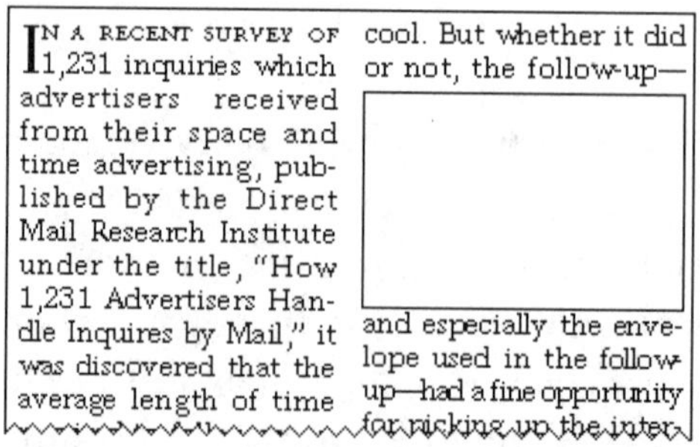

IN A RECENT SURVEY OF 1,231 inquiries which advertisers received from their space and time advertising, published by the Direct Mail Research Institute under the title, "How 1,231 Advertisers Handle Inquires by Mail," it was discovered that the average length of time

cool. But whether it did or not, the follow-up—

and especially the envelope used in the follow up—had a fine opportunity for picking up the inter-

Here, Maintain Leading is turned off; the columns don't match.

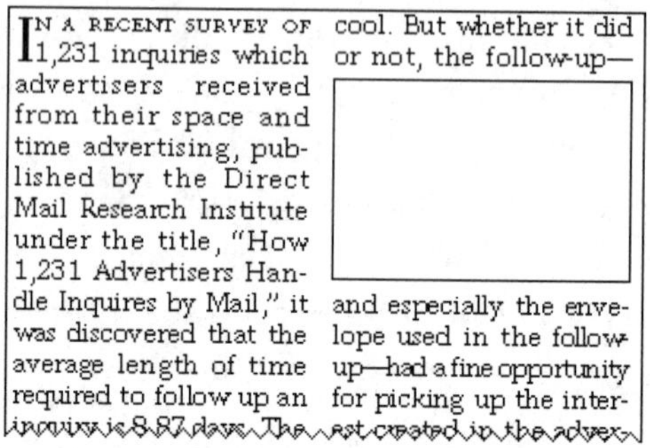

IN A RECENT SURVEY OF 1,231 inquiries which advertisers received from their space and time advertising, published by the Direct Mail Research Institute under the title, "How 1,231 Advertisers Handle Inquires by Mail," it was discovered that the average length of time required to follow up an inquiry is 8.87 days. The

cool. But whether it did or not, the follow-up—

and especially the envelope used in the follow up—had a fine opportunity for picking up the inter-

Here, Maintain Leading is turned on, and the columns align.

Show/Hide Baseline Grid. This last item is less a typographic preference than an aid in page layout. You can display the usually-invisible baseline grid (see page 235) by selecting Show Baseline Grid from the View menu. You can hide it again by selecting Hide Baseline Grid from the same menu. Like many other features in QuarkXPress, this is a great candidate for a QuicKey macro. You can also change the color of the baseline grid guidelines in the Application Preferences dialog box (see "Application Preferences," above).

Note that the baseline grid guides you see when you select Show Baseline Grid act just like ruler guides. They follow the guides control in the General Preferences dialog box (Command-Y) as to whether they appear in front of or behind page items. Plus, when Snap to Guides is on, page items snap to the baseline grid guides (when they're showing).

Smart Quotes

This addition in version 3.2 automatically enters open or closed quote characters as you type. You can also select other characters to be used in place of English open and closed quotes. For a detailed description of how Smart Quotes works, see "Application Preferences," above.

Opening Fonts

He's not sure why, but David seems to have trouble remembering to open all the typefaces he needs in a document. For example, if he has a page that has four different fonts on it, he—as often as not—will fail to open one of those fonts using MasterJuggler (which he prefers tenfold over Suitcase) before he starts QuarkXPress. So he's always had to quit QuarkXPress, load that font, then start the program again. But no longer. David's a happy guy, because as of version 3.1, QuarkXPress can use a font as soon as you open it with Suitcase II or MasterJuggler, even if you're still in the program and your document is open. We call this "instant font updating." You may notice that QuarkXPress sometimes pauses longer than usual after you open the font; it's just updating its internal font list.

In QuarkXPress 3.2, you can also change your document's missing fonts into fonts that are available. See "Forbidden Fonts" in the "Mac to PC Transfer" section later in this chapter for more information.

Horizontal and Vertical Scaling

You've been able to apply horizontal scaling to type in QuarkXPress for ages; now version 3.2 adds vertical type scaling as well. In the Style menu, the Horizontal Scale command is now Horizontal/Vertical Scale.

The dialog box is the same, but with the addition of a pop-up menu you can use to choose whether you're specifying horizontal or vertical scaling. As with horizontal scaling, you can enter a value between 25 and 400 percent. Note that you can't apply both horizontal and vertical scaling to a block of type simultaneously. You must apply either one or the other, and, if necessary, change the type's point size to adjust it in the second direction.

Also, the type scaling keyboard shortcuts remain the same, Command-[and Command-], with one change: these keystrokes scale text either horizontally or vertically, depending on which direction is currently selected in the pop-up menu in the dialog box.

Kerning and Tracking Values

And while we're on the subject of character formatting, you should know that QuarkXPress can now take kerning and tracking values up to plus or minus 500 units (it used to be a measly 100 units). Remember, each unit is $\frac{1}{200}$ of an em. This means that you can really space out type. It also means that you can finally place one character right on top of the preceding character without resorting to using both kerning *and* tracking.

The H&Js of Paragraph Formatting

QuarkXPress 3.1 added a few interesting features that pertain to hyphenation and justification (H&J). First of all, Quark added the Single Word Justify feature to the Edit

Hyphenation & Justification dialog box. This checkbox lets you tell QuarkXPress whether you want a word that falls on a justified line by itself to be force-justified (see Figure C-18). Newspapers will probably leave this on. Art directors of fancy foreign magazines might insist that it get turned off. Personally, we don't like how the word looks either way, and we'd just as soon have the sentence rewritten, or play with other character formatting to reflow the paragraph. Note that this feature doesn't apply to the last line of a paragraph; you still need to use the Flush Zone (see Chapter 4, *Type and Typography*, page 229).

Secondly, when you delete an H&J setting, QuarkXPress 3.2 now prompts you for a replacement.

Figure C-18
Single Word Justify

Quietly, he stalked over to the celery and nibbled gently at it's greens. "Oh, you taste so good," he mumbled through the fibrous vegetable.

A knock at the door! Quickly stuffing the long, slender, store-bought foodstuff into a drawer, he sprung blithely to receive his visitor, only to be greeted by thirty-six thousand members of the feared Fruit-and-Vegetablist Majority. He knew he was in trouble now.

"We know you've been objectifying vegetables again, Mr. Harwood. And we've come to put a

Quietly, he stalked over to the celery and nibbled gently at it's greens. "Oh, you taste so good," he mumbled through the fibrous vegetable.

A knock at the door! Quickly stuffing the long, slender, store-bought foodstuff into a drawer, he sprung blithely to receive his visitor, only to be greeted by thirty-six thousand members of the feared Fruit-and-Vegetablist Majority. He knew he was in trouble now.

"We know you've been objectifying vegetables again, Mr. Harwood. And we've come to put a

In the example on the right, Single Word Justify is turned off. Note the word "Fruit-and-Vegetablist."

Forced Justification. Speaking of justification, QuarkXPress 3.2 has a new alignment mode: Forced. When you select Forced Justification (from the Style menu, the Measurements palette, or by typing Command-Shift-M), QuarkXPress forces every line in a paragraph to be justified, including lines that wouldn't ordinarily extend to the margin, such as a single word on the last line, or a single-line paragraph.

Forced Justification has basically the same effect as creating a Hyphenation and Justification setting with a very large Flush Zone (see page 229). It takes a lot of steps to define and apply such an H&J setting, however, so Quark's made it easy with the Forced mode.

Enhanced Hyphenation. The Quark folks haven't been idle in their H&J research, either. They've come up with a hyphenation scheme that breaks more words better. They call it (surprise) Enhanced Hyphenation. For example, "academy," "appendix," and "electromechanical" all now break the way you'd hope they would. To switch to this mode, select Enhanced in the Typographic Preferences dialog box (Command-Option-Y).

Custom H&J. Before we move on, we should just quickly mention that Quark has included hooks into its H&J controls for XTension developers. What this means is that various third parties can now create their own hyphenation modules. So if you have a particular religious preference for Houghton Mifflin's hyphenation style, you can badger them into developing a special XTension that uses it. None of these modules exist as of this writing, but by the time you read it, something may have been developed.

▼ ▼

Copy Flow

Versions 3.1 and 3.2 of QuarkXPress add a number of new Style Sheets features. There's a Style Sheets palette, you can now specify a Next Style, and it's easier to append styles. Let's look at each of these features and how you can use them.

Style Sheets Palette

We glossed right past a mention of the Style Sheets palette earlier, as if it were hardly of importance. Now we're back to tell you how important this new feature really is. Wow. This is a feature we wish QuarkXPress had had since the beginning. PageMaker users will recognize the Style Sheets palette instantly, as that program has had one for years. The principle is simple: whenever you're working with text, you can apply, edit, and view style sheets on the fly by using the Style Sheets palette (see Figure C-19). The palette lists all the style sheets in your document (if you have lots of styles, you can make the palette larger or just scroll through them), along with their keyboard shortcuts if they have any.

Figure C-19
The Style Sheets palette

The beauty of this floating palette is that you can put it right next to your text box while you work. To apply any style to a paragraph, just put the text cursor somewhere in that paragraph, and click on the desired style in the palette. To apply No Style to a paragraph, just click on No Style in the palette. As you move through your text, the style sheet for each paragraph is highlighted in the Style Sheets palette; you can quickly see what styles are applied. This is especially helpful if local formatting overrides styles (especially in version 3.2; see "Local Formatting," below), or if you have two styles that are similar and you want to know if a paragraph is tagged with one or the other.

To edit a style, click on that style in the palette while holding down the Command key. This brings up the Style Sheets dialog box with the style highlighted. Just click on Edit, or type Return or Enter to edit that style sheet.

▼ ▼

Tip: Creating New Styles. Note that because Command-clicking on a style in the Style Sheets palette brings you to the Style Sheets dialog box, you can quickly create a new style by clicking on the New or Duplicate buttons instead of on the Edit button. This is faster than selecting Style Sheets from the Edit menu, but perhaps not quite as fast as creating a QuicKey macro to do it for you (depending on how you work best).

▼ ▼

Local Formatting

In version 3.2, if there are any local paragraph-formatting or character attributes in the selected text or paragraph containing the insertion point (formatting that overrides the current style's formatting,) a plus sign appears to the right of the style's name in the palette. This is a handy way of knowing if you're looking at a paragraph formatted according to its style, or at formatting that's been applied locally (see Figure C-20).

Figure C-20
Local formatting flag

□ Style Sheets	
No Style	
Call outs	F7
catch line	F12
DID YOU KNOW Heads+	**F8**
FIRST WORDS	F5
LABELS	F9
MAIN TEXT	F6
Normal	

▼ ▼

Tip: Totally Overriding Local Formatting. As we noted back in Chapter 5, *Copy Flow* (see page 289), any paragraph that has No Style applied to it loses all local formatting (including bold and italic) when it's tagged with another style. This, more often than not, is a pain in the butt and causes much confusion. However, there are some powerful uses for this feature, such as stripping out all local formatting that some dumbbell put in for no good reason.

Always on the lookout for a faster way to do something, we were pleased to find that we could apply No Style to a paragraph and then apply a style sheet in one stroke by Option-clicking on the style.

▼ ▼

Next Style

Word processors have had this feature for years, and we're delighted to see it now in version 3.2. In the Edit Style Sheet dialog box, there's a pop-up menu you can use to select the style that QuarkXPress will automatically apply to the next paragraph you create after one with the style you're defining. For example, if you've created a style called Heading to be followed by one called Normal, you can apply the Heading style to a paragraph, and when you press Return after you've typed your heading copy, the new paragraph will have the Normal style.

Note that this only works if the insertion point at the very end of a paragraph when you press Return. If the insertion point is in the middle of a paragraph when you press Return, you'll simply break that paragraph in two, and both new paragraphs will have the same style as the original one.

Also, note that when you're defining a new style, one of the choices in the Next Style pop-up menu is "Self." It's only available when you're creating a new style and haven't yet named it.

Appending Styles

Prior to version 3.2, if you wanted to import styles into your document that had the same name as a currently defined style, you were out of luck. QuarkXPress wouldn't do it (and wouldn't even alert you to the problem) until you first deleted the style with the same name in your target document. Since this would replace that style with No Style wherever you'd applied it, deleting a style was a pretty drastic step (you had to go through and restyle all the paragraphs; see "Tip: Deleting Styles," below). It was usually easier to simply redefine the style by hand in your target document rather than to delete it and import the style with the same name.

Well, in version 3.2, Quark has taken the first step towards solving this problem. Now, if you bring styles into a document by using the Append command, QuarkXPress checks to see if there are styles in your target document with the same name as any you're importing (see Figure C-21). If it finds such a conflict, it displays a dialog box showing the name and characteristics of the conflicting styles, and gives you the option of renaming the style that's being imported, or simply ignoring it and using the existing style. If you rename the style, QuarkXPress appends an asterisk to its name, and imports it.

Note that if you import a style sheet by dragging a page or a text box from one document to another, QuarkXPress won't alert you that there is a style-name conflict.

Although this is a step in the right direction, we'd still love to see QuarkXPress allow you to actually replace style definitions when there are style-name conflicts (see "Tip: Overwriting Existing Styles," below). Most word processors let you do it, and it's a handy way to quickly change all the formatting in a document.

Figure C-21
Conflicting style sheets
dialog box

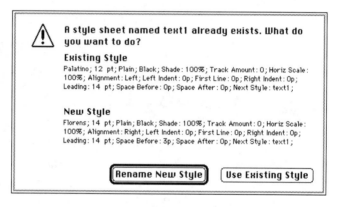

> ⚠ **A style sheet named text1 already exists. What do you want to do?**
>
> **Existing Style**
> Palatino; 12 pt; Plain; Black; Shade: 100%; Track Amount: 0; Horiz Scale: 100%; Alignment: Left; Left Indent: 0p; First Line: 0p; Right Indent: 0p; Leading: 14 pt; Space Before: 0p; Space After: 0p; Next Style: text1;
>
> **New Style**
> Florens; 14 pt; Plain; Black; Shade: 100%; Track Amount: 0; Horiz Scale: 100%; Alignment: Right; Left Indent: 0p; First Line: 0p; Right Indent: 0p; Leading: 14 pt; Space Before: 3p; Space After: 0p; Next Style: text1;
>
> [Rename New Style] [Use Existing Style]

Tip: Deleting Styles. Okay, we're going to go out on a limb here. Quark has told us that in the final release of QuarkXPress 3.2, when you delete a style sheet, the program will ask you if you want to replace it with another one. That is, all the text that is tagged with the deleted style would be assigned a new style sheet, rather than going to No Style. The dialog box that you'll see is similar to the one you now get when you delete a color or an H&J setting. We think this is one of the coolest features about style sheets in version 3.2.

Tip: Style Sheet Page Breaks. PageMaker has a kind of cool feature that we like: you can specify a paragraph style that breaks to a new page. That is, any paragraph that is tagged with this attribute will always start at the top of a page or column. As it turns out, you can do a similar thing in Quark-XPress. Many readers pointed out that you can simply make the Space Before value in the Paragraph Formats dialog box as large as the text column is tall. For example, if your text box is 45 picas tall, make the Space Before value 45 picas. You can set this as a paragraph style or as local formatting.

▼ ▼

Xstyle

The Style Sheets palette is great, but this discussion wouldn't be complete if we didn't mention Em Software's Xstyle XTension. This add-on takes the Style Sheets palette concept and runs with it, adding all sorts of functionality (see Figure C-22). For example, it has pop-up menus that work the way all pop-up menus should: just type the first couple of letters of the style sheet's name and it figures out which one you want. Plus, you can quickly add or change local paragraph and character formatting. There's even a built-in method for creating pseudo-character styles (similar to Frank Kubin's CopySpecs XTension, but handled differently). This XTension still has its limitations, but it's made life a lot nicer for us. For example, check out "Tip: Overwriting Existing Styles," below.

Figure C-22
Xstyle's floating
palettes

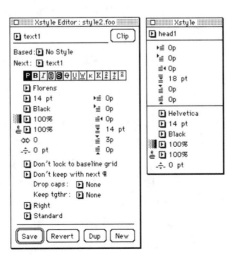

▼ ▼

Tip: Overwriting Existing Styles. As we said earlier, we wish that there were a little more control over how QuarkXPress handles importing style sheets. But take heart: there are always workarounds. Here's a great one from our friend Mike Arst that lets you import style sheets that override the ones within your document. He does it by merging styles using the Xstyle XTension.

1. Import the new style sheets from another document using the Append button in the Style Sheets dialog box. When it asks you whether you want to rename the incoming styles or not, click on Rename. As we said earlier, QuarkXPress adds an asterisk after the name of each new style.

2. Click on Save to exit that dialog box, and then open Xstyle's Style Editor palette.

3. Select the new style in the Style Editor palette. For example, select "Text*".

4. Click on the Clip button in that palette. This saves the style sheet's formatting to a buffer area, so you can reapply it later.

5. Select the old style in the Style Editor palette. In this case, that'd be "Text" (without the asterisk).

6. Now, hold down the Option key, and select *Clipped "Text*"* from the Style Editor palette's pop-up menu.

7. Click on the palette's Save button.

Now the old style is the same as the newly imported style, and you can delete the newly imported style. In effect, the old style sheet name has been overwritten by the new one. We know that this sounds like a lot of steps, but it's actually really easy and fast.

▼ ▼

Pictures

Earlier in this appendix, we looked at various Application Preferences such as the bit-depth options for color and gray-scale TIFFs. These aren't the only new features in QuarkXPress that have to do with pictures. There are a few others; each of them is minor, but useful nonetheless. Let's take a look.

Previews

It's not that these first two features aren't useful, it's just that they don't shake the very foundations of how we've come to know QuarkXPress. The first is a TIFF/RIFF previewer. This means that when you are importing pictures, you can now see a preview of TIFF or RIFF pictures as well as EPS and PICT graphics. Quark has done a pretty good job of optimizing the preview speed, but if you don't need to see the picture to pick it, you're still better off not turning the Picture Preview checkbox on.

The second new picture-oriented feature is a Picture Preview window in the Find Missing Picture dialog box, for when you need to find missing pictures (see Figure C-23). This previewer works in the same way as the Picture Preview in the Get Picture dialog box: the checkbox in the upper right corner turns it on and off.

Turning Off Printing from Picture Usage

Sometimes a change in QuarkXPress doesn't seem like a big deal until you realize how much time it can save you under the right circumstances. One of these sleeper changes is version 3.2's addition to the Picture Usage dialog box. There's now a column at the far right which you can use to turn on or off the printing of each picture individually (see Figure C-24). When you think of a document that has lots of pictures, some that you want to print sometimes, others that you want to print other times, you can see how valuable this feature really is.

Figure C-23

The picture previewer

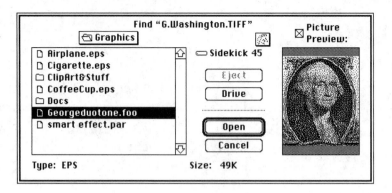

Find "G.Washington.TIFF"

☒ Picture
    Preview:

Graphics

☐ Airplane.eps
☐ Cigarette.eps
☐ ClipArt&Stuff
☐ CoffeeCup.eps
☐ Docs
☐ Georgeduotone.foo
☐ smart effect.par

⊖ Sidekick 45

Eject

Drive

Open

Cancel

Type: EPS

Size: 49K

▼ ▼

Tip: Overprinting TIFFs. We really like the way Adobe Photoshop handles duotones (or tritones or quadtones). They're simple to make, they separate beautifully from QuarkXPress as EPS files (as long as you have the spot colors' names the same in both programs), and you can see what they look like in color. However, if you can't—or won't—use Photoshop for this, you can now create duotones within QuarkXPress using a simple—albeit klunky—technique.

The method relies on overprinting one TIFF image on another. We generally import a gray-scale TIFF into a picture box, size it, and position it where we want it. Then we clone it (see "Tip: Clone Item," on page 62), change the color and the contrast curve for this second image, and make sure that the background color of the overprinting image is set to None. Last, we set the trap for the picture box background to overprint in the Trap Information palette.

Lithographers have all sorts of methods for creating duotones (they're the ones who have traditionally made them). Some change the line screen of one plate. Others change the contrast curve slightly. We recommend the latter.

New Picture File Formats

Just in case someone gives you a picture in one of those strange DOS or Windows file formats, QuarkXPress is now flexible enough to handle them. We don't want to spend a lot of time on these, because we think you'd be crazy to use

Figure C-24

The Picture Usage
dialog box

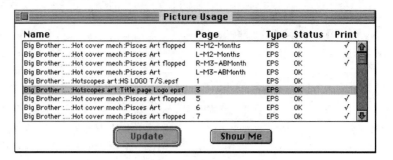

them in a professional graphic arts setting. They're not reliable or powerful enough to do high-quality work. As we said back in Chapter 5, *Pictures*, we recommend TIFF and EPS much more.

Windows Bitmap. Windows Bitmap (.BMP) is the bitmap format native to Windows Paint, but isn't usually encountered outside of Windows and OS/2 Presentation Manager. We still prefer TIFF to this format.

Windows Metafile. Closely tied to graphics technology underlying Windows, Windows Metafile (.WMF) is a reliable object-oriented format to use in Windows. However, when you take it out of that environment and on to the Macintosh, things get a little weird. Fonts that are embedded in the graphic really get messed up, and colors can get screwy, too. We suggest leaving this at home on the PC.

Scitex CT & LW files. Starting with version 3.1, QuarkXPress can import both Scitex CT (continuous tone) and LW (line work) files. However, it can only separate CT files. Note that when we say CT files, we are actually referring to CT HandShake files. We know of at least one guy who got burned because he asked a color house for CT files and got Scitex's proprietary format instead of the open-format CT HandShake files.

PhotoCD. If you have the PhotoCD XTension loaded in your QuarkXPress folder, you'll be able to open images saved in Kodak's PhotoCD format through the Get Picture dialog box.

▼ ▼

System 7 Subscription

Marketing blitz! Everybody hit the ground!

Seriously, the hoopla that surrounded the introduction of System 7 has still got our heads spinning, but we were never sure that it was worth the dizziness. Of course QuarkXPress 3.1 and 3.2 work fine under System 7. In fact, they even have one feature that works only under System 7: Subscribe.

In the last edition of this book, we took a pretty hard line with Publish and Subscribe; we didn't think it was worth its weight in RAM. But the developments over the past year are making us change our minds. Let's take a look at how this system feature can be a powerful asset to you.

Publish and Subscribe Lesson #1

Let's start out with a quick vocabulary lesson. Subscribe is the second half of "Publish and Subscribe." The concept—in case you haven't been bombarded with information like we have—is that you can publish a picture in one program, subscribe to it in QuarkXPress, and then whenever that picture is updated, QuarkXPress can automatically update itself. The file itself is called an "edition."

The original problem with Publish and Subscribe was (and is) that most edition files are PICT files, which we like using about as much as being bludgeoned by blunt objects. PICT files and PICT editions are just plain inconsistent when it comes to fonts, line weights, tints, and so on, making them less than useful for graphic arts production work.

However, edition files can now be in the form of an EPS. An EPS edition is much, much more consistent and useful. We'll look at just how useful in a moment. Note that the only programs that we know of which can publish EPS editions at this time are Adobe Photoshop, Aldus FreeHand, Adobe Illustrator, and Brøderbund's TypeStyler.

How to Be a Publisher

Here's a (very) quick lesson in how to publish an edition. Create a picture in your graphics application. You can select all of it, or a portion of it, and publish it (usually done by selecting Create Publisher from the Edit menu). When you publish it, you create an "intermediate" file, called an edition file. You can't edit this file, but whenever you save a change to the source document, the edition file gets automatically updated. When you create the edition, you sometimes have to specifically ask that the program create it as an EPS edition rather than as a PICT edition.

In QuarkXPress, subscribing to an edition file is much the same as importing a picture, except that you use the Subscribe To command under the Edit menu, rather than the Get Picture command. Why they put it in the Edit menu, we'll never know; but there it is. The edition looks like a picture, it acts like a picture, it even shows up in the Picture Usage dialog box like a picture. In fact, there's only one little clue that tells you it's an edition: if you go to the Subscriber Options dialog box (see below), there's a little gray square next to the graphic's name, indicating that it's an edition.

Subscriber Options

So what is Subscriber Options? Subscriber Options is a dialog box that lets you do a number of nifty things (see Figure C-25). You get to it by choosing Subscriber Options from the Edit menu or by double-clicking on the picture box with the Content tool (you have to have the picture box selected first to do either of these).

Figure C-25
The Subscriber Options
dialog box

Subscriber to:	☐ FigureC-23 ▼	
Get Editions:		Cancel Subscriber
○ Automatically		Open Publisher
● Manually	Get Edition Now	
Latest Edition:	Thursday, May 6, 1993 3:07:15 PM	
Last Received:	Friday, January 1, 1904 12:00:00 AM	Cancel OK

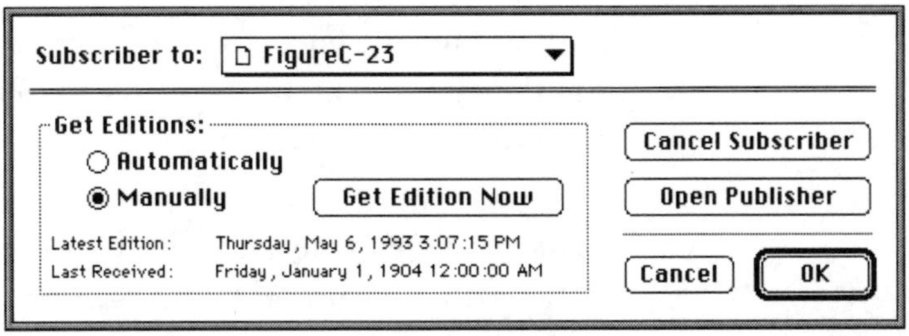

At the top of the dialog box is a pop-up menu showing the path to the selected picture. Sometimes this can be handier than puzzling out a picture's path from the often-truncated listing in the Picture Usage window. You can tell whether the image is an edition or a regular file by what icon is sitting next to its name. A little icon of a document page means it's a regular picture. A little gray square means it's an edition.

There are several important features in the Subscriber Options dialog box, including Get Editions, Cancel Subscriber, and Open Publisher.

Get Editions. Below the path display are two radio buttons in the Get Editions area. These buttons determine whether QuarkXPress automatically updates that picture every time the edition file is changed, or whether you must update the picture manually.

The Subscriber Options dialog box shows you the last time that QuarkXPress imported or updated the picture (Latest Edition). If you select the Manual button, then QuarkXPress also gives you the Last Received information. To tell you the truth, we can't figure out when this value would be different from the Latest Edition value, so we just ignore it.

If you tell a picture to update manually, then the only time the picture gets updated is when you select the Get Edition Now button in this dialog box.

Cancel Subscriber. The Cancel Subscriber button in the Subscriber Options dialog box supposedly breaks the links between the picture in your QuarkXPress document and the edition upon which it's based, but it actually doesn't appear to do anything at all. Well, it's always nice to have an extra button lying around.

Open Publisher. Eric's favorite button in this dialog box is the Open Publisher button. When you press this button, QuarkXPress automatically launches the application that created the picture, and loads the original picture file upon which the edition is based. You can change the picture, and when you save your changes, the edition is updated for you. When you return to QuarkXPress, you'll see that the program has automatically updated your picture (unless you've selected manual updating; then you'll have to click on the Get Edition button in the Subscriber Options dialog box).

The only real problem with Open Publisher is that you have to have a lot of RAM for it to work.

▼ ▼

Tip: Use Subscriber Options for Any Picture. What David likes most about the Subscriber Options dialog box in QuarkXPress 3.2 is that it works with *all* kinds of imported pictures, not just with edition files. That's right, you can access Subscriber Options for any picture you've imported into your document using the Get Picture command as well as the Subscribe To command. Therefore, Auto Update can work for any picture, rather than just for editions. Subscriber Options makes working with all of your pictures easier and faster.

▼ ▼

Auto Picture Import vs. Get Edition Automatically

At first glance, the Auto Picture Import (see Chapter 6, *Pictures*, page 336) and the Get Edition Automatically features seem so similar that you might think they're basically equivalent. Not so! Here's the difference. Auto Picture Import only updates pictures when you open your document. You can have your document open for seven hours during a day while you or someone else changes the images, and QuarkXPress never gets the chance to update its pictures.

However, if you turn on Get Edition Automatically for a given picture box, QuarkXPress updates the image anytime it "sees" that the picture has changed on your hard drive.

While Get Editions Automatically might seem like the clear winner here (who wants to wait to have pictures updated?), we think there are good reasons for being judicious with its use. First of all, if you have a document with dozens or hundreds of pictures all set to be automatically updated, QuarkXPress could become so busy checking and rechecking for changed artwork, it might begrudge giving you time for trivial tasks such as editing your page.

Another good reason to not use Get Editions Automatically is that there are many times when you don't want images to be changing in your document (especially if the changed images have different aspect ratios—height to width—than the originally imported images). For example, if you've imported images for position only (FPO), then you don't want them suddenly changing and messing up your text runaround and so on.

▼ ▼

Tip: Subscribing to Non-Native Formats. Since the Open Publisher command works equally well on artwork you've imported or subscribed to, what's the advantage of subscribing? Not much, if your graphics program can directly edit the file you've brought into your QuarkXPress document. Let's say that you have an EPS image from Adobe Illustrator and you import that onto your QuarkXPress page. If you select Open Publisher from the Subscriber Options dialog box, the system launches Adobe Illustrator and opens the file up so that you can change it. When you're done, you simply save it again, and QuarkXPress can update the picture. This works because Adobe Illustrator can properly open its own EPS files.

But some programs, such as Aldus FreeHand or Type-Styler, can't properly read their own EPS format. They can export the EPS file with no problem, but if you try to open that EPS from within the program, they often get confused. Instead, you have to open the original file, make changes, and then export a new EPS that can be updated in QuarkXPress.

If you try using Open Publisher on an EPS file from FreeHand or TypeStyler from within QuarkXPress, the program launches, but it either opens the picture wrong or doesn't open it at all. Again, you'll have to find and change your original file, and then re-export as EPS.

However, like many things, there's a simple solution. If you *publish* your picture from FreeHand or TypeStyler as an

EPS rather than *exporting* it as EPS, the Open Publisher command usually works just like it does with an Illustrator or Photoshop EPS.

So while subscribing to editions from Adobe Illustrator or Adobe Photoshop is an often-needless complication, publishing and subscribing from programs such as Aldus FreeHand or Brøderbund's TypeStyler can be quite effective.

▼ ▼

Tip: Out of One, Many. We can think of one good reason to use Publish and Subscribe with applications such as Illustrator. The reason lies in the ability to create many editions from a single file. Suppose you have a large, complicated Illustrator picture, and you want to get different parts of it into different places within your QuarkXPress document. You could just import the entire picture to each location, and crop it as desired. But that's wasteful, as your printer still has to image the whole picture, no matter what's cropped out. You could cut and paste each element from the main picture into smaller picture files, but that's quite inefficient.

An easier solution is to simply select each discrete area of the picture you want to bring into your document, and publish it as an edition. Whenever you change the master, all the published editions get updated, and then are automatically updated in your QuarkXPress document as well.

▼ ▼

Don't Publish or Subscribe to PICTs

We've told you a few reasons why you should consider using Publish and Subscribe, but there's one very major reason why you shouldn't. Most programs that publish graphics only publish in PICT format. By now you know how we feel about PICT, much as the child in the famous New Yorker cartoon did about broccoli. Check the Publisher Options dialog box or user manual of the application from which you want to publish, and see if it supports publishing as EPS. If it doesn't, don't bother publishing. Odds are you'll have only grief when it comes time to print. As nifty as Publish and Subscribe can be, don't publish an Excel spreadsheet or

Word table as a PICT and expect it to look acceptable after you subscribe to it and print it from QuarkXPress.

Printing Editions

Note that editions act just like EPS or TIFF images when you print them. That is, QuarkXPress doesn't embed the whole picture into your document, it only creates a link from the document to the picture on your disk. If you send your document to a service bureau to print it, you need to send that edition file, too. No, you don't have to send the original picture file.

Color

When we ask people why they use QuarkXPress, the answer (as often as not) is, "It's the program to use for color work, and that's what we do." It's true that QuarkXPress has become the leader in color page layout, but it's still not perfect for working with color. Some of these imperfections have been addressed with the addition of the Colors and Trapping Information palettes, new trapping preferences, and two new color models to work with. In this section we'll look at each of these new features. Later, in "Printing," we'll cover the newest QuarkXPress addition in printing color separations: OPI. We discuss the capabilities added by the EfiColor XTension in Appendix D, *EfiColor*.

Colors Palette

Just like style sheets, you can apply and edit colors with a click, using the new Colors palette (see Figure C-26). This floating palette contains a list of every available color (see Chapter 9, *Color*), along with a tint-percentage control and three icons. These icons change, depending on what object you have selected. When you select a text box, the icons represent frame color, text color, and background color for that box. When you select a line, two icons gray out, and only the line color icon remains.

Figure C-26
The Colors palette

To apply a color to an object, first click on the correct icon for what you want to change, then click on the desired color in the color list. If you want a tint of that color, first change the percentage in the upper right corner, then type Return or Enter to apply the change. You can also just click somewhere other than on the palette. For example, let's say you want to change one word in a text box to 30 percent cyan. First, select the word in the text box. Second, click on the center icon in the Colors palette, which represents text. Third, click on Cyan in the colors list. Fourth, change the percentage to 30 and press Enter. It's funny, but those four steps are often much faster than selecting a color and tint from the Style menu.

Note that you can change the color of a text or picture box frame, even if the box doesn't have a frame. If you later add a frame, it will be the color you designated.

You can also edit or create new colors by Command-clicking on a color in the Colors palette. This brings up the Colors dialog box, in which you can edit, duplicate, append, or delete colors. This is also the fastest way to the Edit Trap dialog box.

▼ ▼

Tip: Drag-and-Drop Color Application. Sometimes we think the folks at Quark like to toss in features just because they're cool—for example, drag-and-drop color application. Try it: hold your mouse down on one of the tiny color squares on the

Colors palette, and drag it over your page. Notice that as you drag, the image of that color square stays attached to your pointer. As you move the pointer over objects, their color changes to the color you're dragging. Move the pointer past an object, and its color reverts to whatever it was before. It really doesn't add a tremendous amount of what we in the software-pontificating business like to call "functionality," but it's a heck of a lot of fun to play with.

To apply a color to an object, just let go of the mouse button. Note that you can apply a color in this way to backgrounds and borders, but not to text, even if you have the text icon selected in the Color palette. And since the palette is grayed out until you select an object, you can't drag anything until you've selected at least one object. Of course, if you have a black-and-white monitor, those color squares aren't displayed, so you can't use this tip.

▼ ▼

Cool Blends

The Colors palette is also the home of the new blends feature. The linear blend was added in 3.1; five others arrived with 3.2. Blends are often called vignettes, fountains, or graduated fills, but the concept is always the same: the background of a text or picture box can make a gradual transition from one color to another (see Figure C-27). Unlike some other programs that create graduated fills, in QuarkXPress you can blend any combination of spot colors, process colors, white, black, or registration.

With Version 3.2, Quark's added a dizzying array of blends, not just Linear, but also Mid-Linear (goes from one color to another, then back again), Rectangular, Diamond, Circular, and Full Circular. See Figure C-28 and Figure D in the color plates for examples of these various blends.

Creating a blend is easy. Just follow these steps.

1. Select the text or picture box to which you want to apply the blend.

Figure C-27
Color blends

2. Click on the background icon in the Colors palette, if it's not already selected.

3. Select the blend you want from the pop-up menu in the Colors palette.

4. Make sure button #1 is selected, then click on the beginning color of the blend (you can adjust the tint level, too).

5. Click on button #2, and select the ending color of the blend (and adjust the tint, if necessary).

6. Specify the angle of the blend. For linear and mid-linear blends, zero degrees (the default value) puts color #1 on the left and color #2 on the right. Increasing the value rotates the blend counter-clockwise (so that at 75 degrees, color #1 is almost at the bottom of your box). Surprisingly, the angle value you enter has an effect on any kind of blend. It rotates diamond and rectangular blends, and affects how the circular blends spread out within a box.

That's it. If you don't see the blend on your screen, it means one of two things. First, you performed this procedure wrong. Second, you have the Contents tool selected. When the Contents tool is selected, the active item (the text or picture box you have selected) only shows you the beginning color of the blend. This is so screen redraw can take place quickly and efficiently. To see the blend, either deselect the active picture or text box, or select the Item tool.

Figure C-28
New blends in 3.2

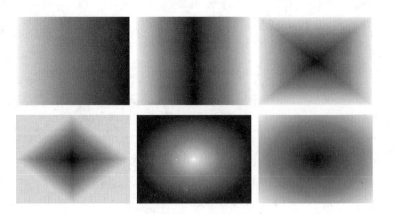

If you want to change one of the colors of the blend, simply click on radio button #1 or #2, then select the color, change its tint, or adjust the angle.

A warning for those placing blends behind gray-scale TIFFs: our experience has shown that this usually results in something that looks as pleasant as a baboon's behind. Proceed at your own risk.

▼ ▼

Tip: A New Dimension. Okay, maybe we're just easily amused, but we think this trick for creating three-dimensional buttons in QuarkXPress is pretty keen.

1. Draw a rectangle or oval (we think it looks best with a square or circle).

2. Give it a straight linear blend. We like to set it at 45 degrees, but it's up to you.

3. Duplicate the object, and make it smaller. The amount you make it smaller is up to you. Remember that if you want to reduce it to 80 percent, you can simply type *.8 in the width and height boxes.

4. Make the blend angle for the second object the angle of the first object's, blend minus 270. So if the first object had a 45-degree blend, the second object should have a 225-degree blend (270–45). You don't have to do the math if you don't want to; just type 270–45 in the angle box of the Color palette.

5. Space/Align the two objects so that their centers are equal (set Vertical and Horizontal alignment to zero offsets from the objects' centers in the Space/Align dialog box).

You can really see the effect best when the page guides are turned off (see Figure C-29). It's even nicer when you add a .3-point white frame around the inside object (sort of a highlight to the button's ridge).

Figure C-29
Three-dimensional buttons

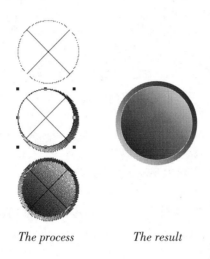

The process   *The result*

Trapping Preferences

Back in Chapter 9, *Color*, on page 427, we talked about the Auto Trap Preferences that first became available with the QuarkFreebies 3.0 XTension package. Like many other features that first saw life as a free XTension from Quark, these, too, have been incorporated into the application itself. However, some controls are now handled differently, so let's rehash the discussion. To keep the Application Preferences dialog box from getting too crowded, Quark broke out trapping preferences into its own dialog box in version 3.2.

The Trap Preferences dialog box contains six controls: Auto Method, Auto Amount, Indeterminate, Overprint Limit, Ignore White, and Process Trap. These let you get pretty specific about how you want QuarkXPress's trapping to act.

Auto Method. The Auto Method control is a two-item pop-up menu that determines how automatic trapping should be handled. Your two choices are Proportional and Absolute. The first choice, Proportional, tells QuarkXPress to handle automatic trapping in the way we described back in Chapter 9: "the width of the trap is determined by which color is darker and how much darker it is." The maximum trap amount is the value in the Auto Amount field. Note that we use the word "darkness" rather than "blackness," as we did back in Chapter 9, *Color*. QuarkXPress 3.1 now "looks" at how dark the two colors are, rather than how much black is in them.

The second choice, Absolute, tells QuarkXPress to always use the same trapping value. This trapping amount is the value in the Auto Amount Field. As far as we're concerned, there's rarely a reason to use Proportional trapping, so we always leave the Auto Method set to Absolute. But then again, we try to avoid using automatic trapping as much as possible anyway (and we think you should, too).

Auto Amount. The value that you set in the Auto Amount field tells QuarkXPress the maximum value that Proportional automatic trapping can use, and the specific value that Absolute automatic trapping should use. The default value of .144 point (about two thousandths of an inch) seems a little small to us, so we usually change this to .25 point. However, remember to check with your lithographer first.

Indeterminate. The value that you set in the Indeterminate field sets the amount of trap that QuarkXPress uses for objects which are placed over indeterminate colors (see Chapter 9, *Color*, page 425). Note that this is an absolute (not relative) value. That is, any object that sits over an indeterminate color is trapped by this amount (unless you specifically change it in the Edit Trap dialog box); it doesn't change depending on luminance or blackness. For those of you who have used QuarkXPress 3.0, note that the definition of "Indeterminate" changed slightly in version 3.1. We'll use examples to show the difference.

In version 3.0, a red circle that is placed half over a blue box and half over the white page would be considered to have an indeterminate background. In version 3.1, this became an option (see "Ignore White," below). In version 3.0, if that red circle is placed half over a blue box and half over a green box, it's considered to have an indeterminate background. QuarkXPress checks to see what the red/blue and the red/green trapping values are set to. If they're both set to spread or to choke, QuarkXPress uses the smaller of the two values. If one is set to spread by some amount and the other is set to choke, then QuarkXPress uses Indeterminate trapping.

▼ ▼

Tip: Knockout Lettering from Rich Black. Back in Chapter 9, *Color*, on page 429, we talked about creating a rich black (black with 40 percent cyan in it), and noted that when you have text or an object knocking out the black, any misregistration on press results in the cyan peeking out horribly from behind the black. The engineers at Quark have built a very cool internal solution to this problem.

Now, QuarkXPress checks to see if an object is knocking out a rich black. If it is, it only spreads the cyan, magenta and yellow plates of that rich black color, leaving the black plate alone.

You need this kind of help most when you're placing a white object (such as white, reversed text) over a rich black. QuarkXPress now handles this trapping for you automatically, spreading the cyan, magenta, and yellow plates by the amount specified in the Auto Amount field.

If you don't understand what we're talking about, try it yourself with proofs from a laser printer (but change the trap to something enormous like 3 points).

▼ ▼

Overprint Limit. Just because a color is set to overprint in the Edit Trap dialog box doesn't mean that it'll really overprint. The key is this Overprint Limit value in the Trapping Preferences dialog box. QuarkXPress overprints the color black and any other color that is set to overprint only when their tint levels are above the Overprint Limit. For example, let's say you have the color green set to overprint. If you screen it back to 50 percent, QuarkXPress knocks the color out rather than overprinting it, because the tint falls below the Overprint Limit. Likewise, when the color black is set to Automatic, it always overprints any color, as long as the black is above this Overprint Limit.

Ignore White. When a page item such as a picture box only partially overlaps another page item (see Figure C-30), QuarkXPress 3.0 gets confused about what color is in the background, so it calls it "Indeterminate." Now you have a say in the matter. When the Ignore White checkbox is turned on in the Trapping Preferences dialog box, QuarkXPress won't call a partial overlap "Indeterminate" because it just ignores the white page background. If you turn this off, however, it "sees" the white background page, and considers the mix of background colors to be Indeterminate.

Process Trap. At last! Someone has finally taken a step toward making process colors trap correctly. This new feature is called Process Trap. If you're used to the way QuarkXPress 3.0 trapped process colors, you might be pleasantly surprised at how newer versions trap when you turn Process Trap on.

Take a look at the two process colors (foreground and background) listed in Table C-3. If you spread this foreground color (a yellow) into the background color (a

Figure C-30
Ignore White

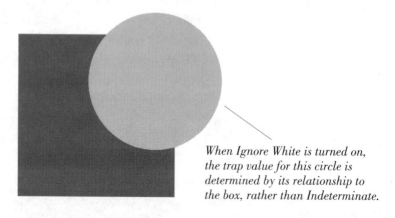

When Ignore White is turned on, the trap value for this circle is determined by its relationship to the box, rather than Indeterminate.

	Color	Foreground box	Background box
Table C-3 Color breakdown for trapping example	cyan	0	30
	magenta	20	50
	yellow	100	90
	black	5	0

muddy brown) using version 3.0, the trap area doesn't mesh the two colors the way you'd want. That is, the trap area is the same as the foreground color on each process color plate except for the cyan plate, on which—because the foreground has no cyan in it—the background shows through. Now you might say: For a quarter-point trap, who cares? No one will see it anyway. Think again. The greenish line that results stands out clearly.

However, when Process Trap is turned on, QuarkXPress spreads some process colors and chokes others. Here's how it works. Any process color in the foreground object that is darker than the same color in the background object is spread by half the trapping value (if you're using automatic trapping, it's half the value in the Auto Amount field; otherwise it's half of whatever trapping value you specify). Any process color that's lighter is choked by half that value. In the example listed in Table C-3, the cyan plate is choked by half the trapping value (let's say half of .25 point, or .125 point) because there is less cyan in the foreground box than in the background box. Magenta also chokes. However, the yellow and black plates spread by .125 point.

The result is a trap area as wide as the specified trapping value (in the example above, .25 point), centered on the edge of the foreground object, that has the darkest process colors of each of the objects.

If you don't understand this, read the last few paragraphs over several times. If you still don't understand it, then give up and believe us when we tell you that it's a really good thing. Leave Process Trap turned on.

A couple of notes on this feature. When all the process colors in the foreground object are darker or they're all lighter than in the background object, then QuarkXPress doesn't trap at all. This is because it doesn't need to. Also, Process Trap doesn't do anything for spot colors, again because it doesn't need to.

Trap Information Palette

This is the moment we've all been waiting for since Quark announced they were planning on including trapping in QuarkXPress: object-by-object trapping. That's right, you now have the option of trapping a particular object to its background rather than trapping one color in a document to another color. It's still not a perfect system (we'll discuss why in just a bit), but it's a big step in the right direction.

Unlike most palettes in QuarkXPress, where you have the option either to use them or to use menu items, the Trap Information palette is the only way that you can use object-by-object trapping. Let's take a gander at this palette's anatomy (see Figure C-31).

The Trap Information palette shows you the current trap information for a selected page object, gives you "reasons" for why it's trapping the object that way, and lets you change that object's trap value. You can change the trap values, depending on the object you have selected. For example, for a text box with no frame, you can adjust the trap for the background color of the box and the text in the box. For a box with a frame, you can set the trap for the inside of the frame (trapping to the background color of the box) and the outside of the frame (trapping to anything behind that box).

Unless you've changed the trap value, the Trap Information palette displays all objects at their Default trap.

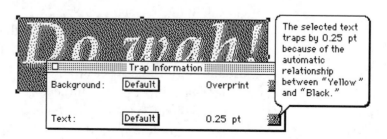

Figure C-31
The Trap
Information palette

This means that the objects trap at whatever value is set in the Edit Trap dialog box (see Chapter 9, *Color*, page 424). QuarkXPress displays the trap value to the right of the word "Default," and then displays a gray button labeled with a question mark. If you click on this button (and hold it down), QuarkXPress gives you a balloon message explaining why it's trapping the object this way. For example, if you have a black line selected, the balloon might tell you that it's overprinting the black line because of the relationship between black and the background color. It doesn't usually go into much more detail than that, but it's better than just leaving you up in the air.

To change the trap value for part of an object (e.g., the inside frame of a picture box), you use the mini-pop-up menu in the Trap Information palette. The menu is usually set to Default, but you can change this to Overprint, Knockout, Auto Amount (+), Auto Amount (–), or Custom. Overprint and Knockout are pretty self-explanatory. The two Auto Amount values use the value in the Auto Amount field of the Application Preferences dialog box (the value is either positive or negative, denoting a spread or a choke). When you select the last item—Custom—QuarkXPress gives you a field in which to type any trap value you want (from -36 to +36 points).

Note that text can be trapped character by character (see Figure C-32), and that one black object can be overprinted where another black object knocks out (this kills the need for our tricky tip for a non-overprinting black).

Taking Custom Traps On the Road

One of the niftiest features added in version 3.0 was its ability to include custom kerning, tracking, and H&J information within a document, so that information doesn't get lost when you send your work to a service bureau or color prepress house for high-resolution output (see "Saving the XPress Data," earlier in this appendix). One thing that Quark forgot to send along with your work was any custom trapping preferences you may have defined. That oversight's been fixed in Version 3.2, we're happy to report.

Figure C-32
Text can be trapped
character by character

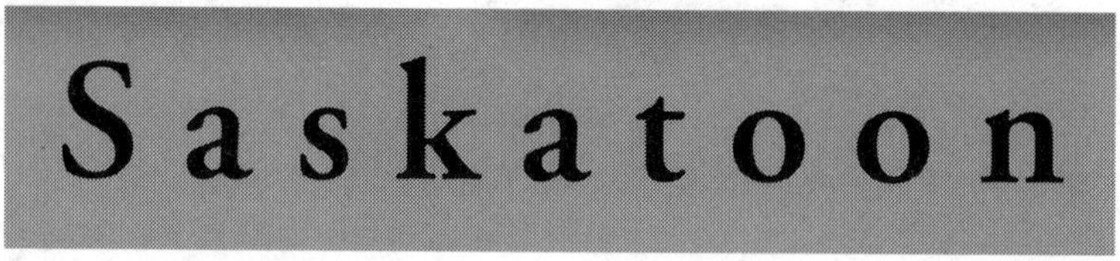

Saskatoon

Color Models

QuarkXPress lets you choose colors from among five more color swatch books: FocolTone, TruMatch, Pantone Process, Pantone ProSim, and Pantone Uncoated. These are all process-color swatch systems. This means that they're like Pantone spot colors insofar as you use a swatch book to choose colors that can easily be communicated to a lithographer, but they're based on the four process colors rather than on solid "spot" colors. The first two are alternatives to the Pantone system we've all become familiar with; the last three are from Pantone and are also designed to work in a process-color environment. As we've said three hundred times before: if you use these, don't rely on the screen representation of the colors. It is almost assuredly wrong. Buy the swatch books (see Appendix B, *Resources*), and use those. Okay, now let's take a look at each of these color models.

FocolTone. Developed in Wales, the FocolTone matching system is used widely in Europe, and very little in North America. After buying the rather expensive FocolTone cross-referenced swatch books, you have to wade through them to find the color you want (you have a choice of 763 colors). These are similar to the Pantone books, which are also in disarray (at least from a user's standpoint). We can't explain FocolTone's numbering system or color sequence to you, because we just can't figure them out.

TruMatch. When QuarkXPress 3.1 was first announced, we noticed a little comment saying that TruMatch, a new color-matching system, was going to be included. In retrospect, we feel a little ashamed that we didn't pay it much attention. We figured, hey, we've got process-color swatch books; why do we need anything else? Then we saw the TruMatch swatch books, and we saw the light.

TruMatch was built by people who know and use color from the desktop (especially color from QuarkXPress, as it turns out). This is more important than it might seem. Creating tint builds from the desktop has a particular advantage over having a printer build tints traditionally: we can specify (and a properly calibrated imagesetter can provide us with) a tint value of any percentage, not just in five- or 10-percent increments. The folks at TruMatch took advantage of this and created a very slick, very easy-to-use system with over 2,000 evenly gradated colors (see the sample swatch in Figure C in the color plates).

The TruMatch swatch books tuck this information away, so we want to explain the TruMatch system here. The colors in the swatch book (and in the TruMatch color selector in the Edit Color dialog box) are arranged in the colors of the spectrum: from red through yellow to green through blue to violet and back to red. The first number in a TruMatch code indicates a color's hue (its place on the spectrum). These numbers range from 1 to 50.

The second item in a color's TruMatch code indicates its tint (its value strength, ranging from "a"—saturated, 100-percent value strength—to "h"—faded, unsaturated, 5-percent value strength). The third item, a number, indicates the color's brightness (the amount of black). Black is always added in 6 percent increments. The brightness code ranges from 1 (6 percent black) to 7 (42 percent black). If there's no black in a color, this third code is left off.

So, why is this so great? Well, first of all, you can quickly make decisions on the relativity of two colors. For example, you can say, "No, I want this color to be a little darker, and a little more green." When you go back to the Edit Color dialog box, you can quickly find a color that suits your desires. Compare this to the Pantone or FocolTone matching systems and you'll understand. TruMatch gives us hope that there really is a positive evolution in electronic publishing.

Pantone Process, ProSim, and Uncoated. Not to be outdone by upstart color-swatch systems, Pantone has introduced some new color-swatch systems of its own. The idea started with the ProSim system, which is a set of process colors designed to simulate as closely as possible the Pantone system's spot colors on coated stock. Pantone Uncoated also tries to simulate spot colors, but it's designed for uncoated papers.

There are three problems with these systems. The first problem is that it's really hard to simulate spot colors with the four process colors. The second problem is that the team of people Pantone hired to create these simulations included one person who was (in Steve Job's infamous words) brain-damaged. It's very strange...many of the simulations are as good as they could be. Others are so far off the mark that we really had to marvel at the scheme (even *we* could find better process color simulations). The third problem is that these systems still use the incredibly strange numbering system that Pantone spot colors use.

Pantone Process, on the other hand, has a new numbering scheme, but it's hardly worth describing because it doesn't appear to be consistent. This system has a few things going for it besides its new numbers. First, it's generally easier to find colors in it (they're arranged with some semblance of order). Second, there are more colors to choose from than in any previous process color matching system. Third, everybody knows the Pantone name, so your printer won't look at you strangely when you say, "I used TruMatch on this job."

As we've always done, we encourage you to use Pantone for spot colors, and whenever you want to specify a process color...well, you can avoid the strange look if you don't tell your printer that you used TruMatch; just specify the CMYK values.

Printing

Let us not forget the ultimate feat of electronic publishing: printing out our documents. Versions 3.1 and 3.2 of Quark-

XPress add a few new features to our printing possibilities. For some people, the best news is the loss of the XPress Data file (see "Saving the XPress Data," earlier in this appendix). This makes sending your documents to a service bureau easier. For others, the Low Resolution printing mode will be the greatest news. If you work with color a lot, you'll like the new PostScript options such as OPI and increased DCS support, as well as the new CMYK TIFF compatibility.

New PostScript Options

PostScript has always been plain, simple, and easy to understand, right? Well, QuarkXPress's PostScript options just got more complicated and powerful in version 3.2. So here's a rundown on the changes from version 3.0, and how they affect you.

ASCII or Binary. Version 3.2 gives you control over the data format QuarkXPress uses when it creates PostScript: ASCII or Binary. When you select one of these, QuarkXPress writes all bitmap image information in one form or the other.

What's the difference? ASCII is plain text; you could read and edit it with any text processor.

Binary, on the other hand, reduces the PostScript code from bitmaps in QuarkXPress to a bunch of ones and zeros. You can't edit it or even figure out what it means from looking at it, but the PostScript code for bitmapped images (black-and-white, gray-scale, or color) is half the size of ASCII. There are two places where QuarkXPress offers you this choice. In the Save Page as EPS dialog box, there's a pop-up menu labeled Data, from which you can choose ASCII or Binary. Similarly, the Page Setup dialog box has a Data Format menu from which you can make the same choices.

Why select one or the other? Bitmapped images are typically very large. And since in binary the image data is half the size, you'll create smaller EPS files when you save a page as EPS; when you print, your data will travel to your printer faster (as there's less data to be sent); and print-to-disk PostScript files will also be smaller. ASCII format is larger, but it's often more compatible when you're moving files between multiple platforms and programs, and over various networks and communication lines.

Open Prepress Interface

Although Ole Kvern (author of *Real World FreeHand*, co-author of *Real World PageMaker*, and cool guy down the hall in David's and Steve's office) is obviously wrong on which page-layout program to devote one's life to, he has a good point about how silly all the uproar is about OPI versus DCS. For those of you who came in late, OPI stands for Open Prepress Interface, and was created by Aldus (creators of PageMaker and PrePrint). DCS stands for Desktop Color Separation, and was created by Quark.

The press loves a good story, and soon after the two companies started talking about their ideas, histrionic tales of competing standards were bandied about. The truth of the matter is that both DCS and OPI are here to stay, they're not competing, you can use either system (or both, even in the same document), and there are certainly times when you'd want to use one over the other.

Both DCS and OPI are methods of separating color TIFF and bitmapped PICT images. And both DCS and OPI rely on a program outside of QuarkXPress (or PageMaker, or whatever) to handle color separations for the images, including undercolor removal, color correction, and so on. The difference is primarily in who's doing the separations, what's being separated, and when the separations are being made.

DCS. We talked a little about Desktop Color Separation (DCS) back in Chapter 9, *Color*, but let's go over it here one more time. The DCS method is based on preseparating color images into five separate EPS files (which is why DCS is sometimes called EPS-5). Four of the files contain high-resolution information for the process colors (cyan, magenta, yellow, and black). The fifth file contains a low-resolution composite image (for proofing), a screen representation of the picture, and pointers to the four higher-resolution files. This fifth file is the file that gets imported into QuarkXPress.

When you print your file, QuarkXPress replaces this representation file (sometimes called the "main file") with the four high-resolution files. This means you can print the separations directly from QuarkXPress to an imagesetter. This is great for situations where the color images are not huge, and can be transmitted in a reasonable amount of time over a small bandwidth network such as AppleTalk.

Now there is the DCS 2.0 file format, which is basically a revised version of the DCS specification. In DCS 2.0 images, the four process plates and the preview "master" image are all rolled into one big file. Plus, DCS 2.0 lets you include spot-color plates, varnish plates—as many plates as you want. That means that you can create an image in Photoshop that includes spot colors, export it with PlateMaker from In Software as a DCS 2.0 file, and separate the whole thing from QuarkXPress.

QuarkXPress 3.2 not only understands DCS documents, it also creates them when you save a page as EPS (see "Saving a Page as EPS," below).

OPI. The OPI method is based on postseparating full-color pages that include color bitmapped images—especially scanned images. For example, you can import a single low-resolution RGB TIFF file into a QuarkXPress document, save that page as EPS, and separate it on a high-end color system such as Hell or Crosfield. The low-resolution image is replaced in the EPS by OPI comments that say what the name of the scanned image file is, and where the separation program can find it.

As it turns out, however, the OPI method also works very well for separating pages to an imagesetter such as the Linotronic 330 or the Agfa SelectSet 5000. You can export an EPS file with OPI comments in it, and print that EPS file with Aldus PrePrint directly to the imagesetter. Aldus PrePrint "strips in" and separates the high-resolution color image at print time. Compumation also has some very good OPI servers.

This is nice for a couple of reasons. First, Aldus PrePrint has much better registration marks than QuarkXPress (unless you've built your own; see page 474). Secondly, it's often nice to have the option to move a small EPS page file around separately from the large TIFF files. (In a DCS image, when you make a PostScript dump or save the page as EPS, the image is encapsulated with it.) A third reason for using OPI and Aldus PrePrint is that you don't have to separate each TIFF image into four big files until you want to print it.

Using OPI

Up until now, Quark said XPress could handle OPI, but it really couldn't (at least not reliably). Now (as of version 3.1) it really can. The trick to building a PostScript file with OPI comments is the new OPI pop-up menu in the Save Page as EPS and Print dialog boxes (see Figure C-33). You have three choices in this menu: Include Images, Omit TIFF, and Omit TIFF & EPS.

Include Images. When Include Images is selected in the OPI pop-up menu, QuarkXPress acts naturally. That is, it works the way it always has, and prints all the TIFF and EPS pictures (or includes them in an EPS).

Omit TIFF. This is the basic setting for OPI comments. When Omit TIFF is selected, QuarkXPress replaces all TIFF images with OPI comments that can be read by an OPI "reader" such as Aldus PrePrint.

Omit TIFF & EPS. Apparently the OPI specs talk about OPI comments for EPS images as well as for TIFF images. However, at this time, no software pays any attention to those specs. So this selection (as far as we can tell) is useless for the time being. Well, it's always nice to have the option....

Saving a Page as EPS

All of the above options—data format, DCS and OPI—come into play when saving a page from QuarkXPress as an EPS

Figure C-33
OPI pop-up menu

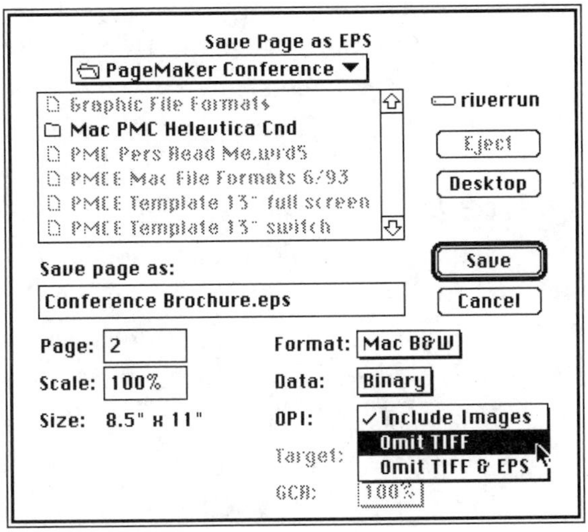

```
                    Save Page as EPS
        📁 PageMaker Conference ▼
    □ Graphic File Formats          ⇧      □ riverrun
    □ Mac PMC Helvetica Cnd
    □ PMC Pers Read Me.wrd5                    Eject
    □ PMEE Mac File Formats 6/93
    □ PMEE Template 13" full screen          Desktop
    □ PMEE Template 13" switch       ⇩

    Save page as:                            Save
    Conference Brochure.eps                  Cancel

    Page:  2              Format:  Mac B&W
    Scale: 100%           Data:    Binary
    Size:  8.5" x 11"     OPI:   ✓ Include Images
                                   Omit TIFF
                          Target:  Omit TIFF & EPS
                          GCR:    100%
```

file, along with still more options. In Version 3.2, when you save a page as EPS, the dialog box gives you the option of saving the file in eight—count 'em, eight—different formats: Macintosh color, Macintosh black and white, Macintosh DCS, Macintosh DCS 2.0, PC color, PC black and white, PC DCS and PC DCS 2.0. Let's look at some of these.

Macintosh Color/B&W. If you choose Macintosh Color or Macintosh B&W, you get a normal ol' encapsulated PostScript file, just like we described back on page 341. One addition, though: we said that the choice between Color and B&W (black and white) is only for the screen image. As it turns out, the choice also affects the way that QuarkXPress writes the PostScript code. If you choose B&W, color items are actually changed into black and white (or gray) items.

DCS. Choosing DCS results in QuarkXPress saving five files to your disk: one master file that contains a preview image, and four process-color files that contain the actual image data. If you set the Target Profile in the Save as EPS dialog box to SWOP-Coated (or to some other process-color profile), the EfiColor processor converts RGB TIFF and PICT images into CMYK (see Appendix D, *EfiColor*). That means you can save an EPS file that will separate properly in other programs.

Note that because the DCS file format only handles the four process colors, any spot colors you assign end up getting separated via EfiColor and placed on the CMYK plates.

DCS 2.0. As we said earlier, DCS 2.0 handles cyan, magenta, yellow, black, and as many spot colors as you want. The cool part about this is that all your spot colors get put on their own plates. The not-so-cool part about this is that RGB images may not get separated correctly. We use the word "may" because this might actually just be a bug in the program. Perhaps by the time you read this, QuarkXPress and EfiColor will separate RGB images properly in DCS 2.0. On the other hand, another solution is simply to use CMYK (TIFF or DCS) instead of RGB images.

And, as we also noted earlier, selecting DCS 2.0 results in only one file on your hard drive, rather than five.

PCs. Back in Chapter 5, *Pictures*, we skipped over the whole notion of EPS images for the PC because we didn't think it was really relevant. However, now it most certainly is. Preview images on the Mac work by including a low-resolution image in the resource fork of the picture's file. However, on the PC, files don't have resource forks, so this method doesn't work. Instead, the preview image is placed as a header in the beginning of the EPS file. In other words, it's kind of like putting a low-resolution TIFF at the beginning of the EPS file.

QuarkXPress 3.2 can create EPS and DCS images in a format that can not only be transferred to the PC, but will retain its preview image. Don't forget to give your image a name that's not longer than eight letters (see "Mac/PC File Transfers," later in this appendix).

OPI. As mentioned above in "Using OPI," you have three choices for OPI format: Include Images, Omit TIFF, and Omit TIFF & EPS. Finally, as described in "ASCII or Binary," above, you have those two choices available for the file's data format. We figure that gives you a whopping 48 different ways to save a page as OPI; have fun experimenting!

CMYK TIFFs

What we can't figure out is why people aren't jumping up and down with excitement over the CMYK TIFF format. The TIFF format was developed primarily by folks at Aldus, but it's always used an RGB color model. Now, Aldus has come up with a partial specification for a TIFF format based on CMYK values (they say it's not a "completed spec," but they've released it anyway). It's been a long time coming, and we think it's the hot new thing in color prepress.

The good news is that QuarkXPress 3.1 can separate a CMYK TIFF image all by itself. No preprocessing, no post-processing—just import the picture and print.

The bad news is that not many programs create CMYK TIFFs yet. It's just too new. But the way this technology moves, by the time you read this, everything might support it. Right now, though, the only software packages we know of that can create CMYK TIFFs are Adobe Photoshop 2.0, ColorStudio 1.5, and Aldus PrePrint 1.5.

Our suggestion is to bring an image (whether it be PICT or RGB TIFF) into Adobe Photoshop 2.0, convert it to CMYK (by changing modes), and then save it as either EPS (to create a DCS file) or TIFF (to create a CMYK TIFF file).

Page Setup Changes

There are a few new options in the Page Setup dialog box (see Figure C-34). First of all, if you have EfiColor installed you can select the EfiColor profile you want to use for your printer (see Appendix D, *EfiColor*)

Other changes have to do with information available in the PDF for the printer you've selected. For high-resolution imagesetters, such as the Linotronic 330, EfiColor lets you select a GCR, or gray component replacement percentage. Also, the dialog box now has a field that displays screen angles for each process color. The defaults are: cyan 105°, magenta 75°, yellow 90°, and black 45°. If the PDF for the printer you've chosen contains alternate screening information, and you've checked the "Use PDF Screen Values" box, the new screen angles and halftone screen appear in this

Figure C-34
New Page Setup
dialog box

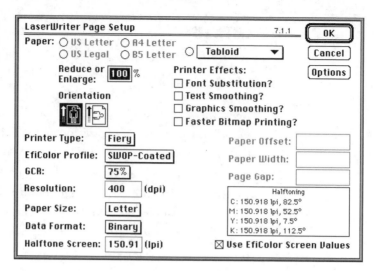

field. Sometimes this means that QuarkXPress will override the line-screen value you've entered in the Halftone Screen field. For example, the LaserWriter IIf-g PDF uses a halftone screen of 106 lpi (to take advantage of Apple's PhotoGrade technology in those printers). Also, see "EfiColor or PDF Screen Values" in Appendix D, *EfiColor*.

Print Dialog Box Changes

The Print dialog box in QuarkXPress 3.2 contains four new print-related features: Low Resolution, Blank Pages, Calibrated Output, and Print Status. One of these saves money, the other three save frustration. First, we should mention that in Version 3.2, Quark cleaned up the dialog box considerably. Gone are the many radio buttons, replaced by a cleaner array of pop-up menus for many familiar options (of course, if you don't like pop-up menus, you're out of luck; the good news is that QuicKeys now has an extension which lets you select items from pop-up menus).

Low Resolution Output. Like many other additions, the new Low Resolution printing feature may not seem like much at first glance, but it can be a tremendous time-saver. If you check Low Resolution in the Print dialog box, QuarkXPress prints a document using the picture preview image built into the document, rather than the source picture file. If you've imported a huge, high-resolution TIFF or EPS, Low Resolution mode prints the document using the low-resolution (36- or 72-dpi) screen image that QuarkXPress creates when you import the picture and position it on your page.

This is a godsend if you have to make many proofs to a low-resolution desktop printer. We can't tell you how much time we've wasted either sending documents with high-resolution pictures to low-resolution devices (it takes forever for them to print), or manually hiding the pictures somewhere on our hard disks so QuarkXPress can't find them, then telling it to print anyway (that was the old trick for making QuarkXPress use the internal low-res image).

Blank Pages. As we write, our white-paper recycling bin overfloweth. We go through so much paper that we feel guilty every time we drive through a forest (which is difficult to avoid in the Pacific Northwest). Therefore, whenever we have the chance to save a tree here and there, we jump at it. QuarkXPress is giving us just this chance with the inclusion of the Blank Pages control in the Print dialog box. When you turn Blank Pages on (the default setting), QuarkXPress prints as it always has: every page, no matter what's on it (or what isn't on it). When you turn Blank Pages off, QuarkXPress won't print a page if there isn't anything printable on it. This includes pages whose only objects are colored white, or are set to suppress printout.

Calibrated Output. If you've ever printed a 50-percent gray box on your desktop laser printer, you've probably noticed that the box doesn't come out 50 percent gray. This is because of QuarkXPress's built-in printer calibration settings. When you select the LaserWriter printer in the Page Setup dialog box, QuarkXPress alters all its gray levels when printing. Fortunately, enough people threw fits, and Quark has now made this an option. When the Calibrated Output checkbox in the Print dialog box is turned on, QuarkXPress performs as it always has (it calibrates for the printer it's set to). When you turn this checkbox off, QuarkXPress doesn't change a thing. There are benefits to both sides, we suppose, but we'd just as soon leave this on as we'd use Microsoft Word to produce books (yeah, we've done it, but we didn't want to).

By the way, turning Calibrated Output off is just the same as temporarily resetting the printer calibration curves to straight lines using the Printer Calibration XTension that comes with the QuarkXTras package.

Print Status. We don't know, but we have an inkling that Print Status is another feature that former PageMaker users talked Quark into throwing in so they'd feel more at home. The concept is as simple as its execution. Concept: we want Quark-XPress to show us its progress as it downloads a print job to a PostScript printer. Execution: just print. In version 3.1, you needed to hold down the Shift key as you clicked on the Print button. Now in version 3.2 it's just the opposite: you get Print Status automatically every time you print, unless you hold down the Shift key. The Print Status dialog box not only tells you what page it's printing, but also what color plate, tile, and EPS/TIFF images it's working on (see Figure C-35).

Remember that no program can know how long a page will take to print on a PostScript printer, so there's no way to show how much longer the print job will take. Instead, the status bar in the Print Status dialog box only displays the percentage of pages that have been printed (for example, if you have two pages in your document, the status bar is 50 percent full after the first page, even if the second page takes ten times longer than the first one to print). Nonetheless, this is a nice intermediate step, and often makes us feel better when we're waiting for those long jobs to print.

Collect for Output. Another welcome addition in version 3.2, "Collect for Output," first saw life as one of the free XTensions from Quark for version 3.1. This command (available under the File menu) copies your document and all the picture files necessary for its output to a folder of your choice. It also creates a report containing detailed information about your document, from fonts and pictures used to

Figure C-35
Print Status dialog box

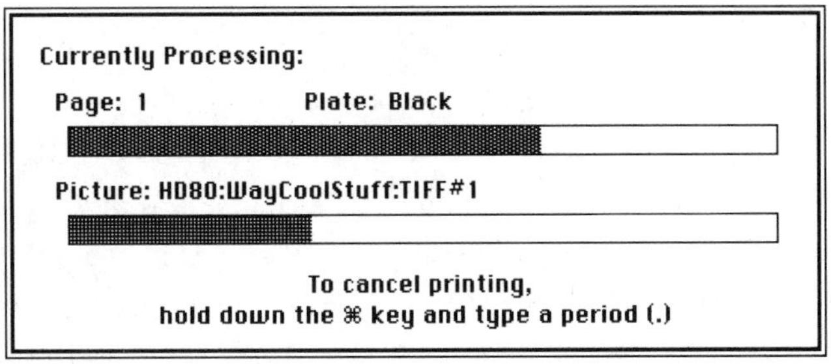

```
┌─────────────────────────────────────────────────────┐
│  ┌───────────────────────────────────────────────┐   │
│  │  Currently Processing:                         │   │
│  │                                                │   │
│  │     Page: 1              Plate: Black          │   │
│  │  ┌──────────────────────────────────────────┐  │   │
│  │  │████████████████████████████████          │  │   │
│  │  └──────────────────────────────────────────┘  │   │
│  │     Picture: HD80:WayCoolStuff:TIFF#1          │   │
│  │  ┌──────────────────────────────────────────┐  │   │
│  │  │██████████████████                        │  │   │
│  │  └──────────────────────────────────────────┘  │   │
│  │                                                │   │
│  │           To cancel printing,                  │   │
│  │     hold down the ⌘ key and type a period (.)  │   │
│  └───────────────────────────────────────────────┘   │
└─────────────────────────────────────────────────────┘
```

trapping information. Then all you have to do is get the folder to your service bureau or color prepress house by modem, messenger, or carrier pigeon.

Using this command is simplicity itself. When you select it, it prompts you to find a folder, and asks you to specify a name for the report. We typically just use QuarkXPress's default name; it's simply the name of your document with "report" stuck on the end. Once you've selected a folder, QuarkXPress copies your document and all picture files, wherever they might reside, to that target folder. You must save your file first or Quark will prompt you to do it. Note that to avoid potential copyright problems, QuarkXPress doesn't copy any fonts to the folder. That's up to you to do yourself, if necessary. The legal ramifications are between you, your service bureau, and your font vendor. We don't blame Quark for wanting to stay out of this one!

Collecting files for output often takes longer than manually copying each file, as QuarkXPress does a very thorough search for each file it needs. This may take a bit more time, but the process does give you the satisfaction of knowing you haven't forgotten to copy that little bitty logo illustration hidden at the bottom of page 32.

More on Printing. No matter how hard we try to tuck all the newest and greatest pieces of information into their proper chapters and sections, there always seem to be a few bits left straggling at the end. Well, here are the remainders of the printing section, in no particular order.

Print to Disk. Here's a tip aimed at anyone using the LaserWriter driver that comes with System 7. There's a new item in the Print dialog box that people often overlook: Destination. You have two choices here: Printer or PostScript file. This is the new way of creating PostScript dumps or print-to-disk files. Don't bother to try holding down the F or the K key. They don't work anymore. Just click on the PostScript file button and press OK. The Mac gives you the option of where you want the file to go and what you want to name it. The file that the Mac saves contains the entire PostScript LaserPrep header (as holding down the K key would do). This is a hassle in some cases, because the PostScript files are larger than they would be otherwise.

▼ ▼

Tip: Laserchecking with LaserCheck. Of course QuarkXPress isn't the only thing that's changed in the past sixteen months since the second edition of this book came out. Steve and Susie had baby Dia, Danuloff and McLelland wrote another sixty-three books, and we started using Systems of Merritt's LaserCheck software. LaserCheck lets you print a document on your desktop laser printer that was meant for an imagesetter. That is, you can actually set up the Page Setup and Print dialog boxes just as though you were printing on an imagesetter, and your laser printer not only handles it correctly, it tells you—with the help of LaserCheck—more than you'd ever want to know about the PostScript file it printed. We've found this handy for checking whether our tabloid-sized pages were going to come out lengthwise or widthwise on the L330, and for seeing whether a file would just plain print. Generally, if it prints with LaserCheck, there's a good chance it'll print on the imagesetter.

If it doesn't print on either, you might look into two PostScript error handlers: PinPoint XT from the Cheshire Group, and the Advanced PostScript Error Handler from Systems of Merritt (see Appendix B, *Resources*). David loves these, but he's a PostScript hacker and likes to muck about in moveto's and curveto's. If you're not ready to jump into this sort of troubleshooting, perhaps you can talk your service bureau into it.

▼ ▼

Mac/PC File Transfers

 Although many hard-core Macintosh users may prefer to wear cloves of garlic (or rubber gloves) when working with Windows machines, the fact can't be denied that there are lots more Windows boxes out there than Macs, and an increasing number of them are running the Windows version of QuarkXPress. From the outset, QuarkXPress for Windows could open files saved by QuarkXPress for Macintosh version 3.1. But it was a one-way trip until QuarkXPress for Macintosh version 3.2 came out. Now, at last, there's two-way transferability of files between Macs and Windows machines.

Or is there? While bringing files from your Mac to someone else's PC and back again is possible, it certainly isn't a no-brainer. In this section we want to take a quick tour of the obstacles in your way when transferring files. By the way, if you're using QuarkXPress for Windows, you'll find even more information on the subject in *The QuarkXPress Book, Windows Edition*.

You Can Get There From Here

There are many ways of transferring files between Macs and PCs, and QuarkXPress is happy with the result no matter how you move your files. If your Mac and PC share a hard drive on a network, you can just copy the file or open it directly. If you have a modem link between the machines, you can use your communication program's file-transfer capabilities.

However, the most popular way to transfer files is via floppy disk. This is easy enough to do if your Mac has a SuperDrive (almost every Mac sold in recent years does). The SuperDrive can read from and write to DOS-formatted floppies as well as to Mac-formatted ones. It's far easier to read a DOS disk on a Macintosh than the other way around (although the software product Mac-in-DOS works well for some people).

Just because the disk drive can read the disk doesn't mean the operating system can. The cheapest way to actually get information off the disk is Apple File Exchange, which comes with your system software. First, launch Apple File Exchange. *Then* insert the DOS disk. Typically, the default translation setting works just fine. On the other hand, if you have a utility that mounts DOS floppies on your desktop, such as DOS Mounter or AccessPC, you can simply drag the file onto or off of the floppy. This is the method that we prefer, although it does cost some extra money.

If you're moving a file from your Macintosh and you don't have a DOS formatted floppy handy, you'll have to format one. Any 3.5-inch floppy will do. All the above programs can do this for you, or you can just use the DOS Format command.

▼ ▼

Tip: Translations vs. Universal File Formats. While you can now move QuarkXPress files between Macs and PCs, there's still no such thing as a "universal" QuarkXPress document format that's identical on both platforms. Each time QuarkXPress opens a document saved on the opposite platform, it must translate the file, and it becomes a new, unsaved document. The file name doesn't change, but (as our favorite Quark tech-support person puts it), "the dirty bit is on," so you should immediately save the file. And since some information gets lost (as we'll describe) or needs to be fixed when you translate files, we'd recommend you keep your cross-platform transfers to the minimum necessary to finish a job. Remember: fewer translations equals less clean-up.

▼ ▼

File Names, Types, and Creators.

The first hassle (though minor) in moving files from one platform to another is that Macintoshes and PCs "see" files differently. On the Macintosh, every file has several attributes attached to it, including file type and creator.

These are mysterious four-letter keys that tell the Macintosh what sort of file it is and what program generated it. For example, when you double-click on a file, the Mac looks at the file's creator to see what application to start up.

In the PC world, everything is different. There are no file types, no file creators...there are only file names. PC files all have names that are eight-dot-three. That means that the name can be no longer than eight letters, followed by a period, and ending with a three-letter extension. This extension provides all the information (and it ain't much) about the file's type and creator.

Moving from PC to Mac. When you're trying to open a QuarkXPress for Windows document on your Mac, you must make certain that the document has either the correct three-letter extension or the correct file type and creator. If the file doesn't have one or both of these correct, it's invisible to QuarkXPress. Unfortunately, if you try to simply move a QuarkXPress for Windows document to your Mac, it probably won't get the correct file type and creator. On the other hand, the three-letter extension almost always comes across fine, and although you don't get the proper-looking icons, QuarkXPress can read the file just fine.

If you want the file to open when you double-click on it in the Finder, you'll have to actually change the file type and creator. To do this, you can use utilities such as CE Software's DiskTop (in the Technical mode), Apple File Exchange, ResEdit, or the shareware program FileTyper. Also, utilities such as DOS Mounter and AccessPC have a cool feature that lets you automatically assign a proper file type and creator based on the PC file's three-letter extension (see "Mac to PC: Names and Extensions," below).

So what are the appropriate file types and creators? All documents created by QuarkXPress on the Macintosh have a creator code of XPR3. The file type depends on what kind of file it is: documents are XDOC, templates are XTMP, and libraries are XLIB. These are the *only* kinds of documents on your Mac that will ever show up in QuarkXPress's file-opening dialog box; you'll never see a Microsoft Word or FileMaker Pro file in there, because QuarkXPress filters out all files except those which have these three specific file types.

Note that when you open a QuarkXPress for Windows file on the Macintosh, the Open dialog box tells you that it's a PC file.

Mac to PC: Filenames and Extensions. If you're a Macintosh user used to 31-character names, you'll find the eight-dot-three filename limit for PC files absolutely infuriating. It's one of the reasons why David's PC has a big dent in its side, right about at kicking level. You can use almost any combination of characters you want in a PC filename, but you can't use spaces, question marks, asterisks, backslashes, or angle brackets in DOS filenames, and we recommend you avoid using colons as well (the Mac operating system chokes on them).

It's really easy to change the file type and creator for a PC file while on either a Macintosh or a PC: just change the three-letter extension. The eight-character file name can be whatever you want, but the relevant extensions are .QXD for documents, and .QXT for templates. If you assign a legal name to a document using these extensions, it should be easily opened by QuarkXPress for Windows, either by double-clicking in the Windows File Manager, or from QuarkXPress for Windows. As it turns out, you actually can open a file in QuarkXPress for Windows even if the extension is wrong, but it's kind of a hassle.

Note that if you don't give a proper DOS name and extension to a document while it's still on the Macintosh, its name may appear strangely altered and truncated when it's transferred over to the PC.

What Does (and Doesn't) Transfer

Physically moving your QuarkXPress files between platforms and successfully opening them is only half the job of transferring files. In general, all page layout, text, and picture information comes across just fine in either direction, as do ferring files. In general, all page layout, text, and picture information comes across just fine in either direction, as do any changes you've made to the General, Typographic, and Tool preferences. Also, any colors, style sheets, and H&J settings you've defined in the document generally transfer without a hitch. However, you'd better be aware of what doesn't get transferred. QuarkXPress documents on each platform are almost identical, but that "almost" can trip you up if you're not careful.

Frames. We have very mixed feelings about the Frame Editor program on the Macintosh. It can do some nice things, but mostly we think it fits best in the Trashcan. But who listens to us? Lots of people are using custom frames and getting reasonable results. However, do note that Frame Editor doesn't exist in QuarkXPress for Windows. In fact, custom frames won't even show up correctly on the screen. Any special frames you've created or assigned on your Mac will travel over to the PC, and usually print fine, but they only show up as heavy black borders on your PC screen.

Color-Contrast Adjustment. In QuarkXPress for Windows, you can't adjust the contrast of color bitmap images, as you can in the Macintosh version. However, any brightness/contrast adjustments you've made to a bitmap in the Mac version won't be lost when you transfer your file to Windows; you just can't change them unless you bring them back to your Mac. But let's get serious for a moment: why would you want to use QuarkXPress's color-contrast functions?

Character Set Remapping. Probably the biggest hassle in transferring files between platforms is character-set remapping. The problem here is that Macintosh and Windows font character sets don't match completely. All the basic "low-ASCII" characters (letters, numbers, punctuation) map just fine, but special characters can really get messed up. If a special character shows up in both Macintosh and Windows typefaces, QuarkXPress does its very best to map them correctly. But there's only so far it can go. Table C-4 shows a list of characters that are commonly found in Windows fonts that just have no equivalent on the Mac (unless you switch to a special pi typeface).

One of the biggest losses in going from Mac to PC is ligatures. The "fi" and "fl" ligatures on the Macintosh are not to be found on the PC. That's right: any ligatures used in your Mac document will go bye-bye when they're opened by QuarkXPress for Windows. There are two solutions to this problem. First, just don't use the special ligature characters. Instead, just type the normal letters and let QuarkXPress create automatic ligatures for you (see "Automatic Ligatures," earlier in this appendix). When you move a Mac file that has automatic ligatures turned on over to Windows, you don't have ligatures anymore. But at least you have fi, fl, or ffi, rather than some strange little character that you have to search for and replace.

The second solution is to use a program like Fontographer or FontMonger to either mess around with the ASCII IDs assigned to ligatures in Window fonts, or create new fonts on the PC that include the ligatures. We only recommend the latter if you're particularly brave, and aren't working on a deadline. Or you can resort to Adobe's expert set fonts, and use the Find/Change dialog to replace fi's and fl's with expert set characters.

Font Metrics. Font metrics describe the width of each character in a font, and the kerning pairs for those characters. On the Macintosh, information about a font's metrics is located in either the screen font (for PostScript Type 1 fonts) or in an outline font (for TrueType). On the PC, the font metrics are located in .PFM files (more of those fun three-letter extensions!). However, no matter where the metrics of a font may reside, you need to be aware that the metrics of a PC font may be different from the metrics of a Macintosh font, even if they're from the same company. We don't know why this is,

Table C-4	Character	ASCII/ANSI Code	Character	ASCII/ANSI Code
Windows special characters with no Mac equivalent	Š	138	½	189
	š	154	¾	190
	¦	166	Đ	208
	²	178	×	215
	³	179	Ý	221
	¹	185	ß	223
	¼	188	ý	253

can easily reflow. Sometimes this is hardly a problem, and other times it can spell hours of work.

It's a good idea to have a printed proof of a Windows document handy after you've imported it into your Mac version of QuarkXPress, and also to send along a printout of any Mac document along with the file itself to Windows users. That way you can check to see if the layout got altered in the transfer. When proofing the document, look for any widows or orphans that may result from minute differences in font metrics. If you notice a problem, you can sometimes adjust the spacing parameters through kerning or tracking to compensate for the differences in font metrics.

Forbidden Fonts. There are certain typefaces that exist only on Macs or only on Windows machines. You should never use them on documents that you intend to shuffle between platforms, unless you enjoy spending a lot of time staring at the Font Usage dialog box. On the Mac, avoid using system fonts such as Chicago, Geneva, Monaco, and New York (a good rule, with some exceptions, is never to use a font named after a city). On the PC, avoid fonts such as Ariel, Helv, System, or Tms Rmn.

If you open a file and its document fonts are missing, QuarkXPress gives you a chance to immediately change them. If you click on Continue, it ignores the missing fonts and replaces them with a default font. If you click on List Fonts, you get the Missing Fonts dialog box (see Figure C-36). You can then select fonts that you want changed, and replace them with a font that you *do* have available.

Figure C-36
Missing Fonts
dialog box

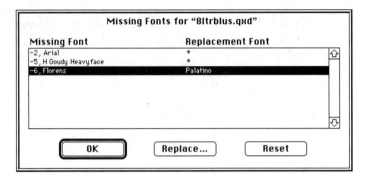

Note that QuarkXPress catches missing fonts if you've used them anywhere in your document, including in style sheets. In other words, even if you don't use a particular style sheet anywhere in your document, if the style sheet description includes a missing font, you get notified.

Transferring Graphics. The last (but certainly not the least) of your problems when transferring files between platforms is graphics. In fact, this is one of the least-understood issues in cross-platform compatibility. The basic problem is that graphics, like fonts, are described in different formats on the two platforms. Fortunately, QuarkXPress is smart enough to do some of the translation work for you, but if you're using pictures in your documents, you've probably got some solid work ahead of you.

The first and most basic problem is that links to EPS and TIFF images almost always get messed up in the transfer. That means you have to relink them using the Picture Usage dialog box. Note that this process is greatly eased if the pictures are in the same location as the QuarkXPress document (the same folder on the Mac, the same subdirectory on a PC).

If you send a document to the PC temporarily, perhaps for a quick proof, the picture links are retained when the file is returned to the Macintosh (as long as they weren't changed on the PC). Similarly, Windows documents will remember links made on their native machines as long as you don't change them. So the trick there is to update a picture only if you're certain you won't be sending the QuarkXPress file back to its original location, or if you absolutely must print with current versions of artwork regardless of the platform.

The next thing you need to be careful of is how images are transferred between the Macintosh and PC. Aside from the name problem that we described a little earlier, there's the issue of screen previews. If you create an EPS in Aldus FreeHand or Adobe Illustrator on the Mac and then move it to the PC, you'll no longer have a screen preview. It typically gets lost in the translation. However, many programs now let you create EPS files in a PC format. These files save their screen preview in the data fork rather than the resource fork, so it doesn't get thrown away (see "Saving a Page as EPS," earlier in this appendix).

Without a screen preview, all you see on the screen is a gray box where the picture should be. The picture often prints just fine if the links are updated properly. But without a preview, most automatic text runarounds are screwed up (no preview, no runaround).

Most Windows graphics programs don't give you the option of saving EPS files in Mac format. They can't, since there's no such thing as a resource fork in the PC world. So you'll certainly run into problems importing a Windows document that uses PC EPS files to your Mac. Your only option is to use the Mac version of the application that created the illustration to open the picture and then save it in a Mac EPS format.

Just as QuarkXPress documents need to have their names changed, graphics that get transferred to the PC also need appropriate file extensions. That means they'll often need to be renamed to have a three-letter ".TIF", ".EPS", or ".PCT" extension (see *The QuarkXPress Book, Windows Edition* for more information on this).

Some formats to avoid: PICTs contained in Mac documents and transferred to PCs sometimes print poorly or not at all (just like on Macs!), and WMF pictures in PC documents may (similarly) not print correctly on the Mac. Sometimes EPS images from the Mac look wrong on screen after they're transferred. Often if you simply reimport the picture, it'll clear up any problems. And when it comes to edition files, forget it. If you've subscribed to an edition file on your Mac, that link gets lost for all time as soon as the file is opened by QuarkXPress for Windows. Similarly, if a Windows user has made OLE links (Windows version of Publish and Subscribe) within a Windows document, that information will be lost when the document's opened on a Macintosh.

▼ ▼

The Big 3.2 Picture

What we don't understand is why Quark persists in numbering its new versions only in .1 increments. With all the new features introduced in 3.1 and 3.2, we feel we should be up to 3.6 or 3.7 by now! It's impressive how the increased functionality (over 3.0) has speeded up our production work. And with features such as separation of CMYK TIFFs and the new palettes, it's easier and easier to create high-quality artwork.

But this isn't the end of the line! The future of Quark-XPress is bright. Products like QuarkPrint and the Quark Publishing System are making printing and networking more efficient. And then there are the many XTension developers who are making our lives even easier (see Appendix B, *Resources*). And as quickly as the world of electronic publishing changes, we'll be right there, acting as your all-night consultants.

EFICOLOR

For years, "What You See Is What You Get," or WYSIWYG (pronounced "wizzywig") was one of the key buzzwords of desktop publishing. It meant that the page layout you saw on your computer screen was, more or less, what you'd get out of your printer. WYSIWYG works fine for a page with any color of ink, so long as it's black (to paraphrase Henry Ford), but it's significant that nobody's felt the need to come up with a similarly cute acronym for describing color fidelity between computer and printer. We did consider "Color You See Is Color You Get," but we wouldn't want to be responsible for unleashing "kissykig" upon the world.

Silliness aside, the main reason nobody's come up with such an acronym is that until fairly recently, it would have described a condition that simply didn't exist. If you've ever tried creating color pages, you've learned—probably with no little pain—that the colors you see on your computer have little more than a passing resemblance to what comes out of your printer or off a printing press. In fact, a major part of working with color on Macs has been learning through trial and error that when you see color A on your Mac screen, you'll actually get color B out of your color proofing printer, and color C off of a four-color press run. Your only guides were process color swatchbooks, test prints, and bitter experience.

▼ ▼

Managing Color

Well, the times they are a-changing, and the hottest things on the Mac market today are color management systems (CMSes) that promise to provide fidelity between the colors on your computer screen and those of your printed output. Apple, Kodak, and Electronics for Imaging (EFI), among others, have management systems that sometimes actually cooperate with each other. Frankly, we're more than a little skeptical of some of the claims made by marketers of these products ("No more Matchprints; proof colors right on your computer screen!"), but color management systems are clearly a step in the right direction.

And if you've purchased or upgraded to QuarkXPress 3.2, you already own one such system, or at least major components of it: EfiColor from Electronics for Imaging, supported in QuarkXPress by the EfiColor XTension.

What Does EfiColor Try to Do?

As a color management system, EfiColor is designed to make the colors on your document's page consistent—from your Macintosh screen to a color proof to your final output device. If you're creating a document to be output on a four-color press, EfiColor makes the colors on your screen look more like those that will emerge from your press run. If you use a color printer such as a QMS ColorScript or Canon CLC 500 with an EFI Fiery raster image processor for comps, EfiColor ensures that your color printout also bears more than a passing resemblance to your final four-color output. Note that we're saying "look like" and "passing resemblance." EfiColor can remove a lot of the guesswork from working with color. So instead of a fifty-percent chance of having a color on your screen look like your final output, you might have an eighty- or ninety-percent chance of seeing what you'll be getting.

Why Color Management "Can't" Work

If there's one thing we want you to get out of reading this appendix, it's that it's just plain not possible for computer monitors, thermal-wax color printers, color copier/printers and four-color printers to exactly match each other, color for color. Each device uses different technology to create color, and each uses differing methods of specifying its colors. Monitors display colors as values of red, green and blue (RGB). Printers usually use cyan, magenta, yellow, and black (CMYK). The colors emitted from a monitor use light and are additive: the more color you add, the closer to white the screen gets. On the other hand, printers that apply ink, wax, or toner to paper generally create colors by combining values of cyan, magenta, yellow, and black. This color model is subtractive: the more of each component you add, the darker your final color becomes. When you create a color with two different methods, there's really no way that the two can look exactly the same.

Plus, the same RGB values on two different monitors might not look like each other at all, because the screen phosphors and technology might be slightly different. Similarly, the same CMYK values printed on a thermal wax transfer printer such as a QMS ColorScript look very different from "identical" values printed on a four-color press on coated stock or newsprint.

We call each of these color systems "device dependent" because the color is specific to only one device—a brand of monitor, color printer, or whatever. EfiColor tries its best to create consistency among various devices, but you need to understand that it's not entirely possible.

"I Only Paint What I See"

Matching colors might be a hopeless comparison of apples, oranges, and grapefruits, except that there's one constant shared by every method of creating colors: the human eye.

The fact is that your eyes don't care what technology a monitor or printer uses to create a color; they just see colors. Just as monitors and printers are device dependent, your eyes are device *independent*. They're the one constant in this whole *mishegoss*, and not surprisingly, they're the key to many color management systems such as EfiColor.

No, EfiColor doesn't try to calibrate your eyes with some sort of cybernetic gizmo. Rather, it uses a color-space model based on scientific analysis of how the eye perceives color. This model was designed by the Commission Internationale de l'Eclairage (International Commission on Color, or CIE for short) in the 1930s, and is appropriately referred to as CIE. The CIE color space describes every color the human eye can see, using a mathematical model that isn't dependent on fickle things like the density of phosphor coatings or the amount of ink spread on certain paper stocks.

Unlike RGB or CMYK values, which don't really describe a color (the same values might look quite different on different devices), CIE values actually describe a color's appearance, not just the values that make it up.

Color Management Concepts

Before we go too much further into this discussion, we have to take a break and define a couple of important words: gamuts and profiles. We'll use these words a lot throughout this chapter.

Gamuts. A device's color "gamut" describes the range of colors that device can create or sense. Since the CIE color space describes every color you can see, by default it has the largest gamut. No device—monitor, scanner, or printer—can come close to reproducing this range of colors, and so the gamut of any specific device is smaller than the CIE gamut.

Profiles. EfiColor uses files called "device profiles" to keep track of not only the color gamut of particular devices, but also other information about their capabilities and limitations. To be specific, EfiColor is a color characterization system, not a color calibration system. Rather than providing you with a color calibrator to map the range of colors available on your hardware, EfiColor uses device profiles created by EFI or a device's manufacturer that describe or characterize each device.

From Device to Device

EfiColor actually adjusts colors depending on what it knows about certain printers and monitors. It does this by converting color information to and from its native CIE color-space format (see Figure D-1). If you've installed the appropriate device profiles on your Mac, EfiColor can transform the color you see on your screen into CIE color, then turn around and convert it to a similar color on your color printer. Moreover, EfiColor's color transformations can even make your proofing printer, such as a Canon CLC 500, simulate the range of colors available on a four-color press.

Figure D-1
EfiColor's
transformations

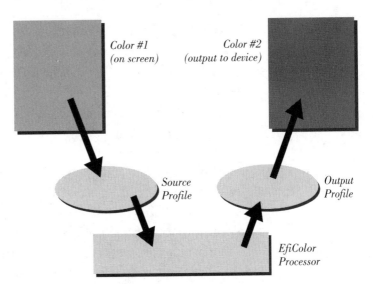

Color #1
(on screen)

Color #2
(output to device)

Source
Profile

Output
Profile

EfiColor
Processor

Note that a color monitor can display more colors than a desktop color printer, which, in turn, has a greater gamut than a four-color press. EfiColor's color transformations work best when they reduce one device's gamut to match another;

it's just not possible to *increase* a device's gamut to match another's, although there are ways of faking it.

Perhaps the most important aspect of this technology is the conversion between RGB and CMYK color models. Once EfiColor transforms a color into its internal CIE color space, it can transform it to any other color model it knows about. And while the RGB-to-CMY conversion is relatively simple (see Chapter 8, *Color*, page 407), converting to CMYK has traditionally been quite difficult. EfiColor does this for you behind the scenes.

Whether you want EFI to do this conversion is a legitimate question; people have argued for years over which program does the best conversion. Some say Photoshop, some say EfiColor, and some say forget all desktop solutions and hire a traditional color separator to do it for you. You'll forgive us if we just stay out of this argument. But do note that EfiColor gives you the choice by letting you turn its transformations on or off.

Metric Color Tags

If all the colors you ever use are created on your own Mac using QuarkXPress, then the color transformations we just described would be all you'd ever need. But life (and desktop publishing) is more complicated than that. Most of the time you'll be importing artwork created or scanned elsewhere. How will you (or rather, your EfiColor XTension) know on what sort of display this artwork was created, and for what kind of printer it was designed? By using a tagging format called Metric Color Tag (MCT), applications that support EfiColor can attach profile information to a graphics file. Then, when you import a picture into QuarkXPress, the EfiColor XTension automatically reads the MCT information from the picture and uses the appropriate device profile to transform the picture's colors when it's displayed and printed, to simulate the colors of the output device you've specified. At least that's the way it's supposed to work.

The important thing to understand here is that specifying a color with RGB or CMYK values alone doesn't really mean anything. For example, it's meaningless to say "This color has such-and-such RGB values," because there's no basis for comparison. The RGB values as displayed on one device are totally different from those values displayed or printed on other devices. However, if you say "This color is defined by these RGB values *as displayed on this particular device*," then you've got something to work with. Knowing both the values and the device profile sets the groundwork for knowing what the color really looks like.

Using EfiColor

OK, so now that you have an idea what EfiColor's supposed to do, let's talk about how it works with QuarkXPress 3.2, and how you tell it what you want it to do.

Installing EfiColor

In order to use EfiColor, you must first install it. When you run QuarkXPress's Installer, one of the first dialog boxes you'll see asks you which file sets you want to install. All you need to do is check the EfiColor XTension checkbox, and let the Installer do the rest. Later in the installation process, you'll be prompted to insert the EfiColor floppy, and asked to specify whether you want the EfiColor XTension and its help file to be installed. Since you've already told the Installer that you want the system installed, you'd better tell it that you want the XTension and help file as well.

What You Get

The main components of the EfiColor system are the EfiColor Processor file and the EfiColor DB folder, both of which live in your Mac's System folder. The EfiColor Processor file is accessed by any application on your Mac which uses EfiColor, such as QuarkXPress's EfiColor XTension or Cachet. The EfiColor DB folder contains folders for all the profiles currently installed on your Mac, as well as ancillary files used by EfiColor. In your QuarkXPress folder are the EfiColor XTension and its help file (EfiColor help is found under the Balloon Help menu; this is another one of those weird and unfortunate standards that Apple is trying to promote). Note that the EfiColor processor is backward compatible, so that you don't have to worry if your copy of EFI's Cachet already loaded one into your System folder.

QuarkXPress ships with a number of profiles, including profiles for two scanners, five printing devices, and a bunch of different monitors. If your monitor's or printer's profile is not included with QuarkXPress, then you should either contact the manufacturer or EFI. The profiles cost anywhere from $129 to $329 each. For example, QuarkXPress comes with the SWOP-Coated profile, but there's no profile for uncoated stock. You can purchase that profile separately, or you can get it by buying EFI's Cachet program. Monitor profiles may be available free from online services and user groups. Monitor calibrators, such as the SuperMatch Display Calibrator, let you create custom profiles for your monitor.

Remember that in order to transform colors correctly, the EfiColor XTension must have profiles available for whatever monitors, color printers, and whatnot that you're using.

The EfiColor XTension

The EfiColor XTension adds many dialog boxes and commands to QuarkXPress. Rather than tackle them on an item-by-item basis, we'll take you on a tour of how we think you'll most likely use the XTension's features.

Although the range of choices you can specify with EfiColor seems daunting, you can break EfiColor's choices into three broad categories: telling it about your monitor, telling it about your printer(s), and telling it how it should modify colors within your document. When the EfiColor XTension knows all these variables, then it can correctly transform color between color spaces and gamuts, resulting in closer color matching between all the devices.

Telling EfiColor About Your Monitor

The first step in getting consistent color is to tell EfiColor about your monitor. When EfiColor is turned on, the Display Correction checkbox is active in the Application Preferences dialog box under the Edit menu (or type Command-Option-Shift-Y). You can then turn Display Correction on or off, and select the profile for your monitor from the pop-up menu (see Figure D-2).

Figure D-2
Display correction in the Application Preferences dialog box

Because EFI's monitor profiles are designed to work with properly calibrated monitors, your screen color looks the best when you have calibrated your monitor to match the values specified in the reference card for your monitor's profile (these reference cards come with the profiles and with the EfiColor XTension's documentation). On most monitors, in fact, if you haven't calibrated properly, or if you're using an Apple 13-inch monitor, chances are that turning Display Correction on won't help much.

Telling EfiColor About Your Printers

The next step in the consistent color game is to tell EfiColor what printer you're printing to. Of course you don't need to do this until you're actually ready to print a proof or your final piece. You give EfiColor this information in the Page Setup dialog box (see Figure D-3). The EfiColor XTension adds two items to the Page Setup dialog box: one pop-up menu for selecting the desired EfiColor profile, and another for specifying the percentage of gray component replacement (GCR) you want to use. In some circumstances, it also changes the Use PDF Values checkbox to Use EfiColor Screen Values.

Figure D-3
EfiColor in the Page
Setup dialog box

EfiColor output controls

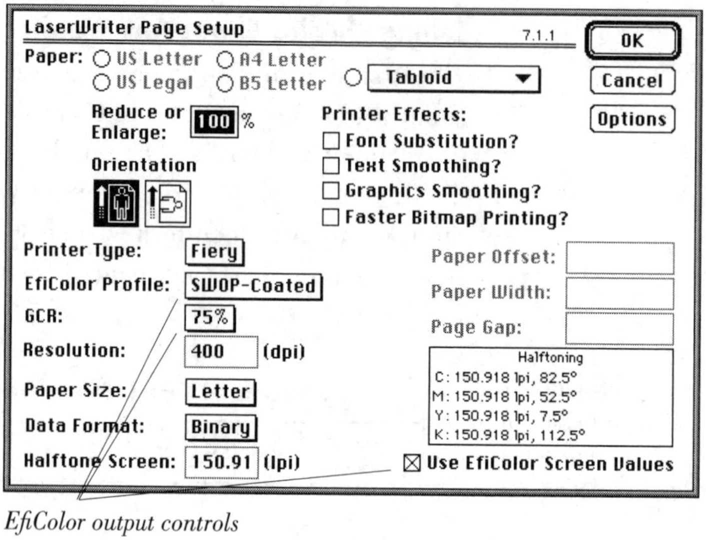

EfiColor Profile. After you use the Printer Type pop-up menu to select your printer, you can use the EfiColor Profile pop-up menu immediately below to select that device's profile. However, note that you should always choose the profile associated with the printer you've selected. If you select the QMS ColorScript from the Printer Type pop-up menu, then you should always pick a ColorScript profile, too (EfiColor helps you out by making an educated guess as to which profile you want). If you select a profile that isn't set up for the printer—for example, if you select SWOP-Coated—you'll probably end up with garbage.

In the future, you may be able to choose a different profile so that one printer can simulate another—like a CLC500 outputting colors that look like they're from an offset press. Note that the EfiColor Profile pop-up menu changes, depending on what printer type you have selected. If you're printing to a black-and-white imagesetter, you can't select a color profile.

Gray Component Replacement. If you select a SWOP-Coated or other four-color process profile, QuarkXPress lets you specify a value for Gray Component Replacement (GCR). You can choose 0, 25, 50, 75, or 100 percent. This process replaces areas of neutral gray that are made up of cyan, magenta, and yellow inks with equivalent tints of black. The two greatest benefits of GCR are saving ink on long press runs and creating richer, crisper dark areas. Typically, you should set this to about 75 percent.

The key to GCR—curiously enough, they don't talk about this in the documentation—is that it only works for RGB to CMYK conversions. That is, CMYK colors and images don't get adjusted at all. If you specify a GCR value, QuarkXPress either applies those GCR values to your process color separations or simulates the effect when printing to a color printer.

In the future, QuarkXPress might support a more robust gray component replacement method—one, perhaps, that works with CMYK as well. But that's a ways off.

EfiColor or PDF Screen Values. Whenever you select a color printer in the Printer Type pop-up menu, QuarkXPress changes the Use PDF Screen Values checkbox in the Page Setup dialog box to Use EfiColor Screen Values. When this checkbox is turned on, QuarkXPress prints your document using the halftone screen frequency and angle values built into the EfiColor profile, rather than using either QuarkXPress's built-in values or those in the PDF. We prefer to use the EfiColor values, but it's really up to you.

No matter what you pick in this checkbox, the angles and screen frequencies are displayed in the Halftoning field at the lower-right corner of the dialog box.

▼ ▼

Tip: QuickDraw Printers. If you're using a QuickDraw (rather than PostScript) printer, you can still specify an EfiColor profile. Once you've selected a QuickDraw printer in the Chooser, you can access an abbreviated Page Setup dialog box. Turn color printing on with the radio buttons, and select the EfiColor Profile you want from the EfiColor Profile pop-up menu. If the profile reference card for your printer profile has instructions for Special (or Printer) effects, make sure to apply them in this dialog box before proceeding with printing. Also, you'll get more accurate color if you use the inks and papers specified on the printer's profile reference card.

▼ ▼

Tip: Turn Calibrated Output Off. If you're using the EfiColor XTension, we recommend that you turn off Calibrated Output in the Print dialog box. Some people use the calibrated output feature to adjust for dot gain, but the way that QuarkXPress handles it just isn't as powerful as other calibration software such as the Precision Imagesetter Linearization Software from Kodak. Whatever the case, if you leave Calibrated Output on, then it may further adjust your color correction, messing up what the EfiColor XTension is trying to do.

▼ ▼

Telling EfiColor About Pictures

Once you've told EfiColor about your monitor and printer, you need to tell it a little about the pictures you're importing. You can do this in several ways, but when you import a picture, typically you'll assign it a profile and rendering method in the Get Picture dialog box.

The EfiColor XTension adds two pop-up menus to the Get Picture dialog box (see Figure D-4). These pop-up menus let you assign both an EfiColor profile and a rendering style to pictures as you import them (we'll explain what rendering style is in just a moment). If a picture didn't have a profile or rendering style assigned to it, then EfiColor couldn't transform its colors because it wouldn't know what to transform *from* (it doesn't know what the colors are *supposed* to look like). Therefore, no color matching would be possible. Again, the point is that when you tell EfiColor where the image came from, here in the Get Picture dialog box or elsewhere, you're telling it how the colors should really look.

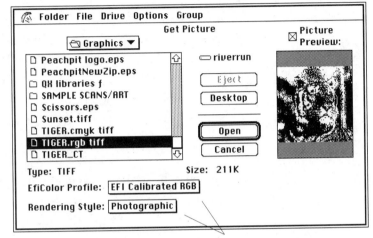

EfiColor picture import controls

Selecting a Profile

The first step you need to take (after selecting the picture in the Get Picture dialog box) is choosing an EfiColor profile for the picture. In general, you should select a profile that corresponds to how the picture was saved. EfiColor is smart enough to examine the format of a file and only display acceptable profiles. That is, it lets you choose process-color profiles such as SWOP-Coated only when you're importing a CMYK image, and RGB color profiles when the image is stored in an RGB mode.

You can change the default settings (the ones that come up automatically) by going to the EfiColor Preferences dialog box (see "EfiColor Preferences," later in this appendix).

Note that if the picture you're importing has a Metric Color Tag (MCT) attached to it, the profiles pop-up menu automatically changes to that profile. Also, its name is displayed with an underline, just to show you that it's a special case. You can change it if you want to, but it's typically not advisable.

Rendering Style

What are rendering styles, anyway, and how do you know what kind to assign to a picture? The rendering style of a picture tells EfiColor how to convert colors in a picture when the gamut of your printer isn't big enough to print those colors. For example, it's easy to pick an RGB color that cannot be printed in CMYK on a press. So the EfiColor XTension can transform that color into a color that a press can print. EfiColor has two methods for converting colors like this: Photographic and Solid Color.

Photographic. If the image you're importing is a scanned photograph, you probably want to use the Photographic rendering method. That seems obvious enough. But why?

When EfiColor needs to transform a color into a smaller gamut, it has to deal with colors that fall outside that gamut—and their relationships to other colors. Photographic rendering compresses the entire color range of your picture to fit into your printer's gamut (see Figure D-5), maintaining the balance of color throughout the picture. All the colors in the picture change, but they maintain their relationships to each other, which results in a more true-to-life rendition of color photographs.

Figure D-5
Solid versus
Photographic rendering

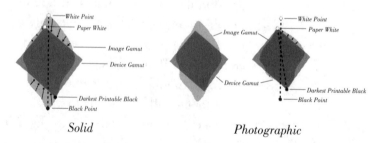

Solid   Photographic

Balance, it turns out, is often more important to maintain in photographic images than the colors themselves. For example, the colors in a picture of a face can be pretty far off, but as long as the colors maintain a relative balance, our eyes adjust to it fine.

Solid Color. If your picture contains only a few colors that must be matched as closely as possible between your proofs and your final output, select Solid Color for the rendering style. When Solid Color is selected, colors in your image that are within the output device's gamut stay just the same; no color adjustment is made. Any color that is outside the printer's gamut gets mapped to the nearest possible color.

You end up with fewer colors using the Solid Color rendering method, because some colors are mapped to the same values as existing colors, but most colors don't change at all, and every color is mapped to its closest equivalent. The relationship between colors changes, but that's less important with a non-photographic image.

Images from FreeHand or Illustrator that have been turned into TIFFs are often perfect for Solid Color rendering, because you want the colors to be as close as possible to your original specifications. On the other hand, if you specify that a photograph should be transformed with Solid Color rendering, the colors in the picture that are inside the printer's gamut will be maintained perfectly, whereas any color outside the printer's gamut will be mapped, throwing the balance way off.

Changing the Profiles for a Picture

What happens if you've imported a picture, and then realize you've chosen the wrong profile or rendering style for it? You could reimport the picture and spend a lot of time (importing pictures takes somewhat longer with EfiColor; see "Before You Use EfiColor," later in this chapter), or you could simply select the picture and choose the Profile command from the Style menu. The Picture Profile dialog box (see Figure D-6), has the same two pop-up menus—Profiles and Rendering Styles—as the Get Picture dialog box. Simply change the values to whatever you want.

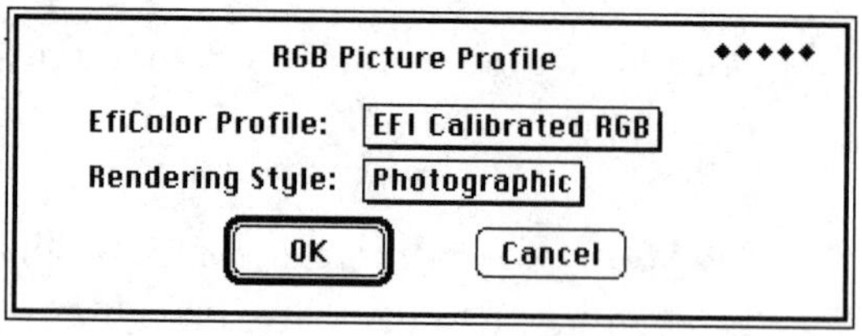

Figure D-6
The Picture Profile
dialog box

```
          RGB Picture Profile        ◆◆◆◆◆
  EfiColor Profile:  [ EFI Calibrated RGB ]
  Rendering Style:  [ Photographic ]
        ( OK )          ( Cancel )
```

If you want to change a lot of pictures at the same time, you can use the Profile Usage dialog box (see Figure D-7), found under the Utilities menu. You look for and replace profiles in much the same way that you identify and update missing pictures or fonts.

The Profile Usage dialog box contains information about your document's pictures and profiles, and lets you replace profiles quickly.

Profile. The first column in the Profile Usage dialog box lists all the profiles used in the current document. Even if you don't have any items in a document, the default profiles for RGB and CMYK images are always listed in the dialog box. Note that a profile can be listed more than once, depending on the kinds of objects to which it's applied. For example, all the QuarkXPress items that have a profile assigned to them are listed, as are all the pictures that have a certain profile, and so on. That makes it easy to change all of one kind of object from one profile into another.

Objects. These are the kinds of color models to which a profile's been applied in a document. The possibilities are pictures, RGB/HSB colors, and CMYK colors. Note that you can't apply the same profile to both RGB/HSB and CMYK colors.

Status. Status in the Profile Usage dialog box means almost the same thing as in the Picture Usage dialog box. However, instead of pictures, QuarkXPress is looking for the availability of profiles. "OK" means that the necessary device profile has been installed in your EfiColor DB folder (usually in the System folder); "Missing" means it's not there (see "Missing Profiles," later in this chapter).

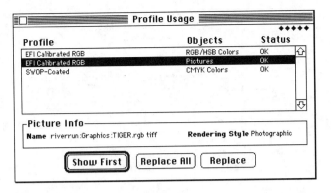

Figure D-7
Profile Usage
dialog box

Show First. The Show First button is active only when you've selected a profile that's applied to pictures. Clicking on it takes you to the first picture in a document that uses the profile you've selected. After you've displayed the first picture, the button changes to Show Next, so you can use it to cycle through all the pictures that use a specific profile. Of course, if there's only one picture in a document that uses that profile, the button remains Show First. And, just like in the Find/Replace dialog box, you can change the button back to Show First at any time by holding the Option key down.

Replace All. This button lets you automatically replace a profile you've selected for the entire object class it's listed next to. When you click the Replace All button, the Replace Profile dialog box appears (see Figure D-8). You can only change the profiles of objects that aren't pictures using this method, or by changing the profiles listed in the EfiColor Preferences dialog box.

This dialog box has the familiar pop-up menus for selecting profiles and rendering styles. If you've selected a profile that's missing, it appears grayed-out in the menu. If you've chosen "Replace All" for several pictures which use different rendering styles, then the word Mixed appears in the Rendering Style pop-up menu. Note that when you replace profiles assigned to RGB/HSB and CMYK colors, the default profiles as displayed in the EfiColor Preferences dialog box also change.

```
┌─────────────────────────────────────────────────┐
│  Replace Profile "EFI Calibrated RGB"   ◆◆◆◆◆    │
│             for TIGER.rgb tiff                    │
│                                                   │
│  EfiColor Profile:  ┌─────────────┐               │
│                     │ Apple 13" RGB│              │
│  Rendering Style:   ┌─────────────┐               │
│                     │ Solid Color │               │
│                                                   │
│        ┌──────────┐     ┌──────────┐              │
│        │    OK    │     │  Cancel  │              │
│        └──────────┘     └──────────┘              │
└─────────────────────────────────────────────────┘
```

Replace. This button is only active when you've selected a profile that is applied to pictures. First, use the Show First or Show Next button to select the picture you want to change. Next, click on the Replace button. This brings up the Replace Profile dialog box.

Picture Info. Underneath the profiles section of the Profile Usage dialog box are two pieces of information titled Picture Info. These fields display the path leading to a selected picture, and the rendering style applied to it. Note that you can only see Picture Info after you've selected a picture with Show First or Show Next.

Pictures that EfiColor Understands

The thing you have to understand about the EfiColor XTension is that it really only works with images that Quark-XPress itself can change. If you remember Chapter 8, *Modifying Images*, QuarkXPress can only modify TIFF, Paint, and bitmap-only PICTs. That means that EfiColor won't even attempt to transform any EPS, DCS, or object-oriented PICTs.

Although the EfiColor XTension can recognize EPS and DCS images that have had MCTs assigned to them, you can't change the profile for these pictures, nor can you assign a profile to EPS or DCS files that don't already have one. Also note that the profile name for an MCT file will appear grayed out if it's a profile not available on your system.

By the way, the EfiColor documentation says that when you print your document using the preview image of an EPS or DCS picture—that is, if either the high-res picture is missing or if you turn Low Resolution on in the Print dialog box—then EfiColor transforms the colors of the preview image. They're wrong. Apparently, that's the way that it was originally supposed to work, but it doesn't yet. Oh well. Perhaps someday.

▼ ▼

Editing Colors in QuarkXPress

Objects that are built or colored directly in QuarkXPress can always be transformed by the EfiColor XTension. The key to making this work is correctly setting up the Edit Color dialog box for each color (see Figure D-9). The EfiColor XTension adds a few new features to this dialog box: Target, Gamut Alarm, and Rendering Style.

Figure D-9
Edit Color dialog box
with EfiColor's
additions

Device gamut

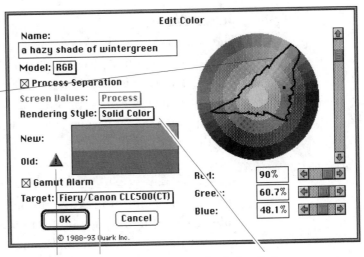

Gamut Alarm   Target pop-up menu   Rendering Style pop-up menu

Note that every color you create in the Edit Color dialog box is automatically assigned a profile based on what you have selected in the EfiColor Preferences dialog box. If the color is set using CMYK, TruMatch, FocolTone, or Pantone ProSim, the assigned profile is the default for CMYK models.

If the color is set using RGB, HSB, or one of the Pantone spot-color models, the profile is the default for RGB/HSB models.

Target

Before you even begin to pick a color, you should select a profile from the Target pop-up menu; the profile that you select should be for your final output device. If your final artwork is from a Canon CLC500 with a Fiery RIP, then select Fiery. If your final destination is a four-color press run, then select SWOP-Coated or another four-color process.

You want to set the target profile because that's how EfiColor figures out whether colors are within the device's gamut (see "Gamut Alarm," below). If Gamut Alarm is turned off, then you don't need to set the Target—in fact, you can't; it's grayed out.

Gamut Alarm

The Gamut Alarm checkbox lets you turn on and off one of the neatest features of the EfiColor XTension: the Gamut Alarm. The Gamut Alarm actually shows you whether the color you specify can be printed on the target printer. There are two ways to see if your color is within gamut: the alarm and the gamut map.

Alarm. The alarm shows up as a little triangular icon with an exclamation point in it, sitting to the left of the New or Old color field. When either the old color (if you're editing a color) or the new color is out of gamut, the Gamut Alarm icon appears to warn you that it cannot be printed on the target printer you've selected.

The Gamut Alarm takes two profiles into consideration: the default color profile and the target profile. The EfiColor XTension essentially compares the two profiles to see if a color created with the default profile (the one set up in the EfiColor Preferences dialog box) falls inside the gamut of the target profile. If it doesn't, then the Gamut Alarm shows up.

Gamut outline. The second part of the gamut alarm system is the gamut outline, which is basically a graphic representation of the available color gamut. If you're specifying an HSB, RGB, or CMYK color, the EfiColor XTension displays a red border on the color wheel that shows you where the edges of the gamut are (see Figure D-10). Note that if you select a color near the border of the gamut outline, the border and the triangular gamut alarm might disagree. The gamut alarm is always the final judge in these disputes. If you're using color swatches—such as TruMatch, Pantone, or FocolTone—diagonal lines cross out swatches that don't fit in the gamut.

Figure D-10
Gamut outlines

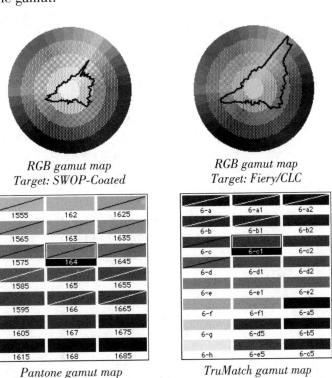

RGB gamut map
Target: SWOP-Coated

RGB gamut map
Target: Fiery/CLC

Pantone gamut map
Target: CLC/Fiery

TruMatch gamut map
Target: QMS ColorScript

Once again, this gamut outline takes into account both the default color profile (the one being used to assign the color) and the target printer. If you change one or the other, the gamut outline changes, too.

Rendering Style

There are times that you want to specify a color, even if the gamut alarm says it won't print correctly. Perhaps you don't have the correct profile to select in the Target pop-up menu, or perhaps you trust yourself more than you trust the Gamut Alarm. (Who are we to stop you if you know what you're doing?) If the color you pick *is* inside the gamut, you can just leave Rendering Style set to Solid (see "Rendering Style," earlier in this chapter). However, if it isn't, you need to think for a moment about which rendering style you want.

You can determine which rendering style to choose based on the source of the color, and how you'd like it to finally appear. If you're specifying a color using a matching system such as TruMatch or Pantone, you probably want your final output to appear to be as close to those colors as possible. In that case, you should probably select Solid Color in the Rendering Style pop-up menu. Likewise, if you're trying to match your color to a color in an imported graphic to which the Solid Color rendering style is assigned, you should also apply the Solid Color rendering style to your color. Otherwise, the picture's color and the color you're creating may not match properly.

On the other hand, if you're creating a color that matches one in a continuous-tone image (a scanned photograph or artwork), you should use the Photographic rendering style (see "Matching Colors in Pictures" below). EFI advises that if your color doesn't fit in your device's gamut, you should use the Photographic rendering style. However, while this does maintain the overall color balance of your document's colors, it may not provide the best match to that one particular color.

Note that Rendering Style is only available when your color is set to Process Separation. That's because EFI figures that if you're creating a Pantone solid spot color, you're always going to want Solid rendering. So that's what it gives you. We can't think of a reason why you wouldn't want this, but if you like, you can call them and complain.

▼ ▼

Tip: Matching Colors in Pictures. Suppose you've imported a picture into your QuarkXPress document, and you want to create a color in QuarkXPress that exactly matches a color in the picture. If you've used named colors such as TruMatch or Pantone to define a color in a graphics program, all you need to do in QuarkXPress is specify the same color with exactly the same name, and assign to it the same rendering style and device profile as you've used for the picture.

However, if you're matching colors in a scanned photograph, you have a little more work cut out for you. The problem is that your graphics program probably defines color differently than QuarkXPress does. Therefore, you have to convert the color from the way it's described in your graphics program to the way it's described in QuarkXPress.

1. Open the image in a program like Photoshop or ColorStudio.

2. Use the eyedropper tool to find the exact RGB or CMYK values of the color you want to match. Write those values down (yes, you may have to actually use a pen—so much for the paperless office).

3. In QuarkXPress, create a color based on those RGB or CMYK values and set it to the Photographic rendering style. Note that some photomanipulation programs define RGB colors as numbers on a scale from 0 to 255, and QuarkXPress defines them as percentages from 0 to 100. To convert the former to the latter, divide the color's value by 255 and multiply by 100; for example, the color value 129 divided by 255 and multiplied by 100 gives you 50.6 percent (see "Tip: QuarkXPress as a Calculator," below).

4. Make sure that the Process Separation checkbox is turned on.

▼ ▼

Tip: QuarkXPress as a Calculator. If for some obscure reason you don't have a calculator around (remember that there's usually a calculator on the Apple menu) and you still have night-mares about math class, you can use QuarkXPress to figure out the conversion described in the last tip.

1. Change your measurements in the General Preferences dialog box to Points.

2. Draw a line on your page or pasteboard and set the Line Mode to Left Point in the Measurements palette.

3. Type the equation into the length field of the line's Measurements palette. In the example above, you'd type "129/255*100."

4. When you press Enter or Return, the length of the line shown in the Measurements palette is the percentage value you want.

5. Delete the line.

We know that this is a really twisted way to get this number (you could just pop up a calculator DA on screen, or pull one out of your desk drawer), but sometimes you really have to stretch to get your work done!

▼ ▼

EfiColor Preferences

The EfiColor Preferences dialog box found under the Edit menu is the Command Central of the EfiColor XTension (see Figure D-11). Here's where you get to set both the default EfiColor settings and also tell EfiColor how and when to do its thing. Note that this preferences dialog box works just like QuarkXPress's: if a document is open, then any changes you make in the EfiColor Preferences dialog box change only that document. If no documents are open when you change something, then that change is good for all subsequent

documents you open (older documents retain their settings).Let's examine what the various options in this dialog
box do.

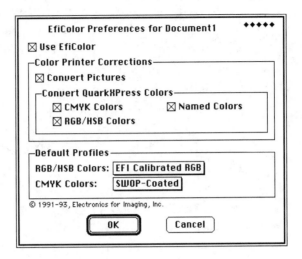

Use EfiColor. The first item in the EfiColor Preferences dialog
box is Use EfiColor. This is almost entirely self-explanatory:
check this box to turn EfiColor on; uncheck it to turn
EfiColor off. When EfiColor is off, the XTension doesn't
transform any colors at import, on screen, or during printing.
Note that any pictures you've already imported into your
document look the same even after you turn EfiColor off. You
can't reset them to a pre-EfiColor screen rendition without
re-importing them. However, if EfiColor is turned off, the
picture won't get transformed when you print the document.

Convert Pictures. At the time of this writing, the upper half of
the EfiColor Preferences dialog box is labeled "Color Printer
Corrections," which is really a misnomer because it's not just
color printers that this affects. The changes you make in this
area of the EfiColor Preferences dialog box alter the way that
EfiColor transforms colors anytime you use a profile. Perhaps
they'll have changed the name by the time you see it, though.

The first checkbox in the Color Printer Corrections section is Convert Pictures. Check this box to have EfiColor
convert colors in imported TIFF and PICT format pictures.

Convert QuarkXPress Colors. The three checkboxes in the Convert QuarkXPress Colors section let you tell EfiColor which kinds of colors created within QuarkXPress to convert. Turning these on or off won't change anything except tint builds or colors that you actually specify in QuarkXPress. The three checkboxes are labeled CMYK Color, RGB/HSB Colors, and Named Colors.

The trick here is that while Pantone is a named color, TruMatch and FocolTone are not. Why? Because the Pantone system actually defines a set of distinct, named ink colors, whereas TruMatch and FocolTone colors are built from CMYK inks.

Default Profiles. The Default Profiles section of the EfiColor Preferences dialog box lets you set which profiles the EfiColor XTension will use whenever you create new colors or import artwork. Of course, you can always override these profiles for individual pictures later on. Also, pictures that already have profiles assigned to them via an MCT ignore the default profiles on import. If you don't want CMYK colors that you specify within QuarkXPress to be modified at all on your final output device, be sure to select that device's profile as your CMYK default.

▼ ▼

Missing Profiles

Progress is never without a price. When you use a new typeface, you have the burden of making sure your service bureau and other people who receive your documents have that typeface as well. It turns out that EfiColor profiles are the same way. When you send a file to another QuarkXPress user, you must make certain that your recipient has legal copies of all the EfiColor profiles you've used in your document (see "Tip: Moving Profiles," below). Just as with fonts, the Collect for Output feature (see "Collect for Output," Appendix C, *Using*

QuarkXPress) doesn't automatically assemble all the profiles used in a document. You're on your own.

What to Do

So let's say you've received a document without all the needed profiles. How will you know? What can you do about it? If you're familiar with the ways QuarkXPress handles missing fonts and pictures, you should have no trouble coping with missing profiles.

When you open a document that uses one or more profiles that are not in your EfiColor DB folder, an error message appears indicating the missing profile or profiles (see Figure D-12). If you can obtain the proper profile from someone—perhaps the person who sent you the QuarkXPress document, or from EFI, or maybe even the manufacturers of the device—then do it (see "Tip: Moving Profiles," below). You just have to put that profile in your EfiColor DB folder (usually in the System folder), and relaunch QuarkXPress.

Figure D-12
Missing profile when
opening alert

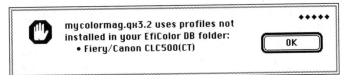

However, if you can't obtain the profile, you can either go ahead and do nothing about it, or replace it with a profile that is active in your system. If you're only interested in a fast and dirty proof—let's say you're proofing page geometry or type—then there's no need to replace profiles. But if you need EfiColor's color matching, you must replace the missing profiles (see "Changing the Profiles for a Picture," earlier in this chapter).

▼ ▼

Tip: Moving Profiles. EfiColor profiles are little pieces of software. And, like most pieces of software, they're copyrighted. Like fonts, you're not really supposed to copy them from one machine to another; you're supposed to buy a profile for each machine you use. However, EFI is being somewhat generous: they're encouraging people to freely pass around monitor and scanner profiles. But restraint is the name of the game when it comes to output device profiles.

While this isn't supposed to be a commercial plug, EFI really makes its money through sales such as these, and we shouldn't begrudge them that. If you need a profile, call them (their number is in Appendix B, *Resources*) and order one. By the time you read this, they might even be doing a special subscription deal so that service bureaus have all the state-of-the-art profiles at good prices.

▼ ▼

Printing with Missing Profiles

If you attempt to print a file which uses profiles that are missing from your system, you'll get an alert very similar to the one displayed when you try to print a document with missing or modified pictures (see Figure D-13, below).

Figure D-13
Missing profile
when printing alert

You've got three options in this dialog box: click on the Cancel button to cancel the print job, the OK button to proceed with printing despite the missing profiles, or the List Profiles button to display the missing profiles. If you choose the third option, you get the Missing Profiles dialog box, which is almost identical in appearance and function to the Profile Usage dialog box, with a few changes.

First of all, it only displays missing profiles and the items associated with them. There's also an OK button, to let you proceed with printing the file regardless of the number of profiles you've replaced. And there's a Cancel button, to stop replacing profiles; however, this also stops your print job.

▼▼▼▼▼▼▼▼▼▼▼▼▼▼▼▼▼▼▼▼▼▼▼▼▼▼▼▼

Tip: Pre-EfiColor Documents. It's pretty simple to take advantage of EfiColor's capabilities in a document created by previous versions of QuarkXPress. When you open an old document, the EfiColor XTension may be turned off. So the first thing you should do is go to the EfiColor Preferences dialog box and make sure it's turned on. Once you turn on EfiColor and choose appropriate profiles for the colors in your document, EfiColor will convert the document's colors when you print. If you're not happy with the results, and would rather have the colors print as they did in previous versions of QuarkXPress, simply turn EfiColor off in the Preferences dialog box.

▼▼▼▼▼▼▼▼▼▼▼▼▼▼▼▼▼▼▼▼▼▼▼▼▼▼▼▼▼▼

Before You Use EfiColor...

If EfiColor is so great and wonderful, why would you ever *not* want to use it? There are lots of reasons, from speed to consistency. In this last section of this appendix, we want to look at a few things that you should think about before you jump in and start using EfiColor.

Performance

Every time EfiColor transforms a color to look right on your screen or your proofing printer or your final output device, the color gets *processed*. That takes time. And time is something we often don't have enough of.

Imagine converting a thirty-megabyte image from RGB mode to CMYK mode in Photoshop or Cachet. It takes a long time, doesn't it? EfiColor can't do it any faster than those programs can, and that's just what it's doing when you print an RGB TIFF from QuarkXPress with EfiColor turned on.

Similarly, when you import any sort of TIFF or PICT image, EfiColor has to convert the screen preview to look correct on the screen. That can easily make importing pictures take four or five times as long as without EfiColor. You can speed the process a little by holding down the Shift key while clicking Open in the Get Picture dialog box; that imports the picture at half the screen resolution. However, you then get a low-resolution image to look at on the screen, which sort of defeats the purpose anyway.

▼ ▼

Tip: Don't Remove the XTension. With most XTensions, if you don't want to use what they have to offer, you can just delete them, or better yet, move them into another folder so that QuarkXPress can't "see" them. However, you shouldn't do this with the EfiColor XTension. That's because Quark actually uses part of the XTension to make preview images for pictures on your screen. So if you don't want EfiColor to function, don't move the XTension; just turn it off in the EfiColor Preferences dialog box. By the way, QuarkXPress still functions fine if you *do* move the XTension. It's just that it functions even better when the XTension is around.

▼ ▼

Incompatible File Formats

What happens when you import a color EPS image from Aldus FreeHand or Adobe Illustrator onto your page, and surround it with colors that you've matched exactly within QuarkXPress? You can throw the words "matched exactly" out of your vocabulary. The colors you assign in QuarkXPress are transformed according to the profiles you choose. The colors in the EPS image are not transformed at all. Why? Because the EfiColor XTension never transforms EPS or DCS images. Never ever. Well, maybe their screen preview renditions.

You have to understand the philosophy of EPS images. The whole idea of Encapsulated PostScript was originally that a program should never need to look "inside" them, and should certainly never change anything inside them. Therefore, according to this school of thought, EfiColor should never adjust the color inside an EPS or DCS image.

The problem is that people use these images all the time, and go nuts when the colors don't match what comes out of QuarkXPress. Unfortunately, we don't really have a good answer for how to handle this situation right now. If you're using images built with Photoshop or Cachet, you can assign either an MCT or an EfiColor profile to the image (EFI is selling color separation sets for Photoshop that help you do this). This allows EfiColor to adjust the screen preview image to more closely match what will come out of the printer. It has no effect on the printed output, however.

Until Aldus and Adobe decide that color management is really worth their time (read: their customers want it), we'll all just have to hold our breath and wait for a whole, integrated color-management system.

▼ ▼

Tip: Don't Convert Pantone Colors. A funny thing happens if you convert a Pantone color to RGB and then try to print it using EfiColor: you get a different color. Now theoretically, this shouldn't happen. However, because of the way that EfiColor "sees" Pantone colors, you get a more accurate Pantone color by leaving it in Pantone mode (you *can* change the name if you want) rather than converting it to RGB or CMYK.

▼ ▼

The Problem with OPI

Trying to manage color with OPI images (see "OPI" in Appendix C, *What's New in QuarkXPress 3.2*) is even more difficult than with EPS, because QuarkXPress never even touches the final image. Remember that with OPI, you export PostScript from QuarkXPress without image data; only little tags are inserted in the PostScript saying what the name of the image is and how it should be adjusted (rotation, cropping, and so on). That's why QuarkXPress is only called an OPI writer.

The PostScript that comes from QuarkXPress gets passed on to another program—an OPI reader—that interprets the PostScript and strips in high-resolution images where appropriate. Until OPI readers include the EfiColor color management system, those images will never get adjusted properly. The solution, again, is to adjust for the target printer when the image is scanned or saved from a image-manipulation program.

Quality of Character

Blends, vignettes, fountains...whatever you want to call them, they're a hassle when it comes to color management. The problem, put simply, is that you can get a nice clean blend, but the colors may be slightly different than you want. Or you can get a weird looking blend, but the colors all along the blend will be as close as they can be to the original colors. EfiColor takes the first path, making the blend look smooth. We agree that this is probably what people want, but you need to at least be aware of it so that you don't get snagged down the road.

Pros and Cons

When it comes right down to it, we think that the EfiColor XTension is not only really cool, but it can be incredibly useful. However, it obviously has limits and isn't for everyone all the time. One of the most important things to note is that color management works best when you're comparing apples to oranges rather than to salmons or coffee beans. What we mean is, you'll get a better idea of a final color by looking at a printed color proof than at the screen. You can calibrate all you want, and you'll still always get a more reliable image from a printer than from the screen. It still won't be a perfect match to your final output, of course, but it's that much closer.

The last thing we need to say is that everyone works differently, and so you need to set up the EfiColor XTension's preferences to best suit your needs.

Index

Bold numbers indicate illustrations.

▼ ▼

The QuarkXPress Book Doesn't Stop Here Anymore

We couldn't do it. We just couldn't steer though the twists and turns of all those wild jungle roads just to stroll off at the end of the line. So we ain't stoppin' here! We've hijacked the bus, we're painting it pink and green and we won't stop drivin' until we reach the top. Stay on board! Give us a shout from time to time and let us know how you've liked the ride so far. Tell us if you've picked up any new XPress Demon machete techniques that make the driving easier. We're always looking out for a new trick or two from a young tyro or a seasoned pro. You can write to David at the following addresses.

c/o Peachpit Press
2414 Sixth Street
Berkeley, CA 94710

CompuServe: 72647, 3302
America Online: Parallax1

DON'T **B** E CRUEL

Examples of what can (but shouldn't) be done with QuarkXPress's polygon tool. ©1993 Carlos Sosa

Colophon

▼ ▼

If anything shows that we practice what we preach, it's this book. *The QuarkXPress Book* was created using almost every technique and many of the tips that we divulge throughout the chapters.

Text

Text was written using various word processors, including QuarkXPress, Microsoft Word, MacWrite II, and WordStar (on an Epson PX-8). The text was copy-edited entirely in Microsoft Word. Style sheets were applied to most of the text in Word and then imported into QuarkXPress template. Any styles that could not easily be created in Word were then applied using QuicKeys and XPress Tags.

The table of contents and index were developed the old fashioned way—by hand—though we also used Sonar Bookends for text searches.

Artwork

We created all the artwork in QuarkXPress, Adobe Illustrator, and Aldus FreeHand. Every screen shot in the book was created with Exposure and then converted to TIFF format with DeskPaint. Each figure was imported, cropped, sized, and labelled within QuarkXPress, and saved in a library (one library per chapter). For fast access to each figure, we labelled them using the library's labelling feature to speed up page production.

Output

We set the body copy in Adobe's Bodoni Book and heads in Bitstream's Futura Condensed Bold. PostScript examples were set in Adobe's Optima. Chapter heads were set in Adobe's Bodoni Poster Compressed.

The pages were sent as PostScript files to Seattle Image-Setting, and Datatype and Graphics in Seattle, where they were imageset on Linotronic 300s and 330s at 1270 dpi. The color plates were output by CMYK Digital Prepress on a Agfa SelectSet 5000. The book was printed on 60 lb. Starbright Smooth Opaque.

More from Peachpit Press...

Art of Darkness (with disk)
Erfert Fenton

This book is the perfect companion to AFTER DARK, the world's most popular screen saver and one of the top-selling utility programs of all time. It explains how to install, operate, and customize the program, as well as how to create modules for new screen savers. Included are nine new AFTER DARK modules created exclusively for this book. *(128 pages)*

Canvas 3.0: The Book
Deke McClelland

This book takes you on a fact-filled tour of Canvas 3.0. It includes essential information about using the program with System 7, creating dynamic illustrations and text effects, and much more. *(384 pages)*

Desktop Publisher's Survival Kit
David Blatner

Here is a book that provides insights into desktop publishing on the Macintosh: troubleshooting print jobs, working with color, scanning, and selecting fonts. A disk containing 12 top desktop publishing utilities, 400K of clip art, and two fonts is included in this package. *(176 pages)*

Illustrator Illuminated
Clay Andres

This book is for people who want to know more about Adobe Illustrator than the manuals can tell them. *Illustrator Illuminated* uses full-color graphics to show how professional artists use Illustrator's tools to create a variety of styles and effects. Each chapter shows the creation of a specific illustration from concept through completion. Additionally, it covers using Illustrator in conjunction with Adobe Streamline and Photoshop. *(200 pages)*

The Little Mac Book, 3rd Edition
Robin Williams

Praised by scores of magazines and user group newsletters, this concise, beautifully written book covers the basics of Macintosh operation. It provides useful reference information, including charts of typefaces, special characters, and keyboard shortcuts. Totally updated for System 7. *(336 pages)*

The Little Mac Word Book
Helmut Kobler

Here's a fast way to learn Word 5.0 basics. This book provides concise and clear information about formatting text; using Word with Apple's new System 7 operating system; taking advantage of Word's writing tools; setting up complex tables, and much more! *(240 pages)*

The Little QuicKeys Book
Steve Roth and Don Sellers

This handy guide to CE Software's QuicKeys 2.0 explores the QuicKeys Keysets and the different libraries QuicKeys creates for each application; shows how to link together functions and extensions; and provides an abundance of useful macros. *(288 pages)*

The Macintosh Bible, 4th Edition
Arthur Naiman, Nancy E. Dunn, Susan McAllister, John Kadyk, and a cast of thousands

It's more than just a book—it's a phenomenon. Even Apple's own customer support staff uses it. Now the Fourth Edition is here, and its 1,248 pages are crammed with tips, tricks, and shortcuts to get the most out of your Mac. And to make sure the book doesn't get out-of-date, three 30-page updates are included in the price (we mail them to you free of charge). Every Mac owner should have one. *(1,248 pages)*

The Macintosh Bible Software Disks
Dave Mark

This three-disk companion to *The Macintosh Bible, 4th Edition* offers Mac users an introduction to the very best public-domain software and shareware that exists for the Mac. The disks include useful utilities, modem software, sounds, games, and fonts.

The Macintosh Bible Guide to FileMaker Pro 2.0
Charles Rubin

Claris's FileMaker Pro product manager enthusiastically declared this book a "must for every FileMaker Pro user." Best-selling author Charles Rubin offers fast relief for FileMaker users of all levels, providing clear and understandable solutions for scores of the most common problems. *(464 pages)*

The Macintosh Bible "What Do I Do Now?" Book, 2nd Edition
Charles Rubin

Completely updated through System 7, this bestseller covers just about every sort of basic problem a Mac user can encounter. The book shows the error message exactly as it appears on screen, explains the problem (or problems) that can produce the message, and discusses what to do. This book is geared for beginners and experienced users alike. *(352 pages)*

The Mac is not a typewriter
Robin Williams

This best-selling, elegant guide to typesetting on the Mac has received rave reviews for its clearly presented information, friendly tone, and easy access. Twenty quick and easy chapters cover what you need to know to make your documents look clean and professional. *(72 pages)*

Photoshop 2.5: Visual QuickStart Guide
Elaine Weinmann and Peter Lourekas

The author of our award-winning *QuarkXPress 3.1: Visual QuickStart Guide* does it again. This is an indispensable guide for Mac users who want to get started in Adobe Photoshop but who don't have a lot of time to read books. Covers how to use masks, filters, colors, tools, and much more. *(264 pages)*

QuarkXPress 3.1: Visual QuickStart Guide (Mac Edition)
Elaine Weinmann

Winner of the 1992 Benjamin Franklin Award, this book is a terrific way to get introduced to QuarkXPress in just a couple of hours. Lots of illustrations and screen shots make each feature of the program absolutely clear. *(200 pages)*

Real World FreeHand 3
Olav Martin Kvern

The ultimate insider's guide to FreeHand, this authoritative and entertaining book first lays out the basics and then concentrates on advanced techniques. *(528 pages)*

Silicon Mirage
Steve Aukstakalnis and David Blatner

Virtual reality is the amazing new technology of "pretend worlds," where individuals can completely immerse themselves in computer-generated environments. *Silicon Mirage* provides an easily understandable explanation of the "virtual senses" already possible, the strikingly broad array of fields where virtual reality is having an impact, and the breathtaking horizons yet to be discovered. *(300 pages)*

Zen and the Art of Resource Editing (with disk)
Derrick Schneider et al.

This book introduces the beginner to ResEdit 2.1, one of the most useful tools ever designed for the Macintosh. It covers ResEdit from a nonprogrammer's point of view, and shows how to customize the Finder, menus, keyboard map and icons. The book contains a disk with the lastest version of ResEdit and 1400K of sample resources. *(240 pages)*

Order Information:

How soon will I get my books?

UPS Ground orders arrive within 10 days on the West Coast and within three weeks on the East Coast. UPS Blue orders arrive within two working days anywhere in the U.S., provided we receive a fax or a phone call by 11 a.m. Pacific Time.

What about backorders?

Any book that is not available yet will be shipped separately when it is printed. *Requesting such books will not hold up your regular order.*

What if I don't like it?

Since we're asking you to buy our books sight unseen, we back them with an *unconditional money-back guarantee*. Whether you're a first time or a repeat customer, we want you to be completely satisfied in all your dealings with Peachpit Press.

What about shipping to Canada and overseas?

Shipping to Canada and overseas is via air mail. Orders must be prepaid in U.S. dollars.

Order Form

To order, call:

(800) 283-9444 or (510) 548-4393 (M-F) • (510) 548-5991 fax

#	Title	Price	Total
	Art of Darkness (with disk)	19.95	
	Canvas 3.0: The Book	21.95	
	Desktop Publisher's Survival Kit (with disk)	22.95	
	Illustrator Illuminated	24.95	
	The Little Mac Book, 3rd Edition	16.00	
	The Little Mac Word Book	15.95	
	The Little QuicKeys Book	18.95	
	The Macintosh Bible, 4th Edition	32.00	
	The Macintosh Bible Disks, 4th Edition	25.00	
	The Macintosh Bible Guide to FileMaker Pro 2.0	22.00	
	The Macintosh Bible "What Do I Do Now?" Book	15.00	
	The Mac is not a typewriter	9.95	
	Photoshop 2.5: Visual QuickStart Guide (Mac Edition)	18.00	
	The QuarkXPress Book, 3rd Edition (Macintosh)	28.00	
	QuarkXPress 3.1: Visual QuickStart Guide (Mac Edition)	14.95	
	QuarkXPress Tips and Tricks	21.95	
	Real World FreeHand	27.95	
	Silicon Mirage	15.00	
	Zen and the Art of Resource Editing	24.95	

SHIPPING:	First Item	Each Additional		
			Subtotal	
UPS Ground	$4	$1	8.25% Tax (CA only)	
UPS Blue	$7	$2		
Canada	$6	$4	Shipping	
Overseas	$14	$14	**TOTAL**	

Name	
Company	
Address	
City	State Zip
Phone	Fax
❑ Check enclosed	❑ Visa ❑ MasterCard
Company purchase order #	
Credit card #	Expiration Date

Peachpit Press, Inc. • 2414 Sixth Street • Berkeley, CA • 94710
Your satisfaction is guaranteed or your money will be cheerfully refunded!

Raves for *The QuarkXPress Book*

These guys obviously know QuarkXPress inside and out. If you use XPress, you need this book.
—*Daniel Brogan, Editor,* Personal Publishing

The QuarkXPress Book is tops for reference and tips.
—*Ric Ford and Rick LePage,* MacWeek

This book is loaded with tips and techniques that have never seen print before. These guys really know QuarkXPress.
—*Tim Gill, Founder, Quark, Inc.*

The book is chock-full of TIPS, TIPS, and more TIPS. It s hard to put down.
—*Perry Koenig,* PostEvent

I want to thank you for the wonderful QuarkXPress book that you wrote. I've been a teacher for 30 years, and I just want to tell you: you're a great teacher.
— *Ruth Snyder, Teacher, Los Angeles*

Creative and inspiring.
—*Osmo Leivo, MacMaailma*

Authors Blatner and Stimely present a comprehensive tour through version 3.0 of QuarkXPress, their pithy discussions peppered with offbeat humor.
—*Computer Publishing*

The QuarkXPress Book—great, great, great! You guys really went the distance. Even the style of prose is entertaining—funny, light, but deadly accurate and informative. A truly great opus. Bravo. I'm ordering a copy for my mom.
—*Dave Schultz, Creative Director, Typesettra, San Diego, CA*

Kudos *in extremis* on *The QuarkXPress Book*! The info on creating PS dumps in exactly what I would hope our customers would do. I've almost come to regard the name Steve Roth on the cover of a book as a guarantee of quality—now I'm almost ready to add David Blatner's and Keith Stimely's names to that category.
—*Scott Walker, Admasters, Atlanta, GA*

Recently there was a discussion of the various XPress books on the Desktop Publishing Forum of CompuServe, and *The QuarkXPress Book* topped most hard-core Quark fans' lists. That's a big endorsement.
—*Anne-Marie Concepcion, Mac/Chicago*

With its lively style, frequent screen shots, and intelligent design, this book is a welcome addition to the growing group of materials on XPress. Reading it will bring you much pleasure; using it will make you more proficient.

—*Suzanne Thomas*, Desktop Connections

The QuarkXPress Book is the best! Finally a book that doesn't rehash the manual! Kudos to all involved!

—*Caryl Felicetta, President, Argyle Studio, Edison, NJ*

If I'd had this book in the past, I wouldn't have had to work until 3 a.m. all those nights.

—*Mike Arst, Senior Typesetter, LaserGraphics*

Absolutely terrific! There aren't enough superlatives to describe it. *The QuarkXPress Book* is definitely a must have. I cannot believe how much really good stuff you crammed between those two covers. Quite honestly I don't see how any Quark user—regardless of their supposed expertise—can afford to be without this book.

—*Jerry Sapperstein, President, Font Bank, Evanston, IL*

To begin with, these guys have a sense of humor. That alone is a welcome change of pace from the remarkably dreary Mac books that line my shelf. But don t let the tongue-in-cheek humor fool you into thinking that this book is a puff job. What we have here is a very fine software manual. It's certainly the most entertaining I've ever read, and among the most useful. I strongly recommend it.

—*Craig Federhen*, Mac Monitor

The QuarkXPress Book is a great book. Not only will it tell you everything you could ever want to know about XPress 3.0, it also covers elements of page design, typography and printing that you really should learn elsewhere, but probably won't.

—*Lawrence I. Charters*, Resources

The QuarkXPress Book is loaded with tips. It will really help with the training of our staff.

—*Valerie Brewster, Seattle Weekly*

The QuarkXPress Book is highly recommended to XPress users of every level. Beginners will welcome its clarity and easy style. Advanced users will discover enough gems among the familar stuff to make it worthwhile. And the price is right!

—*Paul Cohen*, GetInfo!

To paraphrase Blatner in the introduction, having *The QuarkXPress Book* on hand is like having a computer-, graphic design-, and XPress-literate consultant on call for a flat fee. Such a deal!

—*Anne-Marie Concepcion*, Mac/Chicago

The text is so clearly written and cleanly laid out that non-techies can understand it; but the book is so versatile that no matter what your level of expertise, *The QuarkXPress Book* will augment your skills.

—*Camille Ranker*, Small Publishers Exchange